ISABEL BURTON

THE LIFE OF
CAPTAIN
SIR RICHARD F. BURTON

Volume I

Elibron Classics
www.elibron.com

Elibron Classics series.

ISBN 1-4021-1339-0 (paperback)
ISBN 1-4021-0669-6 (hardcover)

This Elibron Classics Replica Edition is an unabridged facsimile of the edition published in 1893 by Chapman & Hall, Ltd., London.

THE LIFE

OF

SIR RICHARD F. BURTON,

K.C.M.G., F.R.G.S.

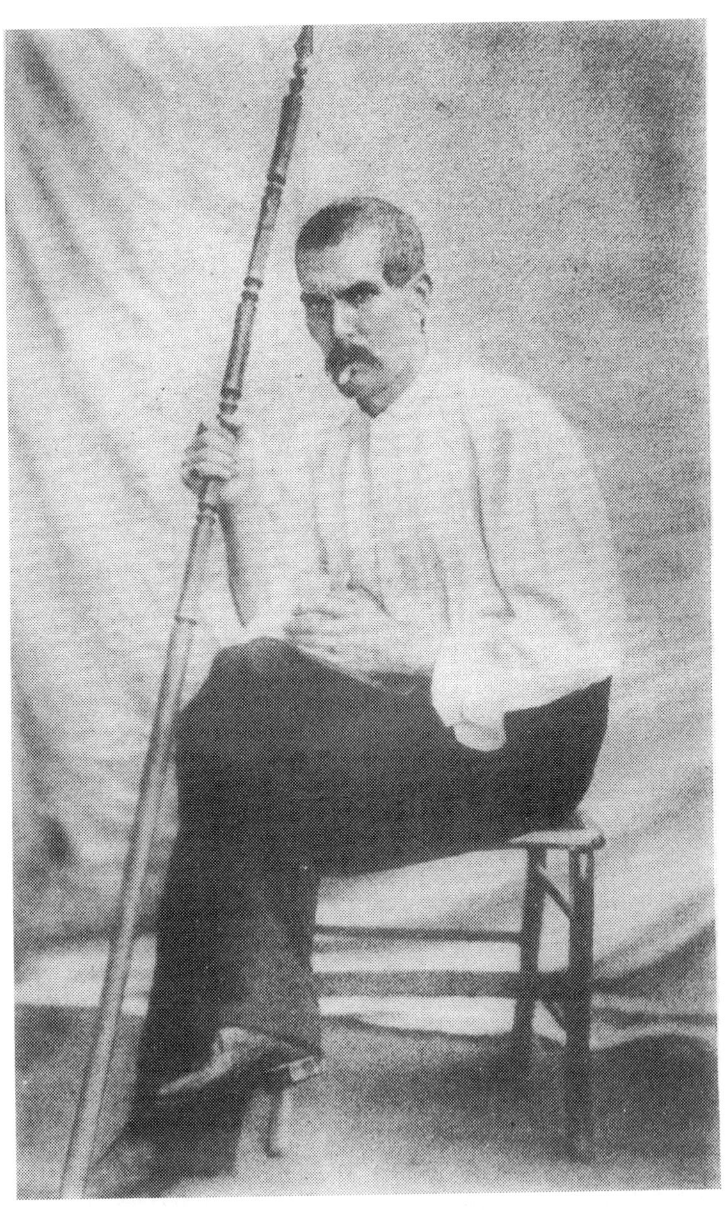

RICHARD BURTON IN HIS TENT IN AFRICA.

THE LIFE OF

CAPTAIN
SIR RICH[D] F. BURTON,

K.C.M.G., F.R.G.S.

BY HIS WIFE,

ISABEL BURTON.

WITH NUMEROUS PORTRAITS, ILLUSTRATIONS, AND MAPS.

IN TWO VOLUMES.

VOL. I.

LONDON: CHAPMAN & HALL, LD.

1893.

CONSECRATION.

TO MY EARTHLY MASTER,

WHO IS WAITING FOR ME ON HEAVEN'S FRONTIERS.

Whilst waiting to rejoin you, I leave as a message to the World we inhabited, the record of the Life into which both our lives were fused. Would that I could write as well as I can love, and do you that justice, that honour, which you deserve! I will do my best, and then I will leave it to more brilliant pens, whose wielders will feel less—and write better.

Meet me soon—I wait the signal!

ISABEL BURTON.

FOREWORD.

"No man can write a man down except himself."

In speaking of my husband, I shall not call him "Sir Richard," or "Burton," as many wives would; nor yet by the pet name I used for him at home, which for some reason which I cannot explain was "Jemmy;" nor yet what he was generally called at home, and what his friends called him, "Dick;" but I will call him Richard in speaking of him, and "I" where he speaks on his own account, as he does in his private journals. I always thought and told him that he destroyed much of the interest of his works by hardly ever alluding to himself, and now that I mention it, people may remark it, that in writing he seldom uses the pronoun *I*. I have therefore drawn, not from his books, but from his private journals. It was one of his asceticisms, an act of humility, which the world passed by, and probably only thought one of his eccentricities. In his works he would generally speak of himself as the Ensign, the Traveller, the Explorer, the Consul, and so on, so that I often think that people who are *not* earnest readers never understood *who* it was that did this, thought that, or saw the other. If I make him speak plainly for himself, as he does in his private journals, but never to the public, it will give twenty times the interest in relating events; so I shall throughout let him speak for himself where I can.

In early January, 1876, Richard and I were on our way to India for a six months' trip to visit the old haunts. We divided our intended journey into two lots. We cut India down the middle, the long way on the map, from north to south, and took the western side, leaving the eastern side for a trip which was deferred, alas! for our old age and retirement. We utilized the voyage out (which occupied thirty-three days in an Austrian Lloyd, used as a Haj, or pilgrim-ship), and also the voyage back, in the part of the following pages which refers to his early life, he dictating and I writing.

In 1887, when my husband was beginning to be a real invalid, he lent some of these notes to Mr. Hitchman (who asked leave to write his biography), Richard promising not to tread upon his heels by his own Autobiography till he should be free from service in 1891. It will not, I think, do any harm to the reading public to reproduce it with more detail, because only seven hundred people got Mr. Hitchman's, who did not by any means use the whole of the material before he returned it, and what I give is the original just as Richard dictated it, and it is more needful, because it deals with a part of his life that was only known to himself, to me only by dictation; because everything that he wrote of himself is infinitely precious, and because to leave to the public a sketch of an early Richard Burton is desirable, otherwise readers would be obliged to purchase Mr. Hitchman's, as well as this work, in order to make a perfect whole.

I must take warning, however, that when Mr. Hitchman's book came out, part of the Press found this account of my husband's boyhood and youth charming, and another part of the Press said that I was too candid, and did nothing to gloss over the faults and foibles of the youthful Burtons; they doubted the accuracy of my information—I was informed that my style was too rough-and-ready, and of many others of my shortcomings. In short, I was considered rather as writing against my own husband, whilst both sides of the Press in their reviews assumed that I wrote it; this charmed Richard, and he would not let me refute. Not one word was mine—it was only dictation, and peremptory dictation when I objected to certain self-accusations. I beg leave to state that I did not write one single word; I could not, for I did not know it—and all that the family objected to, or considered exaggerated, will not be repeated here. Before entering on these pages, I must warn the reader not to expect the goody-goody boy nor yet the precocious vicious youth of 1893. It is the recital of a high-spirited lad of the old school, full of animal spirits and manly notions, a lively sense of fun and humour, reckless of the consequences of playing tricks, but without a vestige of vice in the meaner or lower forms—a lad, in short, who *would* be a gentleman and a man of the world in his teens, and who, from his foreign travel, had seen more of life than boys do brought up at home.

I do not begin this work—the last important work of my life—without fear and trembling. If I can perform this sacred duty—this labour of love—well,—I shall be glad indeed, but I begin it with unfeigned humility. I have never needed any one to point out to me that my husband was on a pedestal far above *me*, or anybody else in the world. I have known it from 1850 to 1893, from a young girl to an old widow, *i.e.* for forty-three years. I feel that I cannot do justice to his scientific life, that I may miss points in travel that would have been more brilliantly treated by a clever man. My only comfort is, that his travels and services are already more or less known to the public, and that other books will be written about them. But if I am so unfortunate as to disappoint the public in *this* way, there is one thing that I feel I *am* fit for, and that is to lift the veil as to the *inner* man. He was misunderstood and unappreciated by the world at large, during his life. No one ever thought of looking for the real man beneath the cultivated mask that generally hid all feelings and belief—but now the world is beginning to know what it *has* lost. The old, old, sad story.

He shall tell his own tale till 1861, the first forty years, annotated by me. Whilst dictating to me I sometimes remarked, "Oh, do you think it would be well to write this?" and the answer always was, "Yes! I do not see the use of writing a biography at all, unless it is the exact truth, a very photograph of the man or woman in question." On this principle he taught me to write quite openly in the unconventional and personal style—being the only way to make a biography interesting, which we *now* class as the Marie

Bashkirtcheff style. As you will see, he always makes the worst of himself, and offers no excuse. As a lad he does not know what to do to show his manliness, and all that a boy should, ought, and does think brave and honourable, be it wild or not, all that he does.

What appals me is, that the task is one of such magnitude—the enormous quantity of his books and writings that I have to look through, and, out of eighty or more publications, to ascertain what has seen the light and what has not, because it is impossible to carry the work of forty-eight years in one's head; and, again, the immense quantity of subjects he has studied and written upon, some in only a fragmentary state, is wonderful. My wish would be to produce this life, speaking only of him—and afterwards to reproduce everything he has written that has not been published. I propose putting all the heavier matter, such as pamphlets, essays, letters, correspondence, and the *résumé* of his works—that is, *what portion shows his labours and works for the benefit of the human race*—into two after-volumes, to be called "Labours and Wisdom of Richard Burton." After his biography I shall renew *his* "Arabian Nights" with his Forewords, Terminal Essay, and Biography of the book in such form that it can be copyrighted—it is now protected by *my* copyright. His "Catullus" and "Pentamerone" are now more or less in the Press, to be followed by degrees by all his unpublished works. His hitherto published works I shall bring out as a Uniform Library, so that not a word will be lost that he ever wrote for the public. Fortunately, I have kept all his books classified as he kept them himself, with a catalogue, and have separate shelves ticketed and numbered; for example, "Sword," "Gypsy," "Pentamerone," "Camoens," and so on.

If I were sure of life, I should have wished for six months to look through and sort our papers and materials before I began this work, because I have five rooms full. Our books, about eight thousand, only got housed in March, 1892, and they *are* sorted—but not the papers and correspondence; but I fancy that the public would rather have a spontaneous work sooner, than wait longer. If I live I shall always go on with them. I have no leisure to think of style or of polish, or to select the best language, the best English, —no time to shine as an authoress. I must just think aloud, so as not to keep the public waiting.

From the time of my husband's becoming a real invalid—February, 1887—whilst my constant thoughts reviewed the dread To Come—the catastrophe of his death—and the subsequent suffering, I have been totally incapable, except writing his letters or attending to his business, of doing any good literary work until July, 1892, a period of five years, which was not improved by four attacks of influenza.

Richard was such a many-sided man, that he will have appeared different to every set of people who knew him. He was as a diamond with so many facets. The tender, the true, the brilliant, the scientific,—and to those who deserved it, the cynical, the hard, the severe. Loads of books will be written about him, and every one will be different; and though perhaps it is an unseemly boast, I venture to feel sure that mine will be the truest one, for I have no interest to serve, no notoriety to gain, belong to no party, have nothing to sway me, except the desire to let the world understand what it once possessed, what it has lost. With many it will mean *I*. With me it means *HIM*.

When this biography is out, the public will, theoretically, but not practically, know him as well as I can make them, and all of his friends will be able after that to put forth a work representing that particular facet of his character which he turned on to them, or which they drew from him. He was so great, so world-wide, he could turn a fresh facet and sympathy on to each world. I always think that a man is one character to his wife at his fireside corner, another man to his *own* family, another man to *her* family, a fourth to a mistress or an amourette—if he have one,—a fifth to his men friends, a sixth to his boon companions, and a seventh to his public, and so on *ad infinitum;* but I think the wife, if they are happy and love each other, gets the pearl out of the seven oyster-shells.

I fear that this work will be too long. I cannot help it. When I embarked on it I had no conception of the scope: it was a labour of love. I thought I could fly over it; but

I have found that the more I worked, the more it grew, and that the end receded from me like the mirage in the desert. I only aim at giving a simple, true recital without comment, and at fairness on all questions of whatever sort. I am very personal, because I believe the public like it. I want to give Richard as I knew him at home. I apologize in advance to my readers if I am sometimes obliged to mention myself oftener than they and I care about; but they will understand that our lives were so interwoven, so bound together, that I should very often spoil a good story or an anecdote or a dialogue were I to leave myself out. It would be an affectation that would spoil my work.

I am rather disheartened by being told by a literary friend that the present British public likes its reading "in sips." How *can* I give a life of seventy years, every moment of which was employed in a remarkable way, "in sips"? It is impossible. Though I must not detail much from his books, I want to convey to the public, at least, what they were about; striking points of travel, his schemes, wise warnings, advice, and plans for the benefit of England—then what about "sips"? It must not be dry, it must not be heavy, nor tedious, nor voluminous; so it shall be personal, full of traits of character, sentiments and opinions, brightened with cheerful anecdotes, and the more serious part shall go into the before-mentioned two volumes, the "Labours and Wisdom of Richard Burton."

I am not putting in many letters, because he generally said such personal things, that few would like them to be shown. His business letters would not interest. To economize time he used to get expressly made for him the smallest possible pieces of paper, into which he used to cram the greatest amount of news—telegram form. He only wrote much in detail, if he had any literary business to transact.

One of my greatest difficulties, which I scarcely know how to express, is, that which I think the most interesting, and which most of my intimates think well worth exploring; it is that of showing the dual man with, as it were, two natures in one person, diametrically opposed to each other, of which he was himself perfectly conscious. I had a party of literary friends to dinner one night, and I put my manuscript on the table before them after dinner, and I begged them each to take a part and look over it. Feeling as I do that the general public never understood him, and that his mantle after death seemed to descend upon my shoulders, that everything I say seems to be misunderstood, and that, in some few eyes, I can do nothing right, I said at the end of the evening, "If I endeavour to explain, will it not be throwing pearls to swine?" (not that I meant, dear readers, to compare *you* to swine—it is but an expression of thought well understood). And the answer was, "Oh, Lady Burton, *do* give the world the ins and outs of this remarkable and interesting character, and let the swine take care of themselves." "If you leave out by order" (said one) "religion and politics, the two touchstones of the British public, you leave out the great part of a man." "Mind you gloss over nothing to please anybody" (said a second). I think they are right—one set of people see one side, and another see another side, and neither of the two will comprehend (like St. Thomas) anything that they have not seen and felt; or, to quote one of Richard's favourite mottoes from St. Augustine, "Let them laugh at me for speaking of things which they do not understand, and I must pity them, whilst they laugh at me." So I must remain an unfortunate buffer amidst a cyclone of opinions. I can only avoid controversies and opinions *of my own*, and quote his and his actions.

These words are forced from me, because I have received my orders, if not exactly from the public, from a few of the friends who profess to know him best. I am ordered to describe Richard as a sort of Didérot (a disciple of Voltaire's), who wrote "that the world would never be quiet till the last king was strangled with the bowels of the last priest,"—whereas there was no one whom Richard delighted more to honour than a worthy King, or an honest straightforward Priest.

There *are* people who are ready to stone me, if I will not describe Richard as being absolutely without belief in anything; yet I really cannot oblige them, without being absolutely untruthful. He was a spade-truth man, and he honestly used to say that he examined every religion, and picked out its pearl to practise it. He did not scoff at them, he was perfectly sincere and honest in what he said, nor did he change, but he *grew.* He always *said,* and innumerable people *could* come forward, if they had the courage—I could name some—to say that they have heard him declare, that at the end of all things there were only two points to stand upon—NOTHING and CATHOLICISM; and many *could,* if they *would,* come forward and say, that when they asked him what religion he was, he answered Catholic.

He *never was,* what is called *here* and *now* in England, an Agnostic; he was a Master-Sufi, he practised Tasáwwuf or Sufi-ism, which combines the poetry and prose of religion, and is mystic. The Sufi is a profound student of the different branches of language and metaphysics, is gifted with a musical ear, indulges in luxuriant imagery and description. They have a simple sense—a *double entendre* understood amongst themselves—God in Nature,—Nature in God—a mystical affection for a Higher Life, dead to excitement, hope, fear, etc. He was fond of quoting Sayyid Mohammad Hosayn's motto, "It is better to restore one dead heart to Eternal Life, than Life to a thousand dead bodies."

I have seen him receive gratuitous copies of an Agnostic paper in England, and I remember one in particular—I do not know who wrote it,—it was very long, and all the verses ended with "Curse God the Father, Son, and Holy Ghost." I can see him now reading it—and stroking his long moustache, and muttering, "Poor devil! Vulgar beast!" He was quite satisfied, as his friends say, that we are not gifted with the senses to understand the origin of the Mysteries by which we are surrounded, and in this nobody agrees more thoroughly than I do. He likewise said he believed there was a God, but that he could not define Him; neither can I, neither can you, but *I* do not want to. Great minds tower above and see into little ones, but the little minds never climb sufficiently high to see into the Great Minds, and never did Lord Beaconsfield say a truer thing, speaking of religion than when he said, "*Sensible men never tell.*" As I want to make this work both valuable and interesting, I am not going into the unknown or the unknowable, only into what he knew—what I know; therefore I shall freely quote his early training, his politics, his Mohammedanism, his Sufiism, his Brahminical thread, his Spiritualism, and all the religions which he studied, and nobody can give me a sensible reason why I should leave out the Catholicism, except to point the Spanish proverb, "that no one pelts a tree, unless it has fruit on it," but were I to do so, the biography would be incomplete.

Let us suppose a person residing inside a house, and another person looking at the house from the opposite side of the street; you would not be unjust enough to expect the person on the outside to describe minutely its inner chambers and everything that was in it, because he would have to take it on trust from the person who resided inside, but you *would* take the report of the man living outside as to the *exterior* of the house. That is exactly the same as my writing my husband's history. Do you want an edition of the inside or an edition of the outside? If you do not want the truth, if you order me to describe a Darwin, a Spencer, a John Stuart Mill, I can do it; but it will not be the home-Richard, the fireside-Richard whom *I* knew, the two perfectly distinct Richards in one person; it will be the man as he was at lunch, at dinner, or when friends came in, or when he dined out, or when he paid visits; and if the world—or, let us say, a small portion of the world,—is so unjust and silly as to wish for untrue history, it must get somebody else to write it. To me there are only two courses: I must either tell the truth, and lay open the "inner life" of the man, by a faithful photograph, or I must let it alone, and leave his friends to misrepresent him, according to their lights.

It has been threatened to me that if I speak the truth I am to reap the whirlwind, because others, who claim to know my husband *well*, see him quite in a different light. (I know many people intimately, but I am quite incompetent to write their lives—I am only fit to do that for the man with whom I lived night and day for thirty years; there are three other people who could each write a small section of his life, and after those nobody; I do not accept the so-called general term "friend.") I shall be very happy indeed to answer anybody who attacks me, who is brave enough to put his or her name; but during the two years I have been in England I have hardly had anything but anonymous communications and paragraphs signed under the brave names of "Agnostic," or "One who knows," so I have no man or woman to deal with, but empty air, which is beneath my contempt. This is a very old game, perhaps even more ancient than "Prophesy, O Christ, who it was that struck Thee!" but it is cowardly and un-English—that is, if England "stands where she did." I would also remind you of the good old Arab proverb, that "a thousand curses never tore a shirt."

I would have you remember that I gain *nothing* by trying to describe my husband as belonging to *any particular religion.* If I would describe him as an English Agnostic—the last new popular word—the small band of people who call themselves his intimate friends, and who think to honour him by injuring me, would be perfectly satisfied. I should have all their sympathy, and my name would be at rest, both in Society and in the Press. I have no interest to serve in saying he was a Catholic more than anything else; I have no bigotry on the question *at all.* If he did something Catholic I shall say it, and if he did something Mohammedan or Agnostic I shall equally say it.

It is also a curious fact, that the people who are most vexed with me on this score, are men who, before their wives, mothers, sisters, are good Protestants, and who go twice to the Protestant church on Sundays, but who are quite scandalized that my husband should be allowed a religion, and are furious because I will not allow that Richard Burton was their Captain. No, thank you! it is not good enough: he was not, never *was* like *any* of you—nor can I see what it can possibly be to you what faith, or no faith, Richard Burton chose to die in, and why you threaten me if I speak the truth! *We* only knew *two* things—the beautiful mysticism of the East, which, until I lived here, I thought was Agnosticism, and I find it is *not;* and calm, liberal-minded Roman Catholicism. The difference between you and Richard is—you, I mean, who admired my husband—that you are not going anywhere,—according to your own creed you have nowhere to go to,—whilst *he* had a God and a continuation, and said he would wait for me; he is only gone a long journey, and presently I shall join him; we shall take up where we left off, and we shall be very much happier even than we have been here.

Of the thousands that have written to me since his death, everybody writes, "What a marvellous brain your husband had! How modest about his learning and everything concerning himself! He was a man never understood by the world." It is no wonder he was *not* understood by the World; his friends hindered it, and when one who knew him thoroughly, offers to *make* him understood, it is resented.

The Press has recently circulated a paragraph saying that "I am not the fittest person to write my husband's life." After I have finished these two volumes, it will interest me very much to read those of the competent person, who will be so kind as to step to the front,—with a name, please, not anonymously,—and to learn all the things I do not know.

He, she, or it, will write what he said and wrote; I write what he *thought* and *did.*

ISABEL BURTON.

29th May, 1893.

NOTE.—I must beg the reader to note, that a word often has several different spellings, and my husband used to give them a turn all round. Indeed, I may say that during the latter years of his life he adopted quite a different spelling, which he judged to be correcter. In many cases it is caused by the English way of spelling a thing, and the real native way of spelling the same. For English Meeanee, native way Miani. The battle of Dabba (English) is spelt Dubba, Dubbah, by the natives. Fulailee river (English) is spelt Phuleli (native). Mecca and Medina have sometimes an *h* at the end of them. Karrachee is Karáchi. Sind is spelt Sind, Sindh, Scind, Scinde; and what the Anglo-Indians call Bóbagees are really Babárchis, and so on. I therefore beg that the spelling may not be criticized. In quoting letters, I write as the author does, since I must not change other people's spelling.—I. B.

CONTENTS.

CHAPTER VI.

MY PUBLIC LIFE BEGINS.

CHAPTER VII.

THE REMINISCENCES WRITTEN FOR MR. HITCHMAN IN 1888—INDIA.

CHAPTER VIII.

ON RETURN FROM INDIA.

CHAPTER IX.

HARAR—THE MOSLEM ABYSSINIA—THE TIMBUCTOO OF EAST AFRICA, THE EXPLORATION OF WHICH HAD BEEN ATTEMPTED IN VAIN BY SOME THIRTY TRAVELLERS.

CHAPTER X.

WITH BEATSON'S HORSE.

CHAPTER XI.

BETWEEN THE CRIMEA AND THE LAKE REGIONS OF CENTRAL AFRICA.

CHAPTER XII.

HIS EXPLORATION OF THE LAKE REGIONS, TAKING CAPTAIN SPEKE AS SECOND IN COMMAND.

CHAPTER XIII.

THE REAL START FOR TANGANYIKA IN THE INTERIOR.

CHAPTER XIV.

OUR REWARD—SUCCESS.

CHAPTER XV.

RICHARD AND I MEET AGAIN.

CHAPTER XVI.

WEST COAST OF AFRICA—RICHARD'S FIRST CONSULATE.

CHAPTER XVII.

HIS FIRST LEAVE.

CHAPTER XVIII.

HOME.

CHAPTER XIX.

SANTOS, SÃO PAULO, BRAZIL—RICHARD'S SECOND CONSULATE.

CHAPTER XX.

DAMASCUS—HIS THIRD CONSULATE.

CHAPTER XXI.

RELIGION.

LIST OF ILLUSTRATIONS.

THE

LIFE OF SIR RICHARD BURTON.

CHAPTER I.

THE EARLY DAYS OF RICHARD F. BURTON.

By himself. Copied from his private Journals.

"He travels and expatriates; as the bee
From flower to flower, so he from land to land,
The manners, customs, policy of all
Pay contributions to the store he gleans;
He seeks intelligence from every clime,
And spreads the honey of his deep research
At his return—a rich repast for *me!*"

GENEALOGY AND FAMILY.

AUTOBIOGRAPHERS generally begin too late.

Elderly gentlemen of eminence sit down to compose memories, describe with fond minuteness babyhood, childhood, and boyhood, and drop the pen before reaching adolescence.

Physiologists say that a man's body changes totally every seven years. However that may be, I am certain that the moral man does, and I cannot imagine anything more trying than for a man to meet himself as he was. Conceive his entering a room, and finding a collection of himself at the several decades. First the puking squalling baby one year old, then the pert unpleasant school-boy of ten, the collegian of twenty who, like Lothair, "knows everything and has nothing to learn." The *homme fait* of thirty in the full warmth and heyday of life, the reasonable man of forty, who first recognizes his ignorance and knows his own mind, of fifty with white teeth turned dark, and dark hair turned white, whose experience is mostly disappointment with regrets for lost time and vanished opportunities. Sixty when the man begins to die and mourns for his past youth, at seventy when he *ought* to prepare for his long journey and never does. And at all these ages he is seven different beings not one of which he would wish to be again.

First I would make one or two notes on family history.

My grandfather was the Rev. Edward Burton, Rector of Tuam, in Galway (who with his brother, eventually Bishop Burton, of Killala, were the first of our branch to settle in Ireland). They were two of the Burtons of Barker Hill, near Shap, Westmoreland, who own a common ancestor with the Burtons of Yorkshire, of Carlow, and Northamptonshire. My grandfather married Maria Margaretta Campbell, daughter, by a Lejeune, of Dr. John Campbell, LL.D., Vicar-General of Tuam. Their son was my father, Lieut.-Colonel Joseph Netterville Burton, of the 36th Regiment, who married a Miss (Beckwith) Baker, of Nottinghamshire, a descendant, on her mother's side, of the Scotch Macgregors. The Lejeune above mentioned was related to the Montmorencys and Drelincourts, French Huguenots of the time of Louis XIV. To this hangs a story which will be told by-and-by. This Lejeune, whose real name was Louis Lejeune, is supposed to have been a son of Louis XIV. by the Huguenot Countess of Montmorency. He was secretly carried off to Ireland. His name was translated to Louis Young, and he eventually became a Doctor of Divinity. The royal, or rather morganatic, marriage contract was asserted to have existed, but has disappeared. The Lady Primrose of that date, who was a very remarkable personage, and a strong ally of the Jacobites, protected him and conveyed him to Ireland.

The Burtons of Shap derive themselves from the Burtons of Longnor, like Lord Conyngham and Sir Charles Burton of Pollacton, and the two above named were the collateral descendants of Francis Pierpoint Burton, first Marquis of Conyngham, who gave up the name of Burton. The notable man of the family was Sir Edward Burton, a desperate Yorkist who was made a Knight Banneret by Edward IV. after the second battle of St. Albans, and who added to his arms the Cross and four roses.

The Bishop of Killala's son was Admiral J. Ryder Burton, who entered the Navy in 1806. He served in the West Indies, and off the North Coast of Spain, when in an attack on the town of Castro, July, 1812, he received a gunshot wound in the left side, from which the ball was never extracted. From 1813 to 1816 he served in the Mediterannean and Adriatic, and was present at the bombardment of Algiers, when he volunteered to command one of the gunboats for destroying the shipping inside the Mole. His last appointment was in May, 1820, to the command of the *Cornelian* brig, in which he proceeded in early 1824 to Algiers, where, in company with the *Naiad* frigate, he fell in with an Algerine corvette, the *Tripoli*, of eighteen guns and one hundred men, which, after a close and gallant action under the batteries of the place, he boarded and carried. This irascible veteran at his death was in receipt of a pension for wounds. He was Rear Admiral in 1853, Vice Admiral in 1858, and Admiral in 1863. He married, in 1822, Anna Maria, daughter of the thirteenth Lord Dunsany; she died in 1850, leaving one son, Francis Augustus Plunkett Burton, Colonel of the Coldstream Guards. He married the great heiress Sarah Drax, and died in 1865, leaving one daughter, Erulí, who married her cousin, John Plunkett, the future Lord Dunsany.

My father, Joseph Netterville Burton, was a lieutenant-colonel in the 36th Regiment. He must have been born in the latter quarter of the eighteenth century, but he had always a superstition about mentioning his birthday, which gave rise to a family joke that he was born in Leap Year. Although of very mixed blood, he was more of a Roman in appearance than anything else, of moderate height, dark hair, sallow skin, high nose, and piercing black eyes. He was considered a very handsome man, especially in uniform, and attracted attention even in the street. Even when past fifty he was considered the best-looking man at the Baths of Lucca. As handsome men generally do, he married a plain woman, and, "Just like Provy," the children favoured, as the saying is, the mother.*

In mind he was a thorough Irishman. When he received a commission in the army it was on condition of so many of his tenants accompanying him. Not a few of the younger sort volunteered to enlist, but when they joined the regiment and found that the "young master" was all right, they at once ran away.

The only service that he saw was in Sicily, under Sir John Moore, afterwards of Corunna, and there he fell in love with Italy. He was a duellist, and shot one brother officer twice, nursing him tenderly each time afterwards. When peace was concluded he came to England and visited Ireland. As that did not suit him he returned to his regiment in England. Then took place his marriage, which was favoured by his mother-in-law and opposed by his father-in-law. The latter, being a sharp old man of business, tied up every farthing of his daughter's property, £30,000, and it was well that he did so. My father, like too many of his cloth, developed a decided

* N.B.—This I deny. Richard was the handsomest and most attractive man I have ever seen, and Edward, though smaller, was very good-looking, but there is no doubt that Richard grew handsomer every year of his life, and I can remember Maria exceedingly attractive so far back as 1857.—I. B.

taste for speculation. He was a highly moral man, who would have hated the idea of *rouge et noir*, but he gambled on the Stock Exchange, and when railways came out he bought shares. Happily he could not touch his wife's property, or it would speedily have melted away; yet it was one of his grievances to the end of his life that he could not use his wife's money to make a gigantic fortune. He was utterly reckless where others would be more prudent. Before his wedding tour, he passed through Windermere, and would not call upon an aunt who was settled near the Lakes, for fear that she might think he expected her property. She heard of it, and left every farthing to some more dutiful nephew.

He never went to Ireland after his marriage, but received occasional visits from his numerous brothers and sisters.

The eldest of the family was the Rev. Edward Burton, who had succeeded to the living. He wasted every farthing of his property, and at last had the sense to migrate to Canada, where he built a little Burtonville. In his younger days he intended to marry a girl who preferred another man. When she was a widow with three children, and he a widower with six children, they married, and the result was eventually a total of about a score. Such families do better than is supposed. The elder children are old enough to assist the younger ones, and they seem to hang together. My father's sisters, especially Mrs. Mathews, used to visit him when in England, and as it was known that he had married an heiress, they all hung to him, apparently, for themselves and their children. They managed to get hold of all the Irish land that fell to his share, and after his death they were incessant in their claims upon his children. My mother was Martha Baker, one of three sister co-heiresses, and was the second daughter. The third daughter married Robert Bagshaw, Esq., M.P. for Harwich, and died without issue. The eldest, Sarah, married Francis Burton, the youngest brother of my father. He had an especial ambition to enter the Church, but circumstances compelled him to become military surgeon in the 66th Regiment. There was only one remarkable event in his life, which is told in a few very interesting pages by Mrs. Ward, wife of General Ward, with a short comment by Alfred Bate Richards, late editor of the *Morning Advertiser*, who, together with Andrew Wilson, author of the "Abode of Snow," who took it up at his death, compiled and put together a short *résumé* of the principal features of my life, of which some three hundred copies were printed in pamphlet form and circulated to private friends.

"FACTS CONNECTED WITH THE LAST HOURS OF NAPOLEON.

"On the night of the 5th of May, 1821, a young ensign of the 66th Regiment, quartered at St. Helena, was wending his solitary way along the path leading from the plain of Deadwood to his barracks, situated on a patch of table-land called Francis Plain. The road was dreary, for to the left yawned a vast chasm, the remains of a crater, and known to the islanders as the 'Devil's Punchbowl;' although the weather had been perfectly calm, puffs of wind occasionally issued from the neighbouring valleys; and, at last, one of these puffs having got into a gully, had so much ado to get out of it, that it shrieked, and moaned, and gibbered, till it burst its bonds with a roar like thunder—and dragging up in its wrath, on its passage to the sea, a few shrubs, and one of those fair willows beneath which Napoleon, first Emperor of France, had passed many a peaceful, if not a happy, hour of repose, surrounded by his faithful friends in exile.

"This occurrence, not uncommon at St. Helena, has given rise to an idea, adopted even by Sir Walter Scott, that the soul of Napoleon had passed to another destiny on the wings of the Storm Spirit; but, so far from there being any tumult among the elements on that eventful night, the gust of wind I have alluded to was only heard by the few whose cottages dotted the green slopes of the neighbouring mountains. But as that fair tree dropped, a whisper fell among the islanders that Napoleon was dead! No need to dwell upon what abler pens than mine have recorded; the eagle's wings were folded, the dauntless eyes were closed, the last words, '*Tête d'armée*,' had passed the faded lips, the proud heart had ceased to beat . . . !!

"They arrayed the illustrious corpse in the attire identified with Napoleon even at the present day; and among the jewelled honours of earth, so profusely scattered upon the breast, rested the symbol of the faith he had professed. They shaded the magnificent brow with the unsightly cocked hat,* and stretched down the beautiful hands in ungraceful fashion; every one, in fact, is familiar with the attitude I describe, as well as with a death-like cast of the imperial head, from which a fine engraving has been taken. The cast is true enough to Nature, but the character of the engraving is spoiled by the addition of a laurel-wreath on the lofty but insensate brow.

"About this cast there is a *historiette* with which it is time the public should become more intimately acquainted; it was the subject of litigation, the particulars of which are detailed in the *Times* newspaper of the 7th September, 1821, but to which I have now no opportunity of referring. Evidence, however, was unfortunately wanting at the necessary moment, and the complainant's case fell to the ground. The facts are these:—

"The day after Napoleon's decease, the young officer I have alluded

* "The coffin being too short to admit this array in the order proposed, the hat was placed at the feet before interment."

to, instigated by emotions which drew vast numbers to Longwood House, found himself within the very death-chamber of Napoleon. After the first thrill of awe had subsided, he sat down, and on the fly-leaf torn from a book, and given him by General Bertrand, he took a rapid but faithful sketch of the deceased Emperor. Earlier in the day, the officer had accompanied his friend, Mr. Burton, through certain paths in the island, in order to collect material for making a composition resembling plaster of Paris, for the purpose of taking the cast with as little delay after death as possible. Mr. Burton having prepared the composition, set to work and completed the task satisfactorily. The cast being moist, was not easy to remove; and, at Mr. Burton's request, a tray was brought from Madame Bertrand's apartments, Madame herself holding it to receive the precious deposit. Mr. Ward, the ensign alluded to, impressed with the value of such a memento, offered to take charge of it at his quarters till it was dry enough to be removed to Mr. Burton's; Madame Bertrand, however, pleaded so hard to have the care of it, that the two gentlemen, both Irishmen and soldiers, yielded to her entreaties, and she withdrew with the treasure, which she *never afterwards would resign.*

"There can scarcely, therefore, be a question that the casts and engravings of Napoleon, now sold as emanating from the skill and reverence of Antommarchi, are from the original taken by Mr. Burton. We can only rest on circumstantial evidence, which the reader will allow is most conclusive. It is to be regretted that Mr. Burton's cast and that *supposed* to have been taken by Antommarchi were not *both* demanded in evidence at the trial in 1821.

"The engraving I have spoken of has been Italianized by Antommarchi, the name inscribed beneath being *Napoleone.*

"So completely was the daily history of Napoleon's life at St. Helena a sealed record, that, on the arrival of papers from England, the first question asked by the islanders and the officers of the garrison was, 'What news of Buonaparte?' Under such circumstances it was natural that an intense curiosity should be felt concerning every movement of the mysterious and ill-starred exile. Our young soldier one night fairly risked his commission for the chance of a glimpse behind the curtain of the Longwood windows, and, after all, saw nothing but the imperial form from the knees downwards. Every night at sunset a *cordon* of sentries was drawn round the Longwood plantations. Passing between the sentinels, the venturesome youth crept, under cover of trees, to a lighted window of the mansion. The curtains were not drawn, but the blind was lowered. Between the latter, however, and the window-frame were two or three inches of space; so down knelt Mr. Ward! Some one was walking up and down the apartment, which was brilliantly illuminated.* The footsteps drew nearer, and Mr. Ward saw the diamond buckles of a pair of thin shoes, then two well-

* "Napoleon's dining-room lamp, from Longwood, is, I believe, still in the possession of the 91st Regiment, it having been purchased by the officers at St. Helena in 1836."

formed lower limbs, encased in silk stockings; and, lastly, the edge of a coat, lined with white silk. On a sofa at a little distance was seated Madame Bertrand, with her boy leaning on her knee; and some one was probably writing under Napoleon's dictation, for the Emperor was speaking slowly and distinctly. Mr. Ward returned to his guard-house satisfied with having *heard the voice of Napoleon Buonaparte.*

"Mr. Ward had an opportunity of seeing the great captive at a distance on the very last occasion that Buonaparte breathed the outer air. It was a bright morning when the serjeant of the guard at Longwood Gate informed our ensign that 'General Buonaparte' was in the garden on to which the guard-room looked. Mr. Ward seized his spy-glass, and took a breathless survey of Napoleon, who was standing in front of his house with one of his Generals. Something on the ground attracted his notice; he stooped to examine (probably a colony of ants, whose movements he watched with interest), when the music of a band at a distance stirred the air on Deadwood Plain; and he who had once led multitudes forth at his slightest word now wended his melancholy way through the grounds of Longwood, to catch a distant glimpse of a British regiment under inspection.

"We have in our possession a small signal book which was used at St. Helena during the period of Napoleon's exile. The following passages will give some idea of the system of vigilance which it was thought necessary to exercise, lest the world should again be suddenly uproused by the appearance of the French Emperor on the battle-field of Europe. It is not for me to offer any opinion on such a system, but I take leave to say that I never yet heard any British officer acknowledge that he would have accepted the authority of Governor under the burden of the duties it entailed. In a word, although every one admits the difficulties and responsibilities of Sir Hudson Lowe's position, all deprecate the system to which he considered himself obliged to bend.

"But the signal-book! Here are some of the passages which passed from hill to valley while Napoleon took his daily ride within the boundary prescribed:—

"'General Buonaparte has left Longwood.'

"'General Buonaparte has passed the guards.'

"'General Buonaparte is at Hutt's Gate.'

"'General Buonaparte is missing.'

"The latter paragraph resulted from General Buonaparte having, in the course of his ride, turned an angle of a hill, or descended some valley beyond the ken, for a few minutes, of the men working the telegraphs on the hills!

"It was not permitted that the once Emperor of France should be designated by any other title than '*General* Buonaparte;' and, alas! innumerable were the squabbles that arose between the Governor and his captive, because the British Ministry had made this puerile order peremptory. I have now no hesitation in making known the great Duke's opinion on this subject, which was transmitted to me two years ago, by one who for some months every year held daily intercourse with his Grace, but who could not, while the Duke was living, permit me to publish what had been expressed in private conversation.

"'I would have taken care that he did not escape from St. Helena,' said Wellington: 'but he might have been addressed by any name he pleased.'

"I cannot close this paper without saying a word or two on the condition of the buildings once occupied by the most illustrious and most unfortunate of exiles.

"It is well known that Napoleon never would inhabit the house which was latterly erected at Longwood for his reception; that, he said, 'would serve for his tomb;' and that the slabs from the kitchen *did* actually form part of the vault in which he was placed in his favourite valley beneath the willows, and near the fountain whose crystal waters had so often refreshed him.

"This abode, therefore, is not invested with the same interest as his real residence, well named the 'Old House at Longwood;' for a more crazy, wretched, filthy barn, it would scarcely be possible to meet with; and many painful emotions have filled my heart during nearly a four years' sojourn on 'The Rock,' as I have seen French soldiers and sailors march gravely and decorously to the spot, hallowed in their eyes, of course, by its associations with their invisible but unforgotten idol, and degraded, it must be admitted, by the change it has undergone.

"Indeed, few French persons can be brought to believe that it ever was a decent abode; and no one can deny that it must outrage the feelings of a people like the French, so especially affected by associations, to see the bedchamber of their former Emperor a dirty stable, and the room in which he breathed his last sigh, appropriated to the purpose of winnowing and thrashing wheat! In the last-named room are two pathetic mementoes of affection. When Napoleon's remains were exhumed in 1846, Counts Bertrand and Las Casas carried off with them, the former a piece of the boarded floor on which the Emperor's bed had rested, the latter a stone from the wall pressed by the pillow of his dying Chief.

"Would that I had the influence to recommend to the British Government, that these ruined and, I must add, desecrated, buildings should be razed to the ground; and that on their site should be erected a convalescent hospital for the sick of all ranks, of *both* services, and of *both* nations. Were the British and French Governments to unite in this plan, how grand a sight would it be to behold the two nations shaking hands, so to speak, over the grave of Napoleon!

"On offering this suggestion, when in Paris lately, to one of the nephews of the first Emperor Napoleon, the Prince replied that 'the idea was nobly philanthropic, but that England would never listen to it.' I must add that his Highness said this 'rather in sorrow than in anger;' then, addressing Count L——, one of the faithful followers of Napoleon in exile, and asking him which mausoleum *he* preferred,—the one in which we then stood, the dome of the *Invalides*, or the rock of St. Helena,—he answered, to my surprise, 'St. Helena; for no grander monument than that can ever be raised to the Emperor!'

"Circumstances made one little incident connected with this, our visit to the *Invalides*, most deeply interesting. Comte D'Orsay was of the party; indeed it was in his elegant *atélier* we had all assembled, ere starting, to survey the mausoleum then being prepared for the ashes of Napoleon. Suffering and debilitated as Comte D'Orsay was, precious, as critiques on art, were the words that fell from his lips during our progress through the work-rooms, as we stopped before the sculptures intended to adorn the vault wherein the sarcophagus is to rest. Ere leaving the works, the Director, in exhibiting the solidity of the granite which was finally to encase Napoleon, struck fire with a mallet from the magnificent block. 'See,' said Comte D'Orsay, 'though the dome of the *Invalides* may fall, France may yet light a torch at the tomb of her Emperor.' I cannot remember the exact words, but such was their import. Comte D'Orsay died a few weeks after this.

"Since the foregoing was written, members of the Burton family have told me, that, after taking the cast, Mr. Burton went to his regimental rounds, leaving the mask on the tray to dry; the back of the head was left on to await his return, not being dry enough to take off, and was thus overlooked by Madame Bertrand. When he returned he found that the mask was packed up and sent on board ship for France in Antommarchi's name. From a feeling of deep mortification he took the back part of the cast, reverently scraped off the hair now enclosed in a ring, and, overcome by his feelings, dashed it into a thousand pieces. He was afterwards offered by Messrs. Gall and Spurzheim (phrenologists), one thousand pounds sterling for that portion of the cast which was wanting to the cast so called Antommarchi's. Amongst family private papers there was a correspondence, read by most members of it, between Antommarchi and Mr. Burton, in which Antommarchi stated that he knew Burton had made the plaster and taken the cast. Mrs. Burton, after the death of her husband and Antommarchi, thought the correspondence useless and burnt it; but the hair was preserved under a glass watch-case in the family for forty years. There was an offer made about the year 1827 or 1828 by persons high in position in France who knew the truth to have the matter cleared up, but Mr. Burton was dying at the time, and was unable to take any part in it, so the affair dropped.

"THE BUST OF BUONAPARTE.

"*Extract from the 'New Times' of September 7th,* 1821.

"On Wednesday a case of a very singular nature occurred at the Bow Street Office.

"Count Bertrand, the companion of Buonaparte in his exile at

St. Helena (and the executor under his will), appeared before Richard Birnie, Esq., accompanied by Sir Robert Wilson, in consequence of a warrant having been issued to search the residence of the Count for a bust of his illustrious master, which, it was alleged, was the property of Mr. Burton, 66th Regiment, when at St. Helena.

"The following are the circumstances of the case :—

"Previous to the death of Buonaparte, he had given directions to his executors that his body should not be touched by any person after his death; however, Count Bertrand directed Dr. Antommarchi to take a bust of him; but not being able to find a material which he thought would answer the purpose, he mentioned the circumstances to Mr. Burton, who promised that he would procure some if possible.

"The Englishman, in pursuance of this promise, took a boat and picked up raw materials on the island, some distance from Longwood. He made a plaster, which he conceived would answer this purpose. When he showed it to Dr. Antommarchi he said it would not answer, and refused to have anything to do with it, in consequence of which Mr. Burton proceeded to take a bust himself, with the sanction of Madame Bertrand, who was in the room at the time. An agreement was entered into that copies should be made of the bust, and that Messieurs Burton and Antommarchi were to have each a copy.

"It was found, however, that the plaster was not sufficiently durable for the purpose, and it was proposed to send the original to England to have copies taken.

"When Mr. Burton, however, afterwards inquired for the bust, he was informed that it was packed and nailed up; but a promise was made, that upon its arrival in Europe, an application should be made to the family of Buonaparte for the copy required by Mr. Burton.

"On its arrival, Mr. Burton wrote to the Count to have his promised copy, but he was told, as before, that application would be made to the family of Buonaparte for it.

"Mr. Burton upon this applied to Bow Street for a search warrant in order to obtain the bust, as he conceived he had a right to it, he having furnished the materials and executed it.

"A warrant was issued, and Taunton and Salmon, two officers, went to the Count's residence in Leicester Square. When they arrived, and made known their errand, they were remonstrated with by Sir Robert Wilson and the Count, who begged they would not act till they had an interview with Mr. Birnie, as there must be some mistake. The officers politely acceded to the request, and waived their right of search.

"Count Bertrand had, it seems, offered a pecuniary compensation to Mr. Burton for his trouble, but it was *indignantly refused by that officer*, who persisted in the assertion of his right to the bust as his own property, and made application for the search warrant.

"Count Bertrand, in answer to the case stated by Mr. Burton, said that the bust was the property of the family of the deceased, to whom he was executor, and he thought he should not be authorized in giving it up. If, however, the law of this country ordained it otherwise, he must submit; but he should protest earnestly against it.

"The worthy magistrate, having sworn the Count to the fact that he was executor under the will of Buonaparte, observed that it was a case out of his jurisdiction altogether, and if Mr. Burton chose to persist in his claim, he must seek a remedy before another tribunal.

"The case was dismissed, and the warrant was cancelled.

"The sequel to the Buonaparte story is short; Captain Burton (in 1861) thinking that the sketch, which was perfect, and the lock of hair which had been preserved in a family watch-case for forty years, would be great treasures to the Buonapartes, and should be given to them, begged the sketch of General and Mrs. Ward, and the hair from the Burtons; he had the hair set in a handsome ring, with a wreath of laurels and the Buonaparte bees. His wife had a complete set of her husband's works very handsomely bound, as a gift, and in January, 1862, Captain Burton sent his wife over to Paris, with the sketch, the ring, and the books, to request an audience with the Emperor and Empress, and offer them these things, simply as an act of civility—for Captain and Mrs. Burton in opinion and feeling were Legitimists. Captain Burton was away on a journey, and Mrs. Burton had to go alone. She was young and inexperienced, and had not a single friend in Paris to advise her. She left her letter and presents at the Tuileries. The audience was not granted. His Imperial Majesty declined the presents, and she never heard anything more of them. They were not returned. Frightened and disappointed at the failure of this, her first little mission at the outset of her married life, she returned to London directly, where she found the Burton family anything but pleased at her failure and her want of *savoir faire* in the matter, having unwittingly caused their treasure to be utterly unappreciated. She said to me on her return, 'I never felt so snubbed in my life, and I shall never like Paris again;' and I believe she has kept her word.

"OXONIAN."

Francis Burton, alluded to in these pages, returned to England after the death of Napoleon, married one of the three co-heiress (Baker) sisters, and died early, leaving only two daughters. One died, and the other, Sarah, became Mrs. Pryce-Harrison.

Nor was this the only little romance in our Burton family, as the following story taken from family documents tends to show. Here is the Louis XIV. history—

"With regard to Louis XIV. there are one or two curious and interesting legends in the Burton family, well authenticated, which make Richard Burton great-great-great-grandson of Louis XIV. of France, by a morganatic marriage; and another which would entitle him to an English baronetcy, dating from 1622.

"One of the documents in the family is entitled, 'A Pedigree of the Young family, showing their descent from Louis XIV. of France,' and which runs as follows:—

"Louis XIV. of France took the beautiful Countess of Montmorency from her husband and shut him up in a fortress. After the death of (her husband) the Constable de Montmorency, Louis morganatically *married* the Countess. She had a son called Louis le Jeune, who 'was brought over to Ireland by Lady Primrose,' then a widow. This Lady Primrose's maiden name was Drelincourt, and the baby was named Drelincourt after his godfather and guardian, Dean Drelincourt (of Armagh), who was the father of Lady Primrose. He grew up, was educated at Armagh, and was known as Drelincourt Young. He married a daughter of Dean Drelincourt, and became the father of Hercules Drelincourt Young, and also of Miss (Sarah) Young, who married Dr. John Campbell, LL.D., Vicar-General of Tuam (*ob.* 1772). Sarah Young's brother, the above-mentioned Hercules Young, married and had a son George, a merchant in Dublin, who had some French deeds and various documents, which proved his right to property in France.

"The above-named Dr. John Campbell, by his marriage with Miss Sarah Young (rightly Lejeune, for they had changed the name from French to English), had a daughter, Maria Margaretta Campbell, who was Richard Burton's grandmother. The same Dr. John Campbell was a member of the Argyll family, and a first cousin of the 'three beautiful Gunnings,' and was Richard Burton's great-grandfather.

"These papers (for there are other documents) affect a host of families in Ireland—the Campbells, Nettervilles, Droughts, Graves, Burtons, Plunketts, Trimlestons, and many more.

"In 1875 *Notes and Queries* was full of this question and the various documents, but it has never been settled.

"The genealogy runs thus:—

"Louis XIV.

"*Son*, Louis le Jeune (known as Louis Drelincourt Young), by Countess Montmorency; adopted by Lady Primrose * (see Earl of Rosebery), and subsequently married to a daughter of Drelincourt, Dean of Armagh.

"*Daughter*, Sarah Young; married to Dr. John Campbell, LL.D., Vicar-General of Tuam, Galway.

"*Daughter*, Maria Margaretta Campbell; married to the Rev. Edward Burton, Rector of Tuam, Galway.

---

* "This Lady Primrose was a person of no small importance, and was the centre of the Jacobite Society in London, and the friend of several distinguished people; and as she was connected on her own side and her husband's with the French Calvinists, she may very likely have protected Lejeune from France to Ireland, and he would probably have, when grown up, married some younger Drelincourt—as such were undoubtedly the names of the parents of Sarah Young, who married Dr. John Campbell. We can only give the various documents as we have seen them."

"*Son*, Lieutenant-Colonel Joseph Netterville Burton, 36th Regiment.

"*Son*, Richard Burton, whose biography I am now relating.

"There was a Lady Primrose buried in the Rosebery vaults, by her express will, with a little casket in her hands, containing some secret, which was to die with her; many think that it might contain the missing link.

"The wife of Richard Burton received, in 1875, two very tantalizing anonymous letters, which she published in *Notes and Queries*, but which she has never been able to turn to account, through the writer declining to come forward, *even secretly*.

"One ran thus:—

"'MADAM,—There is an old baronetcy in the Burton family to which you belong, dating from the reign of Edw. III.*—I rather believe *now in abeyance*—which it was thought Admiral Ryder Burton would have taken up, and which after his death can be taken up by your branch of the family. All particulars you will find by searching the Heralds' Office; but I am positive my information is correct.—From one who read your letter in *N. and Q.*'

"She shortly after received and published the second anonymous letter; but, though she made several appeals to the writer in *Notes and Queries*, no answer was obtained, and Admiral Ryder Burton eventually died.

"'MADAM,—I cannot help thinking that if you were to have the records of the Burton family searched carefully at Shap, in Westmoreland, you would be able to fill up the link wanting in your husband's descent, from 1712 to 1750, or thereabouts. As I am *quite positive* of a baronetcy *being in abeyance* in the Burton family, and that *an old one*, it would be worth your while getting all the information you can from Shap and Tuam—the Rev. Edward Burton, Dean of Killala and Rector of Tuam, whose niece he married was a Miss Ryder, of the Earl of Harrowby's family, by whom he had no children. His second wife, a Miss Judge, was a descendant of the Otways, of Castle Otway, and connected with many leading families in Ireland. Admiral James Ryder Burton could, if he *would*, supply you with information respecting the missing link in your husband's descent. I have always heard that *de Burton* was the proper family name, and I saw lately that a *de Burton* now lives in Lincolnshire.

"'Hoping, madam, that you will be able to establish your claim to the baronetcy,

"'I remain, yours truly,

"'A READER OF *N. and Q.*

"'P.S.—I rather think also, and advise your ascertaining the *fact*,

---

* "This is an error of the anonymous writer. Baronetcies were first created in 1605."—I. B.

that the estate of Barker Hill, Shap, Westmoreland, by the law of *entail*, will devolve, at the death of Admiral Ryder Burton, on your husband, Captain Richard Burton.'

"From the Royal College of Heralds, however, the following information was forwarded to Mrs. Richard Burton :—

"'There *was* a baronetcy in the family of Burton. The first was Sir Thomas Burton, Knight, of Stokestone, Leicestershire; created July 22nd, 1622, a baronet, by King James I. Sir Charles was the last baronet. He appears to have been in great distress—a prisoner for debt, 1712. He is supposed to have died without issue, when the title became extinct—at least nobody has claimed it since. If your husband can prove his descent from a younger son of any of the baronets, he would have a right to the title. The few years must be filled up between 1712 and the birth of your husband's grandfather, which was about 1750; and you must prove that the Rev. Edward Burton, Rector of Tuam in Galway, your husband's grandfather (who came from Shap, in Westmoreland, with his brother, Bishop Burton, of Tuam), was descended from any of the sons of any of the baronets named.'" *

* N.B.—We never had the money to pursue these enquiries. But should they ever be sifted, the proper heir, since my husband is dead, will be Captain Richard St. George Burton, of the "Black Watch." We made out all the links, except twelve years from 1712. It is said that Admiral Ryder Burton himself was the author of those two anonymous letters to me. My husband often used to say there were only two titles he would care to have. Firstly, the old family baronetcy, and the other to be created Duke of Midian.—ISABEL BURTON.

CHAPTER II.

RICHARD'S BIRTH AND CHILDHOOD.

I WAS born at 9.30 p.m., 19th March (Feast of St. Joseph in the calendar), 1821, at Barham House, Herts, and suppose I was baptized in due course at the parish church. My birth took place in the same year as, but the day before, the grand event of George IV. visiting the Opera for the first time after the Coronation, March 20th. I was the eldest of three children. The second was Maria Catherine Eliza, who married Henry, afterwards General Sir Henry Stisted, a very distinguished officer, who died, leaving only two daughters, one of whom, Georgina Martha, survives. Third, Edward Joseph Netterville, late Captain in the 37th Regiment, unmarried.

The first thing I remember, and it is always interesting to record a child's first memories, was being brought down after dinner at Barham House to eat white currants, seated upon the knee of a tall man with yellow hair and blue eyes; but whether the memory is composed of a miniature of my grandfather, and whether the white frock and blue sash with bows come from a miniature of myself and not from life, I can never make up my mind.

Barham House was a country place bought by my grandfather, Richard Baker, who determined to make me his heir because I had red hair, an unusual thing in the Burton family. The hair soon changed to black, which seems to justify the following remarks by Alfred Bate Richards in the pamphlet alluded to. They are as follows:—

"Richard Burton's talents for mixing with and assimilating natives of all countries, but especially Oriental characters, and of becoming as one of themselves without any one doubting or suspecting his origin; his perfect knowledge of their languages, manners, customs, habits, and religion; and last, but not least, his being gifted by nature with an Arab head and face, favoured this his first enterprise" (the pilgrimage to Mecca). "One can learn from that versatile poet-traveller, the excellent Théophile Gautier, why Richard Burton is an Arab in appearance; and account for that incurable restlessness that is unable to wrest from fortune a spot on earth wherein to repose when weary of wandering like the desert sands.

"'There is a reason,' says Gautier, who had studied the Andalusian and the Moor, 'for the fantasy of nature which causes an Arab to be born in Paris, or a Greek in Auvergne; the mysterious voice of blood which is silent for generations, or only utters a confused murmur, speaks at rare intervals a more intelligible language. In the general confusion race claims its own, and some forgotten ancestor asserts his rights. Who knows what alien drops are mingled with our blood? The great migrations from the table-lands of India, the descents of the Northern races, the Roman and Arab invasions, have all left their marks. Instincts which seem *bizarre* spring from these confused recollections, these hints of distant country. The vague desire of this primitive Fatherland moves such minds as retain the more vivid memories of the past. Hence the wild unrest that wakens in certain spirits the need of flight, such as the cranes and the swallows feel when kept in bondage—the impulses that make a man leave his luxurious life to bury himself in the Steppes, the Desert, the Pampas, the Sáhara. He goes to seek his brothers. It would be easy to point out the intellectual Fatherland of our greatest minds. Lamartine, De Musset, and De Vigny are English; Delacroix is an Anglo-Indian; Victor Hugo a Spaniard; Ingres belongs to the Italy of Florence and Rome.'

"Richard Burton has also some peculiarities which oblige one to suspect a drop of Oriental, perhaps gipsy, blood. By gipsy we must understand the pure Eastern."

My mother had a wild half-brother—Richard Baker, junior, a barrister-at-law, who refused a judgeship in Australia, and died a soap-boiler. To him she was madly attached, and delayed the signing of my grandfather's will as much as possible to the prejudice of her own babe. My grandfather Baker drove in his carriage to see Messrs. Dendy, his lawyers, with the object of signing the will, and dropped dead, on getting out of the carriage, of ossification of the heart; and, the document being unsigned, the property was divided. It would now be worth half a million of money.

When I was sent out to India as a cadet, in 1842, I ran down to see the old house for the last time, and started off in a sailing ship round the Cape for Bombay, in a frame of mind to lead any forlorn hope wherever it might be. Warren Hastings, Governor-General of India, under similar circumstances threw himself under a tree, and formed the fine resolution to come back and buy the old place; but *he* belonged to the eighteenth century. The nineteenth is far more cosmopolitan. I always acted upon the saying, *Omne solum forti patria*, or, as I translated it, "For every region is a strong man's home."

Meantime my father had been obliged to go on half-pay by the Duke of Wellington for having refused to appear as a witness against Queen Caroline. He had been town mayor at Genoa when she lived there, and her kindness to the officers had greatly prepossessed them in her favour; so, when ordered by the War Office to turn Judas, he flatly refused. A great loss to himself, as Lord William Bentinck, Governor-General of India, was about to take him as aide-camp, and to his family, as he lost all connection with the army, and lived entirely abroad, and, eventually coming back, died with his wife at Bath in 1857. However, he behaved like a gentleman, and none of his family ever murmured at the step, though I began life as an East Indian cadet, and my brother in a marching regiment, whilst our cousins were in the Guards and the Rifles and other crack corps of the army.

The family went abroad when I was a few months old, and settled at Tours, the charming capital of Touraine, which then contained some two hundred English families (now reduced to a score or so), attracted by the beauty of the place, the healthy climate, the economy of living, the facilities of education, and the friendly feeling of the French inhabitants, who, despite Waterloo, associated freely with the strangers.

They had a chaplain, the Rev. Mr. Way (whose son afterwards entered the Indian army; I met him in India, and he died young); their schoolmaster was Mr. Clough, who bolted from his debts, and then Mr. Gilchrist, who, like the Rev. Edward Irving, Carlisle's friend (whom the butcher once asked if he couldn't assist him), caned his pupils to the utmost. The celebrated Dr. Brettoneau took charge of the invalids. They had their duellist, the Honourable Martin Hawke, their hounds that hunted the Forest of Amboise, and a select colony of Irishmen, Messrs. Hume and others, who added immensely to the fun and frolic of the place.

At that period a host of these little colonies were scattered over the Continent nearest England; in fact, an oasis of Anglo-Saxondom in a desert of continentalism, somewhat like the society of English country towns as it was in 1800, not as it is now, where society is confined to the parson, dentist, surgeon, general practitioners, the bankers, and the lawyers. And in those days it had this advantage, that there were no snobs, and one seldom noticed the *aigre discorde*, the *maladie chronique des ménages bourgeoises.* Knowing nothing of Mrs. Grundy, the difference of the foreign colonies was that the *weight* of English respectability appeared to be taken off them, though their lives were respectable and respected. The Mrs. Gamps and Mrs. Grundys were not so rampant. The English of these little colonies were intensely patriotic, and cared comparatively little for party politics. They stuck to their own Church because it *was* their Church, and they knew as much about the Catholics at their very door, as the average Englishman does of the Hindú. Moreover, they honestly called themselves Protestants in those days, and the French called themselves Catholics. There was no quibble about "their being Anglo-Catholics, and the others Roman-Catholics." They subscribed liberally to the Church, and did not disdain to act as churchwardens. They kept a sharp look-out upon the parson, and one of your Modern High Church Protestants or Puseyites or Ritualists would have got the sack after the first sermon. They were intensely national. Any Englishman in those days who refused to fight a duel with a Frenchman was sent to Coventry, and bullied out of the place. English girls who flirted with foreigners, were looked upon very much as white women who permit the addresses of a nigger, are looked upon by those English who have lived in black countries. White women who do these things lose caste. Beauséjour, the château taken by the family, was inhabited by the Maréchale de Menon in 1778, and eventually became the property of her *homme d'affaires*, Monsieur Froguet. The dear old place stands on the right bank of the Loire, halfway up the heights that bound the stream, commanding a splendid view, and fronted by a French garden and vineyards now uprooted. In 1875 I paid it a last visit, and found a friend from Brazil, a Madame Izarié, widow of my friend the French Consul of Bahia, who had come to die in the house of his sister, Madame Froguet.

Tours was in those days (1820–30) the most mediæval City in France. The western half of the city, divided from the eastern by the Rue Royale, contained a number of old turreted houses of freestone, which might have belonged to the fifteenth century. There also was the tomb of the Venerable St. Martin in a crypt, where lamps are ever burning, and where the destroyed cathedral has not yet been rebuilt. The eastern city contained the grand Cathedral of St. Garcien, with its domed towers, and the Archévêché or Archbishop's palace with beautiful gardens. Both are still kept in the best order. In forty-five years the city has grown enormously. The southern suburbs, where the Mall and Ramparts used to be, has become Boulevarts Heurteloup and Béranger; and "Places," such as that of the Palais de Justice, where cabbage gardens fenced with paling and thorn hedges once showed a few pauper cottages defended by the fortifications, are now Crescents and Kiosks for loungers, houses with tall mansarde roofs, and the large railway station that connects Tours with the outer world. The river, once crossed by a single long stone bridge, has now two suspension bridges and a railway bridge, and the river-holms, formerly strips of sand, are now grown to double their size, covered with trees and defended by stone dykes.

I remember passing over the river on foot when it was frozen, but with the increased population that no longer happens. Still there are vestiges of the old establishments. The Boule d'Or with its Golden Ball, and the Pheasant Hotel, both in the Rue Royale, still remain. You still read, "Maison Piernadine recommended for *is* elegance, *is* good taste, *is* new fashions of the first choice." Madame Fisterre, the maker of admirable apple-puffs, has disappeared and has left no sign. This was, as may be supposed, one of my first childish visits. We young ones enjoyed ourselves very much at the Château de Beauséjour, eating grapes in the garden, putting our Noah's ark animals under the box hedges, picking snail-shells and cowslips in the lanes, playing with the dogs—three black pointers of splendid breed, much admired by the Duke of Cumberland when he afterwards saw them in Richmond Park, named Juno, Jupiter, and Ponto. Charlotte Ling, the old nurse, daughter of the lodge-keeper at Barham House, could not stand the absence of beef and beer and the presence of kickshaws and dandelion salad, and after Aunt Georgina Baker had paid us a visit, she returned with her to Old England. A favourite amusement of us children was swarming up the tails of our father's horses, three in number, and one—a horse of Mecklenburg breed—was as tame as an Arab. The first story Aunt Georgina used to tell of me was of my lying on my back in a broiling sun, and exclaiming, "How I love a bright burning sun!" (Nature speaking in early years). Occasional drawbacks were violent storms of thunder and lightning, when we children were hustled out of our little cots under the roof, and taken to the drawing-room, lest the lightning should strike us, and the daily necessity of learning the alphabet and so forth, multiplication table, and our prayers.

I was intended for that wretched being, the infant phenomenon, and so began Latin at three and Greek at four. Things are better now. Our father used to go out wild-boar hunting in the *Forêt d'Amboise*, where is the château in which Abd-el-Kadir was imprisoned by the French Government from 1847 to 1852, when he was set free by Napoleon III., at the entreaties of Lord Londonderry. (It is said that his Majesty entered his prison in person and set him free. Abd-el-Kadir, at Damascus, often expressed his obligations to the English, and warmly welcomed any English face. On one occasion I took a near relation of Lord Londonderry's to see him, and he was quite overcome.) My father was periodically brought home hurt by running against a tree. Sport was so much in vogue then as to come between the parson and his sermon.

This pleasant life came to a close one day. We were three: I was six, Maria four, and Edward three. One morning saw the hateful school-books fastened with a little strap, and we boys and our little bundle were conveyed in a small carriage to the town, where we were introduced into a room with a number of English and French boys, who were sitting opposite hacked and ink-spotted desks, looking as demure as they could, though every now and then they broke out into wicked grins and nudges. A lame Irish schoolmaster (Clough) smiled most graciously at us as long as our father was in the room, but was not half so pleasant when we were left alone. We wondered "what we were doing in that *Galère*," especially as we were sent there day after day, and presently we learnt the dread truth that we were at school at the ripe ages of six and three. Presently it was found that the house was at an inconvenient distance from school, and the family transferred itself to the Rue de l'Archévêché, a very nice house in the north-eastern corner of what is still the best street in the town (Rue Royale being mostly commercial). It is close to the Place and the Archbishop's palace, which delighted us, with small deer feeding about the dwarf lawn.

Presently Mr. Clough ran away, leaving his sister to follow as best she could, and we were transferred to the care of Mr. John Gilchrist, a Scotch pedagogue of the old brutal school, who took an especial delight in caning the boys, especially with a rattan or ferula across the palm of the hand; but we were not long in discovering a remedy, by splitting the end of the cane and inserting a bit of hair. We took lessons in drawing, dancing, French, and music, in which each child showed its individuality. Maria loved all four; Edward took to French and music and hated drawing; I took to French and drawing, and hated music and dancing. My brother and I took to the study of Arms, by nature, as soon as we could walk, at first with popguns and spring pistols and tin and wooden sabres, and I can quite well remember longing to kill the porter at five years old, because he laughed at our *sabres de bois* and *pistolets de paille*.

I was a boy of three ideas. Usually if a child is forbidden to eat the sugar or to lap up the cream he simply either obeys or does the contrary; but I used to place myself before the sugar and cream and carefully study the question, "Have I the courage not to touch them?" When I was quite sure of myself that I had the courage

I instantly rewarded resolution by emptying one or both. Moreover, like most boys of strong imagination and acute feeling, I was a resolute and unblushing liar; I used to ridicule the idea of my honour being any way attached to telling the truth, I considered it an impertinence the being questioned, I never could understand what moral turpitude there could be in a lie, *unless it was told for fear of the consequences* of telling the truth, or one that would attach blame to another person. That feeling continued for many a year, and at last, as very often happens, as soon as I realized that a lie was contemptible, it ran into quite the other extreme, a disagreeable habit of scrupulously telling the truth whether it was timely or not.*

The school was mostly manned by English boys, sprinkled with French, and the mixture of the two formed an ungodly article, and the Italian proverb—

> "Un Inglese Italianato
> È un Diavolo incarnato"

may be applied with quite as much truth to English boys brought up in France. To succeed in English life, boys must be brought up in a particular groove. First the preparatory school, then Eton and Oxford, with an occasional excursion to France, Italy, and Germany, to learn languages, not of Stratford-atte-Bowe, and to find out that England is not the whole world. I never met any of my Tours schoolfellows save one—Blayden Edward Hawke, who became a Commander in the Navy, and died in 1877.

We boys became perfect devilets, and played every kind of trick despite the rattan. Fighting the French gutter-boys with sticks and stones, fists, and snowballs was a favourite amusement, and many a donkey-lad went home with ensanguined nose, whilst occasionally we got the worst of it from some big brother. The next favourite game was playing truant, passing the day in utter happiness, fancying ourselves Robinson Crusoes, and wandering about the strip of wood (long since doomed to fuel) at the top of the Tranchée. Our father and mother went much into the society of the place, which was gay and pleasant, and we children were left more or less to the servants. We boys beat all our bonnes, generally by running at their petticoats and upsetting them. There was one particular case when a new nurse arrived, a huge Norman girl, who at first imposed upon this turbulent nursery by her breadth of shoulder and the general rigour of her presence. One unlucky day we walked to the Faubourg at

* N.B.—From that he became a man wholly truthful, wholly incorruptible, who never lost his "dignity," a man whose honour and integrity from the cradle to the grave was unimpeachable.—I. B.

the south-east of the town, the only part of old Tours now remaining; the old women sat spinning and knitting at their cottage doors, and remarked loud enough for us boys to hear, "Ah ça! ces petits gamins! Voilà une honnête bonne qui ne leur laissera pas faire des farces!" Whereupon Euphrosyne became as proud as a peacock, and insisted upon a stricter discipline than we were used to. That forest walk ended badly. A jerk of the arm on her part brought on a general attack from the brood; the poor bonne measured her length upon the ground, and we jumped upon her. The party returned, she with red eyes, torn cap, and downcast looks, and we hooting and jeering loudly, and calling the old women "Les Mères Pomponnes," who screamed predictions that we should come to the guillotine.

Our father and mother had not much idea of managing their children; it was like the old tale of the hen who hatched ducklings. By way of a wholesome and moral lesson of self-command and self-denial, our mother took us past Madame Fisterre's windows, and bade us look at all the good things in the window, during which we fixed our ardent affections upon a tray of apple-puffs; then she said, "Now, my dears, let us go away; it is so good for little children to restrain themselves." Upon this we three devilets turned flashing eyes and burning cheeks upon our moralizing mother, broke the windows with our fists, clawed out the tray of apple-puffs, and bolted, leaving poor mother a sadder and a wiser woman, to pay the damages of her lawless brood's proceedings.

Talking of the guillotine, the schoolmaster unwisely allowed the boys, by way of a school-treat, to see the execution of a woman who killed her small family by poisoning, on condition that they would look away when the knife descended; but of course that was just the time (with such an injunction) when every small neck was craned and eyes strained to look, and the result was that the whole school played at guillotine for a week, happily without serious accidents.*

The residence at Tours was interrupted by occasional trips, summering in other places, especially at St. Malo. The seaport then

* N.B.—This kind of *indulgence* should never be allowed by parents or tutors. During our eighteen years in Austria, there were some parents up the Slav district who allowed their two eldest children, boy and girl, six and seven, to see the pigs killed for a treat. They saw everything, to the hanging up of the pigs ready for buying. Next day the mother went down to the Trieste market, father to work, and the children were left in charge of the cottage. When the parents got near the cottage in late afternoon, the two children ran out and said, "We have had such fun, mamma; we have played all day at killing pigs, and we have done baby beautifully, and he squealed at first just like a real pig." The horrified parents rushed in, and found truly that baby was beautifully done, hanging up by the legs, his poor little stomach kept open by a bit of wood just like a real pig, and had been dead for hours.—I. B.

thoroughly deserved the slighting notice, to which it was subjected by Captain Marryat, and the house in the Faubourg was long remembered from its tall avenue of old yew trees, which afforded abundant bird's-nesting. At Dieppe the gallops on the sands were very much enjoyed, for we were put on horseback as soon as we could straddle. Many a fall was of course the result, and not a few broken heads, whilst the rival French boys were painfully impressed by the dignity of spurs and horsewhips.

At times relations came over to visit us, especially Grandmamma Baker (Grandmamma Baker was a very peculiar character). Her arrival was a signal for presents and used to be greeted with tremendous shouts of delight, but the end of a week always brought on a quarrel. Our mother was rather thin and delicate, but our grandmother was a thorough old Macgregor, of the Helen or the Rob Roy type, and was as quick to resent an affront as any of her clan. Her miniature shows that she was an extremely handsome woman, who retained her good looks to the last. When her stepson, Richard Baker, jun., inherited his money, £80,000, he went to Paris and fell into the hands of the celebrated Baron de Thierry. This French friend persuaded him to embark in the pleasant little speculation of building a bazaar. By the time the walls began to grow above ground the Englishman had finished £60,000, and, seeing that a million would hardly finish the work, he sold off his four greys and fled Paris post-haste in a post-chaise. The Baron Thierry followed him to London, and, bold as brass, presented himself as an injured creditor at grandmamma's pretty little house in Park Lane. The old lady replied by summoning her servants and having him literally kicked downstairs in true Highland fashion. That Baron's end is well known in history. He made himself king of one of the Cannibal Islands in the South Sea, and ended by being eaten by his ungrateful subjects.

Grandmamma Baker was determined to learn French, and, accordingly, secured a professor. The children's great delight was to ambuscade themselves, and to listen with joy to the lessons. "What is the sun?" "Le soleil, madame!" "La solelle." "Non, madame. Le so—leil." "Oh, pooh! La solelle." After about six repetitions of the same, roars of laughter issued from the curtains—we of course speaking French like English, upon which the old lady would jump up and catch hold of the nearest delinquent and administer condign punishment. She had a peculiar knack of starting the offender, compelling him to describe a circle of which she was the centre, whilst, holding with the left hand, she administered smacks and cuffs with the right; but, as every mode of attack has its own defence, it was soon found out that the proper corrective was to throw one's self on one's back, and give vigorous kicks with both legs. It need hardly be said that Grandmamma predicted that Jack Ketch would make acquaintance with the younger scions of her race, and that she never arrived at speaking French like a Parisian.

Grandmama Burton was also peculiar in her way. Her portrait shows the regular Bourbon traits, the pear-shaped face and head which culminates in Louis Philippe's. Although the wife of a country clergyman, she never seemed to have attained the meekness of feeling associated with that peaceful calling. The same thing is told of her as was told of the Edgeworth family. On one occasion during the absence of her husband, the house at Tuam was broken into by thieves, probably some of her petted tenantry. She lit a candle and went upstairs to fetch some gunpowder, loaded her pistols, and ran down to the hall, when the robbers decamped. She asked the raw Irish servant girl who had accompanied her what had become of the light, and the answer was that it was standing on the barrel of "black salt" upstairs; thereupon Grandmamma Burton had the pluck to walk up to the garret and expose herself to the risk of being blown to smithereens. When my father returned from service in Sicily, at the end of the year, he found the estate in a terrible condition, and obtained his mother's leave to take the matter in hand. He invited all the tenants to dinner, and when speech time came on, after being duly blarneyed by all present, he made a little address, dwelling with some vigour upon the necessity of being for the future more regular with the "rint." Faces fell, and the only result was, that when the rent came to be collected, he was fired at so frequently (showing that this state of things had been going on for some sixty or seventy years), that, not wishing to lead the life of the "Galway woodcock," he gave up the game, and allowed matters to take their own course.

Another frequent visitor was popularly known as "Aunt G."—Georgina Baker, the younger of the three sisters, who was then in the heyday of youth and high spirits. An extremely handsome girl, with blue eyes and dark hair and fine tall figure, she was the life of the house as long as her visits lasted. Her share of the property being £30,000, she had of course a number of offers from English as well as foreigners. On the latter she soon learned to look shy, having heard that one of her rejected suitors had exclaimed to his friend, "Quelle dommage, avec cette petite ferme a vendre," the wished-for farm, adjoining his property, happening then to be in the market. Heiresses are not always fortunate, and she went on refusing suitor after suitor, till ripe middle age, when she married Robert Bagshaw, Esq., M.P. for Harwich. She wanted to adopt me, intending to accompany me to Oxford and leave me her property, but this project had no stay in it. At the time she was at Tours, Aunt G. had a kind of "fad" that she would marry one of her brother-in-law Burton's brothers. Her eldest sister Sarah had married my uncle Burton, elder brother of my father, who, sorely against his wish, which pointed to the Church, had been compelled by the failure of the "rint" to become an army surgeon—the same who had the disappointment at St. Helena.

At last it became apparent that Tours was no longer a place for us who were approaching the ticklish time of teens. All Anglo-French boys generally were remarkable young ruffians, who, at ten years of age, cocked their hats and loved the ladies. Instead of fighting and fagging, they broke the fine old worked glass church windows, purloined their fathers' guns to shoot at the monuments in the churchyards, and even the shops and bazaars were not safe from their impudent raids. The ringleader of the gang was a certain Alek G——, the son of a Scotchmen of good family, who was afterwards connected with or was the leading spirit of a transaction, which gave a tablet and an inscription to Printing House Square. Alek was very handsome, and his two sisters were as good looking as himself. He died sadly enough at a hospital in Paris. Political matters, too, began to look queer. The revolution which hurled Charles X. from the throne, produced no outrages in quiet Tours, beyond large gatherings of the people with an immense amount of noise, especially of "*Vive la Chatte!*" (for La Charte), the good *commères* turning round and asking one another whom the Cat might be that the people wished it so long a life; but when Casimir Périer had passed through the town, and "the three glorious days of July" had excited the multitude, things began to look black, and cries of "*À bas les Anglais!*" were not uncommon. An Englishmen was threatened with prison because the horse he was driving accidentally knocked down an old woman, and a French officer of the line, who was fond of associating with English girls, was grossly insulted and killed in a dastardly duel by a pastrycook.

At last, after a long deliberation, the family resolved to leave Tours. Travelling in those days, especially for a large family, was a severe infliction. The old travelling carriages, which had grown shabby in the coachhouse, had to be taken out and furbished up, and all the queer receptacles, imperial, boot, sword-case, and plate-chest, to be stuffed with miscellaneous luggage. After the usual sale by auction, my father took his departure, perhaps mostly regretted by a little knot of Italian exiles, whom he liked on account of his young years spent in Sicily, and whose society not improbably suggested his ultimate return to Italy. Then began the journey along the interminable avenues of the old French roads, lined with parallel rows of poplars, which met at a vanishing point of the far distance. I found exactly the same thing, when travelling through Lower Canada in 1860. Mighty dull work it was, whilst the French postilion in his seven-league boots jogged along with his horses at the rate of five miles an hour, never dreaming of increasing the rate, till he approached some horridly paved town, when he cracked his whip, like a succession of pistol shots, to the awe and delight of all the sabots. Very slow hours they were, especially as the night wore on, and the road, gleaming white between its two dark edges, looked of endless length. And when at last the inn was reached, it proved very unlike the inn of the present day. A hard bargain had to be driven with a rapacious landlady, who, if you objected to her charges, openly roared at you with arms akimbo, "that if you were not rich enough to travel, you ought to stay at home." Then the beds had to be inspected, the damp sheets to be aired, and the warming-pans to be ordered, and, as dinner had always to be prepared after arrival, it was not unusual to sit hungry for a couple of hours.

The fatigues of the journey seriously affected my mother's health, and she lost no time in falling very ill at Chartres. Then Grandmamma Baker was sent for to act *garde-malade*, and to awe the children, who were wild with delight at escaping school and masters, with the weight of her sturdy Scotch arm. The family passed through Paris, where the signs of fighting, bullets in the walls, and burnt houses, had not been wholly obliterated, and were fortunate enough to escape the cholera, which then for the first time attacked Europe in its very worst form. Grandmamma Baker was very nearly as bad, for she almost poisoned her beloved grandchildren, by stuffing our noses and mouths full of the strongest camphor whenever we happened to pass through a town. The cold plunge into English life was broken by loitering on the sands of Dieppe. A wonderful old ramshackle place it was in those days, holding a kind of intermediate place between the dulness of Calais and the liveliness of "Boolone," as the denizens called it. It wanted the fine hotels and the *Établissement*, which grew up under the Second Empire, but there was during the summer a pleasant, natural kind of life, living almost exclusively upon the sands and dipping in the water, galloping about on little ponies, and watching the queer costumes of the bathers, and discussing the new-comers. Though railways were not dreamt of, many Parisians used to affect the place, and part of the French nature seems to be, to rush into the sea as soon as they see it.

CHAPTER III.

THE CHILDREN ARE BROUGHT TO ENGLAND.

LANDING in England was dolorous. Grandmamma Baker inflated her nostrils, and, delighted at escaping from those *crapauds* and their kickshaws, quoted with effusion her favourite Cowper, "England, with all thy faults, I love thee still." The children scoffed. The air of Brighton, full of smoke and blacks, appeared to them unfit for breathing. The cold grey seas made them shudder. In the town everything appeared so small, so prim, so mean, the little one-familied houses contrasting in such a melancholy way with the big buildings of Tours and Paris. We revolted against the coarse and half-cooked food, and, accustomed to the excellent Bordeaux of France, we found port, sherry, and beer like strong medicine; the bread, all crumb and no crust, appeared to be half baked, and milk meant chalk and water. The large joints of meat made us think of Robinson Crusoe, and the vegetables *cuite à l'eau*, especially the potatoes, which had never heard of "*Maître d'hôtel*," suggested the roots of primitive man. Moreover, the national temper, fierce and surly, was a curious contrast to the light-hearted French of middle France. A continental lady of those days cautioned her son, who was about to travel, against ridicule in France and the *canaille* in England. The little children punched one another's heads on the sands, the boys punched one another's heads in the streets, and in those days a stand-up fight between men was not uncommon. Even the women punched their children, and the whole lower-class society seemed to be governed by the fist.

My father had determined to send his boys to Eton to prepare for Oxford and Cambridge. In the mean time some blundering friend had recommended him a preparatory school. This was kept by the Rev. Charles Delafosse, who rejoiced in the title of Chaplain to the Duke of Cumberland, a scion of royalty, who had, apparently, very little to do with the Church. Accordingly, the family went to

Richmond, the only excitement of the journey being the rage of the post-boys, when we boys on the box furtively poked their horses with long sticks. After sundry attempts at housing themselves in the tiny doll-rooms in the stuffy village, they at last found a house, so called by courtesy, in "Maids of Honour Row," between the river and the Green, a house with a strip of garden fronting it, which a sparrow could hop across in thirty seconds. Opening upon the same Green, stood that horror of horrors, the school, or the "Establishment," as it would *now* be called. It consisted of a large block of buildings (detached), lying between the Green and the Old Town, which has long been converted into dwelling-houses. In those days it had a kind of paling round a paddock, forming a long parallelogram, which enclosed some fine old elm trees. One side was occupied by the house, and the other by the school-room. In the upper stories of the former, were the dormitories with their small white beds, giving the idea of the Lilliput Hospital; a kind of outhouse attached to the dwelling was the place where the boys fed at two long tables stretching the whole length of the room. The only decoration of the palings were names cut all over their inner surfaces and rectangular nails at the top, acting as *chevaux de frise.* The school-room was the usual scene of hacked and well-used benches and ink-stained desks, everything looking as mean and uncomfortable as possible.

This was the kind of Dotheboys Hall, to which, in those days, gentlemen were contented to send their sons, paying a hundred a year, besides "perquisites" (plunder): on the Continent the same treatment would be had for £20.

The Rev. Charles was a bluff and portly man, with dark hair and short whiskers, whose grand aquiline nose took a prodigious deal of snuff, and was not over active with the rod; but he was no more fit to be a schoolmaster than the Grand Cham of Tartary. He was, however, rather a favourite with the boys, and it was shrewdly whispered, that at times he returned from dining abroad half-seas over. His thin-lipped wife took charge of the *ménage*, and looked severely after the provisions, and swayed with an iron sceptre the maid-servants, who had charge of the smaller boys. The ushers were the usual consequential lot of those days. There was the handsome and dressy usher, a general favourite with the fair; the shabby and mild usher, despised by even the smallest boy; and the unfortunate French usher, whose life was a fair foretaste of Purgatory.

Instead of learning anything at this school, my brother and I lost much of what we knew, especially in French, and the principal acquisitions were, a certain facility of using our fists, and a general development of ruffianism. I was in one perpetual scene of fights; at one time I had thirty-two affairs of honour to settle, the place of meeting being the school-room, with the elder boys sitting in judgment. On the first occasion I received a blow in the eye, which I thought most unfair, and having got my opponent down I proceeded to hammer his head against the ground, using his ears by way of handles. My indignation knew no bounds when I was pulled off by the bystanders, and told to let my enemy stand up again. "Stand up!" I cried, "after all the trouble I've had to get the fellow down." At last the fighting went on to such an extent, that I was beaten as thin as a shotten herring, and the very servant-maids, when washing me on Saturday night, used to say, "Drat the child! what has he been doing? he's all black and blue." Edward fought just as well as I did, but he was younger and more peaceable. Maria says that I was a thin, dark little boy, with small features and large black eyes, and was extremely proud, sensitive, shy, nervous, and of a melancholy, affectionate disposition. Such is the effect of a boys' school after a few months' trial, when the boys learn to despise mother and sisters, and to affect the rough as much as possible, and this is not only in England, but everywhere where the boy first escapes from petticoat government. He does not know what to do to show his manliness. There is no stronger argument in favour of mixed schools, up to a *certain age*, of boys and girls together.

At the little Richmond theatre we were taken to see Edmund Kean, who lived in a cottage on the Green. He had gentle blood in his veins, grandson (illegitimate) of George Savile, Marquis of Halifax, and that accounted for his Italian, or rather un-John-Bull appearance, and for his fiery power. I saw him in his famous Richard III. *rôle*, and remember only what old Colley Grattan described, "Looks bloated with brandy, nose red, cheeks blotched, and eyes blood-shot." He was drinking himself to death. His audience appeared not a little afraid of him; perhaps they had heard of the Guernsey scene, where he stood at the footlights and flashed out, "Unmannered dogs! stand ye where *I* command."

Our parents very unwisely determined to correct all personal vanity in their offspring by always dwelling upon our ugliness. My nose was called cocked; it was a Cross which I had to carry, and was a perpetual plague to me; and I was assured that the only decent feature in my face was my teeth. Maria, on account of her fresh complexion, was called Blousabella; and even Edward, whose features were perfect, and whom Frenchmen used to stop and stare at in the streets, and call him "Le petit Napoleon," was told to nauseousness that "handsome is as handsome does." In later life we were dressed in a marvellous fashion; a piece of yellow nankin would be bought to dress the whole family, like three sticks of barley sugar. Such was the discipline of the day, and nothing could be more ill-judged; it inflicted an amount of torment upon sensitive children which certainly was not intended, but which had the very worst effect.

If we children quarrelled, and turned up our noses at the food in English hotels, what must have been our surprise at the food of an English school? Breakfast at 8 a.m., consisting of very blue milk and water, in chipped and broken-handled mugs of the same colour. The boys were allowed tea from home, but it was a perpetual battle to get a single drink of it. The substantials were a wedge of bread with a glazing of butter. The epicures used to collect the glazing to the end of the slice in order to convert it into a final *bonne bouche.* The dinner at one o'clock began with stickjaw (pudding) and ended with meat, as at all second-rate schools. The latter was as badly cooked as possible, black out and blue inside, gristly and sinewy. The vegetables were potatoes, which could serve for grapeshot, and the hateful carrot. Supper was a repetition of breakfast, and, at an age when boys were making bone and muscle, they went hungry to bed.

Occasionally the pocket-money and tips were clubbed, and a "room" would go in for a midnight feed of a quartern loaf, ham, polony, and saveloys, with a quantity of beer and wine, which generally led to half a dozen fights. Saturday was a day to be feared on account of its peculiar pie, which contained all the waifs and strays of the week. On the Sunday there was an attempt at plum-pudding of a peculiarly pale and leaden hue, as if it had been unjustly defrauded of its due allowance of plums. And this dull routine lasted throughout the scholastic year. School hours were from seven till nine, and ten to one, and three to five, without other changes, save at the approach of the holidays, when a general burst of singing, locally called "challenging," took place. Very few were the schoolfellows we met in after life. The ragged exceptions were Guildford Onslow, the Claimant's friend. Tuckey Baines, as he was called on account of his exploits on Saturday pie, went into the Bombay army, and was as disagreeable and ill-conditioned as when he was a bully at school. He was locally celebrated for hanging the wrong Mahommad, and for his cure for Sindee litigiousness, by making complainant and defendant flog each other in turn. The only schoolboy who did anything worthy, was Bobby Delafosse (who was appointed to the 26th Regiment, N.I.), who showed immense pluck, and died fighting bravely in the Indian Mutiny.

I met him in Bombay shortly before I went off to the North-West Provinces, but my remembrances of the school were so painful, that I could not bear to recognize him. In fact, that part of life, which most boys dwell upon with the greatest pleasure, and concerning which, most autobiographers tell the longest stories—school and college—was ever a nightmare to us. It was like the "Blacking-shop" of Charles Dickens.

Before the year concluded, an attack of measles broke out in the school, several of the boys died, and it was found necessary to disperse the survivors. We were not hard-hearted, but we were delighted to get home. We worked successfully on the fears of Aunt G., which was assisted by my cadaverous appearance, and it was resolved to move us from school, to our infinite joy. My father had also been thoroughly sick of "Maids of Honour Row" and "Richmond Green." He was sighing for shooting and boar-hunting in the French forests, and he felt that he had done quite enough for the education of the boys, which was turning out so badly. He resolved to bring us up abroad, and picked up the necessary assistance for educating us by tutor and governess. Miss Ruxton, a stout red-faced girl, was thoroughly up in the three R's, and was intended to direct Maria's education. Mr. Du Pré, an undergraduate at Exeter College, Oxford, son of the Rector of Berkhampstead, wanted to see life on the Continent, and was not unwilling to see it with a salary. He was an awkward-looking John Bull article, with a narrow forehead, eyes close together, and thick lips, which secured him a perpetual course of caricaturing. He used to hit out hard whenever he found the caricatures, but only added bitterness to them. Before he had been in the family a week, I obliged him with a sketch of his tomb and the following inscription :—

"Stand, passenger! hang down thy head and weep,
A young man from Exeter here doth sleep;
If any one ask who that young man be,
'Tis the Devil's dear friend and companion—Du Pré"—

which was merely an echo of Shakespeare and John à Combe, but it showed a fine sense of independence.

I really caught the measles at school, and was nursed by Grand-mamma Baker in Park Street. It was the only infantine malady that I ever had. The hooping-cough only attacked me on my return from Harrar, when staying with my friend Dr. Steinhaüser at Aden, in 1853. As soon as I was well enough to travel, the family embarked at the Tower Wharf for Boulogne. We boys scandalized every one on board. We shrieked, we whooped, we danced for joy. We shook our fists at the white cliffs, and loudly hoped we should never see them again. We hurrah'd for France, and hooted for England, "The Land on which the Sun ne'er sets—nor rises," till the sailor who was hoisting the Jack, looked upon us as a pair of little monsters. In our delight at getting away from school and the stuffy little island, we had no idea of the disadvantages which the new kind of life would inflict on our future careers. We were too young to know. A man who brings up his family abroad, and who lives there for years, must expect to lose all the friends who could be useful to him when he wishes to start them in life. The conditions of society in England are so complicated, and so artificial, that those who would make their way in the world, especially in public careers, must be broken to it from their earliest day. The future soldiers and statesmen must be prepared by Eton and Cambridge. The more English they are, even to the cut of their hair, the better. In consequence of being brought up abroad, we never thoroughly understood English society, nor did society understand us. And, lastly, it is a *real* advantage to belong to some parish. It is a great thing, when you have won a battle, or explored Central Africa, to be welcomed home by some little corner of the Great World, which takes a pride in your exploits, because they reflect honour upon itself. In the contrary condition you are a waif, a stray; you are a blaze of light, without a focus. Nobody outside your own fireside cares.

No man ever gets on in the world, or rises to the head of affairs, unless he is a representative of his nation. Taking the marking characters of the last few years—Palmerston, Thiers, Cavour, and Bismarck—what were they but simply the types of their various nationalities? In point of intellect Cavour was a first-rate man, Thiers second-rate, Palmerston third-rate, whilst Bismarck was strength, Von Moltke brain. Their success in life was solely owing to their representing the failings, as well as the merits of their several nationalities. Thiers, for instance, was the most thoroughbred possible *épicier*, and yet look at his success. And his death was mourned even in England, and yet he was the bitterest enemy that England ever had. His Chauvinism did more than the Crimean War to abolish the prestige of England. Unhappily for his Chauvinism, it also thoroughly abolished France.

Mr. Du Pré, the tutor, and Miss Ruxton, the governess, had their work cut out for them. They attempted to commence with a strict discipline; for instance, the family passing through Paris lodged at the Hôtel Windsor, and they determined to walk the youngsters out school fashion. The consequence was that when the walk extended to the boulevards, the young ones, on agreement, knowing Paris well, suddenly ran away, and were home long before the unfortunate strangers could find their way, and reported that their unlucky tutor and governess had been run over by an omnibus. There was immense excitement till the supposed victims walked in immensely tired, having wandered over half Paris, not being able to find their way. A scene followed, but the adversaries respected each other more after that day.

The difficulty was now where to colonize. One of the peculiarities of the little English colonies was the unwillingness of their denizens to return to them when once they had left them. My father had been very happy at Tours, and yet he religiously avoided it. He passed through Orleans—a horrid hole, with as many smells as Cologne—and tried to find a suitable country house near it, but in vain; everything seemed to smell of goose and gutter. Then he drifted on to Blois, in those days a kind of home of the British stranger, and there he thought proper to call a halt. At last a house was found on the high ground beyond the city, which, like Tours, lies mainly on the left bank of the river, and where most of the English colonists dwelt. There is no necessity of describing this little bit of England in France, which was very like Tours. When one describes one colony, one describes them all. The notables were Sir Joseph Leeds, Colonel Burnes, and a sister of Sir Stamford Raffles, who lived in the next-door villa, if such a term may be applied to a country house in France in 1831. The only difference from Tours was, there was no celebrated physician, no pack of hounds, and no parson. Consequently service on Sundays had to be read at home by the tutor, and the evening was distinguished by one of Blair's sermons. This was read out by us children, each taking a turn. The discourse was from one of Blair's old three volumes, which appeared to have a soporific effect upon the audience. Soft music was gradually heard proceeding from the nasal organs of father and mother, tutor and governess; and then we children, preserving the same tone of voice, entered into a conversation, and discussed matters, until the time came to a close.

At Blois we were now entering upon our teens; our education was beginning in real earnest. Poor Miss Ruxton soon found her task absolutely impossible, and threw up the service. A school-room was instituted, where time was wasted upon Latin and Greek for six or seven hours a day, besides which there was a French master—one of those obsolete little old men, who called themselves *Professeurs-ès-lettres*, and the great triumph of whose life was that he had read Herodotus in the original. The dancing-master was a large and pompous oldster, of course an *ancien militaire*, whose kit and whose capers were by contrast peculiarly ridiculous, and who quoted at least once every visit, "Oh, Richard! oh, mon roi!" He taught, besides country dances, square and round, the Minuet de la Cour, the Gavotte de Vestris, and a Danse Chinoise, which consisted mainly in turning up thumbs and toes. The only favourite amongst all those professors was the fencing-master, also an old soldier, who had lost the thumb of his right hand in the wars, which of course made him a *gauché* in loose fencing. We boys gave ourselves up with ardour to this study, and passed most of our leisure hours in exchanging thrusts. We soon learned not to neglect the mask: I passed my foil down Edward's throat, and nearly destroyed his uvula, which caused me a good deal of sorrow. The amusements consisted chiefly of dancing at evening parties, we boys choosing the tallest girls, especially a very tall Miss Donovan. A little fishing was to be had, my father being a great amateur. There were long daily walks, swimming in summer, and brass cannons, bought in the toy shops, were loaded to bursting.

The swimming was very easily taught; in the present day boys and girls go to school and learn it like dancing. In our case Mr. Du Pré supported us by a hand under the stomach, taught us how to use our arms and legs, and to manage our breath, after which he withdrew his hand and left us to float as we best could.

This life lasted for a year, till all were thoroughly tired of it. Our father and mother were imperceptibly lapsing into the category of professed invalids, like people who have no other business in life, except to be sick. This was a class exceptionally common in the unoccupied little English colonies that studded the country. It was a far robuster institution than the Parisian invalid, whose object in life was to appear *maladive et souffrante*. The British *malade* consumed a considerable quantity of butcher's meat, but although he or she always saw death in the pot, they had not the moral courage to refuse what disagreed with them. They tried every kind of drug and nostrum known, and answered every advertisement, whether it agreed with their complaint or not. Their *table de nuit* was covered with bottles and gallipots. They dressed themselves three or four times a day for the change of climate, and insensibly acquired a horror of dining out, or passing the evening away from home. They had a kind of rivalry with other invalids; nothing offended them more than to tell them that they were in strong health, and that if they had been hard-worked professionals in England, they would have been ill once a year, instead of once a month. Homœopathy was a great boon to them, and so was hydropathy. So was the grape-cure and all the humbug invented by non-professionals, such as hunger-cure and all that nonsense.

Our parents suffered from asthma, an honest and respectable kind of complaint, which if left to itself, allows you, like gout, to last till your eightieth year, but treated systematically, and with the aid of the doctor, is apt to wear you out. Grandmamma Baker, who came over to Blois, compared them in her homely Scotch fashion to two buckets in a well. She was very wroth with my father, when, remembering the days of his youth, he began to hug the idea of returning to Italy and seeing the sun, and the general conclusion of her philippics ("You'll kill your wife, sir") did not change his resolution. She even insinuated that in the olden day there had been a Sicilian young woman who received the Englishman's pay, and so distributed it as to keep off claims. So Grandmamma Baker was sent off to her beloved England, "whose faults she still loved."

The old yellow chariot was brought out of the dusty coach-house once more, and furbished up, and, after farewell dinners and parties all round, the family turned their back on Blois. The journey was long, being broken by sundry attacks of asthma, and the posting and style of travel were full of the usual discomforts. In crossing over the Tarare a drunken postilion nearly threw one of the carriages over the precipice, and in shooting the Pont de St. Esprit the steamer nearly came to grief under one of the arches. We stayed a short time in Lyons, in those days a perfect den of thieves. From Avignon my tutor and I were driven to the Fountain of Vaucluse, the charming blue well in the stony mountain, and the memories of Petrarch and Laura were long remembered. The driver insisted upon a full gallop, and the protests of the unfortunate Englishman, who declared every quarter of an hour that he was the father of a large family, were utterly disregarded.

The first view of Provence was something entirely new, and the escape was hailed from the flat fields and the long poplar avenues of Central France. Everything, even the most squalid villages, seemed to fall into a picture. It was something like a sun that burst upon the rocks. The olive trees laden with purple fruit were a delight after the apples and pears, and the contrast between the brown rock and the blue Mediterranean, was quite a new sensation. At Marseilles we embarked for Leghorn, which was then, in Italy, very much what Lyons was in France. It was the head-quarters of brigands. Indeed it was reported that a society existed, whose members were pledged to stab their fellow-creatures, whenever they could do it safely. And it was brought to light by the remorse of a son, who had killed his father by mistake. The Grand Duke of Tuscany, with his weak benevolence, was averse to shedding blood, and the worst that these wretches expected was to be dressed in the red or the yellow of the Galeotti, and to sweep the streets and to bully the passenger for *bakshish*. Another unpleasant development was the quantity of vermin,—even the washerwoman's head appeared to be walking off her shoulders. Still there was a touch of Italian art about the place, in the days before politics and polemics had made Italian art, with the sole exception of sculpture, the basest thing on the Continent: the rooms were large, high, and airy, the frescoes on the ceiling were good, and the pictures had not been sold to Englishmen, and replaced by badly coloured daubs, and cheap prints of the illustrated paper type.

After a few days, finding Leghorn utterly unfit to inhabit, my father determined to transfer himself to Pisa. There, after the usual delay, he found a lodging on the wrong side of the Arno—that is to say, the side which does not catch the winter sun—in a huge block of buildings opposite the then highest bridge. Dante's old "Vituperio delle gante" was then the dullest abode known to man, except perhaps his sepulchre. The climate was detestable (Iceland on the non-sunny, Madeira on the sunny side of the river), but the doctors thought it good enough for their patients; consequently it was the hospital of a few sick Britishers upon a large scale. These unfortunates had much better have been left at home instead of being sent to die of discomfort in Tuscany, but there they would have died upon the doctor's hands. The dullness of the place was something preternatural.

The Italians had their own amusements. The principal one was the opera, a perfect den of impurity, where you were choked by the effluvia of *pastrane* or the brigands' cloaks, which descended from grandfather to grandson. The singing, instrumentation, and acting were equally vile, but the Pisani had not the critical ferocity of the Livornesi, who were used to visit the smallest defect with "Torni in iscena, bestia!" The other form of amusement was the conversazione. Here you entered about six o'clock, and found an enormous room, with a dwarf sofa and an avenue of two lines of chairs projecting from it perpendicularly. You were expected to walk through the latter, which were occupied by the young women, to the former, upon which sat the dowagers, and after the three *saluts d'usage* and the compliments of the season, you backed out by the way you came in, and then passed the evening leaning over the back of the chair of the fair dame whose *cavaliere servente* you were supposed to be. Refreshments were an occasional glass of cold water; in luxurious houses there were water ices and sugared wafers. They complain that we English are not happy in society without eating, and I confess that I prefer a good beefsteak to cold water and water ices.

There was no bad feeling between the Italians and English; they simply ignored one another. Nothing could be shadier than the English colony at Pisa. As they had left England, the farther they were the more wretched they became, till they reached the climax at Naples. They had no club, as at Tours, and they met to read their *Gagliani* at a grocer's shop on the Lung' Arno. They had their parson and doctor and their tea-caddies, but the inhospitable nature of the country—and certainly Italy is the least given to the savage virtue—seemed to have affected the strangers. Equally unknown were the dinner-parties of Tours and the hops of Blois. No one shot and no one fished. A madman used to plunge through the ice on the Lung' Arno in midwinter, but most of them contented themselves with promenading the Quai and basking in its wintry sun till they returned to their stuffy rooms. A good many of them were half-pay officers. Others were Jamaican planters, men who had made their fortunes in trade; the rest were nondescripts whom nobody knew. At times some frightful scandal broke out in consequence of some gentleman who had left his country for his country's good.

The discomforts of Pisa were considerable. The only fireplace in those days was a kind of brazier, put in the middle of the room. The servants were perfect savages, who had to be taught the very elements of service, and often at the end of the third day a great burly peasant would take leave, saying, "Non mi basta l'anima!" My father started a fearful equipage in the shape of a four-wheeled trap, buying for the same a hammer-headed brute of a horse which at once obtained the name of "Dobbin." Dobbin was a perfect demon steed, and caused incalculable misery, as every person was supposed to steal his oats. One of us boys was sent down to superintend his breakfast, dinner, and supper. On journeys it was the same, and we would have been delighted to see Dobbin hanged, drawn, and quartered. We tried riding him in private, but the brute used to plant his forelegs and kick up and down like a rocking-horse. The trap was another subject of intense misery. The wheels were always supposed to be wanting greasing, and as the natives would steal the grease, it was necessary that one of us should always superintend the greasing. There is no greater mistake than that of trying to make boys useful by making them do servant's work.

The work of education went on nimbly, if not merrily. To former masters was added an Italian master, who was at once dubbed "Signor No," on account of the energy of his negation. The French master unfortunately discovered that his three pupils had poetic talents; the consequence was that we were set to write versical descriptions, which we hated worse than Telemachus and the *Spectator*.

And a new horror appeared in the shape of a violin master. Edward took kindly to the infliction, worked very hard, and became an amateur almost equal to a professional; was offered fair pay as member of an orchestra in Italy, and kept it up after going into the Army, till the calls of the Mess made it such a nuisance that he gave it up; but took to it again later in life *con amore*. I always hated my fiddle, and after six months it got me into a terrible scrape, and brought the study to an untimely end. Our professor was a thing like Paganini, length without breadth, nerves without flesh, hung on wires, all hair and no brain, except for fiddling. The creature, tortured to madness by a number of false notes, presently addressed his pupil in his grandiloquent Tuscan manner, "Gli altri scolari sono bestie, ma voi siete un Arci-bestia." The "Arci" offended me horribly, and, in a fury of rage, I broke my violin upon my master's head; and then my father made the discovery that his eldest son had no talent for music, and I was not allowed to learn any more.

Amongst the English at Pisa we met with some Irish cousins, whose names had been Conyngham, but they had, for a fortune, very sensibly added "Jones" to it, and who, very foolishly, were ashamed of it ever after. There was a boy, whose face looked as if badly cut out of a half-boiled potato, dotted with freckles so as to resemble a goose's egg. There was a very pretty girl, who afterwards became Mrs. Seaton. The mother was an exceedingly handsome woman of the Spanish type, and it was grand to see her administering correction to "bouldness." They seemed principally to travel in Italy for the purpose of wearing out old clothes, and afterwards delighted in telling how many churches and palaces they had "done" in Rome per diem. The cute Yankee always travels, when he is quite unknown, in his best bib and tucker, reserving his old clothes for his friends who appreciate him. Altogether the C.J.'s were as fair specimens of Northern barbarians invading the South, as have been seen since the days of Brennus.

The summer of '32 was passed at Siena, where a large rambling old house was found inside the walls. The venerable town, whose hospitality was confined to an inscription over the city gate, was perhaps one of the dullest places under heaven. No country in the world shows less hospitality—even Italians amongst themselves—than Italy, and in the case of strangers they have perhaps many reasons to justify their churlishness.

Almost all the English at Siena were fugitives from justice, social or criminal. One man walked off with his friend's wife, another with his purse. There was only one old English lady in the place who was honourable, and that was a Mrs. Russell, who afterwards killed herself with mineral waters. She lived in a pretty little *quinta* outside the town, where moonlight nights were delightful, and where the nightingales were louder than usual. Beyond this amusement we had little to do, except at times to peep at the gate of Palone, to study very hard, and to hide from the world our suits of nankin. The weary summer drew to a close. The long-surviving chariot was brought out, and then Dobbin, with the "cruelty van," was made ready for the march.

Travelling in *vetturino* was not without its charm. It much resembled marching in India during the slow old days. It is true you seldom progressed along more than five miles an hour, and uphill at three. Moreover, the harness was perpetually breaking, and at times a horse fell lame; but you saw the country thoroughly, the *vetturino* knew the name of every house, and you went slowly enough to impress everything upon your memory. The living now was none of the best; food seemed to consist mostly of omelettes and pigeons. The pigeons, it is said, used to desert the dove-cotes every time they saw an English travelling-carriage approaching. And the omelettes showed more hair in them than eggs usually produce. The bread and wine, however, were good, and adulteration was then unknown. The lodging was on a par with the food, and insect powder was not invented or known. Still, taking all in all, it is to be doubted whether we are more comfortable in the Grand Hotel in these days when every hotel is grand, when all mutton is *pré salé*, when all the beer is bitter, when all the sherry is dry.

It was now resolved to pass the Holy Week at Rome, and the only events of the journey, which went on as usual, were the breaking down of Dobbin's "cruelty van" in a village near Perugia, where the tutor and boys were left behind to look after repairs. We long remembered the peculiar evening which we passed there. The head ostler had informed us that there was an opera, and that he was the *primo violino*. We went to the big barn, that formed the theatre. A kind of "Passion play" was being performed, with lengthy intervals of music, and all the mysteries of the faith were submitted to the eyes of the faithful. The only disenchanting detail was, that a dove not being procurable, its place was supplied by a turkey-cock, and the awful gabbling of the ill-behaved volatile caused much more merriment than was decorous.

We, who had already examined Voltaire with great interest, were delighted with the old Etruscan city of Perugia, and were allowed a couple of hours' "leave" to visit Pietro di Aretino's tomb, and we loitered by the Lake Thrasimene.

The march was short, and the family took a house on the north side of the Arno, near the Boboli Gardens, in Florence. The City of Flowers has always had a reputation beyond what it deserved. Though too fair to be looked upon except upon holidays, it has discomforts of its own. The cold, especially during the *Tramontana* blowing from the Appenines, is that of Scotland. The heat during the dog-days, when the stone pavements seem to be fit for baking, reminds one of Cairo during a *Khamsin*, and the rains are at times as heavy and persistent as in Central Africa. The Italians and the English, even in those days, despite all the efforts of the amiable Grand Duke, did not mix well.

Colonies go on as they begin, and the Anglo-Florentine flock certainly has contained, contains, and ever will contain some very black sheep. They were always being divided into cliques. They were perpetually quarrelling. The parson had a terrible life. One of the churchwardens was sure to be some bilious old Indian, and a common character was to be a half-pay Indian officer who had given laws, he said, to millions, who supported himself by gambling, and induced all his cronies to drink hard, the whispered excuse being, that he had shot a man in a duel somewhere. The old ladies were very scandalous. There were perpetual little troubles, like a rich and aged widow being robbed and deserted by her Italian spouse, and resident old gentlemen, when worsted at cards, used to quarrel and call one another liars. Amongst the number was a certain old Dr. Harding who had a large family. His son was sent into the army, and was dreadfully wounded under Sir Charles Napier in Sind. He lived to be Major-General Francis Pim Harding, C.B., and died in 1875.

Another remarkable family was that of old Colonel de Courcy. He had some charming daughters, and I met his son John when he was in the Turkish Contingent and I was Chief of the Staff of Irregular Cavalry in the Crimea.

Still Florence was always Florence. The climate, when it was fine, was magnificent. The views were grand, and the most charming excursions lay within a few hours' walk or drive. The English were well treated, perhaps too well, by the local Government, and the opportunities of studying Art were first-rate. Those wonderful Loggie and the Pitti Palace contained more high Art than is to be found in all London, Paris, Berlin, and Vienna put together, and we soon managed to become walking catalogues. A heavy storm, however, presently broke the serenity of the domestic atmosphere at Siena.

We boys had been allowed to begin regular shooting with an old single-barrelled Manton, a hard-hitter which had been changed from flint to percussion. We practised gunnery in secret every moment we could, and presently gave our tutor a specimen of our proficiency. He had been instituting odious comparisons between Edward's length and that of his gun, and went so far as to say that for sixpence he would allow a shot at fifty yards. On this being accepted with the firm determination of peppering him, he thought it better to substitute his hat, and he got away just in time to see it riddled like a sieve. We then began to despise shooting with small shot.

Our parents made a grand mistake about the shooting excursions, especially the mother, who, frightened lest anything should occur, used to get up quarrels to have an excuse to forbid the shooting parties, as punishment. It was soon found out and resented accordingly.

We hoarded the weekly francs which each received, we borrowed Maria's savings, *i.e.* the poor girl was never allowed to keep it for a day, and invested in what was then known as a "case of pistols." My father—who, when in Sicily with his regiment, had winged a brother-officer, an Irishman, for saying something unpleasant, had carefully and fondly nursed him, and shot him again as soon as ever he recovered, crippling him for life—saw the turn that matters were taking, and ordered the "saw-handles" to be ignominiously returned to the shop. The shock was severe to the *pun d'onor* of we two Don Quixotes.

I have a most pleasant remembrance of Maria Garcia, a charming young girl, before she became wife and "divine devil" to the old French merchant Morbihan. Both she and her sister (afterwards Madame Viardot) were going through severe training under the old Tartar of a father Garcia, who was, however, a splendid musician and determined to see his girls succeed. They tell me she had spites and rages and that manner of thing in after life, but I can only remember her as worthy of Alfred de Musset's charming stanza.

After a slow but most interesting drive we reached the Eternal City, and, like all the world, were immensely impressed by the entrance at the Porto del Popolo. The family secured apartments in the Piazza di Spagna, which was then, as it is now, the capital of English Rome. Everything in it was English, the librarian, the grocer, and all the other little shops, and mighty little it has changed during the third of a century. In 1873, when my wife and I stayed there, the only points of difference observed were the presence of Americans and the large gilded advertisements of the photographers. The sleepy atmosphere was the same, and the same was the drowsy old fountain.

At Rome sight-seeing was carried on with peculiar ardour. With "Mrs. Starke" under the arm, for "Murray" and "Baedeker" were not invented in those days, we young ones went from Vatican to the Capitol, from church to palazzo, from ruin to ruin. We managed to get introductions to the best studios, and made acquaintance with all the shops which contained the best collections of coins, of cameos, of model temples, in rosso-antico, and giallo-antico, and of all the treasures of Roman Art, ancient and modern. We passed our days in running about the town, and whenever we found an opportunity, we made excursions into the country, even ascending Mount Soracte. In those days Rome was not what it is now. It was the ghost of the Imperial City, the mere shadow of the Mistress of the world. The great Forum was a level expanse of ground, out of which the half-buried ruins rose. The Coliseum had not changed for a century. The Palatine hill had never dreamt of excavation. The greater part of the space within the old walls, that represents the ancient City, was a waste, what would in Africa be called bush, and it was believed that turning up the ground caused fatal fevers. It had no pretensions to be a Capital. It wanted fortifications; the walls could be breached with six-pounders. The Tiber was not regulated, and periodically flooded the lower town. The Ghetto was a disgrace. Nothing could be fouler than the Trastevere: and the Leonine City, with the exception of St. Peter's and the Vatican, was a piggery.

At Rome there was then very little society. People met when doing the curiosities, and the principal amusements were conversaziones, when the only conspicuous object was some old Cardinal sitting in red, enthroned upon a sofa. Good old Gregory XVI. did not dislike foreigners, and was even intimate with a certain number of heretics, but *that* could not disperse the sleepy atmosphere of the place, whilst the classes of society were what the satirical French duchesse called, 'une noblesse de Sacrament'—and yet it was the season of the year. Then, as now, the wandering world pressed to Rome to see ceremonies of the Holy Week, to hear the music of the Sistine Chapel, to assist at the annual conversion of a Jew at St. John of Lateran, to walk gaping about at the interior of St. Peter's, and to enjoy the magnificent illuminations, which were spoiled by a high wind, and a flood of rain. Nothing could be more curious than the contrast between the sons of the Holy City and the barbarians from the North, and the far West, when the Pope stood in the balcony delivering his benediction *urbi et orbi*; the English and Irish Catholics seemed to be overwhelmed with awe whilst the Romans delivered themselves of small jokes, very audible withal, upon the mien and the demeanor of the Vecchierello. Inside the great cathedral the crowd used to be of the most pushing kind, and young priests attempted to scale one's shoulders. Protestant ladies consumed furtive sandwiches, and here and there an aged sightseer was thrown down and severely trampled upon. In fact, there was a perfect opposition between the occasion of the ceremony and the way it was carried out.

It was necessary to leave Rome in time to reach Naples before the hot season began, and return to summer quarters. In those days the crossing of the Pontine Marshes was considered not a little dangerous. Heavy breakfasts were eaten to avoid the possible effect of malaria upon an empty stomach, and the condemned pistols were ostentatiously loaded to terrify the banditti, who were mostly the servants and hangers-on of the foul little inns.

At Terracina we found an Englishman temporarily under arrest. This was Mr. St. John, who had just shot in a duel Count Controfiani. The history of the latter was not a little curious. He was a red-haired Neapolitan, extremely plain in appearance, and awkward in manner, but touchy and sensitive in the extreme. His friends and his acquaintances chose to make a butt of him, little fancying how things were going to end. One day he took leave of them all, saying that he was going to travel for some years. He disguised himself with a wig, and hid in the suburbs, practising pistol-shooting, foil, and broadsword. When satisfied with his own progress, he reappeared suddenly in society, and was received with a shout of ironical welcome, "Ecco il nostro bel Controfiani." He slapped the face of the ringleader, and in the duel which followed cut him almost to pieces. After two or three affairs of the kind, his reputation was thoroughly made, even in a City where duelling was so common as Naples. At last, by some mischance, he met St. John at Rome, and the two became intimate. They used to practise pistol-shooting together, and popular report declares that both concealed their game. At last a quarrel arose about some young person, and Controfiani was compelled to fight at the pleasure of a member of the Royal family of Naples, of whose suite he was. The duel was to be *à la barrière*, first shot at twenty-five paces, and leave to advance twelve, after standing the fire. The delay was so great that the seconds began to show signs of impatience, when St. John levelled his pistol, and hit his adversary in the flank, above the hip. Controfiani had the courage to plug his wound with the forefinger of his left hand, and had the folly to attempt advancing, mortally wounded as he was. The movement shook him, his hand was unsteady; his bullet whizzed past St. John's head, and he was dead a few hours later.

The family halted a short while at Capua, then a quiet little country town, equally thoughtless of the honours of the past, or the fierce scenes that waited it in the future; many years afterwards my friend Blakely of the Guns, and I, offered the Government of King Francis, to go out to rifle the cannon, which was to defend them against Garibaldi and his banditti. Unfortunately the offer came too late. It would have been curious had a couple of Englishmen managed, by shooting Garibaldi, to baffle the plans which Lord Pam. had laid with so much astuteness and perseverance.

At Naples a house was found upon the Chiaja, and after trying it for a fortnight, and finding it perfectly satisfactory and agreeing to take it for the next season, the family went over to Sorrento. This, in those days, was one of the most pleasant *villegiature* in Italy. The three little villages that studded the long tongue of rock and fertile soil, were separated from one another by long tracts of orchard and olive ground, instead of being huddled together, as they are now. They preserved all their rural simplicity, baited buffalo-calves in the main squares, and had songs and sayings in order to enrage one another. The villas scattered about the villages were large rambling old shells of houses, and Aunt G. could not open her eyes sufficiently wide when she saw what an Italian villa really was. The bathing was delightful; break-neck paths led down the rocks to little sheltered bays with the yellowest of sands, and the bluest of waters, and old smugglers' caves, which gave the coolest shelter after long dips in the tepid seas. There was an immense variety of excursion. At the root of the tongue arose the Mountain of St. Angelo, where the snow harvest, lasting during summer, was one perpetual merry-making. There were boating trips to Ischia, to Procida, to romantic Capri, with its blue grotto and purple figs, to decayed Salerno, the splendid ruin, and to the temples of Pæstum, more splendid still. The shooting was excellent during the quail season; tall poles and immense nets formed a *chevaux de frise* on the hilltops, but the boys went to windwards, and shot the birds before they were trapped in the nets, in the usual ignoble way. In fact, nothing could be more pleasant than Sorrento in its old and uncivilized days. Amongst the amusements at Sorrento, we indulged ourselves with creeping over the Natural Arch, simply because the Italians said, "Ma non è possibile, Signorini." It was a dangerous proceeding, as the crumbling stone was ready at every moment to give way.

Amongst other classical fads, we boys determined to imitate Anacreon and Horace. We crowned ourselves with myrtle and roses, chose the prettiest part of the garden, and caroused upon the best wine we could afford, out of cups, disdaining to use glasses. Our father, aware of this proceeding, gave us three bottles of sherry, upon the principle that the grocer opens to the young shopboy his drawers of figs and raisins. But we easily guessed the meaning of the kind present, and contented ourselves with drinking each half a bottle a day, as long as it lasted, and then asked for more, to the great disgust of the donor. We diligently practised pistol-shooting, and delighted in cock-fighting, at which the tutor duly attended. Of course the birds fought without steel, but it was a fine game-breed, probably introduced of old by the Spaniards. It not a little resembles the Derby game-cock, which has spread itself half over South America.

There was naturally little variety in amusements. The few English families lived in scattered villas. Old Mrs. Starke, Queen of Sorrento, as she loved to be called, and the authoress of the guide book, was the local "lion," and she was sketched and caricatured in every possible way in her old Meg Merrilies' cloak. Game to the last, she died on the road travelling. An Englishman, named Sparkes, threw himself into one of the jagged volcanic ravines that seam the tongue of Sorrento; but there is hardly a place in Italy, high or low, where some Englishman has not suicided himself. A painter, a Mr. Inskip, brought over an introduction, and was very tipsy before dinner was half over. The Marsala wine supplied by Iggulden & Co. would have floored Polyphemus. The want of excitement out of doors, produced a correspondent increase of it inside. We were getting too old to be manageable, and Mr. Du Pré taking high grounds on one occasion, very nearly received a good thrashing. My father being a man of active mind, and having nothing in the world to do, began to be unpleasantly chemical; he bought Parke's "Catechism;" filled the house with abominations of all kinds, made a hideous substance that he called soap, and prepared a quantity of filth that he called citric acid, for which he spoiled thousands of lemons. When his fit passed over it was succeeded by one of chess, and the whole family were bitten by it. Every spare hour, especially in the evening, was given to check and checkmating, and I soon learned to play one, and then two games, with my eyes blindfolded. I had the sense, however, to give it up completely, for my days were full of Philidor, and my dreams were of gambits all night.

The dull life was interrupted by a visit from Aunt G. She brought with her a Miss Morgan, who had been governess to the three sisters, and still remained their friend. She was a woman of good family in Cornwall, but was compelled, through loss of fortune, to take service.

Miss Morgan was very proud of her nephew, the Rev. Morgan Cowie, who was senior Wrangler at Cambridge. He had had the advantage of studying mathematics in Belgium, where in those days the entering examination of a College was almost as severe as the passing examination of an English College. She was also very well read, and she did not a little good in the house. She was the only one who ever spoke to us children as if we were reasonable beings, instead of scolding and threatening with the usual parental brutality of *those days*. That unwise saying of the wise man, "Spare the rod and spoil the child," has probably done more harm to the junior world than any other axiom of the same size, and it is only of late years that people have begun to "spoil the rod and spare the child." So Miss Morgan could do with the juniors what all the rest of the house completely failed in doing. The only thing that was puzzling about her was, that she could not play at Chess. Aunt G. waxed warm in defence of her friend, and assured the scoffers that "Morgan, with her fine mind, would easily learn to beat the whole party." "Fine mind!" said the scoffers. "Why, we would give her a Queen."

Naples after Sorrento was a Paris. In those days it was an exceedingly pleasant City, famous as it always has been for some of the best cooks in Italy. The houses were good, and the servants and the provisions were moderate. The Court was exceedingly gay, and my father found a cousin there, old Colonel Burke, who was so intimate with the King, known as "Old Bomba," as to be admitted to his bedroom. There was also another Irish cousin, a certain Mrs. Phayre, who for many years had acted duenna to the Miss Smiths (Penelope and Gertrude). Penelope had always distinguished herself in Paris by mounting wild horses in the Bois de Boulogne, which ran away with her, and shook her magnificent hair loose. She became a favourite at the Court of Naples, and amused the dull royalties with her wild Irish tricks. It is said that, on one occasion, she came up with a lift instead of the expected *vol au vent*, or pudding. She ended by marrying the Prince of Capua, greatly to the delight of the King, who found an opportunity of getting rid of his brother, and put an end to certain scandals. It was said that the amiable young Prince once shot an old man, whom he found gathering sticks in his grounds, and on another occasion that he was soundly thrashed by a party of English grooms, whom he had insulted in his cups. The happy pair had just run away and concluded the "triple alliance," as it was called (this is a marriage in three different ways, in order to make sure of it; Protestant, Catholic, and Civil), when our family settled in Naples, and they found Mrs. Phayre and Gertrude Smith, the other sister, in uncomfortable State, banished by the Court, and harassed by the police. All their letters had been stopped at the post-office, and they had had no news from home for months. My father saw them carefully off to England, where Gertrude, who had a very plain face and a very handsome figure, presently married the rich old Lord Dinorben. Poor Miss Morgan also suffered considerably at Naples from the stoppage of all her letters; she being supposed at least to be a sister of Lady Morgan, the "wild Irish girl," whose writings at that time had considerably offended the Italian Court.

Naples was perhaps the least strict of all the Italian cities, and consequently it contained a colony, presided over by the Hon. Mrs. Temple, Lady Eleanor Butler, Lady Strachan, and Berkeley Craven, who would somewhat have startled the proprieties of another place. The good-natured Minister was the Hon. Mr. Temple, Lord Palmerston's brother, who cared nothing for a man's catechism provided he kept decently clear of scandal. The Secretary of Legation was a Mr. Kennedy, who married a Miss Briggs, and died early. These were great friends of the family. On the other hand, the Consul, Captain Galway, R.N., was anything but pleasant. He was in a perpetual state of rile because his Consular service prevented his being received at Court; moreover, he heard (possibly correctly) that Mrs. Phayre and her two *protégées* were trying to put Colonel Burton in his place. He was also much troubled by his family, and one of them (the parson) especially troubled him. This gentleman having neglected to provide for a young Galway whose mamma he had neglected to marry, the maternal parent took a position outside the church, and as the congregation streamed out, cried in a loud voice, pointing to the curate, "Him the father of my child." Another element of confusion at Naples was poor Charley Savile, Lord Mexborough's son, who had quarrelled himself out of the Persian Legation. He was a good hand with his sword, always ready to fight, and equally ready to write. He always denied that he had written and sent about some verses which all Naples attributed to him, and they were certainly most scandalous. Of one lady he wrote—

> "Society courts her, wicked old sinner,
> Yet what won't man do for the sake of a dinner?"

Of another he wrote—

> "You look so demure, ma'am,
> So pious, so calm,
> Always chanting a hymn,
> Or singing a psalm.
> Yet your thoughts are on virtue and heav'n no more
> Than the man in the moon—you dreadful young bore."

This pasquinade led to some half-dozen challenges and duels. It was severe, but not worse than society deserved. Naples has never been strict; and about the forties it was, perhaps, the most dissolute City on the Continent. The natives were bad, but the English visitors were worse. In fact, in some cases their morals were unspeakable.

There was a charming family of the name of Oldham. The father, when an English officer serving in Sicily, had married one of the beauties of the island, a woman of high family and graceful as a Spaniard. The children followed suit. The girls were beautiful, and the two sons were upwards of six feet in height, and were as handsome men as could well be seen. They both entered the army. One, in the 2nd Queen's, was tortured to death by the Kaffirs when his cowardly soldiers ran away, and left him wounded. The other, after serving in the 86th in India, was killed in the light cavalry charge of Balakalava. The families became great friends, and I met them both in India.

Naples was a great place for excursions. To the north you had Ischia and the Solfatara, a miniature bit of Vulcanism somewhat like the Geyser ground in Iceland, where ignoramuses thought themselves in the midst of untold volcanic grandeur. Nothing could be more snobbish than the visit to the Grotto del Cane, where a wretched dog was kept for the purpose of being suffocated half a dozen times a day. There I was determined to act dog, and was pulled up only in time to prevent being thoroughly asphyxiated. The Baths of Nero are about equal to an average Turkish *Hammám*, but nothing more. To the south the excursions were far more interesting.

Beyond Herculaneum, dark and dingy, lay Pompeii, in those days very different from the tame Crystal Palace affair that it is now. You engaged a cicerone as best you could; you had nothing to pay because there were no gates; you picked up what you liked, in shapes of bits of mosaic, and, if you were a swell, a house or a street was opened up in your honour. And overlaying Pompeii stood Vesuvius, which was considered prime fun. The walking up the ash cone amongst a lot of seniors, old men dragged up by *lazzaroni*, and old women carried up in baskets upon *lazzaroni's* backs, was funny enough, but the descent was glorious. What took you twenty minutes to go up took four minutes to go down. Imagine a dustbin magnified to ten thousand, and tilted up at an angle of thirty-five degrees; in the descent you plunged with the legs to the knees, you could not manage to fall unless you hit a stone, and, arrived at the bottom, you could only feel incredulous that it was possible to run at such a rate. We caused no end of trouble, and I was found privily attempting to climb down the crater, because I had heard that an Englishman had been let down in a basket. Many of these ascents were made; on one occasion during an eruption, when the lava flowed down to the sea, and the Neapolitans with long pincers were snatching pieces out of it to stamp and sell, we boys, to the horror of all around, jumped on the top of the blackening fire stream, burnt our boots, and vilely abused all those who would not join us.

At Naples more was added to the work of education. Caraccioli, the celebrated marine painter, was engaged to teach oil-painting; but he was a funny fellow, and the hours which should have been spent in exhausting palettes passed in pencil-caricaturing of every possible friend and acquaintance. The celebrated Cavalli was the fencing-master; and in those days the Neapolitan school, which has now almost died out, was in its last bloom. It was a thoroughly business-like affair, and rejected all the elegances of the French school; and whenever there was a duel between a Neapolitan and a Frenchman, the former was sure to win. We boys worked at it heart and soul, and generally managed to give four hours a day to it. I determined, even at that time, to produce a combination between the Neapolitan and the French school, so as to supplement the defects of the one by the merits of the other. A life of very hard work did not allow me any leisure to carry out my plan; but the man of perseverance stores up his resolve, and waits for any number of years till he sees the time to carry it out. The plan was made in 1836, and was completed in 1880 (forty-four years).*

My father spared no pains or expense in educating his children. He had entered the army at a very early age. Volunteers were called for in Ireland, and those who brought a certain number into the field received commissions gratis. The old Grandmamma

* "The Sword," in three large works nobly planned out, when after the first part was brought out, death frustrated the other two.—I. B.

Burton's tenants' sons volunteered by the dozen. They formed a very fair company, and accompanied the young master to the wars; and when the young master got his commission, they all, with the exception of one or two, levanted, bolted, and deserted. Thus my father found himself an officer at the age of seventeen, when he ought to have been at school; and recognizing the deficiencies of his own education, he was determined that his children should complain of nothing of the kind. He was equally determined they none of them should enter the army; the consequence being that both the sons became soldiers, and the only daughter married a soldier. Some evil spirit, probably Mr. Du Pré, whispered that the best plan for the boys would be to send them to Oxford, in order that they might rise by literature, an idea which they both thoroughly detested. However, in order to crush their pride, they were told that they should enter "Oxford College as sizars, poor gentlemen who are supported by the alms of the others." Our feelings may be imagined. We determined to enlist, or go before the mast, or to turn Turks, banditti, or pirates, rather than undergo such an indignity.

Parthenope was very beautiful; but so true is English blood, that the most remarkable part of it was "Pickwick," who happened to make his way there at the time of the sojourn of our family. We read with delight the description of the English home. We passed our nights, as well as our days, devouring the book, and even "Ettore Fieramosca" and the other triumphs of Massimo d'Azelio were mere outsiders compared with it; but how different the effect of the two books—"Pickwick," the good-humoured caricature of a boy full of liquor and good spirits, and the "Disfida di Barletta," one of the foundation-stones of Italian independence.

At last the house on the Chiaja was given up, and the family took a house inside the City for a short time. The father was getting tired and thinking of starting northwards. The change was afflicting. The loss of the view of the Bay was a misfortune. The only amusement was prospecting the streets, where the most extraordinary scenes took place. It was impossible to forget a beastly Englishman, as he stood eating a squirting orange surrounded by a string of gutter-boys. The dexterity of the pickpockets, too, gave scenes as amusing as a theatre. It was related of one of the Coryphæi that he had betted with a friend that he would take the pocket-handkerchief of an Englishman, who had also betted that no man born in Naples could pick his pocket. A pal walked up to the man as he was promenading the streets, flower in button-hole, solemnly spat on his cravat, and ran away. The principal, with thorough Italian politeness, walked up to the outraged foreigner, drew his pocket-handkerchief and proceeded to remove the stain, exhorted the outraged one to keep the fugitive in sight, and in far less time than it takes to tell, transferred the handkerchief to his own pocket, and set out in pursuit of the *barbaro.*

The *lazzaroni,* too, were a perpetual amusement. We learned to eat maccaroni like them, and so far mastered their dialect, that we could exchange chaff by the hour. In 1869 I found them all at Monte Video and Buenos Ayres, dressed in *cacciatore* and swearing "M'nnaccia l'anima tua;" they were impressed with a conviction that I was myself a *lazzarone* in luck. The shady side of the picture was the cholera. It caused a fearful destruction, and the newspapers owned to 1300 a day, which meant say 2300. The much-abused King behaved like a gentleman. The people had determined that the cholera was poison, and doubtless many made use of the opportunity to get rid of husbands and wives and other inconvenient relationships; but when the mob proceeded to murder the doctors, and to gather in the market square with drawn knives, declaring that the Government had poisoned the provisions, the King himself drove up in a phaeton and jumped out of it entirely alone, told them to put up their ridiculous weapons, and to show him where the poisoned provisions were, and, seating himself upon a bench, ate as much as his stomach would contain. Even the *lazzarone* were not proof against this heroism, and viva'd and cheered him to his heart's content.

My brother and I had seen too much of cholera to be afraid of it. We had passed through it in France, it had followed us to Siena and Rome, and at Naples it only excited our curiosity. We persuaded the Italian man-servant to assist us in a grand escapade. He had procured us the necessary dress, and when the dead-carts passed round in the dead of the night, we went the rounds with them as some of the *croquemorts.* The visits to the pauper houses, where the silence lay in the rooms, were anything but pleasant, and still less the final disposal of the bodies. Outside Naples was a large plain, pierced with pits, like the silos or underground granaries of Algeria and North Africa. They were lined with stone, and the mouths were covered with one big slab, just large enough to allow a corpse to pass. Into these flesh-pots * were thrown the unfortunate bodies of the poor, after being stripped of the rags which acted as their winding-sheets. Black and rigid, they were thrown down the apertures like so much rubbish, into the festering heap below, and the decay caused a kind of lambent blue flame about the sides of the

* There are three hundred and sixty-five of these pits, one for every day in the year.—I. B.

pit, which lit up a mass of human corruption, worthy to be described by Dante.

Our escapades, which were frequent, were wild for strictly brought up Protestant English boys—they would be nothing now, when boys do so much worse—but there were others that were less excusable. Behind the Chiaja dwelt a multitude of syrens, who were naturally looked upon as the most beautiful of their sex. One lady in particular responded to the various telegraphic signs made to her from the flat terrace of the house, and we boys determined to pay her a visit. Arming ourselves with carving-knives, which we stuffed behind our girdles, we made our way jauntily into the house, introduced ourselves, and being abundant in pocket-money, offered to stand treat, as the phrase is, for the whole neighbourhood. The orgie was tremendous, and we were only too lucky to get home unhurt, before morning, when the Italian servant let us in. The result was a correspondence, consisting in equal parts of pure love on our side and extreme debauchery on the syrens'. These letters, unfortunately, were found by our mother during one of her Sunday visitations to our chambers. A tremendous commotion was the result. Our father and his dog, Mr. Du Pré, proceeded to condign punishment with the horsewhip; but we climbed up to the tops of the chimneys, where the seniors could not follow us, and refused to come down till the crime was condoned.

This little business disgusted our father of Naples, and he resolved to repair to a pure moral air. Naples is a very different place now; so is all the Italy frequented by travellers, and spoiled by railways and officialdom.

In 1881 a distinguished officer, and a gentleman allied to Royalty, wrote as follows: "You threw some doubts on the efficiency of the Italian posts, and I believe you; I don't think I was ever so glad to get home. At Malta it looks so clean after the filth of Naples. I think Italy, the Italians, their manners, customs, and institutions, more damnable every time I see them, and feel sure you will meet with less annoyance during your travels on the Gold Coast, than I met with coming through Italy. Trains crowded, unpunctual; starvation, filth, incivility, and extortion at every step; and, were it not that there are so many works of art and of interest to see, I doubt if any one would care to visit the country a second time."

(Here is an account of a purchase made to transfer home.) "A small table was packed in a little case, and firmly nailed down. At the station they refused to let it go in the luggage van, unless it were corded, *lest it might be opened en route.* The officials offered to cord it for *bakshish,* which was paid, but the cord not put on. They cut open my leather bag, and tried to open my portmanteau, but when I called this fact to the notice of the station-master at Rome, he simply turned on his heel and declined to answer. At Naples they opened the little case, because furniture was subject to octroi; and, on leaving, the case was again inspected, lest it might contain a picture (they were not allowed to leave the country)." It is no longer the classical Italy of Landor, nor the romantic Italy of Leigh Hunt, nor the ideal Italy of the Brownings, nor the spiritualized Italy of George Eliot, nor the everyday Italy of Charles Lever. They thought they were going to be everything when they changed Masters, but they have only succeeded in making it a noisy, vulgar, quarrelsome and contentious, arrogant, money-grasping Italy, and the sooner it receives a sound drubbing from France or Austria the better for it. It will then reform itself.

The family left Naples in the spring of 1836. The usual mountain of baggage was packed in the enormous boxes of the period, and the Custom House officers never even opened them, relying, as they said—and did in those good old days—upon the word of an Englishman, that they contained nothing contraband. How different from the United Italy, where even the dressing-bag is rummaged to find a few cigars, or an ounce of coffee. The voyage was full of discomforts. My mother, after a campaign of two or three years, had been persuaded to part with her French maid Eulalie, an old and attached servant, who made our hours bitter, and our faces yellow. The steamer of the day was by no means a floating palace, especially the English coasting steamers, which infested the Mediterranean. The machinery was noisy and offensive. The cabins were dog-holes, with a pestiferous atmosphere, and the food consisted of greasy butter, bread which might be called dough, eggs with a perfume, rusty bacon, milkless tea and coffee, that might be mistaken for each other, waxy potatoes, graveolent greens *cuite à l'eau*, stickjaw pudding, and cannibal haunches of meat, charred without, and blue within.

The only advantage was that the vessels were manned by English crews, and in those days the British sailor was not a tailor, and he showed his value when danger was greatest.

We steamed northwards in a good old way, puffing and panting, pitching and rolling, and in due time made Marseille.

The town of the Canebière was far from being the splendid City that it is now, but it always had one great advantage, that of being in Provence. I always had a particular propensity for this bit of Africa in Europe, and in after life in India for years, my greatest friend, Dr. Steinhaüser, and myself indulged in visions of a country cottage, where we would pass our days in hammocks, and our nights in bed, and never admit books or papers, pens or ink, letters or telegrams. This retreat was intended to be a rest for middle age, in order to prepare for senility and second childhood. But this vision passed into the limbo of things imagined (in fact, the vision of two hard-working and overworked men), and I little thought that at fifty-five I should be a married man, still in service, still knocking about the world, working hard with my wife, and poor Steinhaüser dead fifteen years ago.

To return. However agreeable Provence was, the change from Italians to French was not pleasant. The subjects of Louis Philippe, the Citizen-King, were rancorous against Englishmen, and whenever a fellow wanted to get up a row he had only to cry out, "These are the *misérables* who poisoned Napoleon at St. Helena." This pleasant little scene occurred on board a coasting steamer, between Marseille and Cette, when remonstrance was made with the cheating steward, backed by the rascally captain. Cette was beginning to be famous for the imitation wines composed by the ingenuity of Monsieur Guizot, brother of the *austère intrigant.* He could turn out any wine, from the cheapest Marsala to the choicest Madeiran Bual.

But he did his counterfeiting honestly, as a little "G" was always branded on the bottom of the cork, and Cette gave a good lesson about ordering wines at hotels. The sensible traveller, when in a strange place, always calls for the *carte*, and chooses the cheapest; he knows by sad experience, by cramp and acidity of stomach, that the dearest wines are often worse than the cheapest, and at best that they are the same with different labels. The proprietor of the hotel at Cette, had charged his *dâme de comptoir* with robbing the till. She could not deny it, but she replied with a *tu quoque:* "If I robbed you I only returned tit for tat. You have been robbing the public for the last quarter of a century, and only the other day you brought a bottle of ordinaire and *escamoté*'d it into sixteen kinds of *vins fin.*" The landlord thought it better to drop the proceedings. From Cette we travelled in hired carriages (as Dobbin and the carriages had been sold at Naples) to Toulouse. We stayed at Toulouse for a week, and I was so delighted with student life there, that I asked my father's leave to join them. But he was always determined on the Fellowship at Oxford. Our parents periodically fell ill with asthma, and we young ones availed ourselves of the occasion, by wandering far and wide over the country. We delighted in these journeys, for though the tutor was there, the books were in the boxes. My chief remembrances of Toulouse were, finding the mistress of the hotel correcting her teeth with *table d'hôte* forks, and being placed opposite the model Englishman of Alexandre Dumas and Eugène Sue. The man's face never faded from my memory. Carroty hair, white and very smooth forehead, green eyes, a purple-reddish lower face, whiskers that had a kind of crimson tinge, and an enormous mouth worn open, so as to show the protruding teeth.

In due time we reached Pau in the Pyrenees, the capital of the Basses Pyrénées, and the old Bearnais. The little town on the Gave de Pau was no summer place. The heats are intense, and all who can, rush off to the Pyrenees, which are in sight, and distant only forty miles. Our family followed suit, and went off to Bagnières de Bigorres, where we hired a nice house in the main Square. There were few foreigners in the Bagnières de Bigorres; it was at that time a thoroughly French watering-place. It was invaded by a mob of Parisians of both sexes, the men dressed in fancy costumes intended to be "truly rural," and capped with Basque bonnets, white or red. The women were more wonderful still, especially when on horse-back; somehow or other the Française never dons a riding-habit without some solecism. Picnics were the order of the day, and they were organized on a large scale, looking more like a squadron of cavalry going out for exercise than a party of pleasure. We boys obtained permission to accompany one of those caravans to the Brêche de Roland, a nick in the mountain top clearly visible from the plains, and supposed to have been cut by the good sword "Joyeuse."

Here we boys were mightily taken with, and tempted to accept the offer made to us by, a merry party of *contrabandistas*, who were smuggling to and fro chocolate, tobacco, and *aguardienta* (spirits). Nothing could be jollier than such a life as these people lead. They travelled *au clair de la lune*, armed to the teeth; when they arrived at the hotels the mules were unloaded and turned out to grass, the guitar, played *à la Figaro*, began to tinkle, and all the young women, like "the Buffalo girls," came out to dance. Wine and spirits flowed freely, the greatest good humour prevailed, and the festivities were broken only sometimes by "knifing or shooting."

We also visited Tarbes, which even in those days was beginning to acquire a reputation for "le shport;" it presently became one of the centres of racing and hunting in France, for which the excellent climate and the fine rolling country admirably adapted it. It was no wonder that the young French horse beat the English at the same age. In the Basque Pyrénées a colt two years old is as well grown as a Newmarket weed at two and a half.

When the great heat was over, the family returned to Pau, where they found a good house over the arcade in the Place Gramont. Pau boasts of being the birthplace of Henry IV., Gaston de Foix, and Bernadotte. Strangers go through the usual routine of visiting the Castle, called after the Protestant-Catholic King, Henry IV.; driving to Ortez, where Marshal Soult fought unjustifiably the last action of the Peninsular War; and of wandering about the flat, moor-like *landes*, which not a little resemble those about Bordeaux. The society at Pau was an improvement upon that of Naples. The most remarkable person was Captain (R.N.) Lord William Paget, who was living with his mother-in-law (Baroness de Rothenberg), and his wife and children, and enjoying himself as usual. Though even impecunious, he was the best of boon companions, and a man generally loved. But he could also make himself feared, and, as the phrase is, would stand no nonsense. He had a little affair with a man whom we will call Robinson, and as they were going to the meeting-place he said to his second, "What's the fellow's pet pursuit?" "Well!" answered the other, "I don't know —but, let me see—ah, I remember, a capital hand at waltzing." "Waltzing!" said Lord William, and hit him accurately on the hip-bone, which spoilt his saltations for many a long month. Years and years after, when both were middle-aged men, I met at Shepherd's Hotel, Cairo, his son, the boy whom I remembered straddling across a diminutive donkey—General Billy Paget. He had also entered the Anglo-Indian army, and amongst other things had distinguished himself by getting the better (in an official correspondence) of General John Jacob, the most obstinate and rancorous of men. "Billy" had come out to Egypt with the intention of returning to India, but the Red Sea looked so sweltering hot and its shores so disgustingly barren, that he wrote to Aden to recall his luggage, which had been sent forward, then and there retired from the service, married a charming woman, and gave his old friends a very excellent dinner in London.

There were also some very nice L'Estranges, one of the daughters a very handsome woman, some pretty Foxes, an old Captain Sheridan, with two good-looking daughters, and the Ruxtons, whom we afterwards met at Pisa and the Baths of Lucca. Certain elderly maidens of the name of Shannon lived in a house almost overhanging the Gave de Pau. Upon this subject O'Connell, the Agitator, produced a *bon mot*, which is, however, not fit for the drawing-room. Pau was still a kind of invalid colony for consumptives, although the native proverb about its climate is, "that it has eight months winter, and four of the Inferno." Dr. Diaforus acts upon the very intelligible system of self-interest. He does not wish his patients to die upon his hands, and consequently he sends them to die abroad. In the latter part of the last century he sent his moribunds to Lisbon and to Montpellier, where the *vent de bise* is as terrible as a black east wind is in Harwich.

Then he packed them off to Pisa, where the tropics and Norway meet, and to damp, muggy, reeking Madeira, where patients have lived a quarter of a century with half a lung, but where their sound companions and nurses suffer from every description of evil which attend biliousness. They then found out that the dry heat of Teneriffe allowed invalids to be out after sunset, and, lastly, they discovered that the dry cold of Canada and Iceland, charged with ozone, offers the best chance of a complete cure. I proposed to utilize the regions about the beautiful Dead Sea, about thirteen hundred feet below the level of the Mediterranean, where oxygen accumulates, and where, run as hard as you like, you can never be out of breath. This will be the great Consumptive Hospital of the future.

At Pau the education went on merrily. I was provided with a French master of mathematics, whose greasy hair swept the collar of the *redingote* buttoned up to the chin. He was a type of his order. He introduced mathematics everywhere. He was a red republican of the reddest, hating rank and wealth, and he held that *Le Bon Dieu* was not proven, because he could not express Him by a mathematical formula, and he called his fellow-men *Bon-Dieusistes.* We were now grown to lads, and began seriously to prepare for thrashing our tutor, and diligently took lessons in boxing from the Irish groom of a Captain Hutchinson, R.N. Whenever we could escape from study we passed our hours in the barracks, fencing with the soldiers, and delighting every *piou-piou* (recruit) by our powers of consuming the country spirit (the white and unadulterated cognac). We also took seriously to smoking, although, as usual with beginners in those days, we suffered in the flesh. In the later generation, you find young children, even girls, who, although their parents have never smoked, can finish off a cigarette without the slightest inconvenience, even for the first time.

Smoking and drinking led us, as it naturally does, into trouble. There was a Jamaica Irishman with a very dark skin and a very loud brogue, called Thomas, who was passing the winter for the benefit of his chest at Pau. He delighted in encouraging us for mischief sake. One raw snowy day he gave us his strongest cigars, and brewed us a bowl of potent steaming punch, which was soon followed by another. Edward, not being very well, was unusually temperate, and so I, not liking to waste it, drank for two. A walk was then maliciously proposed, and the cold air acted as usual as stimulant to stimulant. Thomas began laughing aloud, Edward plodded gloomily along, and I got into half a dozen scrimmages with the country people. At last matters began to look serious, and the too hospitable host took his two guests back to their home. I managed to stagger upstairs; I was deadly pale, with staring eyes, and compelled to use the depressed walk of a monkey, when I met my mother. She was startled at my appearance, and as I pleaded very sick she put me to bed. But other symptoms puzzled her. She fetched my father, who came to the bedside, looked carefully for a minute at his son and heir, and turned upon his heel, exclaiming, "The beast's in liquor." The mother burst into a flood of tears, and next morning presented me with a five-franc piece, making me promise to be good for the future, and not to read Lord Chesterfield's "Letters to his Son," of which she had a dreadful horror. It need hardly be said that the five francs soon melted away in laying in a stock of what is popularly called "a hair of the dog that bit."

What we learnt last at Pau was the Bearnais dialect. It is a charmingly naïve dialect, mixture of French, Spanish, and Provençale, and containing a quantity of pretty, pleasant songs. The country folk were delighted when addressed in their own lingo. It considerably assisted me in learning Provençale, the language of Le Geysaber; and I found it useful in the most out-of-the-way corners of the world, even in Brazil. Nothing goes home to the heart of a man so much as to speak to him in his own *patois*. Even a Lancashire lad can scarcely resist the language of "Tummas and Mary."

At length the wheezy, windy, rainy, foggy, sleety, snowy winter passed away, and the approach of the warm four months, warned strangers to betake themselves to the hills. This time the chosen place was Argélés. In those days it was a little village, composed mainly of one street, not unlike mining Arrayal in Brazil, or a negro village on the banks of the Gaboon. But the scenery around it was beautiful. It lay upon a brawling stream, and the contrast of the horizontal meadow-lands around it, with the backing of almost vertical hills and peaks, thoroughly satisfied the eye. It had cruel weather in winter time, and a sad accident had just happened. A discharged soldier had reached it in midwinter, when the snow lay deep and the wolves were out, and the villagers strongly dissuaded him from trying to reach his father's home in the hills. He was armed with his little *briquet*, the little curved sword then carried by the French infantry soldiers, and he laughed all caution to scorn. It was towards nightfall; he had hardly walked a mile, before a pack came down upon him, raging and ravening with hunger. He put his back to a tree, and defended himself manfully, killing several wolves, and escaped whilst the carcases were being devoured by their companions; but he sheathed his sword without taking the precaution to wipe it, and when he was attacked again it was glued to the scabbard. The wolves paid dearly for their meal, for the enraged villagers organized a battue, and killed about a score of them as an expiatory sacrifice for the poor soldier.

We two brothers, abetted by our tutor, had fallen into the detestable practice of keeping our hands in by shooting swifts and swallows, of which barbarity we were afterwards heartily ashamed. Our first lesson was from the peasants. On one occasion, having shot a harmless bird that fell among the reapers, the latter charged us in a body, and being armed with scythes and sickles, caused a precipitous retreat. In those days the swallow seemed to be a kind of holy bird in the Bearnais, somewhat like the pigeons of Mecca and Venice. I can only remember that this was the case with old Assyrians and Aramæans, who called the swift or devilling the destiny, or foretelling bird, because it heralded the spring.

There was a small society at Argèlès, consisting chiefly of English and Spaniards. The latter were mostly refugees, driven away from home by political changes. They were not overburdened with money, and of course looked for cheap quarters. They seemed chiefly to live upon chocolate, which they made in their own way, in tiny cups so thick and gruelly, that sponge-cake stood upright in it. They smoked cigarettes with maize-leaf for paper, as only a Spaniard can. The little cylinder hangs down as if it were glued to the smoker's lower lip. He goes on talking and laughing, and then, by some curious movement of a muscle developed in no other race, he raises the weed to the horizontal and puffs out a cloud of smoke. They passed their spare time in playing the guitar and singing party songs, and were very much disgusted when asked to indulge the company with Riego el Cid. There was a marriage at Argèlès, when a Scotch maiden of mature age married M. Le Maire, an old French *mousquetaire*, a man of birth, of courtly manners, and who was the delight of the young ones, but his *plaisanteries* are utterly unfit for the drawing-room. There was also a Baron de Meydell, his wife, her sister, and two very handsome daughters. The eldest was engaged to a rich young planter in the Isle of Bourbon. We two lads of course fell desperately in love with them, and the old father, who had served in the Hessian Brigade in the English army, only roared with laughter when he saw and heard our *polissoneries*. The old man liked us both, and delighted in nothing more than to see us working upon each other with foil and sabre. The parting of the four lovers was something very sad, and three of us at least shed tears. The eldest girl was beyond such childishness.

As the mountain fog began to roll down upon the valley, our father found that his poor chest required a warmer climate. This time we travelled down the Grand Canal du Midi in a big public barge, which resembled a Dutch *trekschuyt.* At first, passing through the locks was a perpetual excitement, but this very soon palled. The L'Estranges were also on board, and the French part of the company were not particularly pleasant. They were mostly tourists returning home, mixed with a fair proportion of *commis-voyageurs,* a class that corresponds with, but does not resemble, our commercial traveller. The French species seems to have but two objects in social life : first, to glorify himself, and secondly, to glorify Paris.

Monsieur Victor Hugo has carried the latter mania to the very verge of madness, and left to his countrymen an example almost as bad as bad can be. The peculiarity of the *commis-voyageur* in those days, was the queer thin varnish of politeness, which he thought it due to himself to assume. He would help himself at breakfast or dinner to the leg, wing, and part of the breast, and pass the dish to his neighbour when it contained only a neck and a drumstick, with a pleased smile and a ready bow, anxiously asking " Madame, veut elle de la volaille ? " and he was frightfully unprogressive. He wished to " let sleeping dogs lie," and hated to move quiet things. It almost gave him an indigestion to speak of railways. He found the diligence and the canal boat quite fast enough for his purpose. And in this to a certain extent he represented the Genius of the Nation.

With the excellent example of the Grand Canal du Midi before them, the French have allowed half a century to pass before they even realized the fact that their rivers give them most admirable opportunities for inland navigation, and that by energy in spending money they could have a water line leading up from Manches to Paris, and down from Paris to the Mediterranean. In these days of piercing isthmuses, they seem hardly to have thought of a canal that would save the time and expense of running round Spain and Portugal, when it would be so easy to cut the neck that connects their country with the Peninsula. The rest of the journey was eventless as usual. The family took the steamer at Marseille, steamed down to Leghorn, and drove up to Pisa. There they found a house on the south side or the Lung' Arno, belonging to a widow of the name of Pini. It was a dull and melancholy place enough, but it had the advantage of a large garden that grew chiefly cabbages. It was something like a return home ; a number of old acquaintances were met, and few new ones were made.

The studies were kept up with unremitting attention. I kept up drawing, painting, and classics, and it was lucky for me that I did.

I have been able to make my own drawings, and to illustrate my own books. It is only in this way that a correct idea of unfamiliar scenes can be given. Travellers who bring home a few scrawls and put them into the hands of a professional illustrator, have the pleasure of seeing the illustrated paper style applied to the scenery and the people of Central Africa and Central Asia and Europe. Even when the drawings are carefully done by the traveller-artist, it is hard to persuade the professional to preserve their peculiarities. For instance, a sketch from Hyderabad, the inland capital of Sind, showed a number of mast-like poles which induced the English artist to write out and ask if there ought not to be yards and sails. In sending a sketch home of a pilgrim in his proper costume, the portable Korán worn under the left arm narrowly escaped becoming a revolver. On the chocolate-coloured cover of a book on Zanzibar, stands a negro in gold, straddling like the Colossus of Rhodes. He was propped crane-like upon one leg, supporting himself with his spear, and applying, African fashion, the sole of the other foot to the perpendicular calf.

But music did not get on so well. We all three had good speaking voices, but we sang with a "*voce di gola,*" a throaty tone which was terrible to hear. It is only in England that people sing without voices. This may do very well when chirping a comic song, or half-speaking a ballad, but in nothing higher. I longed to sing, began singing with all my might at Pau in the Pyrenees, and I kept it up at Pisa, where Signor Romani (Mario's old master) rather encouraged me, instead of peremptorily or pathetically bidding me to hold my tongue. I wasted time and money, and presently found out my mistake and threw up music altogether. At stray times I took up the flageolet, and other simple instruments, as though I had a kind of instinctive feeling how useful music would be to me in later life. And I never ceased to regret that I had not practised sufficiently, to be able to write down music at hearing. Had I been able to do so, I might have collected some two thousand motives from Europe, Asia, Africa, and America, and have produced a musical note-book which would have been useful to a Bellini, or Donizetti, or a Boito.

We had now put away childish things; that is to say, we no longer broke the windows across the river with slings, or engaged in free fights with our coevals. But the climate of Italy is precocious, so, as the Vicar of Wakefield has it, "we cocked our hats and loved the ladies." And our poor father was once appalled by strange heads being put out of the windows, in an unaccustomed street, and with the words, "Oh! S'or Riccardo, Oh! S'or Edoardo."

Madame P——, the landlady, had three children. Sandro, the

son, was a tall, gawky youth, who wore a *cacciatore* or Italian shooting jacket of cotton-leather, not unlike the English one made loose, with the tails cut off. The two daughters were extremely handsome girls, in very different styles. Signorina Caterina, the elder, was tall, slim, and dark, with the palest possible complexion and regular features. Signorina Antonia, the younger, could not boast of the same classical lines, but the light brown hair, and the pink and white complexion, made one forgive and forget every irregularity. Consequently I fell in love with the elder, and Edward with the latter. Proposals of marriage were made and accepted. The girls had heard that, in her younger days, mamma had had half a dozen strings to her bow at the same time, and they were perfectly ready to follow parental example. But a serious obstacle occurred in the difficulty of getting the ceremony performed. As in England there was a popular but mistaken idea that a man could put a rope round his wife's neck, take her to market, and sell her like a quadruped, so there was, and perhaps there is still, in Italy, a legend that any affianced couple standing up together in front of the congregation during the elevation of the Host, and declaring themselves man and wife, are very much married. Many inquiries were made about this procedure, and at one time it was seriously intended. But the result of questioning was, that *promessi sposi* so acting, are at once imprisoned and punished by being kept in separate cells, and therefore it became evident, that the game was not worth the candle. This is like a Scotch marriage, however—with the Italian would be binding in religion, and the Scotch in law.

Edward and I made acquaintance with a lot of Italian medical students, compared with whom, English men of the same category were as babes, and they did us no particular good. At last the winter at Pisa ended, badly—very badly. The hard studies of the classics during the day, occasionally concluded with a revel at night. On one hopeless occasion a bottle of Jamaica gin happened to fall into the wrong hands. The revellers rose at midnight, boiled water, procured sugar and lemons, and sat down to a steaming soup tureen full of punch. Possibly it was followed by a second, but the result was that they sallied out into the streets, determined upon what is *called* a "spree." Knockers did not exist, and Charleys did not confine themselves to their sentry-boxes, and it was vain to ring at bells, when every one was sound asleep. Evidently the choice of amusements was limited, and mostly confined to hustling inoffensive passers-by. But as one of these feats had been performed, and cries for assistance had been uttered, up came the watch at the double, and the revellers had nothing to do but to make tracks. My legs were the longest, and I escaped; Edward was seized and led off, despite his fists and heels, ignobly to the local *violon*, or guard-house. One may imagine my father's disgust next morning, when he was courteously informed by the prison authorities that a *giovinotto* bearing his name, had been lodged during the night at the public expense. The father went off in a state of the stoniest severity to the guard-house, and found the graceless one treating his companions in misfortune, thieves and ruffians of every kind, to the contents of a pocket-flask with which he had provided himself in case of need. This was the last straw; our father determined to transfer his head-quarters to the Baths of Lucca, and then to prepare for breaking up the family. The adieux of Caterina and Antonia were heartrending, and it was agreed to correspond every week. The journey occupied a short time, and a house was soon found in the upper village of Lucca.

In those days, the Lucchese baths were the only place in Italy that could boast of a tolerably cool summer climate, and a few of the comforts of life. Sorrento, Montenero, near Leghorn, and the hills about Rome, were frequented by very few; they came under the category of "cheap and nasty." Hence the Bagni collected what was considered to be the distinguished society. It had its parson from Pisa, even in the days before the travelling continental clergyman was known, and this one migrated every year to the hills, like the flight of swallows, and the beggars who desert the hot plains and the stifling climate of the lowlands. There was generally at least one English doctor who practised by the kindly sufferance of the *then* Italian Government. The Duke of Lucca at times attended the balls; he was married, but his gallant presence and knightly manner committed terrible ravages in the hearts of susceptible English girls.

The queen in ordinary was a Mrs. Colonel Stisted, as she called herself, the "same Miss Clotilda Clotworthy Crawley who was" so rudely treated by the wild Irish girl, Lady Morgan. I was also obliged to settle an old score with her in after years in "Sinde, or the Unhappy Valley." And so I wrote, "She indeed had left her mark in literature, not by her maudlin volume, 'The Byeways of Italy,' but by the abuse of her fellow authors." She was "the sea goddess with tin ringlets and venerable limbs" of the irrepressible Mrs. Trollope. She also supplied Lever with one of the characters which he etched in with his most corrosive acid. In one season the Baths collected Lady Blessington, Count D'Orsay, the charming Lady Walpole, Mrs. Elizabeth Barrett Browning, the poetess, whose tight *sacque* of black silk gave us youngsters a series of caricatures. There, too, was old Lady Osborne, full of Greek and Latin, who married her daughter to Captain Bernal, afterwards Bernal Osborne. Amongst the number was Mrs. Young, whose daughter became Madame Matteucci, wife of the celebrated scientist and electrician of Tuscany. She managed, curiously to say, to hold her own in her new position. Finally, I remember Miss Virginia Gabriell, daughter of old General Gabriell, commonly called the "Archangel Gabriel." Virginia Gabriell, "all white and fresh, and virginally plain," afterwards made a name in the musical world, composed beautiful ballads, published many pieces, and married, and died in St. George's Hospital by being thrown from a carriage, August 7, 1877. She showed her *savoir faire* at the earliest age. At a ball given to the Prince, all appeared in their finest dresses and richest jewellery. Miss Virginia was in white, with a single necklace of pink coral. They danced till daylight; and when the sun arose, Miss Virginia was like a rose amongst faded dahlias and sunflowers.

There was a very nice fellow of the name of Wood, who had just married a Miss Stisted, one of the nieces of the "Queen of the Baths," with whom all the "baths" were in love. Another marking young person was Miss Helen Crowley, a girl of the order "dashing," whose hair was the brightest auburn, and complexion the purest white and red. Her father was the Rev. Dr. Crowley, whose Jewish novel "Salathiel" made a small noise in the world; but either he or his wife disliked children, so Miss Helen had been turned over to the charge of aunts. These were two elderly maiden ladies, whose agnosticism was of the severest description. "Sister, what is that noise?" "The howling of hymns, sister." "The beastly creatures," cried she, as "Come across hill and dale" reached her most irreverent ears. I met both of these ladies in later life, and it was enough to say that all three had terribly changed.

Amongst the remarkable people we knew were the Desanges family, who had a phenomenon in the house. A voice seemed to come out of it of the very richest volume, and every one thought it was a woman's. It really belonged to Master Louis, who afterwards made for himself so great a name for battle-scenes (The Desanges' Crimea and Victoria Cross Gallery) and also for portraits.* The voice did not recover itself thoroughly after breaking, but sufficient remained for admirable comic songs, and no man who ever heard them came away from "Le Lor Maire" and "Vilikens et sa Dinah" without aching sides. There was another learned widow of the name of Graves, whose husband had been a kinsman of my father. Her daughter prided herself upon the breadth

* In 1861 he painted Richard's and my portraits as a wedding gift.—I. B.

of her forehead and general intellectuality. She ended by marrying the celebrated historian Von Ranke. Intellectual Englishwomen used to expect a kind of intellectual paradise in marrying German professors. They were to share their labours, assist in their discoveries, and wear a kind of reflected halo or gloria, as the moon receives light from the sun; but they were perfectly shocked when they were ordered to the kitchen, and were addressed with perhaps "Donner—Wetter—Sacrament" if the dinner was not properly cooked.

These little colonies like the "Baths of Lucca" began to decline about 1850, and came to their Nadir in 1870. Then they had a kind of resurrection. The gambling in shares and stocks and loans lost England an immense sum of money, and the losses were most felt by that well-to-do part of the public that had a fixed income and no chance of ever increasing it. The loss of some five hundred millions of pounds sterling, rendered England too expensive for a large class, and presently drove it abroad. It gained numbers in 1881, when the Irish Land Bill, soon to be followed by a corresponding English Land Bill, exiled a multitude of landowners. So the little English colonies, which had dwindled to the lowest expression, gradually grew and grew, and became stronger than they ever did.

It was evident that the Burton family was ripe for a break up. Our father, like an Irishman, was perfectly happy as long as he was the only man in the house, but the presence of younger males irritated him. His temper became permanently soured. He could no longer use the rod, but he could make himself very unpleasant with his tongue. "Senti come me li rimangia quei poveri ragazzi!" (Hear how he is chawing-up those poor lads!) said the old Pisan-Italian lady's-maid, and I do think now that we were not pleasant inmates of a household. We were in the "Sturm und drang" of the teens. We had thoroughly mastered our tutor, threw our books out of the window if he attempted to give a lesson in Greek or Latin, and applied ourselves with ardour to Picault Le Brun, and Paul de Kock, the "Promessi Sposi," and the "Disfida di Barletta." Instead of taking country walks, we jodelled all about the hillsides under the direction of a Swiss scamp. We shot pistols in every direction, and whenever a stray fencing-master passed, we persuaded him to give us a few hours of "point." We made experiments of everything imaginable, including swallowing and smoking opium.

The break-up took place about the middle of summer. It was comparatively tame. Italians marvelled at the Spartan nature of the British mother, who, after the habits of fifteen years, can so easily part with her children at the cost of a lachrymose last embrace, and watering her prandial beefsteak with tears. Amongst Italian families, nothing is more common than for all the brothers and sisters to swear that they will not marry if they are to be separated from one another. And even now, in these subversive and progressive days, what a curious contrast is the English and the Italian household. Let me sketch one of the latter, a family belonging to the old nobility, once lords of the land, and now simple proprietors of a fair Estate. In a large garden, and a larger orchard of vines and olives, stands a solid old house, as roomy as a barrack, but without the slightest pretension of comfort or luxury. The old Countess, a widow, has the whole of her progeny around her—two or three stalwart sons, one married and the others partially so, and a daughter who has not yet found a husband. The servants are old family retainers. They consider themselves part and parcel of the household; they are on the most familiar terms with the family, although they would resent with the direst indignation the slightest liberty on the part of outsiders. The day is one of extreme simplicity, and some might even deem it monotonous. Each individual leaves his bed at the hour he or she pleases, and finds coffee, milk, and small rolls in the dining-room. Smoking and dawdling pass the hours till almost mid-day, when *déjeuner à la fourchette*, or rather a young dinner, leads very naturally up to a siesta. In the afternoon there is a little walking or driving, and even shooting in the case of the most energetic. There is a supper after nightfall, and after that dominoes or cards, or music, or conversazione, keep them awake for half the night. The even tenor of their days is broken only by a festival or a ball in the nearest town, or some pseudo Scientific Congress in a City not wholly out of reach; and so things go on from year to year, and all are happy because they look to nothing else.

Our journey began in the early summer of 1840. My mother and sister were left at the Baths of Lucca, and my father, with Mr. Du Pré, and Edward and I, set out for Switzerland. We again travelled *vetturino*, and we lads cast longing eyes at the charming country which we were destined not to see again for another ten years. How melancholy we felt when on our way to the chill and dolorous North! At Schinznach I was left in charge of Mr. Du Pré, while my father and brother set out for England direct. These Hapsburg baths in the Aargau had been chosen because the abominable sulphur water, as odorous as that of Harrogate, was held as sovereign in skin complaints, and I was suffering from exanthémata, an eruption brought on by a sudden check of perspiration. These eruptions are very hard to cure, and they often embitter a man's life. The village consisted of a single Establishment, in which all nationalities met. Amongst them was an unfortunate Frenchman, who had been attacked at Calcutta with what appeared to be a leprous taint. He had tried half a dozen places to no purpose, and he had determined to blow his brains out if Schinznach failed him. The only advantage of the place was, its being within easy distance of Schaffhausen and the falls of the Rhine.

When the six weeks' cure was over, I was hurried by my guardian across France, and Southern England, to the rendezvous. The Grandmother and the two aunts, finding Great Cumberland Place too hot, had taken country quarters at Hampstead. Grandmamma Baker received us lads with something like disappointment. She would have been better contented had we been six feet high, bony as Highland cattle, with freckled faces, and cheek-bones like horns. Aunt Georgina Baker embraced and kissed her nephews with effusion. She had not been long parted from us. Mrs. Frank Burton, the other aunt, had not seen us for ten years, and of course could not recognize us.

We found two very nice little girl-cousins, who assisted us to pass the time. But the old dislike to our surroundings, returned with redoubled violence. Everything appeared to us so small, so mean, so ugly. The faces of the women were the only exception to the general rule of hideousness. The houses were so unlike houses, and more like the Nuremberg toys magnified. The outsides were so prim, so priggish, so utterly unartistic. The little bits of garden were mere slices, as if they had been sold by the inch. The interiors were cut up into such wretched little rooms, more like ship-cabins than what was called rooms in Italy. The drawing-rooms were crowded with hideous little tables, that made it dangerous to pass from one side to the other. The tables were heaped with nick-nacks, that served neither for use or show. And there was a desperate neatness and cleanness about everything that made us remember the old story of the Stoic who spat in the face of the master of the house because it was the most untidy place in the dwelling.

Then came a second parting. Edward was to be placed under the charge of the Rev. Mr. Havergal, rector of some country parish. Later on, he wrote to say that "Richard must not correspond with his brother, as he had turned his name into a peculiar form of ridicule." He was in the musical line, and delighted in organ-playing. But Edward seemed to consider the whole affair a bore, and was only too happy when he could escape from the harmonious parsonage.

In the mean time I had been tried and found wanting. One of my father's sisters (Mrs. General D'Aguilar, as she called herself) had returned from India, after an uninterrupted residence of a score of years, with a large supply of children of both sexes. She had. settled herself temporarily at Cambridge, to superintend the education of her eldest son, John Burton D'Aguilar, who was intended for the Church, and who afterwards became a chaplain in the Bengal Establishment. Amongst her many acquaintances was a certain Professor Sholefield, a well-known Grecian. My father had rather suspected that very little had been done in the house, in the way of classical study, during the last two years. The Professor put me through my paces in Virgil and Homer, and found me lamentably deficient. I did not even know who Isis was! worse still, it was found out that I, who spoke French and Italian and their dialects like a native, who had a considerable smattering of Bearnais, Spanish, and Provençale, barely knew the Lord's Prayer, broke down in the Apostles' Creed, and had never heard of the Thirty-nine Articles—a terrible revelation!

CHAPTER IV.

OXFORD.

As it was Long Vacation at Oxford, and I could not take rooms at once in Trinity College, where my name had been put down, it was necessary to place me somewhere out of mischief. At the intervention of friends, a certain Doctor Greenhill agreed to lodge and coach me till the opening term. The said doctor had just married a relation of Dr. Arnold, of Rugby, and he had taken his bride to Paris, in order to show her the world and to indulge himself in a little dissecting. Meanwhile I was placed *pro tem.* with another medical don, Dr. Ogle, and I enjoyed myself in that house. The father was a genial man, and he had nice sons and pretty daughters. As soon as Dr. Greenhill returned to his house in High Street, Oxford, I was taken up there by my father, and was duly consigned to the new tutor. Mr. Du Pré vanished, and was never seen again.

The first sight of Oxford struck me with a sense of appal. "O Domus antiqua et religiosa," cried Queen Elizabeth, in 1664, standing opposite Pembroke College, which the Dons desecrated in 1875. I could not imagine how such fine massive and picturesque old buildings as the colleges could be mixed up with the mean little houses that clustered around them, looking as if they were built of cardboard. In after days, I remembered the feeling, when looking at the Temple of the Sun in Palmyra, surrounded by its Arab huts, like swallows' nests planted upon a palace wall. And everything, *except* the colleges, looked so mean.

The good old Mitre was, if not the only, at least the chief hostelry of the place, and it had the outward and visible presence of a pothouse. The river with the classical name of Isis, was a mere moat, and its influent, the Cherwell, was a ditch. The country around, especially just after Switzerland, looked flat and monotonous in the extreme. The skies were brown-grey, and, to an Italian nose, the smell of the coal smoke was a perpetual abomination. Queer beings walked the streets, dressed in aprons that hung behind, from their shoulders, and caps consisting of a square, like that of a lancer's helmet, planted upon a semi-oval to contain the head. These queer creatures were carefully shaved, except, perhaps, a diminutive mutton-cutlet on each side of their face, and the most serious sort were invariably dressed *in vestibus nigris aut sub fuscis.*

Moreover, an indescribable appearance of donnishness or incipient donnishness pervaded the whole lot. The juniors looked like schoolboys who aspired to be schoolmasters, and the seniors as if their aspirations had been successful. I asked after the famous Grove of Trinity, where Charles I. used to walk when tired of Christ Church meadows, and which the wits called Daphne. It had long been felled, and the ground was covered with buildings.

At last term opened, and I transferred myself from Dr. Greenhill to Trinity College.

Then my University life began, and readers must be prepared not to be shocked at the recital of my college failures, which only proves the truth of what I said before, that if a father means his boy to succeed in an English career, he must put him to a preparatory school, Eton or Oxford, educate him for his coming profession, and not drag his family about the Continent, under governesses and tutors, to learn fencing, languages, and become wild, and to belong to nowhere in particular as to parish or county.

In the autumn term of 1840, at nineteen and a half, I began residence in Trinity College, where my quarters were a pair of dog-holes, called rooms, overlooking the garden of the Master of Balliol. My reception at College was not pleasant. I had grown a splendid moustache, which was the envy of all the boys abroad, and which all the advice of Drs. Ogle and Greenhill failed to make me remove. I declined to be shaved until formal orders were issued to the authorities of the college. For I had already formed strong ideas upon the Shaven age of England, when her history, with some brilliant exceptions, such as Marlborough, Wellington, or Nelson, was at its meanest.

As I passed through the entrance of the College, a couple of brother collegians met me, and the taller one laughed in my face. Accustomed to continental decorum, I handed him my card and called him out. But the college lad, termed by courtesy an Oxford man, had possibly read of duels, had probably never touched a weapon, sword or pistol, and his astonishment at the invitation exceeded all bounds. Explanations succeeded, and I went my way sadly, and felt as if I had fallen amongst *épiciers.* The college porter had kindly warned me against tricks played by the older hands, upon "fresh young gentlemen," and strongly advised me to "sport my oak," or, in other words, to bar and lock my outer door. With dignity deeply hurt, I left the entrance wide open, and thrust a poker into the fire, determined to give all intruders the warmest possible reception. This was part and parcel of that unhappy education abroad. In English public schools, boys learn first "to take," and then "to give." They begin by being tossed, and then by tossing others in the blanket. Those were days when practical jokes were in full force. Happily it is now extinct. Every greenhorn coming to college or joining a regiment, was liable to the roughest possible treatment, and it was only by submitting with the utmost good humour, that he won the affection of his comrades, and was looked upon as a gentleman. But the practice also had its darker phase. It ruined many a prospect, and it lost many a life. The most amusing specimen that *I* ever saw was that of a charming youngster, who died soon after joining his Sepoy regiment. The oldsters tried to drink him under the table at mess, and had notably failed. About midnight, when he was enjoying his first sleep, he suddenly awoke and found a ring of spectral figures dancing round between his bed and the tent-walls. After a minute's reflection, he jumped up, seized a sheet, threw it over his shoulders, and joined the dancers, saying, "If this is the fashion I suppose I must do it also." The jokers, baffled a second time, could do nothing but knock him down and run away.

The example of the larky Marquis of Waterford, seemed to authorize all kinds of fantastic tricks. The legend was still fresh, that he had painted the Dean of Christ Church's door red, because that formidable dignitary had objected to his wearing "pink" in High Street. Another, and far more inexcusable prank, was his sending all the accoucheurs in the town, to the house of a middle-aged maiden lady, whose father, a don, had offended him. In the colleges they did not fly at such high game, but they cruelly worried everything in the shape of a freshman. One unfortunate youth, a fellow who had brought with him a dozen of home-made wine, elder and cowslip, was made shockingly tight by brandy being mixed with his port, and was put to bed with all his bottles disposed on different parts of his person. Another, of æsthetic tastes, prided himself upon his china, and found it next morning all strewed in pieces about his bed. A third, with carroty whiskers, had them daubed with mustard, also while in a state of insensibility, and had to have them fall, yellow, next morning under a barber's hands.

I caused myself to be let down by a rope into the Master of Balliol's garden, plucked up some of the finest flowers by the roots, and planted in their place great staring marigolds. The study of the old gentleman's countenance when he saw them next morning was a joy for ever. Another prank was to shoot with an air-cane, an article strictly forbidden in college, at a brand-new watering-pot, upon which the old gentleman greatly prided himself, and the way which the water spirted over his reverend gaiters, gave an ineffable delight to the knot of mischievous undergraduates who were prospecting him from behind the curtain. I, however, always had considerable respect for the sturdy common sense of old Dr. Jenkins, and I made a kind of amends to him in "Vikram and the Vampire," where he is the only Pundit who objected to the tiger being resurrectioned. Another neat use of the air-cane, was to shoot the unhappy rooks, over the heads of the dons, as they played at bowls; the grave and reverend signiors would take up the body, and gravely debate what had caused the sudden death, when a warm stream of blood, trickling into their shirts, explained it only too clearly. No undergraduate in college could safely read his classics out loud after ten o'clock p.m., or his "oak" was broken with dumb-bells, and the dirty oil lamp, that half lit the stairs, was thrown over him and his books.

I made amends to a certain extent for my mischief by putting my fellow-collegians to bed, and I always maintain that the Welshmen were those who gave me the most trouble.

The Oxford day, considered with relation to the acquisition of knowledge, was a "fast" pure and simple—it began in the morning with Chapel, during which time most men got up their logic. We then breakfasted either in our rooms, or in large parties, where we consumed an immense quantity of ham, bacon, eggs, mutton chops, and indigestible muffins. We then attended a couple of lectures, and this was Time completely thrown away. We were then free for the day, and every man passed his time as he best pleased. I could not afford to keep horses, and always hated the idea of riding hired hacks. My only amusements therefore were walking, rowing, and the school-at-arms. My walks somehow or other always ended at Bagley Wood, where a pretty gypsy girl (Selina), dressed in silks and satins, sat in state to receive the shillings and the homage of the undergraduates. I worked hard, under a coach, at sculling and rowing; I was one of the oars in the College Torpid, and a friend and I challenged the River in a two-oar, but unfortunately both of us were rusticated before the race came off.

My friend in misfortune belonged to an eminent ecclesiastical family, and distinguished himself accordingly. Returning from

Australia, he landed at Mauritius without a farthing. Most men under the circumstances would have gone to the Governor, told their names, and obtained a passage to England. But the individual in question had far too much individuality to take so commonplace a step. He wrote home to his family for money, and meanwhile took off his coat, tucked up his sleeves, and worked like a coolie on the wharf. When the cheque for his passage was sent, he invited all his brother coolies to a spread of turtle, champagne, and all the luxuries of the season, at the swell hotel of the place, and left amidst the blessings of Shem and the curse of Japhet. Another of my college companions—the son of a bishop, by-the-by—made a cavalry regiment too hot to hold him, and took his passage to the Cape of Good Hope in an emigrant ship. On the third day he brought out a portable roulette table, which the captain sternly ordered off the deck. But the ship was a slow sailer, she fell in with calms about the Line, and the official rigour was relaxed. First one began to play, and then another, and at last the ship became a perfect "hell." After a hundred narrow escapes, and all manner of risks by fire and water, and the fists and clubs of the enraged losers, the distinguished youth landed at Cape Town with almost £5000 in his pocket.

The great solace of *my* life was the fencing-room. When I first entered Oxford, its only *salle d'armes* was kept by old Angelo, the grandson of the gallant old Italian, mentioned by Edgeworth, but who knew about as much of fencing as a French collegian after six months of *salle d'armes*. He was a priggish old party too, celebrated for walking up to his pupils and for whispering stagely, after a salute with the foil, "This, sir, is not so much a School of Arms as a *School of Politeness*." Presently a rival appeared in the person of Archibald Maclaren, who soon managed to make his mark. He established an excellent saloon, and he gradually superseded all the wretched gymnastic yard, which lay some half a mile out of the town. He was determined to make his way; he went over to Paris, when he could, to work with the best masters, published his systems of fencing and gymnastics, and he actually wrote a little book of poetry, which he called "Songs of the Sword." He and I became great friends, which friendship lasted for life. The only question that ever arose between us was touching the advisability or non-advisability of eating sweet buns and drinking strong ale at the same time. At the fencing-rooms I made acquaintance, which afterwards became a life-long friendship, with Alfred Bates Richards. He was a tall man, upwards of six feet high, broad in proportion, and very muscular. I found it unadvisable to box with him, but could easily master him with foil and broadsword. He was one of the few who would take the trouble to learn. Mostly Englishmen go to a fencing school, and, after six weeks' lessons, clamour to be allowed to fence loose, and very loose fencing it is, and is fated always to be. In the same way, almost before they can fix their colours they want to paint *tableaux de genre*, and they have hardly learnt their scales, when they want to attempt *bravura* pieces. On the Continent men work for months, and even years, before they think themselves in sight of their journey's end. A. B. Richards and I often met in after life and became intimates.* His erratic career is well known, and he died at a comparatively early age, editor of the *Morning Advertiser*. He had raised the tone of the Licensed Victuallers' organ to such a high pitch that even Lord Beaconsfield congratulated him upon it.

A. B. Richards was furious to see the treatment my services received; he always stood up bravely for me—his fellow-collegian, both with word and pen—in leaders too.

The time for "Hall," that is to say for college dinner, was five p.m., and the scene was calculated to astonish a youngster brought up on the Continent. The only respectable part of it was the place itself, not a bad imitation of some old convent refectory. The details were mean in the extreme, and made me long for the meanest *table d'hôte*. Along the bottom of the Hall, raised upon a dwarf dais, ran the high table, intended for the use of fellows and fellow-commoners. The other tables ran along the sides. Wine was forbidden, malt liquor being the only drink. The food certainly suited the heavy strong beers and ales brewed in the college. It consisted chiefly of hunches of meat, cooked after Homeric or Central African fashion, and very filling at the price. The vegetables, as usual, were plain boiled, without the slightest aid to digestion. Yet the college cooks were great swells. They were paid as much as an average clergyman, and put most of their sons into the Church. In fact, the stomach had to do the whole work, whereas a good French or Italian cook does half the work for it in his saucepans. This cannibal meal was succeeded by stodgy pudding, and concluded with some form of cheese, Cheshire or double Gloucester, which painfully reminded one of bees'-wax, and this was called dinner. Very soon my foreign stomach began to revolt at such treatment, and I found out a place in the town, where, when I could escape Hall, I could make something of a dinner.

The moral of the scene offended all my prepossessions. The fellow-

* He began and wrote the "Career of R. F. Burton," printed by Waterlow, and brought it up to 1876. We deeply regretted him.—I. B.

commoners were simply men, who by paying double what the commoners paid, secured double privileges. This distinction of castes is odious, except in the case of a man of certain age, who would not like to be placed in the society of young lads. But worse still was the gold tuft, who walked the streets with a silk gown, and a gorgeous tassel on his college cap. These were noblemen, the offensive English equivalent for men of title. *Generosus nascitur nobilis fit.* The Grandfathers of these noblemen may have been pitmen or grocers, but the simple fact of *having* titles, entitled them to most absurd distinctions. For instance, with a smattering of letters, enough to enable a commoner to squeeze through an ordinary examination, gold tuft took a first class, and it was even asserted that many took their degrees by merely sending up their books. They were allowed to live in London as much as they liked, and to condescend to college at the rare times they pleased. Some Heads of Colleges would not stoop to this degradation, especially Dean Gaisford of Christ Church, who compelled Lord W—— to leave it and betake himself to Trinity; but the place was, with notable exceptions, a hotbed of toadyism and flunkeyism. When Mr. (now Sir Robert) Peel first appeared in the High Street, man, woman, and child stood to look at him because he was the son of the Prime Minister.

After dinner it was the custom to go to wine. These desserts were another abomination. The table was spread with a vast variety of fruits and sweetmeats, supplied at the very highest prices, and often on tick, by the Oxford tradesmen,—model sharks. Some men got their wine from London, others bought theirs in the town. Claret was then hardly known, and port, sherry, and Madeira, all of the strong military ditto type, were the only drinks. These wines were given in turn by the undergraduates, and the meal upon meal would have injured the digestion of a young shark. At last, about this time, some unknown fellow, whose name deserved to be immortalized, drew out a cigar and insisted on smoking it, despite the disgust and uproar that the novelty created. But the fashion made its way, and the effects were admirable. The cigar, and afterwards the pipe, soon abolished the cloying dessert, and reduced the consumption of the loaded wines to a minimum.

But the English were very peculiar about smoking. In the days of Queen Anne it was so universal that dissident jurymen were locked up without meat, drink, or tobacco. During the continental wars it became un-English to smoke, and consequently men, and even women, took snuff. And for years it was considered as disgraceful to smoke a cigar out of doors as to have one's boots blacked, or to eat an orange at Hyde Park Corner. "Good gracious! you don't mean to say that you smoke in the streets?" said an East Indian Director in after years, when he met me in Pall Mall with a cigar in my mouth. Admiral Henry Murray, too, vainly endeavoured to break through the prohibition by leading a little squad of smoking friends through Kensington Gardens. Polite ladies turned away their faces, and unpolite ladies muttered something about "snobs." At last the Duke of Argyll spread his plaid under a tree in Hyde Park, lighted a cutty pipe, and beckoned his friends to join him. Within a month every one in London had a cigar in his mouth. A pretty lesson to inculcate respect for popular prejudice!

After the dessert was finished, not a few men called for cognac, whisky, and gin, and made merry for the rest of the evening. But what else was there for them to do? Unlike a foreign University, the theatre was discouraged; it was the meanest possible little house, decent actors were ashamed to show themselves in it, and an actress of the calibre of Mrs. Nesbitt appeared only every few years. Opera, of course, there was none, and if there had been, not one in a thousand would have understood the language, and not one in a hundred would have appreciated the music. Occasionally there was a concert given by some wandering artists, with the special permission of the college authorities, and a dreary two hours' work it was. Balls were unknown, whereby the marriageable demoiselles of Oxford lost many an uncommon good chance. A mesmeric lecturer occasionally came down there and caused some fun. He called for subjects, and amongst the half-dozen that presented themselves was one young gentleman who had far more sense of humour than discretion. When thrown into a deep slumber, he arose, with his eyes apparently fast closed, and, passing into the circle of astonished spectators, began to distribute kisses right and left. Some of these salutations fell upon the sacred cheeks of the daughters of the Heads of Houses, and the tableau may be imagined.

This dull, monotonous life was varied in my case by an occasional dinner with families whose acquaintance I had made in the town. At Dr. Greenhill's I once met at dinner Dr. (afterwards Cardinal) Newman and Dr. Arnold. I expected great things from their conversation, but it was mostly confined to discussing the size of he Apostles in the Cathedral of St. Peter's in Rome, and both these eminent men showed a very dim recollection of the subject. I took a great fancy to Dr. Newman, and used to listen to his sermons, when I would never give half an hour to any other preacher. There was a peculiar gentleness in his manner, and the matter was always suggestive. Dr. Newman was Vicar of St. Mary's, at Oxford, and used to preach, at times, University sermons; there was a stamp and seal upon him, a solemn music and sweetness in his tone and manner, which made him singularly attractive, yet there was no change of inflexion in his voice; action he had none; his sermons were always read, and his eyes were ever upon his book; his figure was lean and stooping, and the *tout ensemble* was anything but dignified or commanding, yet the delivery suited the matter of his speech, and the combination suggested complete candour and honesty; he said only what he believed, and he induced others to believe with him.* On the other hand, Dr. Pusey's University sermons used to last for an hour and a half; they were filled with Latin and Greek, dealt with abstruse subjects, and were delivered in the dullest possible way, and seemed to me like a *mauvais rêve* or nightmare.

At Dr. Greenhill's, too, I met Don Pascual de Gayangos, the Spanish Arabist. Already wearying of Greek and Latin, I had attacked Arabic, and soon was well on in Erpinius's Grammar; but there was no one to teach me, so I began to teach myself, and to write the Arabic letters from left to right, instead of from right to left, *i.e.* the wrong way. Gayangos, when witnessing this proceeding, burst out laughing, and showed me how to copy the alphabet. In those days, learning Arabic at Oxford was not easy. There was a Regius Professor, but he had other occupations than to profess. If an unhappy undergraduate went up to him, and wanted to learn, he was assured that it was the duty of a professor to teach a class, and not an individual. All this was presently changed, but not before it was high time. The Sundays used generally to be passed in "outings." It was a pleasure to get away from Oxford, and to breathe the air which was not at least half smoke.

Another disagreeable of Oxford was, the continuous noise of bells. You could not make sure of five minutes without one giving tongue, and in no part of the world, perhaps, is there a place where there is such a perpetual tinkling of metal. The maddening jangle of bells seems to have been the survival of two centuries ago. In 1698 Paul Heutzner wrote: "The English are vastly fond of great noises that fill the air, such as the firing of cannon, drums, and the ringing of bells, so that it is common for a number of them that have got a 'glass' in their heads, to go up into some belfry, and ring the bells for hours together for the sake of exercise."

A favourite Sunday trip used to be to Abingdon, which, by the wisdom of the dons in those days, was the railway station of Oxford.

* Richard always said that if *all* Catholics were like Dr. Newman, nearly every thinking person would become Catholic.—I. B.

Like most men of conservative tendency, who disliked to move quiet things, who cultivated the *status quo*, because they could hardly be better off, and might be worse off, and who feared nothing more than innovations, because these might force on enquiring into the disposal of the revenues and other delicate monetary questions, they had fought against the line with such good will, that they had left it nearly ten miles distant from the town. Their conduct was by no means exceptional; thousands did the same. For instance, Lord John Scott, determined to prevent the surveyor passing through his estate, engaged a company of "Nottingham Lambs," and literally strewed the floor of the porter's lodge with broken surveying instruments. Mrs. Partington cannot keep out the tide with her rake, and the consequence was that Oxford was obliged to build a branch line, and soon had to lament that she had lost the advantage of the main line.

The Rev. Thomas Short was at that time doing Sunday duty at Abingdon. He was not distinguished for ability as a college tutor, but he was a gentlemanly and kind-hearted man; he was careful not to be too sharp-eyed when he met undergraduates at Abingdon. They generally drove out in tandems, which the absurd regulations of the place kept in fashion, by forbidding them. No one would have driven them had they not possessed the merits of stolen fruit. I, having carefully practised upon "Dobbin" in my earlier days, used thoroughly to enjoy driving. In later years I met with my old tutor, the Rev. Thomas Short, who lived to a great age, and died universally respected and regretted by all who knew him.*

At last the lagging autumnal term passed away, and I went up to my grandmother and aunts in Great Cumberland Place. It was not lively; a household full of women only, rarely is.

The style of Society was very promiscuous. The Rev. Mr. Hutchins, the clergyman under whom the family "sat" in the adjoining Quebec Chapel, introduced me to the eccentric Duke of Brunswick, who used to laugh consumedly at my sallies of high spirits. Lady Dinorben, with whom Mrs. Phayre still lived, gave me an occasional invitation. The aunts' near neighbours were old General Sutherland of the Madras Army, whose son Alick I afterwards met in the Neilgherry Hills. Mr. Lawyer Dendy was still alive, and one of his sons shortly after followed me to India as a Bombay civilian. Another pleasant acquaintance was Mrs. White, wife of the colonel of the 3rd Dragoons, whose three stalwart sons were preparing for India, and gave me the first idea of going there.

* I can remember, in later years, Richard going to see him, and when he was so old he had almost to be supported, gazing at him with affection and moist eyes.—I.B.

A man who dances, who dresses decently, and who is tolerably well introduced, rarely wants invitations to balls in London, and I found some occupation for my evenings.

But I sadly wanted a club, and in those days the institution was not as common as it is now. At odd times I went to the theatres, and amused myself with the humours of the little "Pic" and the old Cocoa-Nut Tree. But hazard is a terrible game. It takes a man years to learn it well, and by that time he has lost all the luck with which he begins. I always disliked private play, although I played a tolerable hand at whist, *écarté*, and piquet, but I found it almost as unpleasant to win from my friends as to lose to my friends. On the other hand, I was unusually lucky at public tables. I went upon a principle, not a theory, which has ruined so many men. I noted as a rule that players are brave enough when they lose, whereas they begin to fear when they win. My plan, therefore, was to put a certain sum in my pocket and resolve never to exceed it. If I lost it I stopped, one of the advantages of public over private playing; but I did not lay down any limits to winning when I was in luck; I boldly went ahead, and only stopped when I found fortune turning the other way.

My grandmother's house was hardly pleasant to a devoted smoker; I was put out on the leads, leading from the staircase, whenever I required a weed. So I took lodgings in Maddox Street, and there became as it were a "man about town." My brother Edward joined me, and we had, as the Yankees say, "A high old time." It appeared only too short, and presently came on the Spring Term, when I returned to my frouzy rooms in Trinity College; and I had not formed many friendships in Trinity itself. It had made a name for fastness amongst the last generation of undergraduates, and now a reaction had set in. They laughed at me, at my first lecture, because I spoke in Roman Latin—real Latin—I did not know the English pronunciation, only known in England. The only men of my own college I met in after life, were Father Coleridge, S.J., and Edward A. Freeman, of Somerleaze, the historian.

Mrs. Grundy had then just begun to reign, inaugurated by Douglas Jerrold with "What will Mrs. Grundy say?" This ancient *genitrix* highly disapproved of my foreign ways, and my expressed dislike to school and college, over which I ought to have waxed sentimental, tender, and æsthetic; it appeared to her little short of blasphemy. I had a few friends at "Exeter," including Richards, and three at Brasenose, then famous for drinking heavy beers and ales as Bonn or Heidelberg, especially on Shrove Tuesday, when certain verses chaffingly called the "Carmen seculare" used to be sung. But I delighted in "Oriel," which, both as regards fellows and undergraduates, was certainly the nicest college of *my* day. There I spent the chief part of my time with Wilberforce, Foster, and a little knot, amongst whom was Tom Hughes (afterwards Tom Brown). We boxed regularly, and took lessons from Goodman, ex-pugilist and pedestrian, and actual tailor, who came down to Oxford at times. We had great fun with Burke—the fighting man—who on one occasion honoured Oxford with his presence. The "Deaf 'un," as he was called, had a face that had been hammered into the consistency of sole-leather, and one evening, after being too copiously treated, he sat down in a heavy armchair, and cried out, "Now, lads! half a crown a hit." We all tried our knuckles upon his countenance, and only hurt our own knuckles.

Balliol (it was chiefly supplied from Rugby) then held her head uncommonly high. As all know, Dr. Arnold had made the fortune of Rugby, and caused it to be recognized among public schools. During his early government the Rugbyites had sent a cricket challenge to Eton, and the Etonians had replied "that they would be most happy to send their scouts;" but as scholarship at Eton seemed to decline, so it rose in Rugby and Oxford. Scholarship means *£ s. d.* At Balliol I made acquaintance with a few men, whose names afterwards made a noise in the world. They all belonged to a generation, collegically speaking, older than myself. Coleridge (now Lord Coleridge) was still lingering there, but he had taken his bachelor's degree, and his brother, afterwards a Jesuit and author of many works, was a scholar at Trinity. Ward of Balliol, who also became a Catholic, was chiefly remarkable for his minute knowledge of the circulating library novels of the Laura-Matilda type. He suffered from insomnia, and before he could sleep, he was obliged to get through a few volumes every night. Lake of Balliol, then a young don, afterwards turned out a complete man of the world; and there is no need to speak of Jowett, who had then just passed as B.A., and was destined to be Master of Balliol.

Oxford between 1840 and 1842 was entering upon great changes. The old style of "fellow," a kind of survival of the Benedictine monks, was rapidly becoming extinct, and only one or two remained. Men who lived surrounded by their books on vertical stands, were capable of asking you if "cats let loose in woods would turn to tigers," and tried to keep pace with the age by reading up the *Times* of eight years past. But a great deal of reform was still wanted. Popular idea about Oxford was, that the Classic groves of Isis were hotbeds for classical *Scholasticism*, whilst Cambridge succeeded better in Mathematics, but I soon found out that one would learn more Greek and Latin in one year at Bonn and Heidelberg than in three at Oxford. The college teaching, for which one was obliged to pay, was of the most worthless description. Two hours a day were regularly wasted, and those who read for honours were obliged to choose and to pay for a private coach. Amongst the said coaches were some *drôles*, who taught in very peculiar ways, by Rhymes, not always of the most delicate description. One celebrated coach, after lecturing his blockheads upon the subject, we will say, of Salmanizer, would say to them, "Now, you fellows, you'll forget in a day everything that I've been teaching you for the last hour. Whenever you hear this man's name, just repeat to yourselves * * * * * and you'll remember all about it."

The worst of such teaching was, that it had no order and no system. Its philology was ridiculous, and it did nothing to work the reasoning powers. Learning foreign languages, as a child learns its own, is mostly a work of pure memory, which acquires, after childhood, every artificial assistance possible. My system of learning a language in two months was purely my own invention, and thoroughly suited myself. I got a simple grammar and vocabulary, marked out the forms and words which I knew were absolutely necessary, and learnt them by heart by carrying them in my pocket and looking over them at spare moments during the day. I never worked more than a quarter of an hour at a time, for after that the brain lost its freshness. After learning some three hundred words, easily done in a week, I stumbled through some easy book-work (one of the Gospels is the most come-atable), and underlined every word that I wished to recollect, in order to read over my pencillings at least once a day. Having finished my volume, I then carefully worked up the grammar minutiæ, and I then chose some other book whose subject most interested me. The neck of the language was now broken, and progress was rapid. If I came across a new sound like the Arabic *Ghayn*, I trained my tongue to it by repeating it so many thousand times a day. When I read, I invariably read out loud, so that the ear might aid memory. I was delighted with the most difficult characters, Chinese and Cuneiform, because I felt that they impressed themselves more strongly upon the eye than the eternal Roman letters. This, by-and-by, made me resolutely stand aloof from the hundred schemes for transliterating Eastern languages, such as Arabic, Sanscrit, Hebrew, and Syriac, into Latin letters, and whenever I conversed with anybody in a language that I was learning, I took the trouble to repeat their words inaudibly after them, and so to learn the trick of pronunciation and emphasis.

The changes which followed 1840 made an important difference in the value of fellowships. They were harder to get and harder to keep. They were no longer what the parlous and supercilious youth defined them, "An admirable provision for the indigent members of the middle classes." The old half-monk disappeared, or rather he grew his moustachios, and passed his vacations "sur le Conti-nong." But something still remains to be done. It is a scandal to meet abroad in diplomacy, and other professions, a gentleman belonging to the *bene nati, bene vestiti, modice docti* of "All Souls'," drawing, moreover, his pay for doing nothing. The richest University in the world is too poor to afford the host of professors still required, and it is a disgrace that an English University, whose name means the acquisition of universal knowledge, should not be able to teach Cornish, Gaelic, Welsh, and Irish, the original languages of the island. Again, the endowment of research, a *sine quâ non*, is simply delayed because money is not forthcoming. A little sensible economy would remedy this, and make Oxford what she ought to be, a Seat of Learning—not, as the old fellows of Christ Church define it, "A place to make rather ignorant gentlemen." The competition fellowships at Oxford were started in 1854, which changed the whole condition of things.

During this term I formally gave up my intention to read for a first class. *Aut primus aut nullus* was ever my motto, and though many second-class men have turned out better than many first-class men, I did not care to begin life with a failure. I soon ascertained the fact that men who may rely upon first classes are bred to it from their childhood, even as horses and dogs are trained. They must not waste time and memory upon foreign tongues. They must not dissipate their powers of brain upon anything like general education. They may know the -isms, but they must be utterly ignorant of the -ologies; but, above all things, they must not indulge themselves with what is popularly called "*The World.*" They must confine themselves to one straight line, a college curriculum, and even then they can never be certain of success. At the very moment of gaining the prize their health may break down, and compel them to give up work. I surprised Dr. Greenhill by my powers of memory when I learned Adam's "Antiquities" by heart. But the doctor, who had not taken a class himself, threw cold water on my ambition—perhaps the best thing he could do—and frankly told me that, though I *could* take a first class, he could by no means answer that I *would.* The fellows of Trinity were nice gentlemanly men, but I by no means wished to become one of the number. My father had set his heart upon both sons being provided for by the Universities, and very often "when fathers propose, sons dispose."

My disgust at the idea of University honours was perhaps not decreased by my trying for the two scholarships, and failing to get them.

I attributed my non-success at University College (where I was beaten by a man who turned a chorus of Æschylus into doggerel verse) chiefly to my having stirred the bile of my examiners with my real (Roman) Latin. At times, too, the devil palpably entered into me, and made me speak Greek Romaically by accent, and not by quantity, even as they did and still do at Athens. I had learnt this much from one of the Rhodo-Kanakis Greek merchants at Marseille, so that I could converse in Latin and Greek as spoken as well as ancient Latin and Greek.

The history of the English pronunciation of Latin is curious. In Chaucer it was after the Roman fashion, in Spencer the English A appears, and the change begins to make itself felt under the succession of Queen Elizabeth. It is most probable that this was encouraged by the leaders of education, in order more thoroughly to break with Rome. The effect was, that after learning Greek and Latin for twenty years, a lad could hardly speak a sentence, because he had never been taught to converse in the absurdly *called* Dead Languages, and if he did speak, not a soul but an Englishman could understand him. The English pronunciation of Latin vowels, happens to be the very worst in the world, because we have an O and an A which belongs peculiarly to English, and which destroys all the charms of those grand-sounding vowels.

Years after I was laughed at at Oxford, public opinion took a turn, and Roman pronunciation of Latin was adopted in many of the best schools. I was anxious to see them drop their absurd mispronunciation of Greek, but all the authorities whom I consulted on the subject, declared to me that schoolmasters had quite enough to do with learning Italianized Latin, and could not be expected to trouble themselves with learning Athenianized Greek. I had another most quixotic idea, which was truly breaking one's head against a windmill. I wanted the public to pronounce Yob for Job, Yericho for Jericho, Yakoob for Jacob, and Yerusalem for Jerusalem. The writers of the Anglican version, must certainly have intended this, and it is inconceivable how the whole English public dropped the cognate German pronunciation of J, and took to that of France and Italy.

At last the dreary time passed away, and a happy family meeting was promised. My father brought my mother and sister from Pisa to Wiesbaden in Germany, and we boys, as we were still called, were invited over to spend the Long Vacation. We were also to escort

Mrs. D'Aguilar, who with two of her daughters were determined to see the Rhine. One of the girls was Emily, who died soon. The other was Eliza, who married a clergyman of the name of Pope, and whose son, Lieutenant Pope of the 24th Queen's, died gallantly at Isandula; though surrounded by numbers, he kept firing his revolver and wounding his enemies, till he received a mortal wound by an assegai in the breast. This was on January 22nd, 1879. In the end of 1875 he came to Folkestone, to take leave of my wife and me, who were going out to India. We both liked him very much.

In those days travellers took the steamer from London Bridge, dropped quietly down the Thames, and, gaining varied information about the places on both sides of it, dined as usual on a boiled leg of mutton and caper sauce, and roast ribs of beef with horse-radish, and slept as best they could in the close boxes called berths or on deck; if the steamer was in decent order, and there was not too much head wind, they could be in the Scheldt next morning.

Our little party passed a day at Antwerp, which looked beautiful from the river. The Cathedral tower and the tall roofs and tapering spires of the churches around it made a matchless group. We visited the fortifications, which have lately done such good work, and we had an indigestion of Rubens, who appeared so gross and so fleshy after the Italian school. Mrs. D'Aguilar was dreadfully scandalized, when, coming suddenly into a room, she found her two nephews at romps with a pretty little *soubrette*, whose short petticoats enabled her to deliver the sharpest possible kicks, while she employed her hands in vigorously defending her jolly red cheeks. The poor lady threw up her hands and her eyes to heaven when she came suddenly upon this little scene, and she was even more shocked when she found that her escort had passed the Sunday evening in the theatre.

From Antwerp we travelled to Bruges, examined the belfry, heard the chimes, and then went on to Cologne. A marvellous old picturesque place it was, with its combination of old churches, crumbling walls, gabled houses, and the narrowest and worst-paved streets we had ever seen. The old Cathedral in those days was not finished, and threatened never to be finished. Still there was the grand solitary tower, with the mystical-looking old crane on the top, and a regular garden growing out of the chinks and crannies of the stonework. Coleridge's saying about Cologne, was still emphatically true in those days, and all travellers had recourse to "Jean Marie Farina *Gegenüber*." What a change there is now, with that hideous Gothic railway bridge, and its sham battlements, and loopholes to defend nothing, with its hideous cast-iron turret over the centre of the church, where the old architect had intended a light stone lantern-tower, with the ridiculous terrace surrounding the building, and with the hideous finials with which the modern German architects have disfigured the grand old building!

At Cologne we took the steamer and ran up the river. A far more sensible proceeding than that of these days, when tourists take the railway, and consequently can see only one side of the view. The river craft was comfortable, the meals were plentiful, the Pisporter was a sound and unadulterated wine, and married remarkably well with Knaster tobacco, smoked in long pipes with painted china bowls. The crowd, too, was good-tempered, and seemed to enjoy its holiday. Bonn, somehow or other, always managed to show at least one very pretty girl, with blue porcelain eyes and gingerbread-coloured hair. Then came the Castle Crag of Drachenfels and the charming Siebengebirge, which in those days were not spoiled by factory chimneys. We landed at Mainz, and from there drove over to thc old Fontes Mattiace, called in modern day Wiesbaden.

It has been said that to enjoy the Rhine one must go to it *from* England, not the other way from Switzerland; and travellers' opinions are very much divided about it, some considering it extremely grand, and others simply pretty. I was curious to see what its effect upon me would be after visiting the four quarters of the globe; so, in May, 1872, I dropped down the river from Basle to the mouth. The southern and the northern two-thirds were uninteresting, but I found the middle as pretty as ever, and, in fact, I enjoyed the beautiful and interesting river more than when I had seen it as a boy.

I found the middle, beginning at Bingen, charming. Bishop Hatto's Tower had become a cockneyfied affair, and the castles, banks, and islands were disagreeably suggestive of Richmond Hill. But Drachenfels, Nonnenswerth, and Rolandseck, were charming, and I quite felt the truth of the saying, that this is one of the paradises of Germany. At Düsseldorf the river became old and ugly, and so continued till Rotterdam.

Wiesbaden in those days was intensely "German and ordinary," as Horace Walpole says. It was a kind of Teutonic Margate, with a *chic* of its own. In the days before railways, this was the case with all these "Baths," where people either went to play, or to get rid of what the Germans call *eine sehr schöne corpulenz*, a corporation acquired by stuffing food of three kinds, salt, sour, or greasy, during nine or ten months of the year. It was impossible to mistake princely Baden-Baden and its glorious Black Forest, for invalid Kissingen or for Homberg, which combined mineral waters and gambling tables. Wiesbaden was so far interesting that it showed the pure and unadulterated summer life of middle-class Germans. There you see in perfection the grave blue-green German eye.

You are surprised at the frequency of the name of Johann. Johann was a servant; Johannes, a professor; Schani, a swell; Jean, a kind of *fréluqué;* Hans, a peasant; and Hansl, a village idiot. Albrecht, with flat occiput, and bat-like ears, long straight hair and cap, with unclean hands, and a huge signet ring on his forefinger, with a pipe rivalling the size of a Turkish *chibouque*, took his regular seat on one of the wooden benches of the promenade, with Frau Mutter mending his stockings on one side, and Fraülein Gretchen knitting mittens on the other. This kind of thing would continue perhaps for ten seasons, but on the eleventh you met Albrecht, *au petit soins*, with Mütze as his bride, and Gretchen being waited upon by her bridegroom Fritz, and then everything went on as before. Amongst the women the *kaffee-gesellschaft* flourished, when coffee and scandal took the place of scandal and tea, the beverage which I irreverently call "chatter-water." The lady of the house invites two or three friends to come and bring their work and drink a cup of coffee. Before the hour arrives the invitations most likely number twenty. They dress in afternoon promenade toilette, which was very unadorned at Wiesbaden, and they drop in one by one—much kissing and shaking of hands and uncloaking; then each one pulls out knitting, or various pieces of work, which are mutually admired, and patterns borrowed, and then they fall to upon children, servants, toilettes, domestic economy, and the reputations of such of their friends as are not there. This goes on for hours, only interrupted by the servant wheeling in a table covered with coffee, cakes, sweetmeats, jam, and *kugelhupf*.

In the evening there was often a dance at the Kursaal—admirable waltzing, and sometimes quadrilles with steps. Here the bald old Englishman, who in France would collect around him all the old ladies in the room to see him dance, was little noticed. The hearty and homely Germans danced themselves, even when they had grey hair.

Our family found a comfortable house at Wiesbaden, and the German servants received the "boys," as we were still called, with exclamations of "Ach! die schöne schwarze kinder." We paid occasionally furtive visits to the Kursaal, and lost a few sovereigns like men. But our chief amusement was the fencing-room. Here we had found new style of play, with the *schläger*, a pointless rapier with razor-like edges. It was a favourite student's weapon, used to settle all their affairs of honour, and they used it with the silly hanging guard. Some of them gave half an hour every day to working at the post, a wooden pillar stuck up in the middle of the room and bound with vertical ribbons of iron.

When we were tired of Wiesbaden, we amused ourselves with wandering about the country. We visited the nearer watering-places. The first was Schwalbach, "the Swallows' Brook," where the rusty waters turned all our hair red. We then went off to Schlangenbad, "the Snakes' Bath," whose Kalydor made the Frenchman fall in love with himself. These waters had such a reputation, that one lady (of course she was called a Russian Princess) used to have them sent half across Europe for daily use.

In those days there were not many English in these out-of-the-way places, and the greater number were Oxford and Cambridge men. They were learning German and making the most extraordinary mistakes. One gentleman said that the German particles were difficult, but he made a great confusion of the matter. Amongst others, there were the daughters of Archbishop Whately, at that time very nice girls. We then returned to Wiesbaden, and went over to Heidelberg, which is so charmingly picturesque. Here we found a little colony of English, and all fraternized at once.

We "boys" wanted to enter one of the so-called brigades, and chose the Nassau, which was the fightingest of all. An Irish student, who was one of the champions of the corps, and who had distinguished himself by slitting more than one nose, called upon us, and, over sundry *schoppes* of beer, declared that we could not be admitted without putting in an appearance at the Hirschgasse. This was a little pot-house at the other side of the river, with a large room where monomachies were fought. The appearance of the combatants was very ridiculous. They had thick felt caps over their heads, whose visors defended their eyes. Their necks were swathed in enormous cravats, and their arms were both padded, and so were their bodies from the waist downwards. There was nothing to hit but the face and the chest. That, however, did not prevent disagreeable accidents. Sometimes too heavy a cut went into the lungs, and at other times took an effect upon either eye. But the grand thing was to walk off with the tip of the adversary's nose, by a dexterous upward snick from the hanging guard. A terrible story was told of a duel between a handsome man and an ugly man. Beauty had a lovely nose, and Beast so managed that presently it was found on the ground. Beauty made a rush for it, but Beast stamped it out of all shape. There was a very little retreating in these affairs, for the lines were chalked upon the ground. The seconds stood by, also armed with swords and protected with masks, to see that there was nothing like a *sauhieb* or unfair cut. A medical student was always present, and when a cut went home, the affair was stopped to sew it up. Sometimes, however, the artery shrank, and its patient was marked with a cross, as it was necessary to open his cheek above and below in order to tie it up.

A story is told of a doctor who attended a students' duel, when the mask fell, and one of them lost his nose. The doctor flew at it and picked it up, and put it in his mouth to keep it warm, whipped out his instruments, needle and thread, and so skilfully stitched on the nose, and stopped it with plaster, that the edges united, and in a few weeks the nose was as handsome and useful as ever.

We boys did not see the fun of this kind of thing, and when our Irish friend told us what the ordeal was, we said that we were perfectly ready to turn out with foils or rapiers, but that we could not stand the paddings. Duels with the broadsword, and without protection, were never fought except on desperate occasions. Our friend promised to report it to the brigade, and the result was that some time afterwards we were introduced to a student, who said that he knew a little fencing, and should like to try a *botte* with us. We smelt a rat, as the phrase is, and showed him only half of what we could do. But apparently that was enough, for our conditions were not accepted, and we were not admitted into the Nassau Brigade.

At Heidelberg I told my father that Oxford life did not in any way suit me. I pleaded for permission to go into the Army, and, that failing, to emigrate to Canada or Australia. He was inexorable. He was always thinking of that fellowship. Edward, too, was deadly tired of Dr. Havergal, and swore that he would rather be a "private" than a fellow of Cambridge. However, he was sent *nolens volens* to the University on the Cam, and there he very speedily came to grief. It was remarked of him, before the end of the first term, that he was never seen at Chapel. His tutor sent for him, and permitted himself strong language on this delinquency. "My dear sir," was the reply, "no party of pleasure ever gets me out of bed before ten o'clock, and do you *really, really* think that I am going to be in Chapel at eight o'clock?" "Are you joking, or is that your mature decision?" said the tutor. "My very ripest decision," said Edward, and consequently he was obliged to leave college without delay.

When the visit was over, and the autumnal term was beginning, I left Germany and steamed down the Rhine. Everything that I saw made me less likely to be pleased at the end of my journey. However, there was no choice for it. I arrived in London, and found my grandmother and aunts still at the seaside, in a house over the cliff at Ramsgate. Ramsgate I rather liked. There were some very handsome girls there, the Ladies P—t, and the place had a kind of distant resemblance to Boulogne. The raffles at the libraries made it a caricature of a German Bath. I wandered about the country; I visited Margate, where the tone of society was perfectly marvellous, and ran about the small adjacent bathing-places, like Broadstairs and Herne Bay. This brought on the time when I was obliged to return to Oxford.

I went there with no good will, and as my father had refused to withdraw me from the University, I resolved to withdraw myself.

My course of action was one of boyish thoughtlessness. Reports of wine-parties were spread everywhere, whispers concerning parodies on venerable subjects, squibs appeared in the local papers—in those days an unpardonable offence—caricatures of Heads of Houses were handed about, and certain improvisations were passed from mouth to mouth. I had a curious power of improvising any number of rhymes, without the slightest forethought; but the power, such as it was, was perfectly useless to me, as it was accompanied with occasional moments of nervousness, when I despaired, without the slightest reason whatever, of finding the easiest rhyme. Probably the professional Italian, who declaims a poem or a tragedy, labours under the perfect conviction that nothing in the world can stop him. And then it is so much easier to rhyme in Italian than in English; so my efforts were mostly confined to epigrams and epitaphs, at wines and supper-parties, and you may be sure that these brilliant efforts did me no good.

This was the beginning of the end. My object was to be rusticated, not to be expelled. The former may happen in consequence of the smallest irregularity, the latter implies ungentlemanly conduct. I cast about in all directions for the safest line, when fortune put the clue into my hands. A celebrated steeplechaser, Oliver the Irishman, came down to Oxford, and I was determined to see him ride. The collegiate authorities, with questionable wisdom, forbad us all to be present at the races, and especially at what they called "the disgraceful scenes of 'race ordinaries.'" Moreover, in order to make matters sure, they ordered all the undergraduates to be present at the college lecture, at the hour when the race was to be run.

A number of high-spirited youngsters of the different colleges swore that they would not stand this nonsense, that it was infringing the liberty of the subject, and that it was treating them like little boys, which they did not deserve. Here, doubtless, they were right. But, well foreseeing what would be the result, they acted according to the common saying, "In for a penny, in for a pound;" so the tandem was ordered to wait behind Worcester College, and when they should have been attending a musty lecture in the tutor's room, they were flicking across the country at the rate of twelve miles an hour. The steeplechase was a delight, and Oliver was very amusing at the race ordinary, although he did not express much admiration for the riding of what he called "The Oxford lads."

Next morning there was eating of humble-pie. The various culprits were summoned to the Green Room and made conscious of the enormity of the offence. I secured the respect of the little knot by arguing the point with the college dignitaries. I boldly asserted that there was no moral turpitude at being present at a race. I vindicated the honour and dignity of collegiate men by asserting that they should not be treated as children. I even dropped the general axiom "that trust begets trust," and "they who trust us elevate us." Now, this was too much of a good thing, to commit a crime, and to declare it a virtuous action. Consequently, when all were rusticated, I was singled out from the *Hoi polloi*, by an especial recommendation not to return to Oxford from a Rus. Stung by a sense of injustice, I declared at once that I would leave the college, and expressed a vicious hope, that the caution-money deposited by my father would be honestly returned to him. This was the climax. There was a general rise of dignitaries, as if a violent expulsion from the room was intended. I made them my lowest and most courtly bow, Austrian fashion, which bends the body nearly double, wished them all happiness for the future, and retired from the scene. I did not see Oxford again till 1850, when, like the prodigal son, I returned to Alma Mater with a half-resolution to finish my terms and take my bachelor degree.* But the idea came too late. I had given myself up to Oriental studies, and I had begun to write books. Yet I was always glad, during my occasional visits home, to call at my old college, have a chat with the Reverend and Venerable Thomas Short, and to breakfast and dine with the dons who had been bachelors or undergraduates at the time of my departure.

The way in which I left Oxford was characteristic of the rest. One of my rusticated friends, Anderson of Oriel, had proposed that we should leave with a splurge—"go up from the land with a soar." There was now no need for the furtive tandem behind Worcester College. It was driven boldly up to the college doors. My bag

---

* How often I have heard him regret that he did not do this, and I can testify that at the bottom of his heart he loved Oxford, but he could not obey his father, and also carry out the destiny for which he was best fitted and obliged to follow.—I. B.

and baggage were stowed away in it, and with a cantering leader and a high-trotting shaft-horse, which unfortunately went over the beds of the best flowers, we started from the High Street by the Queen's Highway to London, I artistically performing upon a yard of tin trumpet, waving adieu to my friends, and kissing my hand to the pretty shop-girls. In my anger I thoroughly felt the truth of the sentiment—

"I leave thee, Oxford, and I loathe thee well,
Thy saint, thy sinner, scholar, prig, and swell."

Alfred Bates Richards, Dick's college mate, wrote in after years: "It is a curious reflection at school for any boy or any master, 'What will become of the boy? Who will turn out well? who ill? Who will distinguish himself? who will remain in obscurity? Who live? who die?' I am sure, though Burton was brilliant, rather wild, and very popular, none of us foresaw his future greatness, nor knew what a treasure we had amongst us."

CHAPTER V.

GOING TO INDIA.

ARRIVING in London, I was received by the family harem with some little astonishment, for they already knew enough of "terms" to be aware that the last was unfinished. I was quite determined to have two or three days in peace, so I thoroughly satisfied all the exigencies of the position by declaring that I had been allowed an extra vacation for taking a double-first with the very highest honours. A grand dinner-party was given, quite the reverse of the fatted calf. Unfortunately, amongst the guests was the Rev. Mr. Phillips, a great friend of mine, who grinned at me, and indirectly ejaculated, "Rusticated, eh?" The aunts said nothing at the time, but they made inquiries, the result of which was a tableau.

This Phillips was the brother of Major-General Sir B. T. Phillips, who served long and well in the Bengal army, was rather a noted figure as a young-old man in London, and died in Paris in 1880.

You will say that these are wild oats with a vengeance, but most thus sow them, and it is better that they should sow them in early youth. Nothing is more melancholy than to see a man suddenly emancipated from family rule, and playing tricks when the heyday is passed. Youth is like new wine that must be allowed to ferment freely, or it will never become clear, strong, and well flavoured.

I was asked what I intended to do, and I replied simply that I wished to go into the Army, but that I preferred the Indian service, as it would show me more of the world, and give me a better chance of active service. There was no great difficulty in getting a commission. The Directors were bound not to sell them, but every now and then they would give a nomination to a friend, and my friend did not throw away the chance. My conviction is that the commission cost £500.

It was arranged that I should sail in the spring, and meanwhile I determined to have a jolly time. I made a number of new acquaintances, including old Mr. Varley, the artist, of whom I was very fond. He had just finished a curious book that he called "Zodiacal Physiognomy," in order to prove that every man resembled, after a fashion, the sign under which he was born. Readers will kindly remember, that in the old Zodiacs, all the figures were either human or bestial. Mr. Varley was a great student of occult science, and perhaps his favourite was astrology. It is curious how little London knows of what goes on in the next-door house. A book on "Alchemy" was printed, and the curious fact came out, that at least one hundred people in London were studying the philosopher's stone.

Mr. Varley drew out my horoscope, and prognosticated that I was to become a great astrologer; but the prophesy came to nothing, for, although I had read Cornelius Agrippa and others of the same school at Oxford, I found Zadkiel quite sufficient for me. Amongst the people that I met was the Rev. Robert, popularly called Satan Montgomery, who had come up from Scotland deadly tired of Glasgow punch, and was making a preaching campaign. He had written a quantity of half-nonsense verses, which were very much admired by his feminine devotees, and which were most savagely mangled by Lord Macaulay in the *Quarterly*. He was an effective figure in the pulpit; he had a very pale face, and tolerably straight features, very black hair, and very white hands, with a large diamond and a very white pocket-handkerchief.

He had, to a marvellous extent, what is vulgarly called the "gift of the gab;" he spoke for an hour without a moment's hesitation. But there was something solid below all this froth, and he had carefully read up all the good old theological works. The women, including the aunts, went literally mad; they crowded the little Gothic chapel, they mobbed as he came in and went out, and they literally overwhelmed him with slippers, chest-protectors, and portable articles to administer the Sacrament. His reign was short; he married, came up to London, took a chapel, subsided into the average popular preacher, and soon died. Amongst others that I met was a certain Robert Bagshaw from Calcutta, who was destined afterwards to marry my aunt Georgina Baker. I managed to offend him very much. He was rather boasting of a new dress-coat, when I delicately raised the tail, and said, "You don't mean to say that you call *this* a coat?"

With all this wasting of time, I kept my eye steadily fixed upon the main chance. I gave up boxing at Owen Swift's, and fencing at Angelo's, and spent all my spare time in learning Hindostani with old Duncan Forbes. A very curious old Scotchman it was. He had spent a year or so in Bombay, and upon the strength of it, he was perfect master of Oriental languages. He had two passions: one was for smoking a huge meerschaum, stuffed with the strongest possible tobacco, and the other was for chess, concerning which he published some, at that time, very interesting and novel studies.

Perhaps his third passion was not quite so harmless; it was simply for not washing. He spoke all his Eastern languages with the broadest possible Scotch accent; and he cared much more for telling anecdotes, than for teaching. However, he laid a fair foundation, and my *then* slight studies of Arabic, secured me the old man's regard. He published a number of books, and he certainly had not the *suaviter in modo.* He attacked Eastwick, the Orientalist, in the most ferocious style.

Presently the day came when I was to be sworn in at the India House. In those days the old building stood in Leadenhall Street, and gave Thackeray a good opportunity of attacking it as the "Hall of Lead;" a wonderful dull and smoky old place it was, with its large and gorgeous porter outside, and its gloomy, stuffy old rooms inside, an atmosphere which had actually produced "The Essays of Elia." In those days it kept up a certain amount of respect for itself. If an officer received a gift of a sword, he was conducted by the tall porter to the general meeting of the Directors, and duly spoken to and complimented in form; but as times waxed harder, the poor twenty-four Kings of Leadenhall Street declined from Princes into mere *Shayhks.* They actually sent a Sword of Honour to one of their officers by a street messenger, and the donee returned it, saying, he could not understand the *manner* of the gift; and so it went on gradually declining and falling, till at last the old house was abandoned and let for offices. The shadowy Directors flitted to the West End, into a brand-new India House, which soon brought on their Euthanasia.

My bringing-up caused me to be much scandalized by the sight of my future comrades and brother officers, which I will presently explain. The Afghan disaster was still fresh in public memory. The aunts had been patriotic enough to burst into tears when they heard of it; and certainly it was an affecting picture, the idea of a single Englishman, Dr. Brydone, riding into Jellalabad, the only one of thirteen thousand, he and his horse so broken as almost to die at the gates.

Poor General Elphinstone, by-the-by, had been my father's best man at his marriage, and was as little fitted for such field service, as Job was at his worst. Alexander Burns was the only headpiece in the lot. He had had the moral courage to report how critical the position was; but he had not the moral courage to insist upon his advice being taken, and, that failing, to return to his regiment as a Captain.

MacNaghten was a mere Indian civilian. Like too many of them, he had fallen into the dodging ways of the natives, and he distinctly deserved his death. The words used by Akbar Khan, by-the-by, when he shot him, were, "Shumá mulk-e-má mí gírid" ("So you're the fellow who've come to take our country").

But the result of the massacre was a demand for soldiers and officers, especially Anglo-Indians. Some forty medical students were sent out, and they naturally got the name of the "Forty Thieves." The excess of demand explained the curious appearance of the embryo cadets when they met to be sworn in at the India House. They looked like raw country lads, mostly dressed in home-made clothes, and hair cut by the village barber, country boots, and no gloves. So my friend, Colonel White's son, who was entering the service on the same day, and I looked at one another in blank dismay. We had fallen amongst young Yahoos, and we looked forward with terror to such society. I was originally intended for Bengal, but, as has been seen, I had relations there. I was not going to subject myself to surveillance by my uncle by marriage, an old general of invalids. Moreover, one of my D'Aguilar cousins was married to a judge in Calcutta. I was determined to have as much liberty as possible, and therefore I chose Bombay. I was always of opinion that a man proves his valour by doing what he likes; there is no merit in so doing when you have a fair fortune and independent position, but for a man bound by professional ties, and too often lacking means to carry out his wishes, it is a great success to choose his own line and stick to it.

The next thing to do was to obtain an outfit. This was another great abuse in those days. As the friends of the Directors made money by the cadets' commissions to the friends, the friends made money by sending them to particular houses. The unfortunate cadets, or rather their parents, were in fact plundered by everything that touched them. The outfit, which was considered *de rigueur*, was absurdly profuse. Dozens upon dozens of white jackets and trousers, only fit to give rheumatism—even tobacco, niggerhead and pigtail, as presents for the sailors. Even the publishers so arranged that their dictionaries and grammars of Hindostani should be forced upon the unhappy youths.* The result was absolutely ridiculous. As a rule, the bullock trunks were opened

* Our boxes were stuffed with Wellington's despatches, Army Regulations, Mill's ponderous "History of India," and whatever the publisher chose to agree upon with the outfitter.

during the voyage, the kit was displayed, and on fast ships it was put down as a stake at cards. Stories are told of sharp hands landing in India after winning half a dozen outfits, which literally glutted the market. Guns, pistols, and swords, and saddles were of the most expensive and useless description, and were all to be bought much better, at a quarter the price, in any Indian port.

The average of the voyage lasted four months. Two or three changes of suits only, were necessary, and the £100 outfit was simply plunder to the outfitter.

An unusual article of outfit was ordered by me, and that was a wig from Winter in Oxford Street. In early life I found the advantage of shaving my head, enabling me to keep it cool, when it was usually in the other condition.

An old Joe Miller was told in Bombay about a certain Duncan Grey, a Scotch doctor, who was famous for selling hog-mane ponies to new-comers. He was in medical attendance upon the cadets, and took the opportunity of pocketing his wig, and persuading them that shaved heads were the official costume. He accompanied them for the first official visit, and as they were taking off their caps he whipped on his wig, and presented to the astonished Commanding Officer half a dozen utterly bald pates, which looked as if they belonged to as many lunatics.

My only companion was a bull-terrier of the Oxford breed, more bull than terrier. Its box-head and pink face had been scratched all over during a succession of dog-fights and various tussles with rats. It was beautifully built in the body, and the tail was as thin as a little finger, showing all the vertebræ. The breed seems to have become almost extinct, but I found it again at Oxford when I went there in 1850. The little brute bore a fine litter of pups, and died in Gujarat, as usual with every sign of old age, half-blind eyes, and staggering limbs. The pups grew up magnificently. One, which rejoiced in the name of Bachhûn, received the best of educations. He was entered necessarily on mice, rats, and *Gilahris*, or native squirrels, which bite and scratch like cats. He was so thoroughly game, that he would sally out alone in the mornings, and kill a jackal single-handed. He was the pride of the regiment, and came as usual to a bad end. On one of my journeys, dressed as a native, I had to leave him behind in charge of my friend Dr. Arnold, surgeon of the regiment. Dr. Arnold also, when absent, confided him to the care of a brother-medico, Dr. Pitman, who had strict opinions on the subject of drugs. The wretch actually allowed the gallant little dog to die of some simple disease, because he would not give him a dose of medicine belonging to the Company.

CHAPTER VI.

MY PUBLIC LIFE BEGINS.

"Wanted: Men.
Not systems fit and wise,
Not faiths with rigid eyes,
Not wealth in mountain piles,
Not power with gracious smiles,
Not even the potent pen;
Wanted: Men.

"Wanted: Deeds.
Not words of winning note,
Not thoughts from life remote,
Not fond religious airs,
Not sweetly languid prayers,
Not love of scent and creeds;
Wanted: Deeds.

"Men and Deeds.
Men that can dare and do;
Not longing for the new,
Not pratings of the old:
Good life and action bold—
These the occasion needs,
Men and Deeds."

DUNCAN MACGREGOR.

THE next thing was to choose a ship, and the aunts were directed by their friend of the commission, to the *John Knox* (Captain Richard B. Cleland), sailing barque, belonging to Messrs. Guy and Co. I was to embark at Greenwich; the family harem went down with me. I was duly wept over, and I dropped down the river with the scantiest regret (except for my relatives) for leaving Europe, on June 18th, 1842.

My companions were Ensign Boileau, of the 22nd Regiment, Ensign Thompson, of the Company (line), and Mr. Richmond, going out to a commercial house in Bombay.*

* The general orders of the Commander-in-Chief—

"To rank from date of sailing from Gravesend to the ship by which they proceeded in the following order, viz.:—

"Charles Thompson, per barque *John Knox* ..	June 18, 1842.
Richard Francis Burton, per barque *John Knox* ..	June 18, 1842.
The latter appointed to the 14th Regiment B.N.I.	Sept. 24, 1842.
The latter transferred to 18th B.N.I.	Oct. 25, 1842.
No. 106, date of arrival at Bombay	Oct. 28, 1842."

There was an equal number of the other sex—a lady calling herself Mrs. Lewis, and three sturdy wives of sergeants. Fortunately also, there were three native servants who spoke Hindostani.

The voyage began as usual by a straight run down the Channel, and a June weather passage along the coasts of Europe and Africa. There were delays in the Doldrums and calms near the Line. Neptune came on board as usual, but there was very little fun, the numbers being too small. At such times troubles are apt to break out on board. The captain, Richard Cleland, was one of the best seamen that ever commanded a ship, yet his career had been unlucky—as Vasco da Gama said to Don Manoel, "Men who are unfortunate at sea should avoid the affairs of the sea." He had already lost one ship, which was simply ill-fortune, for no seaman could be more sober or more attentive to his duty. He managed, however, to have a row on board, called upon the cadets to load their pistols and accompany him to the forecastle, where he was about to make a mutineer a prisoner. These were very disagreeable things to interfere with, and the Supreme Court of Bombay always did its best to hang an officer if a seaman was shot on these occasions; one man in particular had a narrow escape.

The discipline on the ship was none of the best. Captain Cleland had begun early, and determined to establish a raw, and invited me to put on the gloves with him. The result was that the tall lanky Scotchman, who was in particularly bad training, got knocked into a cocked hat. Then arose the usual troubles amongst the passengers. Normally on such voyages, all begin by talking together, and end by talking with themselves. Of course there were love passages, and these only made matters worse. The chief mate, a great hulking fellow, who ought to have hit like Tom Spring, but whose mutton fist could not dent a pat of butter, was solemnly knocked down on quarter-deck for putting in his oar. Then followed a sham duel, the combatants being brought up at midnight, and the pistols loaded with balls of blackened cork instead of bullets. During the day there were bathings along the ship in a sail, to keep out the sharks; catching of sharks and flying-fish, and massacring of unhappy birds. I, however, utilized my time by making the three native servants who were on board, talk with me, and by reading Hindostani stories from old Shakespeare's text-book. I made a final attempt to keep up musical notation, and used the flageolet to the despair of all on board; but the chief part of my time was passed in working at Hindostani, reading all the Eastern books on board, gymnastics, and teaching my brother youngsters the sword. There was also an immense waste of gunpowder, for were not all these young gentlemen going out to be Commanders-in-Chief?

The good ship *John Knox* ran past the Cape in winter, and a magnificent scene it was. Waves measuring miles in length came up from the South Pole, in lines as regular as those of soldiers marching over a dead plain. Over them floated the sheep-like albatrosses, whom the cadets soon tired of shooting, especially when they found that it was almost impossible to stuff the bird. The little stormy petrels were respected, but the Cape pigeons were drawn on board in numbers, with a hook and a bit of bait. Nothing could be brighter than the skies and seas, and the experience of what is called "a white gale" gave universal satisfaction. It came down without any warning, except ploughing up the waters, and had not Captain Cleland been on deck and let go his gear, most of the muslin would have been on the broad bosom of the Atlantic.

There was little interest in sailing up the eastern coast of South Africa. We saw neither the coast nor Madagascar, but struck north-east for the western coast of India. The usual tricks were played upon new-comers. They had been made to see the Line by a thread stretched over a spy-glass, and *now* they were told to smell India after a little oil of cloves had been rubbed upon the bulwarks!

When the winds fell, the cadets amused themselves with boarding the *pattymars*, and other native craft, and went ferreting all about the cabins and holes, to the great disgust of the owners. They gaped at the snakes, which they saw swimming about, and were delighted when the *John Knox*, one fine night, lumbered on her way through nets and fishing stakes, whose owners set up a noise like a gigantic frog concert. Next morning, October 28th, the Government pilot came on board; excited questions were put to him, "What was doing in Afghanistan? What of the war?" At his answer all hopes fell to zero. Lord Ellenbrough had succeeded Lord Auckland. The avenging army had returned through the Khaybar Pass. The campaign was finished. Ghuzni had fallen, the prisoners had been given up. Pollock, Sale, and Pratt had been perfectly successful, and there was no chance of becoming Commanders-in-Chief within the year.

I never expected to see another Afghan War, and yet I did so before middle age was well over.

> "Thy towers, Bombay! gleam bright, they say,
> Against the dark blue sea,"

absurdly sings the poet. It was no picture like this we saw on the morning of the 28th of October, 1842, when our long voyage ended.

The bay so celebrated appeared anything but beautiful. It was a great splay thing, too long for its height, and it had not one of the beautiful perpendiculars that distinguish Parthenope.

The high background is almost always hid by the reek that rises during the day, and the sun seems to burn all the colour out of the landscape. The rains had just ceased, yet the sky seemed never clear, and the water wanted washing. After this preliminary glance, the companions shook hands, and, not without something of soreness of heart, separated, after having lived together nearly five months. I went to the British Hotel in the Fort, then kept by an Englishman named Blackwell, who delegated all his duty to a Parsee, and never troubled himself about his guests. A Tontine Hotel had been long proposed, but there is a long interval between sayings and doings in India. The landing in a wretched shore-boat at the unclean Apollo Bunder, an absurd classicism for Palawa Bunder, was a complete disenchanter. Not less so to pass through the shabby doorway in the dingy old fortifications, which the Portuguese had left behind them when the island was ceded to Charles II. The bright Towers were nowhere, and the tower of a cathedral that resembled a village church, seemed to be splotched and corroded as if by gangrene.

Bombay was in those days the most cosmopolitan City in the East, and the Bhendi Bazaar, the centre of the old town, was the most characteristic part of all—perhaps more characteristic than were those of Cairo or Damascus. It was marvellously picturesque with its crowds of people from every part of the East, and its utter want of what is called civilization, made it a great contrast to what it became a score of years afterwards. Englishmen looked at it with a careless eye, as a man scours his own property, but foreigners (Frenchmen like Jacquemont, and Germans like Von Orlich) were delighted with its various humours, and described them in their most picturesque style. Everything looked upon a pauper scale.

The first sight of a Sepoy nearly drove me back to the *John Knox.* I saw an imitation European article; I saw a shako, planted on the top of a dingy face, and hair as greasy as a Chinese's. The coat of faded scarlet seemed to contain a mummy with arms like drumsticks, and its legs, clad in blue dungaree, seemed to fork from below its waist; and yet this creature in his national dress, was uncommonly picturesque, with his long back hair let down, his light jacket of white cotton, his salmon-coloured waistcloth falling to his ankles, in graceful folds, and his feet in slippers of bright cloth, somewhat like the *piéd d'ours* of the mediæval man-at-arms. The hotel was an abomination. Its teas and its curries haunted the censorium of memory for the rest of man's natural life. The rooms were loose boxes, and at night intoxicated acquaintances stood upon chairs and amused themselves by looking over the thin cloth walls. I stood this for a few days till I felt sick with rage. I then applied to the garrison surgeon, in those days Dr. J. W. Ryan, popularly known as Paddy Ryan.* He was a good-natured man; he enquired copiously about my Irish relations and connections, knew something of Lord Trimleston, and removed me from the foul hotel, to what in those days was called the Sanitarium.

The Sanitarium was a pompous name for a very poor establishment. About half a dozen bungalows of the semi-detached kind, each with its bit of compound or yard, fronted in a military line Back Bay, so famous for wrecks. The quarters consisted of a butt and ben, an outer room and an inner room, with unattached quarters for servants. They were places in which an Englishman tolerably well off would hardly kennel his dogs, and the usual attendants were lizards and bandicoot rats. As each tenant went away he carried off his furniture, so it was necessary to procure bed, table, and chairs. That, however, was easily done by means of a little Parsee broker, who went by the name of "The General," and who had plundered generations after generations of cadets. He could supply everything from a needle to a buggy, or ten thousand rupees on interest, and those who once drank his wine never forgot it. He was shockingly scandalized at the sight of my wig. Parsees must touch nothing that come from the human body.

He recommended as *moonshee*, or language-master, a venerable old Parsee priest, in white hat and beard, named Dosabhai Sohrabji, at that time the best-known coach in Bombay. Through his hands also generations of griffins have passed. With him, as with all other Parsees, Gujarati was the mother tongue, but he also taught Hindostani and Persian, the latter the usual vile Indian article. He had a great reputation as a teacher, and he managed to ruin it by publishing a book of dialogues in English and these three languages, wherein he showed his perfect unfitness. He was *very* good, however, when he had no pretensions, and in his hands I soon got through the Akhlak-i-Hindi and the Tota-Kaháni. I remained friends with the old man till the end of his days, and the master always used to quote his pupil, as a man who could learn a language running.

The Sanitarium was not pleasantly placed. In latter days the foreshore was regulated, and a railroad ran along the sea. But in

* He was assistant garrison surgeon, serving under Superintendent Surgeon A. C. Kane. The latter's name evidently subjected him to a variety of small witticisms, especially when he was called in to treat a certain A. Bell.

1842 the façade was a place of abominations, and amongst them, not the least, was the *Smashán*, or Hindu burning-ground. The fire-birth was conducted with very little decency; the pyres were built up on the sands, and heads and limbs were allowed to tumble off, and when the wind set in the right quarter, the smell of roast Hindú was most unpleasant. The occupants of the Sanitarium were supposed to be invalids, but they led the most roystering and rackety life. Mostly they slept in the open, under mosquito curtains, with a calico ceiling, and a bottle of cognac under the bed. One of these, who shall be nameless, married shortly after, and was sturdily forbidden by his wife to indulge in night draughts when he happened to awake. He succumbed, but pleaded permission to have an earthen gugglet of pure water. The spouse awoke one night in a state of thirst, which she proceeded to quench, and was nearly choked by a draught of gin-and-water compounded in what are called nor'-wester proportions, three of spirit to one of water. One of the invalids led me into all kinds of mischief, introducing me to native society of which the less said the better.

The Governor of Bombay at the time was Colonel Sir George Arthur, Bart., K.C.H., who appears in "Jack Hinton, the Guardsman." He was supposed to be connected with the Royal Family through George IV., and had some curious ideas about his visitors "backing" from the "Presence." The Commander-in-Chief was old Sir Thomas Macmahon, popularly called "Tommy." He was one of the old soldiers who had served under the Duke of Wellington, who had the merit of looking after his friends, as well as looking up his enemies; but he was utterly unfit for any command, except that of a brigade. It would be impossible to tell one tithe of the stories current about him. One of his pet abominations was a certain Lieutenant Pilfold, of the 2nd Queen's, whose commanding officer, Major Brough, was perpetually court-martialling. Pilfold belonged to that order of soldiers which is popularly called "the lawyer," and invariably argued himself out of every difficulty. Pilfold was first court-martialled in 1840, then 1841, and 1844, when, after being nearly cashiered, he changed into a regiment in Australia, and died. At last he revenged himself upon the Commander-in-Chief by declaring that "as hares go mad in March, so Major-Generals go mad in May"—the day when "Tommy" confirmed one of the court-martials, that was quashed from home.

The Bombay Marine, or, as the officers preferred it to be called, "The Indian Navy," had come to grief. Their excellent superintendent, Admiral Sir Charles Malcolm, was a devoted geographer; in fact, he was the man who provoked the saying, "Capable of speaking evil, even of the Equator." Under his rule, when there was peace at sea, the officers were allowed ample leave to travel and explore in the most dangerous countries, and they did brilliant service. Their names are too well known to require quotation. But Sir Charles was succeeded by a certain Captain Oliver, R.N., a sailor of the Commodore Trunnion type, and a martinet of the first water. He made them stick to their monotonous and wearisome duties in the Persian Gulf, and in other places, popularly said to be separated by a sheet of brown paper. He was as vindictive as he was one-ideaed, and the service will never forget the way in which he broke the heart of an unfortunate Lieutenant Bird.

Captain Cleland, of the *John Knox*, had introduced me to his sister, Mrs. Woodburn, who was married to an adjutant of the 25th Regiment of Sepoys, and she kindly introduced me to Bombay society. I stood perfectly aghast in its presence. The rank climate of India, which produces such a marvellous development of vegetation, seems to have a similar effect upon the Anglo-Indian individuality. It shot up, as if suddenly relieved of the weight with which society controls it in England. The irreligious were marvellously irreligious, and the religious no less marvellously religious. The latter showed the narrowest, most fanatic, and the most intolerant spirit; no hard-grit Baptist could compare with them. They looked upon the heathen around them (very often far better than themselves) as faggots ready for burning.* They believed that the Parsees adored the sun, that the Hindús worshipped stocks and stones, and that the Mohammedans were slaves to what they called "the impostor Mahomet." They were not more lenient to those of their own blood who did not run on exactly the same lines with them. A Roman Catholic, as they called him, was doomed to perdition, and the same was the case with all non-church-going Protestants. It is hardly to be wondered at if, at times, they lost their wits. One man, who was about the wildest of his day, and who was known as the "Patel" of Griffin-gaon, suddenly got a "call." He used to distinguish himself by climbing a tree every morning, and by shouting with all his might, "Dunga Chhor-do, Jesus Christ, Pakro," meaning, "Abandon the world, and catch hold of the Saviour." This lasted for years, and it ended in his breaking down in the moral line, and dying in a mad-house.

The worst of all this was, that in 1842, there were very few white faces in Bombay, and every man, woman, and child knew his, her, or its religious affairs, as well as their own. It was, in fact, a garrison,

* Amongst natives, caste is so powerful in India that it even affects Mlenchha, or outcast races.

not a colony. People lived in a kind of huge barracks. Essentially a middle-class society, like that of a small county town in England, it was suddenly raised to the top of a tree, and lost its head accordingly. Men whose parents in England were small tradesmen, or bailiffs in Scotland, found themselves ruling districts and commanding regiments, riding in carriages, and owning more pounds a month than their parents had pounds a year. Those who had interest, especially in Leadenhall Street, monopolized the best appointments, and gathered in clans at the Residency, as head-quarters were called. They formed the usual ring—a magic circle into which no intruder was admitted, save by the pain *fort et dure* of intermarriage. The children were hideously brought up, and, under the age of five, used language that would make a porter's hair stand on an end. The parents separated, of course, into cliques. At that time Bombay was ruled by two Queens, who in subaltern circles went by the name of "Old Mother Plausible," and "Old Mother Damnable."

To give a taste of "Mother Damnable's" quality : I had been waltzing with a girl, who, after too much exertion, declared herself fainting. I led her into what would at home be called the cloak-room, fetched her a glass of water, and was putting it to her lips, when the old lady stood at the door. "Oh dear ! I never intended to interrupt you," she said, made a low bow, and went out of the room, positively delighted. "Mother Plausible's" style was being intensely respectable. She was terribly "exercised" about a son at Addiscombe, and carefully consulted every new cadet about his proficiency in learning. "But does he prefer the classics ?" she asked a wild Irishman. "I don't know that he does," was the answer. "Or mathematics ?" The same result. "Or modern languages ?" "Well, no !" "Then what does he do ?" "Faix," said the informant, scratching his head for an idea, "he's a very purty hand at football."

But it was not only Society that had such an effect upon me. I found the Company's officers, as they were called, placed in a truly ignoble position. They had double commissions, and signed by the Crown, and yet they ranked with, but after, their brothers and cousins in the Queen's service. Moreover, with that strange superciliousness, which seems to characterize the English military service, and that absence of brotherhood which distinguishes the Prussian and Austrian, all seemed to look down upon their neighbours. The Queen's despised the Company, calling them armed policemen, although they saw as much, if not much more service, than the Queen's in India. The Artillery held its head above the Cavalry, the Cavalry above the Line, and, worse still, a Company's officer could not, except under very exceptional circumstances, rise above a certain rank. Under the circumstances, I ventured to regret that I had not entered the Duke of Lucca's Guards. India had never heard of the Duke of Lucca, or his Guards, and when they heard the wild idea—

> "Their inextinguished laughter rent the skies."

For instance, they had no hopes of becoming local Commanders-in-Chief, and the General Commander-in-Chief of the East Indies was carefully put out of their reach. None but Englishmen would have entered such a service under such conditions. A French *piou-piou*, with his possible marshal's bâton in his knapsack, would have looked down upon it with contempt; but England, though a fighting nation, is not a military people, or rather *was* not until Louis Napoleon made it necessary that they should partially become so. At the end of six weeks or so, I received orders to join my regiment, which was then stationed at Baroda, in Gujarat. In those days there were no steamers up the coast, and men hired what were called *pattymars.** As the winds were generally northerly, these tubs often took six weeks over what a civilized craft now does in four days.

The happy family embarked from Bombay. I preferred engaging Goanese-Portuguese servants, as they were less troublesome than Hindús and Mussulmans. I had engaged an excellent *buttrel*, named Salvador Soares, who was *major domo* over the establishment, for at that time a subaltern never had less than a dozen servants. The sail northwards, with all its novelties, was delightful, and I made a point of landing every evening to see all that I could see upon the way. And so I had my first look at Bassein, Broach, and Surat, the latter a kind of nursery of the Anglo-Indian Empire. After a fortnight or so the *pattymar* reached the Tankaria-Bunder, the mud-bank where travellers landed to reach Baroda. Then came the land march of four days, which was full of charms for a Griffin. I had utterly rejected the so-called Arab horses—bastard brutes from the Persian Gulf—which were sold at the Bombay bomb-proofs then at extravagant prices of five hundred rupees, now doubled, and had contented myself with Kattywar horses. This was a bright dun, with black stripes and stockings, a very vicious brute, addicted to all the sins of horseflesh, but full of spirit as a thoroughbred. Master and horse got on thoroughly well, and the gallant animal travelled everywhere, till it was killed on the Neilgherry Hills by a heavy fall on its side on the slippery clay. The marching was at the rate of about twelve or fifteen miles a day,

* For description of *pattymar*, see "Goa and Blue Mountains," by R. F. Burton.

and the leisure hours gave ample opportunity of seeing everything on and off the road.

To the traveller from Europe, Gujarat in winter was a novel spectacle. The ground, rich black earth, was almost flat, and was covered with that vivid leek-like verdigris green, which one associates with early spring in the temperates. The little villages, with their leafy huts, were surrounded and protected by hedge milk-bush, green as emeralds, and nothing could be more peaceful or charming than the evening hour, when the flocks and herds were returning home, and the villagers were preparing for supper and sleep, with a sky-blue mist overhanging the scene. A light veil, coloured like Damascene silver, hung over each settlement, and the magnificent trees, compared with which the oaks in Hyde Park appeared like shrubs, were tipped by peacocks screaming their good-night to the sun. How curious that the physiologist will assert that the nose has no memory! That light cloud was mostly composed of cow-chips smoke, and I could never think of Gujarat without recalling it; even the bazar always suggested spices and cocoa-nut oil.

Again I was scandalized by the contrast of the wretched villages under English rule, and those that flourished under the Gaikwar. After the boasting of Directorial speeches, and their echoes in the humbug press, I could not understand this queer contrast of fiction and fact. I made inquiries about it from every one, and immensely disgusted the Company's Resident, Mr. Boyd, by my insistance, but a very few weeks explained the matter to me. The Anglo-Indian rule had no elasticity, and everything was iron-bound; it was *all rule* without exception. A crack young Collector would have considered himself dishonoured had he failed to send in the same amount of revenues during a bad season, as during the best year. It was quite different with the natives. After a drought or an inundation, a village would always obtain remission of taxes, it being duly understood that a good harvest would be doubly taxed, and this was the simple reason why the natives preferred their own to foreign rule. In the former case they were harried and plundered whenever anything was to be got out of them, but in the mean time they were allowed to make their little piles. Under the English they were rarely tortured, and never compelled to give up their hardly won earnings, but they had no opportunity of collecting the wherewithal for plunder.

On the fourth day I arrived at my head-quarters, Baroda, and found myself lodged in the comfortless travellers' bungalow. Here I was duly inspected by my brother officers—Major H. James, then commanding the 18th Bombay Native Infantry, Captain Westbrooke, second in command, Lieutenant MacDonald, who was married,

Lieutenant and Adjutant Craycroft, Lieutenant J. J. Coombe, Ensign S. N. Raikes, and Assistant-Surgeon Arnott, and a few others present. One wing of the corps, containing a greater number of officers, had been stationed for some time at Mhow, on the borders of the Bengal Presidency, and the rest, as usual in those days, were on the Staff, that is, on detached employment, some in Civil employ, and others in the Corps called Irregulars.

The first night at Mess was an epoch, and the old hands observed that I drank no beer. This was exceptional in those days. Malt liquor had completed the defeat of brandy pawnee and the sangaree (sherry, etc., with water, sugar, and spices) affected by a former generation, and beer was now king. The most moderate drank two bottles a day of strong bottled stuff supposed to have been brewed by Bass and Allsopp, but too often manipulated by the Parsee importer. The immoderate drank a round dozen, not to speak of other liquors. The messes in those days were tolerably rich, and their *godowns*, or stores, generally contained a fair supply of port, sherry, and Madeira. "Drink beer, think beer" is essentially true in India. Presently the bloating malt liquor began to make way for thin French wines, claret, and Burgundy, and a quarter of a century afterwards, the Anglo-Indian returned to brandy pawnee with a difference. The water was no longer plain water, but soda-water, that is, carbonic-acid gas pumped into well water, and every little station had its own manufactory. Consequently the price declined from eighteenpence to twopence a bottle, and most men preferred the "peg," as it is called, which is probably one of the least harmful. I adhered manfully to a couple of glasses of port a day. Paddy Ryan at Bombay had told me that the best tonic after fever, was a dozen of good port. I soon worked out the fact, that what would cure fever, might also prevent it, and consequently drank port as a febrifuge. It was the same with me on the West Coast of Africa, where during four years of service I came off well, when most other men died.

I was duly introduced to the drill-ground, where I had not much to learn. Yet I studied military matters with all my might, for the ominous words "tail of the Afghan storm" were in many men's mouths. I had taught myself, with the assistance of books, the mysteries of goose-step and extension movements, and perpetual practice with the sword had made the other manœuvres easy to me. Having lodged myself in what was called a bungalow, a thatched article not unlike a cowshed, and having set up the slender household, I threw myself with a kind of frenzy upon my studies. I kept up the little stock of Arabic that I had acquired at Oxford, and gave some twelve hours a day to a desperate tussle with

Hindostani. Two *moonshees* barely sufficed for me. Sir Charles J. Napier in 1842 was obscurely commanding at Poonah. Presently he was appointed to the Command in Sind, and all those who knew the old soldier looked forward to lively times. Brevet-Major Outram, of the 23rd N.I., had proceeded to England on December 13th, 1842, and had returned to India in February, 1843. This rapid movement also had an ominous sound. The military day was then passed in India as follows :—

Men rose early, for the sun in India keeps decent hours (not like the greater light in England, which in summer seems to rise shortly after midnight, and in winter shortly before noon). The first proceeding was a wash in cold water and a cup of tea. After that the horse was brought round saddled, and carried the rider to the drill-ground. Work usually began as soon as it was light, and lasted till shortly after sunrise. In the Bengal Presidency the officers used to wash their teeth at three a.m., and scarcely ever saw the face of the sun. Consequently the Qui-hyes, or Bengalís, died like sheep upon a march where much exposure was necessary.

In India the sun requires a little respect. It is not wise, for instance, to wade through cold water with the rays beating upon the upper part of the body, but it is always advisable to accustom one's self to sunshine. After the parade was over, the officers generally met at what was called a coffee shop, where one of the number hung out *Choti-hazri* or little breakfast—tea or *café au lait*, biscuit, bread and butter, and fruit. After that, the heavy work of the day being done, each proceeded to amuse himself as he best could; some to play at billiards, others for a day's sport.

Some few youths in the flush of Griffinhood used to mount their tattoos (ponies) and go out "peacocking," that is to say, calling upon officers' wives. With the usual Indian *savoir vivre*, visiting hours were made abominable. Morning calls began at eleven o'clock, when the *beau sexe* was supposed to be in war-paint, and ended at two, when it was supposed to sit down to tiffin. The ride through the burning sun, followed by a panting *ghorewalla*, and the self-preservation in a state of profuse perspiration, were essentials of peacocking, which soon beat off the most ardent admirers of the white fair sex. The latter revenged itself for anything like neglect in the most violent way, and the consequence was that, in those days, most men, after their first year, sought a refuge in the society of the dark fair. Hence in the year of grace 1842 there was hardly an officer in Baroda who was not more or less morganatically married to a Hindí or a Hindú woman. This could be a fertile ground for anecdote, but its nature forbids entering into details.

These irregular unions were mostly temporary, under agreement to cease when the regiment left the station. Some even stipulated that there were to be no children. The system had its advantages and disadvantages. It connected the white stranger with the country and its people, gave him an interest in their manners and customs, and taught him thoroughly well their language. It was a standing joke in my regiment that one of the officers always spoke of himself in the feminine gender. He had learnt all his Hindostani from his harem. On the other hand, these unions produced a host of half-castes, mulattos, "neither fish nor fowl, nor good red herring," who were equally despised by the races of both progenitors.

Baroda was not a great place for pig-sticking. The old grey boars abounded, but the country was too much cut up by deep and perpendicular hillocks, which were death to horse and man. I invested in an old grey Arab, which followed the game like a bloodhound, with distended nostrils, and ears viciously laid back. I began, as was the cruel fashion of the day, by spearing pariah dogs for practice, and my first success brought me a well-merited accident. Not knowing that the least touch of the sharp leaf-like head is sufficient to kill, I made a mighty thrust with my strong-made bamboo shaft, which was carried under the arm, Bombay fashion, not overhand, as in Bengal. The point passed through the poor brute and deep into the ground. The effect of the strong elastic spear was to raise me bodily out of the saddle, and to throw me over the horse's head. It was a good lesson for teaching how to take first blood. The great centres for pig-sticking were in the Deccan and in Sind. The latter, however, offered too much danger, for riding through tamarisk bushes is much like charging a series of well-staked fishing-nets. Baroda, however, abounded in wild beasts; the jackals screamed round the bungalows every night, and a hyæna once crossed, in full day, the parade ground. One of the captains (Partridge) cut it down with his regimental sword, and imprudently dismounted to secure it. The result was a bite in the arm which he had reason long to remember.

The sport all about Baroda was excellent, for in the thick jungle to the east of the City, tigers were to be shot, and native friends would always lend their elephants for a day's work. In the broad plains to the north, large antelopes, called the *nilghai,* browsed about like cows, and were almost as easy to shoot, consequently no one shot them. It was different with the splendid black buck, sly and wary animals, and always brought home in triumph. Cheetahs, or hunting leopards, were also to be had for the asking. As for birds, they were in countless numbers, from the huge adjutant crane, and the *sáras* (*antigoni*), vulgarly called *Cyrus Gries antigone*, which dies if its mate be shot, and the peacock, which there, as in most parts of India, is a sacred bird, to the partridge, which no one eats because it feeds on the road, the wild duck, which gives excellent shooting, and the snipe, equal to any in England. During the early rains quails were to be shot in the compounds, or yards, attached to the bungalows. In fact, in those days, sensible men who went out to India took one of two lines—they either shot, or they studied languages.

Literature was at a discount, although one youth in the Bombay Rifles was addicted to rhyme, and circulated a song which began as follows :—

"'Tis merry, 'tis merry in the long jungle grass,
When the Janwars around you fly,
To think of the slaughter that you will commit,
On the beasts that go passing by" —

this being the best stanza of the whole.

The 18th Bombay Infantry was brigaded with the 4th Regiment, *alias* Rifles, under the command of Major C. Crawley. These Sepoys, in their dingy green uniform, which seemed to reflect itself upon their chocolate-coloured cheeks, looked even worse than those dressed in red.

There was also a company called Golandaz, a regular native artillery, commanded by a Lieutenant Aked. Gunners are everywhere a peculiar race, quite as peculiar as sailors. In India they had the great merit of extreme attachment to their weapons, which, after a fashion, they adored as weapons of destruction. "One could hit a partridge with a gun like this," said a pink-faced youngster to a grizzly old cannonier. "A partridge!" cried the veteran. "This does not kill partridges; it smashes armies, slaughters Cities, and it would bring down Shiva himself." And in Baroda City the Gaikwar had two guns, to which regular adoration was offered. They were of massive gold, built around steel tubes, and each was worth about £100,000. Yet the company of Native Artillery was utterly absurd in European eyes. Nothing more beautiful than the Gujarat bullocks, with their noble horns and pure white coats. Europe has seen them in the *cascine* of Tuscany. But it was truly absurd to see these noble animals dragging a gun into position at a shambling and dislocated trot. Satirical subalterns spoke of the "cow batteries." In these days all, of course, are horsed.

There was no such thing as society at Baroda. The Station was commanded by an old Brigadier, named Gibbons, who had no wife, but a native family. He was far too infirm to mount a horse ; he never received, ignored dinners either at home or abroad, and lived as most General Officers did in those days. But he managed to get into a tremendous row, and was removed from his Command for losing his temper, and beating a native Chief of the Bazar about the head, with a leg of mutton.

Hospitalities used to be exchanged between the corps on certain ceremonious occasions, but a Mess dinner was the extent of sociability. As in all small Societies, there were little tiffs, likings, and dislikings. But the age of duelling had passed away, especially after the fatal affairs of Colonel Fawcet of the 55th Regiment, and his brother-in-law, Mr. Monro.

A most pernicious practice, common in those days, was that of eating "tiffin"—in other words, a heavy luncheon—at two, which followed the normal breakfast, or *pakki-hazri*, at nine. Tiffin was generally composed of heavy meats and the never-failing curry, washed down with heavy bottled beer, was followed by two or three Manilla cheroots, and possibly by a siesta. Nothing could be more anti-hygienic than this. It is precisely the same proceeding by which the liver of the Strasbourg goose is prepared for *pâté de foie gras.* The amount of oxygen present in the air of India, is not sufficient to burn up all this carbon, hence the dingy complexions and the dull dark hair which distinguished Anglo-Indians on their return home. I contented myself with a biscuit and a glass of port, something being required to feed the brain, after the hard study of many hours.

The French in India manage these things much better. They keep up their natural habits, except that they rise very early, take a very light meal, chiefly consisting of *café noir*, and eat a heavy breakfast at eleven. Between that and dinner, which follows sunset, they rarely touch anything, and the consequence is that they return with livers comparatively sound. But Anglo-Indian hours of meals were modelled upon those of England, and English hours are laid down by the exigencies of business. Hence the Briton, naturally speaking, breakfasts at nine. As he rises late and has little appetite at that hour, he begins the work of the day upon such a slender basis as tea, bread and butter, an egg, or a frizzle of bacon. It was very different in the days of Queen Elizabeth, as certainly the beefsteaks and beer produced a stronger race. But in those days all rose early and lived much in the open air.

During the fine weather there was generally something to do on the parade ground, shortly before sunset, after which the idlers mounted their nags and took a lazy ride. The day ended at Mess, which was also characteristically Indian. It was a long table in the Mess bungalow, decorated with the regimental plate, and surmounted by creaking punkahs, that resembled boards horizontally slung, with a fringe along the lower part. A native, concealed behind the wall, set these unpleasant articles in movement, generally holding the rope between two toes. At the top of the table sat the Mess President, at the bottom the Vice, and their duty was to keep order, and especially to prevent shop-talking. The officers dressed like so many caterpillars in white shell-jackets, white waistcoats, and white overalls, were a marvellous contrast to the gorgeous Moslem *Khidmatgars*, who stood behind them, with crossed arms, turbans the size of small tea-tables, waist-shawls in proportion. The dinner consisted of soup, a joint of roast mutton at one end, and boiled mutton or boiled fowls at the other, with vegetables in the side dishes. Beef was never seen, because the cow was worshipped at Baroda, nor was roast or boiled pork known at native messes, where the manners and customs of the unclean bazar pig were familiar to all, and where there were ugly stories about the insults to which his remains were exposed on the part of the Mohammedan scullions. At times, however, a ham made its appearance, disguised under the name of "Wilayati Bakri," *Anglicè* "Europe mutton."

This substantial part of the dinner always concluded with curry, accompanied by dry fish, Bombay ducks, and *papris* (assafœtida cake). Anglo-Indians appreciate curry too much to allow it, as in England, to precede other dishes, and to rob them of all their flavour. After this came puddings and tarts, which very few men touched, as they disagreed with beer, and cheese, which was a universal favourite. Coffee, curious to say, was unknown, ice was rare, except at the Residency, and tin vegetables, like peas and asparagus, had only lately been invented. Immediately after cheese, all lit their cigars, which in those days were invariably Manillas. They cost only twenty rupees a thousand, so few were driven to the economy of the abominable Trichinopoly, smoked in Madras. Havanas were never seen, pipes were as little known, and only the oldsters had an extensive article, with a stand two feet high and a pipe twenty feet long, in which they smoked a mixture called Guraku. This was a mingling of tobacco, with plantains, essence of roses, and a dozen different kinds of spices, that gave a very peculiar perfume. The Hookah was, however, then going out of fashion, and presently died the death. It is now as rarely seen in Anglo-India, as the long *chibouque* at Constantinople.

The Mess dinner sometimes concluded with a game of whist, but a wing of a native Corps had not officers enough to make it interesting. After a *quantum sufficit* of cheroots and spirits and water, the members of the Mess broke up, and strolled home, immensely enjoying the clear moonlight, which looked as if frost were lying on the emerald green of Gujarat. On festive occasions there was a *Nach,* which most men pronounced "Nautch." The scene has often been described in its picturesque aspect. But it had a dark side. Nothing could be more ignoble than the two or three debauched and drunken musicians, squealing and scraping the most horrible music, and the *figurantes* with Simiad or apish faces, dressed in magnificent brocades, and performing in the most grotesque way. The exhibition gave one a shiver, yet not a few of the old officers, who had been brought up to this kind of thing, enjoyed it as much as the Russians, of the same epoch, delighted in the gypsy *soirées* of Moscow, and ruined themselves with Madeira and Veuve Cliquot.

It was very different during the rains, which here, as in most parts of the western lowlands of India, were torrential, sometimes lasting seven days and seven nights, without an hour's interruption. The country was mostly under water, and those who went to Mess had to protect themselves with waterproofs; and if they wished to save their horses from the dangerous disease called *barsáti*, had to walk to and fro with bare legs and feet.

This even tenor of existence was varied by only two things. The first was the annual reviews, when old General Morse came over from Ahmedabad to inspect the Corps, preparations for which ceremony had been going on for a couple of months. These old officers were greatly derided by the juniors, chiefly because their brains seemed to have melted away, and they had forgotten almost everything except drill, which they had learnt in their youth. This old General in particular prided himself upon his Hindostani, and suffered accordingly. "How would you say 'Tell a plain story,' General?" "Maydan-ki bát bolo"—which means, "Speak a word of a level country."

Another great event were the annual Races. Even here, however, there was a division of the small Society. They were encouraged by the Company's Resident, Mr. Boyd, and by Major Henry Corsellis, who had come up with his wife to take command of the regiment. They were discouraged, on the other hand, by Major Crawley, of the 4th Rifles, who invariably had a picnic during the Race week. The reason, however, was not "principle," but some quarrel about an old bet. I was one of the winners at the Welter Stakes, having beaten an experienced rider, Lieutenant Raikes.

The state of things at Baroda was not satisfactory. The French govern their colonies too much, the English too little. The latter, instead of taking their stand as the Masters, instead of declaring, *Sic volo, sic jubeo, sit pro ratione voluntas,* seemed, in Baroda at least, to rule on sufferance: they were thoroughly the Masters of the position; they could have superseded the Gaikwar, or destroyed the town in a week. But the rule of the Court of Directors was not a rule of honour.

The officers in Cantonments, distant only half an hour's ride from the Palace, were actually obliged to hire *rámosis* (Paggis) to protect their lives and properties. These men were simply professed thieves, who took blackmail to prevent their friends and relations from plundering. In the bungalows, on the borders of the camp, a couple of these scoundrels were necessary. In two bungalows, officers had been cut down, and the one in which I lived showed, on the door-lintel, sabre cuts. Officers were constantly robbed and even murdered when travelling in the districts, and the universally expressed wish was, that some Director's son might come to grief, and put an end to this miserable state of things. Now, these things *could* have been put a stop to by a single dispatch of the Court of Directors to the Resident at Baroda. They had only to make the Gaikwar and the Native Authorities answerable for the lives and property of their officers. A single hanging and a few heavy fines would have settled the business once and for ever; but, I repeat, the Government of the Court of Directors was not a rule of honour, and already the hateful doctrine was being preached, that "prestige is humbug."

The officers marvelled at the proceedings of their Rulers, and marvelled without understanding things. Little could they know what was going on at home. Here Mr. Richard Cobden, one of the most single-sided of men, whose main strength was that he embodied most of the weakness, and all the prejudice, of the British middle-class public, was watching the affairs of India with a jealous and unfriendly eye, as a Military and Despotic Government, as an acquisition of impolitic violence and fraud, and as the seat of unsafe finance. India appeared to him utterly destitute of any advantage either to the natives or to their foreign masters.

He looked upon the East India Company in Asia as simply monopoly, not merely as regards foreigners, but against their own countrymen. He openly asserted that England had attempted an impossibility in giving herself to the task of governing one hundred millions of Asiatics. Rumours of an Asiatic war were in the air, especially when it was known that Lieut.-Colonel Stoddart and Captain Conolly had been foully murdered by the Amir of Bokhara. He declared (as if he had been taken into supernatural confidence), that God and His visible Natural Laws have opposed insuperable obstacles to the success of such a scheme. His opinion as a professional reformer was, that Hindostan must be ruled by those that live on that side of the globe, and that its people will prefer to be ruled badly by its own colour, kith, and kin, than subject itself to the humiliation of being better governed by a succession of transient intruders from the Antipodes. He declared that ultimately, of course, Nature (of which he knew nothing) will assert the supremacy of her laws, and the white skins will withdraw to their own latitudes, leaving the Hindús to the enjoyment of the climate, for which their dingy skins are suited.

All this was the regular Free-trade bosh, and the Great Bagsman would doubtless have been thunderstruck, had he heard the Homeric shouts of laughter with which his mean-spirited utterances were received by every white skin in British India. There was not a subaltern in the 18th Bombay N.I. who did not consider himself perfectly capable of governing a million Hindús. And such a conviction realizes itself—

> " By the sword we won the land,
> And by the sword we'll hold it still ; "

for every subaltern felt (if he could not put the feeling into words) that India had been won, *despite England*, by the energy and bravery of men like himself. Every history tells one so in a way that all can understand. The Company began as mere traders, and presently they obtained the right of raising guards to defend themselves. The guards naturally led to the acquisition of territory. The territory increased, till its three centres, Bengal, Madras, and Bombay, became centres of little Kingdoms.

The native Princes were startled and frightened. They attacked their energetic neighbours, with more or less success, and the intruders became more intrusive than before. Next day they began to elect Governors, and Governor-Generals. Whenever a new man was sent out from England, the natives, after the fashion of their kind, thought that they saw an opportunity, and, losing their fear of the old Governor, declared war against the new one. The latter assembled an army, and duly reported the fact home. It took from eight to nine months before the document was received and answered. The general tone of the reply was a fierce diatribe against territorial aggrandizement, but in the mean time a great battle or two had been fought, a province had been conquered and duly plundered, and a large slice of territory had been added to Anglo-Indian rule. This is the way in which British Empire in the

East arose, and probably this was the least objectionable way. For when the Company rose to power, it began to juggle native Princes out of their territory, to deny the right of adopting a sacred privilege amongst the Hindús, and to perpetrate all kinds of injustice. A fair example was the case of the Rajah of Patara, and the same proceedings in Oudh, led to the celebrated Mutiny in 1857, and nearly wrecked British dominion in India.

At last a bright day dawned. The whole of the little Cantonment was electrified by the news of the battle of Meeanee, which had been fought on February 21st, 1843. After a number of reverses truly humiliating to British self-esteem, the Sun of Victory had at last shone upon her bayonets. Sir Charles Napier had shown that, with a little force of mixed Englishmen and Sepoys, he could beat the best and bravest army that any Native Power could bring into the field. It was a gallant little affair, because the few white faces had done nearly the whole work. The Sepoys, as usual, had behaved like curs, and five of their officers had been killed, to one of the Queen's service.

Then, on March 25th, followed the battle of Dabba, and Sind fell into the power of the English, and Major Outram returned to England on April 1st. Then arose the great quarrel between the two great men. The general opinion of the time was, that the Bayard of India, as his future enemy had called him, wished *himself* to depose the Ameers, and resented the work being done by another. His (Major Outram's) own writings show, that he found them unfitted to rule, and that he had proposed the most stringent remedies. But when these were carried out by another man, he ranged himself in the ranks of the opposition. Sir Charles Napier and his free-spoken brother, Sir William, had been bitterly opposed to the twenty-four little Kings in Leadenhall Street, and had never hesitated to express their opinions. One of their energetic dicta was, that every rupee has a blood-spot on it, and that wash as you will, the cursed spot will not out. Talking of which, by-the-by, I, in one of those pungent epigrams, which brought me such abundance of "good will (?)," wrote as follows, referring to the £60,000 which Sir Charles Napier cleared by way of prize money :—

"Who, when he lived on shillings, swore
Rupees were stained with Indian gore,
And 'widows' tears' for motto bore,
But Charley?

"And yet who, in the last five years,
So round a sum of that coin clears,
In spite of 'gore' and 'widows' tears,'
As Charley?"

Major Outram again left India for England. The Court of Directors persuaded him to become their champion, against their old enemy, Sir Charles Napier. The latter was very strong, for he was thoroughly supported by the new Governor-General (Lord Ellenborough), in opposition to all others, and thoroughly identified himself with the Army, and the Army adored him accordingly. One of his sayings, "*Kacheri* (or Court-House) hussar," alluding to the beards or the mustachios of the civilians, caused a perfect tornado of wrath amongst the black coats of India. He was equally free-spoken in his condemnation of the politicals. The Court of Directors did not dare to recall him at once, but they riled with impotent rage.

Amongst other cabals that they brought against him was the affair of the Somnath Gates. Few people understood the truth of the question in that day, and most who did, have not forgotten it. These famous doors, which had been carried off in the year A.D. 1023 from a Hindú temple in Gujarat by the great warrior, Mahmoud of Ghazni, had been matters of dispute years before Lord Ellenborough's time. As early as 1831, when Shah Shuja was in treaty with Runjeet Singh, of the Panjab, for aid to recover his throne, one of the conditions of the latter, was the restoration of the Gates of Somnath. Probably the Rajah, like the Governor-General, was utterly ignorant of the fact that the ruins of the Moon Temple have entirely perished. On that occasion, however, the Shah reminded the Hindú of an old prophesy which foreboded the downfall of the Sikh empire, or the withdrawal of the Gates from the warrior's tomb at Ghazni. They were removed to India at the end of 1842, and in September, 1843, the Sikh empire practically collapsed with the murder of Sher Singh—a curious case of uninspired prophecy. The Gates were removed by General Mott, acting under the orders of the Governor-General, on March 10th, 1843; they were deposited in Agra, where they were kept, and may even now be kept, in an old palace in the Fort, formerly used as an arsenal by the British.* The venerable relics ought long ago to have been sent to the South Kensington Museum.

The feud between Sir Charles Napier and Major Outram, divided Western Anglo-India into two opposing camps. Major Outram belonged to a family of mechanics, from whose name came the tramways, and he had begun his service in the Bombay marine. He was presently transferred to the Native Infantry, and carved out a career for himself. His peculiar temperament gave him immense

* Colonel Yule gives an illustration of these gates in his second volume of "Marco Polo."

power amongst the wild Bhíls and other tribes, whom he had been sent, as it were, to civilize. He was a short, stout man, anything but prepossessing in appearance, but of immense courage and most violent temper. A story is told concerning him and his brother, who, in a dispute at a tiger-hunt, turned their rifles against each other. He hated to be outdone, or even to be equalled. On one occasion, when he found a man who could spring into the lake, off the house terrace, like himself, he made a native raise him upon his shoulders, and so managed to outdo the rival jumper. He was immensely generous and hospitable, living quite in the native way, with a troupe of *Nach* girls to pass the evening. He always acted upon impulse, and upon generous impulses. On one occasion, when marching past, at the head of his troops, he was grossly insulted by a villager, whereupon he turned to and administered condign chastisement to the villagers. When transferred to Sind, he had denounced the Ameers in the severest way; in fact, his account of them, as political, seemed to justify their being dethroned. But, as I said, when that operation was performed by another than himself, he suddenly turned round and denounced the deed. He was a Scotchman, and was by no means wanting in that canniness which teaches a man which side his bread carries the butter. He was thoroughly impressed with the axiom that "bluid is thicker than water," and always promoted, if he could, the interests of a countryman, to the detriment of others. Sir Charles Napier, on the other hand, belonged to that exceptional order of Scotchmen, who are chiefly remarkable for having nothing of the Scotchman about them. He was utterly deficient in prudence, he did not care a fig how many enemies he made, and his tongue was like a scorpion's sting. He spoke of Sir James Hogg as "that Hogg," alluding to the Hindostani word *suar* ("pig"), one of the most insulting words in the language. He spoke of Dr. Buist, a Scotch editor at Bombay, as "the blatant beast of the Bombay *Times*." In fact, he declared war to the knife.

On the other hand, Outram's friends were not idle. He had a large party of his own. Men liked his courage, his generosity, his large-heartedness, and his utter disregard for responsibility. He could also write, in a dull, thick style, it is true, but thoroughly intelligible to the multitude, and quite unlike the style, like polished steel, that was so doughtily used by Sir William Napier. Become a politician, the "Bayard" did not improve; in fact, two or three dodges were quoted about him which added very little to his reputation. I had no reason to like him. In his younger days, thirsting for distinction, Outram was ambitious to explore the Somáli country, then considered the most dangerous in Africa, but when I proposed to do so, he openly opposed me. This was, however, perhaps natural, as he was then commanding at Aden.

As soon as I had passed my drill I was placed in charge of a Company, and proceeded to teach what I had just learnt. I greatly encouraged my men in sword exercise, and used to get the best players to my quarters for a good long bout every day. The usual style in India is a kind of single-stick, ribbonded with list cloth, up to the top, and a small shield in the left hand. The style of work seems to have been borrowed from the sword-dance of some civilized people, like the Bactrian-Greeks. The swordsman begins with "renowning it," vapouring, waving his blade, and showing all the curious *fantasie* that distinguish a Spanish Espada. Then, with the fiercest countenance, he begins to spring in the air, to jump from side to side, to crouch and to rush forwards and backwards, with all the action of an excited baboon. They never thought of giving "point:" throughout India the thrust is confined to the dagger. The cuts, as a rule, were only two—one in the shoulder, and the other, in the vernacular called *kalam*, at the lower legs. Nothing was easier than to guard these cuts, and to administer a thrust that would have been fatal with steel. I gave a prize every month, to the best swordsman, wrestler, and athlete, generally some gaudy turban. But, although I did my best, I never could teach them to use a foil.

These proceedings excited not a little wonder amongst my brother subs, but much more when I sent for a *Chábu Sawar*, or native jockey, and began to learn the Indian system of riding, and of training the horse. As a rule, this was absurdly neglected in India. Men mostly rode half-broken Arabs, and many an annual review showed the pleasant spectacle of a commanding officer being run away with in one direction, and the second in command in another. And when it came to meeting Indians in the field, the Englishman was at a terrible disadvantage. An old story is told of an encounter between an Indian and English cavalry officer, who had been offended by the remarks of the former. They charged, sword in hand, in presence of their regiments, and both were equally skilful in parrying the enemy's attack; presently, however, the Britisher found himself in a fix, the native with his sharp light blade having cut the horse's reins, without hurting either horse or man. This is a favourite native ruse. Whereupon the English officer drew his pistol and disloyally shot the Indian, who in his lingering illness, which ended fatally, declared that he never meant to hurt the English officer, but only to prove his own words, that he was not his equal in swordsmanship or horsemanship. Light chains were afterwards adopted to accompany the leather bridle. The English officer deeply regretted the event, and it was hushed up; but such acts are never quite buried.

A similar manslaughter took place during one of the Sind campaigns. An officer, who shall be nameless, attacked a Beluch chief, who, being mounted upon a tired mare, made no attempt to fly. The Englishman, who had some reputation as a swordsman, repeatedly bore down upon him, making a succession of cuts, which the opponent received upon his blade and shield. At last, being unable to win fairly, the Englishman, who is now high in command, drew his pistol and shot him, and, curious to say, was not court-martialled!

At last I considered myself thoroughly qualified to pass in Hindostani, and in early April, 1843, obtained leave from the Commander-in-Chief to visit Bombay for the purpose of examination. I made the same march from Baroda to Tankaria-Bunder, and then found a *pattymar* for Bombay. The sail southwards, despite the extraordinary heat of the season, was perfectly charming. The north-east monsoon, about drawing to its end, alternated with the salt sea-breeze and the spicy land-breeze, the former justly called "The Doctor." The sky was deep blue, unflecked by a single cloud, and the sea bluer, still hardly crisped by the wind. There was perfect calm inside and outside the vessel. No posts and no parades. The living was simple enough, consisting chiefly of rice, curry and *chapatis,* with the never-failing tea and tobacco. Tea in India is better than in England, although of inferior quality, because it has less sea voyage. The native servants, however, have a peculiar way of brewing it, and those who have once drunk a sneaker, or double-sized cup, full of Indian tea, will never forget it. Sensible men, therefore, brew their tea for themselves.

Despite landing almost every evening, the voyage down coast occupied only six or seven days. This time I hired a tent, with the aid of the old Parsee General, and pitched in the Strangers' Lines. They extended southwards from the Sanitarium, along the shore of Back Bay, and were not, as now, huddled up into a little space on the other side of the road. With the assistance of old Dosabhai Sohrabji I worked up the last minutiæ of the language, and on May 5th appeared in the Town Hall, where the examinations were held.

These were not without a certain amount of difficulty. The candidate was expected to make a written translation, to read and translate *vivâ voce* from a native book, to read a written letter, often vilely scrawled, and to converse with the *moonshee,* Mohammed Makba, a Concani Mussulman, whose son I afterwards met in 1876. I was fortunate in my examiner. Captain Pope, who formerly held that position, had been made Assistant-Commissary-General, and could no longer indulge his pet propensity of plucking candidates. The committee was composed of Major-General Vans-Kennedy and three or four nobodies. The former was an Orientalist after a fashion, knew a great deal of books, and much more of native manners and customs. In fact, he lived in their society, and was, as usual, grossly imposed upon. Whenever a servant wanted "leave," he always begged permission to leave a *badli*, or substitute, to do his work, and when number one returned, number two remained. Consequently, the old man was eaten up by native drones. He lived amongst his books in a tumble-down bungalow, in a tattered compound, which was never repaired, and he had a slight knowledge of Sanscrit and Arabic, an abundant acquaintance with Hindostani and Persian, and general Oriental literature.

The one grievance of his life was his treatment by Sir John (afterwards Lord) Keane. This Western barbarian came out to India when advanced in years, and, imbued with a fine contempt "of the twenty-years-in-the-country-and-speak-the-language man," he could not understand what was the use of having officers who did nothing but facilitate the study of Orientalism, and he speedily sent off Colonel Vans-Kennedy to join his regiment. The latter was deeply in debt, as usual, under his circumstances; his creditors tolerated him at the Presidency, where they could lay ready claws upon his pay, but before he could march up country, he was obliged to sell, for a mere nothing, his valuable library of books and manuscripts, which had occupied him a lifetime in collecting. He was a curious spectacle, suggesting only a skeleton dressed in a frock-coat of worn-out blue cloth uniform, and he spoke all his languages with a fine broad lowland accent, which is, perhaps, Orientally speaking, the best.

I passed my examination the first of twelve. Next to me was Ensign Robert Gordon, of the 4th Bombay Rifles, and Ensign Higginson, of the 78th Highlanders. The latter brought to the Examination Hall one of the finest Irish brogues ever heard there. I had been humble enough before I passed, but, having once got through, I was ready to back my knowledge against the world. This was no great feat on my part, as I had begun Arabic at Oxford, and worked at Hindostani in London, and on board the ship, and had studied for twelve hours a day at Baroda. Before I quitted the Presidency, I had an unpleasantness with a certain Dr. Bird, a pseudo-Orientalist, who, after the fashion of the day, used the brains of *moonshee* and *pandit* to make his own reputation. I revenged myself by lampooning him, when, at the ripe age of forty-five, he was about to take to himself a spare-rib. The line began—

> "A small grey bird goes out to woo,
> Primed with Persian ditties new;
> To the gardens straight he flew,
> Where he knew the rosebud grew."

We afterwards met in London, and were very good friends.

Dr. Bird only regretted that he had wasted his time on native languages, instead of studying his own profession. He practised medicine for a short time in London, and died.

I left Bombay on May 12th, and rejoined my regiment just before the burst of the south-west monsoon. This was a scene that has often been described in verse and prose. It was a prime favourite with the Sanscrit poets, and English readers are familiar with it through Horace Hayman Wilson's Hindú theatre. But the discomforts of the season in a cowshed-like bungalow were considerable; you sat through the day in a wet skin, and slept through the night with the same. The three months were an alternation of steaming heat and damp, raw cold.

The rains are exceptionally heavy in Gujarat, and sometimes the rainpour lasted without interval for seven days and seven nights. This is mostly the case in the lowlands of India, especially at Bombay and other places, where the Ghâts approach the coast. Throughout the inner plateau, as at Poonah, the wet season, which the Portuguese call winter, with its occasional showers and its bursts of sunshine, is decidedly pleasant. The brown desolation of the land disappears in a moment, and is replaced by a brilliant garb of green. The air is light and wholesome, and the change is hailed by every one; but at Baroda there were torments innumerable. The air was full of loathsome beings, which seemed born for the occasion—flying horrors of all kinds, ants and bugs, which persisted in intruding into meat and drink. At Mess it was necessary to have the glasses carefully covered, and it was hardly safe to open one's mouth. The style of riding to a dinner has been already described. There was no duty, and the parade-ground was a sheet of water. Shooting was impossible, except during the rare intervals of sunshine; and those who did not play billiards suffered from mortal *ennui.*

I now attacked with renewed vigour the Gujarati language, spoken throughout the country, and by the Parsees of Bombay and elsewhere. My teacher was a Nagar Brahman, named Hím Chand. Meanwhile I took elementary lessons of Sanscrit, from the regimental *pandit.*

Every Sepoy Corps, in those days, kept one of these men, who was a kind of priest as well as a schoolmaster, reading out prayers, and superintending the nice conduct of Festivals, with all their complicated observances. Besides these men, the Government also supplied schoolmasters, and the consequence was, that a large percentage of young Sepoys could read and write. I once won a bet from my brother-in-law Stisted, by proving that more men in the 18th Bombay Native Infantry than in the 78th Queen's could read and write. In the latter, indeed, they occasionally had recruits who could not speak English, but only Gaelic.

Under my two teachers I soon became as well acquainted, as a stranger can, with the practice of Hinduism. I carefully read up Ward, Moor, and the publications of the Asiatic Society, questioning my teachers, and committing to writing page after page of notes, and eventually my Hindú teacher officially allowed me to wear the *Janeo* (Brahminical thread). My knowledge, indeed, not a little surprised my friend Dr. H. G. Carter, who was secretary to the Asiatic Society at Bombay. On June 26th, 1843, I was appointed interpreter to my regiment, which added something—a few rupees, some thirty a month—to my income. My brother officers now began to see that I was working with an object. When I returned from Bombay, they had been surprised at my instantly resuming work, and not allowing myself a holiday. They grumbled not a little at having so unsociable a messmate.

About that time, too, I began to acquire the ominous soubriquet of "The White Nigger," and what added not a little to the general astonishment was, that I left off "sitting under" the garrison Chaplain, and transferred myself to the Catholic Chapel of the chocolate-coloured Goanese priest, who adhibited spiritual consolation to the *buttrels* (butlers and head-servants) and other servants of the camp.* At length, on August 22nd, 1843, I again obtained leave "to proceed to Bombay to be examined in the Guzerattee language."

---

* I was at this time a child in the schoolroom; we had no knowledge of each other's existence; I therefore had no part in the matter. He did not tell me of it until we had been married for some time, as he wished, he said, to see if *he* was paramount in *my* mind, and that I would make the sacrifice for him, which was necessary for our marriage later on. He then said, "that if a man *had* a religion, it must be the Catholic; it was the religion of a gentleman—a terrible religion for a man of the world to live in, but a good one to die in." I have often wondered that this step never excited any comment; he wrote of it freely; he spoke of it freely until his latter years; but as he did not like *me* to do so, I never did. Nobody ever dared to question his action till after he was dead; but when the master-mind, the witty tongue was powerless, when the scathing pen the strong right sword-arm could no longer wield, people fell foul of me for speaking of it as a simple and natural fact. I never called him a devout practical Catholic; I only said he was received into the Church, and that he meant to have its rites at the time of his death.—I. B.

This time I was accompanied on the journey by Lieutenant R. A. Manson, who was on like business, to the Presidency. The march was detestable. We could hardly ride our horses through the sticky and knee-deep mud of Gujarat. So we fitted up native carts with waterproof tilts, and jogged behind the slow-paced steers on the high-road to Broach. Here we found a detachment of a native Corps, living the usual dull, monotonous life.

Hence we proceeded to Surat, once the cradle of the British power in India, and afterwards doomed to utter neglect. Its masterful position for trade secured it from utter ruin, but no thanks to its rulers. Here we again took a *pattymar*, and dropped down the river, *en route* to the Presidency. But this time it was very different voyaging. The south-west monsoon was dead against us, and nothing could be more ominous than the aspect of the weather. We reached Bombay on September 26th, just in time to avoid the *Elephanta*, or dangerous break up of the rainy monsoon. Little Manson, who had been wrecked when coming out in Back Bay, was in an extreme state of nervousness, and I was prepared for any risk when I saw the last sheets of lightning hung out by the purple-black clouds. The examination took place on October 16th, 1843, again in presence of old General Vans-Kennedy and the normal three or four nobodies, and I again passed first, distancing my rival, Lieutenant C. P. Rigby, of the 16th Bombay N.I. I wished to remain in Bombay to await my regiment, then under orders for Sind, but on the 10th of November I was ordered north, and yet the corps had received orders to march on November 23rd.

The break up of the Cantonment produced all manner of festivities. The two Corps took leave of one another, and passed the last night in the enjoyment of a stupendous *Nach*, or Nautch.

A March with a regiment in those days was a pleasure. The first bugle sounded shortly after midnight, and presently came the signal—

> "Don't you hear the general say,
> 'Strike your tents and march away'?"

After a few days' practice, the camp was on the ground and ready packed for starting on carts and camels, within a few minutes. Naturally loose marching was the rule. The men were only expected to keep in Companies, and the officers, with rifles in their hands, rode before, behind, or alongside of them. In this way many a head of game made its appearance at the regimental Mess. The Marches seldom exceeded fifteen miles a day; at the end of the stage the Sepoys were drawn up into line, inspected, and told off to pitching the tents. Breakfast was generally eaten by the officers shortly after sunrise, and the morning air gave fine appetites. The food was generally carried in a *dúli*, a kind of portable palanquin, primarily intended for the sick and wounded. After the tents were pitched most men were glad to have a short sleep. They assembled again at Tiffin, and its objectionable properties disappeared during the march. They then amused themselves with shooting, or strolling about the country, till Mess hour. The officers' wives were always present at dinner, and no smoking was allowed until they had disappeared. After mess, men were only too glad to turn in, and to get as much sleep as they could before the morning bugle.

The regiment embarked in a native craft at Tankaria-Bunder, and on December 26th, 1843, encamped on the Esplanade, Bombay. They were in the highest spirits, for all expected to see service. The wing from Mhow had been ordered to rejoin head-quarters, and the same was the case with the Staff officers, Captains Jamieson and Partridge, Lieutenants Macdonald, Hough, Compton, and Ensign Anderson. Needless to say that the latter were in high dudgeon at leaving their fat appointments.

On New Year's Day of 1844, the corps embarked on board the H.E.I. Company's steamship *Semiramis*, generally known as the "Merry Miss." She was commanded by Captain Ethersey, who ended badly. His "'aughtiness," as the crew called it, won him very few friends. And now I come to the time when I began to describe my experiences in print. The first chapter of "Scinde; or the Unhappy Valley" gives a facetious account of this voyage.

On board the *Semiramis* I made a good friend in Captain Walter Scott, of the Bombay Engineers, who had been transferred from Kandesh, to take charge of the Survey in Lower Sind, by general order of November 23rd, 1843. He was a handsome man in the prime of life, with soft blue eyes, straight features, yellow hair, and golden-coloured beard. Withal he not a little resembled his uncle, "The Magician of the North," of whom he retained the fondest remembrance. He preserved also the trick, wholly unintentional, of the burr and the lisp, the former in the humorous parts, and the latter in the tenderer part of his stories. He was an admirable conversationist, and his anecdotes were full of a dry and pawky humour, which comes from north of the Tweed. Yet, curious to say, when he took pen in hand his thoughts seemed to fly abroad. His lines were crooked, and his sentences were hardly intelligible. Something of this was doubtless owing to his confirmed habit of cheroot smoking, whilst he was writing, but it was eminently characteristic of the man.

Walter Scott was a truly fine character. His manners were those of a gentleman of the Old School, and he never said a disagreeable word or did an ungraceful deed. A confirmed bachelor, he was not at all averse to women's society; indeed, rather the contrary. He was generous, even lavish to the extreme, and he was quite as ready to befriend an Englishman, as a "brither Scot." These two latter qualities seemed to distinguish a high-bred Scotchman, whilst the English and Irish gentleman preserved the characteristics of his nationality, of course refining it and raising it to the highest standard. The Scottish gentleman seems to differ not only in degree, but in kind, and to retain only the finer qualities of his race. This is not speaking of the aristocracy, but of the finer nature, which is the nature of a true gentleman. Whereas the common herd errs in excess of canniness and cautiousness, keeps a keen eye upon the main chance, and distrusts everything and everybody. The select few are rather rash than otherwise, think less of gain than of a point of honour, and seem to believe all other men as true-hearted and high-spirited as themselves, as well as utterly destitute of religious fanaticism.

Walter Scott's favourite reading was old history and romance. He was delighted to meet with a man who was acquainted with Hollingshed and Froissart. Moreover, he had sent to Italy for a series of books upon the canalization of the valley of the Po, and was right glad to find a man who had been in that part of the world, and could assist him by his knowledge of Italian. And I capped the good effect I had upon him, by quoting some of the finest of his uncle's lines, which end with—

"I bless thee, and thou shalt be blessed."

The little voyage, beautiful outside the ship, and stiff and prim within, ended on the fourth day. The *Semiramis* ran past Manora Head and anchored near the Bar, which in those days was as bad as bad could be. My first impressions of the country, a marvellous contrast to Gujarat and Bombay, were as follows:—

"In those days Sind was in the most primitive state. The town, or rather village, of Karáchi was surrounded by a tall wall of guy swish, topped with fancy crenelles, and perpendicularly striped with what the Persians call *Da mágheh*, or nostril holes, down which the besieged could pour hot oil, or boiling water. Streets there were none; every house looked like a small fort, and they almost met over the narrow lanes that formed the only thoroughfares. The bazar, a long line of miserable shops, covered over with rude matting of date leaves, was the only place comparatively open. Nothing could exceed the filthiness of the town; sewers there were none. And the deodorization was effected by the dust. The harbour, when the tide was out, was a system of mud-flats, like the lagoons of Venice, when you approach them by the Murazzi. A mere sketch of a road, which in these days would be called a Frere highway, led from the nearest mud-bank to the Cantonment. The latter was in its earliest infancy. The ground of hard clay was still covered with milk-bush and desert vegetation, and only here and there a humble bungalow was beginning to be built. There was no sign of barracks, and two race-courses were laid out before any one thought of church or chapel.

"Yet Karáchi showed abundant sign of life. Sir Charles Napier thoroughly believed in its future, and loudly proclaimed that in a few years it would take the wind out of Bombay sails. The old Conqueror himself was temporarily staying there. He had his wife and two handsome daughters. His personal staff was composed of his two nephews, Captain William Napier and Lieutenant Byng. In his general Staff he had Major Edward Green, Assistant Adjutant-General, for Quarter-Master-General; Captain MacMurdo, who afterwards married his daughter; a civilian named Brown, *alias* 'Beer' Brown; Captain Young, of the Bengal army, as his Judge Advocate-General; and Captain Preedy for his Commissary-General. The latter was the son of a violent old officer in the Bombay army, and of whom many a queer story was told. One of them is as follows:—He was dining at a Dragoon mess at Poonah, when they began to sing a song which had been written by an officer of the regiment, and which had for refrain—

'Here's death to those
Who dare oppose
Her Majesty's Dragoons.'

Old Preedy well knew that in the affair alluded to, the Dragoons, having ventured into a native village, had been soundly thrashed by the villagers. After patiently hearing the song out, he proposed to give the villagers a turn, but he had hardly finished his first verses—

'Success to who
Dare to bamboo
Her Majesty's Dragoons,'

before he was duly kicked out of the Mess.

"Karáchi was then swarming with troops. The 78th Highlanders were cantoned there, and were presently joined by the 86th, or 'County Down Boys.' Both consumed a vast quantity of liquor, but in diametrically different ways. The kilts, when they felt fou, toddled quietly to bed, and slept off the debauch; the brogues quarrelled and fought, and made themselves generally disagreeable, and passed the night in the guard-house. There was horse artillery and foot artillery, and the former, when in uniform, turned out in such gorgeous gingerbread-gold coats, that gave a new point to the old sneer of 'buying a man at your own price, and selling him at his own,' and there were native regiments enough to justify brigade parades on the very largest scale.

The 18th was presently ordered off to Gharra, a desolate bit of rock and clay, which I described as follows :—

"Look at that unhappy hole—it is Gharra.

"The dirty heap of mud-and-mat hovels that forms the native village is built upon a mound, the *débris* of former Gharras, close to a creek which may or may not have been the 'western outlet of the Indus in Alexander's time.' All round it lies a—

"windy sea of land :"—

salt, flat, barren rock and sandy plain, where eternal sea-gales blow up and blow down a succession of hillocks—warts upon the foul face of the landscape—stretching far, far away, in all the regular irregularity of desolation.

"You see the cantonment with its falling brick lines outside, and its tattered thatched roofs peeping from the inside of a tall dense hedge of bright green milk-bush."

We were obliged to pitch tents, for there was no chance of lodging in the foul little village, at the head of the Gharra creek. Under the circumstances, of course, the work was very hard.

A sandstorm astonished an English visitor considerably.

"When we arose in the morning the sky was lowering, the air dark; the wind blew in puffs, and—unusual enough at the time of the year—it felt raw and searching. If you took the trouble to look towards the hills about eight a.m. you might have seen a towering column of sand from the rocky hills, mixed with powdered silt from the arid plains, flying away as fast as it could from the angry puffing Boreas.

"The gale increases—blast pursuing blast, roaring and sweeping round the walls and over the roofs of the houses with the frantic violence of a typhoon. There is a horror in the sound, and then the prospect from the windows! It reminds one of Firdausi's vast idea that one layer has been trampled off earth and added to the coats of the firmament. You close every aperture and inlet, in the hope of escaping the most distressing part of the phenomenon. Save yourself the trouble, all such measures are useless. The finer particles with which the atmosphere is laden would pass without difficulty through the eye of a needle; judge what comfortable thoroughfares they must find the chinks of these warped doors and the crannies of the puttyless munnions.

"It seems as though the dust recognized in our persons kindred matter. Our heads are powdered over in five minutes; our eyes, unless we sit with closed lids, feel as if a dash of cayenne had been administered to them; we sneeze like schoolboys after a first pinch of 'blackguard;' our epidermises are grittier than a loaf of provincial French bread, and washing would only be a mockery of resisting the irremediable evil.

"Now, Mr. Bull, if you wish to let your friends and old cronies at home see something of the produce of the East, call for a lighted candle, and sit down to compose an 'overland letter.' It will take you at least two hours and a half to finish the four pages, as the pen becomes clogged, and the paper covered every few minutes; moreover, your spectacles require wiping at least as often as your quill does. By the time the missive comes to hand it will contain a neat little cake of Indus mud and Scinde sand moulded in the form of paper. Tell Mrs. Bull that you went without your tiffin—lunch I mean—that you tried to sleep, but the novel sensation of being powdered all over made the attempt an abortive one—that it is impossible to cook during a dust-storm—and that you are in for a modification of your favourite 'intramural sepulture,' if the gale continues much longer. However, your days are safe enough; the wind will probably fall about five or six in the afternoon,—it is rare that it does not go down with the sun—and even should it continue during the night, it will be a farce compared to what we are enduring now."

There was great excitement on June 20th, 1844, when the Sepoys of the 64th Regiment mutinied at Shikapur and beat their officers. The station was commanded by Major-General Hunter, C.B. Most of his experience was in studs. When campaigning with Sir Charles Napier, the latter sent to him for something to eat, and the reply was a ham and a round of press beef. The "devil's brother," as the Sindís called him, cut a slice out of the ham and another out of the beef, and then sent the remainder back to the owner. On June 27th a general order established vernacular examination, making it every officer's duty to learn something more or less of the language. In September I went down to Bombay to pass an examination in Maharátta, and on October 15th I distanced some six competitors.

Richard produced another Chapter on India when he was sick, in 1888, for Mr. Hitchman, which is the one the biographer used, having objected to some of the other parts, whilst I have used the original manuscript just as it was given to me in 1876.

CHAPTER VII.

THE REMINISCENCES WRITTEN FOR MR. HITCHMAN IN 1888—INDIA.

WHEN I landed at Bombay (October 28th, 1842), "Momba Devi" town was a marvellous contrast with the "Queen of Western India," as she thrones it in 1887; no City in Europe, except perhaps Vienna, can show such a difference. The old Portuguese port-village *temp. Caroli Secundi*, with its silly fortifications and useless esplanade, its narrow alleys and squares like *places d'armes*, had not developed itself into "Sasson-Town," as we may call the olden, and "Frére-Town" the modern moiety.

Under the patriarchal rule of the Court of Directors to the Hon. East Indian Company, a form of torpidity much resembling the paternal government of good Emperor Franz, no arrangements were made for the reception of the queer animals called "cadets." They landed and fell into the knowing hands of some rascals; lodged at a Persian tavern, the British Hotel, all uncleanliness at the highest prices. I had a touch of "seasoning sickness," came under the charge of "Paddy Ryan," Fort Surgeon and general favourite, and was duly drafted into the Sanitary Bungalow—thatched hovels facing Back Bay, whence ever arose a pestilential whiff of roast Hindú, and opened the eyes of those who had read about the luxuries of the East. Life was confined to a solitary ride (at dawn and dusk), a dull monotonous day, and a night in some place of dissipation—to put it mildly—such as the Bhendi bazar, whose attractions consisted of dark young persons in gaudy dress, mock jewels, and hair japanned with cocoa-nut oil, and whose especial diversions were an occasional "row"—a barbarous manner of "town and gown." But a few days of residence had taught me that India, at least Western India, offered only two specialities for the Britisher; first *Shikar* or sport, and secondly, opportunities of studying the people and their languages. These were practically unlimited; I found that it took me some years of hard study before I could walk into a bazar and distinguish the several castes, and know something of them, their manners and customs, religion and superstitions. I at once engaged a venerable Parsee, Dosabhai Sohrabji, also a *mubid*, or priest, as his white cap and coat showed, who had coached many generations of *griffs*, and under his guidance dived deep into the "Ethics of Hind" (Akhlak-i-Hindi) and other such text-books.

This was the year after the heir-apparent was born; when Nott, Pollock, and Sale revenged the destruction of some 13,000 men by the Afghans; when the Chinese War broke out; when Lord Ellenborough succeeded awkward Lord Auckland; and when Major-General Sir Charles J. Napier, commanding at Poonah, was appointed to Sind (August 25th, 1842), and when his subsequent unfriend, Brevet-Major James Outram, was on furlough to England; lastly, and curious to say, most important of all to me, was the fact that "Ensign Burton" was ranked and posted in the G. G. O. of October 15th, 1842, to the 18th Regiment, Bombay N.I.

Nor was I less surprised by the boasting of my brother officers (the Sepoys had thrashed the French in India and elsewhere, they were the flower of the British army, and so forth)—fine specimen of *esprit de corps* run mad, which was destined presently to change its tone, after 1857. Meanwhile this loud brag covered an ugly truth. We officers of the Indian army held her Majesty's commission; but the Company's officers were looked upon by the Queen's troops as mere auxiliaries, locals without general rank, as it were black policemen. Moreover the rules of the service did not allow us to rise above a certain rank. What a contrast to the French private, who carries a Marshal's baton in his knapsack!

Captain Cleland introduced me to his sister, the wife of a field-officer, and she to sundry of her friends, whose tone somewhat surprised me. Here and there a reference was made to my "immortal soul," and I was overwhelmed with oral treatises upon what was expected from a "Christian in a heathen land." And these ladies "talked shop," at least, so it appeared to me, like non-commissioned officers. After *Shikar* and the linguistics, the only popular pursuit in India is (I should think always was) "Society." But indigestible dinners are not pleasant in a Turkish bath; dancing is at a discount in a region of eternal dog-days; picnics are unpleasant on the "palm-tasselled strand of glowing Ind," where scorpions and cobras come uninvited; horse-racing, like Cicero's "Mercaturi," to be honoured, must be on a large scale; the Mess tiffin is an abomination ruinous to digestion and health; the billiard-table may pass an hour or so pleasantly enough, but it becomes a monotonous waste of time, and the evening bands, or meet at "Scandal Point," is open to the charge of a deadly dullness.

Visits become visitations, because that tyrant Madam Etiquette commanded them about noon, despite risk of sunstroke, and "the ladies" insisted upon them without remorse of conscience. Needless to say that in those days the *Gym-hánah* was unknown, and that the Indian world ignored lawn-tennis, even croquet.

Another point in Bombay Society at once struck me, and I afterwards found it in the Colonies and most highly developed in the United States. At home men and women live under an incubus, a perfect system of social despotism which is intended to make amends for an unnatural political equality, amongst classes born radically unequal. Abroad, the weight is taken off their shoulders, and the result of its removal is a peculiar rankness of growth. The pious become fanatically one-idea'd, pharisaical, unchristian, monomaniacal. The un-pious run to the other extreme, believe nothing, sneer at the holies, "and look upon the mere Agnostic as a 'slow coach.'" Eccentricity develops itself Bedlam-wards. One of my friends had a mania and swore 'By my halidom.'" Another had an image of Gánpati over his door, which he never passed without the prayer, "Shri ganeshayá Hamahá" ("I bow to auspicious Janus"). A third, of whom I heard, had studied Aristotle in Arabic, and when shown the "Novum Organon," asked, indignantly, "who the fellow might be that talked such stuff." And in matters of honesty the social idea was somewhat lax; to sell a spavined horse to a friend was considered a good joke, and to pass off plated wares for real silver was looked upon as only a trifle too "smart." The Press faithfully reflected these nuances with a little extra violence and virulence of its own. By-the-by, I must not forget making the acquaintance of a typical Scot, Dr. Buist (afterwards Sir Charles Napier's "blatant beast of the *Bombay Times*"). He wrote much (so badly that only one clerk could read it) and washed little; and as age advanced he married a young wife.

After a month or so at Bombay, chiefly spent in mugging "Hindostani," and in providing myself with the necessaries of life—servants, headed by Salvador Soares, a handsome Goanese; a horse, in the shape of a dun-coloured Kattywár nag; also a "horsekeeper," a dog, a tent, and so forth—I received my marching orders and set out to "join" my own corps. The simple way of travelling in those days before steam and rail was by palanquin or *pattymar*. I have described the latter article in "Goa," and I may add that it had its advantages. True it was a "slow coach," creeping on seventy or eighty miles a day, and some days almost stationary; it had few comforts and no luxuries. I began by actually missing "pudding," and have often smiled at the remembrance of my stomach's comical disappointment. *En revanche*, the study of the little world within was most valuable to the "young Anglo-Indian," and the slow devious course allowed landing at places rarely visited by Europeans. During my repeated trips I saw Diu, once so famous in Portuguese story, Holy Dwarká, guarded outside by sharks and filled with fierce and fanatic mercenaries, and a dozen less interesting spots.

The end of this trip was Tankária-Bunder, a small landing in the Bay of Cambay, a most primitive locale to be called a port, where a mud-bank, adapted for a mooring-stake, was about the only convenience. It showed me, however, a fine specimen of the *Ghora*, or bore, known to our Severn and other rivers—an exaggerated high tide, when the water comes rushing up the shallows like a charge of cavalry. Native carts were also to be procured at Tankária-Bunder for the three days' short march to Baroda, and a mattress spread below made the rude article comfortable enough for young limbs and strong nerves.

Gujarat, the classical Gujaráhtra, a land of the Gujar clan, which remained the Syrastrena Regio of Arian, surprised me by its tranquil beauty and its vast natural wealth. Green as a card-table, flat as a prairie, it grew a marvellous growth of trees, which stunted our English oaks and elm trees—

> "to ancient song unknown,
> The noble sons of potent heat and flood"—

and a succession of fields breaking the glades, of townlets and villages walled by luxuriant barriers of caustic milk-bush (euphorbia), teemed with sights and sounds and smells peculiarly Indian. The sharp bark of Hanu the Monkey and the bray of the *Shankh* or conch near the bowery pagoda were surprises to the ear, and less to the nose was the blue vapour which settled over the hamlets morning and evening, a semi-transparent veil, the result of *Gobar* smoke from "cow-chips." A stale trick upon travellers approaching India by sea was to rub a little sandal oil upon the gunwale and invite them to "smell India," yet many a time for miles off shore I have noted that faint spicy odour, as if there were curry in the air, which about the abodes of man seems to be crossed with an aroma of drugs, as though proceeding from an apothecary's store. Wondrous peaceful and quiet lay those little Indian villages, outlaid by glorious banyan and pipal trees, topes or clumps of giant figs which rain a most grateful shade, and sometimes provided by the piety of some long-departed Chief with a tank of cut stone, a *baurá* or draw-well of fine masonry and large dimensions. But what "exercised" not a little my "Griffin" thoughts was to note the unpleasant difference between villages under English rule and those belonging to "His Highness the Gaikwar" or cowkeeper; the penury of the former and the prosperity of the latter. Mr. Boyd, the then Resident at the local court, soon enlightened me upon the evils of our unelastic rule of "smart Collectors," who cannot and dare not make any allowance for deficient rainfall or injured crops, and it is better to have something to lose, and to lose it even to the extent "of being ousted of possessions and disseized of freehold," with the likely hope of gaining it again, than to own nothing worth plundering.

The end of the march introduced me to my corps, the 18th Regiment, Bombay Native Infantry, whose head-quarters were in Gujarat, one wing being stationed at Mhow, on the Bengal frontier.

The officer commanding, Captain James (C.V.), called upon me at the Travellers' bungalow, the rudimentary Inn which must satisfy the stranger in India, suggesting the while such sad contrast, and bore me off to his bungalow, formally presented me at Mess—then reduced to eight members besides myself—and the Assistant-Surgeon Arnott put me in the way of lodging myself. The regimental Mess, with its large cool Hall and punkahs, its clean napery and bright silver, its servants each standing behind his master's chair, and the cheroots and hookahs which appeared with the disappearance of the "table"-cloth, was a pleasant surprise, the first sight of comfortable home-life I had seen since landing at Bombay. Not so the Subalterns' bungalow, which gave the idea of a dog-hole at which British Ponto would turn up his civilized nose. The business of the day was mainly goose-step and studying the drill book, and listening to such equivocal words of command as "Tandelees" (stand at ease) and "Fiz-bagnat" (fix bayonets). Long practice with the sword, which I had began seriously at the age of twelve, sometimes taking three lessons a day, soon eased my difficulties, and led to the study of native swordsmanship, whose grotesqueness and buffoonery can be rivalled only by its insufficiency.*

The wrestling, however, was another matter, and not a few natives in my Company had at first the advantage of me, and this induced a trial of Indian training, which consisted mainly of washing down balls of *Gur* (unrefined sugar) with bowls of hot milk hotly spiced. The result was that in a week I was blind with bile. Another set of lessons suggested by common sense, was instruction by a *chábuh-*

---

* Those curious upon the subject will consult my "Book of the Sword," vol. i. p. 163. Remember, young swordsman, these people never give point and never parry it.

sawar, or native jockey. All nations seem to despise one another's riding, and none seem to know how much they have to learn. The Indian style was the merit of holding the horse well in hand, making him bound off at a touch of the heel, stopping him dead at a hand gallop, and wheeling him round as on a pivot. The Hindú will canter over a figure-of-eight, gradually diminishing the dimensions till the animal leans over at an angle of 45°, and throwing himself over the off side and hanging by the heel to the earth, will pick up sword or pistol from the ground. Our lumbering chargers brought us to notable grief more than once in the great Sikh War. And as I was somewhat nervous about snakes, I took lessons of a "Charmer," and could soon handle them with coolness.

The *Bibi* (white woman) was at that time rare in India; the result was the triumph of the *Búbú* (coloured sister). I found every officer in the corps more or less provided with one of these helpmates.

We boys naturally followed suit; but I had to suffer the protestations of the Portuguese *padre*, who had taken upon himself the cure and charge of my soul, and was like a hen who had hatched a duckling. I had a fine opportunity of studying the *pros* and *cons* of the *Búbú* system.

Pros: The "walking dictionary" is all but indispensable to the Student, and she teaches him not only Hindostani grammar, but the syntaxes of native Life. She keeps house for him, never allowing him to save money, or, if possible, to waste it. She keeps the servants in order. She has an infallible recipe to prevent maternity, especially if her tenure of office depends on such compact. She looks after him in sickness, and is one of the best of nurses, and, as it is not good for man to live alone, she makes him a manner of home.

The *disadvantages* are as manifest as the advantages. Presently, as overland passages became cheaper and commoner, the *Bibi* won and the *Búbú* lost ground. Even during *my* day, married men began, doubtless at the instance of their wives, to look coldly upon the half-married, thereby showing mighty little common sense. For India was the classic land of Cicisbeism, where husbands are occupied between ten a.m. and five p.m. at their offices and counting-houses, leaving a fair field and much favour to the sub unattached, and whose duty often keeps the man sweltering upon the plains, when the wife is enjoying the *somer-frisch* upon "the Hills." Moreover, the confirmed hypocrite and the respectable-ist, when in power, established a kind of inquisitorial inquiry into the officer's house, and affixed a black mark to the name of the half-married. At last the *Búbú* made her exit and left a void. The greatest danger in

British India is the ever-growing gulf that yawns between the governors and the governed; they lose touch of one another, and such racial estrangement leads directly to racial hostility.

The day in Cantonment-way is lively. It began before sunrise on the parade-ground, an open space, which any other people but English would have converted into a stronghold. Followed, the baths and the *choti-hazri*, or little breakfast, the *munshi* (language-master), and literary matters till nine o'clock meal. The hours were detestable, compared with the French system—the *déjeuner à la fourchette*, which abolished the necessity of lunch; but throughout the Anglo-American world, even in the places worst adapted, "business" lays out the day. After breakfast, most men went to the billiard-room; some, but very few, preferred "peacocking," which meant robing in white-grass clothes and riding under a roasting sun, as near the meridian as possible, to call upon "regimental ladies," who were gruff as corporals when the function was neglected too long. The dull and tedious afternoon again belonged to *munshi*, and ended with a constitutional ride, or a rare glance at the band; Mess about seven p.m., possibly a game of whist, and a stroll home under the marvellous Gujarat skies, through a scene of perfect loveliness, a paradise bounded by the whity-black line.

There was little variety in such days. At times we rode to Baroda City, which seemed like a Mansion, to which the Cantonment acted as porter's Lodge. "Good Water" (as the Sanskritists translate it) was a walled City, lying on the north bank of the Vishwamitra river, and containing some 150,000 souls, mostly hostile, who eyed us with hateful eyes, and who seemed to have taught even their animals to abhor us. The City is a *mélange* of low huts and tall houses, grotesquely painted, with a shabby palace, and a *Chauk*, or Bazar, where four streets meet. At times H.M. the Gaikwar would show us what was called sport—a fight between two elephants with cut tusks, or a caged tiger and a buffalo—the last being generally the winner—or a wrangle between two fierce stallions, which bit like camels. The cock-fighting was, however, of a superior kind, the birds being of first-class blood, and so well trained, that they never hesitated to attack a stranger. An occasional picnic, for hunting, not society, was a most pleasant treat. The native Prince would always lend us his cheetahs or hunting leopards, or his elephants; the jungles inland of the city swarmed with game, from a snipe to a tiger, and the broad plains to the north were packs of *nilghai* and the glorious black buck. About twenty-eight miles due east, rises high above the sea of verdure the picturesque hill known as Pávangarh, the Fort of Eolus, and the centre of an old Civilization. Tanks and Jain temples were scattered around it, and the ruins of Champenír City cumbered the base. In a more progressive society, this place, 2500 feet high, and cooler by 18° to 20° F., would have become a kind of sanitarium. But men, apparently, could not agree. When the Baroda races came round, Major C. Crawley, commanding the 4th Bombay Rifles, used, in consequence of some fancied slight, to openly ride out of cantonment; and Brigadier Gibbons, the commander, did nothing for society. But the crowning excitement of the season was the report of Sir Charles Napier's battle of Miani (February 21st), followed by the affair of Dubba (March 25th), the "tail of the Afghan War." The account seemed to act as an electric shock upon the English frame, followed by a deep depression and a sense of mortal injury at the hands of Fate in keeping us out of the fray.

At length, in April, 1843, I obtained two months' leave of absence to the Presidency, for the purpose of passing an examination in Hindostani. The function was held at the Town Hall. Major-General Vans-Kennedy presided, a queer old man as queerly dressed, who had given his life to Orientalism, and who had printed some very respectable studies of Hinduism. The examining *munshi*, Mohammed "Mucklá," was no friend to me, because I was coached by a rival, old Dosabhai, yet he could not prevent my distancing a field of eleven. This happened on May 5th, and on May 12th I had laid in a full supply of Gujarati books, and set out by the old road to rejoin.

If Baroda was dull and dreary during the dries, it was mortal during the rains. I had been compelled to change my quarters for a bigger bungalow, close to the bank of the *nullah* which bounded the camp to the east and fed the Vishwamitra. It was an ill-omened place; an English officer had been wounded in it, and the lintel still bore the mark of a sabre which some native ruffian had left, intending to split a serjeant's head. Other quarters in the cantonment were obliged to keep one *ramosi*, *alias* Paggi, a tracker, a temporarily reformed thief who keeps off other thieves; my bungalow required two. An ignoble position for a dominant race, this openly paying blackmail and compounding felony. The rule of the good Company was, however, not a rule of honour, but of expediency, and the safety of its officers was little regarded; they were stabbed in their tents, or cut down by dacoits, even when travelling on the highways of Gujarat. Long and loudly the survivors hoped that some fine day a bishop or a Director's son would come to grief, and *when this happened at last* the process was summarily stopped. Indeed, nothing was easier to find than a remedy. A heavy fine was imposed upon the district in which the outrage was committed. By such means, Mohammed Ali of Egypt made the Suez Desert safer than a London street, and Sir Charles Napier pacified Sind, and made deeds of violence unknown—by means not such as Earl Russell virtually encouraged the robber-shepherds of Greece to plunder and murder English travellers.

The monsoon,* as it is most incorrectly termed, completely changes the tenor of Anglo-Indian life. It is ushered in by a display of "insect youth" which would have astonished Egypt in the age of the plagues, "flying bugs," and so forth. At Mess every tumbler was protected by a silver lid. And when the downfall begins it suggests that the "fountains of the great deep" have been opened up. I have seen tropical rains in many a region near the Line, but never anything that rivals Gujarati. Without exaggeration, the steady discharge of water buckets lasted literally, on one occasion, through seven days and nights without intermission, and to reach Mess we had to send our clothes on, and to wear a single waterproof, and to gallop through water above, around, and below at full speed. This third of the year was a terribly dull suicidal time, worse even than the gloomy month of November. It amply accounted for the card-table surface and the glorious tree-clump of the Gujarat—

> "The mighty growth of sun and torrent-rains."

Working some twelve hours a day, and doing nothing but work, I found myself ready in later August for a second trip to the Presidency, and obtained leave from September 10th to October 30th (afterwards made to include November 10th) for proceeding to Bombay, and being examined in the Guzerattee language.

This time I resolved to try another route, and, despite the warning of abominable roads, to ride down coast *viâ* Baroch and Surat. I had not been deceived; the deep and rich black soil, which is so good for the growth of cotton, makes a mud truly terrible to travellers. Baroch, the Hindu Brighu-Khatia, or Field of Brighú, son of Brahma, is generally made the modern successor of Ptolemy and Arrian's "Barygaza," but there are no classic remains to support the identification of the spot, nor indeed did any one in the place seem to care a fig about the matter. A truly Hindú town of some twelve thousand souls on the banks of the Nerbudda, it boasted of only one sight, the *Kabir-bar*, which the English translated "Big

* The word is a Portuguese "corruption" of *mausim*, in Arabia a season, and *per excellentiam* the sailing season. Thence it was transferred to the dry season, when the north-eastern trade-winds blow upon the Indian Ocean. But popular use transferred the name to the south-western rainy winds, which last from June to September.

† On June 26th, 1843, "Ensign Burton" appeared in orders as "Regimental Interpreter."

Banyan," and which meant, "Banyan-tree of (the famous ascetic and poet, Das Kabir)." I remember only two of his lines—

> "Máyá mare na man mare, mar mar gaya sarir"
> ("Illusion dies; dies not the mind, though body die and die")—

Máyá (illusion) being sensuous matter, and old Fakirs express the idea of the modern Hylozoist,* "All things are thinks." The old tree is hardly worth a visit, although it may have sheltered five thousand horsemen and inspired Milton, for which see the guide-books.

Surat (Surashtra = good region), long time the "Gate of Meccah," where pilgrims embarked instead of at Bombay, shows nothing of its olden splendour.

This was the nucleus of British power on the western coast of India in the seventeenth century, and as early as May, 1609, Captain Hawkins, of the *Hector*, obtained permission at Agra here to found a factory for his half-piratical countrymen, who are briefly described as "Molossis suis ferociores." They soon managed to turn out the Portuguese, and they left a Graveyard which is not devoid of some barbaric interest—Tom Croyate of the Crudities, however, is absent from it. At Surat I met Lieutenant Manson, R.A. He was going down to "go up" in Maharátta, and we agreed to take a *pattymar* together. We cruised down the foul Tapti river —all Indian, like West African, streams seem to be made of dirty water—and were shown the abandoned sites of the Dutch garden and French factory, Vaux's Tomb, and Dormus Island. We escaped an *Elephanta* storm, one of those pleasant September visitations which denote the break up of the "monsoon," and which not unfrequently bestrews the whole coast of Western India with wreckage. This time I found lodging in the Town Barracks, Bombay, and passed an examination in the Town Hall before General Vans-Kennedy, with the normal success, being placed first. The process consisted of reading from print (two books), and handwriting, generally some "native-letter," and of conversing and of writing an "address" or some paper of the kind.

Returning Baroda-wards, whence my regiment was transferred to our immense satisfaction to Sind, I assisted in the farewell revelries, dinners and *Naches*, or native dances—the most melancholy form in which Terpsichore ever manifested herself.

By far the most agreeable and wholesome part of regimental life in India is the march; the hours are reasonable, the work not too

* See "Humanism *versus* Theism, or Solipsism (Egoism)—Atheism," letters by Robert Lewin, M.D. London: Freethought Publishing Company, 1887.

severe, and the results, in appetite and sleep, admirable. At Bombay we encamped on the Esplanade, and on January 1st, 1844, we embarked for Karáchi on board the H.E.I.C.'s steamer *Semiramis*, whose uneventful cruise is told in "Scinde, or the Unhappy Valley," chap. 1, "The Shippe of Helle." Yet not wholly uneventual to me.

On board of the *Semiramis* was Captain Walter Scott, Bombay Engineers, who had lately been transferred from commanding in Candeish to the superintendence of the Sind Canals, a department newly organized by the old Conqueror of "Young Egypt," and our chance meeting influenced my life for the next six years. I have before described him. With short intervals I was one of his assistants till 1849. We never had a diverging thought, much less an unpleasant word; and when he died, at Berlin, in 1875, I felt his loss as that of a near relation.

Karáchi, which I have twice described, was in 1844 a mere stretch of a Cantonment, and nothing if not military; the garrison consisting of some five thousand men of all arms, European and native. The discomfort of camp life in this Sahara,* which represented the Libyan Desert, after Gujarat, the Nile Valley, was excessive, the dust-storms were atrocious,† and the brackish water produced the most unpleasant symptons. Parades of all kinds, regimental and brigade, were the rule, and Sir Charles Napier was rarely absent from anything on a large scale.

The Conqueror of Scinde was a noted and remarkable figure at that time, and there is still a semi-heroic ring about the name. In appearance he was ultra-Jewish, a wondrous contrast to his grand brother, Sir William; his countrymen called him Fagan, after Dickens, and his subjects, Shaytan-á-Bhái, Satan's brother, from his masterful spirit and reckless energy. There is an idealized portrait of him in Mr. W. H. Bruce's "Life" (London, Murray, 1885), but I much prefer the caricature by Lieutenant Beresford, printed in my wife's volume, "A.E.I." Yet there was nothing mean in the Conqueror's diminutive form; the hawk's eye, and eagle's beak, and powerful chin would redeem any face from vulgarity.

Sir Charles, during his long years of Peninsular and European service, cultivated the habit of jotting down all events in his diary, with a *naïveté*, a vivacity, and a fulness which echoed his spirit, and which, with advancing years, degenerated into intemperance of language and extravagance of statement. He was hard, as were most men in those days, upon the great Company he termed the

* "Scinde, or the Unhappy Valley," 2 vols.; and "Sind Revisited," 1877.
† "Scinde," chapter iv.

"Twenty-four Kings of Leadenhall Street"—"ephemeral sovereigns;" he quoted Lord Wellesley about the "ignominious tyrants of the East."

In his sixtieth year he was appointed to the command of Poonah (December 28th, 1841), and he was so lacking in the goods of this world that a Bombay house refused to advance him £500. He began at once to study Hindostani, but it was too late; the lesson induced irrisistible drowsiness, and the *munshi* was too polite to awaken the aged scholar, who always said he would give Rs. 10,000 to be able to address the Sepoys. On September 3rd, 1842, he set off to assume his new command in Upper and Lower Sind, and he at once saw his opportunity. Major Outram had blackened the faces of the Amirs, but he wanted to keep the work of conquest for himself, and he did not relish its being done by another. He, however, assisted Sir Charles Napier, and it was not till his return to England in 1843 that he ranged himself on the side of the Directors, whose hatred of the Conqueror grew with his success, and two factions, Outramists and Napierists, divided the little world of Western India.

The battles of Miani and Dubba were much criticized by military experts, who found that the "butcher's bill" did not justify the magnificent periods of Sir William Napier. This noble old soldier's "Conquest of Scinde" was a work of *fantaisie;* the story was admirably told, the picture was perfect, but the details were so incorrect, that it became the subject of endless "chaff" even in Government House, Karáchi. The corrective was an official report by Major (afterwards General) Waddington, B.O. Eng., which gave the shady, rather than the sunlit side of the picture. And there is still a third to be written. Neither of our authorities tell us, nor can we expect a public document to do so, how the mulatto who had charge of the Amir's guns had been persuaded to fire high, and how the Talpur traitor who commanded the cavalry, openly drew off his men and showed the shameless example of flight. When the day shall come to publish details concerning disbursement of "Secret service money in India," the public will learn strange things. Meanwhile those of us who have lived long enough to see how history is written, can regard it as but little better than a poor romance.

However exaggerated, little Miani taught the world one lesson which should not be forgotten—the sole plan to win a fight from barbarians, be they Belochis, Kafirs, or Burmese. It is simplicity itself; a sharp cannonade to shake the enemy, an advance in line or *échelon* as the ground demands, and a dash of cavalry to expedite the runaways. And presently the victory led to organizing the

"Land Transport Corps" and the "Baggage Corps," two prime wants of the Indian army. Here Sir Charles Napier's skill as an inventor evolved order out of disorder, and efficiency from the most cumbrous of abuses. The pacification of the new Province was marvellóusly brought about by the enlightened despotism of the Conqueror. Outram had predicted ten years of guerilla warfare before peace could be restored; Sir Charles made it safer than any part of India within a year, and in 1844, when levelling down the canals, I was loudly blessed by the peasants, who cried out, "These men are indeed worthy to govern us, as they work for our good."

But Sir Charles Napier began India somewhat too late in life, and had to pay the penalty. His mistakes were manifold, and some of them miserable. When preparing for the "Truhkee campaign," he proposed to content himself with a "*Numero-cent*" tent for a Commander-in-Chief! When marching upon Multan, his idea was to quarter the Sepoys in the villages, which would have been destroyed at once; and it was some time before his Staff dared put it in this light.

From over-deference to English opinion, he liberated all the African slaves in Sind and turned them out to starve; it would have been wiser to "free the womb," and forbid importation. He never could understand the "Badli system," where a rich native buys a poor man to be hanged for him who committed the crime, and terribly scandalized Captain Young, the civilian Judge Advocate-General, by hanging the wrong man. Finding that the offended husband in Sind was justified by public opinion for cutting down his wife, he sent the unfortunate to the gallows, and the result was a peculiar condition of society. On one occasion, the anonymas of Hyderabad sent him a deputation to complain "that the married women were taking the bread out of their mouths."

Sir Charles was a favourite among the juniors, in fact, amongst all who did not thwart or oppose him. He delighted in Rabelaisian, *bon-mots*, and the *Conte grivois*, as was the wont of field-officers in his day; his comment upon a newspaper's "peace and plenty at Karáchi" was long quoted.

After a month of discomfort at Karáchi, rendered more uncomfortable by the compulsory joining of six unfortunate Staff-officers who lost their snug appointments in India,* we were moved to Gharra—"out of the frying-pan into the fire"—a melancholy hole some forty miles by road north of Head-quarters, and within hearing of the evening gun. I have already described its horror.† Our

* "Scinde," vol. i. p. 252.

† Ibid., p. 89.

predecessors had not built the barracks or bungalows, and we found only a parallelogram of rock and sand, girt by a tall dense hedge of bright green milk-bush, and surrounded by a flat of stone and gravel, near a filthy village whose timorous inhabitants shunned us as walking pestilences.

This, with an occasional temperature of 125° F., was to be our "house" for some years. As I had no money wherewith to build, I was compelled to endure a hot season in a single-poled tent, pitched outside the milk-bush hedge; and after, to escape suffocation, I was obliged to cover my table with a wet cloth and pass the hot hours under it. However, energy was not wanting, and the regimental *pandit* proving a good school-master, I threw away Sindi for Maráthá; and in October, 1844, I was able to pass my examination in Maráthá at the Presidency, I coming first of half a dozen. About this time Southern Bombay was agitated by a small mutiny in Sáwantwádi, and the papers contained a long service-correspondence about Colonels Outram and Wallace, the capture of Amanghar, and Lieutenant Brassy's descent on Shiva Drug. I at once laid in a store of Persian books, and began seriously to work at that richest and most charming of Eastern languages.

On return to Karáchi, I found myself, by the favour of my friend Scott, gazetted as one of his four assistants in the Sind "Survey," with especial reference to the Canal Department; my being able to read and translate the valuable Italian works on hydro-dynamics being a point in my favour. A few days taught me the use of compass, theodolite, and spirit-level, and on December 10th, 1844, I was sent with a surveying party and six camels to work at Fulayli (Phuleli) and its continuation, the Guni river. The labour was not small; after a frosty night using instruments in the sole of a canal where the sun's rays seemed to pour as through a funnel, was decidedly trying to the constitution. However, I managed to pull through, and my surveying books were honoured with official approbation. During this winter I enjoyed some sport, especially hawking, and collected material for "Falconry in the Valley of the Indus." * I had begun the noble art as a boy at Blois, but the poor kestrel upon which I tried my "'prentice hand" had died soon, worn out like an Eastern ascetic by the severities of training, especially in the fasting line. Returning northwards, I found my Corps at Hyderabad, and

* It was brought out in 1852, by my friend John Van Voorst, of Paternoster Row, who, after a long and honourable career, retired at the ripe age of eighty-four to take well-merited rest. He has proved himself to me a phœnix amongst publishers. "Half profits are no profits to the author," is the common saying, and yet for the last thirty years I have continually received from him small sums which represented my gains. Oh that all were so scrupulous!

passing through the deserted Gharra, joined the Head-quarters of the Survey at Karáchi in April.

Here I made acquaintance with Mirza Ali Akhbar, who owed his rank (Khan Bahádur) to his gallant conduct as Sir Charles Napier's *munshi* at Miani and Dubba, where he did his best to save as many unfortunate Beloch braves as possible. He lived outside the camp in a bungalow which he built for himself, and lodged a friend, Mirza Dáud, a first-rate Persian scholar. My life became much mixed up with these gentlemen, and my brother officers fell to calling me the "White Nigger." I had also invested in a Persian *munshi*, Mirza Mohammad Musayn, of Shiraz; poor fellow, after passing through the fires of Scinde unscathed, he returned to die of cholera in his native land. With his assistance I opened on the sly three shops at Karáchi,* where cloth, tobacco, and other small matters were sold exceedingly cheap to those who deserved them, and where I laid in a stock of native experience, especially regarding such matters as I have treated upon in my "Terminal Essay" to the "Thousand Nights and a Night," † but I soon lost my *munshi* friends. Mirza Dáud died of indigestion and patent pills at Karáchi; I last saw Mirza Ali Akhbar at Bombay, in 1876, and he deceased shortly afterwards. He had been unjustly and cruelly treated. Despite the high praises of Outram and Napier for the honesty and efficiency of Ali Akhbar,‡ the new commission had brought against the doomed man a number of trumped-up charges, proving bribery and corruption, and managed to effect his dismissal from the service. The unfortunate Mirza, in the course of time, disproved them all, but the only answer to his application for being reinstated was that what had been done could not now be undone. I greatly regretted his loss. He had promised me to write out from his Persian notes a diary of his proceedings during the conquest of Scinde; he was more "behind the curtain" than any man I knew, and the truths he might have told would have been exceedingly valuable.

Karáchi was, for India, not a dull place in those days. Besides our daily work of planning and mapping the surveys of the cold season, and practising latitudes and longitudes till my right eye became comparatively short-sighted, we organized a "Survey Mess" in a bungalow belonging to the office "Compound." There were six of us—Blagrave, Maclagan, Vanrenin, and afterwards Price and Lambert—and local society pronounced us all mad, although I cannot see that we were more whimsical than our neighbours. I

* "Falconry in the Valley of the Indus," pp. 100, 101.

† Vol. x. p. 205, *et seqq.*

‡ See, in vol. i. p. 53 of "Sind Revisited," Sir Charles's outspoken opinion.

also built a bungalow, which got the title of the "Inquisition," and there I buried my favourite game-cock Bhujang (the dragon), who had won me many a victory—people declared that it was the grave of a small human. I saw much of Mirza Husayn, a brother of Agha Khan Mahallati, a scion of the Isma'iliyah, or "Old Man of the Mountain," who, having fled his country, Persia, after a rebellion, ridiculous even in that land of eternal ridiculous rebellions, turned *condottière*, and with his troop of one hundred and thirty ruffians took service with us and was placed to garrison Járak (Jerruch). Here the Belochis came down upon him, and killed or wounded about a hundred of his troop, after which he passed on to Bombay and enlightened the Presidency about his having conquered Scinde. His brother, my acquaintance, also determined to attack Persia *viâ* Makran, and managed so well that he found himself travelling to Teheran, lashed to a gun carriage. The Lodge "Hope" kindly made me an "entered apprentice," but I had read Carlisle, "The Atheistical Publisher," and the whole affair appeared to me a gigantic humbug, dating from the days of the Crusades, and as Cardinal Newman expressed it, "meaning a goose club." But I think better of it now, as it still serves political purposes in the East, and gives us a point against our French rivals and enemies. As the "Scinde Association" was formed, I was made honorary secretary, and had no little correspondence with Mr. E. Blyth, the curator of the Zoological Department, Calcutta. Sir Charles Napier's friends also determined to start a newspaper, in order to answer the Enemy in the Gate, and reply to the "base and sordid Bombay faction," headed by the "Rampant Buist," with a strong backing of anonymous officials.

The *Karrachee Advertiser* presently appeared in the modest shape of a lithographed sheet on Government foolscap, and, through Sir William Napier, its most spicy articles had the honour of a reprint in London. Of these, the best were "the letters of Omega," by my late friend Rathborne, then Collector at Hyderabad, and they described the vices of the Sind Amirs in language the reverse of ambiguous. I did not keep copies, nor, unfortunately, did the clever and genial author.

This pleasant, careless life broke up in November, 1845, when I started with my friend Scott for a long tour to the north of Sind. We rode by the high-road through Gharra and Jarak to Kotri, the station of the Sind flotilla, and then crossed to Hyderabad, where I found my Corps flourishing. After a very jolly week, we resumed our way up the right bank of the Indus and on the extreme western frontier, where we found the Beloch herdsmen in their wildest state. About that time began to prevail the wildest reports about the lost tribes of Israel (who were never lost), and with the aid of Gesenius and Lynch I dressed up a very pretty grammar and vocabulary, which proved to sundry scientists that the lost was found at last. But my mentor would not allow the joke to appear *in print.* On Christmas Day we entered "Sehwán," absurdly styled "Alexander's Camp." Here again the spirit of mischief was too strong for me. I buried a broken and hocussed jar of "*Athenæum* sauce," red pottery with black Etruscan figures, right in the way of an ardent amateur antiquary; and the results were comical. At Larkháná we made acquaintance with "fighting FitzGerald," who commanded there, a magnificent figure, who could cut a donkey in two; and who, although a man of property, preferred the hardships of India to the pleasures of home. He had, however, a mania of blowing himself up in a little steamer mainly of his own construction, and after his last accident he was invalided home to England, and died within sight of her shores.

At Larkháná the following letter was received:—

"Karáchi, January 3, 1846.

"MY DEAR SCOTT,

"The General says you may allow as many of your assistants as you can spare to join their regiments, if going on service, with the understanding that they must resign their appointments and will not be reappointed, etc.

(Signed) "JOHN NAPIER."

This, beyond bazar reports, was our first notice of the great Sikh War, which added the Punjab to Anglo-India. This news made me wild to go. A carpet-soldier was a horror to me, and I was miserable that anything should take place in India without my being in the thick of the fight. So, after a visit to Sahkar Shikarpúr and the neighbourhood, I applied myself with all my might to prepare for the Campaign. After sundry small surveyings and levellings about Sahkar (Sukhur), I persuaded Scott, greatly against the grain, to send in my resignation, and called upon General James Simpson, who was supposed to be in his dotage, and was qualifying for the Chief Command in the Crimea.

My application was refused. Happily for me, however, suddenly appeared an order from Bengal to the purport that all we assistant-surveyors must give sureties. This was enough for me. I wrote officially, saying that no man would be bail for me, and was told to be off to my corps; and on February 23rd, I marched with the 18th from Rohri.

Needless to repeat the sad story of our disappointment.* It was a model army of thirteen thousand men, Europeans and natives, and under "Old Charley" it would have walked into Multan as into a mutton-pie. We had also heard that Náo Mall was wasting his two millions of gold, and we were willing to save him the trouble. Merrily we trudged through Sabzalcote and Khanpur, and we entered Baháwalpur, where we found the heart-chilling order to retire and to march home, and consequently we marched and returned to Rohri on April 2nd; and after a few days' halt there, tired and miserable, we marched south, *viâ* Khayrpur, and, after seventeen marches, reached the old regimental quarters in Mohammad Khan Ká Tándá, on the Fulayli river.†

But our physical trials and mental disappointments had soured our tempers, and domestic disturbances began. Our colonel was one Henry Corsellis, the son of a Bencoolen civilian, and neither his colour nor his temper were in his favour. The wars began in a small matter.

I had been making doggrel rhymes on men's names at Mess, and knowing something of the commanding officer's touchiness, passed him over. Hereupon he took offence, and seeing well that I was "in for a row," I said, "Very well, Colonel, I will write your Epitaph," which was as follows—

"Here lieth the body of Colonel Corsellis;
The rest of the fellow, I fancy, in hell is.'

After which we went at it "hammer and tongs."

I shall say no more upon the subject; it is, perhaps, the part of my life upon which my mind dwells with least satisfaction. In addition to regimental troubles, there were not a few domestic disagreeables, especially complications, with a young person named Núr Jan. To make matters worse, after a dreadful wet night my mud bungalow came down upon me, wounding my foot.‡ The only pleasant reminiscences of the time are the days spent in the quarters of an old native friend § on the banks of the beautiful Phuleli, seated upon a felt rug, spread beneath a shadowy tamarind tree, with beds of sweet-smelling *rayhan* (basil) around, and eyes looking over the broad smooth stream and the gaily dressed groups gathered at the frequent ferries. I need hardly say that these visits were paid in native costume, and so correct was it, that I, on camel's back, frequently passed my Commanding Officer in the Gateway of Fort

---

* "Scinde," vol. ii. p. 258, etc.
† "Sind Revisited," vol. i. p. 256, shows how I found my old home in 1876.
‡ "Scinde," vol. i. p. 151.
§ "Falconry," pp. 103–105.

Hyderabad, without his recognizing me. I had also a host of good friends, especially Dr. J. J. Steinhaüser, who, in after years, was to have accompanied me, but for an accident, to Lake Tanganyika, and who afterwards became my collaborateur in the "Thousand Nights and a Night."

The hot season of 1846 was unusually sickly, and the white regiments at Karáchi, notably the 78th Highlanders, suffered terribly. Hyderabad was also threatened, but escaped better than she deserved. In early July I went into "sick quarters," and left my regiment in early September, with a strong case. At Bombay my friend Henry J. Carter assisted me, and enabled me to obtain two years' leave of absence to the Neilgherries.

My *munshi*, Mohammed Husayn, had sailed for Persia, and I at once engaged an Arab "coach." This was one Haji Jauhur, a young Abyssinian, who, with his wife, of the same breed, spoke a curious Semitic dialect, and was useful in conversational matters. Accompanied by my servants and horse, I engaged the usual *pattymar*, the *Daryá Prashád* ("Joy of the Ocean"), and set sail for Goa on February 20th, 1847. In three days' trip we landed in the once splendid capital, whose ruins I have described in "Goa and the Blue Mountains" (1851). Dom Pestanha was the Governor-General, Senhor Gomez Secretary to Government, and Major St. Maurice chief aide-de-camp, and all treated me with uncommon kindness. On my third visit to the place in 1876, all my old friends and acquaintances had disappeared, whilst the other surroundings had not changed in the least degree.

From Goa to Punány was a trip of five days, and from the little Malabar Port, a terrible dull ride of ten days, halts and excursions included, with the only excitement of being nearly drowned in a torrent, placed me at Conoor, on the western edge of the "Blue Mountains." At Ootacamund, the capital of the sanitarium, I found a friend, Lieutenant Dyett, who offered to share with me his quarters. Poor fellow! he suffered sadly in the Multan campaign, where most of the wounded came to grief, some said owing to the salt in the silt, which made so many operations fatal; after three amputations his arm was taken out of the socket. I have noted the humours of "Ooty" in the book before mentioned, and I made myself independent of society by beginning the study of Telugu, in addition to Arabic.

But the sudden change from dry Scinde to the damp cold mountains induced in me an attack of rheumatic ophthalmia, which began at the end of May, 1847, and lasted nearly two years, and would not be shaken off till I left India in March, 1849. In vain I tried diet and dark rooms, change of place, blisters of sorts, and the whole contents of the Pharmacopœia; it was a thorn in the flesh which determined to make itself felt. At intervals I was able to work hard and to visit the adjacent places, such as Kotagherry, the Orange Valley, and St. Catherine's Falls.* Meanwhile I wrote letters to the *Bombay Times*, and studied Telugu and Toda as well as Persian and Arabic, and worked at the ethnology of Hylobius the Hillman, whose country showed mysterious remains of civilized life, gold mining included.

"Ooty" may be a pleasant place, like a water-cure establishment to an invalid in rude health; but to me nothing could be duller or more disagreeable, and my two years of sick leave was consequently reduced to four months. On September 1st, 1847, glad as a partridge-shooter, I rode down the Ghát, and a dozen days later made Calicut, the old capital of Camoens' "Jamorim," the Samriry Rajah. Here I was kindly received, and sent to visit old Calicut and other sights, by Mr. Collector Conolly, whom a Madras civilianship could not defend from Fate. A short time after my departure he was set upon and barbarously murdered in his own verandah, by a band of villain *Moplahs*,† a bastard race got by Arab sires on Hindú dams. He was thus the third of the gallant brothers who came to violent end.

This visit gave me a good opportunity of studying on the spot the most remarkable scene of "The Lusiads," and it afterwards served me in good stead. The *Seaforth*, Captain Biggs, carried me to Bombay, after passing visits to Mangalore and Goa, in three days of ugly monsoon weather. On October 15th I passed in Persian at the Town Hall, coming out first of some thirty, with a compliment from the examiners; and this was succeeded by something more substantial, in the shape of an "honorarium" of Rs. 1000 from the Court of Directors.

This bright side of the medal had its reverse. A friend, an Irish medico, volunteered to prescribe for me, and strongly recommended frictions of citric ointment (calomel in disguise) round the orbit of the eye, and my perseverance in his prescription developed ugly symptoms of mercurialism, which eventually drove me from India.

My return to Scinde was in the s.s. *Dwárká*, the little vessel which, in 1853, carried me from Jeddah to Suez, and which, in 1862, foundered at the mouth of the Tapti or Surat river. She belonged to the Steam Navigation Company, Bombay, and she had been

---

* "Goa," etc., p. 355.

† See Ibid., p. 339.

brought safely round the Cape by the skipper, a man named Tribe. That "climate" had demoralized him. He set out from Kárách without even an able seaman who knew the Coast; the Captain and his Mate were drunk and incapable the whole way. As we were about to enter the dangerous port, my fellow-passengers insisted upon my taking Command as Senior Officer, and I ordered the *Dwárká's* head to be turned westward under the easiest steam, so that next morning we landed safely.

My return to head-quarters of the Survey was a misfortune to my comrades; my eyes forbade regular work, and my friends had to bear my share of the burden. However, there were painless intervals when I found myself able to work at Sindí under Munshi Nandú, and at Arabic under Shaykh Háshim, a small half-Bedawin, who had been imported by me from Bombay. Under him also I began the systematic study of practical Moslem divinity, learned about a quarter of the Korán by heart, and became a proficient at prayer. It was always my desire to visit Meccah during the pilgrimage season; written descriptions by hearsay of its rites and ceremonies were common enough in all languages, European as well as native, but none satisfied me, because none seemed practically to know anything about the matter. So to this preparation I devoted all my time and energy; not forgetting a sympathetic study of Sufi-ism, the *Gnosticism* of Al-Islam,* which would raise me high above the rank of a mere Moslem. I conscientiously went through the *chillá*, or quarantine of fasting and other exercises, which, by-the-by, proved rather over-exciting to the brain. At times, when overstrung, I relieved my nerves with a course of Sikh religion and literature: the good old priest solemnly initiated me in presence of the swinging *Granth*, or Naná Shah's Scripture. As I had already been duly invested by a strict Hindú with the *Janeo*, or "Brahminical thread," my experience of Eastern faiths became phenomenal, and I became a Master-Sufi.

There was a scanty hope of surveying for weak eyes; so I attempted to do my duty by long reports concerning the country and the people, addressed to the Bombay Government, and these were duly printed in its "Selections," which MSS. I have by me. To the local branch of the Royal Asiatic Society, there were sent two papers, "Grammar of the Játakí or Mulltani Language," and "Remarks on Dr. Dorn's Chrestomathy of the Afghan Tongue."† Without hearing of Professor Pott, the *savant* of Halle (and deceased

* This stuck to him off and on all his life.—I. B.

† Written with the assistance of a fine old Afghan *mullah*, Akhund Burhan al-Din.

lately), I convinced myself that the Játs of Scinde, a race which extends from the Indus's mouth to the plains of Tartary, give a clue to the origin of the Gypsies as well as to the Getæ and Massagetæ (Great Getæ).

And this induced me to work with the Camel men, who belong to that notorious race, and to bring out a grammar and vocabulary.

Indeed the more sluggish became my sight, the more active became my brain, which could be satisfied only with twelve to fourteen hours a day of alchemy, mnemonics, "Mantih," or Eastern logic, Arabic, Sindi, and Panjábi. In the latter, official examinations were passed before Captain Stack, the only Englishman in the country who had an inkling of the subject.

The spring of 1848, that most eventful year in Europe, brought us two most exciting items of intelligence. The proclamation of the French Republic reached us on April 8th, and on May 2nd came the news of the murder of Anderson and his companion by Náo Mall of Multan.

Richard wrote a little bit of autobiography about himself in 1852. In case all may not have seen it, and many may not remember it, I here insert it.

Richard Burton's Little Autobiography.

"The only scrap of autobiography we have from Richard Burton's pen," said Alfred Richard Bates, "was written very early in life, whilst in India, and dates thirty years ago. It is so characteristic it deserves to be perpetuated:—

"I extract the following few lines from a well-known literary journal as a kind of excuse for venturing, unasked, upon a scrap of autobiography. As long as critics content themselves with bedevilling one's style, discovering that one's slang is 'vulgar,' and one's attempts at drollery 'failures,' one should, methinks, listen silently to their ideas of 'gentility,' and accept their definitions of wit, reserving one's own opinion upon such subjects. For the British author in this, our modern day, engages himself as clown in a great pantomime, to be knocked down, and pulled up, slashed, tickled, and buttered *à discrétion* for the benefit of a manual-pleasantry-loving Public. So it would be weakness in him to complain of bruised back, scored elbows, and bumped head.

"Besides, the treatment you receive varies prodigiously according to the temper and the manifold influences from without that operate upon the gentleman that operates upon you. For instance—

"''Tis a *failure* at being *funny*," says surly Aristarchus, when, for some reason or other, he dislikes you or your publisher.

"'It is a *smart* book,' opines another, who has no particular reason to be your friend.

"'Narrated with *freshness of thought*,' declares a third, who takes an honest pride in 'giving the devil his due.'

"'Very *clever*,' exclaims the amiable critic, who for some reason or another likes you or your publisher.

"'There is *wit* and *humour* in these pages,' says the gentleman who has some particular reason to be your friend.

"'Evinces considerable *talent*.'

"And—

"'There is *genius* in this book,' declare the dear critics who in any way identify themselves or their interests with you.

"Now for the extract:—

"'Mr. Burton was, it appears, stationed for several years in Sind with his regiment, and it is due to him to say that he has set a good example to his fellow-subalterns by pursuing so diligently his inquiries into the language, literature, and customs of the native population by which he was surrounded. We are far from accepting all his doctrines on questions of Eastern policy, especially as regards the treatment of natives; but we are sensible of the value of the additional evidence which he has brought forward on many important questions. For a young man, he seems to have adopted some very extreme opinions; and it is perhaps not too much to say, that the fault from which he has most to fear, not only as an author, but as an Indian officer, is a disregard of those well-established rules of moderation which no one can transgress with impunity.'

"The greatest difficulty a raw writer on Indian subjects has to contend with, is a proper comprehension of the *ignorance crasse* which besets the mind of the home-reader and his oracle the critic. What a knowledge these lines *do* show of the opportunity for study presented to the Anglo-Indian subaltern serving with his corps! Part of the time when I did duty with mine we were quartered at Ghárrá, a heap of bungalows surrounded by a wall of milk-bush; on a sandy flat, near a dirty village whose timorous inhabitants shunned us as walking pestilences. No amount of domiciliary visiting would have found a single Sindian book in the place, except the accounts of the native shopkeepers; and, to the best of my remembrance, there was not a soul who could make himself intelligible in the common medium of Indian intercourse—Hindostani. An ensign stationed at Dover Castle might write 'Ellis's Antiquities;' a *sous-lieutenant* with his corps at Boulogne might compose the 'Legendaire de la Morinie,' but Ghárrá was sufficient to paralyse the readiest pen that ever coursed over foolscap paper.

"Now, waiving, with all due modesty, the unmerited compliment of 'good boy,' so gracefully tendered to me, I proceed to the judgment which follows it, my imminent peril of 'extreme opinions.' If there be any value in the 'additional evidence' I have 'brought forward on important questions,' the reader may, perchance, be curious to know how that evidence was collected. So, without further apology, I plunge into the subject.

"After some years of careful training for the Church in the north and south of France, Florence, Naples, and the University of Pisa,

I found myself one day walking the High Street, Oxford, with all the emotions which a Parisian exquisite of the first water would experience on awaking—at 3 p.m.—in 'Dandakaran's tangled wood.'

"To be brief, my 'college career' was highly unsatisfactory. I began a 'reading man,' worked regularly twelve hours a day, failed in everything—chiefly, I flattered myself, because Latin hexameters and Greek iambics had not entered into the list of my studies—threw up the classics, and returned to old habits of fencing, boxing, and single-stick, handling the 'ribbons,' and sketching facetiously, though not wisely, the reverend features and figures of certain half-reformed monks, calling themselves 'fellows.' My reading also ran into bad courses—Erpenius, Zadkiel, Falconry, Cornelius Agrippa, and the Art of Pluck.

"At last the Afghan War broke out. After begging the paternal authority in vain for the Austrian service, the Swiss Guards at Naples, and even the *Légion étrangère*, I determined to leave Oxford, *coûte qui coûte*. The testy old lady, Alma Mater, was easily persuaded to consign, for a time, to 'country nursing' the froward brat who showed not a whit of filial regard for her. So, after two years, I left Trinity, without a 'little go,' in a high dog-cart,—a companion in misfortune too-tooing lustily through a 'yard of tin,' as the dons started up from their game of bowls to witness the departure of the forbidden vehicle. Thus having thoroughly established the fact that I was fit for nothing but to be 'shot at for sixpence a day,' and as those Afghans (how I blessed their name !) had cut gaps in many a regiment, my father provided me with a commission in the Indian army, and started me as quickly as feasible for the 'Land of the Sun.'

"So, my friends and fellow-soldiers, I may address you in the words of the witty thief—slightly altered from Gil Blas—'Blessings on the dainty pow of the old dame who turned me out of her house; for had she shown clemency I should now doubtless be a dyspeptic Don, instead of which I have the honour to be a lieutenant, your comrade.'

"As the Bombay pilot sprang on board, twenty mouths agape over the gangway, all asked one and the same question. Alas! the answer was a sad one!—the Afghans had been defeated—the avenging army had retreated! The twenty mouths all ejaculated a something unfit for ears polite.

"To a mind thoroughly impressed with the sentiment that

> 'Man wants but little here below,
> Nor wants that little long,'

the position of an Ensign in the Hon. E. I. Company's Service is a very satisfactory one. He has a horse or two, part of a house, a pleasant Mess, plenty of pale ale, as much shooting as he can manage, and an occasional invitation to a dance, where there are thirty-two cavaliers to three dames, or to a dinner-party when a chair unexpectedly falls vacant. But some are vain enough to want more, and of these fools was I.

"In India two roads lead to preferment. The direct highway is 'service;'—getting a flesh wound, cutting down a few of the enemy, and doing something eccentric, so that your name may creep into a despatch. The other path, study of the languages, is a rugged and tortuous one, still you have only to plod steadily along its length, and, sooner or later, you must come to a 'staff appointment.' *Bien entendu*, I suppose you to be destitute of or deficient in Interest whose magic influence sets you down at once a heaven-born Staff Officer, at the goal which others must toil to reach.

A dozen lessons from Professor Forbes and a native servant on board the *John Knox* enabled me to land with *éclat* as a griff, and to astonish the throng of palanquin bearers that jostled, pushed, and pulled me at the pier head, with the vivacity and nervousness of my phraseology. And I spent the first evening in company with one Dosabhai Sohrabji, a white-bearded Parsee, who, in his quality of language-master, had vernacularized the tongues of Hormuzd knows how many generations of Anglo-Indian subalterns.

"The corps to which I was appointed was then in country quarters at Baroda, in the land of Gujerat; the journey was a long one, the difficulty of finding good instructors there was great, so was the expense, moreover fevers abounded; and, lastly, it was not so easy to obtain leave of absence to visit the Presidency, where candidates for the honours of language are examined. These were serious obstacles to success; they were surmounted, however, in six months, at the end of which time I found myself in the novel position of 'passed interpreter in Hindostani.'

"My success—for I had distanced a field of eleven—encouraged me to a second attempt, and though I had to front all the difficulties over again, in four months my name appeared in orders as qualified to interpret in the Guzerattee tongue.

"Meanwhile the Ameers of Sind had exchanged their palaces at Haydarábád for other quarters not quite so comfortable at Hazaree-bagh, and we were ordered up to the Indus for the pleasant purpose of acting police there. Knowing the Conqueror's chief want, a man who could speak a word of his pet conquest's vernacular dialect, I had not been a week at Karáchee before I found a language-master and a book. But the study was undertaken *invitâ minervâ*. We were quartered in tents, dust-storms howled over us daily, drills and brigade parades were never ending, and, as I was acting interpreter to my regiment, courts-martial of dreary length occupied the best part of my time. Besides, it was impossible to work in such an atmosphere of discontent. The seniors abhorred the barren desolate spot, with all its inglorious perils of fever, spleen, dysentery, and congestion of the brain, the juniors grumbled in sympathy, and the Staff officers, ordered up to rejoin the corps—it was on field service—complained bitterly of having to quit their comfortable appointments in more favoured lands without even a campaign in prospect. So when, a month or two after landing in the country, we were transferred from Karáchee to Ghárrá—purgatory to the other locale—I threw aside Sindí for Maharattee, hoping, by dint of reiterated examinations, to escape the place of torment as soon as possible. It was very like studying Russian in an English country-town; however, with the assistance of Molesworth's excellent dictionary, and the regimental *pundit*, or schoolmaster, I gained some knowledge of the dialect, and proved myself duly qualified in it at Bombay. At the same time a brother subaltern and I had jointly leased a Persian *moonshee*, one Mirza Mohammed Hosayn, of Shiraz. Poor fellow, after passing through the fires of Sind unscathed, he returned to his delightful land for a few weeks, to die there!—and we laid the foundation of a lengthened course of reading in that most elegant of Oriental languages.

"Now it is a known fact that a good Staff appointment has the general effect of doing away with one's bad opinion of any place whatever. So when, by the kindness of a friend whose name *his* modesty prevents my mentioning, the Governor of Sind was persuaded to give me the temporary appointment of Assistant in the Survey, I began to look with interest upon the desolation around me. The country was a new one, so was its population, so was their language. After reading all the works published upon the subject, I felt convinced that none but Mr. Crow and Captain J. MacMurdo had dipped beneath the superficies of things. My new duties compelled me to spend the cold season in wandering over the districts, levelling the beds of canals, and making preparatory sketches for a grand survey. I was thrown so entirely amongst the people as to depend upon them for society, and the 'dignity,' not to mention the increased allowances of a Staff officer, enabled me to collect a fair stock of books, and to gather around me those who could make them of any use. So, after the first year, when I had Persian at my fingers'-ends, sufficient Arabic to read, write, and converse fluently, and a superficial knowledge of that dialect of Punjaubee which is spoken in the wilder parts of the province, I began the systematic study of the Sindian people, their manners and their tongue.

"The first difficulty was to pass for an Oriental, and this was as necessary as it was difficult. The European official in India seldom, if ever, sees anything in its real light, so dense is the veil which the fearfulness, the duplicity, the prejudice, and the superstitions of the natives hang before his eyes. And the white man lives a life so distinct from the black, that hundreds of the former serve through what they call their 'term of exile' without once being present at a circumcision feast, a wedding, or a funeral. More especially the present generation, whom the habit and the means of taking furloughs, the increased facility for enjoying ladies' society, and, if truth be spoken, a greater regard for appearances, if not a stricter code of morality, estrange from their dusky fellow-subjects every day more and more. After trying several characters, the easiest to be assumed was, I found, that of a half-Arab, half-Iranian, such as may be met with in thousands along the northern shore of the Persian

Gulf. The Sindians would have detected in a moment the difference between my articulation and their own, had I attempted to speak their vernacular dialect, but they attributed the accent to my strange country, as naturally as a home-bred Englishman would account for the bad pronunciation of a foreigner calling himself partly Spanish, partly Portuguese. Besides, I knew the countries along the Gulf by heart from books, I had a fair knowledge of the Shiah form of worship prevalent in Persia, and my poor *moonshee* was generally at hand to support me in times of difficulty, so that the danger of being detected—even by a 'real Simon Pure'—was a very inconsiderable one.

"With hair falling upon his shoulders, a long beard, face and hands, arms and feet, stained with a thin coat of henna, Mirza Abdullah of Bushire—your humble servant—set out upon many and many a trip. He was a *bazzaz*, a vendor of fine linen, calicoes, and muslins—such chapmen are sometimes admitted to display their wares, even in the sacred harem, by 'fast' and fashionable dames—and he had a little pack of *bijouterie* and *virtù* reserved for emergencies. It was only, however, when absolutely necessary that he displayed his stock-in-trade; generally, he contented himself with alluding to it on all possible occasions, boasting largely of his traffic, and asking a thousand questions concerning the state of the market. Thus he could walk into most men's houses, quite without ceremony; even if the master dreamed of kicking him out, the mistress was sure to oppose such measure with might and main. He secured numberless invitations, was proposed to by several papas, and won, or had to think he won, a few hearts; for he came as a rich man and he stayed with dignity, and he departed exacting all the honours. When wending his ways he usually urged a return of visit in the morning, but he was seldom to be found at the caravanserai he specified—was Mirza Abdullah the Bushiri.

"The timid villagers collected in crowds to see the rich merchant in Oriental dress, riding spear in hand, and pistols in holsters, towards the little encampment pitched near their settlements. But regularly every evening on the line of march the Mirza issued from his tent and wandered amongst them, collecting much information and dealing out more concerning an ideal master—the Feringhee supposed to be sitting in State amongst the *moonshees*, the Scribes, the servants, the wheels, the chains, the telescopes, and the other magical implements in which the camp abounded. When travelling, the Mirza became this mysterious person's factotum, and often had he to answer the question how much his perquisites and illicit gains amounted to in the course of the year.

"When the Mirza arrived at a strange town, his first step was to secure a house in or near the bazar, for the purpose of evening *conversazioni*. Now and then he rented a shop, and furnished it with clammy dates, viscid molasses, tobacco, ginger, rancid oil, and strong-smelling sweetmeats; and wonderful tales Fame told about these establishments. Yet somehow or other, though they were more crowded than a first-rate milliner's rooms in town, they throve not in a pecuniary point of view; the cause of which was, I believe, that the polite Mirza was in the habit of giving the heaviest possible weight for their money to all the ladies, particularly the pretty ones, that honoured him by patronizing his concern.

"Sometimes the Mirza passed the evening in a mosque listening to the ragged students who, stretched at full length with their stomachs on the dusty floor, and their arms supporting their heads, mumbled out Arabic from the thumbed, soiled, and tattered pages of theology upon which a dim oil light shed its scanty ray, or he sat debating the niceties of faith with the long-bearded, shaven-pated, blear-eyed, and stolid-faced *genus loci*, the *Mullah*. At other times, when in merrier mood, he entered uninvited the first door whence issued the sounds of music and the dance;—a clean turban and a polite bow are the best 'tickets for soup' the East knows. Or he played chess with some native friend, or he consorted with the hemp-drinkers and opium-eaters in the *estaminets*, or he visited the Mrs. Gadabouts and Go-betweens who make matches amongst the Faithful, and gathered from them a precious budget of private history and domestic scandal.

"What scenes he saw! what adventures he went through! But who would believe, even if he ventured to detail them? *

"The Mirza's favourite school for study was the house of an elderly matron on the banks of the Fulailee River, about a mile from the Fort of Haydarábád. Khanum Jan had been a beauty in her youth, and the tender passion had been hard upon her—at least judging from the fact that she had fled her home, her husband, and her native town, Candahar, in company with Mohammed Bakhsh, a purblind old tailor, the object of her warmest affections.

"'Ah, he is a regular old hyæna now,' would the Joan exclaim in her outlandish Persian, pointing to the venerable Darby as he sat in the cool shade, nodding his head and winking his eyes over a pair of pantaloons which took him a month to sew, 'but you should have seen him fifteen years ago, what a wonderful youth he was!'

"The knowledge of one mind is that of a million—after a fashion. I addressed myself particularly to that of 'Darby;' and many an hour of tough thought it took me before I had mastered its truly Oriental peculiarities, its regular irregularities of deduction, and its strange monotonous one-idea'dness.

"Khanum Jan's house was a mud edifice, occupying one side of a square formed by tall, thin, crumbling mud walls. The respectable matron's peculiar vanity was to lend a helping hand in all manner of *affaires du cœur*. So it often happened that Mirza Abdullah was turned out of the house to pass a few hours in the garden. There

---

* This was the manner in which he excelled in Eastern life and knowledge, and knew more than all your learned Orientalists and men high in office. I wish he would have written a personal novel about these scenes, but I never could induce him to do so. First he thought that they would never suit Mrs. Grundy, and though he could retain a crowd of friends around him till the small hours of the morning to listen to his delightful experiences, in print he never could be got to talk about himself.—I. B.

he sat upon his felt rug spread beneath a shadowy tamarind, with beds of sweet-smelling basil around him, his eyes roving over the broad river that coursed rapidly between its wooded banks and the groups gathered at the frequent ferries, whilst the soft strains of mysterious, philosophical, transcendental Hafiz were sounded in his ears by the other Mirza, his companion; Mohammed Hosayn—peace be upon him!

"Of all economical studies this course was the cheapest. For tobacco daily, for frequent draughts of milk, for hemp occasionally, for four months' lectures from Mohammed Bakhsh, and for sundry other little indulgences, the Mirza paid, it is calculated, the sum of six shillings. When he left Haydarábád, he gave a silver talisman to the dame, and a cloth coat to her protector: long may they live to wear them!

* * * * * *

"Thus it was I formed my estimate of the native character. I am as ready to reform it when a man of more extensive experience and greater knowledge of the subject will kindly show me how far it transgresses the well-established limits of moderation. As yet I hold, by way of general rule, that the Eastern mind—I talk of the nations known to me by personal experience—is always in extremes; that it ignores what is meant by 'golden mean,' and that it delights to range in flights limited only by the *ne plus ultra* of Nature herself. Under which conviction I am open to correction.

"RICHARD F. BURTON."

Richard's works on India are—A grammar of the Játakí, or Belochi dialect. Here I would remark he mixed with the Játs of Sind, a race extending from the mouth of the Indus to the plains of Tartary, and who *he* believed to be the origin and head of the numerous tribes of Oriental gypsies, and he worked with the Camel men to assimilate himself with them. The next work was a grammar of the Mooltanee language, "Notes on the Pushtû, or Afghan Dialect," Reports to Bombay, (1) "General Notes on Sind," (2) "Notes on the Population of Sind."

These were all *preparatory* to becoming an author, and were brought out in 1849 by the Royal Asiatic Society, Bombay branch, and the Government Records. I have a single copy of each, but they must be out of print; meantime he prepared "Goa and the Blue Mountains," 1 vol.; "Scinde, or the Unhappy Valley," 2 vols.; and "Sindh and the Races that inhabit the Valley of the Indus," 1 vol.; but these did not appear until 1851.

"Scinde, or the Unhappy Valley," is, I think, the freshest, most witty and spirited thing I ever read. He had not been to war with the critics and Mrs. Grundy then, and there is all the boy's fun and fire in it. "Falconry in the Valley of the Indus" was produced in 1852, and is worthy of any sportsman's attention. That is Van

Voorst's, now Gurney and Jackson, whom Richard used to say was the only honest publisher he ever met. It is *not* out of print. In 1870 appeared "Vikram and the Vampire," 1 vol. These tales are thoroughly witty, and make those laugh heartily who have lived in the East, but it was a great amusement to Richard and me, when the publisher, having accepted "Vikram," which is full of "chaff," said to me with a long face, "My eldest boy and I read over some of the tales last night, and we were so disappointed we could not laugh." I could not help saying drily, "No, I dare say you couldn't."

The last book on India was "Sind Revisited," 2 vols., 1877. It was written in maturer years and after hard experience of the world. It may be more valuable, but to my mind has not the sparkle of twenty-six years earlier. All these eight or ten books, including my own "A.E.I."—"Arabia, Egypt, and India"—brought out in 1879, I boiled down into Christmas books for boys. I took my manuscript (enough for three Christmas books) to David Bogue, King William Street, Strand, and went abroad, and the next thing I heard was, that David Bogue was bankrupt, and my manuscript had disappeared.

I give a few pages in the appendixes out of his first book on Scinde as a sample. One describes his visit to the village of a Scindian chief, a perfect picture of an Oriental visit; the other is a description of a cock-fight. After his transfer to the Goanese Church, his bungalow was nicknamed the "Inquisition," and there he buried Bhujang, when his favourite game-cock departed this life, and people declared it was a baby's grave. For all that my husband *said* of India, he talked exactly as Mr. Rudyard Kipling writes, and when I read him, I can hear Richard talking; hence I knew how true and to the point are his writings. Also I think Mr. Kipling must have taken his character of "Strickland" from my husband, who mixed with, and knew all about, the natives and their customs, as Strickland did.

During those first seven years in India, Richard passed in Hindostani, Guzaratee, Persian, Maharattee, Sindhee, Punjaubee, Arabic, Telugu, Pushtû (Afghan tongue), with Turkish and Armenian. In 1844 he went to Scinde with the 18th Native Infantry, and Colonel Walter Scott put him on Sir Charles Napier's staff, who soon found out what he was worth, and turned his merits to account, but he accompanied his regiment to Mooltan to attack the Sikhs. He became much attached to his Chief; they quite understood each other, and remained together for five years. Richard's training was of the uncommon sort, and glorious as it was, dangerous as it was, and romantic as it will ever be to posterity, he did not get from dense and narrow-minded Governments those rewards which men who risk their lives deserve, and which would have been given to the man who took care of "number one," and who, with average stupidity, worked on red-tape lines. He was sent out amongst the wild tribes of the hills and plains to collect information for Sir Charles. He did not go as a British officer or Commissioner, because he knew he would see nothing but what the natives chose him to see; he let down a curtain between himself and Civilization, and a tattered, dirty-looking dervish would wander on foot, lodge in mosques, where he was venerated as a saintly man, mix with the strangest company, join the Beloch and the Brahui tribes (Indo-Scythians), about whom there was nothing then known. Sometimes he appeared in the towns; as a merchant he opened a shop, sold stuffs or sweetmeats in the bazar. Sometimes he worked with the men in native dress, "Játs" and Camel men, at levelling canals.

When Richard was in India he at one time got rather tired of the daily Mess, and living with men, and he thought he should like to learn the manners, customs, and habits of monkeys, so he collected forty monkeys of all kinds of ages, races, species, and he lived with them, and he used to call them by different offices. He had his doctor, his chaplain, his secretary, his aide-de-camp, his agent, and one tiny one, a very pretty, small, silky-looking monkey, he used to call his wife, and put pearls in her ears. His great amusement was to keep a kind of refectory for them, where they all sat down on chairs at meals, and the servants waited on them, and each had its bowl and plate, with the food and drinks proper for them. He sat at the head of the table, and the pretty little monkey sat by him in a high baby's chair, with a little bar before it. He had a little whip on the table, with which he used to keep them in order when they had bad manners, which did sometimes occur, as they frequently used to get jealous of the little monkey, and try to claw her. He did this for the sake of doing what Mr. Garner is now doing, that of ascertaining and studying the language of monkeys, so that he used regularly to talk to them, and pronounce their sounds afterwards, till he and the monkeys at last got quite to understand each other. He obtained as many as sixty words, I think twenty more than Mr. Garner—that is, leading words—and he wrote them down and formed a vocabulary, meaning to pursue his studies at some future time. Mr. Garner has now the advantage of phonographs, and all sorts of appliances. Had Richard been alive, he could have helped him greatly. Unfortunately his monkey vocabulary was burnt in Grindlay's fire. He also writes—but this was with his regiment—

"Amongst other remarkable experiments made by me, a Sányasi, whom I knew, talked to me about their manner of burying themselves alive. I said I would not believe it unless I saw it. The native therefore told me that he would prove it, by letting me try it; but that he should require three days for preparation, and hoped for a reward. Accordingly for three days he made his preparations by swallowing immense draughts of milk. I refused to put him in a coffin, or to bury him in the earth, lest he should die; but he lay down in a hammock, rolled his tongue up in his throat, and appeared to be dead. My brother officers and I then slung him up to the ceiling by four large hooks and ropes, lying comfortably in the hammock, and, to avoid trickery, one of us was always on guard day and night, each taking two hours' watch at a time. After three weeks we began to get frightened, because if the man died there would be such a scandal. So we lowered him down, and tried to awake him. We opened his mouth and tried to unroll his tongue into its natural position. He then, after some time, woke perfectly well. We gave him food, paid him a handsome reward, and he went away quite delighted, offering to do it for *three months*, if it pleased us."

Richard would be in a dozen different capacities on his travels, but when he returned, he was rich with news and information for Sir Charles, for he arrived at secrets quite out of the reach of the British Army. He knew all that the natives knew, which was more than British officers and surveyors did. General MacMurdo consulted his journals and Survey books, which were highly praised by the Surveyor-General. He was frequently in the presence of and speaking before his own Colonel without his having the slightest idea that it was Richard.

Sir Charles Napier liked decision; he hated a man who had not an answer ready for him. For instance, a young man would go and ask him for an appointment. Sir Charles would say, "What do you want?" The youth of firm mind would answer, "An Adjutancy, Sir." "All right," said Sir Charles, and he probably got it. But "Anything you please, Sir Charles," would be sure to be contemptuously dismissed. On returning from his native researches, Sir Charles would ask Richard such questions as: "Is it true that native high-class landowners, who monopolize the fiefs about the heads of the canals, neglect to clear out the tails, and allow Government ground and the peasants' fields to lie barren for want of water?"

"Perfectly true, Sir."

"What would be my best course then?"

"Simply to confiscate the whole or part of those estates, Sir."

"H'm! You don't mince matters, Burton."

He once asked Richard how many bricks there were in a newly built bridge (an impossible question, such as are put to lads whom the examiner intends to pluck). Richard, knowing his foible, answered, "229,010, Sir Charles." He turned away and smiled. Another time he ordered a review on a grand scale to impress certain Chiefs—

"Lieutenant Burton, be pleased to inform these gentlemen that I propose to form these men in line, then to break into échelon by the right, and to form square on the centre battalion," and so on, for about five minutes in military technical terms, for which there were no equivalents in these men's dialects.

"Yes, Sir," said Richard, saluting.

Turning to the Chiefs, Richard said, "Oh, Chiefs! our Great Man is going to show you the way we fight, and you must be attentive to the rules." He then touched his cap to Sir Charles.

"Have you explained all?" he asked.

"Everything, Sir," answered Richard.

"A most concentrated language that must be," said Sir Charles, riding off with his nose in the air.

After seven years of this kind of life, overwork, overstudy, combined with the hot season, and the march up the Indus Valley, told on Richard's health, and at the end of the campaign he was attacked by severe ophthalmia, the result of mental and physical fatigue, and he was ordered to take a short rest. He utilized that leave in going to Goa, and especially to Old Goa, where, as he said himself, he made a pilgrimage to the tomb of St. Francis Xavier, and explored the scenes of the Inquisition. At last news reached him that another campaign was imminent in Mooltan, that Sir Charles Napier would take command; Colonel Scott and a host of friends were ordered up. He writes as follows:—

"I applied in almost suppliant terms to accompany the force as interpreter. I had passed examinations in six native languages, besides studying others, Multani included, and yet General Auchmuty's secretary wrote to me that this could not be, as he had chosen for the post Lieutenant X. Y. Z., who had passed in Hindustani.

"This last misfortune broke my heart. I had been seven years in India, working like a horse, volunteering for every bit of service, and qualifying myself for all contingencies. Rheumatic ophthalmia, which had almost left me when in hopes of marching northward, came on with redoubled force, and no longer had I any hope of curing it except by a change to Europe. Sick, sorry, and almost in tears of rage, I bade adieu to my friends and comrades in Sind. At Bombay there was no difficulty in passing the Medical

Board, and I embarked at Bombay for a passage round the Cape, as the Austral winter was approaching, in a sixty-year-old teak-built craft, the brig *Eliza*, Captain Cory.

"My career in India had been in my eyes a failure, and by no fault of my own; the dwarfish demon called 'Interest' had fought against me, and as usual had won the fight."

CHAPTER VIII.

ON RETURN FROM INDIA.

When Richard came home, he first ran down full of joy to visit all his relations and friends. He then went to Oxford with half a mind to take his degree. He was between twenty-eight and twenty-nine years of age. In 1850 he went back to France, and devoted himself to fencing. To this day "the Burton *une-deux*," and notably the *manchette* (the upward slash, disabling the swordarm, and saving life in affairs of honour), earned him his *brevet de pointe* for the

LUNGE AND CUT IN CARTE (INSIDE).

excellence of his swordsmanship, and he became a *Maître d'armes*. Indeed, as horseman, swordsman, and marksman, no soldier of his day surpassed him, and very few equalled him. His family, that is his father, mother and sister, with her two children—her husband being in India, and his brother Edward in the 37th Regiment (Queen's)—went to Boulogne, like all the rest of us, for change, quiet, and economy, and there he joined them.

We did exactly the same, the object being to put me and my sisters into the Sacré Cœur to learn French. Boulogne, in those days, was a very different town to what it is now. It was "the home of the stranger who had done something wrong." The natives were of the usual merchant, or rich *bourgeoisie* class; there was a sprinkling of local *noblesse* in the Haute-Ville; the gem of the natives in the lower class were the Poissardes, who hold themselves entirely distinct from the town, are a cross between Spanish and Flemish, and in *those* days were headed by a handsome "Queen" called Caroline, long since dead. The English colony was very large. The *crême*, who did not mix with the general "smart people," were the Seymours, Dundases, Chichesters, Jerninghams, Bedingfelds, Cliffords, Molyneux-Seels, and ourselves. Maybe I have forgotten many others.

The rest of the colony, instead of living like the colonies that Richard describes at Tours, used to walk a great deal up and down the Grand Rue, which was the fashionable lounge, the Rue de l'Écu, the Quai, and the Pier. The men were handsome and smart, and beautifully dressed, with generally an immense amount of white shirt-front, as in the Park, and the girls were pretty and well dressed. So were the young married women in those days. The Établissement was a sort of Casino, where everybody passed their evening, except the *crême;* they had music, dancing, cards, old ladies knitting, and refreshments, and it was the hotbed, like a club, of all the gossip and flirtation, with an occasional roaring scandal.

The hardship of *my* life and that of my sisters, was, that our mother would never let us set foot inside of it, which was naturally the only thing we longed to do, so that we had awfully dull, slow lives. Here Richard brought out his "Goa," his two books on Scinde, and his "Falconry," and prepared a book that came out in 1853, "A Complete System of Bayonet Exercise," of which, I regret to say, the only copy I possessed has been lost with the manuscript at David Bogue's. People were *now* beginning to say that "Burton was an awfully clever young fellow, a man of great mark, in fact the coming man." Whilst I am speaking of that system of bayonet exercise, I may say that it was, as all he did, undervalued *at the time*, but still it has long been the one used by the Horseguards. Colonel Sykes, who was Richard's friend, sent for him, and sharply rebuked him with printing a book that would do far more harm than good.

It was thought that bayonet exercise would make the men unsteady in the ranks. The importance of bayonet exercise was recognized everywhere *except* in England. Richard detected our weak point in military system, and he knew that it would be the British soldier's forte when properly used. Richard was not "in the ring,"*t* but when that was proved, his pamphlet was taken down from the dusty pigeon-hole, and a few modifications—not improvements—were added, so as to enable a just and enlightened War Office, not to send him a word of thanks, a compliment, an expression of official recognition, which was all his soul craved for, but a huge letter from the Treasury, with a seal the size of a baby's fist, with a gracious permission to draw upon the Treasury for the sum of one shilling.

Richard always appreciated humour. He went to the War Office at once, was sent to half a dozen different rooms, and, to the intense astonishment of all the clerks, after three-quarters of an hour's very hard work he drew his shilling, and instead of framing it, he gave it to the first hungry beggar that he saw as soon as he came out of the War Office.

"Lord love yer, sir," said the beggar.

"No, my man, I don't exactly expect Him to do *that.* But I dare say you want a drink?"

He did not lead the life that was led by the general colony at Boulogne. He had a little set of men friends, knew some of the French, had a great many flirtations, one very serious one. He passed his days in literature and fencing: at home he was most domestic; his devotion to his parents, especially to his sick mother, was beautiful.

My sisters and I were kept at French all day, music and other studies, but were frequently turned into the Ramparts, which would give one a mile's walk around, to do our reading; then we had a turn down the Grande Rue, the Rue de l'Écu, the Quai, and the Pier at the fashionable hour, for a treat, or else we were taken a long country walk, or a long row up the river Liane in the summer time, where we occasionally saw a Guingette; but we were religiously marched home at half-past eight to supper and bed, unless one of the *crême* gave a dull tea-party.

One day, when we were on the Ramparts, the vision of my awakening brain came towards us. He was five feet eleven inches in height, very broad, thin, and muscular;* he had very dark hair,

* He was so broad and muscular that he did not look more than five feet nine —but he really was two inches taller, and the one complaint of his life was not to be able to grow another inch to make six feet.

black, clearly defined, sagacious eyebrows, a brown weather-beaten complexion, straight Arab features, a determined-looking mouth and chin, nearly covered by an enormous black moustache. I have since heard a clever friend say "that he had the brow of a God, the jaw of a Devil." But the most remarkable part of his appearance was, two large black flashing eyes with long lashes, that pierced you through and through. He had a fierce, proud, melancholy expression, and when he smiled, he smiled as though it hurt him, and looked with impatient contempt at things generally. He was dressed in a black, short, shaggy coat, and shouldered a short thick stick as if he was on guard.

He looked at me as though he read me through and through in a moment, and started a little. I was completely magnetized, and when we had got a little distance away I turned to my sister, and whispered to her, "That man will marry *me*." The next day he was there again, and he followed us, and chalked up, "May I speak to you?" leaving the chalk on the wall, so I took up the chalk and wrote back, "No, mother will be angry;" and mother found it,—and *was* angry; and after that we were stricter prisoners than ever. However, "destiny is stronger than custom." A mother and a pretty daughter came to Boulogne, who happened to be a cousin of my father's; they joined the majority in the Society sense, and one day we were allowed to walk on the Ramparts with them. There I met Richard, who—agony!—was flirting with the daughter; we were formally introduced, and the name made me start. I will say why later.

I did not try to attract his attention; but whenever he came to the usual promenade I would invent any excuse that came, to take another turn to watch him, if he was not looking. If I could catch the sound of his deep voice, it seemed to me so soft and sweet, that I remained spell-bound, as when I hear gypsy-music. I never lost an opportunity of seeing him, when I could not be seen, and as I used to turn red and pale, hot and cold, dizzy and faint, sick and trembling, and my knees used to nearly give way under me, my mother sent for the doctor, to complain that my digestion was out of order, and that I got migraines in the street, and he prescribed me a pill which I put in the fire. All girls will sympathize with me. I was struck with the shaft of Destiny, but I had no hopes (being nothing but an ugly schoolgirl) of taking the wind out of the sails of the dashing creature, with whom he was carrying on a very serious flirtation.

In early days Richard had got into a rather strong flirtation with a very handsome and very fast girl, who had a vulgar, middle-class sort of mother. One day he was rather alarmed at getting a polite but somewhat imperious note from the mother, asking him to call upon her. He obeyed, but he took with him his friend Dr. Steinhaüser, a charming man, who looked as if his face was carved out of wood. After the preliminaries of a rather formal reception, in a very prim-looking drawing-room, the lady began, looking severely at him, "I sent for you, Captain Burton, because I think it my dooty to ask what your intentions are with regard to my daughter?" Richard put on his most infantile face of perplexity as he said, "Your dooty, madam——" and, then, as if he was trying to recall things, and after awhile suddenly seizing the facts of the case, he got up and said, "Alas! madam, strictly dishonourable," and shaking his head as if he was going to burst into tears at his own iniquities, "I regret to say, strictly dishonourable;" and bowed himself out with Dr. Steinhaüser, who never moved a muscle of his face. Richard had never done the young lady a scrap of harm, beyond talking to her a little more than the others, because she was so "awfully jolly," but the next time he met her he said, "Look here, young woman, if I talk to you, you must arrange that I do not have 'mamma's dooty' flung at my head any more." "The old fool!" said the girl, "how like her!"

The only luxury I indulged in was a short but heartfelt prayer for him every morning. I read all his books, and was seriously struck as before by the name when I came to the Játs in Scinde—but this I will explain later on. My cousin asked him to write something for me, which I used to wear next to my heart. One night an exception was made to our dull rule of life. My cousins gave a tea-party and dance, and "the great majority" flocked in, and there was Richard like a star amongst rushlights. That was a Night of nights; he waltzed with me once, and spoke to me several times, and I kept my sash where he put his arm round my waist to waltz, and my gloves. I never wore them again. I did not know it then, but the "little cherub who sits up aloft" is not *only* occupied in taking care of poor Jack, for I came in also for a share of it.

Mecca.

Whilst leading this sort of life, on a long furlough, Richard determined to carry out a project he had long had in his head, to study thoroughly the "inner life of the Moslem." He had long felt within himself the qualifications, both mental and physical, which are needed for the exploration of dangerous regions, impossible of access, and of disguises difficult to sustain. His career as a dervish in Scinde greatly helped him. His mind was both practical and imaginative; he set himself to imagine and note down every contingency that *might* arise, and one by one he studied each separate thing until he was master of it. As a small sample he apprenticed himself to a blacksmith; he learned to make horseshoes and shoe his horse.

To accomplish a journey to Mecca and Medinah quite safely in those days (1853) was almost an impossibility, for the discovery that he was *not* a Mussulman would have been avenged by a hundred Khanjars. It meant living with his life in his hand, and amongst the strangest and wildest companions, adopting their unfamiliar manners, and living for perhaps nine months in the hottest and most unhealthy climate, upon repulsive food, complete and absolute isolation from all that makes life tolerable, from all civilization, from all his natural habits—the brain at high tension, never to depart from the *rôle* he had adopted.

He obtained a year's leave on purpose, and left London as a Persian, for, during the time, he had to assume and sustain *several* Oriental characters. Captain Grindlay, who was in the secret, travelled to Southampton and Alexandria as his English interpreter. John Thurburn, who, curiously to say, was also the host of Burckhardt till he died, and was buried in Cairo, received Richard at Alexandria. He and his son-in-law, John Larking, of the Firs, Lee, Kent, were the only persons throughout the perilous expedition who knew of his secret. He went to Cairo as a dervish, and he lived there as a native, till (as he told me) he actually believed himself to be what he represented himself to be, and then he felt he was safe, and he practised on his own country-people the finding out that he was unrecognizable. He had wished to cross the whole length of Arabia, but the Russian War had caused disturbances, which might have delayed him over his year's leave.

In those days it was almost impossible to visit the Holy City as one of the Faithful. First, there was the pilgrim-ship to embark on; then there were long desert caravan marches, with their privations and their dangers; then there was the holy shrine, the Ka'abah, to be visited, and all the ceremonies to be gone through, like a Roman Catholic Holy Week at Rome. Burckhardt, the Swiss traveller, did get in, but he never could see the Ka'abah, and he confessed afterwards that he was so nervous that he was unable to take notes, and unable to write or sketch for fear of being detected, whereas Richard was sketching and writing in his white *burnous* the whole time he was prostrating and kissing the holy Stone. He did not go in mockery, but reverentially. He had brought his brain to believe himself one of them. Europeans, converted Moslems, have of late gone there, but they have been received with the utmost civility, consistent with coldness, have been admitted to outward friendship, but have been carefully kept out of what they most wished to know and see, so that Richard was thus the only European who had beheld the inner and religious life of the Moslems as one of themselves.

Amongst the various Oriental characters that Richard assumed, the one that suited best was half-Arab, half-Iranian, such as throng the northern shores of the Persian Gulf. With long hair falling on his shoulders, long beard, face and hands, arms and legs browned and stained with a thin coat of henna, Oriental dress, spear in hand, and pistols in belt, Richard became Mirza Abdullah, el Bushiri. Here he commenced his most adventurous and romantic life, explored from North to South, from East to West, mixed with all sorts of people and tribes without betraying himself in manners, customs, or speech, when death must often have ensued, had he created either dislike or suspicion.

I here give a slight sketch from his private notes, and for fuller details refer the reader to his "Pilgrimage to Mecca and El Medinah," 3 vols., with coloured illustrations, published in 1855, and which made a great sensation. Although he has been the author of some eighty books and pamphlets, I think that this original edition of three volumes is the one that his name should live by, and it will be the first of the Uniform Library with the Meccan Press. The Uniform Library means a reproduction of all his hitherto published works, and eventually his unpublished ones, so that the world may lose nothing of what he has ever written.

As I have said, on the night of the 3rd of April, 1853, a Persian Mirza, accompanied by an English interpreter, Captain Henry Grindlay, of the Bengal Cavalry, left London for Southampton, and embarked on the P. and O. steamer *Bengal.* The voyage was profitable but tedious; Richard passed it in resuming his Oriental character, with such success, that when he landed at Alexandria, he was recognized and blessed as a true Moslem by the native population.

John Thurburn and his son-in-law, John Larking, received him at their villa on the Mahmudíyah Canal, but he was lodged in an outhouse, the better to deceive the servants. Here he practised the Korán and prayer, and all the ceremonies of the Faith, with a neighbouring Shaykh. He also became a *hakím*, or doctor, and called himself Shaykh Abdullah, preparing to be a dervish. The dervish is a chartered vagabond; nobody asks why he comes, where he goes; he may go on foot, or on horseback, or alone, or with a large retinue, and he is as much respected without arms, as though he were armed to the teeth. "I only wanted," he said, "a little knowledge of medicine, which I *had*, moderate skill in magic, a studious reputation, and enough to keep me from starving." He provided himself with a few necessaries for the journey.

When he had to leave Alexandria he wrote—

"Not without a feeling of regret, I left my little room among the white myrtle blossoms and the rosy oleander flowers with the almond scent. I kissed with humble ostentation my good host's hand, in the presence of his servants. I bade adieu to my patients, who now amounted to about fifty, shaking hands with all meekly, and with religious equality of attention; and mounted in a 'trap' which looked like a cross between a wheelbarrow and a dog-cart, drawn by a kicking, jibbing, and biting mule, I set out for the steamer, the *Little Asthmatic*."

"The journey from Alexandria to Cairo lasted three days and nights. We saw nothing but muddy water, dusty banks, sand, mist, milky sky, glaring sun, breezes like the blasts of a furnace, and the only variation was that the steamer grounded four or five times a day, and I passed my time telling my beads with a huge rosary. I was a deck passenger. The sun burnt us all day, and the night dews were raw and thick. Our diet was bread and garlic, moistened with muddy water from the canal. At Cairo I went to a caravanserai. Here I became a Patháan. I was born in India of Afghan parents, who had settled there, and I was educated at Rangoon, and sent out, as is often the custom, to wander. I knew all the languages that I required to pass me, Persian, Hindostani, and Arabic. It is customary at the shop, on the camel, in the Mosque, to ask, 'What is thy name? Whence comest thou?' and you must be prepared. I had to do the fast of the Ramazan, which is far stricter than the Catholics' Lent, and in Cairo I studied the Moslem faith in every detail. I had great difficulty in getting a passport without betraying myself, but the chief of the Afghan college at the Azhar Mosque contrived it for me. I hired a couple of camels, and put my Meccan boy and baggage on one, and I took the other. I had an eighty-four mile ride in midsummer, on a bad wooden saddle, on a bad dromedary, across the Suez Desert.

"Above, through a sky terrible in its stainless beauty, and the splendours of a pitiless blinding glare, the simoom caresses you like a lion with flaming breath. Around lie drifted sand-heaps, upon which each puff of wind leaves its trace in solid waves, frayed rocks, the very skeletons of mountains, and hard unbroken plains, over which he who rides is spurred by the idea that the bursting of a waterskin, or the pricking of a camel's hoof, would be a certain death of torture; a haggard land infested with wild beasts and wilder men; a region whose very fountains murmur the warning words, 'Drink and away!'

"In the desert, even more than upon the ocean, there is present

Death, and this sense of danger, never absent, invests the scene of travel with a peculiar interest.

"Let the traveller who suspects exaggeration leave the Suez road, and gallop northwards over the sands for an hour or two; in the drear silence, the solitude, and the fantastic desolation of the place, he will feel what the desert *may* be. And then the oases, and little lines of fertility—how soft and how beautiful!—even though the Wady-el-Ward ('the Vale of Flowers') be the name of some stern flat in which a handful of wild shrubs blossom, while struggling through a cold season's ephemeral existence.

"In such circumstances the mind is influenced through the body. Though your mouth glows, and your skin is parched, yet you feel no languor,—the effect of humid heat; your lungs are lightened, your sight brightens, your memory recovers its tone, and your spirits become exuberant. Your fancy and imagination are powerfully aroused, and the wildness and sublimity of the scenes around you, stir up all the energies of your soul, whether for exertion, danger, or strife. Your *morale* improves; you become frank and cordial, hospitable and single-minded; the hypocritical politeness and the slavery of Civilization are left behind you in the City. Your senses are quickened; they require no stimulants but air and exercise; in the desert spirituous liquors excite only disgust.

"There is a keen enjoyment in mere animal existence. The sharp appetite disposes of the most indigestible food; the sand is softer than a bed of down, and the purity of the air suddenly puts to flight a dire cohort of diseases.

"Here Nature returns to Man, however unworthily he has treated her, and, believe me, when once your tastes have conformed to the tranquillity of such travel, you will suffer real pain in returning to the turmoil of civilization. You will anticipate the bustle and the confusion of artificial life, its luxuries and its false pleasures, with repugnance. Depressed in spirits, you will for a time after your return feel incapable of mental or bodily exertion. The air of Cities will suffocate you, and the careworn and cadaverous countenances of citizens will haunt you like a vision of judgment.

"I was nearly undone by Mohammed, my Meccan boy, finding my sextant amongst my clothes, and it was only by Umar Effendi having read a letter of mine to Haji Wali that very morning on Theology, that he was able to certify that I was thoroughly orthodox.

"When I started my intention had been to cross the all but unknown Arabian Peninsula, and to map it out, either from El Medinah to Maskat, or from Mecca to Makallah on the Indian Ocean. I wanted to open a market for horses between Arabia and Central India, to go through the Rubá-el-Khali ('the Empty Abode'), the great wilderness on our maps, to learn the hydrography of the Hejaz, and the ethnographical details of this race of Arabs. I should have been very much at sea without my sextant. I managed to secrete a pocket compass.

"The journey would have been of fifteen or sixteen hundred miles,

Vincent Brooks, Day & Son, lith.

RICHARD BURTON AS HAJÌ ABDULLAH, EN ROUTE TO MECCA.

and have occupied at least ten months longer than my leave. The quarrelling of the tribes prevented my carrying it out. I had arranged with the Beni Harb, the Bedawin tribe, to join them after the Pilgrimage like a true Bedawin, but it *meant* all this above-mentioned work; I found it useless to be killed in a petty tribe-quarrel, perhaps, about a mare, and once I joined them it would have been a point of honour to aid in all their quarrels and raids.

"At Suez we embarked on a *Sambúk*, an open boat of about fifty tons. She had no means of reefing, no compass, no log, no sounding-line, no chart. Ninety-seven pilgrims (fifteen women and children) came on deck. They were all barefoot, bare-headed, dirty, ferocious, and armed. The distance was doubled by detours; it would have been six hundred miles in a straight line. Even the hardened Arabs and Africans suffered most severely. After twelve days of purgatory, I sprang ashore at Yambú; and travelling a fortnight in this pilgrim-boat gave me the fullest possible knowledge of the inner life of El Islam. However, the heat of the sun, the heavy night dews, and the constant washing of the waves over me, had so affected one of my feet that I could hardly put it to the ground.

"Yambú is the port of El Medinah, as Jeddah is that of Mecca. The people are a good type, healthy, proud, and manly, and they have considerable trade. Here I arranged for camels, and our Caravan hired an escort of irregular cavalry—very necessary, for, as the tribes were out, we had to fight every day. They did not want to start till the tribes had finished fighting; but I was resolved, and we went. Here I brought a *shugduf*, or litter, and seven days' provisions for the journey, and here also I became an Arab, to avoid paying the capitation tax, the *Jizyát.*

"We eventually arrived at El Hamra, the 'Red Village,' but in a short while the Caravan arrived from Mecca, and in about four hours we joined it and went on our way. That evening we were attacked by Bedawi, and we had fighting pretty nearly the whole way. We lost twelve men, camels, and other beasts of burden; the Bedawi looted the baggage and ate the camels.

"One morning El Medinah was in sight. We were jaded and hungry; and we gloried in the gardens and orchards about the town. I was met at El Medinah by Shaykh Hamid, who received me into his family as one of the faithful, and where I led a quiet, peaceful, and pleasant life, during leisure hours; but of course, the pilgrimage being my object, I had a host of shrines to visit, ceremonies to perform, and prayers to recite, besides the usual prayers five times a day; for it must be remembered that El Medinah contains the tomb of Mahommad." (For description see Burton's 'Mecca and El Medinah,' 3 vols.)

"The Damascus Caravan was to start on the 27th Zu'l Ka'adah (1st September). I had intended to stay at El Medinah till the last moment, and to accompany the *Kafilat el Tayyárah*, or the 'Flying Caravan,' which usually leaves on the 2nd Zu'l Hijjah, two days after that of Damascus.

"Suddenly arose the rumour that there would be no *Tayyárah*,* and that all pilgrims must proceed with the Damascus Caravan or await the *Rakb*.† The Sheríf Zayd, Sa'ad, the robbers' only friend, paid Sa'ad an unsuccessful visit. Sa'ad demanded back his shaykhship, in return for a safe conduct through his country; 'otherwise,' said he, 'I will cut the throat of every hen that ventures into the passes.'

"The Sheríf Zayd returned to El Medinah on the 25th Zu'l Ka'adah (30th August). Early on the morning of the next day, Shaykh Hamid returned hurriedly from the bazar, exclaiming, 'You must make ready at once, Effendi! There will be no *Tayyárah*. All Hajis start to-morrow. Allah will make it easy to you! Have you your water-skins in order?. You are to travel down the Darb el Sharki, *where you will not see water for three days!*'

"Poor Hamid looked horror-struck as he concluded this fearful announcement, which filled me with joy. Burckhardt had visited and described the Darb el Sultani, the 'High' or 'Royal Road' along the coast; but *no* European had as yet travelled down by Harún el Rashíd's and the Lady Zubaydah's celebrated route through the Nejd Desert. And here was my chance!

"Whenever he was ineffably disgusted, I consoled him with singing the celebrated song of Maysúnah, the beautiful Bedawin wife of the Caliph Muawíyah." (Richard was immensely fond of this little song, and the Bedawin screams with joy when he hears it.)

"'Oh, take these purple robes away,
Give back my cloak of camel's hair,
And bear me from this tow'ring pile
To where the black tents flap i' the air.
The camel's colt with falt'ring tread,
The dog that bays at all but me,
Delight me more than ambling mules,
Than every art of minstrelsy;
And any cousin, poor but free,
Might take me, fatted ass, from thee.' ‡

"The old man was delighted, clapped my shoulder, and exclaimed, 'Verily, O Father of Moustachios, I will show thee the black Tents of my Tribe this year.'

"So, after staying at Medinah about six weeks, I set out with the Damascus Caravan down the Darb el Sharki, under the care of a very venerable Bedawin, who nicknamed me 'Abú Shuwárib,' meaning, 'Father of Moustachios,' mine being very large. I found myself standing opposite the Egyptian gate of El Medinah, surrounded by my friends—those friends of a day, who cross the phantasmagoria of one's life. There were affectionate embraces and parting mementoes.

---

* "The *Tayyârah*, or 'Flying Caravan,' is lightly laden, and travels by forced marches."

† "The *Rakb* is a dromedary-caravan, in which each person carries only his saddle-bags. It usually descends by the road called El Khabt, and makes Mecca on the fifth day."

‡ "By the term 'fatted ass' the intellectual lady alluded to her royal husband.

The camels were mounted; I and the boy Mohammed in the litter or *shugduf*, and Shaykh Nur in his cot. The train of camels with the Caravan wended its way slowly in a direction from north to north-east, gradually changing to eastward. After an hour's travel, the Caravan halted to turn and take farewell of the Holy City.

"We dismounted to gaze at the venerable minarets and the green dome which covers the tomb of the Prophet. The heat was dreadful, the climate dangerous, and the beasts died in numbers. Fresh carcases strewed our way, and were covered with foul vultures. The Caravan was most picturesque. We travelled principally at night, but the camels had to perform the work of goats, and step from block to block of basalt like mountaineers, which being unnatural to them, they kept up a continual piteous moan. The simoom and pillars of sand continually threw them over.

"Water is the great trouble of a Caravan journey, and the only remedy is to be patient and not to talk. The first two hours gives you the mastery, but if you drink you cannot stop. Forty-seven miles before we reached Mecca, at El Zaríbah, we had to perform the ceremony of *El Ihram*, meaning 'to assume the pilgrim garb.' A barber shaved us, trimmed our moustachios; we bathed and perfumed, and then we put on two new cotton cloths, each six feet long by three and a half broad. It is white, with narrow red stripes and fringe, and worn something as you wear it in the baths. Our heads and feet, right shoulder and arm, are exposed.

"We had another fight before we got to Mecca, and a splendid camel in front of me was shot through the heart. Our Sheríf Zayd was an Arab Chieftain of the purest blood, and very brave. He took two or three hundred men, and charged them. However, they shot many of our dromedaries, and camels, and boxes and baggage strewed the place; and when we were gone the Bedawi would come back, loot the baggage, and eat the camels. On Saturday, the 10th of September, at one in the morning, there was great excitement in the Caravan, and loud cries of 'Mecca! Mecca! Oh, the Sanctuary, the Sanctuary!' All burst into loud praises, and many wept. We reached it next morning, after ten days and nights from El Medinah. I became the guest of the boy Mohammed, in the house of his mother.

"First I did the circumambulation at the Haram. Early next morning I was admitted to the house of our Lord; and we went to the holy well Zemzem, the holy water of Mecca,* and then the Ka'abah, in which is inserted the famous black stone, where they say a prayer for the Unity of Allah. Then I performed the seven circuits round the Ka'abah, called the *Tawaf*. I then managed to have a way pushed for me through the immense crowd to kiss it. While kissing it, and rubbing hands and forehead upon it, I narrowly

---

* N.B.—I have still got some of Richard's bottles of this holy water, if any one would wish to analyze it.—I. B.

observed it, and came away persuaded that it is an aerolite. It is curious that almost all agree upon one point, namely, that the stone is volcanic. Ali Bey calls it mineralogically a 'block of volcanic basalt, whose circumference is sprinkled with little crystals, pointed and straw-like, with rhombs of tile-red felspath upon a dark ground like velvet or charcoal, except one of its protuberances, which is reddish.' It is also described as 'a lava containing several small extraneous particles of a whitish and of a yellowish substance.'

"All this time the pilgrims had scorched feet and burning heads, as they were always uncovered. I was much impressed with the strength and steadfastness of the Mohammedan religion. It was so touching to see them; one of them was clinging to the curtain, and sobbing as though his heart would break.* At night I and Shaykh Nur and the boy Mohammed issued forth with the lantern and praying-carpet.

"The moon, now approaching the full, tipped the brow of Abú

---

* N.B.—I found in later years he had recently copied into this part of his journal, from some paper, "The Meditations of a Hindu Prince and Sceptic," by the author of "The Old Pindaree"—

"All the world over, I wonder, in lands that I never have trod,
Are the people eternally seeking for the signs and steps of a God?
Westward across the ocean, and Northward ayont the snow,
Do they all stand gazing, as ever? and what do the wisest know?

"Here, in this mystical India, the deities hover and swarm,
Like the wild bees heard in the treetops, or the gusts of a gathering storm;
In the air men hear their voices, their feet on the rocks are seen,
Yet we all say, 'Whence is the message? and what may the wonders mean?'

"Shall I list to the word of the English, who came from the uttermost sea?
'The secret, hath it been told you? and what is your message to me?'
It is nought but the wide-world story how the earth and the heavens began;
How the gods are glad and angry, and a Deity once a man.

"I had thought, 'Perchance in the cities where the rulers of India dwell,
Whose orders flash from the far land, who girdle the earth with a spell,
They have fathomed the depths we float on, or measured the unknown main:
Sadly they turn from the venture, and say that the quest is vain.

"Is life, then, a dream and delusion? and where shall the dreamer awake?
Is the world seen like shadows on water? and what if the mirror break?
Shall it pass, as a camp that is struck, as a tent that is gathered and gone,
From the sands that were lamp-lit at eve, and at morning are level and lone?

"Is there nought in the heavens above, whence the hail and the levin are hurled,
But the wind that is swept around us by the rush of the rolling world?—
The wind that shall scatter my ashes, and bear me to silence and sleep
With the dirge, and the sounds of lamenting, and the voices of women who weep."

Kubáya, and lit up the spectacle with a more solemn light. In the midst stood the huge bier-like erection—

> 'Black as the wings
> Which some spirit of ill o'er a sepulchre flings!'

except where the moonbeams streaked it like jets of silver falling upon the darkest marble. It formed the point of rest for the eye; the little pagoda-like buildings and domes around it, with all their gilding and framework, faded to the sight. One object, unique in appearance, stood in view—the temple of the one Allah, the God of Abraham, of Ishmael, and of their posterity. Sublime it was, and expressing by all the eloquence of fancy the grandeur of the one idea which vitalized El Islam, and the strength and steadfastness of its votaries.

"One thing I remarked, and think worthy of notice, is that ever since Noah's dove, every religion seems to consider the pigeon a sacred bird; for example, every Mosque swarms with pigeons; St. Mark's, at Venice, and the same exists in most Italian market-places; the Hindoo pandits and the old Assyrian Empire also have them; whilst Catholics make it the emblem of the Holy Ghost.

"The day before I went to Arafat, I spent the night in the Mosque, where I saw many strange sights. One was a negro possessed by the devil. There, too, he prayed by the grave of Ishmael. After this we set out for Arafat, where is the tomb of Adam. (I have seen two since—one at Jerusalem, and one in the mountains behind Damascus.)

"It was a very weary journey, and, with the sun raining fire on our heads and feet, we suffered tortures. The camels threw themselves on the ground, and I myself saw five men fall out and die. On the Mount there were numerous consecrated shrines to see, and we had to listen to an immensely long sermon. On the great festival day we stoned the Devil, each man with seven stones washed in seven waters, and we said, while throwing each stone, 'In the name of Allah—and Allah is Almighty—I do this in hatred of the Devil, and to his shame.' There is then an immense slaughter of victims (five or six thousand), which slaughter, with the intense heat, swarms of flies, and the whole space reeking with blood, produces the most noisome vapours, and probably is the birthplace of that cholera and small-pox which generally devastate the World after the Haj. *Now* we were allowed to doff the pilgrim's garb.

"We all went to barbers' booths, where we were shaved, had our beards trimmed and our nails cut, saying prayers the while; and, though we had no clothes, we might put our clothes over our heads, and wear our slippers, which were a little protection from the heat. We might then twirl our moustachios, stroke our beards, and return to Mecca. At the last moment I was sent for. I thought, 'Now something is going to happen to me; now I am suspected.'

"A crowd had gathered round the Ka'abah, and I had no wish to stand bare-headed and bare-footed in the midday September sun.

At the cry of 'Open a path for the Haji who would enter the House!' the gazers made way. Two stout Meccans, who stood below the door, raised me in their arms, whilst a third drew me from above into the building. At the entrance I was accosted by several officials, dark-looking Meccans, of whom the blackest and plainest was a youth of the Benu Shaybah family, the true blood of the El Hejaz. He held in his hand the huge silver-gilt padlock of the Ka'abah, and presently, taking his seat upon a kind of wooden press in the left corner of the hall, he officially inquired my name, nation, and other particulars. The replies were satisfactory, and the boy Mohammed was authoritatively ordered to conduct me round the building, and to recite the prayers. I will not deny that, looking at the windowless walls, the officials at the door, and a crowd of excited fanatics below—

'And the place death, considering who I was,'

my feelings were of the trapped-rat description, acknowledged by the immortal nephew of his uncle Perez. A blunder, a hasty action, a misjudged word, a prayer or bow, not strictly the right shibboleth, and my bones would have whitened the desert sand. This did not, however, prevent my carefully observing the scene during our long prayer, and making a rough plan with a pencil upon my white *ihram.*

"I returned home after this *quite* exhausted, performed an elaborate toilet, washing with henna and warm water, to mitigate the pain the sun had caused on my arms, shoulders, and breast, head and feet, and put on my gayest clothes in honour of the festival. When the moon rose, there was a second stoning, or lapidation, to be performed, and then we strolled round the coffee-houses. There was also a little pilgrimage to undertake, which is in honour of Hagar seeking water for her son Ishmael.

"I now began to long to leave Mecca; I had done everything, seen everything; the heat was simply unendurable, and the little room where I could enjoy privacy for about six hours a day, and jot my notes down, was a perfect little oven.*

"I slowly wended my way with a Caravan to Jeddah, with donkeys and Mohammed; I must say that the sight of the sea and the British flag was a pleasant tonic. I went to the British Consulate, but the Dragomans were not very civil to the unfortunate Afghan.

"So I was left kicking my heels at the Great Man's Gate for a long time, and heard somebody say, 'Let the dirty nigger wait.' Long inured to patience, however, I did wait, and when the Consul consented to see me, I presented him with a bit of paper, as if it were a money order. On it was written, 'Don't recognize me; I am

* I have only given the barest outlines of what took place, referring my readers to the original, because, as there were between fifty and fifty-five mosques, besides other places, and various interesting ceremonies to be performed in each one, there would be no room for anything else; and the same may be said of El Medinah.—I. B.

Dick Burton, but I am not safe yet. Give me some money' (naming the sum), 'which will be returned from London, and don't take any notice of me.' He, however, frequently afterwards, when it was dark, sent for me, and, once safe in his private rooms, showed me abundance of hospitality. Necessity compelled me living with Shayk Nur in a room (to myself), swept, sprinkled with water, and spread with mats.

"When I went out in gay attire, I was generally mistaken for the Pasha of El Medinah. After about ten days' suspense, an English ship was sent by the Bombay Steam Navigation Company to convey pilgrims from El Hejaz to India, so one day the Afghan disappeared —was supposed to have departed with other dirty pilgrims, but in reality, had got on board the *Dwárká*,* an English ship, with a first-class passage; he had emerged from his cabin, after washing all his colouring off, in the garb of an English gentleman; experienced the greatest kindness from the Commander and Officers, which he much needed, being worn out with fatigue and the fatal fiery heat, and felt the great relief to his mind and body from being able to take his first complete rest in safety on board an English ship; but was so changed that the Turkish pilgrims, who crowded the deck, never recognized their late companion pilgrim."

He ends his personal narrative of his sojourn in El Hejaz thus:—

"I have been exposed to perils, and I have escaped from them; I have traversed the sea, and have not succumbed under the severest fatigues; but they with fatal fiery heat have worn me out, and my heart is moved with emotions of gratitude that I have been permitted to effect the objects I had in view."

An Irish missionary wrote of my husband after he was dead:—

"At Damascus Burton began a new chapter, but he was not permitted to start with a clean page. Two incidents in his previous record foreshadowed him, and hampered him in his efforts to make the best of his new Consulate. He had offended the religious susceptibilities of both Mohammedans and Christians, and he found himself confronted with bitter, unreasoning prejudice.

"It is a question of how far Burton's Oriental disguise concealed the Englishman in his pilgrimage to Mecca. I never conversed with a Mohammedan who had accompanied Burton on that journey,

* On the *Dwárká*, before he had time to go down to the cabin and change his clothes, one of his English brother officers, who was on board the ship, gave him a sly kick, and said, "Get out of the way, you dirty nigger." He often told me how he longed to hit him, but did not dare to betray himself. He was also part of the way in the Red Sea with my cousin William Strickland, a priest, and he used to tease him by sitting opposite to him, reciting his Korán out loud, while William was saying his breviary also out loud. At last one day Strickland got up, saying, "Oh, my God, I can't stand this much more," and afterwards these two became great friends.—I. B.

but I have seen Arabs who saw Palgrave on his way to Nejd, and his attempts to pose as a native were a constant source of amusement to all with whom he came in contact. Burton's Oriental cast of face helped him when putting on the outward appearance of a Bedawin, but at no period of his life could he have passed for an Arab one second after he began to speak.* On the pilgrimage to Mecca, Burton would be known as a devout British Mohammedan, just as easily as we recognize an Arab convert on a missionary platform, notwithstanding the efforts of the schoolmaster and the tailor to transform him into an Englishman. And as a perverted Englishman, Burton would be as welcome in the Hajj as a converted Arab would be in Exeter Hall."

This is a ridiculous paragraph, and spoils an otherwise splendid article. The writer speaks fairly good Syrian Christian Arabic with an Irish accent, but he is not conversant with the Arabic of scholars and high-class Mohammedans, and he does not know a word of Persian, Hindostani, Afghani, Turkish, or any of the other ten Oriental languages, in which my husband passed his pilgrimages. I think native testimony is best. I can remember, at a reception at Lady Salisbury's, the Persian Ambassador and his suite following Richard about the whole evening, and when I joked them about it, they said, "It is such an extraordinary thing to us, to see any foreigner, especially an Englishman, speaking our language like ourselves. He might have never been out of Teheran; he even knows all the slang of the market-place as well as we do." When he arrived in Damascus, his record was perfectly clean with the Mohammedans, and the only bitter, unreasoning prejudice was in the breast of Christian missionaries, and Christian Foreign Office employés, whose friends wanted the post. Burton and Palgrave were quite two different men, as silver and nickel. I know exactly the *sort* of Arabic Palgrave spoke.

In the days that Richard went to Mecca, *no* converted Englishman would have been received as *now*. As to his Arabic, Abd el Kadir told me—and, mind, he was *the* highest cultivated and the most religious Moslem in Damascus; the only Sufi, I believe—that there were only two men in Damascus whose Arabic was worth listening to; one was my husband, and the other was Shaykh Mijwal El Mezrab, Lady Ellenborough's Bedawin husband. We may remember that at Jeddah his life was saved by being mistaken for the Pasha of El Medinah, and when he went to the departure of the Haj at Damascus, as he rode down the lines in frock-coat and fez, he was

* This is absolutely untrue. Since Richard's death, two Englishmen, out of jealousy, have made this remark—one only knew Syrian Christian Arabic; the other, the dialect of Suez.

MECCA AND THE KA'ABAH, OR THE HOLY GRAIL OF THE MOSLEMS.

accosted by more than one as the Pasha of the Haj; and when the mistake was explained, and he told them who he was, they only laughed and said, "Why don't you come along with us again to Mecca, as you did before?" He was looked upon by *all* as a friend to the Moslem. He *never* profaned the sanctuaries of Mecca and Medina, and so far from being unpopular with the Moslems, he received almost yearly an invitation to go back with the Haj, and no opposition would have been made to him had he made another pilgrimage to the jealously guarded Haramayn or the holy Cities of the Moslems. Even *I* am always admitted to the Mosques with the women for *his* sake.

There was no tinsel and gingerbread about anything Richard did; it was always true and real.

In further support of the above I quote two letters, one from *Sporting Truth.*

"I had the pleasure of a slight acquaintance with the late Sir Richard Burton, familiarly known among his friends as 'Ruffian Dick.' Not that there was anything offensive meant by that epithet. Indeed, in his case, it had a playfully complimentary significance. There were, in the old days, as many readers of *Sporting Truth* will recollect, two familiar pugilists who went by the nicknames respectively of the 'Old' and 'Young Ruffian.' The term referred purely to their style of fighting, and was not intended to convey the idea that they were any less decent or civilized members of society than their neighbours. For much the same reason was Sir Richard Burton dubbed 'Ruffian Dick' by his pals. He was, without doubt, a terrible fighter, and fought in single combat more enemies than perhaps any man of his time. A man of peculiar temper, too, and strong individuality, with a wholesome contempt for Mrs. Grundy and all her ways. But his great distinguishing feature was his courage. No braver man than 'Ruffian Dick' ever lived. His daring was of that romantic order which revels in danger for danger's sake. No crisis, however appalling, could shake his splendid nerve. He was as cool when his life hung on a hair's breadth, as when he sat smoking in his own snuggery.

"I know of nothing in the annals of adventure to surpass his memorable journey to Mecca with the Mohammedan pilgrims. None but a follower of the true Prophet had ever penetrated the shrine where the coffin of Mohammed swings between earth and heaven. No eyes but those of the faithful were permitted to gaze upon that holy of holies. Certain and speedy death awaited any infidel who should profane with his footsteps those sacred precincts, or seek to pry into those hidden mysteries. There were secret passwords among the pilgrims, by which they could detect at once any one who was not of the true faith; and detection meant instant death at the hands of the enraged fanatics. Yet all these difficulties and dangers—apparently insurmountable—did not deter Ruffian Dick from undertaking the perilous enterprise. He went through a long course of preparation, studied all the minute ways of the Arabs—he already spoke their language like a native—professed the Mohammedan religion, acquired the secret passwords, and then boldly joined the great annual procession of pilgrims to the shrine of the Prophet.

"How perfect his disguise was, the following anecdote will show. On his return from the pilgrimage to Mecca, his leave had expired, and he had to return to India at once without time to rig himself out with a fresh outfit. One evening a party of officers were lounging outside Shepherd's Hotel, at Cairo. As they sat talking and smoking, there passed repeatedly in front of them an Arab in his loose flowing robes, with head proudly erect, and the peculiar swinging stride of those sons of the desert. As he strode backwards and forwards he drew nearer and nearer to the little knot of officers, till at last, as he swept by, the flying folds of his burnous brushed against one of the officers. 'Damn that nigger's impudence!' said the officer; 'if he does that again I'll kick him.' To his surprise the dignified Arab suddenly halted, wheeled round, and exclaimed, 'Well, damn it, Hawkins, that's a nice way to welcome a fellow after two years' absence.' 'By G—d, it's Ruffian Dick,' cried Hawkins. And Ruffian Dick it was, but utterly transformed out of all resemblance to a European. His complexion was burned by the sun to a deep umber tint, and his cast of features was more Oriental than English, so that in the robes of an Arab he might well pass for one of that nomad race."

Here is the second, from *Allen's Indian Mail.*

"THE LATE SIR RICHARD BURTON.

"To the Editor of the *Times* of India.

"SIR,

"Unlike your correspondent, Mr. Levick (of Suez), questioning Sir Richard's visit to Medinah in 1853, I merely want to say that in Sir Richard the scientific world has lost a bright star. In linguistic attainments there was not his equal in the world. He could not only speak the languages, but act so well that his most intimate friends were often deceived. I was often witness to this feat of his while at Kurrachee in 1847, as I happened to be employed under Dr. Stocks, botanist, in Sind, as his botanical draughtsman. Sir Richard (then a lieutenant) and the doctor occupied the same bungalow. I had necessarily to work in the hall, and consequently had the opportunity of seeing and admiring his ways. He was on special duty, which in his case meant to perfect himself for some political duty, by mastering the languages of the country. When I knew him he was master of half a dozen languages, which he wrote and spoke so fluently that a stranger who did not see him and heard him speaking would fancy he heard a native. His domestic servants were—a Portuguese, with whom he spoke Portuguese and Goanese, an African, a Persian, and a Sindi or Belochee. These spoke their mother tongue to Sir Richard as he was engaged in his studies with *moonshees*, who relieved each other every two hours, from ten to four daily. The *moonshees* would read an hour and converse the next, and it was a treat to hear Sir Richard talk; one would scarcely be able to distinguish the Englishman from a Persian, Arabian, or a Scindian.

"His habits at home were perfectly Persian or Arabic. His hair was dressed *à la Persian*—long and shaved from the forehead to the top of the head; his eyes, by some means or other he employed, resembled Persian or Arabian; he used the Turkish bath and wore a cowl; and when he went out for a ride he used a wig and goggles. His complexion was also thorough Persian, so that Nature evidently intended him for the work he afterwards so successfully performed, namely, visiting the shrine of the Prophet Mohammed—a work very few would have undertaken unless he was a complete master of himself.

"I was a witness to his first essay in disguising himself as a poor Persian, and taking in his friend Moonshee Ali Akbar (the father of Mirza Hossein, solicitor of this City). The *moonshee* was seated one evening in an open space in front of his bungalow in the town of Kurrachee, with a lot of his friends enjoying the evening breeze, and chatting away as Persians are wont to do. Sir Richard, disguised as a Persian traveller, approached them, and after the usual compliments, inquired for the rest-house, and, as a matter of course, gave a long rigmarole account of his travels and of people the *moonshee* knew, and thus excited his curiosity and got him into conversation; and when he thought he acted his part to perfection, bid him the time and left him, but did not go far when he called out to the *moonshee* in English if he did not know him. The *moonshee* was completely taken aback; he did not know where the voice (his friend Burton's) came from, till he was addressed again, and a recognition took place, to the great astonishment of the *moonshee* and his friends. Such a jovial companion Sir Richard was, that his bungalow was the resort of the learned men of the place, amongst whom I noticed Major (afterwards General) Walter Scott, Lieutenant (and now General) Alfred De Lisle, Lieutenant Edward Dansey of Mooltan notoriety, Dr. Stocks, and many others, but who, with the exception of General De Lisle, are all gone to their home above, where Sir Richard has now followed. May their souls rest in peace!

"Some time or other Lady Burton may write a memoir of Sir Richard's life, and a slight incident as the one I have related may be of use to her, and if you think as I do, and consider it worth inserting in a corner of your paper, I shall be very much obliged to you if you will do so.

"Yours, etc.,

"WALTER ABRAHAM.

"October 31, 1891."

On the return journey from Mecca, when Richard could secure any privacy, he composed the most exquisite gem of Oriental poetry, that I have ever heard or imagined, nor do I believe it has its equal, either from the pen of Hafiz, Saadi, Shakespeare, Milton, Swinburne, or any other. It is quite unique; it is called the Kasîdah, or the "Lay of the Higher Law," by Haji Abdu el-Yezdi. It will ride over the heads of most, it will displease many, but it will appeal to all large hearts and large brains for its depth, height, breadth, for its heart, nobility, its pathos, its melancholy, its despair. It is the very perfection of romance, it seems the cry of a Soul wandering through space, looking for what it does not find. I have read it many times during my married life, and never without bitter tears, and when I read it now, it affects me still more; he used to take it away from me, it impressed me so. I give you the poem here in full.

It reminds me more than any other thing of the Rubáiyát of Omar Khayyâm, the astronomer-poet of Khorasán, known as the tent-maker, written in the eleventh century, which poem was made known by Mr. Edward Fitzgerald in about 1861, to Richard Burton, to Swinburne, and Dante Rossetti. Richard at once claimed him as a brother Sufi, and said that all his allusions are purely typical, and particularly in the second verse—

II.

"Before the phantom of False morning died,
Methought a Voice within the Tavern cried,
'When all the temple is prepared within,
Why nods the drowsy Worshipper outside?'"

Yet the "Kasîdah" was written in 1853—the Rubáiyát he did not know till eight years later.

I shall reproduce the "Kasîdah" in its entirety, with its fifteen pages of copious annotations, in the Uniform Library of Sir Richard's works which I am editing. I give the annotations in the Appendix.

It is a poem of extraordinary power on the nature and destiny of Man, anti-Christian and Pantheistic. So much wealth of Oriental learning has rarely been compressed into so small a compass.

"Let his page
Which charms the chosen spirits of the age,
Fold itself for a serener clime
Of years to come, and find its recompense
In that just expectation."

SHELLEY.

"Let them laugh at me for speaking of things which they do not understand; and I must pity them while they laugh at me."—ST. AUGUSTINE.

To the Reader.

The Translator has ventured to entitle a "Lay of the Higher Law" the following Composition, which aims at being in advance of its time; and he has not feared the danger of collision with such unpleasant forms as the "Higher Culture." The principles which justify the name are as follows:—

The Author asserts that Happiness and Misery are equally divided and distributed in the world.

He makes Self-cultivation, with due regard to others, the sole and sufficient object of human life.

He suggests that the affections, the sympathies and the "divine gift of Pity" are man's highest enjoyments.

He advocates suspension of judgment, with a proper suspicion of "Facts, the idlest of superstitions."

Finally, although destructive to appearance, he is essentially reconstructive.

For other details concerning the Poem and the Poet, the curious reader is referred to the end of the volume (*i.e.* the Appendix).

THE KASÎDAH (COUPLETS) OF HAJI ABDU EL-YEZDI.

A Lay of the Higher Law.

The hour is nigh; the waning Queen walks forth to rule the later night;
Crown'd with the sparkle of a Star, and throned on orb of ashen light:

The Wolf-tail * sweeps the paling East to leave a deeper gloom behind,
And Dawn uprears her shining head, sighing with semblance of a wind:

The highlands catch yon Orient gleam, while purpling still the lowlands lie;
And pearly mists, the morning-pride, soar incense-like to greet the sky.

The horses neigh, the camels groan, the torches gleam, the cressets flare;
The town of canvas falls, and man with din and dint invadeth air:

The Golden Gates swing right and left; up springs the Sun with flamy brow;
The dew-cloud melts in gush of light; brown Earth is bathed in morning-glow.

Slowly they wind athwart the wild, and while young Day his anthem swells,
Sad falls upon my yearning ear the tinkling of the Camel-bells:

O'er fiery waste and frozen wold, o'er horrid hill and gloomy glen,
The home of grisly beast and Ghoul,† the haunts of wilder, grislier men;—

With the brief gladness of the Palms, that tower and sway o'er seething plain,
Fraught with the thoughts of rustling shade, and welling spring, and rushing rain;

With the short solace of the ridge, by gentle zephyrs played upon,
Whose breezy head and bosky side front seas of cooly celadon;—

'Tis theirs to pass with joy and hope, whose souls shall ever thrill and fill
Dreams of the Birthplace and the Tomb,—visions of Allah's Holy Hill.‡

But we? Another shift of scene, another pang to rack the heart;
Why meet we on the bridge of Time to 'change one greeting and to part?

We meet to part; yet asks my sprite, Part we to meet? Ah! is it so?
Man's fancy-made Omniscience knows, who made Omniscience nought can know.

Why must we meet, why must we part, why must we bear this yoke of MUST,
Without our leave or askt or given, by tyrant Fate on victim thrust?

That Eve so gay, so bright, so glad, this Morn so dim, and sad, and grey;
Strange that life's Registrar should write this day a day, that day a day!

Mine eyes, my brain, my heart, are sad,—sad is the very core of me;
All wearies, changes, passes, ends; alas! the Birthday's injury!

Friends of my youth, a last adieu! haply some day we meet again;
Yet ne'er the self-same men shall meet; the years shall make us other men:

---

* The false dawn. † The Demon of the Desert. ‡ Arafât, near Mecca.

The light of morn has grown to noon, has paled with eve, and now farewell!
Go, vanish from my Life as dies the tinkling of the Camel's bell.

* * * * * *

In these drear wastes of sea-born land, these wilds where none may dwell but He,
What visionary Pasts revive, what process of the Years we see:

Gazing beyond the thin blue line that rims the far horizon-ring,
Our sadden'd sight why haunt these ghosts, whence do these spectral shadows spring?

What endless questions vex the thought, of Whence and Whither, When and How?
What fond and foolish strife to read the Scripture writ on human brow;

As stand we percht on point of Time, betwixt the two Eternities,
Whose awful secrets gathering round with black profound oppress our eyes.

"This gloomy night, these grisly waves, these winds and whirlpools loud and dread:
What reck they of our wretched plight who Safety's shore so lightly tread?"

Thus quoth the Bard of Love and Wine,* whose dream of Heaven ne'er could rise
Beyond the brimming Kausar-cup and Houris with the white-black eyes;

Ah me! my race of threescore years is short, but long enough to pall
My sense with joyless joys as these, with Love and Houris, Wine and all.

Another boasts he would divorce old barren Reason from his bed,
And wed the Vine-maid in her stead;—fools who believe a word he said! †

And "'Dust thou art to dust returning,' ne'er was spoke of human soul"
The Soofi cries, 'tis well for him that hath such gift to ask its goal.

"And this is all, for this we're born to weep a little and to die!"
So sings the shallow bard whose life still labours at the letter "I."

"Ear never heard, Eye never saw the bliss of those who enter in
My heavenly Kingdom," Isâ said, who wailed our sorrows and our sin:

Too much of words or yet too few! What to thy Godhead easier than
One little glimpse of Paradise to ope the eyes and ears of man?

"I am the Truth! I am the Truth!" we hear the God-drunk gnostic cry
"The microcrosm abides in ME; Eternal Allah's nought but I!"

Mansûr ‡ was wise, but wiser they who smote him with the hurlèd stones;
And, though his blood a witness bore, no wisdom-might could mend his bones.

"Eat, drink, and sport; the rest of life's not worth a fillip," quoth the King;
Methinks the saying saith too much: the swine would say the self-same thing?

Two-footed beasts that browse through life, by Death to serve as soil design'd,
Bow prone to Earth whereof they be, and there the proper pleasures find:

But you of finer, nobler stuff, ye, whom to Higher leads the High,
What binds your hearts in common bond with creatures of the stall and sty?

"In certain hope of Life-to-come I journey through this shifting scene"
The Zâhid § snarls and saunters down his Vale of Tears with confi'dent mien.

Wiser than Amrân's Son ‖ art thou, who ken'st so well the world-to-be,
The Future when the Past is not, the Present merest dreamery;

What know'st thou, man, of Life? and yet, for ever 'twixt the womb, the grave,
Thou pratest of the Coming Life, of Heav'n and Hell thou fain must rave."

The world is old and thou art young; the world is large and thou art small;
Cease, atom of a moment's span, to hold thyself an All-in-All!

* * * * * * *

Fie, fie! you visionary things, ye motes that dance in sunny glow,
Who base and build Eternities on briefest moment here below;

Who pass through Life like cagèd birds, the captives of a despot will;
Still wond'ring How and When and Why, and Whence and Whither, wond'ring still;

Still wond'ring how the Marvel came because two coupling mammals chose
To slake the thirst of fleshly love, and thus the "Immortal Being" rose;

* Hâfiz of Shirâz. † Omar-i-Khayyâm, the tent-maker poet of Persia.
‡ A famous Mystic stoned for blasphemy. § The "Philister" of "respectable" belief.
‖ Moses in the Koran.

Wond'ring the Babe with staring eyes, perforce compell'd from night to day,
Gript in the giant grasp of Life like gale-borne dust or wind-wrung spray;

Who comes imbecile to the world 'mid double danger, groans, and tears;
The toy, the sport, the waif and stray of passions, error, wrath and fears;

Who knows not Whence he came nor Why, who kens not Whither bound and When,
Yet such is Allah's choicest gift, the blessing dreamt by foolish men;

Who step by step perforce returns to countless youth, wan, white and cold,
Lisping again his broken words till all the tale be fully told:

Wond'ring the Babe with quenchèd orbs, an oldster bow'd by burthening years,
How 'scaped the skiff an hundred storms; how 'scaped the thread a thousand shears;

How coming to the Feast unbid, he found the gorgeous table spread
With the fair-seeming Sodom-fruit, with stones that bear the shape of bread:

How Life was nought but ray of sun that clove the darkness thick and blind,
The ravings of the reckless storm, the shrieking of the ravening wind;

How lovely visions 'guiled his sleep, aye fading with the break of morn,
Till every sweet became a sour, till every rose became a thorn;

Till dust and ashes met his eyes wherever turned their saddened gaze;
The wrecks of joys and hopes and loves, the rubbish of his wasted days;

How every high heroic Thought that longed to breathe empyrean air,
Failed of its feathers, fell to earth, and perisht of a sheer despair;

How, dower'd with heritage of brain, whose might has split the solar ray,
His rest is grossest coarsest earth, a crown of gold on brow of clay;

This House whose frame be flesh and bone, mortar'd with blood and faced with skin,
The home of sickness, dolours, age; unclean without, impure within;

Sans ray to cheer its inner gloom, the chambers haunted by the Ghost,
Darkness his name, a cold dumb Shade stronger than all the heav'nly host.

This tube, an enigmatic pipe, whose end was laid before begun,
That lengthens, broadens, shrinks and breaks;—puzzle, machine, automaton;

The first of Pots the Potter made by Chrysorrhoas' blue-green wave;*
Methinks I see him smile to see what guerdon to the world he gave!

How Life is dim, unreal, vain, like scenes that round the drunkard reel;
How "Being" meaneth not to be; to see and hear, smell, taste and feel.

A drop in Ocean's boundless tide, unfathom'd waste of agony;
Where millions live their horrid lives by making other millions die.

How with a heart that would through love, to Universal Love aspire,
Man woos infernal chance to smite, as Min'arets draw the Thunder-fire.

How Earth on Earth builds tow'er and wall, to crumble at a touch of Time;
How Earth on Earth from Shinar-plain the heights of Heaven fain would climb.

How short this Life, how long withal; how false its weal, how true its woes,
This fever-fit with paroxysms to mark its opening and its close.

Ah! gay the day with shine of sun, and bright the breeze, and blithe the throng
Met on the River-bank to play, when I was young, when I was young:

Such general joy could never fade; and yet the chilling whisper came
One face had paled, one form had failed; had fled the bank, had swum the stream;

Still revellers danced, and sang, and trod the hither bank of Time's deep tide,
Still one by one they left and fared to the far misty thither side;

And now the last hath slipt away yon drear Death-desert to explore,
And now one Pilgrim worn and lorn still lingers on the lonely shore.

Yes, Life in youth-tide standeth still; in Manhood streameth soft and slow;
See, as it nears th' abysmal goal how fleet the waters flash and flow!

And Deaths are twain; the Deaths we see drop like the leaves in windy Fall;
But ours, our own, are ruined worlds, a globe collapst, last end of all.

---

* The Abana, River of Damascus.

We live our lives with rogues and fools, dead and alive, alive and dead,
We die 'twixt one who feels the pulse and one who frets and clouds the head :

And,—oh, the Pity !—hardly conned the lesson comes its fatal term ;
Fate bids us bundle up our books, and bear them bod'ily to the worm :

Hardly we learn to wield the blade before the wrist grows stiff and old ;
Hardly we learn to ply the pen ere Thought and Fancy faint with cold :

Hardly we find the path of love, to sink the Self, forget the "I,"
When sad suspicion grips the heart, when Man, *the* Man, begins to die :

Hardly we scale the wisdom-heights, and sight the Pisgah-scene around,
And breathe the breath of heav'enly air, and hear the Spheres' harmonious sound ;

When swift the Camel-rider spans the howling waste, by Kismet sped,
And of his Magic Wand a wave hurries the quick to join the dead.*

How sore the burden, strange the strife ; how full of splendour, wonder, fear ;
Life, atom of that Infinite Space that stretches 'twixt the Here and There.

How Thought is imp'otent to divine the secret which the gods defend,
The Why of birth and life and death, that Isis-veil no hand may rend.

Eternal Morrows make our Day ; our *Is* is aye *to be* till when
Night closes in ; 'tis all a dream, and yet we die,—and then and THEN ?

And still the Weaver plies his loom, whose warp and woof is wretched Man
Weaving th' unpattern'd dark design, so dark we doubt it owns a plan.

Dost not, O Maker, blush to hear, amid the storm of tears and blood,
Man say Thy mercy made what is, and saw the made and said 'twas good ?

The marvel is that man can smile dreaming his ghostly ghastly dream ;—
Better the heedless atomy that buzzes in the morning beam !

O the dread pathos of our lives ! how durst thou, Allah, thus to play
With Love, Affection, Friendship, all that shows the god in mortal clay ?

But ah ! what 'vaileth man to mourn ; shall tears bring forth what smiles ne'er brought ;
Shall brooding breed a thought of joy ? Ah hush the sigh, forget the thought !

Silence thine immemorial quest, contain thy nature's vain complaint
None heeds, none cares for thee or thine ;—like thee how many came and went ?

Cease, Man, to mourn, to weep, to wail ; enjoy thy shining hour of sun ;
We dance along Death's icy brink, but is the dance less full of fun ?

* * * * * * *

What Truths hath gleaned that Sage consumed by many a moon that waxt and waned ?
What Prophet-strain be his to sing ? What hath his old Experience gained ?

There is no God, no man-made God ; a bigger, stronger, crueller man ;
Black phantom of our baby-fears, ere Thought, the life of Life, began.

Right quoth the Hindu Prince of old,† "An Ishwara for one I nill,
Th' almighty everlasting Good who cannot 'bate th' Eternal Ill :"

"Your gods may be, what shows they are ?" Hear China's Perfect Sage declare ; ‡
"And being, what to us be they who dwell so darkly and so far ?"

"All matter hath a birth and death ; 'tis made, unmade and made anew ;
"We choose to call the Maker 'God' :—such is the Zâhid's owly view.

"You changeful finite Creatures strain" (rejoins the Drawer of the Wine) §
"The dizzy depths of Inf'inite Power to fathom with your foot of twine ;"

"Poor idols of man's heart and head with the Divine Idea to blend ;
"To preach as 'Nature's Common Course' what any hour may shift or end."

"How shall the Shown pretend to ken aught of the Showman or the Show ?
"Why meanly bargain to believe, which only means thou ne'er canst know ?

"How may the passing Now contain the standing Now—Eternity ?—
"An endless *is* without a *was*, the *be* and never the *to-be* ?

* Death in Arabia rides a Camel, not a pale horse. † Buddha. ‡ Confucius.
§ The Soofi or Gnostic opposed to the Zâhid.

"Who made your Maker? If Self-made, why fare so far to fare the worse?
"Sufficeth not a world of worlds, a self-made chain of universe?

"Grant an Idea, Primal Cause, the Causing Cause, why crave for more?
"Why strive its depth and breadth to mete, to trace its work, its aid to 'implore?

"Unknown, Incomprehensible, whate'er you choose to call it, call;
"But leave it vague as airy space, dark in its darkness mystical.

"Your childish fears would seek a Sire, by the non-human God defin'd,
"What your five wits may wot ye weet; what *is* you please to dub 'design'd;'

"You bring down Heav'en to vulgar Earth; your Maker like yourselves you make,
"You quake to own a reign of Law, you pray the Law its laws to break;

"You pray, but hath your thought e'er weighed how empty vain the prayer must be,
"That begs a boon already giv'en, or craves a change of Law to see?

"Say, Man, deep learnèd in the Scheme that orders mysteries sublime,
"How came it this was Jesus, that was Judas from the birth of Time?

"How I the tiger, thou the lamb; again the Secret, prithee, show
"Who slew the slain, bowman or bolt or Fate that drave the man, the bow?

"Man worships self: his God is Man; the struggling of the mortal mind
"To form its model as 'twould be, the perfect of itself to find.

"The God became sage, priest and scribe where Nilus' serpent made the vale;
"A gloomy Brahm in glowing Ind, a neutral something cold and pale:

"Amid the high Chaldean hills a moulder of the heavenly spheres;
"On Guebre steppes the Timeless-God who governs by his dual peers:

"In Hebrew tents the Lord that led His leprous slaves to fight and jar;
"Yahveh,* Adon or Elohîm, the God that smites, the Man of War.

"The lovely Gods of lib'ertine Greece, those fair and frail humanities
"Whose homes o'erlooked the Middle Sea, where all Earth's beauty cradled lies,

"Ne'er left its blessèd bounds, nor sought the barb'arous climes of barb'arous gods
"Where Odin of the dreary North o'er hog and sickly mead-cup nods:

"And when, at length, 'Great Pan is dead' uprose the loud and dol'orous cry
"A glamour wither'd on the ground, a splendour faded in the sky.

"Yea, Pan was dead, the Nazar'ene came and seized his seat beneath the sun,
"The votary of the Riddle-god, whose one is three and three is one;

"Whose sadd'ening creed of herited Sin split o'er the world its cold grey spell;
"In every vista showed a grave, and 'neath the grave the glare of Hell;

"Till all Life's Po'esy sinks to prose; romance to dull Real'ity fades;
"Earth's flush of gladness pales in gloom and God again to man degrades.

"Then the lank Arab foul with sweat, the drainer of the camel's dug,
"Gorged with his leek-green lizard's meat, clad in his filthy rag and rug,

"Bore his fierce Allah o'er his sands and broke, like lava-burst upon
"The realms where reigned pre-Adamite Kings, where rose the grand Kayânian throne.†

"Who now of ancient Kayomurs, of Zâl or Rustam cares to sing,
"Whelmed by the tempest of the tribes that called the Camel-driver King?

"Where are the crown of Kay Khusraw, the sceptre of Anûshirwân,
"The holy grail of high Jamshîd, Afrâsiyab's hall?—Canst tell me, man?

"Gone, gone, where I and thou must go, borne by the winnowing wings of Death,
"The Horror brooding over life, and nearer brought with every breath:

"Their fame hath filled the Seven Climes, they rose and reigned, they fought and fell,
"As swells and swoons across the wold the tinkling of the Camel's bell."

* * * * * * *

There is no Good, there is no Bad; these be the whims of mortal will:
What works me weal that call I 'good,' what harm and hurts I hold as 'ill:'

They change with place, they shift with race; and, in the veriest span of Time,
Each Vice has worn a Virtue's crown; all Good was banned as Sin or Crime:

* Jehovah. † Kayâni—of the race of Cyrus; old Guebre heroes.

Like ravelled skeins they cross and twine, while this with that connects and blends;
And only Khizr* his eye shall see where one begins, where other ends:

What mortal shall consort with Khizr, when Musâ turned in fear to flee?
What man foresees the flow'er or fruit whom Fate compels to plant the tree?

For Man's Free-will immortal Law, Anagkê, Kismet, Des'tiny read
That was, that is, that aye shall be, Star, Fortune, Fate, Urd, Norn or Need.

"Man's nat'ural State is God's design"; such is the silly sage's theme;
"Man's primal Age was Age of Gold"; such is the Poet's waking dream:

Delusion, Ign'orance! Long ere Man drew upon earth his earli'est breath
The world was one contin'uous scene of anguish, torture, prey and Death;

Where hideous Theria of the wild rended their fellows limb by limb;
Where horrid Saurians of the sea in waves of blood were wont to swim:

The "fair young Earth" was only fit to spawn her frightful monster-brood;
Now fiery hot, now icy frore, now reeking wet with steamy flood.

Yon glorious Sun, the greater light, the "Bridegroom" of the royal Lyre,
A flaming, boiling, bursting mine; a grim black orb of whirling fire:

That gentle Moon, the lesser light, the Lover's lamp, the Swain's delight,
A ruined world, a globe burnt out, a corpse upon the road of night.

What reckt he, say, of Good or Ill who in the hill-hole made his lair,
The blood-fed rav'ening Beast of prey, wilder than wildest wolf or bear?

How long in Man's pre-Ad'amite days to feed and swill, to sleep and breed,
Were the Brute-biped's only life, a perfect life sans Code or Creed?

His choicest garb a shaggy fell, his choicest tool a flake of stone;
His best of orn'aments tattoo'd skin and holes to hang his bits of bone;

Who fought for female as for food when Mays awoke to warm desire;
And such the lust that grew to Love when Fancy lent a purer fire.

Where ***then*** "Th' Eternal nature-law by God engraved on human heart"?
Behold his simiad sconce and own the Thing could play no higher part.

Yet, as long ages rolled, he learnt from Beaver, Ape and Ant to build
Shelter for sire and dam and brood, from blast and blaze that hurt and killed;

And last came Fire; when scrap of stone cast on the flame that lit his den,
Gave out the shining ore, and made the Lord of beasts a Lord of men.

The "moral sense," your Zâhid-phrase, is but the gift of latest years;
Conscience was born when man had shed his fur, his tail, his pointed ears.

What conscience has the murderous Moor, who slays his guest with felon blow,
Save sorrow he can slay no more, what prick of pen'itence can he know?

You cry the "Cruelty of Things" is myst'ery to your purblind eye,
Which fixed upon a point in space the general project passes by:

For see! the Mammoth went his ways, became a mem'ory and a name;
While the half-reasoner with the hand† survives his rank and place to claim.

Earthquake and plague, storm, fight and fray, portents and curses man must deem
Since he regards his self alone, nor cares to trace the scope, the scheme;

The Quake that comes in eyelid's beat to ruin, level, 'gulf and kill,
Builds up a world for better use, to general Good bends special Ill:

The dreadest sound man's ear can hear, the war and rush of stormy Wind
Depures the stuff of human life, breeds health and strength for humankind:

What call ye them or Goods or Ills, ill-goods, good-ills, a loss, a gain,
When realms arise and falls a roof; a world is won, a man is slain?

And thus the race of Being runs, till haply in the time to be
Earth shifts her pole and Mushtari-‡men another falling star shall see:

---

* Supposed to be the Prophet Elijah. † The Elephant. ‡ The Planet Jupiter.

Shall see it fall and fade from sight, whence come, where gone no Thought can tell,—
Drink of yon mirage-stream and chase the tinkling of the Camel-bell!

* * * * * *

All Faith is false, all Faith is true: Truth is the shattered mirror strown
In myriad bits; while each believes his little bit the whole to own.

What is the Truth? was askt of yore. Reply all object Truth is one
As twain of halves aye makes a whole; the moral Truth for all is none.

Ye scantly-learned Zâhids learn from Aflatûn and Aristû,*
While Truth is real like your good: th' Untrue, like ill, is real too;

As palace mirror'd in the stream, as vapour mingled with the skies,
So weaves the brain of mortal man the tangled web of Truth and Lies.

What see we here? Forms, nothing more! Forms fill the brightest strongest eye,
We know not substance; 'mid the shades shadows ourselves we live and die.

"Faith mountains move" I hear: I see the practice of the world unheed
The foolish vaunt, the blatant boast that serves our vanity to feed.

"Faith stands unmoved"; and why? Because man's silly fancies still remain,
And will remain till wiser man the day-dreams of his youth disdain.

"'Tis blessèd to believe"; you say: The saying may be true enow
An it can add to Life a light:—only remains to show us how.

E'en if I could I nould believe your tales and fables stale and trite,
Irksome as twice-sung tune that tires the dullèd ear of drowsy wight.

With God's foreknowledge man's free will! what monster-growth of human brain,
What pow'ers of light shall ever pierce this puzzle dense with words inane?

Vainly the heart on Providence calls, such aid to seek were hardly wise
For man must own the pitiless Law that sways the globe and sevenfold skies.

"Be ye Good Boys, go seek for Heav'en, come pay the priest that holds the key;"
So spake, and speaks, and aye shall speak the last to enter Heaven,—he.

Are these the words for men to hear? yet such the Church's general tongue,
The horseleech-cry so strong so high her heav'enward Psalms and Hymns among.

What? Faith a merit and a claim, when with the brain 'tis born and bred?
Go, fool, thy foolish way and dip in holy water burièd dead! †

Yet follow not th' unwisdom-path, cleave not to this and that disclaim;
Believe in all that man believes; here all and naught are both the same.

But is it so? How may we know? Happily this Fate, this Law may be
A word, a sound, a breath; at most the Zâhid's moonstruck theory.

Yes Truth may be, but 'tis not Here; mankind must seek and find it There,
But Where nor *I* nor *you* can tell, nor aught earth-mother ever bare.

Enough to think that Truth can be: come sit we where the roses glow,
Indeed he knows not how to know who knows not also how to 'unknow.

* * * * * *

Man hath no Soul, a state of things, a no-thing still, a sound, a word
Which so begets substantial thing that eye shall see what ear hath heard.

Where was his Soul the savage beast which in primeval forests strayed,
What shape had it, what dwelling-place, what part in nature's plan it played?

This Soul to ree a riddle made; who wants the vain duality?
Is not myself enough for me? what need of "I" within an "I"?

---

* Plato and Aristotle.

† I think he is alluding, though he has not expressed it, to the Marcionites' heresy of baptizing for the dead. The Marcionites were heretics who lived at Sinope, A.D. 150. Marcian came to Rome and believed in principles similar to the Manichæans. When a man died, one of the Marcionites sat on his coffin, and another asked him if he were willing to be baptised, and he answered, "Yes," upon which he was baptised. These heretics quoted Paul (1 Cor. xv. 29): "Else what shall they do which are baptised for the dead, if the dead do not rise at all? why are they then baptised for the dead?"—ISABEL BURTON.

Words, words that gender things! The soul is a new-comer on the scene;
Sufficeth not the breath of Life to work the matter-born machine?

We know the Gen'esis of the Soul; we trace the Soul to hour of birth;
We mark its growth as grew mankind to boast himself sole Lord of Earth:

The race of Be'ing from dawn of Life in an unbroken course was run;
What men are pleased to call their Souls was in the hog and dog begun:

Life is a ladder infinite-stepped, that hides its rungs from human eyes;
Planted its foot in chaos-gloom, its head soars high above the skies:

No break the chain of Being bears; all things began in unity;
And lie the links in regular line though haply none the sequence see.

The Ghost, embodied natural Dread of dreary death and foul decay,
Begat the Spirit, Soul and Shade with Hades' pale and wan array.

The Soul required a greater Soul, a Soul of Souls, to rule the host:
Hence spirit-powers and hierarchies, all gendered by the savage Ghost.

Not yours, ye Peoples of the Book, these fairy visions fair and fond,
Got by the gods of Khemi-land * and faring far the seas beyond!

"Th' immortal mind of mortal man"! we hear yon loud-lunged Zealot cry;
Whose mind but means his sum of thought, an essence of atomic "I."

Thought is the work of brain and nerve, in small-skulled idiot poor and mean;
In sickness sick, in sleep asleep, and dead when Death lets drop the scene.

"Tush!" quoth the Zâhid, "well we ken the teaching of the school abhorr'd
"That maketh man automaton, mind a secretion, soul a word."

"Of molecules and protoplasm you matter-mongers prompt to prate;
"Of jelly-speck, development and apes that grew to man's estate."

Vain cavil! all that is hath come either by Mir'acle or by Law;—
Why waste on this your hate and fear, why waste on that your love and awe?

Why heap such hatred on a word, why "Prototype" to type assign,
Why upon matter spirit mass? wants an appendix your design?

Is not the highest honour his who from the worst hath drawn the best;
May not your Maker make the world from matter, an it suit His hest?

Nay more, the sordider the stuff the cunninger the workman's hand:
Cease, then, your own Almighty Power to bind, to bound, to understand.

"Reason and Instinct!" How we love to play with words that please our pride;
Our noble race's mean descent by false forged titles seek to hide!

For "gift divine" I bid you read the better work of higher brain,
From Instinct diff'ering in degree as golden mine from leaden vein.

Reason is Life's sole arbiter, the magic Laby'rinth's single clue:
Worlds lie above, beyond its ken; what crosses it can ne'er be true.

"Fools rush where Angels fear to tread!" Angels and Fools have equal claim
To do what Nature bids them do, sans hope of praise, sans fear of blame!

* * * * * * *

There is no Heav'en, there is no Hell; these be the dreams of baby minds;
Tools of the wily Fetisheer, to 'fright the fools his cunning blinds.

Learn from the mighty Spi'rits of old to set thy foot on Heav'en and Hell;
In life to find thy hell and heav'en as thou abuse or use it well.

So deemed the doughty Jew who dared by studied silence low to lay
Orcus and Hades, lands of shades, the gloomy night of human day.

Hard to the heart is final death: fain would an *Ens* not end in *Nil*:
Love made the senti'ment kindly good: the Priest perverted all to ill.

While Reason sternly bids us die, Love longs for life beyond the grave:
Our hearts, affections, hopes and fears for Life-to-be shall ever crave.

Hence came the despot's darling dream, a Church to rule and sway the State;
Hence sprang the train of countless griefs in priestly sway and rule innate.

---

* Egypt; Kam, Kem, Khem (hierogl.), in the Demotic Khemi.

For future Life who dares reply? No witness at the bar have we;
Save what the brother Potsherd tells,—old tales and novel jugglery.

Who e'er return'd to teach the Truth, the things of Heaven and Hell to limn?
And all we hear is only fit for grandam-talk and nursery-hymn.

"Have mercy, man?" the Zâhid cries, "of our best visions rob us not!
"Mankind a future life must have to balance life's unequal lot."

"Nay," quoth the Magian, "'tis not so; I draw my wine for one for all.
"A cup for this, a score for that, e'en as his measure's great or small:

"Who drinks one bowl hath scant delight; to poorest passion he was born;
"Who drains the score must e'er expect to rue the headache of the morn."

Safely he jogs along the way which "Golden Mean" the sages call;
Who scales the brow of frowning Alp must face full many a slip and fall.

Here èxtremes meet, anointed Kings whose crownèd heads uneasy lie,
Whose cup of joy contains no more than tramps that on the dunghill die.

To fate-doomed Sinner born and bred for dangling from the gallows-tree;
To Saint who spends his holy days in rapt'urous hope his God to see;

To all that breathe our upper air the hands of Dest'iny ever deal,
In fixed and equal parts, their shares of joy and sorrow, woe and weal.

"How comes it, then, our span of days in hunting wealth and fame we spend?
"Why strive we (and all humans strive) for vain and visionary end?"

Reply; mankind obeys a law that bids him labour, struggle, strain;
The Sage well knowing its unworth, the Fool a-dreaming foolish gain.

And who, 'mid e'en the Fools, but feels that half the joy is in the race
For wealth and fame and place, nor sighs when comes success to crown the chase?

Again: In Hind, Chin, Franguestân that accident of birth befell,
Without our choice, our will, our voice: Faith is an accident as well.

What to the Hindu saith the Frank: "Denier of the Laws divine!
However godly-good thy Life, Hell is the home for thee and thine."

"Go strain the draught before 'tis drunk, and learn that breathing every breath,
"With every step, with every gest, some thing of life thou do'est to death."

Replies the Hîndu: "Wend thy way for foul and foolish Mlenchhas fit;
"Your Pariah-par'adise woo and win; at such dog-Heav'en I laugh and spit.

"Cannibals of the Holy Cow! who make your rav'ening maws the grave
"Of Things with self-same right to live;—what Fiend the filthy license gave?"

What to the Moslem cries the Frank? "A polygamic Theist thou!
"From an impostor-Prophet turn; thy stubborn head to Jesus bow."

Rejoins the Moslem: "Allah's one tho' with four Moslemahs I wive,
"One-wife-men ye and (damnèd race!) you split your God to Three and Five."

The Buddhist to Confucians thus: "Like dogs ye live, like dogs ye die;
"Content ye rest with wretched earth; God, judgment, Hell ye fain defy."

Retorts the Tartar: "Shall I lend mine only ready-money 'now,'
For vain usurious 'Then' like thine, avaunt, a triple idiot Thou!"

"With this poor life, with this mean world I fain complete what in me lies;
I strive to perfect this my me; my sole ambition's to be wise."

When doctors differ who decides amid the milliard-headed throng?
Who save the madman dares to cry: "'Tis I am right, you all are wrong"?

"You all are right, you all are wrong," we hear the careless Soofi say,
"For each believes his glimm'ering lamp to be the gorgeous light of day."

"*Thy* faith why false, *my* faith why true? 'tis all the work of Thine and Mine,
"The fond and foolish love of self that makes the Mine excel the Thine."

Cease then to mumble rotten bones; and strive to clothe with flesh and blood
The skel'eton; and to shape a Form that all shall hail as fair and good.

"For gen'erous youth," an Arab saith, "Jahim's* the only genial state;
"Give us the fire but not the shame with the sad, sorry blest to mate."

* Jehannum, Gehenna, Hell.

And if your Heav'en and Hell be true, and Fate that forced me to be born
Force me to Heav'en or Hell—I go, and hold Fate's insolence in scorn.

I want not this, I want not that, already sick of Me and Thee;
And if we're both transform'd and changed, what then becomes of Thee and Me?

Enough to think such things may be; to say they are not or they are
Were folly: leave them all to Fate, nor wage on shadows useless war.

Do what thy manhood bids thee do, from none but self expect applause;
He noblest lives and noblest dies who makes and keeps his self-made laws.

All other Life is living Death, a world where none but Phantoms dwell,
A breath, a wind, a sound, a voice, a tinkling of the Camel-bell.

* * * * * *

How then shall man so order life that when his tale of years is told,
Like sated guest he wend his way; how shall his even tenour hold?

Despite the Writ that stores the skull; despite the Table and the Pen;
Maugre the Fate that plays us down, her board the world, her pieces men?

How when the light and glow of life wax dim in thickly gath'ering gloom,
Shall mortal scoff at sting of Death, shall scorn the victory of the Tomb?

One way, two paths, one end the grave. This runs athwart the flow'ery plain,
That breasts the bush, the steep, the crag, in sun and wind and snow and rain:

Who treads the first must look adown, must deem his life an all in all;
Must see no heights where man may rise, must sight no depths where man may fall.

Allah in Adam form must view; adore the Maker in the made
Content to bask in Mâyâ's smile,† in joys of pain, in lights of shade.

He breaks the Law, he burns the Book, he sends the Moolah back to school;
Laughs at the beards of Saintly men; and dubs the Prophet dolt and fool.

Embraces Cypress' taper-waist; cools feet on wavy breast of rill;
Smiles in the Nargis' love-lorn eyes, and 'joys the dance of Daffodil;

Melts in the saffron light of Dawn to hear the moaning of the Dove;
Delights in Sundown's purpling hues when Bulbul woos the Rose's love.

Finds mirth and joy in Jamshid-bowl; toys with the Daughter of the vine;
And bids the beauteous cup-boy say, "Master I bring thee ruby wine!"‡

Sips from the maiden's lips the dew; brushes the bloom from virgin brow:—
Such is his fleshly bliss that strives the Maker through the Made to know.

I've tried them all, I find them all so same and tame, so drear, so dry;
My gorge ariseth at the thought; I commune with myself and cry:—

Better the myriad toils and pains that make the man to manhood true,
This be the rule that guideth life; these be the laws for me and you:

With Ignor'ance wage eternal war, to know thy self for ever strain,
Thine ignorance of thine ignorance is thy fiercest foe, thy deadliest bane;

That blunts thy sense, and dulls thy taste; that deafs thine ears, and blinds thine eyes;
Creates the thing that never was, the Thing that ever is defies.

The finite Atom infinite that forms thy circle's centre-dot,
So full-sufficient for itself, for other selves existing not,

Finds the world mighty as 'tis small; yet must be fought the unequal fray;
A myriad giants here; and there a pinch of dust, a clod of clay.

Yes! maugre all thy dreams of peace still must the fight unfair be fought;
Where thou may'st learn the noblest law, to know that all we know is nought.

True to thy Nature, to Thyself, Fame and Disfame nor hope nor fear:
Enough to thee the small still voice aye thund'ering in thine inner ear.

From self-approval seek applause: What ken not men thou kennest, thou!
Spurn ev'ry idol others raise: Before thine own Ideal bow:

---

* Emblems of Kismet, or Destiny. † Illusion.
‡ That all the senses, even the ear may enjoy.

Be thine own Deus: Make self free, liberal as the circling air:
Thy Thought to thee an Empire be; break every prison'ing lock and bar:

Do Thou the Ought to self aye owed; here all the duties meet and blend,
In widest sense, withouten care of what began, for what shall end.

Thus, as thou view the Phantom-forms which in the misty Past were thine,
To be again the thing thou wast with honest pride thou may'st decline;

And, glancing down the range of years, fear not thy future self to see;
Resign'd to life, to death resign'd, as though the choice were nought to thee.

On Thought itself feed not thy thought; nor turn from Sun and Light to gaze,
At darkling cloisters paved with tombs, where rot the bones of bygone days:

"Eat not thy heart," the Sages said; "nor mourn the Past, the buried Past;"
Do what thou dost, be strong, be brave; and, like the Star, nor rest nor haste.

Pluck the old woman from thy breast: Be stout in woe, be stark in weal;
Do good for Good is good to do: Spurn bribe of Heav'en and threat of Hell.

To seek the True, to glad the heart, such is of life the HIGHER LAW,
Whose differ'ence is the Man's degree, the Man of gold, the Man of straw.

See not that something in Mankind that rouses hate or scorn or strife,
Better the worm of Izrâil * than Death that walks in form of life.

Survey thy kind as One whose wants in the great Human Whole unite; †
The Homo rising high from earth to seek the Heav'ens of Life-in-Light;

And hold Humanity one man, whose universal agony
Still strains and strives to gain the goal, where agonies shall cease to be.

Believe in all things; none believe; judge not nor warp by "Facts" the thought;
See clear, hear clear, tho' life may seem Mâyâ and Mirage, Dream and Naught.

Abjure the Why and seek the How: the God and gods enthroned on high,
Are silent all, are silent still; nor hear thy voice, nor deign reply.

The Now, that indivis'ible point which studs the length of inf'inite line
Whose ends are nowhere, is thine all, the puny all thou callest thine.

Perchance the law some Giver hath: Let be! let be! what canst thou know?
A myriad races came and went; this Sphinx hath seen them come and go.

Haply the Law that rules the world allows to man the widest range;
And haply Fate's a Theist-word, subject to human chance and change.

This "I" may find a future Life, a nobler copy of our own,
Where every riddle shall be ree'd, where every knowledge shall be known;

Where 'twill be man's to see the whole of what on Earth he sees in part;
Where change shall ne'er surcharge the thought; nor hope deferr'd shall hurt the heart.

But!—faded flow'er and fallen leaf no more shall deck the parent tree;
And man once dropt by Tree of Life what hope of other life has he?

The shatter'd bowl shall know repair; the riven lute shall sound once more;
But who shall mend the clay of man, the stolen breath to man restore?

The shiver'd clock again shall strike; the broken reed shall pipe again:
But we, we die, and Death is one, the doom of brutes, the doom of men.

Then, if Nirwânâ ‡ round our life with nothingness, 'tis haply best;
Thy toils and troubles, want and woe at length have won their guerdon—Rest.

Cease, Abdû, Cease! Thy song is sung, nor think the gain the singer's prize;
Till men hold Ignor'ance deadly sin, till man deserves his title "Wise:" §

In Days to come, Days slow to dawn, when Wisdom deigns to dwell with men,
These echoes of a voice long stilled haply shall wake responsive strain;

Wend now thy way with brow serene, fear not thy humble tale to tell;—
The whispers of the Desert-wind; the Tinkling of the Camel's bell.

שלם

---

* The Angel of Death. † The "Great Man" of the Enochites and the Mormons.
‡ Comparative annihilation. § "Homo sapiens."

But then, again, a year later I find amongst his writings :—

"Man wendeth to his long, long home,
About the streets the mourners go;
Behold the tomb, and hereby mete
The length and depth of mortal woe.
Thou hast nor lover, kin, nor friend!
The deepest grief hath shallows.

"Ah yes, thou hast; but close thine eyes
Upon this world and gaze above.
There, and there only, shalt thou find
Unchanging and unmeasured love.
Then dare the way, and meekly bend
Thy footsteps t'ward the heavenly Friend.

"Dies Iræ!
Lord, Saviour, God, my only stay,
Desert me not that dreadful day."

Richard's idea was that every man, by doing all the good he could in this life, always working for others, for the human race, always acting "Excelsior," should leave a track of light behind him on this World as he passes through. His idea of God was so immeasurably grander than anything people are *usually* taught to think about God. It always seemed to him that we dwindled God down to our own mean imaginations; that we made something like ourselves, only bigger, and far crueller. There is some truth in this; we are always talking about God just as if we understood Him. His idea of a Divine Being was so infinite, so great, that to pray to Him was an impertinence; that it was monstrous that we should expect Him to alter one of His decrees, because *we* prayed for it; that He was a God of big universal love, but so far off, as to be far above anything we can understand. These were the *utmost* extent of his *own* Agnostic fits.

Almost contemporary with these sentiments, I find the following verses :—

1.

"Bright imaged in the glassy lake below,
Crisped by the zephyrs' nimble run,
I saw two sister stars appear.
I looked above, there shone but one;
Then fled the zephyrs, and my eye
The sole reflection could descry.

2.

"Then rising high, the crescent skiff
Thro' the deep azure rolled its way;
On earth a misty shadow lay,
While all of heaven was bright and gay.
Then waxed the night cloud thin and rare,
And died within its home, the air.

3.

"Thus senses that improve the soul
To deadliest error oft give birth;
Dust-born, they grovel and apply
To highest heaven low rubs of earth,
Fell fatal masters where they sway,
Obedient slaves when taught t' obey.

4.

"Nor let th' immortal "I" depend
On Reason, blind and faithless guide,
Who knowing nothing knoweth all
Of mortal folly—human pride;
Not thus may truth be wooed and won—
A *reasonable* creed is none.

5.

"Who then thy falt'ring steps may lead
O'er the wild waste of doubt and fear,
Where sense and reason shed no ray?
The marks and glooms what light may clear?
Shall nature tread a law-girt course,
While man walks earth a living corpse?

6.

"Ah, no! there is a heavenly guide
That leads, directs this fragile clay;
We call it spirit, soul, and life,
Let mortal call it as he may;
Man, go not far, seek not elsewhere;
Search that within—Truth dwelleth *there*."

He was always in one of the two extremes, meaning *All* or *Nothing*. It is what we Catholics call "resisting of Divine grace;" it is what Agnostics would call "resisting a temptation," or the correct shibboleth, I believe, is "upholding his integrity," *i.e.* disbelieving in God and another *world*, which he *never did* at any time of his life.

CHAPTER IX.

HARAR—THE MOSLEM ABYSSINIA—THE TIMBUCTOO OF EAST AFRICA, THE EXPLORATION OF WHICH HAD BEEN ATTEMPTED IN VAIN BY SOME THIRTY TRAVELLLERS.

RICHARD returned up the Red Sea to Egypt, and much enjoyed the rest and safety for a short time, and then returned to Bombay, his leave being up; but the wandering fever was still upon him, and as the most difficult place for a white man to enter was Harar, in Somali-land, Abyssinia, he determined that that should be his object. It is inhabited by a very dangerous race to deal with, and no white man had ever penetrated to Harar. The first white man who went to Abyssinia was kept prisoner till he died. The East India Company had long wished to explore it, because Berberah, the chief port of Somali-land, is the safest and best harbour on the western side of the Indian Ocean—far better than Aden. They went to work with that strange mixture of caution and generosity with which they treated those of their servants who stepped out of what Richard calls their "quarter-deck" routine, that is, to let him go as a private traveller, and the Government to give him no protection, but would allow him to retain the same pay that he would enjoy whilst on leave. Dr. Carter and others refused to do more than to coast along in a cruiser.

Richard applied for Lieutenant Herne, of the 1st Bombay Fusileers, Lieutenant Stroyan, Indian Navy, and Lieutenant Speke, 46th Bengal Native Infantry. Herne was distinguished by his surveys, photography, and mechanics on the west coast of India, in Scinde, and on the Punjaub rivers; Stroyan as amateur surveyor; and Speke, collector of the Fauna of Tibet and the Himalayas and sportsman. Assistant-Surgeon Ellerton Stocks, botanist, traveller, and a first-rate man in all ways, died before the expedition started.

Jealousy, as usual, immediately rose up in opposition. First, Sir James Outram, Political Resident at Aden, called it a tempting of

Providence, and Dr. Buist, the editor of the *Bombay Times*, was told to run down the Somali Expedition, in which task he was assisted by the unpopular chaplain. This was not very gratifying to four high-spirited men; so, instead of using Berberah as a base of operations, then westward to Harar, and then south-east to Zanzibar, the Resident changed the whole scheme and made it fail. Herne was to go to Berberah, where he was joined later by Stroyan. Speke was to land in a small harbour called Bunder Guray, and to trace the watershed of the Wady Nogal, to buy horses and camels, and collect red earth with gold in it; but his little expedition failed through his guide's treachery. Herne and Stroyan succeeded. Richard reserved for himself the post of danger. Harar was as difficult to enter as Mecca. It is the southernmost masonry-built settlement in North Equatorial Africa. He would go as an Arab merchant. Harar had never been visited, has its own language, its own unique history and traditions. The language was unwritten, but he wrote a grammar, and a vocabulary in which the etymology is given, and there he had enough savage anthropology to interest him.

He writes—

"In the first place, Berberah is the true key of the Red Sea, the centre of East African traffic, and the only safe place for shipping upon the Western Erythræan shore, from Suez to Guardafui, backed by lands capable of cultivation, and by hills covered with pine and other valuable trees, enjoying a comparatively temperate climate, with a regular, though thin monsoon. This harbour has been coveted by many a foreign conqueror. Circumstances have thrown it into our arms, and if we refuse a chance, another and a rival nation will not be so blind. [We have since given it away, and kept the far inferior Aden.] We are bound to protect the lives of subjects on this coast. In 1825 the crew of the *Mary Ann* brig was treacherously murdered by the Somal. They continued in that state, and if to-morrow a Peninsular and Oriental Company steamer by any chance fell into their power, it would be the same history. Harar, scarcely three hundred miles distance from Aden, is a counterpart of the ill-famed Timbuctoo. A tradition exists that with the entrance of the first Christian, Harar will fall. All therefore who have attempted it were murdered. It was therefore a point of honour with me to utilize my title of Haji, by entering this City, visiting its Ruler, and returning in safety, after breaking the Guardian's spell."

This exploration of Harar was one of Richard's most splendid and dangerous expeditions, and, for some reason or other, the least known; the reason being, as I think, that his pilgrimage to Mecca was still making a great noise, and that the Crimean War had cropped up, deadening the interest in all *personal* adventure. He therefore thought himself fortunate in being able to persuade Lord Elphinstone, Governor of Bombay, to patronize an expedition into Somali-land.

He was away four months. The journey was useful; at least, it has proved so to the Egyptians, to the English, and now to the Italians. He sailed away, leaving Herne, Stroyan, and Speke, each engaged on his respective work, and arrived at Zayla.

"My ship companions," he writes, "were the wildest of the wild, and as we came into port Zayla a barque came up to give us the bad news. Friendship between the Amir of Harar and the Governor of Zayla had been broken; the road through the Eesa Somal had been closed by the murder of Masúd, a favourite slave and adopted son of Sharmarkay; all strangers had been expelled the City for some misconduct by the Harar chief; moreover, small-pox was raging there with such violence that the Galla peasantry would allow neither ingress nor egress. The tide was out, and we waded a quarter of a mile amongst giant crabs, who showed gristly claws, sharp coralline, and seaweed so thick as to become almost like a mat. In the shallower parts the sun was painfully hot even to my well-tried feet. I was taken immediately to the Governor at Zayla, a fellow Haji, who gave me hospitality.

"The well-known sounds of El Islam returned from memory. Again the melodious chant of the *muezzin*—no evening bell can compare with it for solemnity and beauty—and in the neighbouring Mosque, the loudly intoned 'Amin' and 'Allaho Akbar,' far superior to any organ, rang in my ear. The evening gun of camp was represented by the *nakkarah*, or kettle-drum, which sounded about seven p.m. at the southern Gate; and at ten a second drumming warned the paterfamilias that it was time for home, and thieves and lovers, that it was the hour for bastinado. Nightfall was ushered in by the song, the dance, and the marriage festival—here no permission is required for 'native music in the lines'—and muffled figures flitted mysteriously through the dark alleys.

* * * * * *

"After a peep through the open window, I fell asleep, feeling once more at home.

"I was too much of an Arab to weary of the endless preparations for forming a caravan. I used to provide myself with a Korán and sit receiving visitors, and would occasionally go into the Mosque, my servant carrying the prayer carpet, three hundred pair of eyes staring at me, and after reciting the customary two-bow prayer, in honour of the Mosque, I would place a sword and rosary before me, and, taking the Korán, read the cow-chapter, No. 18, in a loud and twanging voice. This is the character I adopted. You will bear in mind, if you please, that I am a Moslem merchant, a character not to be confounded with the notable individuals seen on ''Change.' Mercator, in the East, is a compound of tradesmen, divine, and T.G. Usually of gentle birth, he is everywhere welcomed and respected; and he bears in his mind and manner that, if Allah please, he may become Prime Minister a month after he has sold you a yard of cloth. Commerce appears to be an accident, not an essential, with him, yet he is by no means deficient in acumen. He is a grave and reverend seignior, with rosary in hand and Korán on lip; is generally a pilgrim; talks at dreary length about Holy Places; writes a pretty hand; has read and can recite much poetry; is master of his religion; demeans himself with respectability; is perfect in all points of ceremony and politeness, and feels equally at home whether Sultan or slave sit upon his counter. He has a wife and children in his own country, where he intends to spend the remnant of his days; but 'the world is uncertain'—'Fate descends, and man's eyes seeth it not'—'the earth is a charnel-house;' briefly, his many old saws give him a kind of theoretical consciousness that his bones may moulder in other places but his fatherland.

"For half a generation we have been masters of Aden, filling Southern Arabia with our calicos and rupees—what is the present state of affairs there? We are dared by the Bedouins to come forth from behind our stone walls and fight like men in the plain,—British *protégés* are slaughtered within the range of our guns,—our allies' villages have been burned in sight of Aden,—our deserters are welcomed and our fugitive felons protected,—our supplies are cut off, and the garrison is reduced to extreme distress, at the word of a half-naked bandit,—the miscreant Bhagi, who murdered Captain Mylne in cold blood, still roams the hills unpunished,—gross insults are the sole acknowledgements of our peaceful overtures,—the British flag has been fired upon without return, our cruisers being ordered to act only on the defensive,—and our forbearance to attack is universally asserted and believed to arise from mere cowardice. Such is, and such will be, the opinion and the character of the Arab!

"I stayed here for twenty-six days, rising at dawn; then went to the Terrace to perform my devotions, and make observation of my neighbours; breakfast at six, then coffee, pipe, and a nap; then receive visitors, who come by dozens with nothing to do or say. When they were only Somal, I wrote Arabic, or extracted from some useful book. When Arabs were there, I would recite tales from the 'Arabian Nights,' to their great delight. At eleven, dinner, more coffee and pipes; then the natives would go to sleep, and I wrote my journals and studies. At about two p.m. more visitors would come, and at sunset again to the Terrace, or walk to a mosque, where games are going on, or stroll to a camp of Bedawi. The Gates are locked at sunset, and the keys are carried to the Haji. It is not safe to be without the City later. Then comes supper.

"After it we repair to the roof to enjoy the prospect of the far Tajarrah Hills and the white moonbeams sleeping upon the nearer sea. The evening star hangs like a diamond upon the still horizon; around the moon a pink zone of light mist, shading off into turquoise blue and a delicate green-like chrysopraz, invests the heavens with a peculiar charm. The scene is truly suggestive; behind us, purpling in the night air and silvered by the radiance from above, lie the wolds and mountains tenanted by the fiercest of savages, their shadowy mysterious forms exciting vague alarms in the traveller's breast. Sweet as the harp of David, the night-breeze and the music of the water comes up from the sea; but the ripple and the rustling sound alternate with the hyæna's laugh, and the jackal's cry, and the wild dog's lengthened howl.

"This journey, which occupied nearly four months, was to be through a savage, treacherous, ferocious, and bloodthirsty people, whose tribes were in a constant state of blood-feud. The party consisted of nine, an *abban* or guide, three Arab matchlock men, two women cooks, who were called Shehrazade and Deenarzade after the 'Arabian Nights,' a fourth servant, and a Bedawin woman to drive a donkey, which camels will follow and which is the custom. We had four or five mules, saddled and bridled, and camels for the baggage. Every one wept over us, and considered us dead men. The *abban* objected to some routes on account of avoiding tribes with which he had a blood-feud."

This was, as I have said, far the most dangerous of Richard's explorations, quite as difficult as Mecca, and far more difficult than anything Stanley has ever done, with his advantages of men, money, and luxuries. The women seemed to be much hardier than the men; they carried the pipe and tobacco, led the camels, adjusted the burdens, at the halt unloaded the cattle, disposed the baggage, covered them with a mat tent, cooked the food, made tea and coffee, and bivouacked outside the tent.

He writes—

"The air was fresh and clear; and the night breeze was delicious after the stormy breath of day. The weary confinement of walls made the weary expanse a luxury to the sight, whilst the tumbling of the surf upon the near shore, and the music of the jackal, predisposed to sweet sleep. We now felt that at length the die was cast. Placing my pistols by my side, with my rifle butt for a pillow, and its barrel as a bed-fellow, I sought repose with none of the apprehension which even the most stout-hearted traveller knows before the start. It is the difference between fancy and reality, between anxiety and certainty; to men gifted with any imaginative powers the anticipation must ever be worse than the event. Thus it happens, that he who feels a thrill of fear before engaging in a peril, exchanges it for a throb of exultation when he finds himself hand to hand with the danger."

The description of the journey is filled in his notes by being hindered and almost captured by Bedawi, lamed with thorns, the camels casting themselves down from fatigue, famishing from hunger, and, worse, from thirst—the only water being sulphurous, which affected both man and beast—and attacks from lions, sleep being disturbed by large ants, three-quarters of an inch long, with venomous stings. Everywhere they went, everybody wept over them, as dead men. He finds time, nevertheless, to remark, that at the height of 3350 feet he found a buttercup and heard a woodpecker tapping, that reminded him of home. He describes a sham attack of twelve Bedawi, who, when they saw what his revolver could do, said they were only in fun.

At one of the kraals he gives an account of how, being surrounded by Somals, they were boasting of their shooting, and of the skill with which they used the shield, but they seemed not to understand the proper use of the sword.

"Thinking it was well to impress them with the superiority of arms, I requested them to put up one of their shields as a mark. They laughed very much, but would not comply. The Somal hate a vulture, because it eats the dead and dying; so, seeing a large brown bare-necked vulture at twenty paces distance, I shot it with my revolver; then I loaded a gun with swan-shot, which they had never seen, and, aiming at a bird that they considered far out of gunshot distance, I knocked it over flying. Fresh screams followed this marvellous feat, and they said, 'Lo! he bringeth down the birds from heaven.' Their Chief, putting his forefinger in his mouth, praised Allah, and prayed to be defended from such a calamity; and always after, when they saw me approach, they said, 'Here comes the Shaykh who knows knowledge.' I then gave a stick to the best man; I provided myself in the same way, and allowed him to cut at me as much as ever he liked, easily warding off the blows with a parry. After repeated failures, and tiring himself enormously, he received a sounding blow from me upon the least bony part of his person. The crowd laughed long and loud, and the knight-at-arms retired in confusion.

"Every now and then we got into difficulties with the Bedawi, who would not allow us to proceed, declaring the land was theirs. We did not deny the claim, but I threatened sorcery, death, and wild beasts, and foraging parties to their camels, children, and women. It generally brought them to their senses. They would spit on us for good luck, and let us depart. Once a Chief was smitten by Shehrazade's bulky charms, and wanted to carry her off. Once in the evening we came upon the fresh trail of a large Habr Awal cavalcade, which frightened my companions dreadfully. We were only nine men and two women, to contend against two hundred horsemen, and all, except the Hammal and Long Guled, would have run away at the first charge. The worst of the ride was over rough and stony road, the thorns tearing their feet and naked legs, and the camels slipping over the rounded pebbles.

"The joy of coming to a kraal was great, where the Chiefs of the village appeared, bringing soft speech, sweet water, new milk, fat sheep and goats, for a *tobe* of Cutch canvas. We passed a quiet, luxurious day of coffee and pipes, fresh cream and roasted mutton. After the great heats and dangers from horsemen on the plain, we enjoyed the cool breeze of the hills, cloudy skies, and the verdure of the glades which refreshed our beasts. Here I shot a few hawks, and was rewarded with loud exclamations of 'Allah preserve thy hand! may thy skill never fail thee before the foe.' A woman ran away from my steam kettle, thinking it was a weapon. They looked upon my sunburnt skin with a favour they denied to the lime-white face. The Somali Bedawi gradually affiliated me to their tribes.

"At one village the people rushed out, exclaiming, 'Lo! let us look at the Kings;' at others, 'Come and see the white man; he is the Governor of Zayla.' My fairness (for, brown as I am, I am fair to them) and the Arab dress made me sometimes the ruler of Aden, the Chief of Zayla, the Haji's son, a boy, an old woman, a man painted white, a warrior in silver armour, a merchant, a pilgrim, a head priest, Ahmed the Indian, a Turk, an Egyptian, a Frenchman, a Banyan, a Sheríf, and, lastly, a calamity sent down from heaven to weary out the lives of the Somal. Every kraal had its own conjecture.

"On December 9th, I rode a little off my way to visit some ruins, Darbíyah Kola, or Kola's Fort, so called on account of its Galla queen. There were once two cities, Aububah, and they fought like the Kilkenny cats till both were eaten up. This was about three hundred years ago, and the substantial ruins have fought a stern fight with Time.

"Remnants of houses cumber the soil, and the carefully built wells are filled with rubbish. The palace was pointed out to me, with its walls of stone and clay, intersected by layers of woodwork. The Mosque is a large, roofless building, containing twelve square pillars of rude masonry, and the *mihrab*, or prayer niche, is denoted by a circular arch of tolerable construction. But the voice of the *muezzin* is hushed for ever, and creepers now twine around the ruined fane. The scene was still and dreary as the grave; for a mile and a half in length all was ruins—ruins—ruins.

"Leaving this Dead City, we rode towards the south-west between two rugged hills. Topping the ridge, we stood for a few minutes to observe the view before us. Beneath our feet lay a long grassy plain—the sight must have gladdened the hearts of our starving mules—and for the first time in Africa horses appeared grazing free amongst the bushes. A little further off lay the Aylonda Valley, studded with graves and dark with verdure. Beyond it stretched the Wady Haráwwah, a long gloomy hollow in the general level. The background was a bold sweep of blue hill, the second gradient of the Harar line, and on its summit, closing the western horizon, lay a golden streak, the Marar Prairie. Already I felt at the end of my journey.

"It was not an unusual thing in the dusk to see a large animal following us with quick stealthy strides, and that I, sending a rifle ball as correctly as I could in the direction, put to flight a large lion.

"The nearer I got to Harar, the more I was stopped by parties of Gallas, and some went on to report evil of me, and many threats were uttered. The 'End of Time' in the last march turned tail. 'Dost thou believe me to be a coward, O Pilgrim?' 'Of a truth I do,' I answered. Nothing abashed, and with joy at his heart, he hammered his mule with his heel, and rode off, saying, 'What hath man but a single life, and he who throweth it away, what is he but a fool?'"

He gives a good account of elephant-hunting, but they did not get near any. The water was in some places so hard it raised lumps like nettle-stings, and they had to butter themselves. At one place the inhabitants flocked out to stare at them. He fired his rifle by way of salute over the head of the prettiest girl. The people, delighted, exclaimed, "Mod! Mod! honour to thee!" and he replied with shouts of "Kullibah! may Heaven aid thee!"

"When there is any danger a Somali watchman sings and addresses himself in dialogue, with different voices, to persuade thieves that several men are watching. Ours was a spectacle of wildness as he sat before the blazing fire. The 'End of Time' conceived the jocose idea of crowning me King of the country, with loud cries of 'Buh! Buh! Buh!' while showering leaves from a gum tree and water from a prayer-bottle over my head, and then with all solemnity bound on my turban. I was hindered and threatened in no end of places, and my companions threatened to desert me, saying, 'They will spoil that white skin of thine at Harar.' Still I pushed on. The Guda Birsi Bedawi number ten thousand spears.

"One night we came upon a sheet of bright blaze, a fire threatening the whole prairie.

"At last came the sign of leaving the Desert. The scene lifted, and we came to the second step of the Ethiopian highlands. In the midst of the valley beneath ran a serpentine of shining waters, the gladdest spectacle we had yet witnessed. Further in front, masses of hill rose abruptly from shady valleys, encircled on the far horizon by a straight blue line of ground resembling a distant sea. Behind us glared the desert. We had now reached the outskirts of civilization, where man, abandoning his flocks and herds, settles, cultivates, and attends to the comforts of life.

"We saw fields, with lanes between, the daisy, the thistle, and the sweet-briar, settled villages, surrounded by strong *abatis* of thorns, which stud the hills everywhere, clumps of trees, to which the beehives are hung, and yellow crops of holcus, or grain. The Harvest-Home-song sounded pleasant to my ears, and, contrasting with the silent desert, the hum of man's habitation was music.

They flocked out to gaze upon us, unarmed, and welcomed us. We bathed in the waters, on whose banks were a multitude of huge Mantidæ, pink and tender green. I now had ample time to see the manners and customs of the settled Somali, as I was conducted to the cottage of the Gerad's pretty wife, and learned the home, and the day, and the food. They spoke Harari, Somali, Galla, Arabic, and dialects. My kettle seems to have created surprise everywhere.

"Here the last preparations were made for entering this dreadful City. All my people, and my camels, and most of my goods, had to be left here for the return journey, and it was the duty of this Chief (Gerad) to accompany me. I happened to hear one of them say, 'Of what use is his gun? Before he could fetch fire I should put this arrow through him.' I wheeled round, and discharged a barrel over their heads, which threw them into convulsions of terror. The man I had now to depend upon was Adan bin Kaushan, a strong wiry Bedawin. He was tricky, ambitious, greedy of gain, fickle, restless, and treacherous, a cunning idiot, always so difficult to deal with. His sister was married to the father of the Amir of Harar, but he said, 'He would as soon walk into a crocodile's mouth as go into the walls of Harar.' He received a sword, a Korán, a turban, an Arab waistcoat of gaudy satin, about seventy *tobes*, and a similar proportion of indigo-dyed stuff—he privily complained to me that the Hammal had given him but twelve cloths. A list of his wants will best explain the man. He begged me to bring him from Berberah a silver-hilted sword and some soap, one thousand dollars, two sets of silver bracelets, twenty guns with powder and shot, snuff, a scarlet cloth coat embroidered with gold, some poison that would not fail, and any other little article of luxury which might be supposed to suit him. In return he was to present me with horses, mules, slaves, ivory, and other valuables: he forgot, however, to do so before he departed.

"Whilst we were discussing the project, and getting on satisfactorily, five strangers well mounted rode in. Two were citizens, and three were Habr Awal Bedawi, high in the Amir's confidence; they had been sent to settle blood-money with Adan. They then told him that I, the Arab, was not one who bought and sold, but a spy; that I and my party should be sent prisoners to Harar. Adan would not give us up, falsely promising to present our salaams to the Amir. When they were gone he told me how afraid he was, and that it was impossible for him to conduct me to the City. I then relied upon what has made many a small man Great, my good star and audacity.

"Driven to bay, I wrote an English letter from the Political Agent at Aden, to the Amir of Harar, intending to deliver it in person; it was 'neck or nothing.' I only took what was necessary, Sherwa the son of Adan, the Bedawi Actidon and Mad Said, and left everything behind me, excepting some presents for the Amir, a change of clothes, an Arab book or two, a few biscuits, ammunition, and a little tobacco. I passed through a lovely country, was stopped by the Gallas, and by the Habr Awal Bedawi, who offered, if we could wait till sunrise, to take us into the City; so I returned a polite answer, leading them to expect that I should wait till eight a.m. for them. I left my journals, sketches, and books in charge of Adan.

"The journey was hard, and I encountered a Harar Grandee, mounted upon a handsomely comparisoned mule, and attended by servants. He was very courteous, and, seeing me thirsty, ordered me a cup of water. Finally arriving, at the crest of a hill, stood the City—the end of my present travel—a long, sombre line, strikingly contrasting with the white-washed towns of the East. The spectacle, materially speaking, was a disappointment; nothing conspicuous appeared but two grey minarets of rude shape; many would have grudged exposing three lives to win so paltry a prize. But of all that have attempted it, none ever succeeded in entering that pile of stones; the thoroughbred traveller will understand my exultation, although my two companions exchanged giances of wonder. Stopping while my companions bathed, I retired to the wayside and sketched the town. We arrived at three p.m., and advancing to the gate, Mad Said accosted a warder whom he knew, sent our salaams to the Amir, saying we came from Aden, and requested the honour of audience. The Habr Awal collected round me *inside* the town, and scowling, inquired why we had not apprised them of our intention of entering the City; but it was 'war to the knife,' and I did not deign to answer.

Ten Days at Harar—the Most Exciting Trial of all.

"We were kept waiting half an hour, and were told by the warder to pass the threshold. Long Guled gave his animal to the two Bedawi, every one advising my attendants to escape with the beasts, as we were going to be killed, on the road to this African St. James. We were ordered to run, but we leisurely led our mules in spite of the guide's wrath, entered the gate, and strolled down the yard, which was full of Gallas with spears, and the waiting gave me an opportunity to inspect the place. I walked into a vast hall, a hundred feet long, between two long rows of Galla spearmen, between whose lines I had to pass. They were large half-naked savages, standing like statues, with fierce movable eyes, each one holding, with its butt end on the ground, a huge spear, with a head the size of a shovel. I purposely sauntered down them coolly with a swagger, with my eyes fixed upon their dangerous-looking faces. I had a six-shooter concealed in my waist-belt, and determined, at the first show of excitement, to run up to the Amir, and put it to his head, if it were necessary, to save my own life.

"The Amir was like a little Indian Rajah, an etiolated youth about twenty-four or twenty-five years old, plain, thin bearded, with a yellow complexion, wrinkled brows, and protruding eyes. His dress was a flowing robe of crimson cloth, edged with snowy fur, and a narrow white turban tightly twisted round a tall conical cap of red velvet, like the old Turkish headgear of our painters. His throne was a common Indian *kursi*, or raised cot, about five feet long, with back and sides supported by a dwarf railing; being an invalid, he rested his elbow upon a pillow, under which appeared the hilt of a Cutch sabre. Ranged in double line, perpendicular to the Amir, stood the 'Court,' his cousins and nearest relations, with right arms bared after the fashion of Abyssinia.

"I entered this second avenue of Galla spearsmen with a loud 'Peace be upon ye!' to which H.H. replying graciously, and extending a hand, bony and yellow as a kite's claw, snapped his thumb and middle finger. Two chamberlains stepping forward, held my forearms, and assisted me to bend low over the fingers, which, however, I did not kiss, being naturally averse to performing that operation upon any but a woman's hand. My two servants then took their turn: in this case, after the back was saluted, the palm was presented for a repetition.* These preliminaries concluded, we were led to, and seated upon a mat in front of the Amir, who directed towards us a frowning brow and an inquisitive eye.

"I made some inquiries about the Amir's health: he shook his head captiously, and inquired our errand. I drew from my pocket my own letter: it was carried by a chamberlain, with hands veiled in his *tobe*, to the Amir, who, after a brief glance, laid it upon the couch, and demanded further explanation. I then represented in Arabic that we had come from Aden, bearing the compliments of our *Daulah*, or Governor, and that we had entered Harar to see the light of H.H.'s countenance: this information concluded with a little speech describing the changes of Political Agents in Arabia, and alluding to the friendship formerly existing between the English and the deceased Chief Abubakr.

"The Amir smiled graciously.

"This smile, I must own, was a relief. We had been prepared for the worst, and the aspect of affairs in the Palace was by no means reassuring.

"Whispering to his Treasurer, a little ugly man with a baldly shaven head, coarse features, pug nose, angry eyes, and stubbly beard, the Amir made a sign for us to retire. The *baisé main* was repeated, and we backed out of the audience-shed in high favour. According to grandiloquent Bruce, 'the Court of London and that of Abyssinia are, in their principles, one;' the loiterers in the Harar palace-yard, who had before regarded us with cut-throat looks, now smiled as though they loved us. Marshalled by the guard, we issued from the precincts, and, after walking a hundred yards, entered the Amir's second palace, which we were told to consider our home. There we found the Bedawi, who, scarcely believing that we had escaped alive, grinned in the joy of their hearts, and we were at once provided from the Chief's kitchen with a dish of *shabta*, holcus cakes soaked in sour milk, and thickly powdered with red pepper, the salt of this inland region.

* In Abyssinia, according to the Lord of Geesh, this is a mark of royal familiarity and confidence.

"When we had eaten, the Treasurer reappeared, bearing the Amir's command that we should call upon his Wazir, the Gerad Mohammad. We found a venerable old man, whose benevolent countenance belied the reports current about him in Somali-land. Half rising, although his wrinkled brow showed suffering, he seated me by his side upon the carpeted masonry-bench, where lay the implements of his craft—reeds, inkstands, and whitewashed boards for paper—politely welcomed me, and, gravely stroking his cotton-coloured beard, desired to know my object in good Arabic.

"I replied almost in the words used to the Amir, adding, however, some details, how in the old day one Madar Faríh had been charged by the late Sultan Abubakr with a present to the Governor of Aden, and that it was the wish of our people to re-establish friendly relations and commercial intercourse with Harar.

"'Khayr Inshallah! it is well, if Allah please!' ejaculated the Gerad. I then bent over his hand, and took leave.

"Returning, we inquired anxiously of the Treasurer about my servants' arms, which had not been returned, and were assured that they had been placed in the safest of storehouses, the Palace. I then sent a common six-barrelled revolver as a present to the Amir, explaining its use to the bearer, and we prepared to make ourselves as comfortable as possible. The interior of our new house was a clean room, with plain walls, and a floor of tamped earth; opposite the entrance were two broad steps of masonry, raised about two feet, and a yard above the ground, and covered with hard matting. I contrived to make upon the higher ledge a bed with the cushions which my companions used as *shabracques*, and after seeing the mules fed and tethered, lay down to rest, worn out by fatigue and profoundly impressed with the *poésie* of our position. I was under the roof of a bigoted prince whose least word was death; amongst a people who detest foreigners; the only European that had ever passed over their inhospitable threshold; and, more than that, I was *the fated instrument of their future downfall.*"

He gives a very detailed account of the City of Harar, its inhabitants, and all he saw during his ten days there, for which I refer people to "First Footsteps in East Africa," one large volume, 1856. He says—

"The explorer must frequently rest satisfied with descrying from his Pisgah, the knowledge which another more fortunate is destined to acquire. *Inside* Harar, I was so closely watched, that it was impossible to put pen to paper. It was only when I got back to Wilensi that I hastily collected the grammatical forms, and a vocabulary which proves that the language is not Arabic; that it *has* an affinity with the Amharic. Harar has its own tongue, unintelligible to any save the citizens. Its little population of eight thousand souls is a distinct race. A common proverb is, 'Hard as the heart of Harar.' They are extremely bigoted, especially against

Christians, and are fond of a religious war, or *jehád*, with the Gallas. They hold foreigners in hate and contempt, and divide them into two classes, Arabs and Somal.

The Somals say that the State dungeon is beneath the palace, and that he who once enters it lives with unkempt beard and untrimmed nails till the day when death sets him free. There is nothing more terrible; the captive is heavily ironed, lies in a filthy dungeon, and receives no food, except what he can obtain from his own family, or buy or beg from his guards. The Amir has bad health; I considered him consumptive. It is something in my favour that, as soon as I departed, he wrote to the acting Political Resident at Aden, earnestly begging to be supplied with a Frank physician, and offering protection to any European who might be persuaded to visit his dominions. His rule was severe, if not just, and it has all the prestige of secrecy. Even the Gerad Mohammad, even the Queen Dowager, are threatened with fetters if they offer uncalled-for advice. His principal occupation is spying his many stalwart cousins, indulging in vain fears of the English and the Turks, amassing treasure by commerce and cheating.

"The Amir Ahmed is alive to the fact that some State should hedge in a Prince. Neither weapons nor rosaries are allowed in his presence; a chamberlain's robe acts as spittoon; whenever anything is given to or taken from him his hand must be kissed; even on horseback two attendants fan him with the hems of their garments. Except when engaged on the Haronic visits, which he, like his father, pays to the streets and byways at night, he is always surrounded by a strong body-guard. He rides to Mosque escorted by a dozen horsemen, and a score of footmen with guns and whips precede him; by his side walks an officer, shading him with a huge and heavily fringed red-satin umbrella—from India to Abyssinia the sign of princely dignity. Even at his prayers, two or three chosen matchlockmen stand over him with lighted fusees. When he rides forth in public, he is escorted by a party of fifty men; the running footmen crack their whips and shout, 'Let! Let!' (Go! go!), and the citizens avoid stripes by retreating into the nearest house, or running into another street.

"Immediately on our arrival we were called upon by all sorts of Arabs; they were very civil to me at first, but when the Amir ceased to send for me, just as at civilized Courts, they prudently cut me. The moment the Amir sent for me, my Habr Awal enemies, seeing the tide of fortune setting in my favour, changed their tactics, and proposed themselves as my escort to return to Berberah, which I politely refused. They did me all the harm they could, but my good star triumphed. After one day's rest, I was summoned to wait upon the Gerad Mohammad, who was Prime Minister. Sword in hand, and, followed by my two attendants, I walked to the Palace, and found him surrounded by six counsellors; they were eating *jat*, which has somewhat the effect of hashish.

He sat me by his right hand on the dais, where I ate *jat*, being, fortunately, used to these things, and fingered the rosary. Then followed prayer, and then a theological discussion, in which, fortunately, I was able to distinguish myself. My theology won general approbation and kind glances from the elders. In a very short time I was sent for by the Amir, and this time was allowed to approach the outer door with covered feet. I entered as ceremoniously as before, and the prince motioned me to sit near the Gerad, on a Persian rug to the right of the throne; my attendants on humble mats at a greater distance. After sundry inquiries of what was going on at Aden, the Resident's letter was suddenly produced by the Amir, who bade me explain its contents, and wished to know if it was my intention to buy and sell at Harar. I replied, 'We are neither buyers nor sellers; we have become your guests to pay our respects to the Amir, who may Allah preserve, and that the friendship between the two Powers may endure.' The Amir was pleased, and I therefore ventured to hope that the Prince would soon permit me to return, as the air of Harar was too dry for me, and that we were in danger of small-pox, then raging in the town, and through the Gerad, the Amir said, 'The reply will be vouchsafed,' and the interview was over.

"I sent my salaam to one of the Ulema, Shaykh Jámi; he accepted the excuse of health and came to see me. He was remarkably well read in the religious sciences, and a great man at Mecca, with much influence with the Sultan, and employed on political Missions amongst the Chiefs. He started with the intention of winning the Crown of Glory by murdering the British Resident at Aden, but he was so struck with the order of justice of our rule, he offered El Islam to that officer, who received it so urbanely, that the simple Eastern, instead of cutting the Kaffir's throat, began to pray fervently for his conversion. We were kindly looked upon by a sick and decrepid eunuch, named Sultán. I used to spend my evenings preaching to the Gallas.

The Gerad Mohammad was now worked upon by the Habr Awal, my enemies, to make inquiries about me, and one of the Ayyal Gedíd clan came up and reported that three brothers * had landed in the Somal country, that two of them were anxiously waiting at Berberah the return of the fourth from Harar, and that, though dressed like Moslems, they were really English spies in Government employ, and orders were issued for cutting off Caravans. We, however, were summoned to the Gerad's, where, fortunately for me, I found him suffering badly from bronchitis. I saw my chance. I related to him all its symptoms, and told him that if I could only get down to Aden, I could send him all the right remedies, with directions. He clung to the hope of escaping his sufferings, and begged me to lose no time. Presently the Amir sent for him, and in a few minutes I was sent for alone. A long conversation ensued about the state of Aden, of Zayla, of Berberah, and of Stamboul. The Chief put a variety of questions about Arabia, and every object there; the answer was that the necessity of commerce, confined us

* "Speke, Herne, and Stroyan."

to the gloomy rock Aden. He used some obliging expressions about desiring our friendship, and having considerable respect for a people who built, he understood, large ships. I took the opportunity of praising Harar in cautious phrase, and especially of regretting that its coffee was not better known amongst the Franks. The small wizen-faced man smiled, as Moslems say, the smile of Umar; * seeing his brow relax for the first time, I told him that, being now restored to health, we requested his commands for Aden. He signified consent with a nod, and the Gerad, with many compliments, gave me a letter addressed to the Political Resident, and requested me to take charge of a mule as a present. I then arose, recited a short prayer, the gist of which was that the Amir's days and reign might be long in the land, and that the faces of his foes might be blackened here and hereafter, bent over his hand, and retired. Returning to the Gerad's levée-hut, I saw by the countenances of my two attendants that they were not a little anxious about the interview, and comforted them with the whispered word, 'Achha!' (all right!)

"Presently appeared the Gerad, accompanied by two men, who brought my servants' arms, and the revolver which I had sent to the prince. This was a *contretemps.* It was clearly impossible to take back the present; besides which, I suspected some *finesse* to discover my feelings towards him. The other course would ensure delay. I told the Gerad that the weapon was intended especially to preserve the Amir's life, and, for further effect, snapped caps in rapid succession, to the infinite terror of the august company. The Minister returned to his Master, and soon brought back the information that, after a day or two, another mule should be given to me. With suitable acknowledgments we arose, blessed the Gerad, bade adieu to the assembly, and departed joyful; the Hammal, in his glee, speaking broken English, even in the Amir's courtyard.

"Shaykh Jámi was rendered joyful by the news he told me when I arrived; he had been informed that in the Town was a man who had brought down the birds from heaven, and the citizens had been thrown into a great excitement by my probable intentions. One of the principal Ulema, and a distinguished Haji, had been dreaming dreams in my favour, and sent their salaams. My long residence in the East had made me grateful to the learned, whose influence over the people, when unbiased by bigotry, is for the good. On January 11th, I was sent for by the Gerad, and given the second mule; he begged me not to forget his remedies as soon as I reached Aden, and I told him that I would start on the morrow. I scarcely had got in, when there were heavy showers and thunder. When I got up to mount early on Friday morning, of course a mule had strayed; then Shaykh Jámi would not go till Monday. Now, as I had been absent from my goods and chattels a whole fortnight, as the people at Harar are immensely fickle, as you never know the moment that the Amir may change his mind, for all African Cities are prisons on a large scale—you enter by your own will, but you

* "Because it was reported that he had never smiled but once."

leave by another's—I longed to start; however, the storms warned me to be patient, and I deferred my departure till next morning.

"Long before dawn on Saturday, January 13th, the mules were saddled, bridled, and charged with our scanty luggage. After a hasty breakfast we shook hands with old Sultán, the eunuch, mounted and pricked through the desert streets. Suddenly my weakness and sickness left me—so potent a drug is joy—and, as we passed the Gates, loudly salaaming to the warders, who were crouching over the fire inside, a weight of care and anxiety fell from me like a cloak of lead.

"Yet I had time, on the top of my mule, for musing upon how melancholy a thing is Success. Whilst failure inspirits a man, attainment reads the sad prosy lesson that all our glories

'Are shadows, not substantial things.'

Truly said the *sayer*, 'Disappointment is the salt of life'—a salutary bitter which strengthens the mind for fresh exertion, and gives a double value to the prize.

"This shade of melancholy soon passed away. We made in a direct line for Kondura. At one p.m. we safely threaded the Gallas' pass, and about an hour afterwards we exclaimed, 'Alhamdulillah,' at the sight of Sagharrah and the distant Marar Prairie. Entering the village, we discharged our firearms. The men gave cordial *poignées de mains*—some danced with joy to see us return alive; they had heard of our being imprisoned, bastinadoed, slaughtered; they swore that the Gerad was raising an army to rescue or revenge us—in fact, had we been their kinsmen, more excitement could not have been displayed. Lastly, in true humility, crept forward the "End of Time," who, as he kissed my hand, was upon the point of tears.

"A pleasant evening was spent in recounting our perils, as travellers will do, and complimenting one another upon the power of our star.

"At eight next morning we rode to Wilensi, and as we approached, all the villagers and wayfarers inquired if we were the party that had been put to death by the Amir of Harar.

"Loud congratulations and shouts of joy awaited our arrival. The Kalendar was in a paroxysm of delight; both Shehrazade and Deenarzade were affected with giggling and what might be blushing. We reviewed our property and found that the One-eyed had been a faithful steward, so faithful indeed that he had wellnigh starved the two women. Presently appeared the Gerad and his sons, bringing with them my books; the former was at once invested with a gaudy Abyssinian *tobe* of many colours, in which he sallied forth from the cottage the admired of all admirers. The pretty wife, Sudíyah, and the good Khayrah were made happy by sundry gifts of huge Birmingham ear-rings, brooches and bracelets, scissors, needles, and thread. The evening as usual ended in a feast.

"We were obliged to halt a week at Wilensi to feed, for both man and beast to lay in a stock of strength for the long desert march before us, to buy onions, tobacco, spices, wooden platters, and a sort of bread called *karanji*. Here I made my grammar and vocabulary of the Harari tongue, under the supervision of Mad Said and Ali the poet, a Somali educated at Harar, who knew Arabic, Somali, Galla, and Harar languages.

On January 21st I wanted to start, but Shaykh Jami appeared with all the incurables of the country. Nobody can form an idea of the difficulties that an Eastern will put in your way when you want to start, and unfortunately in nine cases out of ten the ruses they have resort to, *do* prevent your starting. Now, in this case, I decided that talismans were the best and safest medicines in these mountains. The Shaykh doubted them, but when I exhibited my diploma as a Master-Sufi, a new light broke in upon him and his attendants. 'Verily he hath declared himself this day!' whispered each to his neighbour, sorely mystified. Shaykh Jami carefully inspected the document, raised it reverently to his forehead, muttered prayers, and owned himself my pupil.

Now, however, all my followers had got some reason why they could not go, so I sauntered out alone, attended only by the Hammal, and, in spite of the Chief summoning me to halt, I took an abrupt leave and went off, and entered the Marar Prairie with pleasure. The truants joined us later on, and we met a party whose Chief, a Somali, expressed astonishment at our escaping from Harar, told us that the Berberi were incensed with us for leaving the direct road, advised us to push on that night, to 'ware the bush, whence the Midjans would use their poisoned arrows. The Berberi had offered a hundred cows for our person dead or alive. Then my party sat down to debate; they palavered for three hours. They said that the camels could not walk, that the cold of the prairies was death to man, till darkness came on. Experience had taught me that it was waste of time to debate overnight about dangers to be faced next day, so I ate my dates, drank my milk, and lay down to enjoy sweet sleep in the tranquil silence of the desert. Although I did not know it till after my return from Berberah, Gerad Adan was my greatest danger. If his plotting had succeeded it would have cost him dear, but would also have proved fatal to me. The 23rd of January passed in the same manner, and the explanation I had with my men was, that on the morrow at dawn I would cross the Marar Prairie by myself; and we started at dawn on the 24th, giving a wide berth to the Berberis, whose camp-fires were quite visible at a distance. As we were about to enter the lands of the Habr Awal, our enemies, a week would elapse before we could get protection. We had resolved to reach the coast within the fortnight, instead of which a month's march was in prospect. Suddenly Beuh appeared, and I proposed to him that he should escort the Caravans to Zayla, and that I and the two others who had accompanied me to Harar would mount our mules, only carrying arms and provisions for four days: I pushed through the land of our enemies the Habr Awal. In the land we were to traverse every man's spear would be against us, so I chose the desert roads, and carefully avoided all the kraals.

It was with serious apprehension that I pocketed all my remaining provisions—five biscuits, a few limes, a few lumps of sugar. Any accident to our mules, any delay would starve us; we were traversing a desert where no one would sell us meat or milk, and only one water-bottle in the whole party.

We rode thirty-five miles over awful tracks. Our toil was rendered doubly dreadful by the Eastern traveller's dread—the demon of Thirst rode like Care behind us—for twenty-four hours we did not taste water, the sun parched our brains, the mirage mocked us at every turn, and the effect was a species of monomania. As I jogged along with eyes closed against the fiery air, no image unconnected with the want suggested itself. Water ever lay before me, water lying deep in the shady well, water in streams bubbling icy from the rock, water in pellucid lakes inviting me to plunge and revel in their treasures. Now an Indian cloud was showering upon me fluid more precious than molten pearl, then an invisible hand offered a bowl for which the mortal part would gladly have bartered years of life. Then—drear contrast!—I opened my eyes to a heat-reeking plain, and a sky of that eternal metallic blue so lovely to painter and poet, so blank and death-like to us, whose χάλον was tempest, rain-storm, and the huge purple nimbus. I tried to talk—it was in vain; to sing—in vain; vainly to think; every idea was bound up in one subject—water.*

"As a rule, twelve hours without water in the desert during hot weather kill a man. We had another frightful journey to the next water. I never suffered severely from thirst but on this expedition; probably it was in consequence of being at the time but in weak health so soon after Mecca. A few more hours and the little party would have been food for the desert beasts. We were saved by a bird. When we had been thirty-six hours without water we could go no further, and we were prepared to die the worst of all deaths. The short twilight of the tropics was drawing in, I looked up and saw a *katta*, or sand-grouse, with its pigeon-like flight, making for the nearer hills. These birds must drink at least once a day, and generally towards evening, when they are safe to carry water in their bills to their young. I cried out, 'See, the *katta!* the *katta!*' All revived at once, took heart, and followed the bird, which suddenly plunged down about a hundred yards away, showing us a charming spring, a little shaft of water, about two feet in diameter, in a margin of green. We jumped from our saddles, and men and beasts plunged their heads into the water and drank till they could drink no more. I have never since shot a *katta*.

"With unspeakable delight, after another thirty hours, we saw in the distance a patch of lively green: our animals scented the blessing from afar, they raised their drooping ears, and started with us at

* I often thought Grant Allen, in the third volume of "The Devil's Die," drew his account of the journey of Mohammed Ali and Ivan Royle from Eagle City through the desert to Carthage on the edge of the desert from Richard's journey from Harar; it is so like it—but he told me he did not.—I. B.

a canter, till, turning a corner, we suddenly sighted sundry little wells. To spring from the saddle, to race with our mules, who now feared not the crumbling sides of the pits, to throw ourselves into the muddy pools, to drink a long slow draught, and to dash the water over our burning faces, took less time to do than to recount. A calmer inspection showed a necessity for caution; the surface was alive with tadpoles and insects: prudence, however, had little power at that time—we drank, and drank, and then drank again. As our mules had fallen with avidity upon the grass, I proposed to pass a few hours near the wells. My companions, however, pleading the old fear of lions, led the way before dark to a deserted kraal upon a neighbouring hill. We had marched this time about thirty hours *eastward*, and had entered a safe country belonging to the Bahgoba, our guide's clan.

"There is nothing so dreadful as crossing a country full of blocks and boulders piled upon one another in rugged steps, and it was such a ravine, the Splügen of Somali-land, that we had to dismount. To a laden camel it is almost impossible; the best-fed horses, mules, or asses, having to perform the work of goats instead of their own, are worn out by it after a few hours; and this was what I and my party had to do, and often the boulders were covered with thorns two inches long, tipped with wooden points as sharp as a needle. After three days of hard travelling in this way we saw the face of man—some shepherds, who fled at our approach. We then followed an undulating growth of parched grass, shaping our course for Jebel Almis, to sailors the chief landmark of this coast, and for a certain thin blue stripe on the far horizon,—the sea,—upon which we gazed with gladdened eyes. That night we arrived at a kraal, unsaddled, and began to make ourselves comfortable, when we found we had fallen upon the Ayyal Shirdon, our bitterest enemies. They asked, 'What tribe be ye?' I boldly answered, 'Of Habr Gerhagis.' Thereupon ensued a war of words; they rudely insisted on knowing what had taken us to Harar, when a warrior armed with two spears came forward, recognized the 'End of Time,' and they retired but spoke of fighting. So we made ready with our weapons and bade them come on; but while they were considering, we saddled our mules and rode off. We stopped at three villages, and the Hammal failed to obtain even a drop of water from his relations. It was most distressful, as men and beasts were faint from thirst, so I determined to push forward for water that night. Many times the animals stopped,—a mute hint that they could go no further;—but *I* pushed on, and the rest had learned to follow without a word. The moon arose, and still we tottered on. About midnight—delightful sound!—the murmur of the distant sea. Revived by the music, we pushed on more cheerily. At three in the morning we found some holes which supplied us with bitter water, truly delicious after fifteen hours' thirst. Repeated draughts of this element, and coarse stubbly grass, saved us and our mules. Rain came on, but we slept like the dead. At six, we resumed our march, going slowly along the seacoast, and at noon we were able to sit on the sands and bathe in the sea. Our beasts could hardly move, and slippery mud added to their troubles. At three p.m. we again got a patch of grass, and halted the animals to feed; and a mile further some wells, where we again rested them, watered them, finished our last mouthful of food, and prepared for a long night march.

"We managed to pass all our enemies in the dark, and they cursed the star that had enabled us to slip unhurt through their hands. I was obliged to call a halt within four miles of Berberah; the animals could not move, neither could the men, except the Hammal and I, and they all fell fast asleep on the stones. As soon as we could go on, a long dark line appeared upon the sandy horizon, the silhouettes of shipping showing against sea and sky. A cry of joy burst from every mouth. 'Cheer, boys, cheer! our toils here touch their end.' The 'End of Time' still whispered anxiously lest enemies might arise; we wound slowly and cautiously round the southern portion of the sleeping town, through bone-heaps, and jackals tearing their unsavoury prey, straight into the quarter of the Ayyal Gedíd, our protectors. Anxiously I inquired if my comrades had left Berberah, and heard with delight that they were there. It was two o'clock in the morning, and we had marched forty miles.

"I dismounted at the huts where my comrades were living. A glad welcome, a dish of rice, and a glass of strong waters made amends for past privations and fatigue. The servants and the wretched mules were duly provided for, and I fell asleep, conscious of having performed a feat which, like a certain ride to York, will live in local annals for many and many a year.

"Great fatigue is seldom followed by long sleep. Soon after sunrise I woke, hearing loud voices, seeing masses of black faces, and tawny wigs. The Berberah people, who had been informed of our five-day ride, swore that the thing was impossible, that we *had* never, *could* never have been near Harar, but were astonished when they found it was true. I then proceeded to inspect my attendants and cattle. The former were delighted, having acquitted themselves of their trust; the poor mules were by no means so easily restored. Their backs were cut to the bone by the saddle, their heads drooped sadly, their hams showed dread marks of the spear-point. I directed them to be washed in the sea, to be dressed with cold-water bandages, and copiously fed. Through a broad gap, called Duss Malablay, appear in fine weather the granite walls of Wagar and Gulays, 5700 feet above the level of the sea. Lieutenant Herne found it would make an admirable sanitarium. The emporium of Eastern Africa has a salubrious climate, abundance of sweet water, a mild monsoon, a fine open country, an excellent harbour, a highly productive soil, is the meeting-place of commerce, has few rivals, and for half the money wasted on Aden, might have been covered with houses, gardens, and trees. My companions and I, after a day's rest, made some excursions. We had a few difficulties about our *Abans*, or protectors. We did not choose to be dictated to, so there was a general council of the elders. It took place upon the shore, each Chief forming a semicircle with his followers, all squatting on the sand, with shield and spear planted upright in the ground. entered the circle sword in hand, and sat down in their midst. After much murmuring had gone on the Chief asked, in a loud voice, 'Who is thy protector?' The reply was, 'Burhale Nuh,' followed by an Arabic speech as long as an average sermon, and then, shouldering my blade, I left the circle abruptly. It was a success; they held a peace conference, and the olive waved over the braves of Berberah. On the 5th of February, 1855, I left my comrades *pro tem.*, and went on board *El Kásab*, or the Reed, the ill-omened name of our cranky craft, and took with me the Hammal, Long Guled, and the 'End of Time,' who were in danger, and rejoiced at leaving Berberah with sound skins. I met with opposition at landing. I could not risk a quarrel so near Berberah, and was returning to moralize on the fate of Burckhardt—after a successful pilgrimage refused admittance to Aaron's tomb at Sinai—when a Bedawin ran to tell us that we might wander where we pleased.

"The captain of the *Reed* drew off a great deal further than I ordered, and when I went down to go on board, the vessel was a mere speck upon the sea horizon. He managed to cast anchor at last, after driving his crazy craft through a bad sea. I stood on the shore making signs for a canoe, but he did not choose to see me till about one p.m. As soon as I found myself on quarter-deck—

"'Dawwír el farmán!" (Shift the yard!) I shouted, with a voice of thunder.

"The answer was a general hubbub. 'He surely will not sail in a sea like this?' asked the trembling captain of my companions.

"'He will!' sententiously quoth the Hammal, with a Burleigh nod.

"'It blows wind,' remonstrated the *rais.*

"'And if it blew fire?' asked the Hammal, with the air *goguenard*, meaning that from the calamity of Frankish obstinacy there was no refuge.

"A kind of death-wail rose, during which, to hide untimely laughter, I retreated to a large drawer in the stern of the vessel, called a cabin. There my ears could distinguish the loud entreaties of the crew, vainly urging my attendants to propose a day's delay. Then one of the garrison, accompanied, by the Captain, who shook as with fever, resolved to act forlorn hope, and bring a *feu d'enfer* of phrases to bear upon the Frank's hard brain. Scarcely, however, had the head of the sentence been delivered, before he was playfully upraised by his bushy hair and a handle somewhat more substantial, carried out of the cabin, and thrown, like a bag of biscuit, on the deck.

"The case was hopeless. All strangers plunged into the sea—the popular way of landing in East Africa—the anchor was weighed, the ton of sail shaken out, and the *Reed* began to dip and rise in the yeasty sea laboriously, as an alderman dancing a polka.

"For the first time in my life I had the satisfaction of seeing the Somal unable to eat—unable to eat mutton!! In sea-sickness and needless terror, the Captain, crew, and passengers abandoned to us all the baked sheep, which we three, not being believers in the Evil Eye, ate from head to trotters with especial pleasure. That night the waves broke over us. The 'End of Time' occupied himself in roaring certain orisons which are reputed to calm stormy seas; he desisted only when Long Guled pointed out that a wilder gust seemed to follow, as in derision, each more emphatic period. The Captain, a noted reprobate, renowned on shore for his knowledge of erotic verse and admiration of the fair sex, prayed with fervour; he was joined by several of the crew, who apparently found the charm of novelty in the edifying exercise. About midnight a *sultán el bahr*, or sea-King—a species of whale—appeared close to our counter; and as these animals are famous for upsetting vessels in waggishness, the sight elicited a yell of terror, and a chorus of religious exclamations.

"On the morning of Friday, the 9th of February, 1855, we hove in sight of Jebel Shamsan, the loftiest peak on the Aden crater. And ere evening fell, I had the pleasure of seeing the faces of friends and comrades once more.

"If I had 'let well alone,' I should have done well; but I wanted to make a new expedition Nile-wards, *viâ* Harar, on a larger and more imposing scale. For that I went back to Aden. On April 7th, 1855, I returned successful. Lieutenant King, Indian Navy, commanded the gunboat *Mahi*, and entered the harbour of Berberah with us on board. I was in command of a party of forty-two men, armed, and we established an agency, and selected the site of our camp in a place where we could have the protection of the gunboat; but the Commander of the schooner had orders to relieve another ship, and so could not remain and superintend the departure of the Expedition. It was the time after the Fair, and one might say that Berberah was empty, and that there was scarcely any one but ourselves. Our tents were pitched in one line—Stroyan's to the right, Herne and myself in the middle, and Speke on the left. The baggage was placed between our tents, the camels were in front, the horses and mules behind us. Two sentries all night were regularly relieved and visited by ourselves. We were very well received, and they listened with respectful attention to a letter, in which the Political Resident at Aden enjoined them to treat us with consideration and hospitality. We had purchased fifty-six camels; Ogadayn Caravan was anxious for our escort. If we had departed then, perhaps all would have been well; but we expected instruments and other necessaries by the mid-April mail from Europe. Three days afterwards, a craft from Aden came in with a dozen Somals, who wanted to accompany us, and fortunately I feasted the Commander and the crew, which caused them to remain. We little knew that our lives hung upon a thread, and that had the vessel departed, as she would otherwise have done, the night before the attack, nothing could have saved us. Between two and three a.m. of April 19th, there was a cry that the enemy was upon us, three hundred and fifty strong. Hearing a rush of men, like a stormy wind, I sprang up, and called for my sabre, and sent Herne to ascertain the force of the foray. Armed with a 'Colt,' he went to the rear and left of the camp, the direction of danger, collecting some of the guards—others having already disappeared—and fired two shots into the assailants. Then finding himself alone, he turned hastily towards the tent; in so doing, he was tripped up by the ropes, and, as he arose, a Somali appeared in the act of striking at him with a club. Herne fired, floored the man, and, rejoining me, declared that the enemy was in great force and the guard nowhere. Meanwhile, I had aroused Stroyan and Speke, who were sleeping in the extreme right and left tents. The former, it is presumed, arose to defend himself, but, as the sequel shows, we never saw him alive. Speke, awakened by the report of firearms, but supposing it to be the normal false alarm—a warning to plunderers—remained where he was; presently, hearing clubs rattling upon his tent, and feet shuffling around, he ran to my *rowtie*, which we prepared to defend as long as possible.

"The enemy swarmed like hornets, with shouts and screams, intending to terrify, and proving that overwhelming odds were against us. It was by no means easy to avoid in the shades of night the jobbing of javelins, and the long, heavy daggers thrown at our legs from under and through the opening of the tent. We three remained together; Herne knelt by my right, on my left was Speke guarding the entrance, I stood in the centre, having nothing but a sabre. The revolvers were used by my companions with deadly effect; unfortunately there was but one pair. When the fire was exhausted, Herne went to search for his powder-horn, and, that failing, to find some spears usually tied to the tent-pole. Whilst thus engaged, he saw a man breaking into the rear of our *rowtie*, and came back to inform me of the circumstance.

"At this time, about five minutes after the beginning of the affray, the tent had been almost beaten down—an Arab custom, with which we were all familiar—and had we been entangled in its folds, like mice in a trap, we should have been speared with unpleasant facility. I gave the word for escape, and sallied out, closely followed by Herne, with Speke in the rear. The prospect was not agreeable. About twenty men were kneeling and crouching at the tent entrance, whilst many dusky figures stood further off, or ran about shouting the war-cry, or with shouts and blows drove away our camels. Among the enemy were many of our friends and attendants; the coast being open to them, they naturally ran away, firing a few useless shots, and receiving a modicum of flesh-wounds.

"After breaking through the mob at the tent entrance, imagining that I saw the form of Stroyan lying upon the sand, I cut my way with my sabre towards it amongst dozens of Somal, whose war-clubs worked without mercy, whilst the Balyuz, who was violently pushing me out of the fray, rendered the strokes of my sabre uncertain. This individual was cool and collected. Though incapacitated by a sore right thumb from using the spear, he did not shun danger, and passed unhurt through the midst of the enemy.

His efforts, however, only illustrated the venerable adage, 'Defend me from my friends.' I mistook him in the dark and turned to cut him down; he cried out in alarm. The well-known voice stopped me, and that instant's hesitation allowed a spearman to step forward, and leave his javelin in my mouth, and retire before he could be punished. Escaping as by a miracle, I sought some support. Many of our Somal and servants lurking in the darkness offered to advance, but 'tailed off' to a man as we approached the foe. Presently the Balyuz reappeared, and led me towards the place where he believed my three comrades had taken refuge. I followed him, sending the only man that showed presence of mind, one Golab of the Yusuf tribe, to bring back the *Aynterad* craft from the Spit into the centre of the harbour. Again losing the Balyuz in the darkness, I spent the interval before dawn wandering in search of my comrades, and lying down when overpowered with faintness and pain. As the day broke, with my remaining strength I reached the head of the creek, was carried into the vessel, and persuaded the crew to arm themselves and visit the scene of our disasters.

"Meanwhile, Herne, who had closely followed me, fell back, using the butt-end of his discharged six-shooter upon the hard heads around him. In so doing he came upon a dozen men, who, though they loudly vociferated, 'Kill the Franks who are killing the Somal!' allowed him to pass uninjured.

"He then sought his comrades in the empty huts of the town, and at early dawn was joined by the Balyuz, who was similarly employed. When day broke, he also sent a negro to stop the native craft, which was apparently sailing out of the harbour, and in due time he came on board. With the exception of sundry stiff blows with the war-club, Herne had the fortune to escape unhurt.

"On the other hand, Speke's escape was in every way wonderful. Sallying from the tent, he levelled his 'Dean and Adams' close to an assailant's breast. The pistol refused to revolve. A sharp blow of a war-club upon the chest felled our comrade, who was in the rear and unseen. When he fell, two or three men sprang upon him, pinioned his hands behind, felt him for concealed weapons—an operation to which he submitted in some alarm—and led him towards the rear, as he supposed, to be slaughtered. There, Speke, who could scarcely breathe from the pain of the blow, asked a captor to tie his hands before instead of behind, and begged a drop of water to relieve his excruciating thirst. The savage defended him against a number of the Somal who came up threatening and brandishing their spears. He brought a cloth for the wounded man to lie upon, and lost no time in procuring a draught of water.

"Speke remained upon the ground till dawn. During the interval he witnessed the war-dance of the savages—a scene striking in the extreme; the tallest and largest warriors marching with the deepest and most solemn tones, the song of thanksgiving. At a little distance the grey uncertain light disclosed four or five men lying desperately hurt, whilst their kinsmen kneaded their limbs, pouring water upon their wounds, and placing lumps of dates in their stiffening hands.* As day broke, the division of plunder caused angry passions to rise. The dead and dying were abandoned. One party made a rush upon the cattle, and with shouts and yells drove them off towards the wilds. Some loaded themselves with goods; others fought over pieces of cloth, which they tore with hand and dagger; whilst the disappointed, vociferating with rage, struck at one another and brandished their spears. More than once during these scenes a panic seized them; they moved off in a body to some distance; and there is little doubt that, had our guard struck one blow, we might still have won the day.

"Speke's captor went to seek his own portion of the spoil, when a Somal came up and asked in Hindostani what business the Frank had in their country, and added that he would kill him if a Christian, but spare the life of a brother Moslem. The wounded man replied that he was going to Zanzibar, that he was still a Nazarene, and therefore that the work had better be done at once. The savage laughed, and passed on. He was succeeded by a second, who, equally compassionate, whirled a sword round his head, twice pretending to strike, but returning to the plunder without doing damage. Presently came another manner of assailant. Speke, who had extricated his hands, caught the spear levelled at his breast, but received at the same moment a blow which, paralyzing his arm, caused him to lose his hold. In defending his heart from a succession of thrusts, he received severe wounds on the back of his hand, his right shoulder, and his left thigh. Pausing a little, the wretch crossed to the other side, and suddenly passed his spear clean through the right leg of the wounded man. The latter, 'smelling death,' then leapt up, and, taking advantage of his assailant's terror, rushed headlong towards the sea. Looking behind, he avoided the javelin hurled at his back, and had the good fortune to run, without further accident, the gauntlet of a score of missiles. When pursuit was discontinued, he sat down, faint from loss of blood, upon a sandhill. Recovering strength by a few minutes' rest, he staggered on to the town, where some old women directed him to us. Then, pursuing his way, he fell in with the party sent to seek him, and by their aid reached the craft, having walked and run at least three miles, after receiving eleven wounds, two of which had pierced his thighs. A touching lesson how difficult it is to kill a man in sound health! † My difficulty was, with my comrades' aid, to extract the javelin which transfixed my jaws. It destroyed my palate and four good back teeth, and left wounds on my two cheeks.

* "The Somal place dates in the hands of the fallen to ascertain the extent of injury. He that cannot eat that delicacy is justly decided to be *in articulo.*"

† "In less than a month after receiving such injuries, Speke was on his way to England. He never felt the least inconvenience from the wounds, which closed up like indiarubber."

"When we three survivors had reached the craft, Yusuf, the Captain, armed his men with muskets and spears, landed them near the camp, and ascertained that the enemy, expecting a fresh attack, had fled, carrying away our cloth, tobacco, swords, and other weapons. The corpse of Stroyan was then brought on board. Our lamented comrade was already stark and cold. A spear had traversed his heart, another had pierced his abdomen, and a frightful gash, apparently of a sword, had opened the upper part of his forehead. The body had been bruised with war-clubs, and the thighs showed marks of violence after death. This was the severest affliction that befell us. We had lived together like brothers. Stroyan was a universal favourite, and his sterling qualities of manly courage, physical endurance, and steady perseverance had augured for him a bright career, thus prematurely cut off. Truly melancholy to us was the contrast between the evening when he sat with us full of life and spirits, and the morning when we saw amongst us a livid corpse.

"We had hoped to preserve the remains of our friend for interment at Aden. But so rapid were the effects of exposure that we were compelled most reluctantly, on the morning of the 20th of April, to commit them to the deep, Herne reading the Funeral Service.

"Then, with heavy hearts, we set sail for the near Arabian shore, and, after a tedious two days, carried our friends the news of the unexpected disaster.

"RICHARD F. BURTON."

When Speke wrote the manuscript of this affair, and in *Blackwood*, and also in his book on the "Sources of the Nile," he said that *he* was the Head of the Expedition; *he* had given the order for the night, it was before *him* the spies were brought, *he* was the first to turn out, and no one but *he* had the courage to defend himself. It is hardly worth while to contradict it. It is obvious that this expedition could only be commanded by a man who knew Arabic and some of the other languages, of which he was perfectly ignorant.

So the results of this Expedition, to sum up in short, were, that they barely escaped being caught like mice in a trap, by having their tents thrown down upon them, the four fought bravely against three hundred and fifty Bedawi, poor Stroyan was killed, Herne was untouched, Richard and Speke were desperately wounded, though they all cut their way gallantly through the enemy. Poor Speke had eleven wounds, and Richard, with a lance transfixing his jaws, which carried away four back teeth and part of his palate, wandered up and down the coast suffering from his wounds, fever, hunger, and thirst consequent on the wounds; but they met, they carried off the dead body of their comrade, and were taken on board the native dhow or boat, which the fortunate accident of Richard's hospitality had retained there just half an hour, long enough to save them, and the natives sacked their property. They were so badly wounded, he had to return to England, and here his wounds soon healed and he picked up health. He rendered an account of his explorations before the Royal Geographical Society.* After a month's rest, he obtained leave to volunteer for the Crimea. Here I would rather give his own original manuscript word for word, because it is so fresh, and, in a few pages, gives a better insight into outspoken truth than many other large volumes.

* He began to prepare his public account of Harar in "First Footsteps in East Africa," one large volume, which, however, did not see the light till 1856. It might have been called "Harar," to distinguish it from the trial trip previous to the Great Lake Expedition.

CHAPTER X.

WITH BEATSON'S HORSE.

THE Crimean War is an affair of the last generation; thirty years' distance has given it a certain perspective, and assigned its proper rank and place in the panorama of the nineteenth century. Estimates of its importance, of course, vary; while one man would vindicate its *péripéties* on the plea of being the first genuine attempt to develop the European Concert, to create an International tribunal for the discouragement of the modern revival of *La Force prime le droit*, and for the protection of the weak minority, others, like myself, look upon it as an unmitigated evil to England. It showed up all her characteristic unreadiness, all her defects of organization. It proved that she could not *then* produce a single great *sailor* or *soldier*. It washed her dirty linen in public, to the disgust and contempt of Europe; and, lastly, it taught her the wholly novel and unpleasant lesson of "playing second fiddle" (as the phrase is) to France. Considered with regard to her foreign affairs, this disastrous blunder lost us for ever the affection of Russia, our oldest and often our only friend amongst the continentals of Europe. It barred the inevitable growth of the northern Colossus in a southern direction, and encouraged her mighty spread to the south-east, India-wards, at the same time doubling her extent by the absorption of Turcomania.

The causes which led to the war are manifold enough. Some are trivial enough, like the indiscreet revelation of Czar Nicholas' private talk, talk anent the "Sick Man," by the undiplomatic indiscretion of the diplomatist, Sir Hamilton Seymour. Others are vital, especially the weariness caused by a long sleep of peace which made England, at once the most unmilitary and the most fighting of peoples, "spoil for a row." The belief in the wretched Turk's power of recuperation and even of progress had been diffused by such authorities as Lords Palmerston and Stratford de Redcliffe, and, *en route* to the war, I often heard, to my disgust, British officers exclaim, "If there ever be a justifiable campaign (in support of the unspeakable Turk!) it is this."

Outside England, the main moving cause was our acute ally Louis Napoleon, whose ambition was to figure arm-in-arm in the field with the nation which annihilated his uncle. But he modestly proposed that France should supply the army, England the navy, an arrangement against which, even now, little can be said. Here, however, our jaunty statesman stepped in; Cupidon (Lord Palmerston), the man with the straw in his mouth, the persistent "Chaffer" of wiser men that appreciated the importance of the Fenian movement, the opposer of the Suez Canal,* the Minister who died one day and was forgotten the next, refused to give up the wreath of glory; and, upon the principle that one Englishman can fight three Frenchmen, sent an utterly inadequate force and enabled the French to "revenge Waterloo." French diplomatists were heavily backed against English; a nervous desire to preserve the *entente cordiale* made English Generals and Admirals (as at Alma and the bombardment of Sebastopol) put up with the jockeying and bullying measures of French officers. And the alliance ended not an hour too soon.

After French successes and our failures the *piou-piou* would cry aloud, "Malakoff—yes, yes; Redan—no, no;" whereto Tommy Atkins replied with a growl, "Waterloo, ye beggars!" And the English medal distributed to the *troupier* was pleasantly known as the "Médaille de Sauvetage." At the end of the disastrous year '56 England had come up smiling, after many a knock-down blow, and was ready to go in and win. But Louis Napoleon had obtained all *he* wanted, the war was becoming irksome to *his* fickle lieges; so an untimely peace was patched up, and England was left to pay the piper by the ever-increasing danger to India.

After the disastrous skirmish with the Somali at Berberah, it is no wonder that I returned to England on sick certificate, wounded and sorely discomfited. The Crimean War seemed to me some opportunity of recovering my spirits, and, as soon as my health permitted, I applied myself to the ungrateful task of volunteering. London then was in the liveliest state of excitement about the Crimean

---

* Here, however, "Pam" was in the right. He foresaw that if the Canal was once made, England would cling to Egypt, and never again have a Crimean War. He also appreciated the vast injury which would accrue to our Eastern monopoly. But he never would or could do anything *sérieusement*, and he would humbug his countrymen with such phrases as a "ditch in the sand." He knew as well as any man that the project was feasible, and yet he persuaded Admiral Spratt and poor Robert Stephenson to join in his little dodge. I lost his favour for ever by advocating the Canal, and by proposing to assist the emigration of Fenian emigrants, at the expense of that fatal humbug, the "Coffin Squadron" on the West Coast of Africa.

bungles, and the ladies pitilessly cut every officer who shirked his duty. So I read my paper about Harar before the Royal Geographical Society, and had the pleasure of being assured by an ancient gentleman, who had never *smelt* Africa, that when approaching the town Harar I had crossed a large and rapid river. It was in vain for me to reject this information. Every one seemed to think he must be right.*

Having obtained a few letters of introduction, and remembering that I had served under General James Simpson, at Sakhar, in Sind, I farewelled my friends, and my next step was to hurry through France, and to embark at Marseille on board one of the Messageries Impériales, bound for Constantinople. Very imperial was the demeanour of her officers. They took command of the passengers in most absolute style, and soundly wigged an Englishman, a Colonel, for opening a port, and shipping a sea. I was ashamed of my fellow-countryman's tameness, and yet I knew him to be a brave man. The ship's surgeon was Dr. Nicora, who afterwards became a friend of ours at Damascus, where he died attached to the French sanitary establishment; he talked much, and could not conceal his Anglophobia and hatred of the English. The only pleasant Frenchman on board was General MacMahon, then fresh from his Algerian campaign, and newly transferred to the Crimea, where his fortunes began.

It was a spring voyage on summer seas, and in due time we stared at the Golden Horn, and lodged ourselves at Missiri's Hôtel. The owner, who had been a dragoman to Eöthen, presumed upon his reputation, and made his house unpleasant. His wine, called "Tenedos," was atrocious, his cookery third rate, and his prices first rate. He sternly forbade "gambling," as he called card-playing, in his house, private as well as public; and we had periodically to kick downstairs the impudent dragomans who brought us his insolent messages. However, he had some excuse. Society at Missiri's was decidedly mixed; "bahaduring" was the rule, and the extra military swagger of the juveniles, assistant-surgeons, commissariats, and such genus, booted to the crupper, was a caution to veterans.

At Stamboul, I met Fred Wingfield, who was bound to Balaclava, as assistant under the unfortunate Mr. Commissary-General Filder, and had to congratulate myself upon my good fortune. We steamed together over the inhospitable Euxine, which showed me the reason for its sombre name.

The waters are in parts abnormally sweet, and they appear veiled

---

* How often one has to witness this in learned societies!—I. B.

in a dark vapour. Utterly unknown the blues, amethyst and turquoise, of that sea of beauty, the Mediterranean; the same is the case with the smaller Palus Meotis—Azoff. After the normal three days we sighted the Tauric Chersonese, the land of the Cimmerians and Scythians, the colony of the Greek, the conquest of Janghiz and the Khans of Turkey, and finally annexed by Russia after the wars, in which Charles XII. had taught the Slav to fight. We then made Balaclava (Balik-liwa, "Fish town"), with its dwarf fjord, dug out of dove-coloured limestones, and forming a little port stuffed to repletion with every manner of craft.

But it had greatly improved since October 17, 1854, when we first occupied it and formally opened the absurdly so-called siege, in which we were as often the besieged as the besiegers. Under a prodigiously fierce-looking provost-marshal, whose every look meant "cat," some cleanliness and discipline had been introduced amongst the suttlers and scoundrels who populated the townlet. Store-ships no longer crept in, reported cargoes which were worth their weight of gold to miserables, living

"On coffee raw and potted cat,"

and crept out again without breaking bulk. A decent road had been run through Kadikeui (Kazi's village) to camp and to the front, and men no longer sank ankle-deep in dust, or calf-deep in mud. In tact, England was, in the parlance of the "ring," getting her second wind, and was settling down to her work!

The unfortunate Lord Raglan, with his *courage antique*, his old-fashioned excess of courtesy, and his nervous dread of prejudicing the *entente cordiale* (!) between England and France, had lately died. He was in one point exactly the man *not* wanted. At his age and with one arm and many infirmities, he could not come up to the idea of Sir Charles Napier's model officer under the same circumstances, "eternally on horseback, with a sword in his hand, eating, sleeping, and drinking in the saddle."

But with more energy and fitness for command he might have deputed others to take his place. A good ordinary man, placed by the folly of his aristocratic friends in extraordinary circumstances, he was fated, temporarily, to ruin the prestige of England. He began by allowing himself to be ignobly tricked by that shallow intriguer, Maréchal de Saint Arnaud (*alias* Leroy). At Alma he was persuaded to take the worst and the most perilous position; his delicacy in not disturbing the last hours of his fellow Commander-in-Chief prevented his capturing the northern forts of Sebastopol, which Todleben openly declared were to be stormed by a *coup de main*; and allowed

Louis Napoleon, in the *Moniteur*, to blame England only for the *lâches* of the French, after the "last of European battles fought on the old lines," etc. At Inkermann, where the Guards defended themselves, like prehistoric men, with stones, Lord Raglan allowed his whole army to be surprised by the Russians, and to be saved by General Bosquet, with a host of Zouaves, Chasseurs, and Algerian rifles. No wonder that a Russian general declared, "The French saved the English at Inkermann as the Prussians did at Waterloo, and all Europe believed that France would conquer both Russia and England, the first by arms and the second by contrast." The "thin red line" of Balaclava allowed some national chauvinism, but that was all to be said in its favour, except that the gallantry of the men was to be equalled only by the incompetency of their Chiefs.

I passed a week with Wingfield and other friends, in and about Balaclava, in frequent visits to the front and camp. A favourite excursion from the latter was to the Monastery of St. George, classic ground where Iphigenia was saved from sacrifice. There was a noble view from this place, a foreground of goodly garden, a deep ravine clad with glorious trees, a system of cliffs and needles studding a sandy beach, and a lovely stretch of sparkling sea. No wonder that it had been chosen by a hermit, whose little hut of unhewn blocks lay hard by; he was a man upwards of sixty apparently, unknown to any one, and was fed by the black-robed monks. At Kadikeui also I made the acquaintance of good Mrs. Seacole, Jamaican by origin, who did so much for the comfort of invalids, and whom we afterwards met with lively pleasure at Panámá.

The British cavalry officers in the Crimea were still violently excited by reports that Lord Cardigan was about returning to command; and I heard more than one say, "We will not serve under him." And after a long experience of different opinions on the spot, I came to the following conclusion:—The unhappy charge of the "Six Hundred" was directly caused by my old friend, Captain Nolan of the 15th Hussars. An admirable officer and swordsman, bred in the gallant Austrian Cavalry of that day, he held, and advocated through life, the theory that mounted troops were an overmatch for infantry, and wanted only good leading to break squares and so forth. He was burning also to see the Lights outrival the Heavies, who, under General Scarlett, had charged down upon Russians said to be four times their number. Lord Lucan received an order to take a Russian 12-gun battery on the Causeway Heights, from General Liprandi, and he sent a verbal message by Nolan (General Airey's aide-de-camp) to his brother-in-law, Lord Cardigan, there being bad blood between the two.

Nolan, who was no friend to the hero of the Black Bottle, delivered the order disagreeably, and when Lord Cardigan showed some hesitation, roughly cut short the colloquy with, "You have your commands, my Lord," and prepared, as is the custom, to join in the charge. Hardly did it begin, than he was struck by a shot in the breast, and, as he did not fall at once, some asked Lord Cardigan where he was, and the reply came, "I saw him go off howling to the rear." During the fatal charge Lord Cardigan lost his head, and had that *moment de peur* to which the best soldiers are at times subject. He had been a fire-eater with the "Saw-handles," and the world expected too much of him; again, a man of ordinary pluck, he was placed in extraordinary circumstances, and how few there are who are *born* physically fearless. I can count those known to me on the fingers of my right hand. Believing that his force was literally mown down, he forgot his duty as a Commanding Officer, and instead of rallying the fugitives, he thought only of *sauve qui peut*. Galloping wildly to the rear, he rushed up to many a spectator, amongst others to my old Commander, General Beatson, nervously exclaiming, "You saw me at the guns?" and almost without awaiting a reply, rode on. Presently returning to England, he had not the sound sense and good taste to keep himself in the background; but received a kind of "ovation," as they call it, the ladies trying to secure hairs from his charger's tail by way of keepsake. Of course he never showed his face in the Crimea again. The tale of this ill-fated and unprofessional charge has now changed complexion. It is held up as a *beau fait d'armes*, despite the best bit of military criticism that ever fell from soldier's lips: "*c'est beau, mais ce n'est pas la guerre*," the words of General Bosquet, who saved the poor remnants of the Lights.

At head-quarters I called upon the Commander-in-Chief, General Simpson, whom years before I had found in charge of Sakhar, Upper Sind, held by all as wellnigh superannuated. He was supposed to be one of Lever's heroes, the gigantic Englishman who, during the occupation of Paris, broke the jaw of the duelling French officer, and spat down his throat. But age had told upon him, mentally as well as bodily, and he became a mere plaything in the hands of the French, especially of General Pélissier, the typical Algerian officer, who well knew when to browbeat and when to cajole. "Jimmy Simpson," as the poor old incapable was called, could do nothing for me, so I wrote officially at once to General Beatson, whom I had met at Boulogne, volunteering for the Irregular Cavalry then known as "Beatson's Horse," and I was delighted when my name appeared in orders. Returning to Constantinople,

I called upon the Embassy, then in summer quarters at Therapia, where they had spent an anxious time. The gallant Vukados, Russianized in Boutákoff, a Greek, who, in the nineteenth century, belonged to the heroic days of Thermopylæ and Marathon, and who was actually cheered by his enemies, with the little merchant-brig the *Wladimir*, alias *Arciduca Giovanni*, had shown himself a master-breaker-of-blockades, and might readily have taken into his head to pay the Ambassador a visit.

I looked forward to a welcome and found one; a man who had married my aunt, Robert Bagshaw, of Dovercourt, M.P., and quondam Calcutta merchant, who had saved from impending bankruptcy the house of Alexander and Co., to which Lady Stratford belonged.

Nothing quainter than the contrast between that highly respectable middle-class British peer and the extreme wildness of his surroundings. There were but two exceptions to the general rule of eccentricity—one, Lord Napier and Ettrick with his charming wife, and the other, Odo (popularly called "O don't!") Russell, who died as Lord Ampthill, Ambassador to Berlin. It was, by-the-by, no bad idea to appoint this high-bred and average talented English gentleman to the Court of Prince Bismarck, who disliked and despised nothing more thoroughly than the pert little political, the "Foreign Office pet" of modern days.

Foremost on the roll stood Alison, who died Minister at Teheran. He was in character much more a Greek than an Englishman, with a peculiar *finesse*, not to put too fine a point upon it, which made him highly qualified to deal with a certain type of Orientals. He knew Romaic perfectly, Turkish well, Persian a little, and a smattering of Arabic; so that, most unlike the average order of ignorant secretaries and attachés, he was able to do good work. He seemed to affect eccentricity, went out walking with a rough coat with a stick torn from a tree, whence his cognomen "The Bear with the Ragged Staff," and at his breakfasts visitors were unpleasantly astonished by a weight suddenly mounting their shoulders in the shape of a bear-cub with cold muzzle and ugly claws. He managed to hold his own with his testy and rageous old Chief, and the following legend was told of him:—"Damn your eyes, Mr. Alison, why was not that despatch sent?" "Damn your Excellency's eyes, it went this morning." Miladi also seemed to regard his comical figure with much favour. At Teheran he did little good, having become unhappily addicted to "tossing the elbow," which in an evil hour was reported home by my late friend Edward Eastwick; and he married a wealthy Levantine widow, who predeceased him. On this occasion he behaved uncommonly well, by returning all her large fortune to her family.

Next to him in office, and far higher in public esteem, ranked Percy Smythe, who succeeded his brother as Lord Strangford. Always of the weakest possible constitution, and so purblind that when reading he drew the paper across his nose, he fulfilled my idea of the typical linguist in the highest sense of the word; in fact, I never saw his equal except, perhaps, Professor Palmer, who was murdered by Arábi's orders almost within sight of Suez. Strangford seemed to take in a language through every pore, and to have time for all its niceties and eccentricities: for instance, he could speak Persian like a Shirázi, and also with the hideous drawl of a Hindostani. Yet his health sent him to bed every night immediately after dinner, for which he was more than once taken severely to task by Lady Stratford. He dressed in the seediest of black frock-coats, and was once mightily offended by a Turkish officer, who, overhearing us talking in Persian about "Tasáwaf" (Sufi-ism), joined in the conversation. He treated me with great regard because I was in the gorgeous Bashi-Bazouk uniform, blazing with gold, but looked upon Lord Strangford with such contempt that the latter exclaimed, "Hang the fellow! Can't he see that I am a gentleman?" I then told him that an Eastern judges *entirely* by dress, and that, as I was gorgeous, I was supposed to be the swell, and that, as his coat was very shabby, he was taken for a poor interpreter, probably my dragoman, and induced him to change for the future.

Some years afterwards, when he came to the title, he married Emily Beaufort, the result of reviewing her book "Syrian Shrines," etc. The choice was a mistake; she was far too like him in body and mind, with a strong dash of Israelitish blood, to be a success matrimonially speaking. Had he taken to wife a comely "crummy" little girl with blue eyes, barley-sugar hair, and the rest to match, he might have lived much longer. But the lady was an overmatch for him. When she was a little tot of twelve I saw her at the head of her father's, the hydrographer's table, laying down the law of professional matters to grey-headed Admirals. The last of the Staff was General Mansfield, an ill-conditioned and aggressive man, who held General Beatson in especial dislike for "prostitution of military rank." I have the most unpleasant remembrance of him; he afterwards became Commander-in-Chief of the Army in India, and his conduct in the "Affair of the Pickles" ought to have caused the recall of "Lord Sandhurst."

The Ambassador, whose name was at that time in every mouth,

was as remarkable in appearance as in character and career. When near sixty years of age he had still the clear-cut features and handsome face of his cousin, whom he loved to call the "Great Canning," and under whom, he, like Lord Palmerston, had began official life as private secretary. One of the cleanest and smoothest shaven of old men, he had a complexion white and red as a Westphalia ham, and his silver locks gave him a venerable and pleasing appearance; whilst his chin, that most characteristic feature, showed, in repose, manliness, and his "Kaiser-blue" eye was that of the traditional Madonna, only at excited moments the former tilted up with an expression of reckless obstinacy, and the latter flashed fire like an enraged feline's. The everyday look of the face was diplomatic, an icy impassibility (evidently put on, and made natural by long habit); but it changed to the scowl of a Medusa in fits of rage, and in joyous hours, such as sitting at dinner near the beautiful Lady George Paget—whose like I never saw—it was harmonious and genial as a day in spring.

Such was the personal appearance of the man who, together with the Emperor Nicholas, one equally, if not more remarkable, both in body and in mind, set the whole Western World in a blaze. I heard the origin of the blood-feud minutely told by the late Lord Clanricarde, one of the most charming *raconteurs* and original conversationalists ever met at a London dinner-table. Mr. Stratford Canning became, in early manhood, *Chargé d'affaires* at Constantinople, and took a prominent part in the Treaty of Bucharest, which the Czar found, to speak mildly, unpalatable. However, some years after, when the Embassy at St. Petersburg fell vacant, the Emperor refused to receive this *personâ ingrata*, and aroused susceptibilities which engendered a life-long hatred and a lust for revenge. Lastly, after the affair of 1848, the "Eltchi" persuaded his unhappy tool, the feeble-minded Sultan, Abd Al-Majid, whom he scolded and abused like a naughty schoolboy, now by threats then by promises, to refuse giving up the far-famed Hungarian refugees. This again became well known to all the world, and thus a private and personal pique between two elderly gentlemen of high degree, involved half Europe in hideous war, and was one of the worst disasters ever known to English history, by showing the world how England could truckle to France, and allow her to play the leading part.

Lord Stratford had, as often happens to shrewder men, completely mistaken his vocation. He told me more than once that his inclination was wholly to the life of a *littérateur*, and he showed himself unfit for taking any, save the humblest, *rôle* among the third-rates. He had lived his life in the East without learning a word of Turkish, Persian, or Arabic.

He wrote "poetry," and, amid the jeers of his staff, he affixed to a rustic seat near Therapia, where once Lady Stratford had sat, a copy of verses beginning—

"A wife, a mother to her children dear,"

with rhyme "rested here," and reason to match. After his final return home he printed a little volume of antiquated "verse or *worse*," with all the mediocrity which the gods and the columns disallow, and which would hardly have found admittance to the poet's corner of a country paper. His last performance in this line was a booklet entitled, "Why I am a Christian" (he of all men!), which provoked a shout of laughter amongst his friends. They owned that, mentally, he was a fair modern Achilles—

"Impiger, iracundus, inexorabilis acer;"

but of his "Christianity," the popular saying was, "He is a Christian, and he never forgives." His characteristic was vindictiveness; he could not forget (and here he was right), but also he could not forgive (and here he was wrong). One instance: he tried to hunt out of the service Grenville Murray, whose "Roving Englishman" probably owed much of its charm to Dickens's staff in *Household Words*. Yet Murray, despite all his faults, was a capable man, and a Government more elastic and far-seeing and less "respectable" than that of England, would have greatly profited by his services. Lord Stratford could not endure badinage, he had no sense for and of humour; witness the scene between him and Louis Napoleon's Ambassador, General Baraguay d'Hilliers, recorded by Mr. Consul Skene in his "Personal Reminiscences." He abhorred difference of opinion, and was furious with me for assuring him that "Habash" and "Abyssinia" are by no means equivalent and synonymous terms; he had been enlightening the "Porte" with information that Turkey had never held a foot of ground in "Habash," when the Turk, as my visit to Harar showed, had been an occupant, well hated, as he was well known. And when in a rage he was not pleasant; his eyes flashed fury, his venerable locks seemed to rise like the quills of a fretful porcupine, he would rush round the room like a lean maniac using frightful language—in fact, "langwidge," as the sailor hath it—with his old dressing-gown working hard to keep pace with him, and when the fit was at its worst, he would shake his fist in the offender's face.

The famous Ambassador struck me as a weak, stiff-necked, and violent old man, whose strength physically was in his obstinate chin, together with a "pursed-up mouth and beak in a pet," and morally in an exaggerated "respectability," iron-bound prejudices, and profound self-esteem. He had also a firm respect for rank and the divine right of Kings; witness his rage, when the young naval lieutenant, Prince of Leiningen, was ordered by a superior officer to "swab decks." He lived long enough to repent the last step of his official life. After peace was concluded, a visit to the Crimea greatly disgusted him. With a kind of bastard repentance, he quoted John Bright and the Peace Party in his sorrow at having brought about a Campaign whose horrors contrasted so miserably with its promised advantages.

In the next Russian-Turkish War he remembered that some ten thousand English lives and £80,000,000 had been sacrificed to humble Russia, whose genius and heroism had raised her so high in the opinion of Europe, only to serve the selfish ends of Louis Napoleon, to set up Turkey and the Sultan ("Humpty-dumpty," who refused to be set up), and to humour the grudges of two rancorous old men. So he carefully preached non-intervention to England. He took his seat in the House of Lords, but spoke little, and when he spoke he mostly broke down. Of his literary failures I have already spoken. Yet this was the "Great Eltchi" of Eöthen, a man who gained a prodigious name in Europe, chiefly by living out of it.

After seeing all that was to be seen at Therapia and Constantinople, I embarked on an Austrian Lloyd steamer, and ran down to the Dardanelles, then the head-quarters of the Bashi-Bazouks. The little town shared in the factitious importance of Gallipoli, and other places more or less useful during the war; it had two Pashas, Civil and Military, with a large body of Nizam or Regulars, whilst the hillsides to the north were dotted with the white tents of the Irregulars. General Beatson had secured fair quarters near the old windmills, and there had established himself with his wife and daughters. I at once recognized my old Boulogne friend, although slightly disguised by uniform. He looked like a man of fifty-five, with bluff face and burly figure, and probably grey hair became him better than black. He always rode English chargers of good blood, and altogether his presence was highly effective.

There had been much silly laughing at Constantinople, especially amongst the grinning idiot tribe, about his gold coat, which was said to stand upright by force of embroidery. But here he was perfectly right, and his critics perfectly wrong. He had learnt by many years' service to recognize the importance of show and splendour when dealing with Easterns. And no one had criticised the splendid Skinner or General Jacob of the Sind Horse, for wearing a silver helmet and a diamond-studded sabretache. General Beatson had served thirty-five years in the Bengal army, and was one of the few amongst his contemporaries who had campaigned in Europe during the long peace which followed the long war. In his subaltern days he had volunteered into the Spanish Legion, under the Commander, General Sir de Lacy Evans. After some hard fighting there, and seeing not a few adventures, he had returned to India. When the Crimean War broke out he went to Head-quarters at once, and, for the mere fun of the thing, joined in the Heavy Cavalry charge.

In October, 1854, the Duke of Newcastle, then Minister of War, addressed him officially, directing him to organize a Corps of Bashi-Bazouks, not exceeding in number four thousand, who were to be independent of the Turkish Contingent, consisting of twenty-five thousand Regulars under General Vivian. So, unfortunately for himself, he had made the Dardanelles his Head-quarters, and there he seemed to be settled with his wife and family. Mrs. Beatson was a quiet-looking little woman, who was reputed to rule her spouse with a rod of iron in a velvet case; and the two daughters were charming girls who seemed to have been born on horseback, and who delighted in setting their terriers at timid aides-de-camp, and teaching their skittish little Turkish nags to lash out at them when within kicking distance. General Beatson at once introduced me to his Staff and officers, amongst whom I found some most companionable comrades. There were two ex-Guardsmen, poor Charles Wemyss, who died years after, chronically impecunious, in London, and Major Lennox-Berkeley, who is still living. Of the Home army were Lieut.-Colonel Morgan, ex-cavalry man, and Major Synge. The Indian army had contributed Brigadier-General De Renzi, Brett, Hayman, Money, Grierson, and others. Sankey, whom I had known in Egypt, and whose family I had met at Malta, had been gazetted as lieutenant-colonel. There was also poor Blakeley of the Gun, who afterwards died so unhappily of yellow fever at Chorillos, in Perú.

But there were unfortunately black sheep among the number. Lieut.-Colonel Fardella had only the disadvantage of being a Sicilian, but Lieut.-Colonel Giraud, the head interpreter, was a Smyrniote and a Levantine of the very worst description, and, worse still, there was a Lieut.-Colonel O'Reilly, whose antecedents and subsequents were equally bad. He had begun as a lance-corporal in one of her Majesty's regiments, which he had left under discreditable circumstances. In the Bashi-Bazouks he joined a faction against

General Beatson, and when the war was over he openly became a Mussulman, and entered the Turkish service. He left the worst of reputations between Constantinople and Marocco, and Englishmen had the best reason to be ashamed of him. In subsequent years to the Massacre of Damascus, the English Government had chosen out Fuad Pasha, a witty, unscrupulous, and over-clever Turk, and proposed him as permanent Governor-General of the Holy Land, or to govern in a semi-independent position, like that of the Khedive of Egypt.

No choice could be worse, except that of the French, who favoured with even more inaptitude, by way of a rival candidate, their Algerian captive, the Emir Abd el Kadir, one of the most high-minded, religious, and honourable of men, who was utterly unfit to cope with Turkish roguery and Syrian rascaldom. The project fell through, but till his last day Fuad Pasha never lost sight of it, and kept up putting in an appearance, by causing perpetual troubles amongst the Bedawi and the Druses.

This man O'Reilly was one of his many tools, and at last, when he had brought about against the Turkish Government an absurd revolt of naked Arabs, upon the borders of the Hamah Desert, he was taken prisoner and carried before Rashíd Pasha, then the Governor-General, and in his supplications for pardon he had the meanness to kneel down and kiss the Turk's foot.

But worse still was the position of the affairs which met my eyes at the Dardanelles. Everything had combined to crush our force of Irregulars. First, there was the Greek faction, who naturally hated the English, and adored the Russians, and directed all the national genius to making the foreigners fail. Their example was followed by the Jews, many of them wealthy merchants at the Dardanelles, who in those days, before the Juden-hetze, loved and believed in Russia aud had scanty confidence in England. The two Turkish pashas were exceedingly displeased to see an *Imperium in Imperio*, and did their best to breed disturbance between their Regulars and the English Irregulars. They were stirred up by the German Engineers, who were employed upon the fortifications of the Dardanelles, and who strongly inoculated them with the idea that France and England aimed at nothing less than annexation.

Hence the Pashas not only fomented every disturbance, but they supplied deserters with passports and safe-conducts. The French played the friendly-foelike party; the envy, jealousy, and malice of the *Gr-r-r-ande Nation* had been stirred to the very depths by the failure of their Algerine General Yousouf in organizing a corps of Irregulars, and they saw with displeasure and disgust that an

Englishman was going to succeed. Accordingly Battus, their wretched little French Consul for the Dardanelles, was directed to pack the local Press at Constantinople (which was almost wholly in the French interests) with the falsest and foulest scandals. He had secured the services of the *Journal de Constantinople*, which General Beatson had with characteristic carelessness neglected to square, and his cunningly concocted scandals found their way not only into the Parisian, but even into the London Press.

But our deadliest enemies were of course those nearest home. Mr. Calvert was at that time Vice-Consul for the Dardanelles, and he openly boasted of its having been made by himself so good a thing that he would not exchange it for a Consulate General. I need not enter into the subsequent career of this man, who, shortly after the Crimean War, found his way into a felon's jail at Malta, for insuring a non-existing ship. He had proposed to General Beatson a contract in the name of a creature of his own, who was a mere man of straw, and it was at once refused, because, although Mr. Vice-Consul Calvert might have gained largely thereby, Her Majesty's Government would have lost in proportion. This was enough to make a bitter enemy of him, and he was a manner of Levantine, virulent and scrupulous as he was sharp-witted. He also had another grievance. In his Consulate he kept a certain Lieutenant Ogilvie, who years after fought most gallantly in the Franco-German War, and was looked upon, after he was killed, as a sort of small national hero.

He and his agents were buying up cattle for the public use, and it was a facetious saying amongst the "Buzoukers," as the Bashi-Bazouk officers were called, that they had not left a single three-legged animal in the country. It is no wonder that the reports of these men had a considerable effect upon Lord Stratford, who was profoundly impressed with the opinions of unhappy Lord Raglan, the Commander, who by weak truckling to the French, a nettle fit only to be grasped, had more than once placed us in an unworthy position. He was angrily opposed to the whole scheme; it was contrary to precedent: Irregulars were unknown at Waterloo, and the idea was offensive, because unknown to the good old stock and pipe-clay school. Moreover, but for a Campaign these men are invaluable to act as eyes and feelers for a regular force. The English soldier, unless he be a poacher—by-the-by, one of the best of them—cannot see by night; his want of practice gives him a kind of "noctilypia," and he suffers much from want of sleep. His Excellency already had his own grievance against General Beatson, being enormously scandalized by a letter from the Irregular officer casually proposing to hang the Military Pasha of the Dardanelles, if he continued to intrigue and report falsely concerning his force. And I must confess the tone of the General's letter was peculiar, showing that he was better known to "Captain Sword" than to "Captain Pen." When he put me in orders as "Chief of the Staff" I overhauled his books and stood aghast to see the style of his official despatches. He was presently persuaded, with some difficulty, to let me mitigate their candour under the plea of copying, but on one occasion after the copy was ready I happened to look into the envelope, and I found—

"P.S.—This is official, but I would have your Lordship to know that I also wear a black coat."

Fancy the effect of a formal challenge to combat, "pistols for two and coffee for one," upon the rancorous old man of Constantinople, whose anger burnt like a red-hot fire, and whose revenge was always at a white heat! I took it out, but my General did not thank me for it.

The result of these scandalous rumours was, that Lord Stratford deemed fit to send down the Dardanelles (for the purpose of reporting the facts of the case) a certain Mr. Skene. I have no intention of entering into the conduct of this official, who had been an officer in the English army, and who proposed to make himself comfortable in the Consulate of Aleppo! He has paid the debt of Nature, and I will not injure his memory. Suffice it to say, that he was known on the spot to be taking notes, that every malignant won his ear, and that he did not cease to gratify the Ambassador's prejudices by reporting the worst.

General Beatson was peppery, like most old Indians, and instead of keeping diplomatically on terms with Mr. Skene, he chose to have a violent personal quarrel with him. Consequently Mr. Skene returned to Constantinople, and his place was presently taken by Brigadier T. G. Neil, who shortly appeared in the same capacity—note-taker. His offensive presence and bullying manner immediately brought on another quarrel, especially when he loudly declared that "he represented Royalty," and that he was a universal unfavourite with Beatson's Horse. He afterwards served in the Indian Mutiny, and there he ended well. He made an enormous reputation at home by recklessly daring to arrest a railway clerk, and he was shot before his incapacity could be discovered.

I was also struck with consternation at the condition of Beatson's Horse, better known on the spot as the "Bashi-Bazouks." The correct term in Turkish is *Bāsh Buzuk*, equivalent to *Tête-pourrie*;

it succeeded the ancient *Dillis*, or madmen, who in the good old times represented the Osmanli Irregular Cavalry. It was the habit of those men in early spring, when the fighting season opened, to engage themselves for a term to plunder and loot all they could (and at this process they were first-rate hands), and to return home when winter set in. General Beatson wisely determined that his four thousand sabres should be wholly unconnected with the twenty-five thousand men of the Turkish Contingent. He wished to raise them in Syria, Asia Minor, Bulgaria, and other places, regiment them according to their nationalities, and to officer them, like Sepoy regiments, with Englishmen and Subalterns of their own races.

The idea was excellent, but it was badly carried out, mainly by default of the War Office, which had overmuch to do and could not be at the trouble of sending out officers. So the men, whose camps looked soldier-like enough, were left lying on the hillsides, and Satan found a very fair amount of work for them. This was, however, chiefly confined to duelling, and other such pastimes. The Arnauts or Albanians, who generally fight when they are drunk, had a peculiar style of monomachy. The principals, attended by their seconds and by all their friends, stood close opposite, each holding a cocked pistol in their right hand and a glass of *raki*, or spirits of wine, in their left. The first who drained his draught had the right to fire, and generally blazed away with fatal effect. It would have been useless to discourage this practice, but I insisted on fair play. Although endless outrages were reported at Constantinople, very few really took place: only one woman was insulted, and robbery with violence was exceptionally rare. In fact, the *Tête-pourries* contrasted most favourably with the unruly French detachments at Gallipoli, and with the turbulent *infirmiers* of the Nagara Hospital. With the English invalids at the Abydos establishment no disputes ever arose.

The exaggerated mutinies were mere sky-larking. After a few days' grumbling, a knot of "Rotten Heads" would mount their nags with immense noise and clatter, and, loudly proclaiming that they could stand the dullness of life no longer, would ride away, hoping only to be soon caught. But the worst was, I could see no business doing; there were no morning roll-calls or evening parades, no drilling or disciplining of men, and the General contented himself with riding twice a day through the camp, and listening to many grievances. However, as soon as I was made "Chief of the Staff," I persuaded him that this was not the thing, and induced him to establish all three, and to add thereto a riding school for sundry officers of infantry who were not very firm in the saddle, and also to open a

School of Arms for the benefit of *all* (the last thing a British officer learns is, to use his "silly sword"); and the consequence was, that we soon had a fine body of well-trained sabres, ready to do anything or to go anywhere.

The *Maître d'armes* was an Italian from Constantinople, and he began characteristically by proposing to call out the little Consul Battus, while another purposed making love to Madame! Alas! it was too late. On September 12th, a gunboat, dressed in all her colours, steamed at full speed down the Dardanelles, and caused an immense excitement in camp. The news flew like wildfire that Sebastopol had been captured. It proved, to say the least, premature, and the details filled every Englishman with disgust. I need not describe the grand storming of the Malakoff, which gave Pélissier his *bâton de Maréchal*, or the gallant carrying of the Little Redan by Bourbaki. But our failure at the Great Redan was simply an abomination. Poor old Jemmy Simpson was persuaded by Pélissier to play the second part, and to attack from the very same trench as that which sent forth the unsuccessful assault of June 18th. About half the force required was sent, and these were mostly regiments which had before suffered severely, and the bravest of them could only stand up to be shot down, instead of sneaking, as not a few did, in the trenches. Lastly, instead of leading them himself, the Commander-in-Chief sent General Wyndham, whose gasconade about putting on his gloves under fire seems to be the only item of this disgraceful affair which appears known to and remembered by the British public. The result of our attack was simply a *sauve qui peut*, and (*proh pudor!*) the Piedmontese General Cialdini was obliged to order up one of his brigades to save the British.

Continentals attributed this systematic paucity of our troops to the most urgent emergencies, either to inconsiderate national parsimony, or to overweening contempt for the enemy. It was nothing of the kind; it resulted from the normal appointment of thoroughly incapable Commanders. The private soldier was perfectly right, who volunteered before Lord Raglan that he and his comrades were perfectly ready to take Sebastopol by storm, under the Command of their own officers, if not interfered with by the *Generals.*

I now thought that I saw my way to a grand success, and my failure was proportionally absurd. This was nothing less than the relief of Kars, which was doomed to fall by famine, to the Russians. Pélissier and the Frenchmen were long-sighted enough to know the culminating importance of this stronghold as a *pierre d'échappe* in the way of Russia, and possibly, or rather probably, they had orders from home. However, they managed to keep Omar Pasha and his Turkish troops in the Crimea, where this large force were compelled to lie idle, instead of being sent to attack the Trans-Caucasian provinces, where they might have done good service. So when Omar Pasha, on the 29th of September, gloriously defeated the Russians before the walls of Kars, his victory was useless, and he was compelled to retire. Had the affair been managed in other ways, England might have struck a vital blow at Russia, by driving her once more behind the Caucasus, and by putting off for many a year the threatened advance upon India, which is now one of our *cauchemars.*

Meanwhile the reports concerning the siege of Kars, whose gallant garrison was allowed to succumb to famine, cholera, and the Russians, were becoming a scandal. It was reported that General Williams, who, with the Hungarian General Metz, was taking a prominent part in the defence, addressed upwards of eighty officials to Lord Stratford without receiving a single reply; in fact, as Mr. Skene's book shows, the great man only turned them into ridicule. However, the "Eltchi" feared ultimate consequences, and wrote to Lieut.-General (afterwards Sir) Robert J. Hussey-Vivian, to consult him concerning despatching on secret errand the Turkish Contingent, consisting, as it may be remembered, of twenty-five thousand Nizam or Regulars, commanded by a sufficiency of British officers.

The answer was that *no* carriage could be procured. Vivian, who was a natural son of Lord Vivian's, had seen some active service in his youth, but he was best known as an Adjutant-General of the Madras army, a man redolent of pipe-clay and red tape, and servilely subject to the Ambassador. So I felt that the game was in *my* hands, and proceeded in glorious elation of spirits to submit my project for the relief of Kars to his Excellency. We had already 2640 sabres in perfect readiness to march, and I could have procured *any quantities* of carriage. The scene which resulted passes description. He shouted at me in a rage, "You are the most impudent man in the Bombay Army, Sir!" But I knew him, and understood him like Alison, and did not mind. It ended with, "Of course you'll dine with us to-day?"

* * * * * * *

It was not until some months afterwards that I learnt what my unhappy plan proposed to do. Kars was doomed to fall as a make-weight for the capture of half of Sebastopol, and a Captain of Bashi-Bazouks (myself) had madly attempted to arrest the course of *haute politique.*

The tale of the fall of Kars is pathetic enough. While the British officers dined with General Mouravieff, the gallant Turkish soldiers were ordered to *pile* arms and march off under escort, and, dashing their muskets to the ground, they cried, "Perish our Wazirs who have even shamed us with this shame." And the disastrous and dishonourable result brought about by our political inaptitude has never ceased to weaken our prestige in Central Asia. Civilized Turks simply declared that an officer of artillery, sent out as Commissioner by England, had unwarrantably interfered with the legitimate command of Kars, where Turkey had a powerful army and an important position; and that by keeping the soldiers behind walls, when he knew the City could not be saved, he had lost both Army and City. The criticism was fair and sound.

General (afterwards Sir) W. F. Williams of Kars was at first in huge indignation, and declared that he would persuade the Government to impeach Lord Stratford. But on the way he was met by an offer of the Command at Woolwich, which apparently made him hold his peace. He was somewhat an exceptional man. For years an instructor of the Turkish Artillery, then English member of the mixed Commission for the topography of the Turko-Persian frontier, and finally Queen's Commissioner with the Turkish army at Kars, he had never learnt a word of Turkish. Of course he was hustled into the House of Commons. Whenever a man makes himself known in England that is apparently his ultimate fate. But he fell flatly, as even Kars did, before the sharp tongue of Bernal Osborne. During some debate on the Chinese question, he had assured the House that he was an expert, because he had had much experience of Turkish matters. "Oh, the fall of Kars!" cried the wit; and the ex-Commissioner was extinguished for ever.

Lord Stratford, I suppose by way of consoling *me*, made an indirect offer, through Lord Napier and Ettrick, about commissioning me to pay an official visit to Schamyl, whom some call "The Patriot," and others "The Bandit," of the Caucasus. The idea was excellent, but somewhat surprised me. Schamyl had lately been accused, amongst other atrocious actions, of flogging Russian ladies whom he had taken prisoners, and I could not understand how Lord Stratford, who had an unmitigated horror of all Russian cruelties, and who always expressed it in the rawest terms, could ally himself with such a ruffian. Possibly the political advantages in his opinion counterbalanced his demerits, for, had Schamyl been fairly supported, the Russian conquest of the great mountains might have been retarded for years. I consulted on the subject Alison and Percy Smythe, and both were of the same opinion, namely, that although there were difficulties and dangers, involving a long ride through Russian territory, the task might have been accomplished. They relied greatly upon the ardent patriotism of the Circassian women who then filled the harems of Constantinople. I should not have seen a single face, except perhaps that of a slave-girl, but I should have been warmly assisted with all the interest the fair patriots could make. So I began seriously to think of the matter. But the first visit to Lord Stratford put it entirely out of my head. I asked his Excellency what my reply was to be, should Schamyl ask me upon what mission I came. "Oh, say that you are sent to report to *me.*" "But, my lord, Schamyl will expect money, arms, and possibly troops, and what am I to reply if he asks me about it? Otherwise he will infallibly set me down for a spy, and my chance of returning to Constantinople will be uncommonly small."

However, the "Eltchi." could not see it in that light, and the project fell through.

Here also, although somewhat out of place, I may relate my last chance of carrying out a project upon which I was very warm, namely, to assist Circassia and to attack Georgia.

On returning to London I received a hint that Lord Palmerston had still some project of the kind, and was willing that I should be employed on it. So I wrote a number of letters, which I was allowed to publish in the *Times*, upon the subject of levying a large force of Kurdish Irregular Cavalry, and these being supported by the excellent work of Sir Henry Rawlinson, found favour with the public. But presently came the Franco-Russian peace of 1856. France, who had won all the credit of the mismanaged Campaign because she washed her dirty linen at home, and who had left all the discredit to England, whose practice was the opposite, lost all interest in the war. Louis Napoleon was thoroughly satisfied with what he had done, and Russia, after a most gallant and heroic defence of her territory, wanted time to heal her wounds. Accordingly the Treaty of Paris was entered into, the result being that, fifteen years afterwards, when France was in her sorest straits, Russia, with the consent of England (!), tore up that treaty and threw it in our face.

After this fruitless visit to Constantinople, I returned post haste to the Dardanelles, where I found the Bashi-Bazouks, like the unfortunate Turks at Kars, in a state of siege. On the morning of the 26th of September we were astounded to see the Turkish Regulars drawn out in array against us, Infantry supported by the guns, which were pointed at our camp, and patrols of Cavalry occupying the rear. Three War-steamers commanded the main entrance of the Town, and the enemy's outposts were established within three hundred yards of the 1st Regiment of Beatson's Horse, evidently for the purpose of ensuring a sanguinary affair. The inhabitants had closed their shops, and the British Consulate was deserted. The steamer *Redpole* was sent off in hottest haste to Constantinople with a report that a trifling squabble between the French *infirmiers* and the Bashi-Bazouks had ended in deadly conflict, and that the most terrible consequences were likely to ensue.

General Beatson at once issued an order to his men, who were furious at this fresh insult, and requested permission to punish the aggressors by taking the enemy's guns; and by means of his officers *he restrained the natural anger of his much-suffering men.*

The result was a triumph of discipline, and not a shot was fired that day. About four p.m. the Military Pasha, ashamed of his attitude, marched the Regulars back to their barracks, but he did not fail to complain to Constantinople of General Beatson's order, keeping his men in camp "till the Turkish authorities should have recovered from their panic and *housed* their guns." But the *Redpole* had also carried from the English and French Consuls an exaggerated account of the state of affairs, and earnestly requesting a reinforcement. The reply was an order from Lieut.-General Vivian removing General Beatson from command, and directing him to make it over to Major-General Richard Smith, who appeared at the Dardanelles on September 28th, supported by a fresh body of Nizam; and, lest any insult might be omitted, three hundred French soldiers had been landed at the Nagára Hospital to attack us in the rear.

General Beatson was at the time suffering from an accident, and was utterly unfitted for business. So Major Berkeley and I collected as many of the officers as we could at head-quarters, and proposed to go in a body to General Smith and lay the case before him. We assured him that all the reports were false, and proposed to show him the condition and the discipline of the Bashi-Bazouks; we also suggested that Brigadier-General Brett might be directed to assume temporary Command of the Force, until fresh orders and instructions should be received from General Vivian. Of course General Smith could not comply with our request, so we both declared that we would send in our resignations. After an insult of the kind, we felt that we could no longer serve with self-respect. It was this proceeding, I suppose, which afterwards gave rise to a report that I had done my best to cause a Mutiny.

On the last day of September General Beatson, with his Chief of Staff and military Secretary, left the Dardanelles for ever. Arrived at Buyukdere, a report was sent to General Vivian, and he presently came on board, where a lengthened communication passed between the Generals. Rumours of a Russian attack had induced a most conciliatory tone. General Vivian appeared satisfied with the explanation, and listened favourably to General Beatson's urgent request for permission to return at once to the Dardanelles. He asked expressly if the "Buzouker" could keep his men in order. The answer was a *decided affirmative*, which appeared to have considerable weight with him, and he expressed great regret for having, under a false impression, written an unfavourable letter to Lord Panmure, the tone of whose correspondence had been most offensive. He stated, however, that nothing could be done without the order of her Majesty's Ambassador; and, promising to call upon him for instructions, he left the steamer about midday, declaring that he would return in the course of the afternoon. After a few hours appeared, instead of General Vivian, a stiff official letter, directed to General Beatson. The interview with Lord Stratford had completely altered the tone of his official conduct.

On the 12th of October General Beatson reported officially to Lords Panmure and Stratford the efficient state of his force, concerning which General Smith had written most favourably. An equally favourable view was expressed in the public press by that Prince of War Correspondents, William H. Russell, whose name in those days was quoted by every Englishman. General Beatson begged to be sent on service, offering, upon his own responsibility, to take up transports, and to embark his men for Eupatoria, Yinikali, Batum, Balaclava, or—that unhappy Kars. To this no reply was returned.

Nothing now remained to be done, and on the 18th of October we left Therapia *en route* to England.

The sequel to this affair was sufficiently remarkable. General Beatson came home and attempted to take civil proceedings against his enemies. Chief amongst them was Mr. Skene—one of the Consuls already referred to—who, from the inception of General Beatson's scheme, had shown himself most bitterly opposed to it, and who had used all his influence to make General Beatson's position untenable.

Afterwards he chose to say that, "when General Smith arrived at the Dardanelles, General Beatson assembled the Commanding Officers of the regiments, and actually endeavoured to persuade them to make a mutiny in the regiments against General Smith, and against the authority of Vivian. Two of these Commanding Officers then left the room, saying they were soldiers, and they could not listen to language which they thought most improper and mutinous. These two were Lieut.-Colonels O'Reilly and Shirley. General Beatson subsequently had a sort of round robin prepared by the Chief Interpreter, and sent round to the different officers, in the hope that they would sign it, refusing to serve under any other General than himself. Both of these mutinous attempts are said to have originated from Captain Burton, who it also appears kept the order from Lord Panmure, placing the Irregular Horse under Lieut.-General Vivian, for three whole weeks unknown to any one but General Beatson, and the order was not promulgated until after General Smith had arrived."

General Beatson went into the witness-box and categorically denied the charges made against him.* I followed and gave evidence to the same effect, as did also General Watt; but there was a great difficulty in proving the publication of the libel, the War Office, then represented by Mr. Sidney Herbert, refusing to produce certain letters. Mr. Skene was very ably defended by Mr. Bovill (afterwards Lord Chief Justice), Mr. Lush (afterwards a judge), and Mr. Garth, and he brought forward a considerable number of witnesses, including General Vivian himself. Their evidence, however, tended rather to establish the case against him (Skene), so that he was compelled to plead that his libel was a privileged communication. Mr. Baron Bramwell confined himself in his summing-up strictly to the legal aspects of

---

* Richard was not altogether lucky, as far as promotion went, about his Chiefs. Sir Charles Napier had seen what stuff he was made of, and had utilized and praised him to the utmost, but Napier's patronage was not in those days a recommendation, because he was always fighting some big-wig at home, and high officials who are ruffled up are quite as dangerous as fighting Sikhs or Afghans. He then served under General Beatson, who, like Napier, was always plunging into hot water; but Richard was devoted to his Chiefs, who well deserved his loyalty, and in this instance Richard gave valuable evidence on his old Commander's behalf. He was very amusing in the witness-box; he was so cool and ready, and always worried his cross-examiner into a white heat of rage, playing with him as a cat does a mouse, when the lawyer was doing his best to bewilder him, and make him contradict himself, especially when Richard got him into a network of military terms, the cross-examiner being rather at sea among its technicalities. I can see him now, just as he used to be in the fencing school; he would play with his adversary, just as if he was carving a chicken, and tire him out long before the real play began, so that an ill-tempered man would almost spit himself with rage, if the button had not been on.

It was good to see him under cross-examination. Bovill, subsequently Chief Justice of the Common Pleas, was leading counsel on the other side, and was so ill-advised as to attempt to browbeat Richard. His failure was naturally disastrous. A very simple answer of Richard's quite upset Bovill. "In what regiment did you serve under the plaintiff?" "Eh?" "In what regiment, I say——" "In no regiment." After playing with counsel for a minute or two, Richard let him know that he had served in a "corps." Bovill was still further discomfited in the course of the trial, by a manœuvre of Edwin James, who was managing Beatson's case. James coolly got up while Bovill was speaking for the defence, declared he could not stay and listen to such stuff, and left the court for a while. It is only fair to add that Bovill won the case.—I. B.

the case, but he allowed his view of Mr. Skene's conduct to be very distinctly understood.

The jury (a special one), after half an hour's deliberation, returned a verdict for the defendant on the technical ground, but added a rider to their verdict, expressive of their disgust at Mr. Skene for having refrained from retracting his charges against General Beatson when he found how utterly without foundation they were. The verdict of the jury was confirmed on appeal, but it was generally felt that General Beatson had fully vindicated his character, and had very successfully exposed the conspiracy against the Irregulars, which had ended so disastrously for him and for his officers. The characters of the plaintiff and the defendant respectively may be estimated from one small circumstance. Beatson began his action just as the Indian Mutiny broke out, and being reasonably refused an extension of leave for the purpose of prosecuting it, went out to India. When the Mutiny was suppressed he obtained six months' leave, without pay, for the purpose of prosecuting his case. Mr. Skene had obtained the appointment of Consul at Aleppo, and could have reached England in a fortnight, but he chose to remain at his Consulate, though there would have been no difficulty in obtaining leave of absence on full pay. Under such circumstances, it was perhaps hardly worth while for his counsel to dwell upon the cruelty of pushing on this case in his absence, a complaint for which the presiding judge somewhat emphatically declared *that there was not the smallest foundation.*

CHAPTER XI.

BETWEEN THE CRIMEA AND THE LAKE REGIONS OF CENTRAL AFRICA.

"Aye free, aff-hand your story tell,
When wi' a bosom crony;
But still keep something to yoursel'
Ye scarcely tell to ony."

BURNS.

As soon as Richard was well home from the Crimea, and had attended Beatson's trial, he began to turn his attention to the "Unveiling of Isis," in other words, "Discovering the sources of the Nile, the Lake Regions of Central Africa," on which his heart had long been set, and he passed most of his time in London working it up.

One summer day, in August, 1856, thirty-seven years ago, we had not gone out of town, and I was walking in the Botanical Gardens with my sister, Blanche Pigott, and a friend, and Richard was there, walking with the gorgeous creature of Boulogne—then married. We immediately stopped and shook hands, and asked each other a thousand questions of the four intervening years, and all the old Boulogne memories and feelings which had lain dormant, but not extinct, returned to me. He asked me before I left if I came very often to the Botanical Gardens, and I said, "Oh yes, we always come and read and study here from eleven to one, because it is so much nicer than staying in the hot rooms at this season." "That is quite right," he said. "What are you studying?" I had that day with me an old friend, Disraeli's "Tancred," the book of my heart and tastes, which he explained to me. We were there about an hour, and when I had to leave, as I moved off, I heard him say to his companion, "Do you know that your cousin has grown charming? I would not have believed that the little schoolgirl of Boulogne would have become such a sweet girl;" and I heard her say, "Ugh!" with a tone of disgust.

Next day, when we got there, he was also there—alone—composing poetry to show to Monckton-Milnes on some pet subject, and he came forward, saying laughingly, "You won't chalk up 'Mother will be angry' now, will you, as you did when you were a little girl?" Again we walked and talked. This went on for a fortnight—I trod on air.

At the end of a fortnight he asked me "if I could dream of doing anything so sickly as to give up Civilization, and if he could obtain the Consulate at Damascus, to go and live there." He said, "Don't give me an answer *now*, because it will mean a very serious step for you—no less than giving up your people, and all that you are used to, and living the sort of life that Lady Hester Stanhope led. I see the capabilities in you, but you must think it over." I was so long silent from emotion—it was just as if the moon had tumbled down and said, "I thought you cried for me, so I came"—that he thought I was thinking worldly thoughts, and said, "Forgive me! I ought not to have asked so much." At last I found my voice, and said, "I don't *want* to 'think it over'—I have been 'thinking it over' for six years, ever since I first saw you at Boulogne on the Ramparts. I have prayed for you every day, morning and night. I have followed all your career minutely. I have read every word you ever wrote, and I would rather have a crust and a tent with *you* than be Queen of all the world. And so I say now, Yes! YES! YES!" I will pass over the next few minutes. Then he said, "Your people will not give you to me." I answered, "I know that, but I belong to myself—I give myself away." "That is all right," he answered; "be firm, and so shall I."

After that he came and visited a little at our house as an acquaintance, having been introduced at Boulogne, and he fascinated, amused, and pleasantly shocked my mother, but completely magnetized my father and all my brothers and sisters. My father used to say, "I don't know what it is about that man, but I can't get him out of my head, I dream about *him every night.*"

Cardinal Wiseman and Richard had become friends in early days. Languages had brought them together, and the Cardinal now furnished him with a special passport, recommending him to all the Catholic Missions in wild places all over the World, with special letters describing him as a Catholic Officer.

I now think I must introduce to you two cuttings from the *Journal of the Gypsy Lore Society.* The first was an obituary after his death, January, 1891; the other was a small contribution from me, throwing a light on his Gypsy interests, and this will explain better than any other way why I was so impressed on hearing his name when we were introduced, and why I was so startled at his pursuit and mingling with the Jats, the aboriginal Gypsies in India, mentioned in my Boulogne recital.

OBITUARY IN THE "GYPSY LORE SOCIETY JOURNAL," JANUARY, 1891.

"Not only this Society, but the whole civilized world, has recently had to mourn the death of our distinguished fellow-member, Sir Richard Francis Burton. Of the many events of his eventful life it is needless to speak here. As soldier, explorer, linguist, and man of letters (the writer of about eighty more or less bulky volumes), he made himself separately famous. 'His most famed achievement—the pilgrimage to Mecca and Medina in the character of an Afghan Muslim—was,' says one writer, 'an achievement of the first order. To consider it without a wondering admiration is impossible: so vast is the amount involved of hardihood and self-confidence, of linguistic skill and histrionic genius, or resourcefulness and vigilance and resolve.'

"But the aspect in which he may most suitably be regarded in these pages, is that of a student of the Gypsies, to whom he was affiliated by nature, if not actually by right of descent.

"Whether there may not be also a tinge of Arab, or, perhaps, of Gypsy blood in Burton's race, is a point which is perhaps open to question. For the latter suspicion an excuse may be found in the incurable restlessness which has beset him since his infancy, a restlessness which has effectually prevented him from ever settling long in any one place, and in the singular idiosyncrasy which his friends have often remarked—the peculiarity of his eyes. 'When it (the eye) looks at you,' said one who knows him well, 'it looks through you, and then, glazing over, seems to see something behind you. Richard Burton is the only man (not a Gypsy) with that peculiarity, and he shares with them the same horror of a corpse, death-bed scenes, and graveyards, though caring little for his own life.' When to this remarkable fact he added the scarcely less interesting detail that 'Burton' is one of the half-dozen distinctively Romany names, it is evident that the suspicion of Sir Richard Burton having a drop of Gypsy blood in his descent—crossed and commingled though it be with an English, Scottish, French, and Irish strain—is not altogether unreasonable."

"Unreasonable or not, it can hardly be said that this constitutes a firm basis on which to rear a theory of Gypsy lineage. Yet Burton himself acknowledged a certain Gypsy connection, though, it will be noticed, he does not say the affinity was that of blood, in the following extract from a letter to Mr. J. Pincherle, accepting that gentleman's dedication of his Romany version of the 'Song of Songs' (*I Ghilèngheri Ghilia Salomuneskero*). 'Dear Mr. Pincherle,' writes Sir Richard, 'I accept the honour of your dedication with the same frankness with which you accompanied its offer. And indeed, I am not wholly dissociated from this theme; there is an important family of Gypsies in foggy England, who, in very remote times, adopted our family name. I am yet on very friendly terms with several of these strange people; nay, a certain Hagar Burton, an old fortune-teller (*divinatrice*), took part in a period of my life which in no small degree contributed to determine its course.'

"Whether such slight indications as these really point to a Gypsy line of descent or not, there can be no question as to the interest which Sir Richard Burton took in Gypsy lore. Apart from his various well-known published accounts of the Jats and other tribes of the Indus Valley, he had a work specially entitled 'The Gypsies,' which his biography of 1887 announces as then 'in course of preparation.' The materials of this work are now, we understand, in the possession of Lady Burton, and we trust that they will some day see the light. Sir Richard was himself one of the original members of the Gypsy Lore Society, in which he always took a deep interest; and a letter which he wrote to the secretary, only five days before his death, concludes with the good wish—'All luck to the Society; I will not fail to do what little I can.'

"His death, which was very sudden, took place on October 20th last, while he still held the office of British Consul at Trieste. The high esteem in which he was held by the citizens of Trieste, not only on account of his official position and the great name which he had made for himself in the world of science, but also for those personal qualities which had won their regard, is amply testified by the sincere expressions of regret which accompanied the last honours there paid to his memory. At the time of his death Sir Richard Burton was sixty-nine years of age, having been born at Barham House, Hertfordshire, on March 19th, 1821."

"An Episode from the Life of Sir Richard Burton, by his Wife.

"In our obituary notice of the late Sir Richard Burton, mention was made of a certain Gypsy named Hagar Burton, who, Sir Richard stated, had been instrumental, to some extent, in shaping his destiny. This reference has been fully explained by Lady Burton, who, in favouring us with some account of her illustrious husband, writes as follows:—

"'In the January number of the *Gypsy Lore Journal* a passage is quoted from "a short sketch of the career" of my husband (a little black pamphlet) which half suspects a remote drop of Gypsy blood in him. There is no proof that this was ever the case, but there is no question that he showed many of their peculiarities in appearance, disposition, and speech—speaking Romany like themselves. Nor did we ever enter a Gypsy camp without their claiming him: "What are you doing with a black coat on?" they would say, "why don't you join us and be our King?"

"'He had the peculiar eye, which looked you through, glazed over and saw something behind, and is the only man, not a Gypsy, with that peculiarity. He had the restlessness which could stay nowhere long, nor own any spot on earth—the same horror of a corpse, death-bed scenes, and graveyards, or anything which was in the slightest degree ghoulish, though caring but little for his own life —the same aptitude for reading the hand at a glance. With many, he would drop it at once and turn away, nor would anything induce him to speak a word about it.

"'You quote a letter of his to Mr. James Pincherle, a dear old friend of ours, where he relates the influence that a Gypsy, named Hagar Burton, had upon his life. I will now tell you the story, which will reappear in his biography, if I live to finish it.

"'When I was a girl in the schoolroom in the country, I was enthusiastic about Gypsies, Bedouin Arabs, everything Eastern and mysterious, and especially wild, lawless life. Disraeli's "Tancred" was my second Bible. I was strictly forbidden to associate with the Gypsies in our lanes, which was my delight. When they were only travelling tinkers or basket-menders I was very obedient, but wild horses would not have kept me out of the camps of the Oriental, yet English-named, tribes of Burton, Cooper, Stanley, Osbaldiston, and one other whose name I forget. My particular friend was Hagar Burton, a tall, slender, handsome, distinguished, refined woman, of much weight in the tribe. Many an hour have I passed with her (she called me Daisy), and many a litttle service I did them when any of them were sick, or had got into a scrape with the squires, anent poultry or eggs and other things. At last a time came when we were to go to school in France, and my departure was regretted by them. The last day but one I ever saw Hagar, she cast my horoscope, and wrote it in Romany. The rest of the tribe presented me with a straw flycatcher of many colours, which I still have. The horoscope was translated to me by her, and I give you the most important part concerning my husband—

"'"You will cross the sea, and be in the same town with your Destiny, and know it not. Every obstacle will rise up against you, and such a combination of circumstances, that it will require all your courage and energy and intelligence to meet them. Your life will be like one always swimming against big waves, but God will always be with you, so you will always win. You will fix your eye on your polar star, and you will go for that without looking right or left. *You will bear the name of our Tribe, and be right proud of it. You will be as we are, but far greater than we.* Your life is all wandering, change, and adventure. One soul in two bodies, in life or death; never long apart. Show this to the man you take for your husband. —HAGAR BURTON."

"'In June, 1856, I went to Ascot. I met Hagar and shook hands with her. "Are you Daisy Burton yet?" was her first question. I shook my head—"Would to God I were!" Her face lit up. "Patience, it is just coming." She waved her hand, being rudely thrust from the carriage. I never saw her since, but I was engaged to Richard two months later.

"'After we were engaged, I gave him the horoscope in Romany. It was before he set out in October, 1856, with Speke, for the discovery of Tanganyika. We had been engaged for some weeks. One day in October we had passed several hours together, and he appointed to come next day, at four o'clock in the afternoon. I went to bed quite happy, but I could not sleep at all. At two a.m. the door opened, and he came into my room. A current of warm air came towards my bed. He said, "Good-bye, my poor child. My time is up, and I have gone, but do not grieve. I shall be back in less than three years, and *I am your destiny*. Good-bye."

"'He held up a letter—looked long at me with those Gypsy eyes, and went slowly out, shutting the door. I sprang out of bed to the

SKETCH MAP OF AFRICA.

door, into the passage—there was nothing—and thence into the room of one of my brothers. I threw myself on the ground, and cried my heart out. He got up, asked me what ailed me, and tried to soothe and comfort me. "Richard is gone to Africa," I said, "and I shall not see him for three years." "Nonsense," he replied; "you have only got a nightmare. You told me he was coming at four in the afternoon." "So I did; but I have seen him, and he told me this; and if you wait till the post comes in, you will see I have told you truly." I sat all the night in my brother's armchair, and at eight o'clock, when the post came in, there was a letter to my sister, Blanche Pigott, enclosing one for me. "He had found it too painful to part, and had thought we should suffer less that way, begged her to break it gently to me, and to give me the letter" (which assured me we should be reunited in 1859—as we were, on the 22nd May of that year). He had left London at six o'clock the previous evening, eight hours before I saw him in the night.

"'This is the story of Hagar Burton. We have mixed a great deal since with Gypsies, in all parts of the world, and have sought her in vain. The other Gypsies have chiefly warned us of having to fight through our lives, and to be perpetually on guard against treacheries and calumnies "*chiefly through jealous men and nasty women.*" Well, we have mostly left them to God, and they nearly always come to grief. I may add that all that Hagar Burton foretold came true, and I pray God it may be so to the end, *i.e.* "never long apart" in Life *or* Death.

"'ISABEL BURTON.'"

Richard traced for me a little sketch of what he expected to find in the Lake Regions (see opposite).

That last afternoon I had placed round his neck a medal of the Blessed Virgin upon a steel chain, which we Catholics commonly call "the miraculous medal." He promised me he would wear it throughout his journey, and show it me on his return. I had offered it to him on a gold chain, but he had said, "Take away the gold chain; they will cut my throat for it out there." He did show it me round his neck when he came back; he wore it all his life, and it is buried with him.

What made my position more painful was, that he knew that I should not be allowed to receive any letters from him, and therefore it was not safe to write often, and then only to say what others might read. He left to me, at my request, the task of breaking the fact of my engagement to my people, when, where, and how I pleased, as it would be impossible to marry me until he came back. I would here insert a little poem he wrote on leaving—

"I wore thine image, Fame,
Within a heart well fit to be thy shrine!
Others a thousand boons may gain,
One wish was mine—

"The hope to gain one smile,
To dwell one moment cradled on thy breast,
Then close my eyes, bid life farewell,
And take my rest!

"And now I see a glorious hand
Beckon me out of dark despair!
Hear a glorious voice command,
'Up, bravely dare.

"'And if to leave a deeper trace
'On earth, to thee, Time, Fate, deny;
'Drown vain regret, and have the grace
'Silent to die.'

"She pointed to a grisly land,
Where all breathes death—earth, sea, and air!
Her glorious accents sound once more:
'Go, meet me there!'

"Mine ear will hear no other sound,
No other thought my heart will know.
Is this a sin? 'Oh, pardon, Lord!
'Thou mad'st me so.'

"R. F. B.

"*September*, 1856."

CHAPTER XII.

HIS EXPLORATION OF THE LAKE REGIONS, TAKING CAPTAIN SPEKE AS SECOND IN COMMAND.

MY FOREWORD.

IT was the Royal Geographical Society which induced Lord Clarendon, Secretary of State for Foreign Affairs, to supply Richard with funds for an exploration of the then utterly unknown Lake Regions of Central Africa. In October, 1856, he set out for Bombay, applied for Captain Speke, and landed at Zanzibar on December 19th, 1856. Lieut.-Colonel Hamerton, her Majesty's Consul at Zanzibar, was very good to them; they made a tentative expedition from January 5th to March 6th, 1857, about the Mombas regions. They got a bad coast fever, and returned to Zanzibar. They then set out again into the far interior, into which only one European, Monsieur Maizan, a French naval officer, had attempted to penetrate; he was cruelly murdered at the outset of his journey.

It was the first successful attempt to penetrate that country, and laid the foundation for others. It was the base on which all subsequent journeys were founded; Livingstone, Cameron, Speke and Grant, Sir S. Baker, and Stanley carried it out. Where Richard found the rudest barbarians, Church missions have been established, and commerce, and now a railway is proposed to connect the coast with the Lake Regions. This expedition brought neither honour nor profit to Richard; but the world is not likely to forget it; the future will be more generous and juster than the past or present. During these African explorations, Richard was attacked by fever twenty-one times, by temporary paralysis and partial blindness. On his return he brought out "The Lake Regions of Equatorial Africa," 2 vols., 1860, and the Royal Geographical Society devoted the whole of their thirty-third volume to its recital (Clowes and Son). Richard's book was translated into French by Madame H. Loreau, and republished in New York by Fakir, 1861. It will shortly be added to the Uniform Library in preparation. In May, 1859, the moment he returned to England, he immediately proposed another Expedition, which, however, the Royal Geographical Society gave to his disloyal companion, who completely and wilfully spoiled the first Expedition as far as lay in his power.

Zanzibar; and Two Months in East Africa.

(From his own notes.)

Preliminary Canter.

"Of the gladdest moments, methinks, in human life, is the departing upon a distant journey into *unknown* lands. Shaking off with one effort the fetters of habit, the leaden weight of routine, the cloak of carking care, and the slavery of Civilization, Man feels once more happy. The blood flows with the fast circulation of youth, excitement gives a new vigour to the muscles, and a sense of sudden freedom adds an inch to the stature. Afresh dawns the morn of life, again the bright world is beautiful to the eye, and the glorious face of Nature gladdens the soul. A journey, in fact, appeals to Imagination, to Memory, to Hope—the sister Graces of our moral being.

"The shrill screaming of the boatswain's whistle, and sundry shouts of, 'Stand by yer booms!' 'All ready, for'ard?' 'Now make sail!' sounded in mine ears with a sweet significance.

Zanzibar.

"Our captain decided, from the absence of Friday flags on the Consular Staffs, that some great man had gone to his long home. The *Elphinstone*, however, would not have the trouble of casting loose her guns for nothing; with H.H. the Sayyid of Zanzibar's ensign—a plain red—at the fore, and the Union at the main, she cast anchor in Front Bay, about half a mile from shore, and fired a salute of twenty-one. A gay bunting thereupon flew up to every truck, and the brass cannon of the *Victoria* roared a response of twenty-two. We had arrived on the fortieth, or the last day of mourning.

"When 'chivalry' was explained to the late ruler, Said of Zanzibar (1856), as enlightened a prince as Arabia ever produced, and surrounded by intrigue, he was shrewd enough to remark 'that only the *siflah* (low fellows) interfere between husband and wife.'

"Peace to his soul! he was a model of Arab princes, a firm friend to the English nation, and a great admirer of the 'Malikat el Aazameh,' our most gracious Majesty Queen Victoria.

"The unworthy merchants of Zanzibar, American and European, did their best to secure for us the fate of M. Maizan, both on this and on a subsequent occasion, by spreading all manner of reports amongst the Banyans, Arabs, and Sawahilis.

"Considering the unfitness of the season, we were strongly advised to defer exploration of the interior until we had learned something of the coast, and for that purpose we set out at once, for a two or three months' cruise.

"If we, travellers in transit, had reason to be proud of our countryman's influence at Zanzibar, the European and American merchants should be truly thankful for it. Appointed in 1840 H.B.M.'s Consul and H.E.I. Co.'s agent at the court of H.H. Sayyid Said, and directed to make this island his Head-quarters, Colonel Hamerton found that for nine years not a British cruiser had visited it, and that report declared us to be no longer Masters of the Indian seas. Slavery was rampant. Wretches were thrown overboard, when sick, to prevent paying duty; and the sea-beach before the town, as well as the plantations, presented horrible spectacles of dogs devouring human flesh. The Consul's representations were accepted by Sayyid Said; sundry floggings and confiscation of property instilled into slave-owners the semblance of humanity. The insolence of the negro was as summarily dealt with. The Arabs had persuaded the Sawahilis and blacks that a white man is a being below contempt, and the 'poor African' carries out the theory. Only seventeen years have elapsed since an American Trader-Consul, in consular cocked hat and sword, was horsed upon a slave's back, and solemnly 'bakered' in his own consular house, under his own consular flag. A Sawahili would at any time enter the merchant's bureau, dispose his sandalled feet upon the table, call for a cognac, and if refused, draw his dagger. Negro fishermen would anchor their craft close to a window, and, clinging to the mast, enjoy the novel spectacle of Kafirs feeding.

"*Now* an Englishman here is even more civilly treated than at one of our Presidencies. This change is the work of Colonel Hamerton, who, in the strenuous and unremitting discharge of his duties, has lost youth, strength, and health. The iron constitution of this valuable public servant—I have quoted merely a specimen of his worth—has been undermined by the terrible fever, and at fifty his head bears the 'blossoms of the grave,' as though it had seen its seventieth summer.

"The reader asks, What induced us to take a guide apparently so little fit for rough-and-ready work? In the first place, the presence of Said bin Salim el Lamki was a pledge of respectability. And lastly, a bright exception to the rule of his unconscientious race, he *appears* truthful, honest, and honourable. I have never yet had reason to suspect him of a low action. 'Verily,' was the reply, 'whoso benefiteth the beneficent becometh his Lord; but the vile well-treated turneth and rendeth thee.' I almost hope that he may not deceive us in the end.

"The traveller in Eastern Africa must ever be prepared for three distinct departures—the little start, the great start, and the start.

"On the 10th of January we ran through the paradise of verdant banks and plateaus, forming the approach to Pemba,* and halted a day to admire the Emerald Isle of these Eastern seas. In A.D. 1698 the bold buccaneer, Captain Kidd, buried there his blood-stained

* The distance between Bombay and Zanzibar is two thousand five hundred miles.

hoards of precious stones and metal, the plunder of India and the further Orient. The people of Pemba have found pots full of gold lumps, probably moulded from buttons that the pirate might wear his wealth.

"On the heights of Chhaga, an image or statue of a long-haired woman, seated in a chair and holding a child, is reported to remain. Iconolatry being here unknown, the savages must have derived them from some more civilized race—Catholic missionaries.

"The Mazrui, a noble Arab tribe, placed themselves under British protection in their rebellion against the late Sayyid. They were permitted to fly our flag—a favour for which, when danger disappeared, they proved themselves ungrateful; and a Mr. Reece was placed at Mombas to watch its interests. The travellers lamented that we abandoned Mombas: had England retained it, the whole interior would now be open to us. But such is the history of Britain the Great: hard won by blood and gold, her conquests are parted with for a song.

"The very Hindús required a lesson in civility. With the *Wali*, or Governor, Khalfan bin Ali, an Omani Arab of noble family, we were on the best of terms. But the manifest animus of the public made us feel light-hearted, when, our inquiries concluded, we bade adieu to Mombas.

"The people of Eastern Intertropical Africa are divided by their occupations into three orders. First is the fierce pastoral nomad, the Galla and Masai, the Somal and the Kafir, who lives upon the produce of his cattle, the chase, and foray. Secondly rank the semi-pastoral, as the Wakamba, who, though without fixed abodes, make their women cultivate the ground. And the last degree of civilization, agriculture, is peculiar to the Waníka, the Wasumbára, and the various tribes living between the coast and the interior lakes.

"The Waníka, or Desert race, is composed of a Negritic base, now intimately mixed with Semitic blood.

"When that enlightened Arab statesman, H.E. Ali bin Nasir, H.H. the Imaum of Muscat's Envoy Extraordinary to H.B. Majesty, was Governor of Mombas, he took advantage of a scarcity to feed the starving Waníka from the public granaries. He was careful, however, to secure as pledges of repayment, the wives and children of his debtors, and he lost no time in selling off the whole number. Such a feat was probably little suspected by our countrymen, when, to honour enlightened beneficence, they welcomed the Statesman with all the triumphs of Exeter Hall, presented him with costly specimens of Government, and sent him from Aden to Zanzibar in the H.E.I. Co.'s brig of war *Tigris*. This Oriental votary of free trade came to a merited end. Recognized by the enraged savages, he saw his sons expire in torments; he was terribly mutilated during life, and was put to death with all the refinements of cruelty.

"A report, prevalent in Mombas—even a Sawahili sometimes speaks the truth—and the march of an armed party from the town which denoted belief in their own words, induced my companions and myself to hasten up once more to the Rabai Hills, expecting to find the mission-house invested by savages. The danger had been exaggerated, but the inmates were strongly advised to take temporary shelter in the town. Left Kisulodiny on the 22nd of January, 1857. Some nights afterwards, fires were observed upon the neighbouring hills, and Waníka scouts returned with a report that the Masai were in rapid advance. The wise few fled at once to the *kaza*, or hidden and barricaded stronghold, which these people prepare for extreme danger. The foolish many said, 'To-morrow morning we will drive our flocks and herds to safety.' But ere that morning dawned upon the world, a dense mass of wild spearmen, sweeping with shout and yell, and clashing arms, by the mission-house, which they either saw not or they feared to enter, dashed upon the scattered villages in the vale below, and left the ground strewed with the corpses of hapless fugitives. When driving off their cattle, the Masai, rallying, fell upon them, drove them away in ignominious flight, and slew twenty-five of their number.

"Jack* and I landed at Wásin, and found the shore crowded with a mob of unarmed gazers, who did not even return our salaams: we resolved in future to keep such greetings for those who deserved them. Abd-el-Karím led us to his house, seated us in chairs upon a terrace, and mixed a cooling drink in a vase not usually devoted to such purpose. There is no game on the island, or on the main. In the evening we quitted the squalid settlement without a single regret.

"Our *nakhoda* again showed symptoms of trickery; he had been allowed to ship cargo from Mombas to Wasin, and, Irish-like, he thereupon founded a right to ship cargo from Wasin to Tanga. Unable to disabuse his mind by mild proceedings, I threatened to cut the cable.

"At last, having threaded the *báb*, or narrow rock-bound passage which separates the bluff headland of Tanga Island from Ras Rashíd on the main, we glided into the bay, and anchored in three fathoms of water, opposite, and about half a mile from, the town.

"Tanga Bay extends six miles deep by five in breadth. The entrance is partially barred by a coralline bank, the ancient site of the Arab settlement.

"We landed on the morning of the 27th of January, and were met upon the sea-shore, in absence of the Arab Governor, by the *Diwans* or Sawahili Headmen, the *Jemadar* and his Belochies, the Collector of customs, Mizan Sahib, a daft old Indian, and other dignitaries. They conducted us to the hut formerly tenanted by M. Erhardt; brought coffee, fruit, and milk; and, in fine, treated us with peculiar civility. Here Sheddad built his City of brass, and encrusted the hill-top with a silver dome that shines with various and surpassing colours.

"The mountain recedes as the traveller advances, and the higher he ascends the higher rises the summit. At last blood bursts from the nostrils, the fingers bend backwards, and the most adventurous

* Jack was Speke's christian name.

is fain to stop. Amongst this Herodotian tissue of fact and fable, ran one fine thread of truth: all testified to the intense cold.

"They promised readily, however, to escort me to one of the ancient Cities of the coast.

"Setting out at eight a.m. with a small party of spearmen, I walked four or five miles south of Tanga, on the Tangata road, over a country strewed with the bodies of huge millepedes, and dry as Arabian sand.

"I assumed an Arab dress—a turban of portentous circumference, and a long henna-dyed shirt—and, accompanied by Said bin Salim, I went to inspect the scene.

"The wild people, Washenzy, Wasembára, Wadígo, and Waségeju, armed as usual, stalking about, whilst their women, each with baby on back, carried heavy loads of saleable stuff, or sat opposite their property, or chaffered and gesticulated upon knotty questions of bargain.

"The heat of the ground made my barefooted companions run forward to the shade, from time to time, like the dogs in Tibet. Sundry excursions delayed us six days at Tanga.

"Five hours of lazy sailing ran us into Tangata, an open road between Tanga and Pangany. Here we delayed a day to inspect some ruins, where we had been promised Persian inscriptions and other wonders.

"We spent the remainder of the day and night at Tangata, fanned by the north-east breeze, and cradled by the rocking send of the Indian Ocean.

"At five a.m. on the 3rd of February we hoisted sail, and slipped down with the tepid morning breeze to Pangany, sighting Maziny Island, its outpost, after three hours' run. Soon after arrival I sent Said bin Salim, in all his bravery, on shore with the Sayyid of Zanzibar's circular letter to the *Wali* or Governor, to the *Jemadar*, to the Collector of customs, and the different *Diwans*. All this preparation for a mere trifle! We were received with high honour. The *Diwans* danced an ancient military dance before us with the pomp and circumstance of drawn swords, whilst bare-headed slave-girls, with hair *à la Brutus*, sang and flapped their skirts over the ground, with an affectedly modest and downcast demeanour. After half an hour's endurance, we were led into the upper-storied house of the Wali Meriko, a freedman of the late Sayyid Said, and spent the evening in a committee of ways and means.

"African villages are full of bleared misery by day, and animated filth by night, and of hunting adventures and hair-breadth escapes, lacking the interest of catastrophe.

"We arose early in the morning after arrival at Pangany, and repaired to the terrace for the better enjoyment of the view.

"If it had half-a-dozen white kiosks, minarets, and latticed summer-houses, it would almost rival that gem of creation, the Bosphorus.

"The settlement is surrounded by a thorny jungle, which at times harbours a host of leopards. One of these beasts lately scaled the high terrace of our house, and seized upon a slave-girl. Her master, the burly black *Wali*, who was sleeping by her side, gallantly caught up his sword, ran into the house, and bolted the door, heedless of the miserable cry, 'B'ana, help me!' The wretch was carried to the jungle and devoured. The river is equally full of alligators, and whilst we were at Pangany a boy disappeared.

"Of course the two tribes, Wasumbara and Wazegura, are deadly foes. Moreover, about a year ago, a violent intestine feud broke out amongst the Wazegura, who, at the time of our visit, were burning and murdering, kidnapping, and slave-selling in all directions.

"The timid townsmen had also circulated a report that we were bound for Chhaga and Kilimanjaro: the Masai were 'out,' the rains were setting in, and they saw with us no armed escort. They resolved therefore not to accompany us.

"With abundance of money—say not less than £5000 per annum—an exploring party can trace its own line, pay the exactions of all Chiefs; it can study whatever is requisite; handle sextants in presence of negroes, who would cut every throat for one inch of brass; and, by travelling in comfort, can secure a very fair chance of return. Even from Mombas or from Pangany, with an escort of one hundred matchlock-men, we might have marched through the Masai plunderers to Chhaga and Kilimanjaro. But pay, porterage, and provisions for such a party would have amounted to at least £100 per week; a month and a half would have absorbed our means. Thus it was, gentle reader, that we were compelled to rest contented with a visit on foot to Fuga, for we had only one thousand pounds.

"Presently the plot thickened. Muigni Khatib, son of Sultan Kimwere, a black of most unprepossessing physiognomy, with a 'villanous trick of the eye, and a foolish hanging of the nether lip,' a prognathous jaw, garnished with cat-like moustaches and cobweb beard, a sour frown, and abundant surliness by way of dignity, dressed like an Arab, and raised by El Islam above his fellows, sent a message directing us to place in his hands what we intended for his father. This Chief was travelling to Zanzibar in fear and trembling. He had tried to establish at his village, Kirore, a Romulian asylum for runaway slaves, and, having partially succeeded, he dreaded the consequences. The Beloch *Jemadar* strongly urged us privily to cause his detention at the islands, a precaution somewhat too Oriental for our tastes. We refused, however, the *muigni's* demand in his own tone. Following their Prince, the dancing *Diwans* claimed a fee for permission to reside; as they worded it, '*el adah*'—the habit; based upon an ancient present from Colonel Hamerton; and were in manifest process of establishing a local custom which, in Africa, becomes law to remotest posterity. We flatly objected, showed our letters, and in the angriest of moods threatened reference to Zanzibar. Briefly, all began to beg bakhshish; but I cannot remember any one obtaining it.

"Weary of these importunities, we resolved to visit Chogway, a Beloch outpost, and thence, aided by the *Jemadar* who had preceded us from Pangany, to push for the capital village of Usumbara. We made preparations secretly, dismissed the 'Riami,' rejected the *Diwans* who wished to accompany us as spies, left Said bin Salim and one Portuguese to watch our property in the house of Meriko, the Governor, who had accompanied his *muigni* to Zanzibar, and, under pretext of a short shooting excursion, hired a long canoe with four men, loaded it with the luggage required for a fortnight, and started with the tide at eleven a.m. on the 6th of January, 1857.

"First we grounded; then we were taken aback; then a puff of wind drove us forward with railway speed; then we grounded again.

"And now, while writing amid the soughing blasts, the rain, and the darkened air of a south-western monsoon, I remember with yearning the bright and beautiful spectacle of those African rivers, whose loveliness, like that of the dead, seems enhanced by proximity to decay. We had changed the agreeable and graceful sandstone scenery, on the sea-board, for a view novel and most characteristic. The hippopotamus now raised his head from the waters, snorted, gazed upon us, and sank into his native depths. Alligators, terrified by the splash of oars, waddled down with their horrid claws, dinting the slimy bank, and lay like yellow logs, measuring us with small, malignant, green eyes, deep set under warty brows. Monkeys rustled the tall trees. Below, jungle—men and woman—

> 'So withered, so wild in their attire,
> That look not like th' inhabitants o' th' earth,
> And yet are on't.'

And all around reigned the eternal African silence, deep and saddening, broken only by the curlew's scream, or by the breeze rustling the tree-tops, whispering among the matted foliage, and swooning upon the tepid bosom of the wave.

"We sat under a tree till midnight, unsatiated with the charm of the hour. The moon rained molten silver over the dark foliage of the wild palms, the stars were as golden lamps suspended in the limpid air, and Venus glittered diamond-like upon the front of the firmament. The fireflies now sparkled simultaneously over the earth; then, as if by concerted impulse, their glow vanished in the glooms of the ground. At our feet lay the black creek; in the jungle beasts roared fitfully; and the night wind mingled melancholy sounds with the swelling murmuring of the stream.

"The tide flowing about midnight, we resumed our way. The river then became a sable streak between lofty rows of trees. The hippopotamus snorted close to our stern, and the crew begged me to fire, for the purpose of frightening 'Sultan Momba'—a pernicious rogue. At times we heard the splashing of the beasts as they scrambled over the shoals; at others, they struggled with loud grunts up the miry banks. Then again all was quiet. After a protracted interval of silence, the near voice of a man startled us in the deep drear stillness of the night, as though it had been some ghostly sound. At two a.m., reaching a clear tract on the river side—the Ghaut or landing-place of Chogway—we made fast the canoe, looked to our weapons, and, covering our faces against the heavy, clammy dew, lay down to snatch an hour's sleep. The total distance rowed was about 13·5 miles.

"Fifty stout fellows, with an ambitious leader and a little money, might soon conquer the whole country, and establish there an absolute monarchy.

"These Beloch mercenaries merit some notice. They were preferred, as being somewhat disciplinable, by the late Sayyid Said, to his futile blacks and his unruly and self-willed Oman Arabs. He entertained from one thousand to fifteen hundred men, and scattered them over the country in charge of the forts. The others hate them —divisions even amongst his own children was the ruler's policy— and nickname them 'Kurara Kurara.' The *Jemadar* and the Governor are rarely on speaking terms. Calling themselves Belochies, they are mostly from the regions about Kech and Bampur. They are mixed up with a rabble rout of Afghans and Arabs, Indians and Sudies, and they speak half a dozen different languages. Many of these gentry have left their country for their country's good. A body of convicts, however, fights well. The Mekrani are first-rate behind walls; and if paid, drilled, and officered, they would make as 'varmint' light-bobs as Arnauts. They have a knightly fondness for arms. A 'young barrel and an old blade' are their delight. All use the matchlock, and many are skilful with sword and shield.

"Having communicated our project to the *Jemadar* of Chogway, he promised, for a consideration, all aid; told us that we should start the next day; and, curious to relate, kept his word.

"A start was effected at five p.m., every slave complaining of his load, snatching up the lightest, and hurrying on regardless of what was left behind. This nuisance endured till summarily stopped by an outward application easily divined. The evening belling of deer and the clock-clock of partridge struck our ears. In the open places were the lesses of elephants, and footprints retained by the last year's mud. These animals descend to the plains during the monsoon, and in summer retire to the cool hills. The Belochies shoot, the wild people kill them with poisoned arrows. More than once during our wanderings we found the grave-like trap-pits, called in India, *ogi.*

"Tusks weighing 100 lbs. each are common, those of 175 lbs. are not rare, and I have heard of a pair whose joint weight was 560 lbs.

"At Makam Sayyid Sulayman—a half-cleared ring in the thorny jungle—we passed the night in a small babel of Belochies. One recited his Korán; another prayed; a third told funny stories; whilst a fourth trolled lays of love and war, long ago made familiar to my ear upon the rugged Asian hills. This was varied by slapping lank mosquitoes that flocked to the camp-fires; by rising to get rid of huge black pismires, whose bite burned like a red-hot needle; and by challenging two parties of savages, who, armed with bows and arrows, passed amongst us.

"Tongway is the first offset of the mountain-terrace composing the land of Usumbara. It rises abruptly from the plain, lies north-west of, and nine miles, as the crow flies, distant from, Chogway.

The summit, about two thousand feet above the sea-level, is clothed with jungle, through which, seeking compass-sights, we cut a way with our swords.

"The climate appeared delicious—even in the full blaze of an African and tropical summer; and whilst the hill was green, the land around was baked like bread-crust.

"The escort felt happy at Tongway, twice a day devouring our rice—an unknown luxury; and they were at infinite pains to defer the evil hour.

"Petty pilferers to the backbone, they steal, like magpies, by instinct. On the march they lag behind, and, not being professional porters, they are restive as camels when receiving their load. One of these youths, happening to be brother-in-law—after a fashion—to the *Jemadar*, requires incessant supervision to prevent him burdening the others with his own share. The guide, Muigni Wazira, is a huge broad-shouldered Sawahili, with a coal-black skin; his high, massive, and regular features look as if carved in ebony, and he frowns like a demon in the 'Arabian Nights.'

"A prayerless Sheríf, he thoroughly despises the Makapry or Infidels; he has a hot temper, and, when provoked, roars like a wild beast. He began by refusing his load, but yielded, when it was gently placed upon his heavy shoulder, with a significant gesture in case of recusance.

"Rahewat, the Mekrani, calls himself a Beloch, and wears the title of Shah-Sawar, or the Rider-king. He is the *chelebi*, the dandy and tiger of our party. A 'good-looking brown man,' about twenty-five years old, with a certain girlishness and affectation of *tournure* and manner, which bode no good, the Rider-king deals in the externals of respectability; he washes and prays with pompous regularity, combs his long hair and beard, trains his bushy moustache to touch his eyes, and binds a huge turban. Having somewhat high ideas of discipline, he began with stabbing a slave-boy by way of a lesson.

"The Rider-king, pleading soldier, positively refuses to carry anything but his matchlock, and a private stock of dates, which he keeps ungenerously to himself. He boasts of prowess in vert and venison: we never saw him hit the mark, but we missed some powder and ball.

"The gem of the party is Sudy Mubárak, who has taken to himself the cognomen of 'Bombay.' His sooty skin, and teeth pointed like those of the reptilia, denote his Mhiav origin. He is one of those rare 'Sudies' that delight the passengers in an Indian steamer. Bombay, sold in early youth, carried to Cutch by some Banyan, and there emancipated, looks fondly back upon the home of his adoption, and sighs for the day when a few dollars will enable him to return. He has ineffable contempt for all 'jungly niggers.' His head is a triumph of phrenology. He works on principle, and works like a horse, openly declaring that not love of us, but attachment to his stomach, make him industrious. He had enlisted under the *Jemadar* of Chogway. We thought, however, so highly of his qualifications, that persuasion and paying his debts induced him, after a little coquetting, to take leave of soldiering and follow our fortunes. Sudy Bombay will be our head gun-carrier, if he survives his present fever, and, I doubt not, will prove himself a rascal in the end.

"During the first night all Bombay's efforts were required to prevent a *sauve qui peut.*

"On the 10th of February, after a night of desert silence, we arose betimes, and applied ourselves to the work of porterage. Our luggage again suffered reduction. It was, however, past six a.m. when, forming Indian file, we began to descend the thorn-clad goat-track which spans the north-east spur of Mount Tongway. Overhead floated a filmy canopy of sea-green verdure, pierced by myriads of sunbeams, whilst the azure effulgence above, purified as with fire, from mist and vapour set the picture in a frame of gold and ultramarine. Painful splendours! The men began to drop off. None but Hamdan had brought a calabash. Shaaban clamoured for water. Wazira and the four slave-boys retired to some puddle, a discovery which they wisely kept to themselves, leaving the rest of the party to throw themselves under a tree and bush upon the hot ground.

"As the sun sank westward, Wazira joined us with a mouthful of lies, and the straggling line advanced. Our purblind guide once more lagged in the rear, yielding the lead to old Shaaban. This worthy, whose five wits were absorbed in visions of drink, strode blunderingly ahead, over the Wazira Hills and far away. Jack, keeping him in sight, and I in rear of both, missed the road. Shortly after sunset we three reached a narrow *fiumara*, where stood, delightful sight! some puddles bright with chickweed, and black with the mire below. We quenched our thirst, and bathed our swollen feet, and patted, and felt, and handled the water as though we loved it. But even this charming occupation had an end. Evidently we had lost our way. Our shots and shouts remained unanswered. It would have been folly to thread the thorny jungle by the dubious light of a young moon. We therefore kindled a fire, looked at our arms, lay down upon a soft sandy place, and certain that Shaaban would be watchful as a vestal virgin, were soon lulled to sleep by the music of the night breeze, and by the frogs chanting their ancient querele upon the miry margins of the pools. That day's work had been little more than five leagues. But—

> 'These high wild hills and rough uneven ways
> Draw out the miles.'

"Our guide secured, as extra porters, five wild men, habited in primitive attire. Their only garment was a kilt of dried and split rushes or grass. All had bows and poisoned arrows, except one, who boasted a miserable musket and literally a powder-horn, the vast spoils of a cow. The wretches were lean as wintry wolves, and not less ravenous. We fed them with rice and ghee. Of course they asked for more, till their stomachs, before like shrunken bladders, stood out in the shape of little round bumps from the hoop-work of ribs. We had neglected to take their arms. After feeding, they arose, and with small beady eyes, twinkling with glee, bade us farewell. Though starving they would not work. A few hours afterwards, however, they found a hippopotamus in the open, killed it with their arrows, and soon left nothing but a heap of bones and a broad stain of blood upon the ground.

"Arrived at Kohoday, the elders, as we landed, wrung our hands with rollicking greetings, and those immoderate explosive laughings which render the African family to all appearance so 'jolly' a race.

"We were shown, on the mountain-pass of Usumbara, the watch-fire which is never extinguished; and the Mzegura chief, when supplying us with a bullock, poked his thumb back towards the hills and said, with a roar of laughter, that already we had become the King's guests. Our Beloch guard applauded this kindred soul, patted him upon the shoulder, and declared that, with a score of men of war like themselves, he might soon become lord of all the mountains.

"Our parting was pathetic. He swore he loved us, and promised, on our return, the boat to conduct us down the river; but when we appeared with empty hands, he told the truth, namely, that it is a succession of falls and rapids.

"At five p.m., passing two bridges, we entered Msiky Mguru, a Wazegura village distant twelve miles from Kohoday. It is a cluster of hay-cock huts, touching one another, built upon an island formed by divers rapid and roaring branches of the river. The headman was sick, but we found a hospitable reception. We spent our nights with ants and other little murderers of sleep which shall be nameless. Our hosts expressed great alarm about the Masai. It was justified by the sequel. Scarcely had we left the country when a plundering party of wild spearmen attacked two neighbouring villages, slaughtering the hapless cultivators, and, with pillage and pollage, drove off the cows in triumph.

"After an hour's march we skirted a village, where the people peremptorily ordered us to halt. We attributed this annoyance to Wazira, who was forthwith visited with a general wigging. But the impending rain sharpened our tempers; we laughed in the faces of our angry expostulators, and, bidding them stop us if they could, pursued our road.

"Presently ascending a hill, and turning abruptly to the north-east, we found ourselves opposite, and about ten miles distant from, a tall azure curtain, the mountains of Fuga. Water stood in black pools, and around it waved luxuriant sugar-canes. In a few minutes every mouth in the party was tearing and chewing at a long pole. This cane is of the edible kind. The officinal varieties are too luscious, cloying, and bilious to be sucked with impunity by civilized men. After walking that day sixteen miles, at about four p.m. a violent storm of thunder, lightning, and raw south-west wind, which caused the thermometer to fall many degrees, and the slaves to shudder and whimper, drove us back into the *bandany*, or palaver-house of a large village. The place swarmed with flies and mosquitoes. We lighted fires to keep off fevers.

"Sunday, the 15th of February, dawned with one of those steady little cataclysms, which, to be seen advantageously, must be seen near the Line. At eleven a.m., weary of the steaming *bandany*, our men loaded, and in a lucid interval set out towards the Fuga Hills,* to which we walked for economy sake. As we approached them, the rain shrank to a spitting, gradually ceased, and was replaced by that reeking, fetid, sepulchral heat which travellers in the tropics know and fear. The slippery way had wearied our slaves, though aided by three porters hired that morning; and the sun, struggling through vapour, was still hot enough to overpower the whole party.

"Issuing from the dripping canopy, we followed a steep goat-track, fording a crystal burn, and having reached the midway, sat down to enjoy the rarefied air, and to use the compass and spyglass. The view before us was extensive, if not beautiful. Under our feet the mountains fell in rugged folds, clothed with plantain fields, wild mulberries, custard-apples, and stately trees, whose lustrous green glittered against the ochreous ground. The sarsaparilla vine hung in clusters from the supporting limbs of the tamarind, the toddy palm raised its fantastic arms over the dwarf coco, and bitter oranges mingled pleasant scent with herbs not unlike mint and sage. Below, half veiled by rank streams, lay the yellow Nika or Wazegura wilderness, traversed by a serpentine of trees denoting the course of the Mkomafi affluent. Far beyond we could see the well-wooded line of the Lufu river, and from it to the walls of the southern and western horizon stretched a uniform purple plain.

"The three fresh porters positively refused to rise unless a certain number of cloths were sent forward to propitiate the magnates of Fuga. This was easily traced to Wazira, who received a hint that such trifling might be dangerous. He had been lecturing us all that morning upon the serious nature of our undertaking. Sultan Kimwere was a potent monarch, not a Momba. His Ministers and councillors would, unless well paid, avert from us their countenances. We must enter with a discharge of musketry to awe the people, and by all means do as we are bid. The Belochies smiled contempt, and, pulling up the porters, loaded them, deaf to remonstrance.

"Resuming our march after a short halt, we climbed rather than walked, with hearts beating from such unusual exercise, up the deep zigzag of a torrent. Villages then began to appear perched like eyries upon the hilltops, and the people gathered to watch our approach. At four p.m. we found ourselves upon the summit of a ridge. The Belochies begged us to taste the water of a spring hard by. It was icy cold, with a perceptible chalybeate flavour, sparkled in the cup, and had dyed its head with rust.

"The giant flanks of Mukumbara bound the view. We stood about four thousand feet above the sea-level, distant thirty-seven miles from the coast, and seventy-four or seventy-five along the

* One of the places forbidden to strangers.

winding river. There is a short cut from Kohoday across the mountains; but the route was then waterless, and the heat would have disabled our Belochies.

"After another three-mile walk along the hill flanks, we turned a corner and suddenly sighted, upon the opposite summit of a grassy cone, an unfenced heap of hay-cock huts—Fuga. This being one of the Cities where ingress is now forbidden to strangers, we were led by Wazira through timid crowds that shrank back as we approached, round and below the cone, to four tattered huts, which superstition assigns as the 'travellers' bungalow.' Even the son and heir of great Kimwere must abide here till the lucky hour admits him to the presence and the Imperial City. The cold rain and sharp rarefied air rendering any shelter acceptable, we cleared the huts of sheep and goats, housed our valuables, and sent Sudy Bombay to the Sultan, requesting the honour of an interview.

"Before dark appeared three bareheaded *mdue*, or 'Ministers,' who in long palaver declared that council must squat upon two knotty points—*Primo*, Why and wherefore we had entered the country *viâ* the hostile Wazegura? *Secundo*, What time might be appointed by his Majesty's *mganga*, or medicine-man, for the ceremony? Sharp-witted Hamdan at once declared us to be European wizards, and *waganga* of peculiar power over the moon and stars, the wind and rain. Away ran the Ministers to report the wonder.

"The *mganga*, who is called by the Arabs *tabib*, or doctor, and by us priest, physician, divine, magician, and medicine-man, combines, as these translations show, priestly with medical functions.

"At six p.m. the Ministers ran back and summoned us to the 'Palace.' They led the way through rain and mist to a clump of the usual huts, half hidden by trees, and overspreading a little eminence opposite to and below Fuga.

"Sultan Kimwere half rose from his cot as we entered, and motioned us to sit upon dwarf stools before him. He was an old, old man, emaciated by sickness. His head was shaved, his face beardless, and wrinkled like a grandam's; his eyes were red, his jaws disfurnished, and his hands and feet were stained with leprous spots. Our errand was inquired and we were welcomed to Fuga. As none could read the Sayyid of Zanzibar's letter, I was obliged to act secretary. The centagenarian had heard of our scrutinizing stars, stones, and trees. He directed us at once to compound a draught which would restore him to health, strength, and youth. I replied that our drugs had been left at Pangany. He signified that we might wander about the hills and seek the plants required. After half an hour's conversation, Hamdan being interpreter, we were dismissed with a renewal of welcome.

"On our return to the hovels, the present was forwarded to the Sultan with the usual ceremony. We found awaiting us a fine bullock, a basketful of *sima*—young Indian corn pounded and boiled to a thick hard paste—and balls of unripe bananas, peeled and mashed up with sour milk. Our Belochies instantly addressed themselves to the making of beef, which they ate with such a will that unpleasant symptoms presently declared themselves in camp. We had covered that day ten miles—equal, perhaps, to thirty in a temperate climate and a decent road. The angry blast, the groaning trees, and the lashing rain, heard from within a warm hut, affected us pleasurably, and I would not have exchanged it for the music of Verdi. We slept the sweet sleep of travellers.

"The African Traveller, in this section of the nineteenth century, is an animal overworked. Formerly, the reading public was satisfied with dry details of mere discovery; was delighted with a few latitudes and longitudes. Of late, in this, as in other pursuits, the standard has been raised. Whilst marching so many miles *per diem*, and watching a certain number of hours *per noctem*, the traveller, who is in fact his own general, adjutant, quarter-master, and executive, is expected to survey and observe—to record meteorology, hygrometry, and hypsometry—to shoot and stuff birds and beasts, to collect geological specimens, to gather political and commercial information, to advance the infant study ethnology, to keep accounts, to sketch, to indite a copious legible journal, to collect grammar and vocabularies, and frequently to forward long reports which shall prevent the Royal Geographical Society napping through evening meetings. It is right, I own, to establish a high standard which insures some work being done; but explorations should be distinguished from railway journeys, and a broad line drawn between the feasible and the impossible. The unconscionable physicist now deems it his right to complain, because the explorer has not used his theodolite in the temple of Mecca, and introduced his sympiesometer within the walls of Harar. An ardent gentlemen once requested me to collect beetles, and another sent me excellent recipes for preserving ticks.

"These African explorations are small campaigns, in which the traveller, unaided by discipline, is beset by all the troubles, hardships, and perils of savage war. He must devote himself to feeding, drilling, and directing his men to the use of arms and the conduct of a Caravan, rather than the study of infusoria and barometers. The sight of an instrument convinces barbarians that the stranger is bringing down the sun, stopping rain, causing death, and bewitching the land for ages. Amidst utter savagery such operations are sometimes possible; amongst the semi-civilized they end badly. The climate also robs man of energy as well as health. He cannot, if he would, collect ticks and beetles. The simplest geodesical labours, as these pages will prove, are unadvisable. Jack has twice suffered from taking an altitude. Why is not a party of physicists sent out to swallow the dose prescribed by them to their army of martyrs?

"The rainy monsoon had set in at Fuga. Heavy clouds rolled up from the south-west, and during our two days and nights upon the hills the weather was a succession of drip, drizzle, and drench. In vain we looked for a star; even the sun could not disperse the thick raw vapours that rose from the steamy earth. We did not dare to linger upon the mountains. Our Belochies were not clad to resist the temperature—here 12° lower than on the coast; the rain would make the lowlands a hotbed of sickness, and we daily expected the inevitable 'seasoning-fever.' In the dry monsoon this route might be made practicable to Chhaga and Kilimanjaro. With an escort of a hundred musketeers, and at an expense of £600, the invalid who desires to avail himself of this 'sanitarium,' as it is now called by the Indian papers, may, if perfectly sound in wind, limb, and digestion, reach the snowy region, if it exist, after ten mountain-marches, which will not occupy more than a month.

"The head-quarter village of Usumbara is Fuga, a heap of some five hundred huts, containing, I was told, three thousand souls. It is defenceless, and composed of the circular abodes common from Harar to Timbuctoo.

"On Monday, the 16th of February, we took leave of, and were duly dismissed by, Sultan Kimwere. The old man, however, was mortified that our rambles had not produced a plant of sovereign virtue against the last evil of life. He had long expected a white *mganga*, and now two had visited him, to depart without even a trial! I felt sad to see the wistful lingering look with which he accompanied 'Kuahery!' (farewell!) But his case was far beyond my skill.

"None of Sultan Kimwere's men dared to face the terrible Wazegura.

"We descended the hills in a Scotch mist and drizzle, veiling every object from view. It deepened into a large-dropped shower upon the fœtid lowlands. That night we slept at Pasunga; the next at Msiky Mguru; and the third, after marching seventeen miles—our greatest distance—at Kohoday.

"Our Belochies declared the rate of marching excessive; and Hamdan, who personified 'Master Shoetie, the great traveller,' averred that he had twice visited the Lakes, but had never seen such hardships in his dreams.

"With some toil, however, we coaxed him into courage, and joined on the way a small party bound for Pangany. At one p.m. we halted to bathe and drink, as it would be some time before we should again sight the winding stream. During the storm of thunder and lightning which ensued, I observed that our savage companions, like the Thracians of old Herodotus, and the Bheels and coolies of modern India, shot their iron-tipped arrows in the air.

"About four p.m. we found ourselves opposite Kizanga, a large Wazegura village on the right bank of the river. From Kizanga we followed the river by a vile footpath. The air was dank and oppressive; the clouds seemed to settle upon the earth, and the decayed vegetation exhaled a feverish fœtor. As we advanced, the roar of the swollen stream told of rapids, whilst an occasional glimpse through its green veil showed a reefous surface, flecked with white froth. Heavy nimbi purpled the western skies, and we began to inquire of Wazira whether a village was at hand.

"About sunset, after marching fifteen miles, we suddenly saw tall cocos—in these lands the 'traveller's joy'—waving their feathery heads against the blue eastern firmament. Presently, crossing a branch of the river by a long bridge, we entered an island settlement of Wazegura. This village, being upon the confines of civilization, and excited by wars and rumours of wars, suggested treachery to experienced travellers. Jack and I fired our revolvers into trees, and carefully reloaded them for the public benefit. The sensation was such that we seized the opportunity of offering money for rice and ghee. No provision, however, was procurable. Our escort went to bed supperless; Hamdan cursing this *Safar khâis—Anglicè*, rotten journey. Murad Ali had remained at Msiky Mguru to purchase a slave without our knowledge. A novice in such matters, he neglected to tie the man's thumb, and had the exquisite misery to see, in the evening after the sale, his dollars bolting at a pace that baffled pursuit. We then placed our weapons handy, and were soon lulled to sleep, despite smoke, wet beds, and other plagues, by the blustering wind and the continuous pattering of rain.

"At sunrise on Friday, the 20th of February, we were aroused by the guide; and, after various delays, found ourselves on the road about seven a.m. This day was the reflection of the last march. At nine a.m. we stood upon a distant eminence to admire the falls of the Pangany river. Here the stream, emerging from a dense dark growth of tropical forest, hurls itself in three huge sheets, fringed with flashing foam, down a rugged wall of brown rock. Halfway the fall is broken by a ledge, whence a second leap precipitates the waters into the mist-veiled basin of stone below. These cascades must be grand during the monsoon, when the river, forming a single horseshoe, acquires a volume and a momentum sufficient to clear the step which divides the shrunken stream. Of all natural objects, the cataract most requires that first element of sublimity—size. Yet, as it was, this fall, with the white spray and bright mist, set off by black jungle, and a framework of slaty raincloud, formed a picture sufficiently effective to surprise us.

"As we journeyed onwards the heat became intense. The nimbi hugged the mountain tops. There it was winter; but the sun, whose beams shot stingingly through translucent air, parched the summer plains. At ten a.m. our Belochies, clean worn out by famine and fatigue, threw themselves upon the bank of a broad and deep ravine, in whose sedgy bed a little water still lingered. Half an hour's rest, a cocoa-nut each, a pipe, and, above all things, the *spes finis*, restored their vigour. We resumed our march over a rolling waste of green, enlivened by occasional glimpses of the river, whose very aspect cooled the gazer. Villages became frequent as we advanced, far distancing our Belochies. At three p.m., after marching fourteen miles, we sighted the snake-fence and the pent-houses of friendly Chogway.

"The *Jemadar* and his garrison received us with all the honours of travel, and admired our speedy return from Fuga. As at Harar, a visitor can never calculate upon a prompt dismissal. We were too strong for force, but Sultan Kimwere has detained Arab and other strangers for a fortnight before his *mganga* fixed a fit time for audience. Moreover, these walking journeys are dangerous in one point: the least accident disables a party, and accidents will happen to the best-regulated expedition.

"Our feet were cut by boots and shoes, and we had lost 'leather' by chafing and sunburns. A few days' rest removed these inconveniences. Our first visit was paid to Pangany, where Said bin Salim, who had watched his charge with the fidelity of a shepherd's dog, received us with joyous demonstrations. After spending a day upon the coast, we returned, provided with *munitions de bouche* and other necessaries, to Chogway, and settled old scores with our escort. Then, as the vessel in which we were to cruise southward was not expected from Zanzibar till the 1st of March, and we had a week to spare, it was resolved to try a fall with Behemoth.*

"Captain Owen's officers, when ascending streams, saw their boats torn by Behemoth's hard tusks; and in the Pangany, one 'Sultan Momba,' a tyrant thus dubbed by the Belochies in honour of their friend the Kohoday chief, delighted to upset canoes, and was once guilty of breaking a man's leg.

"Behold us now, O brother in St. Hubert, dropping down the stream in a *monoxyle*, some forty feet long, at early dawn, when wild beasts are tamest.

"As we approach the herds, whose crests, flanked with small pointed ears, dot the mirrory surface, our boatmen indulge in such vituperations as 'Mana marira!' (O big belly!) and 'Hanamkia!' (O tasteless one!) In angry curiosity the brutes raise their heads, and expose their arched necks, shiny with trickling rills. Jack, a man of speculative turn, experiments upon the nearest optics with two barrels of grape and B shot. The eyes, however, are oblique; the charge scatters, and the brute, unhurt, slips down like a seal. This will make the herd wary. Vexed by the poor result of our trial, we pole up the rippling and swirling surface, that proves the enemy to be swimming under water towards the further end of the pool. After a weary time he must rise and breathe. As the smooth water undulates, swells, and breaches a way for the large black head, eight ounces of lead fly in the right direction. There is a splash, a struggle; the surface foams, and Behemoth, with mouth bleeding like a gutter-spout, rears, and plunges above the stream. Wounded near the cerebellum, he cannot swim straight. At last a *coup de grâce* speeds through the air; the brute sinks, gore dyes the surface purple, and bright bubbles seethe up from the bottom. Hippo is dead. We wait patiently for his reappearance, but he appears not. At length, by peculiar good luck, Bombay's sharp eye detects an object some hundred yards down stream. We make for it, and find our "bag" brought up in a shallow by a spit of sand, and already in process of being ogled by a large fish-hawk. The hawk suffers the penalty of impudence. We tow our defunct to the bank, and deliver it to certain savages, whose mouths water with the prospect of

* Hippopotamus.

hippopotamus beef. At sundown they will bring to us the tusks and head picked clean, as a whistle is said to be.

"The herd will no longer rise; they fear this hulking craft; we must try some 'artful dodge.' Jack, accompanied by Bombay, who strips to paddle in token of hot work expected, enters into a small canoe, ties fast his shooting-tackle in case of an upset, and, whilst I occupy one end of the house, makes for the other. Whenever a head appears an inch above water, a heavy bullet 'puds' into or near it; crimson patches adorn the stream; some die and disappear, others plunge in crippled state, and others, disabled from diving by holes drilled through their noses, splash and scurry about with curious snorts, caused by breath passing through their wounds. At last Jack ventures upon another experiment. An infant hippo, with an imprudence pardonable at his years, uprears his crest; off flies the crown of the kid's head. The bereaved mother rises for a moment, viciously regards Jack, who is meekly loading, snorts a parent's curse, and dives as the cap is being adjusted. Presently a bump, a shock, and a heave send the little canoe's bows high in the air. Bombay, describing a small parabola in frog-shape, lands beyond the enraged brute's back. Jack steadies himself in the stern, and as the assailant, with broad dorsum hunched up and hogged like an angry cat, advances for another bout, he rises, and sends a bullet through her side. Bombay scrambles in, and, nothing daunted, paddles towards the quarry, of which nothing is visible but a long waving line of gore. With a harpoon we might have secured her; now she will feed the alligators or the savages.

"The Belochies still take great interest in the sport, as Easterns will when they see work being done. They force the boatmen to obey us. Jack lands with the black woodmen, carrying both 'smashers.' He gropes painfully through mangrove thicket, where parasitical oysters wound the legs with their sharp edges, and the shaking bog admits a man to his knees. After a time, reaching a clear spot, he takes up position behind a bush impending the deepest water, and signals me to drive up the herd. In pursuit of them I see a hole bursting in the stream, and a huge black head rises with a snort and a spirt. 'Momba! Momba!' shout the Belochies, yet the old rogue disdains flight. A cone from the Colt strikes him full in front of the ear; his brain is pierced; he rises high, falls with a crash upon the wave, and all that flesh 'cannot keep in a little life.' Momba has for ever disappeared from the home of hippopotamus; never shall he break nigger's leg again. Meanwhile the herd, who, rubbing their backs against the great canoe, had retired to the other end of the pool, hearing an unusual noise, rise, as is their wont, to gratify a silly curiosity. Jack has two splendid standing shots, and the splashing and circling in the stream below tell the accuracy of the aim.

"We soon learned the lesson that these cold-blooded animals may be killed with a pistol-ball if hit in brain or heart; otherwise they carry away as much lead as elephants. At about ten a.m. we had slain six, besides wounding I know not how many of the animals. They might be netted, but the operation would not pay in a pecuniary sense; the ivory of small teeth, under four pounds each, is worth little. Being perpetually pop-gunned by the Belochies, they are exceedingly shy, and after an excess of bullying they shift quarters. We returned but once to this sport, finding the massacre monotonous, and such cynegetics about as exciting as partridge-shooting.

"On Thursday, the 26th of February, we left 'the bazar.' Jack walked to Pangany, making a route survey, whilst I accompanied the *Jemadar* and his tail in our large canoe.

"For two days after returning to the coast we abstained from exercise. On the third we walked out several miles, in the hottest of suns, to explore a cavern, of which the natives, who came upon it when clearing out a well, had circulated the most exaggerated accounts. Jack already complained of his last night's labour—an hour with the sextant upon damp sand in the chilly dew. This walk finished the work. On entering the house we found the Portuguese lad, who had accompanied us to Fuga, in a high fever. Jack was prostrated a few hours afterwards, and next day I followed their example.

"As a rule, the traveller in these lands should avoid exposure and fatigue beyond a certain point, to the very best of his ability. You might as well practise sitting upon a coal-fire as inuring yourself (which green men have attempted) to the climate. Dr. B——, a Polish divine, who had taken to travelling at the end of a sedentary life, would learn to walk bareheaded in the Zanzibar sun; the result was a sunstroke. Others have paced barefooted upon an exposed terrace, with little consequence but ulceration and temporary lameness. The most successful in resisting the climate are they who tempt it least, and the best training for a long hungry march is repose, with good living. Man has then stamina to work upon; he may exist, like the camel, upon his own fat. Those who fine themselves down by exercise and abstinence before the march, commit the error of beginning where they ought to end.

"Our attacks commenced with general languor and heaviness, a lassitude in the limbs, a weight in the head, nausea, a frigid sensation creeping up the extremities, and dull pains in the shoulders. Then came a mild, cold fit, succeeded by a splitting headache, flushed face, full veins, vomiting, and an inability to stand upright. Like 'General Tazo' of Madagascar, this fever is a malignant bilious-remittent. The eyes become hot, heavy, and painful when turned upwards; the skin is dry and burning, the pulse full and frequent, and the tongue furred; appetite is wholly wanting (for a whole week I ate nothing), but a perpetual craving thirst afflicts the patient, and nothing that he drinks will remain upon his stomach. During the day extreme weakness causes anxiety and depression; the nights are worse, for by want of sleep the restlessness is aggravated. Delirium is common in the nervous and bilious temperament, and if the lancet be used, certain death ensues; the action of the heart cannot be restored. The exacerbations are slightly but distinctly marked (in my own case they recurred regularly between two and three a.m. and p.m.), and the intervals are closely watched for administering quinine, after due preparation. This drug, however, has killed many, especially Frenchmen, who, by overdosing at a wrong time, died of apoplexy.

"Whilst the Persians were at Zanzibar they besieged Colonel Hamerton's door, begging him to administer Warburg's drops, which are said to have a wonderful effect in malignant chronic cases. When the disease intends to end fatally, the symptoms are aggravated; the mind wanders, the body loses all power, and after perhaps an apparent improvement, stupor, insensibility, and death ensue. On the other hand, if yielding to treatment, the fever, about the seventh day, presents marked signs of abatement; the tongue is clearer, pain leaves the head and eyes, the face is no longer flushed, nausea ceases, and a faint appetite returns. The recovery, however, is always slow and dubious. Relapses are feared, especially at the full and change of the moon; they frequently assume the milder intermittent type, and in some Indians have recurred regularly through the year. In no case, however, does the apparent severity of the fever justify the dejection and debility of the convalescence. For six weeks recovery is imperfect; the liver acts with unusual energy, the stomach is liable to severe indigestion, the body is lean, and the strength wellnigh prostrated. At such times change of air is the best of restoratives; removal, even to a ship in the harbour, or to the neighbouring house, has been found more beneficial than all the tonics and the preventatives in the Pharmacopœia.

"In men of strong nervous diathesis the fever leaves slight consequences, in the shape of white hair, boils, or bad toothaches. Others suffer severely from its secondaries, which are either visceral or cerebral. Some lose memory, others virility, others the use of a limb; many become deaf or dim-sighted; and not a few, tormented by hepatitis, dysentery, constipation, and similar disease, never completely recover health.

"Captain Owen's survey of the Mombas Mission, and of our numerous cruisers, proves that no European can undergo exposure and fatigue, which promote the overflow of bile, without undergoing the 'seasoning.' It has, however, one advantage—those who pass the ordeal are acclimatized; even with a year's absence in Europe, they return to the tropics with little danger. The traveller is always advised to undergo his seasoning upon the coast before marching into the interior; but after recovery he must await a second attack, otherwise he will expend in preparation the strength and bottom required for the execution of his journey. Of our party the Portuguese boy came in for his turn at Zanzibar. The other has ever since had light relapses; and as a proof that the negro enjoys no immunity, Seedy * Bombay is at this moment (June 8th) suffering severely.

"The Banyans intended great civility; they would sit with us

* He was originally Sudy, but afterwards they dubbed him Seedy.—I. B.

for hours, asking, like Orientals, the silliest of questions, and thinking withal that they were 'doing the agreeable:' repose was out of the question. During the day, flies and gnats added another sting to the mortifications of fever. At night, rats nibbled at our feet, mosquitoes sang their song of triumph, and a torturing thirst made the terrible sleeplessness yet more terrible. Our minds were morbidly fixed upon one point, the arrival of our vessel; we had no other occupation but to rise and gaze, and exchange regrets as a sail hove in sight, drew near, and passed by. We knew that there would be no failure on the part of our thoughtful friend, who had written to promise us a *battela* on the 1st of March, which did not make Pangany till the evening of the 5th of March.

"After sundry bitter disappointments, we had actually hired a Banyan's boat that had newly arrived, when the expected craft ran into the river. Not a moment was to be lost. Said bin Salim, who had been a kind nurse, superintended the embarkation of our property. Jack, less severely treated, was able to walk to the shore; but I—alas for manliness!—was obliged to be supported like a bedridden old woman. The worst part of the process was the presence of a crowd. The Arabs were civil, and bade a kindly farewell. The Sawahili, however, audibly contrasted the present with the past, and drew dedecorous conclusions from the change which a few days had worked in the man who bore a twenty-four pound gun, my pet four-ounce.*

"All thoughts of cruising along the southern coast were at an end. Colonel Hamerton had warned us not to despise bilious-remittents; and evidently we should not have been justified in neglecting his caution to return, whenever seized by sickness. With the dawn of Friday, the 6th of March, we ordered the men to up sail; we stood over for Zanzibar with a fine fresh breeze, and early in the afternoon we found ourselves once more within the pale of Eastern civilization. *Deo gratias!* our excellent friend at once sent us to bed, whence, gentle reader, we have the honour to make the reverential salaam."

* These two guns I still treasure.—I. B.

CHAPTER XIII.

THE REAL START FOR TANGANYIKA IN THE INTERIOR.

"WHEN we left Zanzibar the Sultan of Zanzibar and the Sawahil and his sons came on board with three letters of introduction. One was to Musa Mzuri, the Indian *doyen* of the merchants settled at Unyamwezi; secondly, a letter to the Arabs there resident, and thirdly, one to all his subjects who were travelling in the interior. I carried, in an *étui* round my neck, the diploma of the Shaykh El Islam of Mecca, and a passport from Cardinal Wiseman to all the Catholic missionaries. His Highness the Sultan Said of Muscat had died on his way from Arabia to Zanzibar. The party, besides Jack and I, were two Goanese boys, two negro gun-carriers, the Seedy Mubárak Mombai (Bombay), his brother, and eight Beloch mercenaries appointed by the Sultan. Lieut.-Colonel Hamerton, her Majesty's Consul at Zanzibar, a friend of mine, gave me all particulars and recommendations, and enlisted in my favour the Sayyid Sulayman bin Hamid bin Said (the noble Omani, 'who never forgets the name of his Grandsire'), landed us upon the coast, and superintended our departure, attended by Mr. Frost, the apothecary attached to the Consulate.

"My desire was to ascertain the limits of the Sea of Ujiji, Tanganyika, or Unyamwezi Lake, to learn the ethnography of its tribes, and determine the export of the produce of the interior. The Foreign Office granted £1000, and the Court of Directors allowed me two years' leave of absence to command the Expedition. Consul Hamerton warned us against Kilwa, where any one attempting to open the interior ran the danger of being murdered.

"We landed at Wale Point, about eighty-four miles distant from the little town of Bagamóyo. We wanted to engage one hundred and seventy porters, but we could only get thirty-six, and thirty animals were found, which were all dead in six months, so we had to leave part of our things behind, greater part of the ammunition, and our iron boat. The Hindoos were faithful to their promise to forward everything, but, great mistake, received one hundred and fifty dollars for the hire of twenty-two men to start in ten days; we went on, obliged to trust, but we did not get them for eleven months. We paid various visits to the hippopotamus haunts, and had our boat uplifted from the water upon the points of two tusks, which made corresponding holes in the bottom. My escort were under the impression that nothing less than one hundred guards, one hundred and fifty guns, and several cannon would enable them to fight a way through the perils of the interior. We were warned that for three days we must pass through savages, who sat on the trees, and discharged poisoned arrows into the air with extraordinary dexterity (meaning the Amazons); that they must avoid trees (which was not easy in a land all forest); that the Wazaramo had sent six several letters forbidding the white man to enter their country, and that they buried their provisions in the jungle, that travellers might starve; that one rhinoceros kills two hundred men; that armies of elephants attack camps by night; that the craven hyæna is more dangerous than a Bengal tiger.

"We owed all our intrigues to a rascal named Ramji, who had his own commerce in view, and often to our *Ras Kaptan*, or Caravan leader, Said bin Salim, who did not wear well. The varnish soon melted, and showed him as great a liar and thief as his men. At times it is good to appear a dupe, to allow people to think and to say that you are a muff, chronicling a vow that they shall change places with you before the end of the game. I confided to Mr. Frost two manuscripts addressed through the Foreign Office, one to Mr. John Blackwood of Edinburgh, the other to Mr. Norton Shaw, of the Royal Geographical Society. Blackwood's arrived safe, Norton Shaw's in six years.* I took a melancholy leave of my warm-hearted friend, Lieut.-Colonel Hamerton, who had death written on his features. He looked forward to death with a feeling of delight, the result of his Roman Catholic religious convictions, and, in spite of my entreaties, he *would* remain near the coast till he heard of our safe transit through the lands of the dangerous Wazaramo. This courage was indeed sublime, an example not often met with. After this affecting farewell we landed at Kaolé. I insisted that Ladha, the Collector of customs, and Ramji, his clerk, should insert in the estimate the sum required to purchase a boat upon the Sea of Ujiji. Being a Hindoo, he thought I was ignorant of Cutchee, so the following conversation took place:—

"*Ladha.* Will he ever reach it?

"*Ramji.* Of course not. What is *he* that he should pass through Ugogo? (a province about halfway).

* Some of these things disappeared in a very singular manner, and one was very curiously fated. It was missed here, and came home to me in six years. Later on, in 1863, it again disappeared for six years. It was stolen at Fernando Po in 1863; it was marked by somebody on a bit of parchment, "Burton's Original Manuscript Diary, Africa, 1857." Colonel Maude, the Queen's Equerry, saw it outside an old book-shop, was attracted by the label on the Letts's Diary. He bought it for a few shillings, called on Lord Derby, and left it in the hall, forgetting it. Lord Derby, coming down, saw the book, recognized my handwriting, wrote to Colonel Maude for permission to restore the private diary to its rightful owner. We happened to be in town. He kindly called and gave it back to us, so that journal twice disappeared for six years, but had to come home. Who shall say there is no destiny in this?

"So I remarked at once that I *did* intend to cross Ugogo, and also the Sea of Ujiji, that I did know Cutchee, and that I was even able to distinguish between the debits and the credits of his voluminous sheets. The worst loss that I had was that my old and valued friend, Dr. Steinhaüser, civil surgeon at Aden, sound scholar, good naturalist, skilful practitioner, with rare personal qualities, which would have been inestimable, was ill and could not come. His Highness the late Sayyid Said, that great ally of the English nation, had made most public-spirited offers to his friend, Lieut.-Colonel Hamerton, for many years. Lieut.-Colonel Hamerton's extraordinary personal qualities enabled him to perform anything but impossibilities amongst the Arabs, and he was dying. Finally, as Indian experience taught me, I was entering the 'unknown land' at the fatal season when the shrinking of the waters after the wet monsoon would render it a hotbed of malaria, but I was tied by scanty means and a limited 'leave;' it was neck or nothing, and I determined to risk it. All the serving men in Zanzibar Island and the East African coast are serviles. There is no word to express a higher domestic. There was no remedy, so that I paid them wages, and treated them as if they were free men. I had no power to prevent my followers purchasing slaves, because they would say, 'We are allowed by our law to do so;' all I could do was to see that their slaves were well fed and not injured; but I informed all the wild people that Englishmen were pledged against slavery, and I always refused all slaves offered as presents.

"In eighteen days we accomplished (despite sickness and every manner of difficulty) a march of one hundred and eighteen indirect statute miles, and entered K'hutu, the safe rendezvous of foreign merchants, on the 14th of July. On the 15th we entered Kiruru, where I found a cottage, and enjoyed for the first time an atmosphere of sweet, warm smoke." (In all Richard's wilder travels in damp places, he laid such a stress upon "sweet, warm smoke.") "Jack (that is, Speke), in spite of my endeavours, would remain in the reeking miry tent, and laid the foundations of the fever which threatened his life in the mountains of Usagára.

"As soon as we reached Dut'húmi, where we were detained nearly a week, the malaria brought on attacks of marsh fever. In my case it lasted twenty days." (In all Richard's fever fits, and for hours afterwards, both now and always, he had a queer conviction of divided identity, never ceasing to be two persons, who generally thwarted and opposed each other, and also that he was able to fly.) "Jack suffered still more; he had a fainting-fit which strongly resembled a sunstroke, and it seemed to affect him more or less throughout our journey. Our sufferings were increased by the losses of our animals, and we had to walk, often for many miles, through sun, rain, mud, and miasmatic putridities. The asses shy, stumble, rear, run away, fight, plunge and pirouette when mounted; they hog and buck till they burst their girths; they love to get into holes and hollows; they rush about like pigs when the wind blows; they bolt under tree-shade when the sun shines; so they have to be led, and if the least thing happens the slave drops the halter and runs away.

"The Zanzibar riding-asses were too delicate and died; we were then reduced to the half-reclaimed beast of Wamyamwezi. As to the baggage animals, they were constantly thrown, and the Beloch only grumbled, sat down, and stared. They stole the ropes and cords; they never were pounded for the night, nobody counted them, and we were too ill to look after it. We were wretched; each morning dawned with a fresh load of care and trouble, and every evening we knew that another miserable morrow was to dawn, but I never relinquished the determination to risk everything, myself included, rather than to return unsuccessful. At Dut'húmi, two Chiefs fought, and the strongest kidnapped five of his weaker neighbour subjects. I could not stand by and see iniquity done without an attempt, so I headed a little Expedition against the strong, and I had the satisfaction of restoring the rescued, the five unhappy stolen wretches, to their hearths and homes, and two decrepit old women, that had been rescued from slavery, thanked me with tears of joy" (Richard lightly calls this "an easy good deed" done), "after which I was able, though with swimming head and trembling hands, to prepare a report for the Geographical Society.

"On the 24th of July we were able to move on under the oppressive rain-sun. From Central K'hutu to the base of the Usagára Mountains there were nothing but filthy heaps of the rudest hovels, built in holes of the jungle. Their miserable inhabitants, whose frames are lean with constant intoxication, and whose limbs are distorted by ulcerous sores, attest the hostility of Nature to Mankind.

"Arrived at Zungomero, we waited a fortnight for the twenty-two promised porters. It was a hotbed of pestilence, where we nearly found wet graves. Our only lodging was the closed eaves of a hut; the roof was a sieve, the walls all chinks, and the floor a sheet of mud. The Beloch had no energy to build a shed, and became almost mutinous because we did not build it for them.

"Our life here was the acme of discomfort; we had pelting showers, followed by fiery sunshine, which extracted steam from the grass, bush, and trees. My Goanese boys got a mild form of 'yellow Jack,' and I was obliged to take them into my hut, already populated with pigeons, rats, flies, mosquitoes, bugs, and fleas. We were weary of waiting for the porters and baggage, so we prepared our papers, and sent them down by a confidential slave to the coast. Jack and I left Zungomero on the 7th of August. We were so weak, we could hardly sit our asses, but we were determined to get to the nearest ascent of the Usagára Mountains, a march of five hours, and succeeded in rising three hundred feet from the plain, ascending its first gradient.

"This is the frontier of the second region, or Ghauts. There was no vestige of buildings, nor sight nor sound of Man. There was a wondrous change of climate at this place, called Mzizi Maogo; strength and health returned as if by magic, even the

Goanese shook off their mild 'yellow Jack.' Truly delicious was the escape from the nebulous skies, the fog-driving gusts, the pelting rain, the clammy mists veiling a gross growth of fœtor, the damp raw cold rising as it were from the earth, and the alternations of fiery and oppressive heat; in fact, from the cruel climate of the river valley, to the pure sweet mountain air, alternately soft and balmy, cool and reviving, and to the aspect of clear blue skies, which lent their tints to highland ridges well wooded with various greens.

"Dull mangrove, dismal jungle, and monotonous grass were supplanted by tall solitary trees, amongst which the lofty tamarind rose conspicuously graceful, and a card-table-like swamp, cut by a network of streams, nullahs, and stagnant pools, gave way to dry healthy slopes, with short steep pitches and gently shelving hills. The beams of the large sun of the Equator—and nowhere have I seen the Rulers of Night and Day so large—danced gaily upon blocks and pebbles of red, yellow, and dazzling snowy quartz, and the bright sea-breeze waved the summits of the trees, from which depended graceful llianas and wood-apples large as melons, whilst creepers, like vine tendrils, rising from large bulbs of brown-grey wood, clung closely to their stalwart trunks. Monkeys played at hide-and-seek, chattering behind the bolls, as the iguana, with its painted scale-armour, issued forth to bask upon the sunny bank; white-breasted ravens cawed when disturbed from their perching places, doves cooed on the well-clothed boughs, and hawks soared high in the transparent sky. The field-cricket chirped like the Italian cicala in the shady bush, and everywhere, from air, from earth, from the hill-slopes above, and from the marshes below, the hum, the buzz, and the loud continuous voice of insect life, through the length of the day, spoke out its natural joy. Our gypsy encampment lay

'By shallow rivers, to whose falls
Melodious birds sing madrigals.'

By night, the soothing murmurs of the stream at the hill's base rose mingled with the faint rustling of the breeze, which at times, broken by the scream of the night-heron, the bellow of the bull-frog in his swamp home, the cynhyæna's whimper, and the fox's whining bark, sounded through the silence most musical, most melancholy. Instead of the cold night rain, and the soughing of the blast, the view disclosed a peaceful scene, the moonbeams lying like sheets of snow upon the ruddy highlands, and the stars hanging like lamps of gold from the dome of infinite blue. I never wearied with contemplating the scene, for, contrasting with the splendours around me, still stretched in sight the 'Slough of Despond,' unhappy Zungomero, lead-coloured above, mud-coloured below, wind-swept, fog-veiled, and deluged by clouds that dared not approach these Delectable Mountains.

"All along our way we were saddened by the sight of clean-picked skeletons, and here and there the swollen corpses of porters who had perished in this place by starvation. A single large body which passed us but yesterday had lost fifty of their number by small-pox, and the sight of their deceased comrades made a terrible impression. Men staggering on, blinded by disease, mothers carrying on their backs infants as loathsome as themselves. The poor wretches would not leave the path, as every step in their state of failing strength was precious. He who once fell would never rise again. No village would admit a corpse into its precincts, no friend or relation would return for them, and they would lie till their agony was ended by the raven, the vulture, and the fox. Near every kraal were detached huts set apart for those seized with the fell disease. Several of our party caught the infection, and must have thrown themselves into some jungle, for when they were missed we came back to look and there was no sign of them. The further we went on, the more numerous were the corpses. Our Moslems passed them with averted faces, and with the low 'La haul!' of disgust, and a decrepit old porter gazed and wept for himself. At the foot of the 'Goma Pass' we found the outlying huts for the small-pox, and an old kraal, where we made comfortable for the night. All around peeped the little beehive villages of the Wakaguru and the Wakwivi.

"When we arrived at Rufuta I found that nearly all our instruments had been spoilt or broken, the barometer had come to grief, no aneroid had been sent from Bombay, and we had chiefly to get on with two bath thermometers. Zonhwe was the turning-point of the expedition's difficulties. The 17th of August, as we went on, the path fell easily westwards down a long grassy jungly incline, cut by several water-courses. At noon I lay down fainting in the sandy bed of the Muhama nullah, meaning the 'Palmetto' or 'Fan-palm,' and keeping Wazira and Mabruki with me, I begged Jack to go on, and send me back a hammock from the halting-place. The men, who were partly mutinous and deserting, suddenly came out well; they reappeared, led me to a place where stagnant water was found, and showed abundant penitence. At three o'clock, as Jack did not send the hammock, I remounted and passed through another 'Slough of Despond' like Zungomero, and found two little villages, and on a hillside my caravan halted, which had been attacked by a swarm of wild bees. At Muhama we halted three days, and forded the Makata, and pursuing our march next day, I witnessed a curious contrast in this strange African nature, which is ever in extremes, and where extremes ever meet, where grace and beauty are seldom seen without a sudden change to a hideous grotesqueness.

"A splendid view charmed me in the morning. Above lay a sky of purest azure, flaked with fleecy opal-tinted vapours floating high in the empyrean, and catching the first roseate smiles of the unrisen sun. Long lines, one bluer than the other, broken by castellated crags and towers of the most picturesque form, girdled the far horizon; the nearer heights were of a purplish-brown, and snowy mists hung like glaciers about their folds. The plain was a park in autumn, burnt tawny by the sun or patched with a darker hue where the people were firing the grass—a party was at work merrily, as if preparing for an English harvest home—to start the animals, to promote the growth of a young crop, and, such is the popular belief, to attract rain. Calabashes, palmyras, tamarinds, and clumps of evergreen trees, were scattered over the scene, each stretching its lordly form over subject circlets of deep dew-fed verdure. Here the dove cooed loudly, and the guinea-fowl rang its wild cry, whilst the peewit chattered in the open stubble, and a little martin, the prettiest of its kind, contrasted by its nimble dartings along the ground, with the vulture wheeling slowly through the upper air. The most graceful of animals, the zebra and the antelope, browsed in the distance; now they stood to gaze upon the long line of porters, then, after leisurely pacing, with retrospective glances, in an opposite direction, they halted motionless for a moment, faced about once more to satiate curiosity, and lastly, terrified by their own fancy, they bounded in ricochets over the plain.

"About noon the fair scene vanished as if by enchantment. We suddenly turned northwards into a tangled mass of tall fœtid reeds, rank jungle, and forest. One constantly feels, in malarious places, suddenly poisoned as if by miasma; a shudder runs through the frame and a cold perspiration, like a prelude for a fainting fit, breaks from the brow. We came upon the deserted—once flourishing—village of Wasagara, called Mbumi. The huts were torn and half burnt, the ground strewed with nets and drums, pestles and mortars, cots and fragments of rude furniture; the sacking seemed to be about ten days old. Two wretched villagers were lurking in the jungle, not daring to revisit the wreck of their own homes. The demon of Slavery reigns over a solitude of his own creation; can it be, that by some inexplicable law, where Nature has done her best for the happiness of Mankind, Man, doomed to misery, must work out his own unhappiness?

"Next day our path was slippery as mud, and man and beast were rendered wild by the cruel stings of a small red ant and a huge black pismire. They are large headed; they cannot spring, but show great quickness in fastening themselves to the foot or ankle as it brushes over them. The pismire is a horse-ant, about an inch in length, whose bulldog head and powerful mandibles enable it to destroy rats and mice, lizards and snakes; its bite burns like a pinch of a red-hot needle. When it sets to work, twisting itself round, it may be pulled in two without relaxing its hold. As the people stopped to drink they were seized by these dreadful creatures, and suddenly began to dance and shout like madmen, pulling off their clothes, and frantically snatching at their lower limbs. In the evening it was like a savage opera scene. One would recite his Korán, another pray; a third told funny stories; a fourth trolled out in a minor key lays of love and war that were familiar to me upon the Scindian hills. This was varied by slapping away the black mosquitoes, ridding ourselves of ants, and challenging small parties of savages who passed us from time to time with bows and arrows.

"Now we also began to suffer severely from the tzetze fly, which is the true *Glossina morsitans*. It extended from Usagara westward as far as the Central Lakes. It has more persistency of purpose than an Egyptian fly; when beaten off, it will return half a dozen times to the charge. It cannot be killed except by a smart blow, and its long sharp proboscis draws blood through a canvas hammock. The sting is like an English horse-fly and leaves a lasting trace. This land is eminently fitted for breeding cattle and for agriculture, which, without animals, cannot be greatly extended. Why this plague should have been placed here, unless to exercise human ingenuity, I cannot imagine. Perhaps some day it will be exterminated by the introduction of some insectiferous bird, which will be the greatest benefactor that Central Africa ever knew. The brown ant has cellular hills of about three feet high, whereas in Somali-land they become dwarf ruins of round towers. When we reached Rumuma the climate was new to us, after the incessant rains of the Maritime Valley, and the fogs and mists of the Rufuta range; but it was in extremes—the thermometer under the influence of dewy gusts sank in the tent to 48° F., a killing temperature in these latitudes to half-naked and houseless men. During the day it showed 90° F.; the sun was fiery, and a furious south wind coursed through skies purer and bluer than I had ever seen in Greece or Italy.

"When we were ill our followers often mutinied, and would do nothing, but stole and lost our goods, and would not work. Sometimes, though they carried the water, they would refuse us any. Jack was as ill as I was. We reached Rubeho, the third and westernmost range of the Usagára Mountains, and here we were welcomed with joy, and given milk and butter and honey, a real treat. Here we were in danger of being attacked by the Wahúmba. Next day a Caravan arrived, under the command of four Arab merchants, of which Isa bin Hijji was most kind, and did us good service. I was always at home when I got amongst Arabs. They always treat me practically as one of themselves. They gave us useful information for crossing the Rubeho range, and superintended our arrangements. When they went away I charged them not to spread reports of our illness. I saw them depart with regret. It had really been a relief to hear once more the voice of civility and sympathy.

"Our greatest labour was before us. Trembling with ague, with swimming heads, ears deafened by weakness, and limbs that would hardly support us, we contemplated with dogged despair the perpendicular scramble over the mountains and the ladders of root and boulder, up which we and our starving, drooping asses had to climb. Jack was so weak that he had three supporters; I, having stronger nerves, managed with one. We passed wall-like sheets of rock, long steeps of loose white soil and rolling stones. Every now and then we were compelled to lie down by cough and thirst and fatigue; and when so compelled, fires suddenly appeared on the neighbouring hills. The War-cry rang loud from hill to hill, and Indian files of archers and spearmen, streaming like lines of black ants, appeared in all directions down the paths.

It was the Wahúmba, who, waiting for the Caravans to depart, were going down to fall fiercely on the scattered villages in the lowlands, kill the people, and to drive off the cattle, and plunder the villages of Inengé. Our followers prepared to desert us, but, strange to say, the Wahúmba did not touch us. By resting every few yards, and clinging to our supporters, we reached the summit of this terrible path after six hours, and we sat down amongst aromatic flowers and bright shrubs, to recover strength and breath. Jack was almost in a state of coma, and could hardly answer. The view disclosed a retrospect of severe hardships past and gone.

"We eventually arrived, after more walking, at a place called the Great Rubeho, where several settlements appeared, and where poor Jack was seized with a fever fit and dangerous delirium; he became so violent that I had to remove his weapons, and, to judge from certain symptoms, the attack had a permanent cerebral effect. Death appeared stamped upon his features, and yet our followers clamoured to advance, *because it was cold.* This lasted two nights, when he was restored and came to himself, and proposed to advance. I had a hammock rigged up for him, and the whole Caravan broke ground. We went on ascending till we reached the top of the third and westermost range of the Usagára Mountains, raised 5700 feet above sea level, and we begin to traverse Ugogi, which is the halfway district between the Coast and Unyanyembe, and stands 2760 feet above sea level, and the climate of Ugogi pleases by its elasticity and its dry healthy warmth.

"The African traveller's fitness for the task of Exploration depends more upon his faculty of chafing under delays and kicking against the pricks than upon his power of displaying the patience of a Griselda or a Job. Another Caravan of coast Arabs arrived. They brought news from the sea-board, and, wondrous good fortune, the portmanteau containing books, which a porter, profiting by the confusion when they were attacked by bees, had deposited in the long grass at the place where I directed the slaves to look for it. Some half-caste Arabs had gone forward and spread evil reports of us. They said we had each one eye and four arms; we were full of magic; we caused rain to fall in advance, and left droughts in our rear; we cooked water-melons, and threw away the seeds, thus generating small-pox; we heated and hardened milk, thus breeding a murrain amongst cattle; our wire, cloth, and beads caused a variety of misfortunes; we were Kings of the Sea, and therefore white-skinned and straight-haired, as are all men who live in salt water, and next year we would seize their land.

"As far as *our* followers were concerned, there was not a soul to stand by Jack and me except ourselves. Had anything happened we must have perished. We should have been as safe with six as with sixty guns, but six hundred stout fellows, well armed, might march through the length and breadth of Central Africa." (Richard said when the Government sent Gordon to Khartoum they failed because they sent him *alone.* Had they sent him with five hundred soldiers there would have been no war.) "And now a word to sportsmen in this part of Africa. Let no future travellers make my mistake. I expected great things without realizing a single hope. In the more populous parts the woodman's axe and the hunter's arrows have melted away game. Even where large tracks of jungle abound with water and forage, the notes of a bird rarely strike the ear, and during the day's march not a single large animal will be seen. In places such as the park-lands of Dut'húmi, the jungles and forests of Ugogi and Mgunda Mk'hali, the barrens of Usukuma, and the tangled thickets of Ujiji, there is abundance of noble game—lions, leopards, elephants, rhinoceroses, wild cattle, giraffes, gnus, zebras, quaggas, and ostriches; but the regions are so dangerous that a sportsman cannot linger. There is miasma, malaria, want of food, rarely water, no camels, and every porter would desert, whilst the extraordinary expense of provision and of carriage would be the work of a very rich man. As for us, we could only shoot on halting days at rare periods, and there is nothing left but the hippopotamus and the crocodile of the seacoast.

"On the 8th of October we fell in with a homeward-bound Caravan headed by Abdullah bin Nasib, who was very, very kind to us. He kindly halted a day that we might send home a mail, and gave me one of his riding animals, and would take nothing for it except a little medicine. We left K'hok'ho, a foul strip of crowded jungle, where we were stung throughout the fiery day by the tzetze fly, swarms of bees, and pertinacious gadflies, where an army of large poisonous ants drove us out of the tent by the wounds which they inflicted between the fingers and other tender parts of the body, till kettles of boiling water persuaded them to abandon us. These ant-fiends made the thin-skinned asses mad with torture. In this ill-omened spot my ass Seringe, the sole survivor of the riding animals brought from Zanzibar, was so torn by a hyæna that it died of its wounds, and fifteen of my porters deserted, so that I thought that it was no use continuing my weary efforts and anxiety about baggage.

"I gave Jack my good donkey, because he was worse than I was, and I took one of the poor ones, and found that I must either walk or leave valuable things behind. Trembling with weakness, I set out to march the length of the Mdáburu jungle. The memory of that march is not pleasant. The burning sun and the fiery reflected heat arising from the parched ground—here a rough, thorny, and waterless jungle, where the jessamine flowered and the frankincense was used for fuel; there a grassy plain of black and sun-cracked earth—compelled me to lie down every half-hour. The water-gourds were soon drained by my attendant Beloch; and the sons of Ramji, who, after reaching the resting-place, had returned with ample stores for their comrades, hid their vessels on my approach. Sarmalla, a donkey-driver, the model of a surly negro, whose crumpled brow, tightened eyes, and thick lips, which shot out on the least occasion of excitement, showed what was going on within his head, openly refused me the use of his gourd, and—thirst is even less to be trifled with than hunger—found ample reason to repent himself of the proceeding. Near the end of the jungle I came upon a party of the Beloch, who, having seized upon a porter belonging to a large Caravan of Wanyamwezi that had passed us on that march, were persuading him, half by promises and half by threats, to carry their sleeping mats and their empty gourds.

"Towards the end of that long march I saw with pleasure the kindly face of Seedy Bombay, who was returning to me in hot haste, leading an ass and carrying a few scones and hard-boiled eggs. Mounting, I resumed my way, and presently arrived at the confines of Mdáburu, where, under a huge calabash, stood our tent, amidst a kraal of grass boothies, surrounded by a heaped-up ridge of thorns.

"We left Ugogi and pursued our way to 'Mgunda Mk'hali,' a very wild part, and at last got to Jiwella Mkoa, the halfway house. We were cheered by the sight of the red fires glaring in the kraal, but Jack's ass, perhaps frightened by some wild beast which we did not see, reared high in the air, bucked like a deer, broke his girths, and threw Jack, who was sick and weak, heavily upon the hard earth. Our people had become so selfish that they always attended to themselves first, and Said bin Salim, the leader, actually refused to give us a piece of canvas to make a tent. Bombay made a memorable speech: 'If you are not ashamed of your Master, O Said, be at least ashamed of his servant,' which had such an effect that he sent the whole awning, and refused the half which I sent back to him.

"The three Tribes of this part are the Wagogo (the Wamasai), the Wahúmba, and the Wakwafi, who are remarkable for their strength and intelligence, and for their obstinate and untamable characters. They only sell their fellow tribesmen when convicted of magic, or from absolute distress, and many of them would rather die under the stick than work. The Wagogo are thieves; they would rob during the day, are importunate beggars, and specify their long lists of wants without stint or shame. An Arab merchant once went out to the Wahúmba to buy asses. He set out from Tura in Eastern Unyamwezi, and traversing the country of the wild Watatúru, arrived on the eighth day at the frontier district, I'ramba, where there is a river which separates the tribes. He was received with civility, but none have ever since followed his example.

"As we neared Unyanyembe the porters became more restive under their light loads, their dignity was hurt by shouldering a pack, and day after day, till I felt weary of life, they left their burdens upon the ground. At Rubuga I was visited by an Arab merchant, who explained something which had puzzled me. Whenever an advance beyond Unyanyembe was spoken of, Said bin Salim's countenance fell. The merchant asked me if I thought the Caravan was strong enough to bear the dangers of the road between that and Ujiji, and I replied that I did, but even if I did not, I should go on. The perpetual risk of loss, discourages the traveller in these lands. In a moment papers which have cost him months of toil may be scattered to the winds. Collectors should *never* make them on the *march upwards*, but on their *leisurely return*. My field and sketch-books were entrusted to an Arab merchant who preceded me to Zanzibar. Jack sent down maps, papers, and instruments, and I my vocabularies, ephemeris, and drawing-books, which ran no danger, except from Hamerton's successor, who seemed careless.

"The hundred and thirty-fourth day from leaving the coast, after marching over six hundred miles, we prepared to enter Kázeh. I was met by Arabs who gave me the Moslem salutation, and courteously accompanied me. I was to have gone to the *tembe* kindly placed at my disposal by Isa bin Hijji and the Arabs met at Inengé, but by mistake we were taken to that of Musa Mzuri, an Indian merchant, for whom I bore an introductory letter, graciously given by H.H. the Sayyid Majjid of Zanzibar. Here I dismissed the porters, who separated to their homes. What a contrast between the open-handed hospitality and the hearty good will of this truly noble race (Arabs), and the niggardliness of the savage and selfish African! It was heart of flesh after heart of stone. They warehoused my goods, disposed of my extra stores, and made all arrangements for my down march on return. During two long halts at Kázeh, Snay bin Amir never failed to pass the evening with me, and, as he thoroughly knew the country all around, I derived immense information from his instructive and varied conversation.

"Here were the times when Jack was at such a disadvantage from want of language; he could join in none of these things, and this made him, I think, a little sour, and partly why he wished to have an expedition of his own. Snay bin Amir was familiar with the language, the religion, the manners, and the ethnology of all the tribes. He was of a quixotic appearance, high featured, tall, gaunt, and large limbed. He was well read, had a wonderful memory, fine perceptions, and passing power of language. He was the stuff of which I could make a friend, brave as all his race, prudent, ready to perish for honour, and as honest as he was honourable. At Unyanyembe the merchants expect some delay, because the porters, whether hired at the coast or at Tanganyika, here disperse, and a fresh gang has to be collected. When Snay bin Amir and Musa Mzuri, the Indian, settled at Kázeh, it was only a desert; they built houses, sunk wells, and converted it into a populous place. The Arabs here live comfortably and even splendidly. The houses are single-storied, but large, substantial, and capable of defence. They have splendid gardens; they receive regular supplies of merchandise, comforts, and luxuries from the coast; they are surrounded by troops of concubines and slaves, whom they train to divers crafts and callings. The rich have riding asses from Zanzibar, and the poorest keep flocks and herds. When a stranger appears he receives *hishmat l'il gharib*, or 'the guest welcome.' He is provided with lodgings, and introduced by the host to the rest of the society at a general banquet. A drawback to their happiness is the failure of constitution. A man who escapes illness for a couple of months boasts, and, as in Egypt, no one enjoys robust health. The residents are very moderate in their appetites, and eat only light dishes that they may escape fever.

"From Unyanyembe there are twenty marches to Ujiji upon the Tanganyika, seldom accomplished under twenty-five days. The two greatest places are, first, Msene; the second is the Malagarázi river; but now I bade adieu for a time to the march, the camp, and the bivouac, and was comfortably housed close to my new friend, Shakyh Snay bin Amir. You are all familiar with the Arab Kafilah and its hosts of litters, horses, camels, mules, and asses; but the porter-journeys in East Africa have, till this year of my arrival, escaped the penman's pen. There are three kind of Caravans. These are the Wanyamwezi, the Wasawahili free men, and lastly that of the Arabs. That of the Arabs is splendid, and next to the Persian, he is the most luxurious traveller in the East. A veteran of the way, he knows the effects of protracted hardship and scarcity upon a wayfarer's health; but the European traveller does not enjoy it, because it marches by instinct rather than reason. It dawdles, it hurries, it lingers, losing time twice. It is fatal to observation, and nothing will induce them to enable an Explorer to strike into an unbeaten path, or to progress a few miles out of the main road. Malignant epidemics attack Caravans, and make you repent joining them. For the rest, the porters, one and all, want to eat, drink, sleep, carry the lightest load or none at all; for the slightest service they want double pay; they lose your mules and your baggage; they steal what they can; they desert when they can; they run away when there is the slightest danger. When it is safe, they are mutinous and insolent, because you are dependent on them. If you come to a comfortable place, you cannot dislodge them; if you come to a dangerous place, they will not give the necessary time for food or sleep, or resting the animals. Everything is done to get as much out of you as possible, to do as little as they can for it; gain and self are almost their only thoughts. Bombay proved more or less an exception. During our journey from start to finish, there was not one, from Said bin Salim, the leader, to the very porter, except Bombay and the two Goanese Catholics, who did not attempt to desert.

"About five p.m. the camp was fairly roused, and a little low chatting commences. The porters overnight have promised to start early, and to make a long wholesome march; but, 'uncertain, coy, and hard to please,' the cold morning makes them unlike the men of the warm evening, and so one of them will have fever. In every Caravan there is some lazy lout and unmanageable fellow whose sole delight is to give trouble. If no march be in prospect, they sit obstinately before the fire, warming their hands and feet, and casting quizzical looks at their fuming and fidgety employer. If all be unanimous it is vain to tempt them; even soft sawder is but 'throwing comfits to cows,' and we return to our tent. If, however, there be a division, a little active stimulating will cause a march. They hug the fire till driven from it, when they unstack the loads piled before our tents and pour out of camp or village. Jack and I, when able, mount our asses; we walk when we can, but when unable for either we are borne in hammocks. The heat of the ground, against which the horniest sole never becomes proof, tries the feet like polished leather boots on a quarter-deck in the dog-days near the Line. Sometimes, when in good humour, they are very sportive. When two bodies meet, that commanded by an Arab claims the road. When friendly caravans meet, the two *kirangozis* sidle up with a stage pace, a stride and a stand, and, with sidelong looks, prance till they arrive within distance; then suddenly and simultaneously 'ducking,' like boys 'giving a back,' they come to loggerheads and exchange a butt violently as fighting rams. Their example is followed by all with a rush and a crush, which might be mistaken for the beginning of a fight; but it ends, if there be no bad blood, in shouts of laughter.

"When a Unyamwezi guide is leader of a Caravan the *kirangozi* deliberately raises his plain blood-red flag, and they all follow him. If any man dares to go before him, or into any but his own place, an arrow is extracted from his quiver to substantiate his identity at the end of the march.

"The Wamrima willingly admit strangers into their villages, and the Wazaramo would do the same, but they are constantly at feud with the Wanyamwezi, and therefore it is dangerous hospitality. My Goanese boys, being 'Christians,' that is to say, Roman Catholics, consider themselves semi-European, and they will not feed with the heathenry, so there are four different messes in the Camp. The dance generally assumes, as the excitement increases, the frantic semblance of a ring of Egyptian dervishes. The performance often closes with a grand promenade, all the dancers being jammed in a rushing mass, a *galop infernale*, with features of satyrs, and gestures resembling aught but human. Sometimes they compose songs in honour of me. I understand them, and the singers know that I do. They sing about the Muzungú Mbáya, 'the wicked white man;' to have called me a '*good* white man' would mean that one was a natural, an innocent, who would be plucked and flayed without flinching; moreover, despite my wickedness, it was always to *me* that they came for justice and redress if any one bullied or ill-treated them.

"The Caravan scene at night is often very impressive. The dull red fires flickering and forming a circle of ruddy light in the depths of the black forest, flaming against the tall trunks, and defining the foliage of the nearer trees, illuminate lurid groups of savage men, in every variety of shape and posture. Above, the dark purple sky, studded with golden points, domes the earth with bounds narrowed by the gloom of night. And, behold, in the western horizon, a resplendent crescent, with a dim, ash-coloured globe in its arms, and crowned by Hesperus, sparkling like a diamond, sinks through the vast space in all the glory and gorgeousness of Eternal Nature's sublimest works. From such a night, methinks, the Byzantine man took his device, the crescent and the star.

"At Kázeh, as in Ugogi and everywhere else, the lodgings are a menagerie of hens, pigeons, rats, scorpions, earwigs (the scorpions are spiteful), and in Ugogi there is a green scorpion from four to five inches long, which inflicts a torturing wound. Here they say that it dies after inflicting five consecutive stings, and kills itself if a bit of stick be applied to the middle of its back. House crickets and cockroaches are plentiful, as well as lizards, and frightful spiders weave their webs. One does not count ticks, flies of sorts, bugs, fleas, mosquitoes, and small ants, and the fatal bug of Miana, which vary in size, after suction, from almost invisible dimensions to three-quarters of an inch. The bite does not poison, but the irritation causes sad consequences. Huts have to be sprinkled with boiling water to do away with some of these nuisances.

"It is customary for Caravans proceeding to the Tanganyika to remain for six weeks or two months at Unyanyembe for repose and recovery from the labours they are supposed to have endured, to enjoy the pleasures of 'civilized society,' to accept the hospitality offered by the Arabs. All our party, except Jack and I, considered Unyanyembi the end of the exploration, but to us it merely meant a second point of departure easier than the first, because we had gained experience. We had, however, a cause of delay. Jack had become strong, but all the rest got ill. Valentine, my Goanese boy, was insensible for three days and nights from bilious fever, and when he recovered Gaetano got it and was unconscious. Then followed the bull-headed slave, Mabruki, and lastly Bombay, while the rest of the following, who had led a very irregular life, began to pay the penalty of excess. They brought us a *mganga*, or witch, who doctored us. However, we got distressing weakness, liver derangement, burning palms, tingling soles, aching eyes, and alternate chills of heat and cold, and we delayed till the 1st of December, during which we learnt a lot of necessary things.

"My good Snay bin Amir sent into the country for plantains and tamarinds, and brewed a quantity of beer and plantain wine. He lent me valuable assistance concerning the country and language, and we were able, through him, to learn all about the Nyanza or Northern Lake, and the maps forwarded from Kázeh to the Royal Geographical Society will establish this fact, as they were subsequently determined, after actual exploration, by Jack. Snay bin Amir took charge of all the letters and papers for home, and his energy enabled me afterwards to receive the much-needed reserve of supplies in the nick of time.

"On the 15th we went on to Yombo, where I remarked three beauties who would be deemed beautiful in any part of the world. Their faces were purely Grecian, they had laughing eyes, their figures were models for an artist, like the bending statue that delights the world, cast in bronze. These beautiful domestic animals smiled graciously when, in my best Kinyamwezi, I did my *devoir* to the sex, and a little tobacco always secured for me a seat in the 'undress circle.'

"On the 22nd of December Jack came back, and we left on the 23rd of December, and marched to the district of Eastern Wilyankuru; and there we again separated, and I went on alone to Muinyi

Chandi, and my people were very troublesome. Said bin Salim, believing that my days were numbered, passed me on the last march without a word. The sun was hot, and he and his party were hastening to shade, and left me with only two men to carry the hammock in a dangerous jungle, where shortly afterwards an Arab merchant was murdered. On Christmas Day I mounted my ass, passed through the western third of the Wilyankuru district, and was hospitably received by one Salim bin Said, surnamed Simba the Lion, who received me with the greatest hospitality. He was a large, middle-aged man, with simple and kindly manners, and an honesty of looks and words which rendered his presence extremely prepossessing.

"The favourite dish in this country is the *pillaw*, or *pilaf*, here called *pulao;* and here I want to digress. For the past century, which concluded with reducing India to the rank of a British province, the proud invader has eaten her rice after a fashion which has secured for him the contempt of the East. He deliberately boils it, and after drawing off the nutritious starch, or gluten, called *conjee*, which forms the perquisite of the Portuguese or his pariah cook, he is fain to fill himself with that which has become little more nutritious than the prodigal's husks. Great, indeed, is the invader's ignorance upon that point. Peace be to the manes of Lord Macaulay, but listen to and wonder at his eloquent words: 'The Sepoys came to Clive, not to complain of their scanty fare, but to propose that all the grain should be given to the Europeans, who required more nourishment than the natives of Asia. The thin gruel, they said, which was strained away from the rice, would suffice for themselves. History contains no more touching instance of military fidelity, or of the influence of a commanding mind.' Indians never fail to drink the *conjee*. The Arab, on the other hand, mingles with his rice a sufficiency of *ghee* to prevent the extraction of the 'thin gruel,' and thus makes the grain as palatable and as nutritious as Nature intended it to be—and dotted over with morsels of fowl, so boiled that they shredded like yarn under the teeth.

"Shaykh Masud boasted of his intimacy with the Sultan Msimbira, whose subjects had plundered our portmanteau, and offered, on return to Unyanyambe, his personal services in ransoming it. I accepted with joy, but it afterwards proved that he nearly left his skin in the undertaking. The climate of Kíríra, where I arrived on the 27th of December, is called by the Arabs a medicine, and I spent a delicious night in the cool Barzah after the unhealthy air of Kázeh. Three marches more brought me to Msene, where I was led to the *tembe* of one Saadullah, a low-caste Msawahili, and there I found Jack, looking very poorly. We were received with great pomp and circumstance; the noise was terrific, and Gaetano, Jack's boy, was so excited by the scene that he fell down in an epileptic fit, which fits returned repeatedly.

"On the 10th of January we left, and arrived at Mb'hali, and passed through dense jungle, and eventually came to Sorora and

Kajjanjeri, and here we were freshly ill from miasma. About three in the afternoon I was forced to lay aside my writing by an unusual sensation of nervous irritability, which was followed by a general shudder as in the cold paroxysm of fevers. Presently my extremities began to weigh, and began to burn as though exposed to a glowing fire, and my jack-boots became too tight and heavy to wear. At sunset the attack reached its height. I saw yawning wide to receive me—

> 'Those dark gates across the wild
> That no man knows.'

My body was palsied, powerless, motionless; the limbs appeared to wither and die; the feet had lost all sensation, except a throbbing and a tingling as if pricked by needle points, the arms refused to be directed by will, and to the hands the touch of cloth and stone was the same. Gradually the attack spread upwards till it seemed to compress my ribs, and stopped short there. This at a distance of two months of any medical aid, and with the principal labour of the expedition still in prospect! If one of us was lost, I said to myself, the other might survive to carry home the results of the exploration, which I had undertaken with the resolve either to do or die. I had done my best, and now nothing appeared to remain for me but to die as well.

"It was partial paralysis, brought on by malaria, well known in India. I tried the usual remedies without effect, and the duration of the attack presently revealed what it was. The contraction of the muscles, which were tightened like ligatures above and below the knees, and those λύταγούνατα, a pathological symptom which the old Greek loves to specify, prevented me from walking to any distance for nearly a year; the numbness of the hands and feet disappeared more slowly, but the *Fundi* predicted that I should be able to move in ten days, and on the 10th I again mounted my ass. At Usagozi, Jack, whose blood had been impoverished, and whose system had been reduced by many fevers, now began to suffer from inflammation of the eyes, which produced an almost total blindness, rendering every object enclouded by a misty veil. Goanese Valentine suffered the same on the same day, and subsequently, at Ujiji, was tormented by inflammatory ophthalmia. I suffered in a minor degree. On the 3rd of February we debouched from a jungle upon the river plain; the swift brown stream, there fifty yards broad, was swirling through the tall wet grasses of its banks on our right hand, hard by our track. Upon the off-side, a herd of elephants in Indian file broke through the reed fence in front of them.

"The Malagarázi, corrupted by speculative geographers to Mdjigidgi—the uneuphonious terminology of the 'Mombas Mission Map'—to 'Magrassie,' and to 'Magozi,' has been wrongly represented to issue from the Sea of Ujiji. According to all travellers in these regions, it rises in the mountains of Urundi, at no great distance from the Kitangure, or river of Karagwah; but whilst the latter, springing from the upper counterslope, feeds the Nyanza, or

Northern Lake, the Malagarázi, rising in the lower slope of the equatorial range, trends to the south-east, till it becomes entangled in the decline of the Great Central African Depression—the hydrographical basin first indicated in his address of 1852 by Sir Roderick I. Murchison, president of the Royal Geographical Society of London.* Thence it sweeps round the southern base of Urundi, and, deflected westwards, it disembogues itself into the Tanganyika. Its mouth is in the land of Ukaranga, and the long promontory behind which it discharges its waters is distinctly visible from Kawele, the head-quarters of Caravans in Ujiji. The Malagarázi is not navigable; as in primary and transition countries generally, the bed is broken by rapids. Beyond the ferry the slope becomes more pronounced, branch and channel islets of sand and verdure divide the stream, and as every village near the banks appears to possess one or more canoes, it is probably unfordable. The main obstacle to crossing it on foot, over the broken and shallower parts near the rock-bars, would be the number and the daring of the crocodiles.

"The *mukunguru* of Unyamwezi is the severest seasoning-fever in this part of Africa; it is a bilious-remittent lasting three days, which reduces the patient to nothing, and often followed by a long attack of tertian type. The consequences are severe and lasting, even in men of the strongest nervous diathesis; burning and painful eyes, hot palms and soles, a recurrence of shivering and flushing fits, extremities alternately icy cold, then painfully hot and swollen, indigestion, sleeplessness, cutaneous eruptions, fever sores, languor, dejection, all resulting from torpidity of liver, from inordinate secre-

---

* "The following notice concerning a discovery which must ever be remembered as a triumph of geological hypothesis, was kindly forwarded to me by the discoverer:—

"'My speculations as to the whole African interior being a vast watery plateau-land of some elevation above the sea, but subtended on the east and west by much higher grounds, were based on the following data:—

"'The discovery in the central portion of the Cape Colony, by Mr. Bain, of fossil remains in a lacustrine deposit of Secondary age, and the well-known existence on the coast of loftier mountains known to be of a Palæozoic or Primary epoch, and circling round the younger deposits, being followed by the exploration of the Ngami Lake, justified me in believing that Africa had been raised from beneath the ocean at a very early geological period; and that ever since that time the same conditions had prevailed. I thence inferred that an interior network of lakes and rivers would be found prolonged northwards from Lake Ngami, though at that time no map was known to me showing the existence of such central reservoirs. Looking to the west as to the east, I saw no possibility of explaining how the great rivers could escape from the central plateau-lands and enter the ocean except through deep lateral gorges, formed at some ancient period of elevation, when the lateral chains were subjected to transverse fractures. Knowing that the Niger and the Zaire, or Congo, escaped by such gorges on the west, I was confident that the same phenomenon must occur upon the eastern coast, when properly examined. This hypothesis, as sketched out in my 'Presidential Address' of 1852, was afterwards received by Dr. Livingstone just as he was exploring the transverse gorges by which the Zambesi escapes to the east, and the great traveller has publicly expressed the surprise he then felt that his discovery should have been thus previously suggested.'"

tion of bile, and shows the poison in the system. Sometimes the fever works speedily; some become at once delirious, and die on the first or second day.

"From Tura to Unyamwezi the Caravans make seven marches of sixty geographical miles. The races requiring notice in this region are two—Wakimbu and the Wanyamwezi."

CHAPTER XIV.

OUR REWARD—SUCCESS.

"At length we sight the Lake Tanganyika, or the 'Sea of Ujiji.' The route before us lay through a howling wilderness laid waste by the fierce Watuta. Mpete, on the right bank of the Malagarázi river, is very malarious, and the mosquitoes are dreadful. We bivouacked under a shady tree, within sight of the ferry. The passage of this river is considered dangerous on account of attacks of the tribes. At one place I could only obtain a few corn cobs, and I left the meat, with messages, for the rear. In the passages of the river our goods and chattels were thoroughly sopped. After a while, from a hillside we saw, long after noon, the other part of our Caravan, halted by fatigue, upon a slope beyond a weary swamp; a violent storm was brewing, and the sky was black, and we were anxious and sorry about them.

"On the 13th February, after about an hour's march, I saw the *Fundi* running forward, and changing the direction of the Caravan, and I followed him to know *why* he had taken this responsibility upon himself. We breasted a steep stony hill, sparsely clad with thorny trees, which killed Jack's riding ass. Our fagged beasts refused to proceed. 'What is that streak of light which lies below?' said I to Bombay. 'I am of opinion,' said Bombay, 'that that *is the* water you are in search of.' I gazed in dismay; the remains of my blindness, the veil of trees, a broad ray of sunshine illuminating but one reach of the lake, had shrunk its fair proportions. I began to lament my folly in having risked life and lost health for so poor a prize, to curse Arab exaggeration, and to propose an immediate return to explore the Nyanza, or Northern Lake.

"Advancing a few yards, the whole scene suddenly burst upon my view, filling me with admiration, wonder, and delight. Nothing in sooth could be more picturesque than this first view of Tanganyika Lake, as it lay in the lap of the mountains, basking in the gorgeous tropical sunshine. There were precipitous hills, a narrow strip of emerald green, a ribbon of glistening yellow sand, sedgy rushes, cut by the breaking wavelets, an expanse of light, soft blue water foam thirty to thirty-five miles wide, sprinkled by crisp tiny crescents of snowy foam, with a background of high broken wall of steel-coloured mountain flecked and capped with pearly mist, sharply pencilled against the azure sky, yawning chasms of plum-colour falling towards dwarf hills, which apparently dip their feet in the wave. One could see villages, cultivated lands, fishermen's canoes on the water, and a profuse lavishness and magnificence of Nature and vegetation. The smiling shores of this vast crevasse appeared doubly beautiful to me after the silent and spectral mangrove-creeks on the East African sea-board, and the melancholy monotonous experience of desert and jungle scenery, tawny rock and sun-parched plain, or rank herbage and flats of black mire. Truly it was a revel for Soul and Sight! Forgetting toils, dangers, and the doubtfulness of return, I felt willing to endure double what I had endured; and all the party seemed to join with me in joy. Poor purblind Jack found nothing to grumble at, except the 'mist and glare before his eyes.' Said bin Salim looked exulting—*he* had procured for me this pleasure; the monoculous *Jemadar* grinned his congratulations, and even the surly Beloch made civil salaams.

As soon as we were bivouacked, I proceeded to get a solid-built Arab craft, capable of containing thirty or thirty-five men, belonging to an absent merchant. It was the second largest on the lake, and being too large for paddling, the crew rowed, and at eight next morning we began coasting along the eastern shore of the lake in a north-westerly direction, towards the Kawele district. The picturesque and varied forms of the mountains rising above and dipping into the lake were clad in purplish blue, set off by the rosy tints of the morning, and so we reached the great Ujiji. A few scattered huts in the humblest beehive shape represent the Port town. This fifth region includes the alluvial valley of the Malagarázi river, which subtends the lowest spires of the highlands of Karagwah and Urundi, the western prolongation of the chain which has obtained, *probably* from African tradition, the name of 'Lunar Mountains.'

"At Ujiji terminates, after twelve stages, the transit of the fifth region. The traveller has now accomplished a hundred stages, which with necessary rests, but not including detentions and long halts, should occupy a hundred and fifty days. The distance, on account of the sinuosities of the road, numbers nine hundred and fifty statute miles, which occupied us seven and a half months on account of our disadvantages and illnesses. Arab Caravans seldom arrive at the Tanganyika, for the same reasons, under six months, but the lightly laden and the fortunate may get to Unyamyembe in two and a half, and to the Tanganyika in four months. It is evident that the African authorities (this was written thirty-five years ago) have hitherto confounded the Nyanza, the Tanganyika, and the Nyassa Lakes. Ujiji was first visited in 1840 by the Arabs, and after that they penetrated to Unyamwesi. They found it conveniently situated as a central point from whence their factors and slaves could navigate the waters, and collect slaves and ivory from the tribes upon its banks, but the climate proved unhealthy, the people dangerous, and the coasting voyages ended in disaster. Ujiji never rose to the rank of Unyamyembe, or Msene. Now, from May to September, flying Caravans touch here, and return to Unyamyembe so soon as they have loaded their porters. The principal tribes are the Wajiji, the Wavínza, the Wakaránga, the Watúta, the Wabuha, and the Wáhha; but the fiercest races in the whole land, and also the darkest, are the Wazarámo, the Wajíji, and the Watatúru. The Lakists are almost an amphibious race, are excellent divers, strong swimmers and fishermen, and vigorous eaters of fish, and in the water they indulge in gambols like sportive water-fowls, whether skimming in their hollow logs, or swimming.

"It is a great mistake not to go as a Trader. It explains the Traveller's motives, which are always suspected to be bad ones. Thus the Explorer can push forward into unknown countries, will be civilly received and lightly fined, because the host expects to see him or his friends again: to go without any motive only induces suspicion, and he is opposed in every way. Nobody believes him to be so stupid as to go through such danger and discomfort for exploring or science, which they simply do not understand.

"The cold damp climate, the over-rich and fat fish diet, and the abundance of vegetables, which made us commit excesses, at first disagreed with us. I lay for a fortnight upon the earth, too blind to read or write, too weak to ride, too ill to converse. Jack was almost as groggy upon his legs as I was, suffering from a painful ophthalmia, and a curious contortion of the face, which made him chew sideways, like an animal that chews the cud. Valentine was the same. Jack and Valentine were always ill of the same things, and on the same days, showing that certain climates affected certain temperaments and not others. Gaetano ate too much and brought on a fever. I was determined to explore the northern extremity of the lake, whence, every one said, issued a large river flowing northwards, so I tried to hire the only dhow or sailing craft, and provision it for a month's cruise, and at last Jack went to look after it, and I was twenty-seven days alone.

"I spent my time chiefly in eating, drinking, smoking, dozing. At two or three in the morning I lay anxiously expecting the grey light to creep through the door-chinks; then came the cawing of crows, and the crowing of the village cocks. When the golden rays began to stream over the red earth, torpid Valentine brought me rice-flour boiled in water with cold milk. Then came the slavey with a leafy branch to sweep the floor and to slay the huge wasps. This done, he lit the fire, the excessive damp requiring it, and sitting over it, he bathed his face and hands—luxurious dog!—in the pungent smoke. Then came visits from Said bin Salim and the *Jemadar* (our two headmen), who sat and stared at me, were disappointed to see no fresh symptoms of approaching dissolution, told me so with their eyes and faces, and went away; and I lay like a log upon my cot, smoking, *dreaming of things past*, *visioning things present*, and indulging myself in a few lines of reading and writing.

"As evening approached, I made an attempt to sit under the

broad eaves of the *tembe*, and to enjoy the delicious spectacle of this virgin Nature, and the reveries to which it gave birth—

> 'A pleasing land of drowsihed it was,
> Of dreams that wave before the half-shut eye,
> And of gay castles in the clouds that pass
> For ever flushing round a summer sky.'

"It reminded me of the loveliest glimpses of the Mediterranean; there were the same 'laughing tides,' pellucid sheets of dark blue water, borrowing their tints from the vinous shores beyond; the same purple light of youth upon the cheek of the earlier evening; the same bright sunsets, with their radiant vistas of crimson and gold opening like the portals of a world beyond the skies; the same short-lived grace and loveliness of the twilight; and, as night closed over the earth, the same cool flood of transparent moonbeams, pouring on the tufty heights and bathing their sides with the whiteness of virgin snow.

"At seven p.m., as the last flush faded from the occident, the lamp—a wick in a broken pot full of palm oil—was brought in. A dreary, dismal day you will exclaim, a day that—

> 'lasts out a night in Russia,
> When nights are longest there.'

"On the 29th of March the rattling of matchlocks announced Jack's return. He was moist, mildewed, and wet to the bone, and all his things were in a similar state; his guns grained with rust, his fireproof powder-magazine full of rain, and, worse than that, he had not been able to gain anything but a promise that, *after three months*, the dhow should be let to us for five hundred dollars. The very dhow that had been promised to me whenever I chose to send for it! The faces of my following were indeed a study.

"I then set to work to help Jack with his diaries, which afterwards appeared in *Blackwood*, September, 1859, when I was immensely surprised to find, amongst many other things, a vast horseshoe of lofty mountains that Jack placed, in a map attached to the paper, near the very heart of Sir R. Murchison's Depression. I had seen the mountains growing upon paper under Jack's hand, from a thin ridge of hills fringing the Tanganyika until they grew to the size given in *Blackwood*, and Jack gravely printed in the largest capitals, 'This mountain range I consider to be the true Mountains of the Moon;' thus men *do* geography, and thus discovery is stultified. The poor fellow had got a beetle in his ear, which began like a rabbit at a hole to dig violently at the tympanum, and maddened him. Neither tobacco, salt, nor oil could be found; he tried melted butter, and all failing, he applied the point of a penknife to its back, and wounded his ear so badly that inflammation set in and affected his facial glands, till he could not open his mouth, and had to feed on suction. Six or seven months after, the beetle came away in the wax. At last I got hold of Kannena the Chief, and after great difficulty and enormous extortion, I promised him a rich reward if he kept his word; for I was resolved at all costs, even if we were reduced to actual want, to visit the mysterious stream. I threw over his shoulders a six-foot length of scarlet broadcloth, which made him tremble with joy, and all the people concerned in my getting the dhow received a great deal more than its worth. I secured two large canoes and fifty-five men.

"On the 11th of April, at four in the morning, I slept comfortably on the crest of a sand-wave, and under a mackintosh escaped the pitiless storm, so as to be ready to start lest they should repent, and at 7.20 on the 12th of April, 1858, my canoe, bearing for the first time on those dark waters—

> 'The flag that braved a thousand years
> The battle and the breeze,'

stood out of Bangwe Bay, and, followed by Jack's canoe, we made for the cloudy and storm-vexed north. The best escort to a European capable of communicating with and commanding them, would be a small party of Arabs, fresh from Hazramaut, untaught in the ways and tongues of Africa. They would save money to the explorer, and also his life. There were great rejoicings at our arrival at Uvira, the *ne plus ultra,* the northernmost station to which merchants have as yet been admitted. Opposite still, rose in a high broken line the mountains of the inhospitable Urundi, apparently prolonged beyond the northern extremity of the waters. Some say the voyage is of two days, some say six hours; the breadth of the Tanganyika here is between seven and eight miles.

"Now my hopes were rudely dashed to the ground. The stalwart sons of the Sultan Maruta, the noblest type of Negroid seen near the lake, visited me. They told me they had been there, and that the Rusizi enters *into* and does not *flow out* of the Tanganyika. I felt sick at heart. Bombay declared that Jack had misunderstood, and *his* (Bombay's) informer *now* owned that he had never been beyond Uvira, and never intended to do so. We stopped there nine days, and there I got such a severe ulceration of the tongue that I could not articulate. An African traveller may be arrested at the very bourne of his journey, on the very threshold of his success, by a single stage, as effectually as if all the waves of the Atlantic or the sands of Arabia lay between him and it. Now Maruta and his young giants claimed their blackmail, and also Kannena, and I had to pay up. Slaves are cheaper here than in the market of Ujiji. Gales began to threaten, and the crews, fearing wind and water, insisted on putting out to sea on the 6th of May.

"We touched at various stages and anchored at Mzimu, our former halting-place, where the crew swarmed up a ladder of rock, and returned with pots of palm oil. We left again at sunset; the waves began to rise, the wind also, and rain in torrents, and it was a doubt whether the cockleshell craft could live through the short chopping sea in heavy weather. The crew was frightened, but held on gallantly, and Bombay, a noted Agnostic in fine weather, spent the length of that wild night in reminiscences of prayer. I sheltered myself under my then best friend, my mackintosh, and thought of the couplet—

> 'This collied night, these horrid waves, these gusts that sweep the whirling deep;
> What reck they of our evil plight, who on the shore securely sleep?'

Fortunately the rain beat down the wind and sea, or nothing could have saved us. The next morning Mabruki rushed into the tent, thrust my sword into my hands, said the Warundi were upon us, and that the crews were rushing to their boats and pushing them off. Knowing that they *would* leave us stranded in case of danger, we hurried in without delay; but presently no enemy appeared, and Kannena, the Chief, persuaded them to re-land, and demand satisfaction of a drunken Chief who had badly wounded a man, and then there was a general firing and drawing of daggers. The crew immediately confiscated the three goats that were for our return, cut their throats, and spitted the meat upon their spears. Thus the lamb died and the wolf dined; the innocent suffered, the plunderer was joyed; the strong showed his strength, the weak his weakness—as usual. I saw the sufferer's wounds washed, forbade his friends to knead and wrench him as they were doing, and gave him a purgative which did him good. On the second day he was able to rise. This did not prevent the report at home that I had killed the man.

"On the 11th of May we paddled round to Wafanya Bay, to Makimoni, a little grassy inlet, where our canoes were defended from the heavy surf. On the 12th we went to Kyasanga, and the next night we spent in Bangwe Bay. We were too proud to sneak home in the dark; we deserved the Victoria Cross, we were heroes, braves of braves; we wanted to be looked at by the fair, to be howled at by the valiant.

"On the 13th of May we appeared at the entrance of Kawele, and had a triumphal entrance; the people of the whole country-side collected to welcome us, and pressed waist-deep into the water. Jack and I were repeatedly 'called for,' but true merit is always modest; it aspires to 'Honour, not honours.'* We regained the old *tembe*, were salaamed to by everybody, and felt like a 'return home.' We had expended upwards of a month boating about the Tanganyika Lake. All the way down, we were like baited bears, mobbed every moment; they seemed to devour us; in an ecstasy of curiosity they shifted from Jack to me, and back again, like the well-known ass between the bundles of hay. Our health palpably improved. Jack was still deaf, but cured of his blindness; the ulcerated mouth, which had compelled me to live on milk for seventeen days, returned to its usual state, my strength increased, my feet were still swollen, but my hands lost their numbness, and I could again read and write. I attribute the change from the days

* This was Richard's favourite and self-composed motto, and Chinese Gordon quoted it in every letter he wrote him to the last day of his life, with a word of congratulation as to its happy choice.—I. B.

and nights spent in the canoe, and upon the mud of the lake. Mind also acted upon matter; the object of my Mission was now effected, and I threw off the burden of grinding care, with which the imminent prospect of a failure had before sorely laden me."

Although Richard did not get the meed of success in England, and it has taken the world thirty-four years to realize the grandeur of that Exploration, he was the Pioneer (without money, without food, without men or proper escort, without the bare necessaries of life, to dare and do, in spite of every obstacle, and every crushing thing, bodily and mentally) who opened up that country. It is to *him* that later followers, that Grant and Speke, and Baker and Stanley, Cameron, and all the other men that have ever followed, owe it, that he opened the oyster-shell for them, and they went in to take the pearl. I do not want to detract from any other traveller's merits, for they are all brave and great, but I *will* say that if Richard Burton had had Mr. Stanley's money, escort, luxuries, porterage, and white comrades, backed by influence, there would not have been one single white spot on the whole map of the great Continent of Africa that would not have been filled up. Owing to shameful intrigues (which prospered none of the doers, but injured him, the man who did all this), he got very few words of praise, and that from a few, yet the World owes it to him now that there are Missions and Schools and Churches, and Commerce, and peaceful Settlements, and that anybody can go there. To *him* you owe "Tanganyika in a Bath-Chair;" but Speke got the cheering of the gallery and the pit, and Stanley inherited them. And here I insert the innocent joy-bells of his own heart, as I found them scribbled on the edge of his private journal, and anybody thinking of what he had done and what he had passed through, can warmly enter into his feelings of self-gratulation, so modestly hidden—

"I have built me a monument stronger than brass,
And higher than the Pyramids' regal site;
Nor the bitterness shown, nor the impotent wind,
Nor the years' long line, nor the ages' flight
Shall e'en lay low!

"Not *all* shall I perish; much of *me*
Shall vanquish the grave, and be living still
When Mr. Macaulay's Zealanders view
The ivied ruin on Tower Hill,
And men shall know

"That when Isis hung, in the youth of Time,
Her veil mysterious over the land,
And defied mankind and men's puny will,
All that lay in the shadow, my daring hand
Was *first* to show.

"Then rejoice thee, superb in the triumph of mind,
And the Delphian bay-leaf, O sweet Muse, bind
Around my brow!"

"The rainy monsoon broke up after our return to Kawele. The climate became truly enjoyable, but it did not prevent the strange inexplicable melancholy which accompanies all travellers in tropical countries. Nature is beautiful in all that meets the eye; all is soft that affects the senses; but she is a syren whose pleasures pall, and one sighs for the rare simplicity of the desert. I never felt this sadness in Egypt and Arabia; I was never without it in India and Zanzibar. We got not one single word from the agents who were to forward our things, and Want began to stare us in the face. We had to engage porters for the hammocks, to feed seventy-five mouths, to fee several Sultans, and to incur the heavy expenses of two hundred and sixty miles' march back to Unyanyembe, so I had to supplement with my own little patrimony. One thousand pounds does not go very far, when it has to be divided amongst a couple of hundred greedy savages in two and a half years. On the 22nd of May musket-shots announced arrivals, and after a dead silence of eleven months arrived a Caravan with boxes, bales, porters, slaves, and a parcel of papers and letters from Europe, India, and Zanzibar. Here we first knew of the Indian Mutiny. This good fortune happened at a crisis when it was really wanted, but as my agent could find no porters for the packages, he had kept back some, and what he had sent me, were the worst. They would take us to Unyamyembe, but were wholly inadequate for exploring the southern end of the Tanganyika, far less for returning to Zanzibar, *viâ* the Nyassa Lake and Kilwa, as I hoped to do.

"At the time I write, the Tanganyika, though situated in the unexplored centre of intertropical Africa, and until 1858 unvisited by any European, has a traditionary history of its own, extending over three centuries. The Tanganyika, 250 miles in length, occupies the centre of the length of the African continent. The general formation suggests the idea of a volcanic depression, while the Nyanza is a vast reservoir formed by the drainage of the mountains. The lay is almost due north and south, and the form a long oval widening at the centre, and contracting at the extremities; the breadth varies from thirty to thirty-five miles, the circumference about 550 miles, and the superficial area covers about 5000 square miles. By the thermometers we had with us, the altitude was 850 feet above sea-level, and about 2000 feet below the Nyanza or Northern Lake, with high hill ranges between the lakes, which precluded a possibility of a connection between the waters. The parallel of the northern extremity of the Tanganyika nearly corresponds with the southern creek of the Nyanza, and they are separated by an arc of the meridian of about three hundred and forty-three miles. The waters of the Nyanza are superior to those of Tanganyika. The Tanganyika has a clear soft blue, like the ultramarine of the Mediterranean, with the light and milky tints of tropical seas. I believe that the Tanganyika receives and absorbs the whole river system, the network of streams, nullahs, and torrents of that portion of the Central African Depression, whose watershed converges towards the great reservoir. I think that the Tanganyika, like the Dead Sea, *as* a reservoir, supplies with humidity the winds which have parted with their moisture in the barren and arid regions of the south, and maintains its general level by the exact balance of supply and evaporation, and I think it possible that the saline particles deposited in its waters may be wanting in some constituent, which renders them evident to the taste; hence the freshness.

"According to the Wajiji, from their country to the Marungú river, which enters the lake at the *south*, there are twelve stages, numbering one hundred and twenty stations, but at most of them provisions are not procurable, and there are sixteen tribes and districts. The people of Usige, *north* of the Tanganyika, say that six rivers fall into the Tanganyika from the *east*, and *westernmost* is the Rusizi, and that it is an *influent.*

"The Chief Kazembe is like a viceroy of the country lying south-west of the Tanganyika, and was first visited by Dr. Lacerda, Governor of the Rios de Sena, in 1798–99. He died, and his party remained nine months in the country, without recording the name and position of this African capital. A second expedition went in 1831, and the present Chief was the grandson of Dr. Lacerda's Kazembe. He is a very great personage in these parts, and many Arabs are said to be living with him in high esteem. Marungú, though dangerous, was visited by a party of Arab merchants in 1842, who assisted Sámá in an expedition against a rival. He compelled the merchants to remain with him; they had found means of sending letters to their friends, they are unable to leave the country, but they are living in high favour with the Kazembe who enriched them. Of course there are people who doubt their good fortune. I collect my details from a mass of Arab *oral* geography.

"The 26th of May, 1858, was the day appointed for our departure *en route* for Unyamyembe. Kannena had been drunk for a fortnight, and was attacked by the Watuta, and fled. I heard of him no more. He showed no pity for the homeless stranger—may the World show none to him! I shall long remember my last sunrise look at Tanganyika, enhanced by the reflection that I might never again behold it. Masses of brown purple clouds covered the sunrise. The mists, luminously fringed with Tyrian purple, were cut by filmy rays, and the internal living fire shot forth broad beams like the spokes of a huge aërial wheel, rolling a flood of gold over the light blue waters of the lake, and a soft breeze, the breath of morn, awoke the waters into life.

"The followers were very tiresome, mutinous, and inconsequent in their anxiety to escape from Kannena and the fighting Watuta. So, desiring the headman to precede me with a headstrong gang to the first stage, and to send back men to carry my hammock and remove a few loose loads, I breakfasted, and waited alone till the afternoon in the empty and deserted *tembe;* but no one came back, and the utter misery depicted in the countenance of the Beloch induced me to mount my *manchil*, and to set out carried by only two men. As the shades of evening closed around us we reached the ferry of the Ruche river, and we found no camp. The mosquitoes were like wasps, and the hippopotamus bellowed, snorted, and grunted; the roars of the crocodiles made the party miserable, as the porters waded through water waist-deep, and crept across plains of mud, mire, and sea-ooze. As it was too dark and dangerous to continue the march, and that, had I permitted, they would have wandered through the outer gloom, without fixed purpose, till permanently bogged, I called a halt, and we snatched, under a resplendent moon and a dew that soaked through the blankets, a few hours of sleep. We were destitute of tobacco and food, and when the dawn broke, I awoke and found myself alone; they had all fled and left me. About two p.m., some of them came back to fetch me; but they were so impertinent, ordering me to endure the midday heat and labour, that I turned them out, and told them to send back their master, Said bin Salim, in the evening or the next morning. Accordingly, the next morning, the 28th of May, at nine o'clock, appeared Said, the *Jemadar*, and a full gang of bearers. He was impertinent too, but I soon silenced him, and then we advanced till evening: for having tricked me he lost two days. Later on, a porter placed his burden upon the ground and levanted, and being cognac and vinegar, it was deeply regretted. Then the Unyamwezi guide (because his newly purchased slave-girl had become footsore and was unable to advance) cut off her head, lest out of his evil should come good to another. The bull-headed Mabruki bought a little slave of six years old. He trotted manfully alongside the porters, bore his burden of hide bed and water gourd upon his tiny shoulders. At first Mabruki was like a girl with a new doll, but when the novelty wore off, the poor little devil was so savagely beaten that I had to take him under my own protection. All these disagreeables I was obliged to smooth down, because a traveller who cannot utilize the raw material that comes to his hand, will make but little progress. Their dread of the Wavinza increased as they again approached the Malagarázi ferry. Here there are magnificent spectacles of conflagration.

"A sheet of flame, beginning with the size of a spark, overspreads the hillside, advancing on the wings of the wind with the roaring rushing sound of many hosts where the grass lay thick, shooting huge forky tongues high into the dark air, where tall trees, the patriarchs of the forest, yielded their lives to the blast, smouldering and darkening, as if about to be quenched, where the rock afforded scanty fuel, then flickering, blazing up and soaring again till, topping the brow of the hill, the sheet became a thin line of fire, and gradually vanished from the view, leaving its reflection upon the canopy of lurid smoke studded with sparks and bits of live braise, which marked its descent on the other side of the buttress.

"We were treated with cruel extortion at the crossing of the

Malagarázi, but the armies of ants, and an earthquake at 11.15 a.m. on the 4th of June, which induced us to consent, was considered a bad omen by my party. They took seven hours to transport us, and at four p.m. we found ourselves, with hearts relieved of a heavy load, once more at Ugogi, on the left bank of the river. Fortunately I arrived just in time to prevent Jack from buying a little pig for which he was in treaty, otherwise we should have lost our good name amongst the Moslem population. On the 8th of June we emerged from the inhospitable Uvinza into neutral ground, where we were pronounced 'out of danger.' The next day, when in the meridian of Usagozi, we were admitted for the first time to the comforts of a village.

"On the 17th of June, in spite of desertions, we came to Irora, the village of Salim bin Salih, who received us very hospitably. Here we saw the blue hills of Unyanyembe, our destination. Next day we got to Yombo, where we met some of our things coming up by the coast, sent by the Consul of France—the French do things smartly—and a second packet of letters. Every one had lost some friend or relation near and dear to him. My father had died on the 6th of last September, afrer a six weeks' illness, at Bath, and was buried on the 10th, and I only knew it on the 18th of June—the following year. Such tidings are severely felt by the wanderer who, living long behind the world, is unable to mark its gradual changes, lulls (by dwelling upon the past) apprehension into a belief that *his* home has known no loss, and who expects again to meet each old familiar face ready to smile upon his return, as it was to weep at his departure.

"We collected porters at Yombo, passed Zimbili, the village of our former miseries, and re-entered Kázeh, where we were warmly welcomed by our hospitable Snay bin Amir, who had prepared his house and everything grateful to starving travellers. Our return from Ujiji to Unyanyembe had been accomplished in twenty-two stations, two hundred and sixty-five miles. After a day's repose, all the Arab merchants called upon me, and I had the satisfaction of finding that my last order on Zanzibar for four hundred dollars' worth of cloth and beads had arrived, and I also recovered the lost table and chair which the slaves had abandoned.

"During the first week following the march, we all paid the penalty of the toilsome trudge through a perilous jungly country in the deadly season of the year, when the waters are drying up under a fiery sun, and a violent *vent de bise* from the east pours through the tepid air like cold water into a warm bath. I again got swelling and numbness of the extremities; Jack was a martyr to deafness and dimness of sight, which prevented him from reading, writing, and observing correctly; the Goanese were down with fever, severe rheumatism, and liver pains; Valentine got tertian type, and was so long insensible that I resolved to try the *tinctura Warburgii.* Oh, Doctor Warburg! true apothecary! we all owe you a humble tribute of gratitude; let no traveller be without you. The result was miraculous; the paroxysms did not return, the painful sickness at once ceased; from a death-like lethargy, sweet childish sleep again visited his aching eyes; chief boon of all, the corroding thirst gave way to appetite, followed by digestion. We all progressed towards convalescence, and in my case, stronger than any physical relief, was the moral effect of Success and the cessation of ghastly doubts and fears, and the terrible wear and tear of mind. I felt the proud consciousness of having done my best, under conditions, from beginning to end, the worst and most unpromising, and that whatever future evils Fate might have in store for me, it could not rob me of the meed won by the hardships and sufferings of the past.

"I had not given up the project of returning to the seaboard *viâ* Kilwa. As has already been mentioned, the merchants had detailed to me, during my first halt here, their discovery of a large lake, lying about sixteen marches to the north; and, from their descriptions and bearings, Jack laid down the water in a hand-map, and forwarded it to the Royal Geographical Society. All agreed in claiming for it superiority of size over the Tanganyika, and I saw that, if we could prove this, much would be cleared up. Jack was in a much fitter state of health to go. There was no need for two of us going, and I was afraid to leave him behind at Kázeh. It is very difficult to associate with Arabs as one of themselves. Jack was an Anglo-Indian, without any knowledge of Eastern manners and customs and religion, and of any Oriental language beyond broken Hindostanee. Now, Anglo-Indians, as everybody knows, often take offence without reason; they expect civility as their *due*, they treat all skins a shade darker than their own as 'niggers,' and Arabs are, or can be, the most courteous gentlemen, and exceedingly punctilious.*

"Jack did not afterwards represent this fairly in *Blackwood*, October, 1859. He said I 'was most unfortunately quite done up, and most graciously consented to wait with the Arabs and recruit my health;' but in July, 1858, *writing on the spot*, he wrote, 'To diminish the disappointment caused by the shortcoming of our cloth, and in not seeing the whole of the Sea of Ujiji, I have proposed to take a flying trip to the unknown lake, while Captain Burton prepares for our return homewards.' Said bin Salim did all he could to thwart the project, and Jack threatened him with the *forfeiture of his reward* after he returned to Zanzibar. Indeed, he told him *it was already forfeited*. He said 'he should certainly recommend the Government *not to pay the gratuity, which the Consul had promised on condition that he worked entirely for our satisfaction, in assisting the expedition to carry out the arranged plans*.' How Jack reconciled himself to misrepresent my conduct about the payment on reaching home, will never be understood.

* The Arabs always gave Richard the most courteous and cordial reception, treating him practically as one of themselves. They could not be expected to think so much of Speke, because he did not know their language or their religion, and he always treated them as an Anglo-Indian treats a nigger. He was burning to escape from Kázeh, and the society of an utterly idle man to one incessantly occupied is always a drawback, and Richard, whose stronger constitution had enabled him to bear up at first with greater success, was gradually but surely succumbing to the awful African climate.—I. B.

"Our followers were to receive *certain* pay in *any case*, which they *did* receive, and a reward in *case they behaved well;* our asses, thirty-six in number, all died or were lost; our porters ran away; our goods were left behind and stolen; specimens of the fine poultry of Unyamwezi, intended to be naturalized in England, were bumped to death in the cases; our black escort were so unmanageable as to require dismissal; the weakness of our party invited attacks, and our wretched Beloch deserted us in the jungle, and throughout were the cause of an infinity of trouble. Jack agreed with me thoroughly, that it would be an *act of weakness* to pay the *reward* of *ill-conduct;* instead of putting it down to generosity, they would have put it down to fear, and they would have played the devil with every future traveller; yet he used this afterwards as a means to procure the Command of the next Expedition for himself, and pointed it at me as a disgrace.

"By dint of severe exertion, Jack was able to leave Kázeh on the 10th of July. These northern kingdoms were Karágwah, Uganda, and Unyoro. The *Mkámá*, or Sultan, of Karágwah was Armaníka, son of Ndagára, who was a very great man. He is an absolute Ruler, and governs without squeamishness. He receives the traveller with courtesy, he demands no blackmail, but you are valued according to your gifts. A European would be received with great kindness, but only a rich man could support the dignity of the white face. Corpulence is a beauty. Girls are fattened to a vast bulk by drenches of curds and cream, thickened with flour, and are beaten when they refuse, and they grow an enormous size.

"From the Kitangure river, fifteen stations conduct the traveller to Kibuga, the capital of Uganda, the residence of its powerful despot, Suna. The Chief of Uganda has but two wants, with which he troubles his visitors. One is a medicine against Death, the other a charm to avert thunderbolts, and immense wealth would reward the man who would give him either of these two things. The army of Uganda numbers three hundred thousand men; each brings an egg to muster, and thus something like a reckoning of the people is made. Each soldier carries one spear, two assegais, a long dagger, and a shield; bows and swords are unknown. The women and children accompany, carrying spare weapons, provisions, and water. They fight to the sound of drums, which are beaten with sticks like ours; should this performance cease, all fly the field.

"Suna, when last visited by the Arabs, was a red man, of about forty-five, tall, robust, powerful of limb, with a right kingly presence, a warrior carriage, and a fierce and formidable aspect. He always carried his spear, and wore a long piece of bark-cloth from neck to ground; he makes over to his women the rich clothes presented by the Arabs. He has a variety of names, all expressing something terrible, bitter, and mighty. He used to shock the Arabs by his natural, unaffected impiety. He boasted to them that he was the God of earth, as their Allah was the Lord of heaven. He murmured loudly against the abuse of lightning, and claimed from his subjects divine honours, such as the facile Romans yielded to their

Emperors. His sons, numbering more than a hundred, were confined in dungeons; the heir *elect* was dragged from his chains to fill a throne, and the cadets linger through their dreadful lives till death releases them. His female children were kept under the most rigid surveillance within the palace; but he had one favourite daughter, named Nasurú, whose society was so necessary to him, that he allowed her to appear with him in public.

"Suna encouraged, by gifts and attentions, the Arab merchants to trade in his capital, but the distance has prevented more than half a dozen caravans from reaching him; yet all loudly praised his courtesy and hospitality. My friend Snay Bin Amir paid him a visit in 1852. He was received in the audience hall, outside which were two thousand guards, armed only with staves. He was allowed to retain his weapons. He saluted the Chief, who motioned his guest to sit in front of him. Two spears were close to his hand. He has a large and favourite dog, resembling an Arab greyhound. The dog was, and is always, by his side. The ministers and the women were also present, but placed so that they could only see the visitor's back. He was eager of news. When the despot rose, all dispersed. At the second visit, Snay presented his blackmail, and it was intimated to the 'King's Stranger' that he might lay hands upon whatever he pleased, animate or inanimate; but Snay was too wise to avail himself of this privilege. There were four interviews, in which Suna inquired much about the Europeans, and was anxious for a close alliance with the Sultan of Zanzibar. He treated Snay very generously; but Snay, when he could without offence, respectfully declined things. Like all African Chiefs, the despot considered these visits as personal honours paid to himself. It would depend, however, upon his ingenuity and good fortune whether a traveller would be allowed to explore further, and perhaps the best way would have been to buy or to build boats upon the nearest western shore, with Suna's permission. During Jack's absence, I collected specimens of the multitudinous dialects. Kisawahili, or coast language, into which the great South African family here divides itself, is the most useful, because most generally known, and, once mastered, it renders the rest easy. With the aid of the slaves, I collected about five hundred words in the three principal dialects upon this line of road—the Kisawahili, the Kizaramo, which included the Kik'hutu, and the Kinyamwezi. It was very difficult, for they always used to answer me, 'Verily in the coast tongue, words never take root, nor do they ever bear branches.' The rest of my time was devoted to preparation for journeying, and absolute work—tailoring, sail-making, umbrella-mending, etc.

"On the 14th of July the last Arab Caravan left Unyanyembe, under the command of Sayf bin Said el Wardi. He offered to convey letters and anything else, and I forwarded the useless surveying instruments, manuscripts, maps, field and sketch books, and reports to the Royal Geographical Society. This excitement over, I began to weary of Kázeh.

DIFFERENCES BEGIN BETWEEN SPEKE AND RICHARD.

"Already I was preparing to organize a little expedition to K'hokoro and the southern provinces, when unexpectedly—in these lands a few cries and gun-shots are the only credible precursors of a Caravan —on the morning of the 25th of August reappeared Jack.

"At length Jack had been successful. His 'flying trip' had led him to the northern water, and he had found its dimensions surpassing our most sanguine expectations. We had scarcely, however, breakfasted before he announced to me the startling fact that 'he had discovered the sources of the White Nile.' It was an inspiration perhaps. The moment he sighted the Nyanza, he felt at once no doubt but that the 'lake at his feet gave birth to that interesting river, which has been the subject of so much speculation and the object of so many explorers.' The fortunate discoverer's conviction was strong. His reasons were weak, were of the category alluded to by the damsel Lucetta, when justifying her penchant in favour of the 'lovely gentleman,' Sir Proteus—

> 'I have no other but a woman's reason—
> I think him so because I think him so;' *

* "The following extract from the *Proceedings of the Royal Geographical Society*, May 9, 1859, will best illustrate what I mean:—

"'Mr. Macqueen, F.R.G.S., said the question of the sources of the Nile had cost him much trouble and research, and he was sure there was no material error either in longitude or latitude in the position he had ascribed to them, namely, a little to the eastward of the meridian of 35° and a little northward of the equator. That was the principal source of the White Nile. The mountains there were exceedingly high, from the equator north to Kaffa Enarea. All the authorities, from east, west, north, or south, now perfectly competent to form judgments upon such a matter, agreed with him; and among them were the officers commanding the Egyptian Commission. It was impossible they could *all* be mistaken. Dr. Krapf had been within a very short distance of it; he was more than a hundred and eighty miles from Mombas, and he saw snow upon the mountains. He conversed with the people who came from them, and who told him of the snow and exceeding coldness of the temperature. The line of perpetual congelation, it is well known, was seventeen thousand feet above the sea. He had an account of the navigation of the White Nile by the Egyptian Expedition. It was then given as 30° 30′ N. lat. and 31° E. long. At this point the expedition turned back for want of a sufficient depth of water. Here the river was 1370 feet broad, and the velocity of the current *one quarter* of a mile per hour. The journals also gave a specific and daily current, the depth and width of the river, and everything, indeed, connected with it. Surely, looking at the current of the river, the height of the Cartoom above the level of the sea, and the distance thence up to the equator, the sources of the Nile must be six or eight thousand feet above the level of the sea, and still much below the line of snow, which was six or eight thousand feet farther above them. He deeply regretted he was unable to complete the diagram for the rest of the papers he had given to the Society, for it was more important than any others he had previously given. It contained the journey over Africa from sea to sea, second only to Dr. Livingstone. But all the rivers coming down from the mountains in question, and running south-eastward, had been clearly stated by Dr. Krapf, who gave every particular concerning them. He should like to know what the natives had said was to the northward of the large lake. Did they say the rivers ran out from or into the lake? How could the Egyptian officers be mistaken?

"'Captain Speke replied. They were not mistaken; and if they had pursued and probably his Sources of the Nile grew in his mind as his Mountains of the Moon had grown under his hand.

"His main argument in favour of the lake representing the great reservoir of the White Nile was that the 'principal men' at the southern extremity ignored the extent northward. 'On my inquiring about the lake's length,' said Jack, 'the man (the greatest traveller in the place) faced to the north, and began nodding his head to it. At the same time he kept throwing forward his right hand, and making repeated snaps of his fingers, endeavouring to indicate something immeasurable; and added that nobody knew, but he thought it probably extended to the end of the world.' Strongly impressed by this valuable statistical information, Jack therefore placed the northern limit about 4° to 5° N. lat., whereas the Egyptian Expedition sent by the late Mohammed Ali Pacha, about twenty years ago, to explore the coy Sources, reached 3° 22′ N. lat. The expedition therefore ought to have sailed fifty miles upon the Nyanza Lake. On the contrary, from information derived on the spot, that expedition placed the fountains at one month's journey—three hundred to three hundred and fifty miles—to the south-east, or upon the northern counterslope of Mount Kenia.

"Whilst marching to the coast, Jack—he tells us—was assured by a 'respectable Sawahili merchant that when engaged in traffic, some years previously, to the northward of the Line and the westward of this lake, he had heard it commonly reported that large vessels frequented the northern extremity of these waters, in which the officers engaged in navigating them used sextants and kept a log, precisely similar to what is found in vessels on the ocean. Query, Could this be in allusion to the expedition sent by Mohammed Ali up the Nile in former years?' (*Proceedings of the Royal Geographical Society*, May 9, 1859). Clearly, if Abdullah bin Nasib, the Msawahili alluded to, had reported these words, he merely erred. The Egyptian Expedition, as has been shown, not only did not find, they never even heard of a lake. But not being present at the

---

their journey fifty miles further, they would undoubtedly have found themselves at the northern borders of this lake.

"'Mr. Macqueen said that other travellers—Don Angelo, for instance—had been within one and a half degrees of the equator, and saw the mountain of Kimborat under the Line, and persisted in the statement, adding that travellers had been up the river till they found it a mere brook. He felt convinced that the large lake alluded to by Captain Speke was not the source of the Nile; it was impossible it could be so, for it was not at a sufficiently high altitude.

"'The paper presented to the Society, when fully read in conjunction with the map, will clearly show that the Bahr-el-Abiad had no connection with Kilimanjaro, that it has no connection whatever with any lake or river to the south of the equator, and that the swelling of the river Nile proceeds from the tropical rains of the northern torrid zone, as was stated emphatically to Julius Cæsar by the Chief Egyptian Priest, Amoreis, two thousand years ago.

"'In nearly 3° N. lat. there is a great cataract, which boats cannot pass. It is called Gherba. About halfway (fifty miles) above, and between this cataract and Robego, the capital of Kuenda, the river becomes so narrow as to be crossed by a bridge formed by a tree thrown across it. Above Gherba no stream joins the river either from the south or south-west.'"

conversation, besides the geographical difficulties which any scientific geographer could see at a glance, I am tempted to assign further explanation. Jack, wholly ignorant of Arabic, was obliged to depend upon 'Bombay.' Bombay misunderstood Jack's bad Hindostani. He then mistranslated the words in Kisawahili to the best African, who, in his turn, passed it on in a still wilder dialect to the noble savages who were under cross-examination. My experience is that words in journeys to and fro are liable to the severest accidents and have often bad consequences, and now I felt that an *influent* of the Nyanza was described as an *effluent*, and the real original and only genuine White Nile would remain thus described for years to our shame, and it is easy to see how the blunder originated.

"The Arabic *bahr* and the Kisawahili *báhari* are equally applicable, in vulgar parlance, to a river or sea, a lake or river. Traditions concerning a Western sea—the to them now unknown Atlantic—over which the white men voyage, are familiar to many East Africans; I have heard at Harar precisely the same report concerning the log and sextants. Either, then, Abdullah bin Nasib confounded, or Jack's '*interrupter*' caused *him* to confound, the Atlantic and the lake. In the maps forwarded from Kázeh by Jack, the river Kivira was, after ample inquiry, made a western *influent* of the Nyanza Lake. In the map appended to the paper in *Blackwood*, before alluded to, it has become an *effluent*, and the only minute concerning so very important a modification is, 'This river (although I must confess at first I did not think so) is the Nile itself.'

"Beyond the assertion, therefore, that no man had visited the north, and the appearance of 'sextants' and 'logs' upon the waters, there is not a shade of proof *pro*. Far graver considerations lie on the *con* side; the reports of the Egyptian Expedition, and the dates of the several inundations which—as will presently appear—alone suffice to disprove the possibility of the Nyanza causing the flood of the Nile. It is doubtless a satisfactory thing to disclose to an admiring public of 'Statesmen, Churchmen, Missionaries, Merchants, and more particularly Geographers,' the 'solution of a problem, which it had been the first geographical desideratum of many thousand years to ascertain, and the ambition of the first Monarchs in the World to unravel' (*Blackwood's Magazine*, October, 1859). But how many times since the days of a certain Claudius Ptolemæius, surnamed Pelusiota, have not the fountains of the White Nile been discovered and re-discovered after this fashion?

"What tended at the time to make me the more sceptical, was the substantial incorrectness of the geographical and other details brought back by Jack. This was natural enough. The first thing reported to me was 'the falsehood of the Arabs at Kázeh, who had calumniated the good Sultan Muhayya, and had praised the bad Sultan Machunda:' subsequent inquiries proved their rigid correctness. Jack's principal informant was one Mansur bin Salím, a half-caste Arab, who had been flogged out of Kázeh by his compatriots; he pronounced Muhayya to be a 'very excellent and obliging person,' and of course he was believed. I then heard a detailed account 'of how the Caravan of Salim bin Rashid had been attacked, beaten, captured, and detained at Ukerewe, by its Sultan Machunda.' The Arabs received the intelligence with a smile of ridicule, and in a few days Salim bin Rashid appeared in person to disprove the report. These are but *two* cases of *many*. And what knowledge of Asiatic customs can be expected from the writer of the following lines?—'The Arabs at Unyanyembe had advised my donning their habit for the trip in order to attract less attention; a vain precaution, which I believe they suggested more to gratify their own vanity in *seeing an Englishman lower himself to their position* (?), than for any benefit that I might receive by doing so' (*Blackwood, loco cit.*). This galamatias of the Arabs! the haughtiest and the most clannish of all Oriental peoples.

"Jack changed his manners to me from this date. His difference of opinion was allowed to alter companionship. After a few days it became evident to me that not a word could be uttered upon the subject of the lake, the Nile, and his *trouvaille* generally without offence. By a tacit agreement it was, therefore, avoided, and I should never have resumed it, had Jack not stultified the results of my expedition by putting forth a claim which no geographer can admit, and which is at the same time so weak and flimsy, that no geographer has yet taken the trouble to contradict it.

"Now, for the first time, although I had pursued my journey under great provocations from time to time, I never realized what an injury I had done the Expedition publicly, as well as myself, by not travelling alone, or with Arab companions, or at least with a less crooked-minded, cantankerous Englishman. He is energetic, he is courageous and persevering. He distinguished himself in the Punjaub Campaign. I first found him in Aden with a three years' furlough. His heart was set on spending two years of his leave in collecting animals north of the Line in Africa. He never *thought* in any way of the Nile, and he was astonished at *my* views, which he deemed impracticable. He had no qualifications for the excursion that he proposed to himself, except that of being a good sportsman. He was ignorant of the native races in Africa, he had brought with him about £400 worth of cheap and useless guns and revolvers, swords and cutlery, beads and cloth, which the Africans would have rejected with disdain. He did not know any of the manners and customs of the East; he did not know any language except a little Anglo-Hindostani; he did not *even* know the names of the Coast Towns. I saw him engage, as protectors or *Abbans*, any Somali donkey-boys who could speak a little English. I saw that he was going to lose his money and his 'leave' and his life. Why should I have cared? I do not know; but as 'virtue is really its own reward,' I did so, and have got a slap in the face, which I suppose I deserve. I first took him to Somali-land; then I applied officially for him, and thus saved his furlough and his money by putting him on full service. You would now think, to see his conduct, that the case was reversed—that he had taken me, not I him; whereas I can confidently say that, except his shooting and his rags of Anglo-Hindostani, I have taught him everything he knows. He had suffered in purse and person at Berberah, and though he does not know French or Arabic, though he is not a man of science, nor an acute astronomical observer, I thought it only just to offer him the opportunity of accompanying me as second in command into Africa. He quite understood that it *was* in a subordinate capacity, as we should have to travel amongst Arabs, Belochs, and Africans, whose language he did not know. The Court of Directors refused me, but I obtained it by an application to the Local Authorities at Bombay. He knew by experience in Somali-land what travelling with *me* meant, and yet he was only too glad to come.

"I have also done more than Jack in the cause. The Royal Geographical Society only allowed us £1000, and sooner than fail I have sacrificed a part of the little patrimony I inherited, and my reward is, that I and my expenditure, and the cause for which I have sacrificed everything, are made ridiculous."

N.B.—Richard's kind-heartedness and forethought for others often militated against himself, owing to the meanness and unworthiness of the objects it was bestowed upon.

A Few Details of the Lakes for Geographers.

"I will here offer to the reader a few details concerning the lake in question; they are principally borrowed from Jack's diary, carefully corrected, however, by Snay bin Amir, Salim bin Rashid,* and other merchants at Kázeh.

"This fresh-water sea is known throughout the African tribes as Nyanza, and the similarity of the sound to 'Nyassa,' the indigenous name of the little Maravi, or Kilwa Lake, may have caused in part the wild confusion in which speculative geographers have involved the Lake Regions of Central Africa. The Arabs, after their fashion

* "When Jack returned to Kázeh, he represented Ukerewe and Mazita to be islands, and although in sight of them, he had heard nothing concerning their connection with the coast. This error was corrected by Salim bin Rashid, and accepted by us. Yet I read in his 'Discovery of the Supposed Sources of the Nile:' 'Mansur, and a native, the greatest traveller of the place, kindly accompanied and gave me every obtainable information. This man had traversed the island, as he called it, of Ukerewe from north to south. But *by his rough mode of describing it, I am rather inclined to think that instead of its being an actual island, it is a connected tongue of land, stretching southwards from a promontory lying at right angles to the eastern shore of the lake*, which being a wash, affords a passage to the mainland during the fine season, but during the wet becomes submerged, and thus makes Ukerewe temporarily an island.' The information, I repeat, was given, not by the 'native,' but by Salim bin Rashid. When, however, the latter proceeded to correct Jack's confusion between the well-known coffee mart Kitara, and 'the island of Kitiri occupied by a tribe called Watiri,' he gave only offence, consequently Kitiri has obtained a local habitation in *Blackwood* and Petermann."

of deriving comprehensive names from local and minor features, call it Ukerewe, in the Kisukuma dialect meaning the 'place of Kerewe' (Kelewe), an islet. As has been mentioned, they sometimes attempt to join by a river, a creek, or some other theoretical creation, the Nyanza with the Tanganyika, the altitude of the former being 3750 feet above sea-level, or 1900 feet above the latter, and the mountain regions which divide the two having been frequently travelled over by Arab and African caravans. Hence the name Ukerewe has been transferred in the 'Mombas Mission Map' to the northern waters of the Tanganyika. The Nyanza, as regards name, position, and even existence, has hitherto been unknown to European geographers; but, as will presently appear, descriptions of this sea by native travellers have been unconsciously transferred by our writers to the Tanganyika to Ujiji, and even to the Nyassa of Kilwa.

M. Brun-Rollet ('Le Nil Blanc et le Soudan,' p. 209) heard that on the west of the Padongo tribe—which he places to the south of Mount Kambirah, or below 1° S. lat.—lies a great lake, from whose northern extremity issues a river whose course is unknown. In a map appended to his volume this water is placed between 1° S. and 3° N. lat., and about 25° 50′ E. long. (Greenwich), and the reservoir is made an influent of the White Nile.

"Bowditch ('Discoveries of the Portuguese,' pp. 131, 132), when speaking of the Maravi Lake (the Nyassa), mentions that the 'negroes or the Moors of Melinde' have mentioned a great water which is known to reach Mombaça, which the Jesuit missionaries conjectured to communicate with Abyssinia, and of which Father Lewis Marianna, who formerly resided at Tete, recommended a discovery, in a letter addressed to the Government at Goa, which is still preserved among the public archives of that city. Here the confusion of the Nyanza, to which there was of old a route from Mombasah, with the Nyassa is apparent.

"At the southern point, where the Muingwira river falls into the tortuous creek, whose surface is a little archipelago of brown rocky islets crowned with trees and emerging from the blue waters, the observed latitude of the Nyanza Lake is 2° 24′ S.; the longitude by dead reckoning from Kázeh is E. long. 33° and nearly due north, and the altitude by B. P. thermometer 3750 feet above sea-level. Its extent to the north is unknown to the people of the southern regions, which rather denotes some difficulty in travelling than any great extent. They informed Jack that from Mwanza to the southern frontier of Karágwah is a land journey of one month, or a sea voyage of five days towards north-north-west, and then to the north. They also pointed out the direction of Unyoro N. 20° W. The Arab merchants of Kázeh have seen the Nyanza opposite Weranhanja, the capital district of Armanika, King of Karágwah, and declares that it receives the Kitangure river, whose mouth has been placed about the equator.

"Beyond that point all is doubtful. The merchants have heard that Suna, the late despot of Uganda, built *matumbi*, or undecked vessels, capable of containing forty or fifty men, in order to attack his enemies, the Wasoga, upon the creeks which indent the western shores of the Nyanza. This, if true, would protract the lake to between 1° and 1° 30′ of N. lat., and give it a total length of about 4°, or 250 miles. This point, however, is still involved in the deepest obscurity. Its breadth was estimated as follows:—A hill about two hundred feet above the water-level, shows a conspicuous landmark on the eastern shore, which was set down as forty miles distant. On the south-western angle of the line from the same point, ground appeared; it was not, however, perceptible north-west. The total breadth, therefore, has been assumed at eighty miles—a figure which approaches the traditions unconsciously chronicled by European geographers. In the vicinity of Usoga, the lake, according to the Arabs, broadens out; of this, however, and in fact of all the formation north of the equator, it is at present impossible to arrive at certainty.

"The Nyanza is an elevated basin or reservoir, the recipient of the surplus monsoon rain, which falls in the extensive regions of the Wamasai and their kinsmen to the east, the Karágwah line of the Lunar Mountains to the west, and to the south Usukuma, or Northern Unyamwezi. Extending to the equator in the central length of the African peninsula, and elevated above the limits of the depression in the heart of the continent, it appeared to be a gap in the irregular chain which, running from Usumbara and Kilima-ngao to Karágwah, represents the formation anciently termed the Mountains of the Moon. The physical features, as far as they were observed, suggest this view. The shores are low and flat, dotted here and there with little hills; the smaller islands also are hill-tops, and any part of the country immediately on the south would, if inundated to the same extent, present a similar aspect.

"The lake lies open and elevated, rather like the drainage and the temporary deposit of extensive floods than a volcanic creation like the Tanganyika, a long narrow mountain-girt basin. The waters are said to be deep, and the extent of the inundation about the southern creek proves that they receive during the season an important accession. The colour was observed to be clear and blue, especially from afar in the early morning; after nine a.m., when the prevalent south-east wind arose, the surface appears greyish or of a dull milky white, probably the effect of atmospheric reflection. The tint, however, does not, according to travellers, ever become red or green like the waters of the Nile. But the produce of the lake resembles that of the river in its purity; the people living on the shores prefer it, unlike that of the Tanganyika, to the highest and clearest springs; all visitors agree in commending its lightness and sweetness, and declare that the taste is rather of river or of rain water, than resembling the soft slimy produce of stagnant, muddy bottoms, or the rough harsh flavour of melted ice and snow.

"From the southern creek of the Nyanza, and beyond the archipelago of neighbouring islets, appear the two features which have given to this lake the name of Ukerewe. The Arabs call them

'Jezirah'—an ambiguous term, meaning equally insula and peninsula—but they can scarcely be called islands. The high and rocky Mazita to the east, and the comparatively flat Ukerewe on the west, are described by the Arabs as points terminating seawards in bluffs, and connected with the eastern shore by a low neck of land—probably a continuous reef—flooded during the rains, but never so deeply as to prevent cattle fording the isthmus. The northern and western extremities front deep water, and a broad channel separates them from the southern shore, Usukuma. The Arabs, when visiting Ukerewe or its neighbour, prefer hiring the canoes of the Wasakuma, and paddling round the south-eastern extremity of the Nyanza, to exposing their property and lives by marching through the dangerous tribes of the coast.

"The altitude, the conformation of the Nyanza Lake, the argilaceous colour and the sweetness of its waters, combine to suggest that it may be one of the feeders of the White Nile. In the map appended to M. Brun Rollet's volume, before alluded to, the large water west of the Padongo tribe, which clearly represents the Nyanza or Ukerewe, is, I have observed, made to drain northwards into the Fitri Lake, and eventually to swell the main stream of the White River. The details supplied by the Egyptian Expedition, which, about twenty years ago, ascended the White River to 3° 22′ N. lat. and 31° 30′ E. long., and gave the general bearing of the river from that point of its source as south-east, with a distance of one month's journey, or from three hundred to three hundred and fifty miles, would place the actual sources 2° S. lat. and 35° E. long., or in 2° eastward of the southern creek of the Nyanza Lake. This position would occupy the northern counterslope of the Lunar Mountains, the upper watershed of the high region whose culminating apices are Kilima-ngao, Kenia, and Doengo Engai. The distance of these peaks from the coast as given by Dr. Krapf must be considerably reduced, and little authority can be attached to his river Tumbiri.* The site, supposed by Mr. Macqueen (*Proceedings of the Geographical Society of London*, January 24th, 1859) to be at least twenty-one thousand feet above the level of the sea, and consequently three or four thousand feet above the line of perpetual congelation, would admirably explain the two most ancient theories concerning the source of the White River, namely, that it arises in snowy regions, and that its inundation is the resuit of tropical rains.

* "The large river Tumbiri, mentioned by Dr. Krapf as flowing towards Egypt from the northern counterslope of Mount Kenia, rests upon the sole authority of a single wandering native. As, moreover, the word *T'humbiri* or *Thumbili* means a monkey, and the people are peculiarly fond of satire in a small way, it is not improbable that the very name had no foundation of fact. This is mentioned, as some geographers—for instance, Mr. Macqueen ('Observations on the Geography of Central Africa,' *Proceedings of the R.G.S. of London*, May 9, 1859)—have been struck by the circumstance that the Austrian missionaries and Mr. Werne ('Expedition to discover the Source of the White Nile, in 1840–41') gave Tubirih as the Bari name of the White Nile at the southern limit of their exploration."

"It is impossible not to suspect that between the upper portion of the Nyanza and the watershed of the White Nile there exists a longitudinal range of elevated ground, running from east to west—a *furca* draining northwards into the Nile and southwards into the Nyanza Lake—like that which separates the Tanganyika from the Maravi or Nyassa of Kilwa. According to Don Angelo Vinco, who visited Loquéck in 1852, beyond the Cataract of Garbo—supposed to be in N. lat. 2° 40′—at a distance of sixty miles lie Robego, the capital of Kuenda and Lokoya (Logoja), of which the latter receives an affluent from the east. Beyond Lokoya the White Nile is described as a *small and rocky mountain river*, presenting none of the features of a stream flowing from a broad expanse of water like the great Nyanza reservoir.

"The periodical swelling of the Nyanza Lake, which, flooding a considerable tract of land on the south, may be supposed—as it lies flush with the basal surface of the country—to inundate extensively all the low lands that form its periphery, forbids belief in the possibility of its being the head-stream of the Nile, or the reservoir of its periodical inundation. In Karágwah, upon the western shore, the *masika*, or monsoon, last from October to May or June, after which the dry season sets in. The Egyptian Expedition found the river falling fast at the end of January, and they learned from the people that it would rise again about the end of March, at which season the sun is vertical over the equator. About the summer solstice (June), when the rains cease in the regions south of and upon the equator, the White Nile begins to flood. From March to the autumnal equinox (September) it continues to overflow its banks till it attains its magnitude, and from that time it shrinks through the winter solstice (December) till March.

"The Nile is, therefore, full during the dry season and low during the rainy season, south of and immediately upon the equator. And as the northern counterslope of Kenia will, to a certain extent, be a lee-land like Ugogi, it cannot have the superfluity of moisture necessary to send forth a first-class stream. The inundation is synchronous with the great falls of the northern equatorial regions, which extend from July to September, and is dependent solely upon the tropical rains. It is therefore probable that the true sources of the 'Holy River' will be found to be a network of runnels and rivulets of scanty dimensions, filled by monsoon torrents, and perhaps a little swollen by melted snow on the northern water-parting of the eastern Lunar Mountains.

Our Return.

"At Kázeh, to my great disappointment, it was settled, in a full Arab conclave, that we must return to the coast by the path with which we were painfully familiar. It was only the state of our finances which prevented us, whilst at Ujiji, from navigating the Tanganyika southwards and arriving, after a journey of three months, at Kilwa. That and 'leave' prevented us from going to Karágwah and Uganda. The rains, which rendered travelling impossible, set in about September; our two years' leave of absence were drawing to a close, and we were afraid to risk it, but we meant to return and do these things, tracing the course of the Rufiji river (Rwaha) and visiting the coast between the Usagára Mountains and Kilwa, an unknown line.

"Musa Mzuri returned with great pomp to Kázeh; he is between forty-five and fifty, tall, gaunt, with delicate extremities, and the regular handsome features of a high-caste Indian Moslem. He is sad and staid, wears a snowy skull-cap, and well-fitting sandals. His abode is a village in size, with lofty gates, spacious courts, full of slaves and hangers-on, a great contrast to the humility of the Semite tenements. His son knew a little English, but he had learnt no Hindostani from his father, who, though expatriated for thirty-five years, spoke his mother tongue purely and well. Musa was a man of quiet, unaffected manner, dashed with a little Indian reserve. One Salim bin Rashid, while collecting ivory to the east-ward of the Nyanza Lake, had recovered a Msawahili porter, who, having fallen sick on the road, had been left by a Caravan amongst the wildest of the East African tribes, the Wahuma (the Wamasai). From this man, who spent two years amongst these plunderers and their rivals in villany, the Warudi, I gained most valuable information. I also was called upon by Amayr bin Said el Shaksi, a strong-framed, stout-hearted Arab, who, when his vessel foundered in the Tanganyika, swam for his life, and lived for five months on roots and grasses, until restored to Ujiji by an Arab canoe. He spent many hours a day with me—he gave me immense information; and Hilal bin Nasur, a well-born Harisi returned from K'hokoro, also gave me most valuable facts.

"It is needless to say that, with all our economy and care, we arrived at the coast destitute. The hospitable Snay bin Amir came personally, although only a convalescent, to superintend our departure, provided us with his own slaves and a charming Arab breakfast; he spent the whole of that day with us, and followed us out of the compound through a white-hot sun and a chilling wind; nay, he did more—he followed us to our next station with Musa, and he helped us to put the finishing touches to the journals. I thanked these kind-hearted men for their many good deeds and services, and promised to report to H.H. the Sayyid Majid the hospitable reception of his subjects generally, and of Snay and Musa in particular. In the evening we took a most affecting farewell.* On the 4th of October, insufficiency of porterage compelled me to send back men for articles left by them at several of the villages, and we at last reached Hanga, our former quarters. Desertions were rife, and so were quarrels, in which I was always

* Richard long mourned the loss of his friend, whom Captain Speke, on his second journey with Colonel Grant—whether unable to assist I know not—left to be killed by the negroes of Mirámbo, his African enemy, in the bush.—I. B.

begged to take an active part, but experience amongst the Bashi-Bazouks in the Dardanelles taught me better.

Little Irons.

"At Hanga, Jack had been chilled on the march from the cruel easterly wind, and at the second march he had ague. At Hanga we were lodged in a foul cowhouse full of vermin, and exposed to the fury of the gales. He had a deaf ear, an inflamed eye, and a swollen face, but worst of all was a mysterious pain, which shifted—he could not say whether it was liver or spleen. It began with a burning sensation as by a branding iron above the right breast, and then extended to the heart with sharp twinges. It then ranged round the spleen, attacked the upper part of the right lung, and finally settled in the liver.

"On the 10th of October, at dawn, he woke with a horrible dream of tigers, leopards, and other beasts, harnessed with a network of iron hooks, dragging him, like the rush of a whirlwind, over the ground. He sat up on the side of his bed, forcibly clasping both sides with his hands. Half stupefied by pain, he called to Bombay, who had formerly suffered from this *kichyomachyoma*, 'the little irons,' who put him in the position a man must lie in, who gets this attack. The next spasm was less severe, but he began to wander. In twenty-four hours, supported by two men, he staggered towards the tent to a chair; but the spasms returning, he was assisted back into the house, where he had a third fit of epileptic description, like hydrophobia. Again he was haunted by crowds of devils, giants, lion-headed demons, who were wrenching with superhuman force, and stripping the sinews and tendons of his legs down to his ankles. With limbs racked by cramps, features drawn and ghastly, frame fixed and rigid, eyes glazed and glassy, he began to bark with a peculiar chopping motion of the mouth and tongue, with lips protruding, the effect of difficulty of breathing, which so altered his appearance that he was not recognizable, and terrified all beholders. When the third and severest spasm had passed away, and he could speak, he called for pen and paper, and wrote an incoherent letter of farewell to his family. That was the crisis. I never left him, taking all possible precautions, never letting him move without my assistance, and always having a resting-place prepared for him; but for some weeks he had to sleep in a half sitting-up position, pillow-propped, and he could not lie upon his side. Although the pains were mitigated, they did not entirely cease; this he expressed by saying, "Dick, the knives are sheathed!'

"During Jack's delirium he let out all his little grievances of fancied wrongs, of which I had not had even the remotest idea. He was vexed that his diary (which I had edited so carefully, and put into the Appendix of 'First Footsteps in Eastern Africa') had not been printed *as* he wrote it—geographical blunders and all; also because he had not been paid for it, I having lost money over the book myself. He asked me to send his collections to the Calcutta Museum of Natural History; now he was hurt because I had done so. He was awfully grieved because in the thick of the fight at Berberah, three years before, I had said to him, 'Don't step back, or they will think we are running.' I cannot tell how many more things I had unconsciously done, and I crowned it by not accepting immediately his loud assertion *that he had discovered the Sources of the Nile;* and I never should have known that he was pondering these things in his heart, if he had not raved them out in delirium. I only noticed that his alacrity had vanished; that he was never contented with any arrangement; that he left all the management to me, and that then he complained that he had never been consulted; that he quarrelled with our followers, and got himself insulted; and, previously to our journey, having been unaccustomed to sickness, he neither could endure it himself, nor feel for it in others. He took pleasure in saying unkind, unpleasant things, and said he could not take an interest in any exploration if he did not command it.

"These illnesses are the effects of fever, and a mysterious manifestation of miasma in certain latitudes; for in some tracts we were perfectly well, in other tracts we were mortally sick, and the changes were instantaneous. Cultivation and Civilization will probably wear these effects out, by planting, clearing jungle, and so on.

"I immediately sent an express back to Snay bin Amir, for the proper treatment, and found that they powdered myrrh with yolk of egg and flour of *mung* for poultices. I saw that, in default of physic, change of air was the only thing for him, and I had a hammock rigged up for him, and by good fortune an unloaded Caravan was passing down to the coast. We got hold of thirteen unloaded porters, who for a large sum consented to carry us to Rubuga, else we should have been left to die in the wilderness. Bombay had long since returned to his former attitude, that of a respectful and most ready servant. He had on one trip broken my elephant gun, killed my riding-ass, and lost his bridle, and did all sorts of irrational things, but for all that he was a most valuable servant, for his unwearied activity, his undeviating honesty, and his kindness of heart. Said bin Salim had long forfeited my confidence by his carelessness and extravagance, and the disappearance of the outfit committed to him at Ujiji—in favour of one of his friends, as I afterwards learned—rendered him unfit for stewardship. The others praised each other openly and without reserve, and if an evil tale ever reached my ear, it was against innocent Bombay, its object being to ruin him in my estimation.

As I knew we should be short of water, I prepared by packing a box with empty bottles, which we could fill at the best springs, and by the result of that after-wisdom which some have termed 'fool's wit,' I commenced the down march happy as a *bourgeois* or a trapper in the Pays Sauvage. Before entering the 'Fiery Field' the hammock-bearers became so exorbitant that I drew on my jackboots and mounted an ass, and Jack had so far convalesced that he wanted to ride too. He had still, however, harassing heartache, nausea, and other bilious symptoms, when exposed to the burning sun; but when he got to K'hok'ho in Ugogi, sleep and appetite came, he could carry a heavy rifle, and do damage amongst the antelope and guineafowl. Now all began to wax civil, even to servility, grumbling ceased, smiles mantled every countenance, and even the most troublesome rascal was to be seen meekly sweeping out our tents with a bunch of thorns. We made seven marches between Hanga and Tura, where we arrived on the 28th of October, and halted six days to procure food. My own party were 10; Said bin Salim's, 12; the Beloch, 38; Ramji's party, 24; the porters, 68—in all 152 souls. We plunged manfully into the 'Fiery Field,' and after seven marches in seven days, we bivouacked at Jiwe la Mkoa, and on the 12th of November, after two days' march, came into the fertile red plain of Mdaduru, in the transit of Ugogi. After that, where I had been taught to expect danger, it reduced itself to large disappearances of cloth and beads. Gul Mahommed was our Missionary, but he was just like the European old lady, who believes that on such subjects all the world must think with her. I have long been suspected of telling lies, when describing the worship of a god with four arms, and the goddesses with two heads. The transit of Ugogi occupied three weeks. At Kanyenye we were joined by a large down-Caravan of Wanyamwezi, who, amongst other news, told us that our former line through Usagára was closed through the fighting of the tribes.

"On the 6th of December we arrived at our old ground in the Ugogi Dhun, and met another Caravan, which presently drew forth a packet of letters and papers. This post brought me rather an amusing official wigging. Firstly, there was a note from Captain Rigby, my friend Hamerton's successor at Zanzibar. Secondly, the following letter:—

"'3, Savile Row.

"'Dear Burton,

"'Go ahead! Vogel and MacGuire dead—murdered. Write often.

"'Yours truly,

"'Norton Shaw.'

"The 'wig' was this. I had paid the Government the compliment of sending it, through the Royal Geographical Society, an account of political affairs in the Red Sea, saying I feared trouble at Jeddah, which I had had from my usual private information from the interior, being fearful that there would be troubles at Jeddah; and the only thanks I got was a letter, stating 'that my want of discretion and due regard for the authorities to whom I am subordinate, has been regarded with displeasure by the Government.' They are cold and crusty to reward a little word of wisdom from their babes and sucklings; but what was so comically sad was this:— The official wig was dated the 1st of July, 1857. Posts are slow in

Africa, so that by the same post I got a newspaper with an account of the massacre of nearly all the Christians at Jeddah on the Red Sea, expressing great fears that the Arab population of Suez also might be excited to commit similar outrages. This took place on the 30th of June, 1858, exactly eleven months after I had warned the Government.

"We loaded on the 7th of December, and commenced the passage of the Usagára Mountains by the Kiringawána line. This is the southern route, separated from the northern by an interval of forty-three miles. It contains settlements like Maroro and Kisanga. It is nineteen short stages; provisions are procurable, water plentiful, and plenty of grass, as long as you can pass the Warori tribe. Mosquitoes are plentiful. The owners of the land have a chronic horror of the Warori, and on sighting our peaceful Caravan they raised the war-cry, and were only quieted on knowing that we were much more frightened than they were. We had wild weather, we stayed at Maroro for food; at Kiperepeta there were gangs of four hundred touters, with their muskets, waiting the arrival of Caravans.

"On Christmas Day, 1858, at dawn, we toiled along the Kikoboga river, which we forded four times. Jack and I had a fat capon instead of roast beef, and a mess of ground nuts sweetened with sugar-cane, which did duty for plum-pudding. The contrast of what was, with what might be, now however suggested pleasurable sensations. We might now see Christmas Day of 1859, whereas on Christmas Day, 1857, we saw no chance of that of 1858. Fourteen marches took us from the foot of Usagára Mountains to Central Zungomero, traversing the districts of Eastern Mbwiga, Marundwe, and Kirengwe. It is a road hideous and grotesque: no animals, flocks, or poultry; the villages look like birds' nests torn from the trees; the people slink away—they are all armed with bows and poisoned arrows. At Zungomero, the village on the left bank of the Mgeta, which we had occupied on the outer march, was razed to the ground. I here offered a liberal reward to get to Kilwa. However, I did not succeed, and there was some intrigue about the pay afterwards, which I never understood, which was annoying to me; but such events are common on the slave-paths in Eastern Africa. Of the seven gangs of porters engaged on this journey, *only one*, an unusually small portion, *left me without being fully satisfied*, and *that one fully deserved to be disappointed.*

"On the 14th of January, 1859, we received Mr. Apothecary Frost's letters, drugs, and medical comforts, for which we had written to him July, 1857. After crossing the Mgeta, we sat down patiently on a bank, in spite of the ants, to await the arrival of a Caravan to complete our gang, but the new medical comforts enabled us to have ether-sherbet and ether-lemonade, and it did not hurt us. On the 17th of January a Caravan came, which I had been longing to meet. The Arab Chiefs Sulayman bin Rashid el Riami and Mohammed bin Gharib, who called upon me without delay, gave me most interesting information. To the south, from Uhehe to Ubena, was a continuous chain of highlands pouring affluents across the road into the Rwaha river, and water was only procurable in the beds of the nullahs and *fiumaras*. If this chain be of any considerable length, it may represent the water-parting between the Tanganyika and Nyassa Lakes, and thus divide by another and a southerly lateral band the great Depression of Central Africa.

"The 21st of January we left Zungomero, and made Konduchi on the 3rd of February in twelve marches. The mud was almost throat-deep near Dut'humi, and we had a weary trudge of thick slabby mire up to the knees. In places, after toiling under a sickly sun, we crept under the tunnels of thick jungle-growth veiling the streams, the dank fœtid cold of which caused a deadly sensation of faintness, which was only relieved by a glass of ether-sherbet or a pipe of the strongest tobacco. By degrees it was found necessary to abandon the greater part of the remaining outfit and luggage. The 27th of January saw us pass safely by the village where M. Maizan was murdered.

"On the 28th there was a report that we were to be attacked at a certain place, and Said bin Salim came to tell me that the road was cut off, and that I must delay till an escort could be summoned from the coast. I knew quite well that it was only an intrigue, but I feared that real obstacles might be placed in our way by the wily little man, and as soon as *bakshish* was mentioned, four naked varlets appeared in a quarter of an hour as escort.

"On the 30th of January the men screamed with delight at the sight of the mango tree, and all their old familiar fruits.

"On the 2nd of February, 1859, Jack and I caught sight of the sea. We lifted our caps, and gave 'three times three and one more.' The 3rd of February saw us passing through the poles decorated with skulls—a sort of negro Temple Bar—at the entrance of Konduchi; they now grin in the London Royal College of Surgeons.

"Our entrance was immense. The war-men danced, shot, shouted; the boys crowded; the women lulliloo'd with all their might; and a general procession conducted us to the hut, swept, cleaned, and garnished for us, by the principal *Banyan* of the Head-quarter village, and there the crowd stared and laughed until they could stare and laugh no more. A boat transferred most of our following to their homes, and they kissed my hand and departed, weeping bitterly with the agony of parting. I sent a note to the Consul at Zanzibar, asking for a coasting craft to explore the Delta and the unknown course of the Rufiji river. I liberally rewarded Zawáda, who had attended to Jack in his illness. We were detained at Konduchi for six days, from the 3rd to the 10th of February.

"On the 9th of February the craft arrived at Konduchi from Zanzibar, and we rolled down the coast with a fair, fresh breeze towards Kilwa, the Quiloa of De Gama and of Camoens. We lost all our crew by cholera, and we were unable to visit the course of the great Rufiji river, a counterpart of the Zambesi in the south, and a water-road which appears destined to become the highway of nations into Eastern Equatorial Africa. The deluge of rain and floods showed me that the travelling season was at an end. I turned the head of the craft northwards, and on the 4th of March, 1859, we landed once more on the island of Zanzibar. Sick and wayworn, I entered the house in sad memory of my old friend, which I was fated to regret still more. The excitement of travel was succeeded by an utter depression of mind and body; even the labour of talking was too great. The little State was in the height of confusion, in a state of Civil war; the eldest brother of the Sultan was preparing a hostile visit to his youngest brother, the Sultan Sayyid Majid of Zanzibar. After a fortnight of excitement and suspense, a gunboat was sent to the elder brother to persuade him to return. His Highness Sayyid Majid had honoured me with an expression of his desire that I should remain until the expected hostilities might be brought to a close. I did so willingly, in gratitude to a Prince to whose good will my success was mainly indebted, but the Consulate was no longer bearable to me. I was too conversant with local politics, too well aware of what was going on, to be a pleasant companion to its new tenant. I was unwilling to go, because so much remained to be done. I wanted to wait for fresh leave of absence and additional funds, but the evident anxiety of Consul Rigby to get rid of me, and Jack's nervous impatience to go on, made me abandon my intentions. Said bin Salim called often at the Consulate, but Captain Rigby agreed with me that he had been more than sufficiently rewarded, and the same with the others. Jack also was of the same opinion, but it suited Jack, with his secret prospects or intentions of returning without me, to change his mind afterwards, and he was evidently able to get Captain Rigby to do the same. There can be little doubt that Jack's intention of returning on the second Expedition, on the lines of the one which he had done so much to spoil, had a great deal to do with his action on this occasion. When H.M.S. *Furious*, carrying Lord Elgin and Mr. Laurence Oliphant, his secretary, arrived at Aden, passage was offered to both of us. I could not start, being too ill. But *he* went, and the words Jack said to me, and I to him, were as follows:—'I shall hurry up, Jack, as soon as I can,' and the last words Jack ever spoke to me on earth were, '*Good-bye, old fellow; you may be quite sure I shall not go up to the Royal Geographical Society until you come to the fore and we appear together. Make your mind quite easy about that.*'

"With grateful heart I bid adieu to the Sultan, whose kindness and personal courtesy will long dwell in my memory, and who expressed a hope to see me again, and offered me one of his ships of war to take me home. However, a clipper-built barque, the *Dragon of Salem*, Captain Macfarlane, was about to sail with the south-west monsoon for Aden. Captain Rigby did not accompany us on board, a mark of civility usual in the East, but Bombay's honest face turned up and seemed peculiarly attractive.

"On the 22nd of March, 1859, the clove shrubs and coco trees of Zanzibar faded from my eyes, and after crossing and recrossing three times the tedious Line, we found ourselves anchored, on the

16th of April, near the ill-omened black walls of the Aden crater. The crisis of my African sufferings had taken place at the Tanganyika; the fever, however, still clung to me.

"I left the Aden coal-hole of the East on the 20th of April, 1859, and in due time greeted with becoming heartiness my native shores.

"The very day after he returned to England, May 9th, 1859, Jack called at the Royal Geographical Society and set on foot the scheme of a new exploration. He lectured in Burlington House, and when I reached London on May 21st I found the ground completely cut from under my feet. Sir Roderick Murchison had given Jack the leadership of a new Expedition; my own long-cherished plan of entering Africa through Somali-land, landing at the Arab town Mombas, was dismissed as unworthy of notice. Jack published two articles in *Blackwood's Magazine*, assumed the whole credit to himself, illustrated a wonderful account of his own adventures and discoveries, with a chart where invention is not in it. He said he did all the astronomical work, and had taught me the geography of the country through which we travelled, which made me laugh. Jack, who literally owed everything to me, habitually wrote and spoke of me to mutual friends in a most disagreeable manner. Many people who professed to be friendly to me said it would be more dignified to say nothing, but I knew how unwise it is to let public sentence pass by default, and how delay may cause everlasting evil, so I wrote the most temperate vindication of my position."*

---

* Richard was a strong-willed, outspoken, and grievously injured man, under the greatest provocation ever put forth. He behaved with dignity, calmness, and generosity, above all praise.—I. B.

CHAPTER XV.

RICHARD AND I MEET AGAIN.

"For life, with all its yields of joy and woe
 And hope and fear,
 Is just our chance o' the prize of learning love—
 How love might be, hath been indeed, and is."
ROBERT BROWNING.

"Dying is easy; keep thou steadfast.
 The greater part, to live and to endure."
MRS. HAMILTON KING, *The Disciples.*

"When Calumny's foul dart thy soul oppresses,
 Think'st thou the venomed shaft could poison me?
 No! the world's scorn, still more than its caresses,
 Shall bind me closer, O my love, to thee.

"Should the days darken, and severe affliction
 Close whelming o'er us like a stormy sea,
 Love shall transform them into benedictions
 Binding me closer, O my love, to thee."

"When truth or virtue an affront endures,
 The affront is mine, my friend, and should be yours;
 Mine as a friend to every worthy mind,
 And mine as man who feels for all mankind."
POPE.

JUST as I was getting into despair, and thinking whether I should go and be a Sister of Charity (May, 1859), as the appearance of Speke alone in London was giving me the keenest anxiety, and as I heard that Richard was staying on in Zanzibar, in the hopes of being allowed to return into Africa, I was very sore.*

---

* "Aussitôt qu'un malheur nous arrive il se recontre toujours un ami prêt à venir nous le dire et à nous fouiller le cœur avec un poignard en nous faisant admirer le manche."—BALZAC. This friend I had, but—

"There are no tricks in plain and simple Faith."—*Julius Cæsar*, iv. ii.

I received only four lines in the well-known hand by post from Zanzibar—no letter.

TO ISABEL.

"That brow which rose before my sight,
 As on the palmers' holy shrine;
 Those eyes—my life was in their light;
 Those lips my sacramental wine;
 That voice whose flow was wont to seem
 The music of an exile's dream."

I knew then it was all right.

On May 22nd, 1859, I chanced to call upon a friend. I was told she was gone out, but would be in to tea, and was asked if I would wait. I said, "Yes;" and in about five minutes another ring came to the door, and another visitor was also asked to wait. The door was opened, and I turned round, expecting to see my friend. Judge of my feelings when I beheld Richard. For an instant we both stood dazed, and I cannot attempt to describe the joy that followed. He had landed the day before, and came to London, and now he had come to call on this friend to know where I was living, where to find me. No one will wonder if I say that we forgot all about her and tea, and that we went downstairs and got into a cab, and took a long drive.

I felt like one stunned; I only knew that he put me in and told the cabman to drive. I felt like a person coming to after a fainting fit or in a dream. It was acute pain, and for the first half-hour I found no relief. I would have given worlds for tears or breath; neither came, but it was absolute content, which I fancy people must feel the first few moments after the soul is quit of the body. The first thing that happened was, that we mutually drew each other's pictures out from our respective pockets at the same moment, which, as we had not expected to meet, showed how carefully they had been kept.

After that, we met constantly, and he called upon my parents. I now put our marriage *seriously* before them, but without success as regards my mother.

I shall never forget Richard as he was then; he had had twenty-one attacks of fever, had been partially paralyzed and partially blind; he was a mere skeleton, with brown yellow skin hanging in bags, his eyes protruding, and his lips drawn away from his teeth. I used to give him my arm about the Botanical Gardens for fresh air, and sometimes convey him almost fainting to our house, or friends' houses, who allowed and encouraged our meeting, in a cab.

The Government and the Royal Geographical Society looked coldly on him; the Indian army brought him under the reduction; he was almost penniless, and he had only a few friends to greet him. Speke was the hero of the hour, the Stanley of 1859–1864. This was *one* of the martyrdoms of that uncrowned King's life, and I think but that for me he would have died.

He told me that all the time he had been away the greatest consolation he had had was my fortnightly journals, in letter form, to him, accompanied by all newspaper scraps and public and private information, and accounts of books, such as I knew would interest him, so that when he did get a mail, which was only in a huge batch now and then, he was as well posted up as if he were living in London.

He never abused Speke, as a mean man would have done; he used to say, "Jack is one of the bravest fellows in the world; if he has a fault it is overweening vanity, and being so easily flattered; in good hands he would be the best of men. Let him alone; he will be very sorry some day, though that won't mend my case." It is interesting *now* to mark in their letters how they descend from "Dear Jack," and "Dear Dick," to "Dear Burton," and "Dear Speke," until they become "Sir!" But I must relate in Speke's favour that the injury once done to his friend, and the glory won for himself, he was not happy with it.

Speke and I had a mutual friend, a lady well known in Society as Kitty Dormer (Countess Dormer)—she would be ninety-four were she now living. She was one of the fashionable beauties of George IV.'s time, and was engaged to my father when they were young.

About a hundred years or more ago, a John Hanning Speke had married one of the Arundells of Wardour, and Lord Arundell always considered the Spekes as sort of neighbours and distant connections, so through this lady's auspices, Speke and I met, and also exchanged many messages; and we nearly succeeded in reconciling Richard and Speke, and would have done so, but for the anti-influences around him. He said to me, "I am so sorry, and I don't know how it all came about. Dick was so kind to me; nursed me like a woman, taught me such a lot, and I used to be so fond of him; but it would be too difficult for me to go back now." *And upon that last sentence he always remained and acted.*

Richard was looking so lank and thin. He was sadly altered; his youth, health, spirits, and beauty were all gone for the time. He fully justified his fevers, his paralysis and blindness, and any amount of anxiety, peril, hardship, and privation in unhealthy latitudes. Never did I feel the strength of my love as then. He returned poorer, and dispirited by official rows and every species of annoyance; but he was still, had he been ever so unsuccessful, and had every man's hand against him, my earthly god and king, and I could have knelt at his feet and worshipped him. I used to feel so proud of him; I used to like to sit and look at him, and to think, "You are mine, and there is no man on earth the least like you."

At one time, when he was at his worst, I found the following in his journal—

"I hear the sounds I used to hear,
The laugh of joy, the groan of pain;
The sounds of childhood sound again.
Death must be near!

"Mine eye reviveth like mine ear;
As painted scenes pass o'er the stage,
I see my life from youth to age.
Ah, Death is near!

"The music of some starry sphere,
A low, melodious strain of song,
Like to the wind-harp sweeps along.
Yes, Death is near!

"A lovely sprite of smiling cheer,
Sits by my side in form of light;
Sits on my left a darker sprite.
Sure, Death is near!

"The meed for ever deemed so dear,
Repose upon the breast of Fame;
(I did but half), while lives my name.
Come then, Death, near!

"Where now thy sting? Where now thy fear?
Where now, fell power, the victory?
I have the mastery over thee.
Draw, Death, draw near!"

I felt bitterly not having the privilege of staying with Richard and nursing him, and he was very anxious that our marriage should take place; so I wrote the following letter to my mother, who was still violently opposing me, and who was absent on some visits:—

"October, 1859.

"MY DEAREST MOTHER,*

"I feel quite grateful to you for inviting my confidence. It is the first time you have ever done so, and the occasion shall not be neglected. It will be a great comfort to me to tell you all; but you must forgive me if I say that I have one tender place too sore to be touched, and that an unkind or slighting word might embitter all our future lives. I know it is impossible for you, with your views for me, both spiritual and temporal, to understand, far less sympathize with me on the present occasion.

* My mother was one of the best and cleverest of women—a queenly woman in manners and appearance (people who have been much at Courts have told me that they always felt as if they were in Royal presence when with her). She had a noble heart and disposition, was generous to a fault, and was exceedingly clever. She was, at the time I write of, still a worldly woman of strong brain, of hasty temper, bigoted, and a Spartan with the elder half of her brood. We trembled before her, but we adored her, and we never got over her death in 1872.

"I feel nothing in common with the world I live in. I dreamt of a Companion and a Life that would suit me exactly, and I them. Like many other people, I suppose, I found my heart yearning, and my tastes developing towards quite opposite things to those which fall naturally in my way. I am rather ashamed to tell you that I fell in love with Captain Burton at Boulogne, and would have married him at any time between this and then, if he had asked me. The moment I saw his brigand-daredevil look, I set him up as an idol, and determined that he was the only man I would ever marry; but he never knew it until three years ago, before he went to Africa. From Boulogne he went to Mecca and Medina, and then to Harar, and then to the Crimea, and on his return home, in 1856, you may remember he came to see us, and I saw him again, and then he fell in love with me and asked me to be his wife, and was perfectly amazed to find that I had cared for him all that time. He was then just going to start for Central Africa; he could not marry me, he could not take me, but we promised to be true to each other, and, as you well know, we met every day. When I came home one day in an ecstasy and told you that I had found the Man and the Life I longed for, that I clung to them with all my soul, and that nothing would turn me, and that all other men were his inferiors, what did you answer me? 'That he was the *only* man you would never consent to my marrying; that you would rather see me in my coffin.' Did you know that you were flying in the face of God? Did you know it was my Destiny? Do you not realize that, because it is not *your* ideal, you want to dash mine from me? He has been away three years, and I have waited for him, feeling sure that in the end you would relent. You have faith in the hand of God in these matters! I called on a friend who was not at home. I was asked to wait; five minutes after the bell rang again, and another visitor was also asked to wait; the door opened, and Captain Burton and I stood face to face. He had disembarked the night before, had just arrived in town, and called there to know where I was living. The year and eight months' silence, which had distressed me so awfully, when you all said he had forgotten me, that he had been eaten by jackals, that he never meant to return, had been spent in the wildest part of the desert, where there was no means of communication. He had had twenty-one fevers, temporary blindness, and partial paralysis of the limbs; he has come back with flying colours, but youth, health, good looks, and spirits temporarily broken up from hardships, privations and dangers, and also many a scar. It surprises me that you should consider mine an infatuation, you who worship talent, and my father bravery and adventure, and here they are both united. Look at his military services—India and the Crimea! Look at his writings, his travels, his poetry, his languages and dialects! Now Mezzofanti is dead he stands first in Europe; he is the best horseman, swordsman, and pistol shot. He has been presented with the gold medal, he is an F.R.G.S., and you must see in the newspapers of his glory, and fame, and public thanks, where he is called 'the Crichton of the day,' 'one of the Paladins of the Age,' 'the most interesting figure of the nineteenth century,' 'the man *par excellence* of brain and pluck.' In his wonderful explorings, he goes where none but natives have ever trod, in hourly peril of his life, often wounded, often without food and water. One day he is a doctor, one day a priest, another he keeps a stall in the bazar, sometimes he is a blacksmith. I could tell you such adventures of him, and traits of determination, which would delight you, were you unprejudiced. It makes me quite ill to see little men boasting of the paltry things that they have done or seen, after this man, who has never been known to speak of himself. He is not at all the man, speaking of his private character, that people take him to be, or what he sometimes, for fun, pretends to be. There is no one whom you would more respect, or attach yourself to, for he is lovable in every way; and what fascinates me is, that every thought, word, or deed is that of a thorough gentleman. I wish I could say the same for all our own acquaintances or relations. There is not a particle of pettiness or snobbery in him; he is far superior to any man I ever met; he has the brain, pluck, and manliness of any hundred of those I have ever seen, united to exceeding sensitiveness, gentleness, delicacy, generosity, and good pride. He is the only being who awes me into respect, and to whose command I bow my head; and any evil opinions you may have ever heard of him, arise from his recklessly setting at defiance conventional people, talking nonsense about religion and heart and principle, which those who do not know him unfortunately take seriously, and he amuses himself with watching their stupid faces. Once he is married to me, he will be the favourite of our family, and you will all be proud of him, and have implicit confidence in him. And let me tell you another thing: you and my father are immensely proud of your families, and we are taught to be the same; but from the present to the future, I believe that our proudest record will be our alliance with Richard Burton. I want to '*Live.*' I hate the artificial existence of London; I hate the life of a vegetable in the country; I want a wild, roving, vagabond life. I am young, strong, and hardy, with good nerves; I like roughing it, and I always want to do something daring and spirited; you will certainly repent it, if you keep me tied up. I wonder that you do not see the magnitude of the position offered to me. His immense talent and adventurous life must command interest. A master-mind like his exercises power and influence over all around him; but I love him because I find in him so much depth of feeling, and a generous heart; because, knowing him to be as brave as a lion, he is yet so gentle, of a delicate, sensitive nature, and the soul of honour. I am fascinated by his manners because they are easy, dignified, simple, and yet so original; there is such a touching forgetfulness of himself and his fame. He appears to me a something so unique and romantic. He unites the wild and daring, with the true gentleman in every sense of the word, and a stamp of a man of the world of the very best sort, having seen things *without* the artificial atmosphere *we* live in, as well as *within.* He has even the noble faults I love in a man, if they can be so called. He is proud, fiery, satirical, ambitious; how could I help looking up to him with fear and admiration? I worship ambition. Fancy achieving a good which affects millions, making your name a national one? It is infamous the way most men in the world live and die, and are never missed, and, like us women, leave nothing but a tombstone. By *ambition* I mean men who have the will and power to change the face of things. I wish I were a man. If I were, I would be Richard Burton; but, being only a woman, I would be Richard Burton's wife. He has not mere brilliancy of talent, but brains that are a rock of good sense, and stern decision of character. I love him purely, passionately, and respectfully; there is no void in my heart, it is at rest for ever with him. It is part of my nature, part of myself, the basis of all my actions, part of my religion; my whole soul is absorbed in it. I have given my every feeling to him, and kept nothing back for myself or for the world. I would this moment sacrifice and leave *all* to follow his fortunes, even if you all cast me out—if the world tabooed me, and no compensation *could* be given to me for *his* loss. Whatever the world may condemn of lawless or strong opinions, whatever he is to the world, he is perfect to me, and I would not have him otherwise than he is.

"That is my side of the business, and now I will turn to your few points. You have said that 'you do not know who he is, that you do not meet him anywhere.' I don't like to hear you say the first, because it makes you out illiterate, and you know how clever you are; but as to your not meeting him, considering the particular sort of society which you seek with a view to marrying your daughters, you are not likely to meet him there, because it bores him, and it is quite out of his line. In these matters he is like a noble, simple savage, and has lived too much in the desert to comprehend the snobberies of our little circles in London. He is a world-wide man, and his life and talents open every door to him; he is a great man all over the East, in literary circles in London, and in great parties where you and I would be part of the crowd, he would be remarkable as a star, also amongst scientific men and in the clubs. Most great houses are only too glad to get him. The only two occasions in which he came out last season it was because I begged him to, and he was bored to death. In public life every one knows him. As to birth, he is just as good as we are; all his people belong to good old families. The next subject is religion. With regard to this he *appears* to disbelieve, pretends to self-reliance, quizzes good, and fears no evil. He leads a good life, has a natural worship of God, innate honour, and does unknown good. *At present* he is following no form; at least, none that he *owns* to. He says there is nothing between Agnosticism and Catholicity. He wishes to be married in the Catholic Church, says that I must practise my own religion, and that our children must be Catholics, and will give such a promise in writing. I myself do not care about people *calling* themselves Catholics, if they are not so in actions, and Captain Burton's life is far more Christian, more gentlemanly, more useful, and more pleasing to God—I am sure—

than many who *call* themselves Catholics, and whom we know. *No.* 3 point is money, and here I am before *you*, terribly crestfallen —there is nothing except his pay. As captain, that is, I believe, £600 a year in India, and £300 in England. We want to try and get the Consulship of Damascus, where we could have a life after both our hearts, and where the vulgarity of poverty would not make itself apparent. If you do not disinherit me, I shall settle my portion on him, and after on any children we may have, in which case he would insure his life. He may have expectations or not, but we can't rely on them.

"Now, dearest mother, I think we should treat each other fairly. Let him go to my father, and ask for me properly. Knowing you as I do, your ideas and prejudices, I know that a man of different religion and no means, would stand in a disagreeable position; so does he, and I will *not* have him insulted. I don't ask you to approve, nor to like it; I don't expect it. I do entreat your blessing, and even a *passive*, reluctant consent to anything that I may do. We shall never marry any one else, and never give each other up, should we remain so all our lives. Do not accuse me of deception, because I shall see him and write to him whenever I get a chance, and if you drive me to it I shall marry him in defiance, because he is by far my first object in life, and the day he (if ever) gives me up I will go straight into a convent. If you think your Catholic friends and relatives will blame you, shut your eyes, give me no wedding, no trousseau, let me get married how I can; but when it is *done*, acknowledge to yourself that I neither *could* nor *would* be dishonourable enough to marry any other man, that God made no law against *poor* people becoming attached to each other, that I am of an age when you can only advise but not hinder me, that your leave once asked my duty ends, that your life is three parts run, and mine is before me, and that if I choose to live out of the 'World' that forms *your* happiness, what is it to you? how does it hurt you? I have got to live with him night and day, for all my life. The man you would choose I should loathe. I see all the disadvantages, and am willing to accept them with him. Why should you object? I do not ask you to share it. You will see that I am so set on it, that the whole creation is as nothing in comparison, that nothing will keep me from it. Do not embitter my whole future life, for God's sake. I would rather die a thousand times than go through again what I have borne for the last five years. Do not quarrel with me, or keep me away from you, and you shall not regret it. I shall have a wide field for a useful, active life, if you do not crush me by an unhappy coldness. When you take the 'World' into your confidence, remember that the day will come when you will forgive and repent, and you will feel quite hurt to find that the 'World' does *not* forgive, that it remembers all you said when you were angry, and that you have debarred your own children from many pleasant things in this life. When we are parted there will be endless regrets. I will not allude to other marriages that you *have* consented to, but you should rejoice that I have got a man who knows how to protect me, and to take care of me. Do think it all over in earnest, and if you love me as you say you do—and I believe it well—do be generous and kind about this. Parents hold so much power to bless or curse the future. Which will you do for me? Let it be a blessing! I look upon him as my future husband; I only wait a kind word from you, the appointment, and Cardinal Wiseman's protection. Do write to me, dearest mother, but write not with *your* views, but entering into *mine.*

"Your fondly attached child,

"ISABEL ARUNDELL."

The only answer to this letter was an awful long and solemn sermon, telling me "that Richard was not a Christian, and had no money." I do not defend my letter to my mother; I should not wish that girls should say or think that this is the way to write to one's mother, nor would mothers in general like to receive such a letter. I print it to show what Richard's character was, and the impression that a girl would receive of it, what views, and what feelings she was capable of entertaining for him. I only plead that I was fighting for my whole future life, and my natural destiny; that I had waited for five years; and that I saw that I had to force my mother's hand, or lose all that made life worth living for. Richard used to say that my mother and I were both gifted with "the noble firmness of the mule." Of course I can see *now* what an aggravating letter it must have been to a woman whose heart was set on big matches for her daughters.

Richard now brought out the "Lake Regions of Equatorial Africa" (2 vols., 1860), and the Royal Geographical Society dedicated the whole of Vol. XXXIII. to the same subject (Clowes and Sons, 1860). My mother still remained obstinate, and Richard thought we should have to take the law into our own hands. I could not bear the thoughts of going against my mother.

One day in April, 1860, I was walking out with two friends, and a tightening of the heart came over me that I had known before. I went home and said to my sister, "I am not going to see Richard for some time." She said, "Why, you will see him to-morrow." "No, I shall not," I said; "I don't know what is the matter." A tap came at the door, and a note with the well-known writing was put into my hand. I knew my fate, and with deep-drawn breath I opened it. He had left—could not bear the pain of saying good-bye; would be absent for nine months, on a journey to see Salt Lake City. He would then come back, and see whether I had made up my mind to choose between him or my mother, to marry me if I *would;* and if I had not the courage to risk it, he would go back to India, and from thence to other explorations, and return no more. I was to take nine months to think about it.

I was for a long time in bed, and delirious. For six weeks I was doctored for influenza, mumps, sore throat, fever, delirium, and everything that I had not got, when in reality I was only heartsick, struggling for what I wanted, a last hard struggle with the suspense of my future before me, and nothing and nobody to help me. I felt it would be my breaking up if circumstances continued adverse, but I determined to struggle patiently, and suffer bravely to the end.

At this juncture, as I was going to marry a poor man, and also to fit myself for Expeditions, I went, for change of air, to a farm-house, where I learnt every imaginable thing that I might possibly want, so that if we had *no* servants, or if servants were sick or mutinous, we should be perfectly independent.

On my return I saw the murder of a Captain Burton in the paper, and *even* my mother pitied me, and took me to the mail office, where a clerk, after numberless inquiries, gave us a paper. My life seemed to hang on a thread till he answered, and then my face beamed so that the poor man was quite startled. It *was* a Captain Burton, murdered by his crew. I could scarcely feel sorry—how selfish we are!—and yet he too, doubtless, had some one to love him.

Richard, meantime, had gone all over the United States, and made a wonderful lot of friends; had gone to Salt Lake City to see Brigham Young, where he stayed with the Mormons and their Prophet for six weeks at great Salt Lake City, visiting California, where he went all over the gold-diggings, and learnt practically to use both pick and pan. He asked Brigham Young if he would admit him as a Mormon, but Brigham Young shook his head, and said, "No, Captain, I think you have done that sort of thing once before." Richard laughed, and told him he was perfectly right.

About this time there was a meeting at the Royal Geographical Society—November 13. I quote from the papers—

"Lord Ashburton (President) in the chair.—Captain J. Grantham, R.E.; R. Lush, Q.C.; J. A. Lockwood, and H. Cartwright, Esqs., were elected Fellows.—The minutes of the former meeting having been confirmed, the Chairman said that a letter would be read from Captain Burton, by the Secretary. It would be a matter of pleasure to all present to know that Captain Burton was in good health. Dr. Shaw then read the following characteristic letter, which had been addressed to him by that officer:—

"'Salt Lake City, Deserat, Utah Territory, September 7.

"'My dear Shaw,

"'You'll see my whereabouts by the envelope; I reached this place about a week ago, and am living in the odour of sanctity,—a pretty strong one it is too,—apostles, prophets, *et hoc genus omne.* In about another week I expect to start for Carson Valley and San Francisco. The road is full of Indians and other scoundrels, but I've had my hair cropped so short that my scalp is not worth having. I hope to be in San Francisco in October, and in England somewhere in November next. Can you put my whereabouts in some paper or other, and thus save me the bother of writing to all my friends? Mind, I'm travelling for my health, which has suffered in Africa, enjoying the pure air of the prairies, and expecting to return in a state of renovation and perfectly ready to leave a card on Muata Yanoo, or any other tyrant of that kind.

"'Meanwhile, ever yours,

"'R. F. BURTON.'

"The paper read was, 'Proposed Exploration in North-Western Australia under Mr. F. Gregory.'—Mr. Galton read letters from Captain Speke, in command of the East African Expedition, conveying the gratifying intelligence that, through the kind assistance of Sir George Grey, Governor at the Cape of Good Hope, the party had been strengthened by the accession of a guard of twelve Hottentot soldiers and £300. Admiral Keppel had conveyed the expedition in her Majesty's steamer *Brisk* to Zanzibar.—A despatch from Sir George Grey on Mr. Chapman's and Mr. Anderson's late journeys in South Africa was read.—The President announced that subscriptions would be received at the Royal Geographical Society, 15, Whitehall Place, in aid of Consul Petherick's Expedition, to cooperate with that under Captains Speke and Grant, *viâ* Khartoum and the Upper Nile."

Richard travelled about twenty-five thousand miles, and then he turned his head homewards. He wrote the "City of the Saints," 1 vol., on the Mormons, and he brought it out in 1861. It was reprinted by Messrs. Harper of New York, and extensively reviewed, especially by the *Tour du Monde.*

It was Christmas, 1860, that I went to stop with my relatives, Sir Clifford and Lady Constable (his *first* wife, *née* Chichester), at Burton Constable,—the father and mother of the present baronet. There was a large party in the house, and we were singing; some one propped up the music with the *Times* which had just arrived, and the first announcement that caught my eye was that "Captain R. F. Burton had arrived from America."

I was unable, except by great resolution, to continue what I was doing. I soon retired to my room, and *sat* up all night, packing, and conjecturing how I should get away,—all my numerous plans tending to a "bolt" next morning,—should I get an affectionate letter from him. I received two; one had been opened and read by somebody else, and one, as it afterwards turned out, had been burked at home before forwarding. It was not an easy matter. I was in a large country-house in Yorkshire, with about twenty-five friends and relatives, amongst whom was one brother, and I had heaps of luggage. We were blocked up with snow and nine miles from the station, and (*contra miglior noler voler mal pugna*) I had heard of his arrival only early in the evening, and twelve hours later I had managed to get a telegram ordering me to London, under the impression that it was of the most vital importance.

What a triumph it is to a woman's heart, when she has patiently and courageously worked, and prayed, and suffered, and the moment is realized that was the goal of her ambition!

As soon as we met, and had had our talk, he said, "I have waited for five years. The three first were inevitable on account of my journey to Africa, but the last two were not. Our lives are being spoiled by the unjust prejudices of your mother, and it is for you to consider whether you have not already done your duty in sacrificing two of the best years of your life out of respect to her. If *once* you *really* let me go, mind, I shall never come back, because I shall know that you have not got the strength of character which *my* wife must have. Now, you must make up your mind to choose between your mother and me. If you choose me, we marry, and I stay; if not, I go back to India and on other Explorations, and I return no more. Is your answer ready?" I said, "Quite. I marry you this day three weeks, let who will say nay."

MINIATURE PORTRAIT.

When we fixed the date of our marriage, I wanted to be married on Wednesday, the 23rd, because it was the Espousals of Our Lady and St. Joseph, but he would not, because Wednesday, the 23rd, and Friday, the 18th, were our unlucky days; so we were married on the Vigil, Tuesday, the 22nd of January.

We pictured to ourselves much domestic happiness, with youth, health, courage, and talent to win honour, name, and position. We had the same tastes, and perfect confidence in each other. No one turns away from real happiness without some very strong temptation or delusion. I went straight to my father and mother, and told them what had occurred. My father said, "I consent with all my heart, if your mother consents," and my mother said, "*Never!*" I said, "Very well, then, mother! I cannot sacrifice our two lives to a mere whim, and you ought not to expect it, so I am going to marry him, whether you will or no." I asked all my brothers and sisters, and they said they would receive him with delight. My mother offered me a marriage with my father and brothers present, my mother and sisters not. I felt that that was a slight upon *him*, a slight upon his family, and a slur upon me, which I did not deserve, and I refused it. I went to Cardinal Wiseman, and I told him the whole case as it stood, and he asked me if my mind was absolutely made up, and I said, "*Absolutely.*" Then he said, "Leave the matter to me." He requested Richard to call upon him, and asked him if he would give him three promises in writing—

1. That I should be allowed the free practice of my religion.
2. That if we had any children they should be brought up Catholics.
3. That we should be married in the Catholic Church.

Which three promises Richard readily signed. He also amused the Cardinal, as the family afterwards learnt, by saying sharply, "Practise her religion indeed! I should rather think she *shall.* A man without a religion may be excused, but a woman without a religion is not the woman for me." The Cardinal then sent for me, promised me his protection, said he would himself procure a special dispensation from Rome, and that he would perform the ceremony himself. He then saw my father, who told him how bitter my mother was about it; that she was threatened with paralysis; that we had to consider her in every possible way, that she might receive no shocks, no agitation, but that all the rest quite consented to the marriage. A big family council was then held, and it was agreed far better for Richard and me, and for every one, to make all proper arrangements to be married, and to be attended by *friends*, and for me to go away on a visit to some friends, that they might not come to the wedding, nor participate in it, in order not to have a quarrel with my mother; that they would break it to her at a suitable time, and that the secret of their knowing it, should be kept up as long as mother lived. "Mind," said my father, "you must never bring a misunderstanding between mother and me, nor between her and her children."

I passed that three weeks preparing very solemnly and earnestly for my marriage day, but yet something differently to what many expectant brides do. I made a very solemn religious preparation, receiving the Sacraments. Gowns, presents, and wedding pageants had no part in it, had no place. Richard arranged with my own lawyer and my own priest that everything should be conducted in a strictly legal and strictly religious way, and the whole programme of the affair was prepared. A very solemn day to me was the eve of my marriage. The following day I was supposed to be going to pass a few weeks with a friend in the country.

At nine o'clock on Tuesday, the 22nd of January, 1861, my cab was at the door with my box on it. I had to go and wish my father and mother good-bye before leaving. I went downstairs with a beating heart, after I had knelt in my own room, and said a fervent prayer that they might bless me, and if they did, I would take it as a sign. I was so nervous, I could scarcely stand. When I went in, mother kissed me and said, "Good-bye, child, God bless you." I went to my father's bedside, and knelt down and said good-bye. "God bless you, my darling," he said, and put his hand out of the bed and laid it on my head. I was too much overcome to speak, and one or two tears ran down my cheeks, and I remember as I passed down I kissed the door outside.

I then ran downstairs and quickly got into my cab, and drove to a friend's house (Dr. and Miss Bird, now of 49, Welbeck Street), where I changed my clothes—not wedding clothes (clothes which most brides of to-day would probably laugh at)—a fawn-coloured dress, a black-lace cloak, and a white bonnet—and they and I drove off to the Bavarian Catholic Church, Warwick Street, London. When assembled we were altogether a party of eight. The Registrar was there for legality, as is customary. Richard was waiting on the doorstep for me, and as we went in he took holy water, and made a very large sign of the Cross. The church doors were wide open, and full of people, and many were there who knew us. As the 10.30 Mass was about to begin, we were called into the Sacristy, and we then found that the Cardinal in the night had been seized with an acute attack of the illness which carried him off four years later, and had deputed Dr. Hearne, his Vicar-general, to be his proxy.

After the ceremony was over, and the names signed, we went back to the house of our friend Dr. Bird and his sister Alice, who have always been our best friends, where we had our wedding breakfast.

During the time we were breakfasting, Dr. Bird began to chaff him about the things that were sometimes said of him, and which were not true. "Now, Burton, tell me; how do you feel when you have killed a man?" Dr. Bird (being a physician) had given himself away without knowing it. Richard looked up quizzically, and drawled out, "Oh, quite jolly! How do you?"

We then went to Richard's bachelor lodgings, where he had a bedroom, dressing-room, and sitting-room, and we had very few pounds to bless ourselves with, but were as happy as it is given to any mortals out of heaven to be. The fact is that the only clandestine thing about it, and that was quite contrary to *my* desire, was that my poor mother, with her health and her religious scruples, was kept in the dark, but I must thank God that, though paralysis came on two years later, it was not I that caused it.

I here insert the beautiful and characteristic letter which my husband wrote to my father on the following day, in case he should wish to give it to my mother. For the first few days of our marriage, Richard used to be so worried at being stared at as a bridegroom, that he always used to say that we had been married a couple of years; but that sort of annoyance soon wore off, and then he became rather proud of being a married man. To say that I was happy would be to say nothing; a repose came over me that I had never known. I felt that it was for Eternity, an immortal repose, and I was in a bewilderment of wonder at the goodness of God, who had almost worked miracles for me.

During this time my brothers visited us, keeping us up in all that was going on. Some weeks later, two dear old aunts, Mrs. Strickland-Standish and Monica, Lady Gerard, who lived at Portobello House, Mortlake, nearly opposite to where I live now, and where I had frequently passed several weeks every year (for they made a sort of family focus), got to hear that I was seen going into a bachelor lodging, and bowled up to London to tell my mother. She wrote in an agony to my father, who was visiting in the country, "that a dreadful misfortune had happened in the family; that I been seen going into a bachelor lodging in London, and could not be at the country house where I was supposed to be." My father telegraphed back to her, "She is married to Dick Burton, and thank God for it;" and he wrote to her, enclosing the letter just inserted, and desired her to send one of my brothers for us, who knew where to find us, and to mind and receive us properly. We were then sent for home. My mother behaved like a true lady and a true Christian. She kissed us both, and blessed us. I shall never forget how shy I felt going home, but I went in very calmly, I kissed them all round, and they received Richard in the nicest way, and then mother embarrassed us very much by asking our pardon for flying in the face of God, and opposing what she now knew to be His will. My husband was very much touched. It was not long before she approved of the marriage more than anybody, and as she grew to know him, she loved him as much as her own sons. And this is the way we came to be married.

In short, mother never could forgive herself, and was always alluding to it either personally or by letter. It always was the same burthen of song—"that she exposed me to such a risk, that my relations might have abandoned me, that Society might not have received me, that I might have been forbidden to put my name down for the Drawing-room, when I had done nothing wrong;" and she said, "All through *me*, and God had destined it, but I could not see it. I never thought you would have the courage to take the law in your own hands;" and I used to answer her, "Mother, if you had all cast me out, if Society had tabooed me, if I had been forbidden to go to Court, it would not have kept me from it—I could not have helped myself—I am quite content with my future crust and tent, and I would not exchange places with the Queen; so do not harass yourself."

However, by the goodness of God, and the justness and kindness of a few great people, none of these catastrophes *did* happen. We used to entreat of her not to say anything more about it, but even on her deathbed she persisted in doing so. I shall never forget that first night when we went home; I went up to my room and changed my things, and ate my dinner humbly and silently. We were a very large family and were all afraid to speak, and as Richard was so very clever, the family stood rather in awe of him; so there was a silence and restraint upon us; but the children were allowed to come down to dessert for a treat, and, with the intuition that children have, they knew that he wanted them, and that they could do what they liked with him. One was a little *enfant terrible,* and very fond of copying our midshipmen brothers' slang. They crowded round my mother with their little doll-tumblers waiting for some wine. He was so constrained that he forgot to pass the wine at dessert as it came round to *him,* when a small voice piped out from the end of the long table, "I say, old bottle-stopper —pass the wine!" He burst out laughing, and that broke the ice, and we all fell to laughing and talking. Mother punished the child by giving him no wine, but Richard looked up and said so sweetly, "Oh, *Mother,* not on my first night *at home!*" that her heart went out to him.

We had seven months of uninterrupted bliss. Through the kindness of Lord John Russell, Richard obtained the Consulship of Fernando Po, in the Bight of Biafra, West Coast of Africa, with a coast line of six or seven hundred miles for his jurisdiction, a deadly climate, and £700 a year. He was too glad to get his foot on the first rung of the ladder, so, though it was called the "Foreign Office Grave," he cheerfully accepted it. It was not quite so cheerful for me, because it was a climate of certain death to white women, and he would not allow me to go out in an unlimited way.

We had a glorious season, and took up our position in Society. He introduced me to all the people he knew, and I introduced him to all the people that I knew. Lord Houghton (Monckton-Milnes), the father of the present Lord Houghton, was very much attached to Richard, and he settled the question of our position by asking his

RICHARD BURTON. (PRESENTED TO HIM, WITH HIS WIFE'S PORTRAIT, AS A WEDDING GIFT.)

By Louis Desanges.

ISABEL BURTON AS A BRIDE.

By Louis Desanges.

عبد الله
الحاج

January 23rd 1861

[illegible]

St. James

My dear Father

I have committed a highway robbery by marrying your daughter Isabel at Warwick St. Church and before the Registrar — the details she is writing to her mother.

It only remains for me to say that I have no ties or liaisons of any sort, that the marriage is perfectly legal and "respectable". I want no money with Isabel: I can

work [illegible] [illegible] be my Care that
Time shall bring you nothing
to regret I am
Yours sincerely
Richd F. Burton

friend Lord Palmerston to give a party, and to let me be the bride of the evening; and when I arrived, Lord Palmerston gave me his arm, and he introduced Richard and me to all the people we had not previously known, and my relatives clustered around us as well. I was allowed to put my name down for a Drawing-room. And Lady Russell, now the Dowager, presented me at Court "on my marriage."

Shortly after this, happened Grindlay's fire, where we lost all we possessed in the world, except the few boxes we had with us. The worst was that all his books, and his own poetry, which was beautiful, especially one poem, called "The Curse of Vishnu," and priceless Persian and Arabic manuscripts, that he had picked up in various out-of-the-way places, and a room full of costumes of every nation, were burnt. He smiled, and said in a philosophical sort of way, "Well, it is a great bore, but I dare say that the world will be none the worse for some of those manuscripts having been burnt" (a prophetic speech, as I now think of it). When he went down to ask for some compensation, he found that Grindlay was insured, but that he was not—not, he said, that any money could repay him for the loss of the things. As he always saw the comic side of a tragedy as well as the pathetic, "the funniest thing was the clerk asking me if I had lost any plate or jewellery, and on my saying, 'No,' the change in his face from sympathy to the utter surprise that I could care so much for any other kind of loss, was amusing."

In 1861, when the Indian army changed hands, Richard suffered, and, as Mr. Hitchman remarked, "his enemies may be congratulated upon their mingled malice and meanness." He just gave the official animus a chance. It was a common thing in times of peace for Indian officers to be allowed to take appointments and remain on the *cadre* of their regiment, temporarily or otherwise. Richard, in remonstrance, would not quote names for fear of injuring other men, but any man who knew Egypt could score off half a dozen. His knowledge of the East, and of so many Eastern languages, would have been of incalculable service in Egypt, upon the Red Sea, in Marocco, Persia, in any parts of the East, and yet he, who in any other land would have been rewarded with at least a K.C.B. and a handsome pension, was glad to get his foot on the lowest rung of the ladder of the Consular service, called the "Foreign Office Grave," the Consulate of Fernando Po, and we could not think enough of, talk enough of, or be grateful enough to Lord John Russell, who gave it him; yet the acceptance of this miserable post was made an excuse to strike his name off the Indian army list, and the rule, which had been allowed to lapse in a score of cases, was revived for Richard's injury under circumstances of discourtesy so great, that it would be hard to believe the affront unintentional. He received no notice whatever, and he only realized, on seeing his successor gazetted, that his military career was actually ended, and his past life become like a blank sheet of paper. It would have been stretching no point to have granted this appointment, and to have been retained in the army on half-pay, but it was refused; they swept out his whole nineteen years' service as if they had never been, without a vestige of pay or pension.

All his services in Sind had been forgotten, all his Explorations were wiped out, and at the age of forty he found himself at home, with the rank of Captain, no pay, no pension, plenty of fame, a newly married wife, and a small Consulate in the most pestilential climate, with £700 a year. In vain he asked to go to Fernando Po *temporarily* till wanted for active service. He wrote—

"It will be an act of injustice on the part of the Bombay Government to solicit my removal on account of my having risked health and life in my country's service.

"They are about to treat me as a man who has been idling away my time and shirking duty; whereas I can show that every hour has been employed for my country's benefit, in study, writings, languages, and explorations. Are my wounds and fevers, and perpetual risk of health and life, not to speak of personal losses, to go for nothing?

"The Bombay Government does not take into consideration one iota of my service, but casts the whole into oblivion. I consider the Bombay Government to be unjustly prejudiced against me on account of the *private piques* of a certain half-dozen individuals. Will the Bombay Government put all its charges against me in black and white, and thus allow me a fair opportunity of clearing myself of my supposed delinquencies? Other men—I will merely quote Colonel Greathed and Lieut.-Colonel Norman—are permitted to take service in England, and yet to retain their military service in India.

"In the time of the Court of Directors, an officer might be serving the Foreign Office and India too, as in the case of Lieut.-Colonel Hamerton, late Consul at Zanzibar; but since the amalgamation, the officers of her Majesty's Indian Army hope that they may take any appointment in any part of the world, as a small recompense for their losses; *i.e.* supercession and inability to sell their commissions, after having paid for steps."

At first he wanted to try me, so he pretended he did not like my going to Confession, and I used to say, "Well, my religion teaches me that my first duty is to obey you," and I did not bother to go; so he at once took off this restraint, and used to send me to Mass, and remind me of fish-days. It astonished me, the wonderful way he knew our doctrine, and frequently explained things to me that I did not know myself. He always wore his medal. I was very much surprised, shortly after we were married, at my husband giving me £5. Whilst he had been away one of my brothers had met with a sudden death; his horse had fallen on him and crushed him in a moment. He said, "Take this and have Masses said with it for your poor brother." I only thought then what generosity and what good taste it was. He was always delighted with the society of priests—not so much foreign priests, as English ones—especially if he got hold of a highly educated, broad theologian of a Jesuit; but in all cases he was most courteous to *any* of them, and protected them and their Missions whenever he was in a position to do so. Once he went with me to a midnight Mass, and he cried all the time. I could not understand it, and he said he could not explain it himself. I had no idea then that he had ever been once received into our Church in India. He *always* bowed his head at "Hallowed be Thy Name," and he did that to the day of his death.

We passed delightful days at country houses, notably at Lord Houghton's (Fryston), where, at his house in the country, and his house in Brook Street, and at Lord Strangford's house in Great Cumberland Place, we met all that was worth meeting of rank and fashion, beauty and wit, and *especially* all the most talented people in the world. I can shut my eyes and mentally look round his (Lord Houghton's) large round table even *now*, which usually held twenty-five guests. I can see Buckle, and Carlyle, and all the Kingsleys, and Swinburne, and Froude, and all the great men that were, and many that are, for the last thirty-two years, and remember a great deal of the conversation. But I am not here to describe them, but to give a description of Richard Burton. I can remember the Duc d'Aumale cheek by jowl with Louis Blanc. The present Lord Houghton, and his two sisters, Lady Fitzgerald and the Hon. Mrs. Henniker, were babes in the nursery. I can remember the good old times in the country, at Fryston, where breakfast was at different little round tables, so people came down when they liked, and sat at one or another, and he would stroll from one table to another, with a book in his hand. Swinburne was then a boy, and had just brought out his "Queen Mother Rosamund," and Lord Houghton brought it up to us, saying, "I bring you this little book, because the author is coming here this evening, so that you may not quote him as an absurdity to himself." I can remember Vambéry telling us Hungarian tales, and I can remember Richard cross-legged on a cushion, reciting and reading "Omar el Khayyám" alternately in Persian and English, and chanting the call to prayer, "Allahhu Akbar."

My Society recollections, my happy days, are all of the pleasantest and most interesting. The evil day came far too soon; this was a large oasis of seven months in my life, and even if I had had no other it would have been worth living for. We went down to Worthing to my family, where we passed a very happy time, and he here gave me a proof of affection which I shall never forget. He had gone to see his cousin, Samuel Burton, at Brighton, and had promised to be back by the last train, but he did not make his appearance. I was in a dreadful state of mind lest anything should have happened to him. He arrived about one in the morning, pale and worn out. He had gone to sleep in the train, and had been carried some twenty miles away from Worthing. He could get no kind of conveyance, being in the night; so, inquiring in what direction Worthing lay, and settling the matter by a pocket compass, he started across country, and between a walk and a sort of long trot, from nine to one, he reached me, instead of waiting, as another man would have done, till the next morning for a train back.

I shall never forget when the time came to part, and I was to go to Liverpool to see him off, for he would not allow me to accompany him till he had seen what Fernando Po was like. It was in August, 1861, when we went down to Liverpool, and we were very sad, because he was not going to a Consulate where we could hope to remain together as a *home*. It was a deadly climate, and we were always going to be climate-dodging. I was to go out, not now, but later, and then, perhaps, not to land, and to return and ply up and down between Madeira and Teneriffe and London, and I, knowing he had Africa at his back, was in a constant agitation for fear of his doing more of these Explorations into unknown lands. There were about eighteen men (West African merchants), and everybody took him away from me, and he had made me promise that if I was allowed to go on board and see him off, that I would not cry and unman him. It was blowing hard and raining; there was one man who was inconsiderate enough to accompany and stick to us the whole time, so that we could not exchange a word (how I hated him!). I went down below and unpacked his things and settled his cabin, and saw to the arrangement of his luggage. My whole life and soul was in that good-bye, and I found myself on board the tug, which flew faster and faster from the steamer. I saw a white handkerchief go up to his face. I then drove to a spot where I could see the steamer till she became a dot.

> "Fresh as the first beam
> Glittering on a sail,
> Which brings our friends up
> From the under world;
> Sad as the last, which reddens over one,
> That sinks with all we love below the verge."

Here I give Richard's description of going out, read later—

"A heart-wrench—and all is over. Unhappily I am not one of those independents who can say, *Ce n'est que le premier pas qui coûte.*

"Then comes the first nightfall on board outward-bound, the saddest time that the veteran wanderer knows. Saadi the Persian, one of the best travellers,—he studied books for thirty years, did thirty of *wanderjahre*, and for thirty wrote and lived in retirement—has thus alluded to the depressing influence of what I suppose may philosophically be explained by an absence of Light-stimulus or Od-force—

> 'So yearns at eve's soft tide the heart,
> Which the wide wolds and waters part
> From all dear scenes to which the soul
> Turns, as the lodestone seeks its pole.'

"We cut short the day by creeping to our berths, without even a 'nightcap,' and we do our best to forget ourselves, and everything about us."

CHAPTER XVI.

WEST COAST OF AFRICA—RICHARD'S FIRST CONSULATE.

In his "Wanderings in West Africa" (2 vols., 1863), Richard describes the whole of his jurisdiction, which was several hundred miles of coast. The ship, after leaving Madeira and Teneriffe, goes to Bathurst on the West Coast, to Sierra Leone, Monrovia, Grand Bassa, Cape Palmas, Half Jack, Grand Baltam, Axim, Elmina, Cape Coast Castle, Salt Pond, Winnebah, Accra, Addah, Quitta, Bagadah, Agwey, Whydah, Lagos, Bonny, Fernando Po, and Old Calabar, one station beyond. He ends up with—"Arriving in these outer places is the very abomination of desolation. I drop, for a time, my pen, in the distinct memory of having felt uncommonly suicidal through that first night at Fernando Po."

It would not suit this book to have large copyings from his works, but I think I should give two which are especially useful—one a description of the Sierra Leone negro, and another on the richness of the Guinea Coast, about which I shall have something to say later on in 1881.

"We parted with our consumptives at Madeira; we leave our Africans at Sierra Leone. For this race there is a descending scale of terminology: 1, European; 2, civilized man; 3, African; 4, man—the Anglo-Americans say, 'pussum'—of colour; 5, negro; 6, darkie; 7, nigger, which last, is actionable. Many a £5 has been paid for the indulgence of *lèse majesté* against the 'man and a brother;' and not a few £50 where the case has been brought into the civil courts. Captain Philip Beaver was justified in declaring that he would 'rather carry a rattlesnake than a negro who has been in London.' Not so Mr. Hazelface, into whose soul or countenance *soggezzione*, or shame, never entered—for was he not of the Almighty Negroes? And shall not the most dishonest of Negroes in these days stand before Kings? The second, our Gorilla, or Missing Link, was the son of an emancipated slave, who afterwards distinguished himself as a Missionary and a Minister. His—the sire's—name has appeared in many books, and he wrote one himself, pitying his own 'poor lost father,' because, forsooth, he died in the religion of his ancestors, an honest Fetishist. Our excellent warm-hearted, ignorant souls at home were so delighted with the report of this Lion of the Pulpit, that it was much debated whether the boy Ajáí had not been providentially preserved for the Episcopate of Western Africa.

"These individuals are out of their *assiettes*. At home they will devour, perforce, *Kankey* and bad fish, washing them down with *Mimbo* and *Pitto*—native and palm wine, and hop-less beer—here they abuse the best of beef, long openly for 'palaver sauce' and 'palm-oil chop,' and find fault with their champagne. At home they will wear breech-clouts and Nature's stockings, only. Here their coats are superfine Saxony, with broadest of silk velvet collars. The elongated cocoa-nut head bears jauntily a black pork-pie felt, with bright azure ribbons, and a rainbow necktie vies in splendour with the loudest of waistcoats from the land of Moses and Son; the pants are tightly strapped down to show the grand formation of the knee, the delicate slimness of the calf, the manly purchase of the heel, and the waving line of beauty that distinguishes the shin-bone.* There are portentous studs upon a glorious breadth of shirt, a small investment of cheap, gaudy, tawdry rings sets off the chimpanzee-like fingers, and when in the open air, lemon-coloured gloves invest the hands, whose horny reticulated skin reminds me of the scaly feet of those cranes which pace at ease over the burning sand, for which strong slippers are not strong enough for us; whilst feet of the same order, but slightly superior in point of proportional size, are tightly packed into patent-leather boats, the latter looking as if they had been stuffed with some inanimate substance, say the halves of a calf's head.

"It is hardly fair to deride a man's hideousness, but it is where personal deformity is accompanied by conceit. Once upon a time we all pitied an individual who by acclamation was proclaimed the ugliest man in the B—— army, which is not saying a little. 'Poor E——!' his friends would exclaim; 'it's no matter if a chap's plain, but *he* is revolting,' and they commiserated him accordingly. Once, however, he was detected by his chums looking into a shaving-glass, and thus soliloquizing: 'Well, E——, I declare you'd be a deuced handsome fellow if you had but a better nose.' The discreet chum, of course, spread the story, and from that moment our compassion departed.

"No one, also, is more hopeless about the civilization of Africa than the semi-civilized African returning to the 'home of his fathers.' One feels how hard has been his own struggle to emerge from barbarism. He acknowledges in his own case a selection of species, and he sees no end to the centuries before there can be a nation

* This is pure chaff—they are woefully defective in all these points; but being ignorant they dress so as to show off what an Englishman would improve or conceal.—I. B.

equal even to himself. Yet in *England*, and in *books*, he will cry up the Majesty of African kings; he will give the people whom he thoroughly despises a thousand grand gifts of morals and industry, and extenuate, or rather ignore, all their faults and shortcomings. I have heard a negro assert, with the unblushing effrontery which animates the negro speechifying in Exeter Hall, or before some learned society, that—for instance, at Lagos, a den of thieves—theft is unknown, and that men leave their money with impunity in the storehouse, or on the highway. After which, he goes home, 'tongue in cheek,' despising the facility with which an Englishman and his money are parted.

"Our Africans left the ship without, on our part, or probably on theirs, a single regret. Not so with the Mandengas. The honest and manly bearing of these Moslems—so wonderful a contrast with those caricatures in pork-pie and peg-topped broadcloth—had prepossessed me strongly in their favour. We shook hands, and in broken Arabic bade each other a kindly Allah-speed.

"The white man's position is rendered far more precarious on the coast than it might be, *if the black man were always kept in his proper place.* A European without stockings or waistcoat, and with ragged slops hanging about his limbs, would not be admitted into the cuddy; an African will. Many of the fellows come on board to make money by picking a quarrel. And what does one think of a dusky belle, after dropping her napkin at Government House, saying to her neighbour, 'Please, Mr. Officer-man, pick up my towel'? Or of such a dialogue as this? The steward has neglected to supply soup to some negro, who at every meal has edged himself higher up towards the top of the table, and whose conversation consists of whispering into the ears of an adjacent negro, and of hyæna-like guffaws.

"'I say, daddee, I want *my* soop; all de passengers, he drink 'im soop; *me* no drink *my* soop: what he mean, dis palaver?'

"The words are uttered in a kind of scream; the steward cannot help smiling, and the nigger resumes—

"'Ah, you laff! And for why you laff? I no laff; no drinkee soop!'

"Here the dialogue ends, and the ladies look their acknowledgments that travelling does throw us into strange society.

"From the moment of our arrival, 'negro palaver' began. A *cause célèbre*, which will be referred home, had just been brought to a close. Mr. M——, a civilian official in the colony, after thrice warning out of his compound a troublesome negro and a suspected thief, had applied a certain *vis à tergo*, and had ejected the trespasser, not, however, with unnecessary violence. In England the case would have been settled by a police magistrate, and the fine, if any, would have been half a crown. At Freetown the negro, assisted by his friends or 'company,' betakes himself to a lawyer. The latter may be a mulatto, possibly a pettifogger, certainly a moneyless man who lives in a wretched climate for the pure purposes of lucre; his interest is of course to promote litigation, and he fills his pockets by what is called 'sharp practice.' After receiving the preliminary fee of £5, he demands exemplary damages. The consequence was that Mr. M—— was lightened of £50.

"These vindictive cases are endless; half an hour's chat will bring out a dozen, and, as at Aden, the Sons of the White Cliff have nothing to do but to quarrel and to recount their grievances. A purser of the African S.S. Company, finding a West Indian negro substituting dead for live turkeys, called him a 'tief.' The 'tief' laid an action for £1000, and the officer was only too happy to escape with the retainer, three guineas. The same, when a black came on board for a package, sent him off to the quarter-deck; the fellow became insolent, when a military man present exclaimed, 'If you gave *me* that cheek, I'd have you overboard!' The negro put off, took two of his friends as witnesses, procured an affidavit that the white man had threatened him, and laid an action for defamation of character, etc.; damages £50—a favourite sum.

THE MAN WHO WINS.

Despite a counter oath, signed by two or three English officers, one of them a colonel, to the effect that no bad language had been used except by the plaintiff, whose insolence had been unbearable, the defendant was compelled to make an apology, and to pay £15 costs. Another told me that for raising a stick to an insolent servant, he was 'actioned' for £50, and escaped by compromise for £12. When the defendant is likely to leave the station, the *modus operanda* is as follows:—A writ of summons is issued. The lawyer strongly recommends an apology for the alleged offence and a promise to pay costs, warning the offender at the same time that judgment will go against him if absent by default. Should the defendant prudently 'stump up,' the thing ends; if not, a *capias* is taken out, and the law runs its course. A jury is chosen. The British Constitution determines that a man must be tried by his peers. His peers at Sierra Leone are perhaps a dozen full-blooded blacks, liberated slaves, half-reformed fetishmen, sometimes with a sneaking fondness for the worship of Shángo, and if not criminals in their own country, at least pauper-clad in dish-clouts and palm oil. To see such peers certainly 'takes pride down a peg,' as the phrase is; no use to think of that ancestor who 'came over' with the Conqueror, or that Barony lost in the days of the Rebellion.

"No one raises the constitutional question, 'Are these half-reclaimed barbarians my peers?' And if he did, justice would sternly answer 'Yes!' The witnesses will forswear themselves—not like our porters, for half a crown, but *gratis*, because the plaintiff is a fellow-tribesman. The judge may be 'touched with the tar-brush,' but be he white as milk, he must pass judgment according to verdict, and when damages are under £200, there is no appeal.

"Sierra Leone contains many sable families—Lumpkins, Lewis, Pratt, Ezidio, Nicols, Macarthy, are a few of their patronymics,—against whom it is useless for a stranger to contend and come off scot and lot free. Besides these, there are seventeen chief and two hundred minor tribes, whilst a hundred languages, according to M. Koelle,—one hundred and fifty, says Bishop Vidal—are spoken in the streets of Freetown. All are hostile to one another; all combine against the white man. After the fashion of the Gold Coast, they have formed themselves into independent republics, called 'companies.' These set aside certain funds for their own advancement, and for the ruin of their rivals. The most powerful and influential races are the Aku and the Ibo.

"If the reader believes that I have exaggerated the state of things at Sierra Leone, he is mistaken; the sketch is under rather than over-drawn. And he will presently see a confirmation of these statements in the bad name which these liberated Africans bear upon the whole of the western coast.

"At breakfast we had been duly primed with good advice, viz. not to notice impudence, and to turn our shoulders—the severest punishment—upon all who tried their hands at annoyance. We rowed to the Government landing, a rickety, slippery flight of wooden stairs, which is positively dangerous at night, or when the waves dash against the jetty. We were careful to carry no luggage; porters fight for the job, and often let the object of emulation drop into the water. One of our mail-bags received this *baptism de Sierra Leone* last night. On such occasion a push or poke is a forbidden luxury; the man might fall down—you have certainly injured him internally—you must pay exemplary damages.

Two stories are related about Richard. I do not vouch for them, but they sound likely. One was, that when he arrived in Africa, he found that the negroes were in the state above described, assuming the upper hand, and treating the white men as an inferior race. They were summoning them before tribunals on the most trivial pretext, forwarding complaints home to pander to different people, which a man who had lived in India, and had passed something like twenty-two years in black countries, was not the least likely to stand. A day or two after his arrival at his post, a very dandified-dressed and full-blooded nigger walked into the Consulate, the window of which was not far from the ground, clapped Richard on the back in the most jovial manner, with his disagreeable "yah-yah" laugh. "How do, Consul? Come to shake hands—how do?" holding out his black paw, as if he were a condescending Royalty. There were some other Englishmen waiting about for different business, looking curiously to see what was going to be the attitude of the new Consul. He looked at the bumptious and loud-mannered nigger, with a quiet stare of surprise, and then shouted, "Hi, Kroo-boys, here; throw this nigger out of the window, will you?" The Kroo-boys, his canoemen (of six oars), rushed in, delighted with the commission, and flung him out. It was only a roll of three or four feet—but no niggers in black coats and button-holes came to clap the new Consul on the back after that, nor did they summon him before the Tribunal.

Another story told was, that the merchants on the West Coast were sorely put to inconvenience by the Captains of ships steaming in, discharging their cargo, and steaming off again without giving the merchants time to read and answer to their correspondence. Commerce, therefore, was at a very low ebb, because the merchants were a fortnight behind the world, there being only two steamers a month at that time. They asked Richard in a body, if there was no means of helping them. Richard got out the contracts, and saw that they said "that the Captain of a ship should stop at the port *eighteen hours' daylight* for that very purpose." The next ship that came in, the Captain came and looked into the Consulate in a jovial way, and said, "Now, Captain, hurry up with my papers; I want to be off; going to clear out." Richard looked up at him with a surprised stare, and drawled out lazily, "Oh, you can't go, for I have not finished my letters!" "Oh, damn your letters, Sir! I'm off." "Stop a bit," said Richard; "let us have a look at your contract?" He pulled it out of the drawer. "The contract says that you shall stop here eighteen hours' daylight, to give the merchants an opportunity of receiving and answering their correspondence, otherwise commerce would be ruined, the merchants being a fortnight behind the world." "Oh yes," he said, "but nobody has ever enforced that; the Consuls have never bothered us about that!" "Ha," said Richard, "more shame for them! Now, are you going to stay?" "No, sir, not I!" "Very well, then; I am going up to the Governor's, and I am going to shot two guns. If you go out *one minute* before your eighteen hours' daylight expires—mind, I shall go up there and stay myself—I shall send the first gun right across your bows, and the second slap into you. Mind, I am a man of my word. Good morning!" He did not go out till half an hour after his eighteen hours' daylight; and as long as Richard was there none of them ever did.

"The Sierra Leone man is an inveterate thief; he drinks, he gambles, he intrigues, he over-dresses himself, and when he has exhausted his means, he makes Master pay for all. With a terrible partiality for summoning and enjoying himself thoroughly in a court of law, he enters into the spirit of the thing like an attorney's clerk; he soon wearies of the less exciting life in the wilder settlements, where debauchery has not yet developed itself; home sickness then seizes him, and he deserts, after probably robbing the house. He is the horror of Europeans; the merchants of the Gaboon river prefer forfeiting the benefits of the African Steam Ship Company to seeing themselves invaded by this locust tribe, whose most beautiful view is apparently that which leads out of Sierra Leone. At Lagos and Abeokuta, Sierra Leone has returned to his natural paganism, and has become an inveterate slave-dealer, impudently placing himself under native protection, and renegading the flag that saved him from life-long servitude. Even during the Blackland's short stay, the unruly, disorderly character of the man often enough showed itself by fisticuffing, pulling hair, and cursing, with a mixture of English and African ideas, that presented a really portentous *tout ensemble.*

"With respect to the relative position of Japhet and Ham—perhaps I had better say Ham and Japhet—at Sierra Leone, I may remark that English ultra-philanthropy has granted at times *almost all* the wishes of the Ethiopian melodist—

'I wish de legislatur would set dis darkie free,
Oh, what a happy place den de darkie world would be!
We'd have a darkie parliament
An' darkie code of law,
An' *darkie judges on de bench*,
Darkie barristers and aw'!'

"I own that 'darkie' must be defended, and well defended, too, from the injustice and cruelty of the class whom he calls 'poor white trash.' But protection should be within the limits of *Reason.* If the white man is not to be protected against the black man, why should the Jamaica negro be protected against the coolie? Because he requires it? I think not. Though physically speaking and mentally weaker than his rival, he can hold quite enough of his own —as Sierra Leone proves—by combination, which enables cattle to resist lions. Displays of this sentiment on the part of the whites must, of course, be repressed. Do so freely, but not unfairly. England, however, is still in the throes of her first repentance. Like a veteran devotee, she is atoning for the coquetries of her hot youth.

But a few years ago she contracted to supply the Spanish colonies for thirty years with four thousand eight hundred slaves per annum, and she waged wars and destroyed Cities for a traffic which Cardinal Cibo, at the end of the seventeenth century, on the part of the Sacred College, to the Congoese missionaries, denounced as 'a pernicious and abominable abuse.' For this, and for the 2,130,000 negroes imported into the West Indian estates between A.D. 1680 and A.D. 1786, Britannia yet mourns, and, Rachel-like, will not be comforted, because those niggers are not. What the inevitable reaction shall be, *quien sabe?*

"I do not for a moment regret our philanthropy, even with its terrible waste of life and gold. But England can do her duty to Africa, without cant and without humbug.* She can contend with a world in arms, if necessary, against the injurious traffic, but she might abstain from violently denouncing all who do not share her opinions upon the subject. Anti-slavery men have hitherto acted rather from sentiment than from reason; and Mr. Buckle—alas! that we should hear from him no more—may be right in determining that morality must not rule, but be ruled by intellect. Let us open our eyes to the truth, and eschewing 'zeal without knowledge,' secure to ourselves the highest merit—perseverance in a good cause when thoroughly disenchanted with it. We have one point in our favour. The *dies atra* between 1810–1820, when a man could not speak or write what he thought upon the subject of slavery, is drawing to a close. Increased tolerance now permits us to express our opinions, which, if in error, will wither like the grass in an African day; if right, will derive fresh increase from time.

"There are several classes interested in pitting black man against white man, and in winning the day for him, *coram publico.* An unscrupulous missionary—it is the general policy of the English propagandist to take violent parts in foreign politics—will for his own ends preach resistance to time-honoured customs and privileges, which the negro himself has conceded.† An unworthy lawyer will urge a lawsuit, with a view to filling his pockets; a dishonourable Judge or police Magistrate will make a name for philanthropy at the

---

* "Of late it has become the fashion for the Missionary and the Lecturer to deny, in the presence of Exeter Hall, the African's recognition of the European's superiority. 'The white man,' writes Mr. Robert Campbell, a mulatto, 'who supposes himself respected in Africa *because* he is white, is grievously mistaken.' I distinctly assert the reverse, and every one who has studied the natural history of man must have the same opinion. The same egregious nonsense was once propounded before the Ethnological Society—where with some ethnology there is no anthropology—by another 'African.' And yet the propounder, the late Mr. Consular Agent Hansen, whose death, by-the-by, was an honour, and the only honour, to his life, had shaved his wool, and at the time was wearing a wig of coal-black hair like a Cherokee's. Is imitation no sign of deference?"

† "And not only the missionary, but also the sex which, I am told, has a Mission. I was at Florence in 1850, when our fair countrywomen added not a little to its troubles by dividing into two factions, the Italian and the Austrian. Some wore national colours, others went so far as to refuse waltzes proposed to them by partisans of the hostile nation."

expense of equity and honour; a weak-minded man will fear the official complaints, the false-memorializings which attend an unpopular decision, and the tomahawking that awaits him from the little army of negrophiles at home. But the worst class of all is the mulatto, under which I include quadroon and octaroon. He is everywhere, like wealth, *irritamenta malorum.* The 'bar-sinister,' and the uneasy idea that he is despised, naturally fill him with ineffable bile and bitterness. Inferior in point of *morale* to Europeans, and as far as regards *physique* to Africans, he seeks strength in making the families of his progenitors fall out. Many such men visiting England are received, by virtue of their woolly hair and yellow skin, into a class that would reject a fellow-countryman of similar, nay, of far higher, position; and there are amongst them infamous characters, who are not found out till too late. London is fast learning to distinguish between the Asiatic *Mir* and the *Munshi.* The real African, however—so enduring are the sentimentalisms of Wilberforce * and Buxton—is still to be understood.

"It is hardly fair to pull down one system without having another ready in its stead. I therefore venture to suggest certain steps toward regenerating—diffidently, though, on account of the amount of change to be made in—our unhappy colony, which for years has been steadily declining.

"Creoles, as children of liberated Africans are called here, should be apprenticed for seven years, with superintendents to see that they clear the soil, plant, and build; otherwise the apprenticeship would be merely nominal. For the encouragement of agriculture, I would take a very heavy tax from small shopkeepers and hucksters, who, by virtue of sitting upon a shady board, before a few yards of calico and strings of beads, call themselves merchants. Another very heavy tax—at least £100 per annum—upon all grog-shop licences, very few of which should be issued in the colony. Police magistrates are perfectly capable of settling disputes amongst these people, and of dealing out punishment to the offenders; moreover, in all cases the fines should go to the Crown, not to the complainant: in civil cases, however, there might be an appeal home for the benefit of the litigious. This measure would wipe off at one sweep inducement to engage in actions which the presence of a judicial establishment suggests, and which causes such heart-burning between Europeans and Africans. I would not allow a black jury to 'sit upon' a white man, or *vice versâ;* and, in the exception of a really

* "Such cant I hold to be in their mouths who talk of the 'sin and crime' of slavery. As the author of 'Six Years in the West Indies' (a brave book, considering the date of its publication, 1825) truly says, that the spirit of Christianity tends to abolish servitude is clear, that it admits of servitude is even still clearer. The Authorized Version of the Bible, like the Constitution of the United States, very prudently shirks the word "slave," and translates by 'servants' the *δοῦλοι*, or bondsmen, whom St. Paul enjoins to be subject to their *κυρίοι*, or masters, and elsewhere *δοῦλος*, a chattel, is opposed to *ἐλεύθερος*, a freeman. How astonished St. Athanasius and St. Augustine would have been, had the idea of an 'underground railway' been presented to them! What fulminations they would have showered upon the inventor of the idea!"

deserving mulatto, I would rather see him appointed Lord Lieutenant or Secretary of Ireland than acting Governor or Secretary at Sierra Leone.

"I am convinced that something of the kind will be done, when the *real* state of affairs in this unfortunate colony is ventilated in England. There are men who are always ready to let bad alone, and to hold that—

> 'What has answer'd so long may answer still;'

but the extension of Steam Navigation, and the increased number of travellers and visitors, will not allow progress, for want of a little energy, even at Sierra Leone, to be arrested.

"It is supposed that women, being less exposed than men, can better resist the climate of Sierra Leone. I believe the fact to be the contrary; in many cases the German missionaries have lived, whilst their wives have died. Here lie three Spanish Consuls, who in four years fell victims to a climate which has slain five Captains-General, or Governors, in five years. A deserted cemetery, without flowers or whitewash, is always a melancholy spectacle. This was something more. The grass and bush grew dense and dank from the remnants of mortality, and the only tree within the low decaying walls was a poisonous oleander. Another sense than the eye was unpleasantly affected; we escaped from the City of the Slain, as from a slave-ship or from a plague hospital.

"Servants in shoals presented themselves, begging 'mas'er' to take them down coast. In vain. The Sierra Leone man is handier than his southern brother; he can mend a wheel, make a coffin, or cut your hair, operations which in other places must remain wanted. Yet no one, at least if not a perfect greenhorn on the coast, will engage him in any capacity. In civility and respectfulness, he is far below the Brazilian or the Cuban *emancipado.* He has learned a 'trick or two;' even a black who has once visited Sierra Leone is considered as spoiled for life, as if he spent a year in England.

"An unexpected pleasure was in store for me. Lagos contains, as has been said, some eight hundred Moslems, but not yet two thousand, as it is reported. Though few, they have already risen to political importance; in 1851, our bravest and most active opponents were those wearing turbans. Among these are occasionally found 'white Arabs.' One had lately died at Ekpe, a village on the 'Cradoo waters,' where the ex-king Kosoko lives, and, though a Pagan, affects the Faith. I was presently visited by the Shaykh Ali bin Mohammed El Mekkáwi. The Reverend man was fair of face, but no Meccan; he called himself a Máliki, as indeed are most Moslems in this part of El Islam, and I guessed him to be a Morocco pilgrim, travelling in the odour of sanctity. He was accompanied by the Kazi Mohammed Ghana, a tall and sturdy Hausa negro, with his soot-black face curiously gashed and scarred; he appeared to me an honest man and a good Moslem. The dignitaries were accompanied by a mob of men in loose trousers, which distinguished them from the Pagan crowd; one of them, by trade a tailor, had learned to speak Portuguese in the Brazil.

"Very delightful was this meeting of Moslem brethren, and we took 'sweet counsel' together, as the Missionaries say. The Shaykh Ali had wandered from Tripoli southwards, knew Bornu, Sokatu, Hausa, and Adamáwá, the latter only by name; and he seemed to have suffered but little from a long journey, of which he spoke favourably. He wished me to return with him, and promised me safe conduct. I refused, with a tightening of the heart, a little alleviated, however, by the hope that Fate may spare me to march at some future day through Central Africa homewards. And in that hope I purified my property, by giving the *zakat*, or legal alms, to the holy man, who palpably could not read or write, but who audibly informed his followers that 'this bondsman' is intimately acquainted with *kull'ilm—omnis res scibilis.*"

N.B.—Benin was a great object of interest, and I quote these few remarks anent the Niger for geographers, and then proceed to the *gold*, in which millions are interested.—I. B.

"Benin was visited by Captain Thomas Wyndham in 1553, and in 1823, Belzoni of the Pyramids left his bones near its banks.

"After Lagos we came to the Oil Rivers, and direct connection of the Bonny river with the true Niger is still a subject of geographical speculation: I hope to solve the problem, despite all its difficulties.

"It is opined that the Niger falls into the Gulf of Guinea by a great delta, the Rio del Rey being the eastern, and the Great Rio Formoso, or Benin,* being its western limits. There are twenty-five streams which discharge themselves into this Great Bight, six of which are Oil Rivers—a disagreeable week's trip. This remarkable hypothesis, right in the main, whilst wrong in detail, and characterized at the time as 'hazardous and uncertain,' was probably suggested by native testimony, the coasts of the Gulf of Guinea being well known to French traders. It is hard indeed to comprehend how an intelligent sailor could pass by these shores without suspecting them to be the delta of some great stream. Caillié, the much-abused discoverer of Timbuktu, wrote in 1828 these remarkable words: 'If I may be permitted to hazard an opinion as to the course of the River Dhioliba, I should say that it empties itself by several mouths into the Gulf of Benin.'

"It is directly connected with the twenty or thirty millions of people in the Sudan; the centres of trade are upon the stream, yet the long and terrible caravan march of four months still supplies articles more cheaply than we can afford to sell them, *viâ* the Niger.

---

* "I quote the above *memoriter*. If correct, the limits of the Nigrotic delta hus given are totally incorrect. The Rio del Rey is wholly unconnected with the Niger; even the nearer Calabar and Cross rivers do not flow from it. The same is the case with the Benin river; its source was placed by Mr. Beecroft in the highlands to the westward of the Niger."

Gold in Africa.

"'Slave of the dark and dirty mine:
What vanity has brought thee here?'
LEYDEN.

"'Gold! gold! gold! gold!
Bright and yellow, hard and cold;
Molten, graven, hammer'd, and roll'd;
Heavy to get and light to hold.'
HOOD.

"I lost all patience with Cape Coast Castle. Will our grandsons believe that in these days a colony which cannot afford £150 per annum for a stipendiary magistrate, that men who live in a state of poverty, nay, of semi-starvation, are so deficient in energy as to be content with sitting down hopelessly, whilst gold is among their sands, on their roads, in their fields, in their very walls? That this Ophir—that this California, where every river is a Tmolus and a Pactolus, every hillock is a gold-hill—does not contain a cradle, a puddling-machine, a quartz-crusher, a pound of mercury? That half the washings are wasted because quicksilver is unknown, and that pure gold, selling in England for £3 17*s.* to £4, is here purchaseable for £3 12*s.*? I shout with Dominie Sampson, 'Prodi-gious!'

"Baron Humboldt first announced the theory that gold is constant in meridional ranges of the paleozoic and metamorphic formations. In this he was followed by Sir R. Murchison, and he was *not* followed by Professor Sedgwick. The latter 'has no faith whatever in the above hypothesis, though it led to a happy anticipation,' which followed erroneous premises. He continues, 'What we seem to know is, that gold is chiefly found among paleozoic rocks of a quartzose type,' and, moreover, that 'some of the great physical agencies of the earth are meridional, and these agencies *may probably*—and in a way we do not comprehend—have influenced the deposit of metals on certain lines of bearing.' He thinks, however, it would be a 'hypothetical misdirection' to say that a quartzose paleozoic rock cannot be auriferous, because its strata is not north and south, and that 'experience must settle this point.' The supporters of the meridional theory may quote as instances East Africa Ghauts, the Oural Mountains, the Sierra Nevada of California—which included the diggings in British Columbia—the Australian Cordillera, the New Zealand ranges, and the Western Ghauts of India. On the other hand, there are two notable exceptions—the Central Indian region, in which Sir R. Martin and others, as long as thirty years ago, were convinced that the natives washed for gold; and, still more remarkable, the highly productive African chain, which, for want of a better name, we still call the Kong Mountains.*

"The fact is that gold is a superficial formation, and has been

* "A similar imperfect generalization is the old theory that gold pertains not to islands. Malachi wore a collar of Irish gold, probably from Wicklow. It has been found in Cornwall and other parts of England, and in Scotland; and there

almost universally distributed over the surface of earth's declivities. This want of depth Sir R. Murchison is fond of illustrating by the hand with the fingers turned downwards; they represent the golden veins, whilst the palm denotes the main deposit. It is the contrary with other metals. Gold-placers, therefore, are now rare, except in newly explored or exploited lands of primitive formation, where it is common, nay, almost universal; the article, whose utility was early recognized, soon disappeared from the older workings. The Californian digger, provided with pick, pan, and shovel, made $10 per diem in 1852; in 1862 he still makes $2·50, and in 1872 he probably will make $0. The anciently auriferous countries, especially Arabia, have been stripped of their treasure, perhaps before the dawn of what is called true history;* and if they linger in Sofala, it is by reason of the people's ignorance;† they never traced the metal to its matrix.

"Setting aside the vexed question of the identity of Ophir and Sofala, and the fact that in early times gold was brought down from the eastern regions of the upper Nilotic basin, Western Africa was the first field that supplied the precious metal to Europe. The French claim to have imported it from Elmina as early as A.D. 1382. In 1442, Gonçales Baldeza returned from his second voyage to the

---

are few Californians who do not believe that Queen Charlotte's Island will form rich diggings.

"Another remark has lately been made, which pretends to no more than to discover a curious coincidence. The Oural chain lies 90° west of the Australian diggings, and the Californian Sierra Nevada 90° west of the Oural. But, on the other hand, the fourth quadrantal division falls into the Atlantic between Western Africa and the Brazil; and Eastern Africa, a highly prolific metallic region, is 20° west of the Oural, and 120° east of California."

* "I allude to the Hammæum littus of Pliny, which appears to coincide with the modern Hazramaut. Perhaps, however, the gold of Arabia is not wholly exhausted: it is difficult to believe that the rude appliances of savages and barbarians can extract anything but the coarsest particles from the dirt.

"Some years ago an English traveller, who had seen gold dust brought to Cairo from the coast of Western Arabia, north of Yambu, applied to Dr. Walne, then her Majesty's Consul, for facilities of exploring the place. The sage reply of that official was that gold appeared to be becoming too common. Other officials, equally sage, have since made the same remark."

[He alludes to Lord John Russell, who, when he offered to send a million a year home if he were made Governor of the Gold Coast, said, "Gold was getting too common."—I. B.]

† "In Eastern, as in parts of Western Africa, the natives have a curious superstition, or, rather, a distorted idea of a physical fact. They always return to the earth whatever nuggets are found, under the idea that they are the seed, or mother of gold, and that, if removed, the washing would be unprofitable. They refuse to dig deeper than the chin, for fear of the earth 'caving in;' and quartz-crushing and the use of quicksilver being unknown, they will not wash, unless the gold appears to the naked eye. As late as Mohammed Ali Pasha's day an Egyptian expedition was sent up through Fayzoghlu in search of the precious metal, brought down by the eastern tributaries of the Nile; it failed, because the ignorant Turks expected to pick up ounces where they found only grains. There are many traditions still extant in Egypt, of mysterious travellers floating down the Nile in craft of antique build, accompanied by women of blackest colour, but with Grecian or Abyssinian features, and adorned with rings, collars, and bracelets of pure gold, in shape resembling those found in the tombs of ancient Egypt."

regions about Bojador, bringing with him the first gold. Presently a company was formed for the purpose of carrying on the gold trade between Portugal and Africa; its leading men were the navigators, Lanzarote and Gilianez, and the great Prince Henry did not disdain to become a shareholder. In 1471 João de Santarem and Pedro Escobar reached a place on the Gold Coast, to which, from the abundance of gold found there, they gave the name of Oura da Mina, the present Elmina. After this a flood of gold poured into the lap of Europe, and at last, cupidity having mastered terror of the Papal Bull, which assigned to Portugal the exclusive right to the Eastern hemisphere, English, French, and Dutch adventurers hastened to share the spoils.

"The Portuguese, probably foreseeing competition in the Atlantic waters, but sure of their power in the Indian seas, determined, about the middle of the sixteenth century, to seek gold, of which those who preceded them had heard, in Eastern Africa. The Rev. Father João dos Santos, of the order of San Domingo, has left us, in his 'History of Eastern Ethiopia,' a detailed account of the first disastrous expedition. According to him, Dom Sebastian was scarcely seated on the throne of Portugal * before he sent to Sofala an expedition under command of Francis Baretto, who 'penetrated into Macoronga,'† and 'Maniça,' discovered mines of gold in these kingdoms, of which, by his prudence and valour, he made himself master. Baretto, having successfully passed through, despite a harassing warfare, the territories of the Quiteva or sovereign of Sofala, who fled from his capital, Zimboe, and having contracted with the Moorish or Arab Sultan ‡ of Maniça a treaty of amity, which included the article that the King of Chicanga should admit the strangers to trade throughout his territories for gold dust and other merchandise, reached at length the goal of his ambition. His proceedings are told as follows:—§

"'The Portuguese were enchanted at having, in so short a time, concluded a treaty of such advantage to their sovereign, and so beneficial to the realm; they, moreover, flattered themselves with the hope of acquiring a store of gold, with which to return enriched to their country; but when they saw what toil was requisite for extract-

* "Dom Sebastian, grandson of Don João III., was born July 20th, 1554, and at three years of age ascended the throne of Portugal. His subsequent romantic history is well known."

† "Mr. Cooley ('Geography of N'yassi,' p. 16) has confounded the 'Mucaranga' with the 'Monomoezi.' Captain Burton ('Lake Regions of Central Equatorial Africa,' pp. 228, 289) found the Wakaranga, a people wholly distinct from the Wanpamwezi; the former being a small tribe living near the Tanganyika Lake, south of the Wajiji. Mr. Cooley still, I believe, keeps his own opinion, and persists in writing these tribal names with an initial, M or Mu, which, being an abbreviation of *mtu*, a man, signifies only the individual."

‡ "In the 'Periplus,' attributed to Arrian (A.D. 64–210), chap. xvi., we are told that Rhapta, probably Kilwa (Quiloa), and the adjacent regions were held by colonists from Muza, *i.e.* Bandar Musa, near Aden. Gold is not mentioned amongst the exports, which are confined to ivory, rhinoceros' horns, and tortoiseshell."

§ "Dos Santos, 'History of the Ethiopians,' book ii. chap. i.–iii."

ing this precious metal from the bowels of the earth, and the danger incurred by those who worked in the mines, they were speedily undeceived, and no longer regarded their fortunes as instantaneously made. At the same time, they were induced to reflect that the labour and risk of digging the gold from the abysses whence it is drawn, are such as to stamp that value on it which it bears from its consequent rarity.

"'These people have divers methods of extracting the gold, and separating it from the earth with which it is blended; but the most common is to open the ground, and proceed towards the spot where, from certain indications, ore is supposed to abound. For this purpose they excavate vaults, sustained at intervals by pillars, and notwithstanding they make use of every possible precaution, it often happens that the vaults give way, and bury the subterranean sappers beneath their ruins. When they reach the vein in which the gold is found, mixed with the earth, they take the ore as it is and put it into vessels full of water, and by dint of stirring about the water the earth is dissolved, and the gold remains at the bottom.*

"'They likewise take advantage of heavy rains, which, occasioning torrents, carry before them whatever loose earth they meet in their way, and thus lay open the spots where gold is embedded in the ravines. This the Caffres collect, and wash with care to purify from the grosser parts of its earthy admixture.

"'These people also, however unpolished they may seem, yet possess a secret, peculiar to themselves, for discovering the gold concealed in certain stones, which they likewise have the ingenuity of extracting, constantly observing the same practice of washing it well to separate all earthy particles from the metal, and thus rendering it equally lustrous with that obtained from the earth. This gold is, however, much cheaper than the other, either owing to its being more common, or to its being obtained with more facility and at less expense than that exfoliated from the bowels of the earth.

"'It is a mere matter of fact that this country is rich in gold and silver mines, but these metals are not so easily obtained as is imagined, for the Caffres are prohibited, under penalty of death and the confiscation of their property, from discovering the site of the mine, either to their neighbours, or to those who pass through their country. When a mine is discovered, the persons finding it make wild outcries, to collect witnesses round them, and cover the spot, above which they place some object to denote the site; and far from being susceptible to be prevailed upon by strangers to point out these spots, they avoid encountering them as much as possible, for fear they should even be suspected of such a deed.

"'The motive of the sovereign for enacting these prohibitory laws, and for exacting a declaration to be made to the Court of all mines

* "The reader will remark that at all times, and in all places, gold has been washed or procured in the same way—a fair instance, like the general similarity of rude stone implements from England to Australia, of the instinctive faculty in mankind."

discovered, is that he may take possession of them,* and by preventing the Portuguese from becoming masters of one portion, give no room for succeeding warfare on their part to seize on the remainder.'

"The melancholy fate of Baretto's expedition deserves mentioning. After passing through Zimbo,† where the Quiteva received him with open arms, Baretto returned to Sofala. Being now on good terms with the sovereigns of that place, and of Chicanga, he resolved to open a road into the kingdom of Mongas, the dominions of the Monomotapa, who opposed him with a large army. Baretto signally defeated the 'Caffres,' and reached Chicona, where he found no gold

---

* "The same was the practice of the Indian Rajahs. Whenever a ryot discovered either treasure or gold *in situ* he was most cruelly treated, to compel him to confess and to give up what he had secreted. As, of course, he had secreted a part of his *trouvaille* it was a hard struggle between his cupidity and the ruler's bastinado. About 1840, some peasants near Baroda, in Guzerat, found lumps of gold, which they carried before his Highness the Gaikwar, and received in return a terrible flogging. The Hindú, with that secretiveness which has ever been his shield against the tyranny of rulers and conquerors, resolved for the future to keep his good fortune to himself. The quality of gold which from time to time has appeared amongst these people, made the shrewder sort of European suspect. But the inertness, or, rather, the terror of new things, that possessed the then rulers of the land, 'threw cold water' upon all attempts to trace the diggings, which, accordingly, were worked by the people till the present year. This is the simple history of 'gold mining in the Deccan.'"

† "Barros, describing the ruins of Zimbo, mentions an inscription over the gateway of a fort built with well-cut stones and no lime, whose surface was twenty-five palms long and a little less in height. Around this building, which, like the Ka'abah, might have been a pagan Arab temple, are bastions—also of uncemented lime—and the remainder of a tower, seventy feet high. The inscription was probably in the Himyaritic character, as 'Moors well versed in Arabic' could not decipher it. This was repeated to Mr. Lyons M. M'Leod ('Travels in Eastern Africa,' vol. i. chap. x.) at Mozambique. Dr. Livingstone ('Travels in South Africa,' chap. xxix.) discovered Zumbo in lat. 15° 37′ 22″ S., long. 30° 32′ E., about 8° W.N.W. of Kilimani. At the confluence of the Loangwe and Zambeze, he found the remains of a church, a cross, and a bell, but no date and no inscription. The people of Rios de Sena also state that there are remains of large edifices in the interior; unfortunately they place them at a distance of five hundred leagues, which would lead them nearly to the equator north, and to the Cape of Good Hope south.

"Dr. Livingstone ('Travels in South Africa,' chap. xxx.) explains the word Monomotapa successfully, I think, to mean the 'Lord' (*mone*, *muene*, *mona*, *mana*, or *morena*, are all dialectic varieties, synonymous with the Kisarahili *muinyi*, which means master, sir, *kyrios*, etc.), and 'Mtapa,' the proper name of the chief. The ancient Portuguese assigned to the Monomotapa the extensive regions between the Zambeze and the Limpopo rivers, 7° from north to south. The African traveller, however, is not so successful in explaining the corrupted term, Monomoizes, Monemuiges, and Monomaizes—for which see *Journal of Royal Geographical Society*, vol. xxix. pp. 166 *et seq.*

"Dr. Beke ('On the Mountains forming the Eastern Side of the Basin of the Nile,' p. 14) defends, against Mr. Cooley and Captain Burton, M. Malte Brun's 'Mono-emugi, ou selons un orthographie plus authentique *Mou-mimigi*.' The defence is operated by enclosing after the latter, in italics, another version in parenthesis, and with an interrogation, thus (Nimougi?); and the French geographer's orthography 'being fortunately based on the theoretic root,' is pronounced 'more authentic than any hitherto proposed in its stead.' How often will it be necessary to repeat, that Mono-emugi and Mou-mimigi are merely corruptions of M'nyamwezi, a man or individual of the land Unyamwezi?"

mines. An artful native, however, buried two or three lumps of silver, which, when discovered, brought large presents to the cheat and dreams of Potosi to the cheated.* Baretto, in nowise disheartened by discovering the fraud, left two hundred men in a fort at Chicona, whilst he and the remainder of his force retired upon Sena, on the Zambeze. The Caffres then blockaded the fort, and having reduced the gallant defenders to a famine, compelled them to make a sortie, in which every man was slain.

"The ruins of Maniça, north-west of Sofala, and west of and inland from the East African ghauts, are described as being situated in a valley enclosed by an amphitheatre of hills, having a circuit of about two miles. According to Mr. M'Leod, the district is called Matouca (the Matuka of Dr. Livingstone's map), and the gold-washing tribes Botongos.† The spots containing the metal are known by the bare and barren surface. The natives dig in any small crevice made by the rains of the preceding winter, and there find gold dust. These pot-holes are rarely deeper than two or three feet, at five or six they strike the ground-rock. In the still portions of the rivers, when they are low, the natives dive for nuggets that have been washed down from the hills. Sometimes joining together in hundreds, they deflect the stream, and find extensive deposits. Mr. M'Leod heard of mines four to five hundred miles from Sofala, where the gold is found in solid lumps, or as veins in the rocks and stones.

"The result of Dr. Livingstone's travels is, that whilst he found no gold in the African interior, frequent washings were met with in the Mashinga Mountains ‡ and on the Zambeze river; no silver, however, was met with, nor could the people distinguish it from tin, which, however, does not establish its non-existence; he heard from a Mashanga man, for the first time, a native name for gold, *Dalama.*§ The limits of the auriferous region are thus laid down: 'If we place one leg of the compasses at Tete, and extend the other 3° 30′, bringing it round from the north-east of Tete by west, and then to the south-east, we nearly touch or include all the known gold-producing country.' This beginning from the north-east would

---

* "A French adventurer tried a similar trick upon the Imam Sayyid Said, father of the present Prince of Zanzibar. He melted a few dollars and ran the fluid upon bits of stone, which were duly shown to his Highness. But the old Imam, whose cupidity was equalled only by his cunning, took them to his friend, Colonel Hamerton, her Majesty's Consul, who, finding the matrix to be coralline, had no difficulty in detecting the fraud."

† "Dr. Livingstone places the Botonga people west of Zumbo, and 4° to 5° north-west of Matuka or Maniça."

‡ "These elevations are on the western frontier of the great Marave people; see the 'Lands of Cazembe.'"

§ "In Kisawahili they have but one word for gold, *zahábú*, which is palpably derived from the Arabic. None of the people living in the interior, or even the tribes beyond the coast-line of Zanzibar, are acquainted with the precious metal; they would prefer to it brass or copper. The appreciation of gold on the part of the so-called 'Kafir' race, points to an extensive intercourse with Arabia, if not to a considerable admixture of Arab and Asiatic blood."

include the Marave country,* the now 'unknown' kingdom of Abutua † placed, however, south of the Zambesi, and coming round by the south-west, Mashona, or Bazizulu, Maniça, and Sofala. Gold from about Maniça is as large as wheat grains, whilst that found in the rivers is in minute scales. The process of washing the latter is laborious. 'A quantity of sand is put into a wooden bowl with water, a half-rotatory motion is given to the dish, which causes the coarser particles of sand to collect on one side of the bottom. These are carefully removed with the hand, and the process of rotation is renewed until the whole of the sand is taken away, and the gold alone remains.‡ Mercury is as usual unknown. Formerly one hundred and thirty pounds of gold were submitted to the authorities at Tete for taxation, but when the slave-trade began, the Portuguese killed the goose with the golden eggs, and the annual amount obtained is now only eight to ten pounds.

"It is evident that gold is by no means half worked in Eastern Africa. As in California, it appears to be found in clay shale, which for large profits requires 'hydraulicking.' The South African traveller heard that at the range Mashinga, the women pounded the soft rock in wooden mortars, previous to washing; it is probably rotten quartz, and the yield would be trebled by quicksilver and crushers.

"It is highly probable that the gold formations in those East African ghauts, which Dr. Beke is compelling to become the 'Lunar Mountains,' are by no means limited to the vicinity of the Zambeze. In gold-prospecting, as every geologist knows, the likeliest places often afford little yield and sometimes none. The author of 'The Lake Regions of Central Africa' describes a cordillera which he struck, about a hundred miles from the eastern coast, as primitive, quartzose, and shaly; unfortunately time and health hindered him from exploring it. The same writer, in 'First Footsteps in East Africa' (p. 395), indicates such formation in the small ghauts, and on the western side of that range he is reported to have found gold. What steps he took do not appear; he was probably disheartened by the reflection that all his efforts would be opposed by might and main in official circles. Possibly he feared the fate of Mr. Hargreaves, of Australia, who obtained a reward of £5000, when one per cent. of export would have made him master of eight millions.

* "Dr. Livingstone gives six well-known washing-places, east and north-east of Tete, viz. Mashinga, Shindúndo, Missála, Kapéta, Máno, and Jáwa."

† "Mr. Cooley ('Geography of N'yassi') questions whether there be such a kingdom as Abutua, or Butwa. He derives it from *batúa*, plural of *motúa* (in Kisawahili *wátu*, plural of *m'tu*) signifying men. The Amazulu, when they attacked Delagoa Bay, were called by the same name; but the Portuguese throwing back the accent changed the word to Vátur, of which Captain Owen made Fetwah. So, in 1822, the tribe that fell upon the Bachwáná (Bechuana) were, we were told, called Batúa, but the missionaries recognized the meaning of the word. Though it is 'now unknown,' Dr. Livingstone has inserted it into his map."

‡ "This is absolutely the present practice on the Gold Coast, and perfectly agrees with Mungo Park's descriptions."

Local jealousies at Aden also certainly would have defeated his plans, if permitted to be carried out; and the Court of Directors had already regarded with a holy terror his proposals to build a little fort, by way of base upon the seaboard near Berberah. Leaving, however, these considerations, we are justified by analogy of formation and bearing in believing that at some future time gold may be one of the exports from Eastern Intertropical Africa.*

"Returning to Western Africa, we find in Leo Africanus, who is supposed to have died about 1526, that the King of Ghana had in his palace 'an entire lump of gold'—a monster nugget it would now be called—not cast nor wrought by instruments, but perfectly formed by the Divine Providence only, of thirty pounds weight, which had been bored through and fitted for a seat before the royal throne.† The author most diffuse upon the subject of gold, is Bosman, who treats, however, solely of the Gold Coast.

"The first region which he mentions is Dinkira, under which were included the conquered provinces of Wásá (our Wassaw, Wossa, Wasau, Warsaw, etc.), Encasse and Juffer, each bordering upon one another, and the last upon Commany (Commanda). There the gold is fine, but much alloyed with 'fetishes,' oddly shaped figures used for ornaments, and composed sometimes of pure mountain gold, but more often mixed with one-third, or even half, of silver and copper and filled inside with half weight of the heavy black earth used for moulding them. The second was Acanny, the people of which brought the produce of their own diggings and of their neighbours of Ashantee and Akim: it was so pure and fine, that the negroes called all the best gold 'Acanny Sika,' or Acanny gold. The third was Akim,‡ which 'furnished as large quantities of gold as any land that I know, and that also the most valuable and pure of any that is carried away from this coast; it is easily distinguished by its deep colour.' The fourth and fifth are Ashanti and Ananse, a small province between the former empire and Dinkira. The sixth and last is Awine, our Aowin,§ which formerly used to export large

* "I cannot, however, understand the final flourish of Dr. Beke's paper, above alluded to. He declares that the discovery of gold in his 'Mountains of the Moon' will occasion a complete and rapid revolution, and ends thus: 'We shall then, too, doubtless see in Eastern Africa, as in California and in Australia, the formation of another new race of mankind.' We have seen nothing of the kind in Western Africa, where for four centuries the richest diggings have been known. In fact, they have rather tended to drive away Europeans. Why then expect this marvel from Eastern Africa?"

† "'Similarly, the king of 'Buncatoo' had a solid gold stool, which caused his destruction at the hands of his neighbours of Ashantee."

‡ "Akim still supplies gold, and will be alluded to later on."

§ "The old traveller, however, is wrong, when he says, 'I take it (Awine) to be the first on the Gold Coast, and to be far above Axim.' Aowin is the region to the west of the Assini river, whereas Axim is to the east of the Ancobra river; thus the two are separated by the territory of Apolonia. He apologizes, however, in the same page for any possible errors. 'I cannot inform you better, because the negroes cannot give any certain account of them (the various diggings), nor do any of our people go so far; wherefore I must beg of you, my good friend, to be contented.' Despite which, however, he may yet be right, and his critic wrong."

quantities of fine and pure gold, and they 'being the civilized and the fairest dealers of all the negroes,' the Dutch 'traded with them with a great deal of pleasure.' They were, however, finally subdued by the Dinkiras.

"According to Bosman ('Letters,' vi.) 'the illustrious metal' was found in three sites. The first and best was 'in or between particular hills:' the negroes sank pits there, and separated the soil adhering to it. The second 'is in, at, and about some rivers and waterfalls, whose violence washeth down great quantities of earth, which carry the gold with it. The third is on the seashore, near the mouths of rivulets, and the favourite time for washing is after violent night rains.* The negro women are furnished with large and small troughs or trays, which they first fill full of earth and sand, which they wash with repeated fresh water till they have cleansed it from all its earth; and if there be any gold its ponderosity forces it to the bottom of the trough, which if they find it is thrown into the small tray, and so they go on washing it again, which operation generally holds them till noon; some of them not getting above the value of sixpence; some of them pieces of six or seven shillings, though not frequently; and often they entirely lose their labour.'

"The gold thus dug is of two kinds, dust gold and mountain gold. The former is 'fine as flour,' and the more esteemed because there is no loss in melting. The latter, corresponding with our modern 'nugget,' varies in weight from a farthing to two hundred guineas; it touches better than gold dust, but it is a loss from the metal adhering to the stone.

"The natives, in Bosman's day—and to the present time—were 'very subtle artists in the sophisticating of gold.' The first sort was the fetish before alluded to.† They also cast pieces so artificially, that whilst outside there was pure gold thick as a knife, the interior was copper, and perhaps iron—then a new trick and the most dangerous, because difficult to detect. The common 'false mountain gold' was a mixture of the precious metal with silver and copper, extremely high coloured, and unless each piece was touched, the fraud passed undetected. Another kind was an artificially cast and tinged powder of coral mixed with copper filings; it became tarnished, however, in a month or two. The official tests of gold were as follows:—If offered at night or in the evening large pieces

---

* "So, 'in Coquimbo of Chili,' says Sir Richard Hawkins, 'it raineth seldom, but every shower of rain is a shower of gold unto them, for with the violence of the water falling from the mountains it bringeth from them the gold.'"

† "We are also informed that the same fetishes were cut by the negroes into small bits, worth one, two, or three farthings, and the people could tell their value at sight. These *kakeraa*, as they were called, formed the small change of the country, as our threepenny and fourpenny bits do now. They were current all over the coast, and seemed to pass backwards and forwards without any diminution. The reason for this was, that they sold in Europe for only forty the ounce: the native mixing them with better gold tried to palm them upon the purchasers, but the clerks were ordered to pick them out. A similar custom down the coast, was to cut dollars into halves and quarters, which thus easily became florins and shillings."

were cut through with a knife, and the smaller nuggets were beaten with a stone, and then tried as above. Gold dust was cast into a copper brazier, winnowing with the fingers, and blown upon with the breath, which causes the false gold to fly away. These are not highly artificial tests. Bosman, however, strongly recommends them to raw, inexpert people (especially seafaring men), whom he bids to remember the common proverb, that 'there is no gold without dross.' These greenhorns, it seems, tested the metal by pouring aquafortis upon it, when ebullition or the appearance of green proved it to be false or mixed. 'A miserable test, indeed!' exclaims old Trunk-hose, justly remarking that an eighth or tenth part of alloy would produce those appearances, and that such useless and niceness, entailing the trouble of drying, and causing the negroes to suffer, is prejudicial to trade.

"With respect to the annual export from the Gold Coast, Bosman reckons it in peaceful times, when trade is prosperous, to be '23 tun.' The 7000 marks are disposed of as below.* Mr. Macqueen estimates this exportation at £3,406,275. The English trade has now fallen to £360,000 to £400,000 per annum.†

"The conclusion of Bosman's sixth letter may be quoted as highly applicable to the present day. 'I would refer to any intelligent metallist, whether a vast deal of ore must not of necessity be lost here, from which a great deal of gold might be separated, from want of skill in the metallic art; and not only so, but I firmly believe that large quantities of pure gold are left behind, for the negroes only ignorantly dig at random, without the least knowledge of the veins of the mines. And I doubt not but if this country belonged to the Europeans, they would soon find it to produce much richer treasures than the negroes obtain from it; but it is not probable that we shall ever possess that liberty here, wherefore we must be content with being so far masters of it as we are at present, which, if well and prudently managed, would turn to a very great account.'

---

*

	Marks.
"The Dutch West Indian Company exported	1500
The English African Company	1200
The Zealand interlopers as much as the Dutch, viz.	1500
The English interlopers about 1000 usually, which they have doubted	1000
The Brandenburghers and Danes together, in time of peace ...	1000
The Portuguese and French, together	800
Which makes	7000

"For several years before Bosman's time, the Dutch export had been reduced by one-half (750 marks). Mr. Wilson, however ('Western Africa,' ch. iv.), is evidently in error, when he makes Bosman to estimate the 'amount of gold exported from the Gold Coast at 800 marks per annum.'"

† "Dr. Clarke ('Remarks,' &c.) gives 100,000 ounces. This was the calculation of Mr. Swanzy before a Parliamentary committee in 1816. Of course it is impossible to arrive at any clear estimate. Allowing the African Steam Ship Company a maximum of 4000 ounces per month, we obtain from that source 48,000 ounces. But considerable quantities are exported in merchant ships, more especially for the American market. Whilst, therefore, some reduce the total to 60,000 ounces, others raise it to half a million of money."

"In several countries, as Dinkira, Tueful, Wásá,* and especially Akim, the hill region lying due north of Accra, the people are still active in digging gold. The pits, varying from two to three feet in diameter, and from twelve to fifty feet deep, are often so near the roads that loss of life has been the result. 'Shoring-up' being little known, the miners are not unfrequently buried alive. The stuff is drawn up by ropes in clay pots, or calabashes, and thus a workman at the bottom widens the pit to a pyriform shape: tunnelling, however, is unknown. The excavated earth is carried down to be washed. Besides sinking these holes, they pan in the beds of rivers, and in places collect quartz, which is roughly pounded. The yield is very uncertain, and the Chief of the district is entitled to one-third of the proceeds. During the busy season, when water is abundant, the scene must resemble that described by Dr. Livingstone, near the gold-diggings of Tete. As in California and Australia, prices rise high, and gunpowder, rum, and cotton goods soon carry off the gold dust.

"During the repeated earthquakes of July, 1862, which laid waste Accra, the strata of the Akim Hills were so much shaken and broken up, that, according to report, all the people flocked to the diggings and dispensed with the shafts generally sunk. There are several parts of the Gold Coast where the precious metal is fetish, and where the people will not dig themselves, though perhaps they would not object to strangers risking their lives. One of the most remarkable is the Devil's Hill, called by Bosman 'Monte da Diabo,' near Winnebah, in the Aguna (Agouna) country. In his time, a Mr. Baggs, English agent, was commissioned by the African Company to prospect it. He died at Cape Coast Castle before undertaking a work which, in those days, would have been highly dangerous. Some authorities fix the Seecom river as the easternmost boundary where gold is found. This is so far incorrect, that I have panned it from the sands under James Fort. Besides which, it is notorious that on the banks of the Upper Volta, about the latitude of the Krobo (Croboe) country, there are extensive deposits, regarded by the people as sacred.

"The Slave Coast is a low alluvial tract, and appears to be wholly destitute of gold.† According to the Rev. Mr. Brown, however, a small quantity has been found in the quartz of Yoruba, north of Abeokuta; but, as in the Brazil, it is probably too much dispersed to be worth working. And the Niger, which flows, as will presently be seen, from the true auriferous centre, has at times been found to roll down stream-gold.‡

* "Wasa has been worked both by Dutch and English; they chose, however, sickly situations, brought out useless implements, and died. The province is divided into eastern and western, and is said to be governed by female chiefs—Amazons?"

† "Some years ago the late Consul Campbell, of Lagos, forwarded to her Majesty's Foreign Office bits of broken pottery, in which he detected gold. When submitted to the School of Mines, the glittering particles proved to be mica."

‡ "Silver is also said to be found near the Niger, but of this I have no reliable notices."

"The soil of Fante-land and the seaboard is, as has been seen, but slightly auriferous.

"As we advance northwards from the Gold Coast the yield becomes richer. In Ashanti the red and loamy soil, scattered with gravel and grey granite, is everywhere impregnated with gold, which the slaves extract by washing and digging. It is said that in the market-place of Kumasi there are sixteen hundred ounces' worth of gold—a treasure reserved for State purposes. The bracelets of rock-gold, which the caboceers wear on State occasions, are four pounds in weight, and often so heavy that they must rest their arms upon the heads of their slave-boys.

"In Gyaman, the region to the north-west of the capital, the ore is found in large nuggets, sometimes weighing four pounds. The pits are sunk nine feet in the red granite and grey granite, and the gold is highly coloured. From eight to ten thousand slaves work for two months every year in the bed of the Barra river. There, however, as on the Gold Coast, the work is very imperfect, and in some places where the metal is sacred to the fetish, it is not worked at all. Judging from analogy, we might expect to find the precious metal in the declivities inland and northwards from Cape Palmas, and in that sister formation of the East African ghauts, the 'Sierra dol Crystal.' The late Captain Lawlin, an American trader settled on an island at the mouth of the Fernão Vaz, carried to his own country, about the year 1843–44, a quantity of granular gold, which had been brought to him by some country-people. He brought back all the necessary tools and implements to the Gaboon river, but the natives became alarmed, and he failed to find the spot. Finally, according to the tradition of native travellers, the unexplored region called Rúmá,* and conjecturally placed south of the inhospitable Waday, is a land of goldsmiths, the ore being found in mountainous and well-watered districts. It is becoming evident that Africa will some day equal half a dozen Californias.

"Mungo Park supplies the amplest notices of gold in the regions visited by him north of the Kong Mountains. The principal places are the head of the Senegal river and its various influents; Dindiko, where the shafts are most deep, and notched, like a ladder; Seronda, which gives two grains from every pound of alluvial matter;† Bambuk and Bambarra. In Kongkadu, the 'mountain land,' where the hills are of coarse riddy granite, composed of red feldspar, white quartz, and black shale, containing orbicular concretions, granular gold is found in the quartz, which is broken with hammers; the grains, however, are flat. The diggings at present best known are those of Mandina-land. The gold, we are told, is found not in

---

* "This may be the 'Runga' of our maps, with whose position Rúmá corresponds. My informant wrote down the name from the mouth of a Waday man at Lagos."

† "This would be $\frac{1}{3500}$ (avoirdupois), whereas the cascalho, or alluvium, of the Brazil is $\frac{1}{15000}$, and remarkably rich and pyritical ores in Europe give $\frac{1}{20000}$. Yet M. d'Aubrie estimates the gold in the bed of Father Rhine at six or seven millions of pounds sterling."

mines or veins, but scattered in sand and clay. They vary from a pin's head to the size of a pea, and are remarkably pure. This is called *sana manko,* or gold-powder, in contradistinction to *sana birro,* or gold-stones—nuggets occasionally weighing five drachms. In December, after the harvest home, when the gold-bearing *fiumaras* from the hills have shrunk, the Mansa or Shaykh appoints a day to begin *sana ku*—gold washing.

"Each woman arms herself with a hoe, two or three calabashes, and a few quills. On the morning before departure a bullock is slaughtered for a feast, and prayers and charms are not forgotten. The error made by these people is digging and washing for years in the same spot, which proves comparatively unfruitful unless the torrent shifts its course. They never follow the lead to the hills, but content themselves with exploring the heads of the watercourse, which the rapid stream denudes of sand and clay, leaving a strew of small pebbles that wear the skin off the finger-tips. The richest yield is from pits sunk in the height of the dry season, near some hill in which gold has been found. As the workers dig through the several strata of sand and clay, they send up a few calabashes by way of experiment for the women, whose peculiar duty it is to wash the stuff, and thus they continue till they strike the floor-rock. The most hopeful formation is held to be a bed of reddish sand, with small dark specks, described as 'black matter, resembling gunpowder,' and called by the people *sana mira,* or gold-rust; it is probably titeria. In Murray's edition of 1816, there are illustrations of the various positions, and a long description (vol. i. p. 450, and vol. ii. p. 75) of the style of panning. I will not trouble the reader with it, as it in no way differs from that now practised on the Gold Coast and Kafirlands. There is art in this apparently simple process. Some women find gold when others cannot discover a particle; and as quicksilver is not used, at least one-third must be wasted, or rather, I may say, it is preserved for a better day.

"The gold dust is stored in quills, stopped with cotton, and the washers are fond of wearing a number of these trophies in their hair. The average of an industrious individual's annual collection may be two slaves. The price of these varies from nine to twelve *mankali,** each of 12*s.* 6*d.*, or its equivalent in goods, viz. eighteen gun-flints, forty-eight leaves of tobacco, twenty charges of gunpowder, a cutlass, and a musket. Part of the gold is converted into massive and cumbrous ornaments, necklaces, and earrings, and when a lady of consequence is in full dress, she bears from £50 to £80. A proportion is put by to defray expenses of travelling to and from the coast, and the greater part is then invested in goods, or exchanged with the Moors for salt and merchandise.

"The gold is weighed in small balances, which the people always carry about with them, and they make, like the Hindus, but little difference between gold dust and wrought gold. The purchaser

* "May not this word be an old corruption of the well-known Arabic weight, *miskál?*"

always uses his own *tilikissi*, beans, probably, of the Abrus, which are sometimes soaked in Shea butter, to increase their weight, or are imitated with ground-down pebbles. In smelting gold, the smith uses an alkaline salt, obtained from a ley of burnt corn-stalks. He is capable, as even the wildest African tribes are, of drawing fine wire. When rings—the favourite form in which the precious metal is carried coastward—are to be made, the gold is run without any flux in a crucible of sun-dried red clay, which is covered over with charcoal or braize. The smith pours the fluid into a furrow traced in the ground, by way of mould. When it has cooled, he reheats it, and hammers it into a little square ingot or bar of the size required. After a third exposure to fire he twists with his pincers the bar into a screw shape, lengthens out the ends, and turns them up to form a circle.

"It must now be abundantly evident to the reader, that the great centre of West African gold, the source which supplies Manding to the north and Ashanti to the south, is the equatorial range called the Kong. What the mineral wealth must be there, it is impossible to estimate, when nearly three millions and a half of pounds sterling have usually been drawn from a small parallelogram, between its southern slopes and the ocean, whilst the other three-quarters of the land—without alluding to the equally rich declivities of the northern versant—have remained as yet unexplored. Even in northern Liberia, colonists have occasionally come upon a pocket of $50, and the natives bring gold in from the banks of streams.

"Mr. Wilson * remarks upon this subject, 'It is best for whites and blacks that these mines should be worked just as they are. The world is not suffering for the want of gold, and the comparative small quantities that are brought to the sea-coast keep the people in continual intercourse with civilized men, and ultimately, no doubt, will be the means of introducing civilization and Christianity among them.'

"I differ from the reverend author, *toto cœlo*. For such vain hope as that of improving Africans by European intercourse, and for all considerations of an 'ultimately' vaguer than the sweet singer of Israel's 'soon,' it is regrettable that active measures for exploitation are not substituted. And if the world, including the reverend gentleman and Lord John Russell, are not suffering for the want of gold, there are those, myself for instance, and many a better man, who would be happy at times to see and to feel a little more of that 'vile yellow clay.'"

* "'Western Africa,' chap. x."

CHAPTER XVII.

HIS FIRST LEAVE.

"Oh, when wilt thou return, my love?
For as the moments glide,
They leave me wishing still for thee,
My husband, by my side;
And ever at the evening hour
My hopes more fondly burn,
And still they linger on that word,
'Oh, when wilt thou return?'"
To a Husband during a Long Absence.

RICHARD left me plenty of occupation during this awfully long absence of sixteen months. Firstly, all kinds of official fights about India, and then for a gunboat and other privileges for Fernando Po. I lived with my father, mother, and family, and then I had a great deal to do for his book, "The City of the Saints," and every letter brought its own work and commissions, people to see and to write to, and things to be done for him, so that I was never idle for a minute. I began to feel, what I have always felt since, that he was the glorious, stately ship in full sail, commanding all attention and admiration; and sometimes, if the wind drops, she still sails gallantly, and no one sees the humble little steam-tug hidden at the other side, with her strong heart and faithful arms working forth, and glorying in her proud and stately ship.

I think a true woman, who is married to her proper mate, recognizes the fully performed mission, whether prosperous or not, and that no one can ever take his place *for her*, as an interpreter of that which is betwixt her and her Creator, *to her* as the shadow of God's protection here on earth.

In winter he made me go to Paris with the Napoleon ring and sketch, mentioned in the little story called "The Last Hours of Napoleon;" and, through want of experience and proper friends and protection, my little mission of courtesy failed. The failure drew down upon me some annoyances, which appeared very disagreeable and important to me at the time; they are not worth mentioning, nor, indeed, had I been older and more experienced, should I have thought them worth fretting about.

The rest of the time of those dreary sixteen months was wearing to a degree, and diversified by ten weeks of diphtheria and its results. One day I betook myself to the Foreign Office, and I cried my heart out to Mr. (afterwards Sir) Henry Layard. He seemed very sorry for me, and he asked me to wait awhile whilst he went upstairs; and, when he came back, he told me that he had got four months' leave home for my husband, and had ordered the despatch to be sent off that very afternoon. I could have thrown my arms round his neck and kissed him, but I did not; he might have been rather surprised. I had to go and sit out in the Green Park till the excitement wore off; it was more to me than if he had given me a large fortune.

At last the happy day came to go and meet Richard at Liverpool, and I shall never forget the joy of our meeting. It was December, 1863, and we had some happy weeks in England—a pleasant Christmas with my people at Wardour, and at Lord Gerard's at Garswood, where the family parties mustered strong, and at Fryston (Lord Houghton's), and several other country-houses; and he brought out two books—"Wanderings in West Africa" (2 vols., 1863), also "Abeokuta and the Cameroons" (2 vols., 1863), which he dedicated to me, with a lovely inscription and motto, of which I am very proud. And then came round the time again to leave. But I told him I could not possibly go on living as I was living; it was too miserable, one's husband in a place where one was not allowed to go, and I living with my mother like a girl—I was neither wife, nor maid, nor widow; so he took me with him. Excepting yachting, it was my first experience of *real* sea-going.

The African steamships were established in January, 1852, by the late Mr. MacGregor Laird, who was the second pioneer of the Niger Exploration, and an enthusiastic improver of Africa. These steamers were seven in number, and went once a month; four of them were of 978 tons. They went out to the West Coast, Fernando Po being their furthest station save one, and the whole round from England and back again caused them to visit twenty-two ports, and cover ten thousand nautical miles at eight knots an hour; but they were built for cargo, not for passengers. There was no doctor, no bath; the conveniences were difficult, and the stewardess only went as far as Madeira, the first port. We sometimes had seven or eight human beings stuffed into a cabin, which had four berths. I speak of 1861–2–3–4; it may be all changed since then. We now started in the worst circumstances. It was the big storm of January, 1863, one of the worst that has ever been known. My mother, who was a very bad sailor, insisted on coming on board to see us off. It was terribly rough, and an ironclad just shaved us going out, as we lay to in the river. There were even wrecks in the Mersey. Our Captain frankly said that he had an accident every January, but he would almost rather sink than have a mark put against his name for not going out on his right day. Mother behaved most pluckily. She went back in the tug, and she just reached Uncle Gerard's, which was three-quarters of an hour from Liverpool, got up to her bedroom, took up the poker to poke the fire, which fell out of her hand—she had the strength to crawl to the bell—and when they came up she was on the floor in that attack of paralysis with which she had been so long threatened, and to stave off which, we had hid my marriage from her just two years before.

Long before we had got past the Skerries, we were in serious trouble, and the passengers implored the Captain to alter his course, and take refuge in some harbour; but he explained to them that it would be awfully dangerous to turn the ship's head round, as the going round might sink her. I had forgotten in my ignorance to secure a berth, and the Captain gallantly gave up his own cabin to me, till Madeira. It was just on the break of the poop, and every wave broke over that before it reached the saloon. The ship appeared quite unmanageable; she bucked and plunged without stopping. There were seven feet of water in the hold, and all hands and available passengers were called on to man the pumps. The under berths were full of water, the bird-cages and kittens and parcels were all floating about, most of the women were screaming, many of the men-passengers were drunk, the lights went out, the furniture came unshipped and rolled about at its own sweet will. The cook was thrown on the galley fire, so there could be nothing to eat. Fortunately the sea put the fire out. It was very difficult for men to get along the deck.

A rich lady gave the stewardess £5 to hold her hand all night, so the rest of us poorer ones had to do without consolation. One most painful scene occurred. There were seven women, missionaries' wives, going out either with or to join their husbands. One, a poor child of sixteen, just married, missed her husband, and she called out in the dark for him. A naval officer who was going out to join his ship, and was tipsy the whole way, called out, "Oh, he has tumbled overboard, and is hanging on outside; you will never see him any more." The poor child believed it, and fell down in an epileptic fit, to which she remained subject as long as I ever heard of her. Her husband and mine were working at the pumps. I crawled to my bunk in the Captain's cabin, sick and terrified, and I thought that the terrible seas breaking against its side were loosening the nails, and that the sea would come in and wash me out. I was far away from any help and quite alone, and I hung on to the door, calling, "Carpenter! carpenter!" He came to my assistance, but a huge wave covered us; it carried him overboard and left me—he was never seen again. We lost two men that night.

As I lay there trembling, and terribly sea-sick, something tumbled against my door, and rolled in and sank down on the floor. It was the tipsy naval officer. I could not rise, I could not shut the door, I could not lug him out, so I lay there. When Richard had finished his work, he crawled along the decks till he got to the cabin, where the sea had swamped through the open door pretty considerably. "Hullo! what's that?" he said. I managed faintly to ejaculate, "The tipsy naval officer." He picked him up by the scruff of his neck, and, regardless of consequences, he propelled him, with a good kick behind, all down the deck, and shut the door. He said, "The Captain says we can't live more than two hours in such a sea as this." At first I was frightened that I should die, but now I was only frightened that I shouldn't, and I uttered feebly, "Oh, thank God it will be over so soon." I shall never forget how angry he was with me, because I was not frightened, and gave me quite a sermon. We were like that mostly three days and nights, and then it got better, and I saw the steward passing with some boiled mutton and caper sauce, and called out, "Oh, stop and give me some." He cut me some slices, and I ate them like a starved dog. I got up and dressed and went on deck, and have never been sea-sick since to speak of. I do not speak of Richard, because he never was sea-sick in his life; he never knew what it was; and I believe if it had not been for spilling the ink, he would have been writing his manuscripts, even if the ship had been going round like a squirrel's cage, as he always did all his life, no matter what the weather, and ate and slept enough for three.

The temperature changed by magic. There was a tropical calm at night; the usual rough north-easterly breeze of the outside subsided into a luxurious, sensual calm, with occasional puffs of soft, exciting westerly zephyrs, or *viento de las mugeres*, formed by the land wind of the night. We arrived in thirteen days at Madeira, having been longer than usual on account of the three days' storm. We could smell the land strong of clover hay long before we reached it. I shall never forget my astonishment and delight when I looked out of the port-hole one morning and found myself at Madeira. We had left a frightful English winter, we had suffered much on the sea journey; here was summer—luxuriant and varied foliage, warmth and splendour, the profusion and magnificence of the tropics, a bright blue sky and sun, a deep blue sea, mountains, hills covered with vines, white villas covered with glorious creepers, and picturesque churches and convents. Here we passed a most delightful six weeks. At that time, for about £200 a year, one could have all the luxuries that one could desire—ponies to ride, a hammock to carry you, boats to sail in, and every comfort and luxury; and as for hospitality, there was hardly a chance of breakfasting, lunching, or dining at home. We found here our best and never-to-be-forgotten friend, Lady Marian Alford, with the first Lord Brownlow, Dr. Frank, and a large party whose society we daily enjoyed immensely. After some weeks we went on to Teneriffe in another West African boat.

When we arrived at Santa Cruz, in Teneriffe, I did not think much of it; it is not only far less pretty than Madeira, but there were no comforts and luxuries. *En revanche*, it was far healthier, because Madeira, like Davosplatz, had been quite used up by consumptives, and was full of germs; but then we had arrived at a wrong moment, as we found that the yellow fever was raging at Santa Cruz, and whilst we were there it carried off three thousand people in as many weeks. There was such a panic, that the moment a person was ill, the coffin was brought in and put under the bed, by way of reassuring the patient, and the moment they got into the state of coma, in which they either die or recover, they were clapped into their coffins, but not locked down, and the key was handed to the nearest relative, and the coffin was put into the ground with only a small quantity of mould over it, so that when the patient came to, and was strong enough, he or she would struggle out and come home.

One woman came back in her graveclothes, and tapped at her cottage door, which, in those parts, opens into what serves as a sitting-room. Her daughter was sitting at the table, by moonlight, weeping for her mother's death, when the tap came; she got up and opened the door, and saw her mother standing in her grave-clothes! Believing it to be her ghost, she fell down insensible. The mother lived for many years, and had more children, but the daughter never recovered her reason. One gentlemen, whom we knew, took it at nine in the morning. We went to inquire after him, and was told he was convalescent, and at eleven, two hours later, we saw his funeral going down the street! English people born at Teneriffe have such an emaciated appearance that I was always condoling with them on having had the yellow fever; and then, to my horror, I found it was their natural appearance.

Richard and I thought it better to move, and not waiting for our baggage, things being at the worst, and transport difficult, we set off with knapsacks to walk across the island, twenty-one miles, to Oratava, where we heard that not a single case had made its appearance. There was a halfway house, a very poor little inn. We slept there. Our room was shaped like a claret-case, white-washed, with a tiny grating near the roof for air. There was no furniture of any kind, but they put a mattress on the floor, and gave us a rug. We lay down in our clothes, taking off our weapons and laying them between us. When we woke in the morning, and got up, intending to breakfast and continue our tramp, we found that although we had closed the door, and stuck something up against it, so that any one coming in would knock it down and make a noise, that some one had stolen our best knife from between us, and we were both remarkably light sleepers. A Spaniard cannot resist a knife, and as everything remained exactly as we had left it, it showed that there was some trap-door, or panel in the wall for ingress, which was not perceptible.

It was not comfortable, so we were not sorry to be once more upon the road. We arrived at Oratava, and found it delightful. In our days (1863) there were no hotels; but we were able to hire a room, the size of a riding-school, in a private house on the Square. One side was our bedroom, one corner our dressing-room, one our drawing-room and dining-room, and the middle our study.

Whilst here (March, 1863) we made a delightful excursion up the Peak of Teneriffe. We were out two days and one night. The Peak is 12,198 feet above sea-level. We bivouacked in the snow at 9600 feet, and slept well. Temp., 16°. Around us were no end of little spirts of steam; we counted thirty-five on the final cone. The view from the top, as the dawn broke, was glorious. The horses slept lower down, further ascent being too steep, and the most distressing thing was that they could have no water. The mules could eat snow, but they could not; and coming into the town, they flew at everybody with water-jars on their heads. At last they heard the trickling of the stream near the little town, and they bolted at full gallop. We drew rein, jumped down, and loosened their girths, and let them drink. The only peculiarity of our journey was that it was the *first* performed in *winter*, and therefore people were anxious about us.

The women of Teneriffe were the most beautiful I have ever seen—a cross between Spanish and Irish, who were shipwrecked here in old times. I used to stop and stare at them until they used to say, "What are you staring at?" and I would answer, "At you, because you are so pretty;" and they used to laugh with delight, and show the most lovely teeth. I allude to the peasant women, whose Spanish is very pretty, but not quite Castilian. Here I wrote my first book on Madeira and Teneriffe; but my husband would not let me print it, because he did not think it was up to the mark. He thought I must study and copy many more years before I tried authorship. And he was right, both in this and not letting me share with him the climate of West Africa. But I thought both very hard at the time.

The time came when he had to go back to his post, but I was not allowed to *sleep* at Fernando Po. I thought it dreadfully hard, and cried and begged, but he was immovable; and he was right. So I turned back again with a heavy heart, and had a passage back, if not quite as bad, very nearly as bad, *viâ* Teneriffe and Madeira. Being alone, I had gone into the ladies' cabin—a very small hole with four berths, and what is called by courtesy a sofa; but there were eight of us packed in it. It was pitch dark; the port-hole being closed on account of the weather, the effluvia was disgusting. I got on a dressing-gown, and crawled out to a stack of arms, which I fondly embraced, to keep myself from rolling overboard, where I was found by one of the officers, who ran off to the Captain; he found there was an empty deck cabin, which they immediately put me into, and in a few hours, having got rid of the noxious vapours, I quite recovered. I again passed a long and dreary time, during which he kept me either with my parents well at work, or at sea coming out and going back, with visits to Madeira and Teneriffe. I had one *very* anxious time, inasmuch as he was sent as her Majesty's Commissioner to the King of Dahomè, in *those days* by no means a safe or easy thing.

Dahomè.

"Beautiful feet are those that go
On kindly ministry to and fro—
Down lowliest ways if God wills so

"Beautiful life is that whose span
Is spent in duty to God and man,
Forgetting 'self' in all that it can.

"Beautiful calm when the course is run,
Beautiful twilight at set of sun—
Beautiful death with a life well done."

Richard, being British Consul for Fernando Po, went to visit Agbome, the capital of the kingdom of Dahomè. Lord Russell, hearing of this, gave him instructions to proceed as her Majesty's Commissioner, on a friendly mission to King Gelele, to impress upon the King the importance the British Government attached to the cessation of the slave-trade, and to endeavour by every possible means to induce him to cease to continue the Dahoman customs. Now the Dahoman customs, as all know, meant the cutting of the throats of prisoners of war, and, in old days, making a little lake of blood on which to sail a boat. Not only this, cruelty was the rule of every day. Throats cuts, to send a message to the king's father in the other world; women cut open alive in a state of pregnancy to see what it was like; animals tied up in every sort of horrible position. He writes—

"There is apparently in this people a physical delight in cruelty to beasts as well as to men. The sight of suffering seems to bring them enjoyment, without which the world is tame. Probably the wholesale murderers and torturers of history, from Phalaris and Nero downwards, took an animal and sensual pleasure—all the passions are sisters—in the look of blood, and in the inspection of mortal agonies. I can see no other explanation of the phenomena which meets my eye in Africa. In almost all the towns on the Oil Rivers, you see dead or dying animals fastened in some agonizing position. Poultry is most common, because cheapest—eggs and milk are *juju* to slaves here—they are tied by the legs, head downwards, or lashed round the body to a stake or a tree, where they remain till they fall in fragments. If a man be unwell he hangs a live chicken round his throat, expecting that its pain will abstract from his sufferings. Goats are lashed head downwards tightly to wooden pillars, and are allowed to die a lingering death. Even the harmless tortoise cannot escape impalement. Blood seems to be the favourite ornament for a man's face, as pattern-painting with some dark colour, like indigo, is the proper decoration for a woman. At funerals, numbers of goats and poultry are sacrificed for the benefit of the deceased, and the corpse is sprinkled with the warm blood. The headless trunks are laid upon the body, and if the fowls flap their wings, which they will do for some seconds after decapitation, it is a good omen for the dead man.

"When male prisoners of war are taken they are brought home for sacrifice and food, whilst their infants and children are sometimes supported by the middle, from poles planted in the canoe. The priest decapitates the men—for ordinary executions each Chief has his own headsman—and no one doubts that the bodies are eaten. Mr. Smith and Dr. Hutchinson both aver that they witnessed actual cases. The former declares that, when old Pepple, father of the present King, took captive King Amakree, of New Calabar, he gave a large feast to the European slave-traders on the river. All was on a grand scale. But the reader might perhaps find some difficulty in guessing the name of the dish placed before his Majesty at the head of the table. It was the bloody heart of the King of Calabar, just as it had been torn from the body. He took it in his hand and devoured it with the greatest apparent gusto, remarking, 'This is the way I serve my enemies!'

"Shortly after my first visit, five prisoners of war were brought in from the eastern country. I saw in the *juju*-house their skulls, which were suspiciously white and clean, as if boiled, and not a white man doubted that they had been eaten. The fact is, that they cannot afford to reject any kind of provisions."

Richard was the bearer of presents from Her Majesty to the King—one forty-feet circular crimson silk damask tent, with pole complete; a richly embossed silver pipe with amber mouthpiece; two richly embossed silver belts, with lion and crane in raised relief; two silver waiters; one coat of mail and gauntlets. This is not the place to introduce the subject very largely into *this* book, as I hope to do in "The Labours and Wisdom of Richard Burton" (two further volumes that I am preparing). But I may say that, with regard to his Mission, the King said that if he renounced the customs of his forefathers his people would kill him; that the slaves represented his fortune, but if the Queen would allow him £50,000 a year, that he would be able to do without it. With regard to the tent, it was exceedingly handsome, but it was too small to sit under in that climate, and the only thing he cared for was the gingerbread lion on the top of the pole. He liked his old red-clay and wooden-stem pipe better than the silver one; he liked the silver waiters very much, but he thought they were too small to use as shields; he could not get his hand into the gauntlet; the coat of mail he hung up and made into a target; and then he explained that the only thing he really *did* want, and would be much obliged to her Majesty for, was a carriage and horses, and a white woman!

He made my husband a Brigadier-General of his Amazons, and I was madly jealous from afar; for I imagined lovely women in flowing robes, armed, and riding thoroughbred Arabs, and opposite is the Amazon as, to my great relief, I found she was (afterwards). The King gave him a string of green beads, which was a kind of Dahoman "Garter," a necklace of human bones for his favourite squaw, and a silver chain and Cross with a Chameleon on it. We traced in it the presence of former missionaries, who doubtless found that their crucifixes were thought to be a delightful invention for the King to crucify men, and therefore they replaced it by the chameleon. I have lost my paper on it, and am afraid to quote Greek without it. The King sent return presents to Her Majesty; they consisted of native pipes and tobacco for Her Majesty's smoking, and loin-cloths for Her Majesty to change while travelling, and an umbrella to be held over Her Majesty's head whilst drinking. The presents arrived one day whilst I was at the Foreign Office, but as there had been a murder at Fernando Po, and Richard had been ordered to send home the clothes of the murdered man, on opening the box they were supposed to be these latter articles,

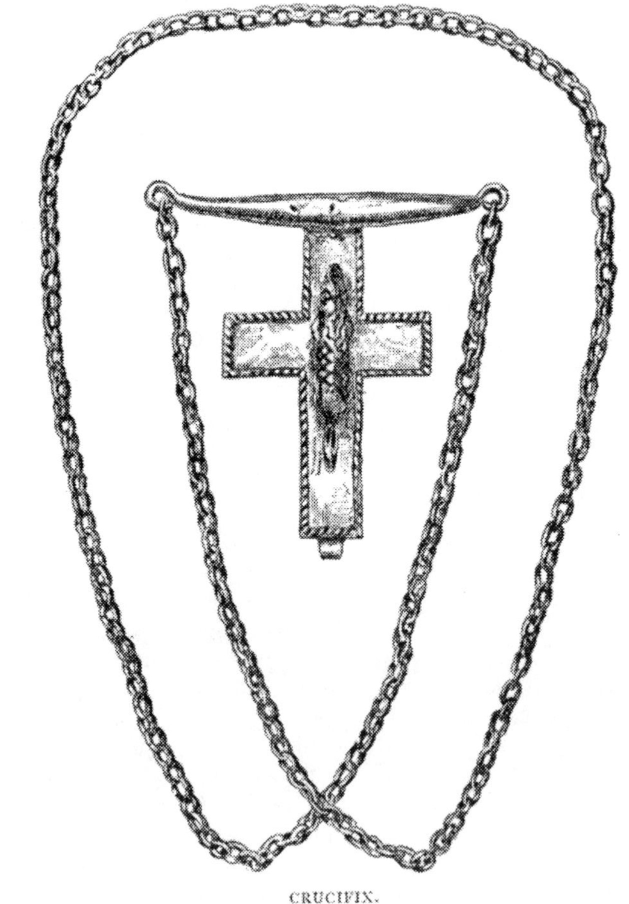

CRUCIFIX.

and were put on one side. I was told they looked quite dirty enough to be that.

The journey occupied three months, during the whole of which time the King made much of him, but holding his life in his hand, and any spiteful moment might have ended it. He told

THE CHIEF OFFICER OF RICHARD'S BRIGADE OF AMAZONS.
Sketched by himself.

me when he came back, that he had seen enough horrid sights to turn a man's brain; and he said, "I used to have to be perfectly calm and dignified whilst seeing these things, or they would have had a contempt for me; but I frequently used to send to the King to say, that if such or such happened again, I should be obliged to leave his Court, as my Government did not countenance such proceedings, which always had the desired effect." On his return, he received no acknowledgment whatever of his services, but Earl Russell wrote me a kind little note, in which he said, "Tell Captain Burton that he has performed his Mission to my utmost and entire satisfaction." I will renew the subject, as I said, in my "Labours and Wisdom of Richard Burton."

The Bight of Biafra, on the West Coast of Africa, extends from Fernando Po to Bathurst, about six hundred miles of coast, and that was Richard's jurisdiction. The lawless conduct of the rum-corrupted natives gave him a good deal of trouble. The traders and the merchants of the coast are called "palm-oil lambs," and they used to call Richard their "shepherd" (supercargoes and skippers are also called "palm-oil ruffians" and "coast-lambs"). I believe he managed them very amicably, and, in spite of business and the dangerous climate, he was supported by all the better class of European agents and supercargoes. He pursued his explorations with ardour. He knew the whole coast from Bathurst (Gambia) to St. Paulo de Loanda (Angola). He marched up to Abeokuta, he ascended the Cameroon Mountains,* the wonderful extinct volcano described by Hanno the Carthagenian and Ptolemy's "Theon Ochema." He wanted the English Government to establish a sanitarium there for the West Coast, and a convict-station for garrotters, the last new crime of *that* day, and to be allowed to use them to construct roads, and in cultivating cotton and chocolate. He told Lord Russell that he would be responsible for them, and should never chain them or lock them up, because, as long as they remained within a certain extent of ring-fence, they would be well and hearty, and the moment they went outside it, they would die without anybody looking after them. The British Government was too tender over their darling human brutes, the cruel, ferocious, and murderous criminals, though the climate was considered quite good enough for Richard and other honourable and active British subjects. He then told Earl Russell that if he would make him Governor of the

* A month ago a black missionary from the Cameroons, with his white wife and her two sisters, paid me a most feeling visit at Mortlake, and visited Richard in his mausoleum, where they showed deep emotion and affection. He had stayed with them on the Cameroons nearly thirty years ago.—I. B.

"Gold Coast," he could send home annually one million pounds sterling; but Lord Russell answered him, "that gold was becoming too common."

He then visited the cannibal Mpangwe, the Fans of Du Chaillu, whose accuracy he had always stood up for when the world had doubted him, and now he was able to confirm it. He then went to Benin City, which was mostly unknown to the Europeans. Belzoni was born in Padua in 1778. During the last eight years of his life he was an African explorer; and he died in Africa, at Benin, in 1823, and he was buried at Gwato, at the foot of a very large tree; guns were fired, and a carpenter from one of the ships put up a tablet to his memory. It is suspected that he was poisoned for the sake of plunder. It was said that some native had inherited his papers: Richard offered £20 for them, but without avail. Belzoni's tree is of a fine spreading growth, which bears a poison apple, and whose boughs droop nearly to the ground. It is a pretty and romantic spot. He writes, "I made an attempt at digging, in order that I might take home his bones and, if possible, his papers, but I was obliged to content myself with sketching his tree, and sending home a handful of wild-flowers to Padua. He died, some say, on the 26th of November, and some say the 3rd of December, 1820." It is remarkable the tender feeling that Richard had for Travellers' graves abroad; indeed, *any* English graves abroad, but especially Travellers or Englishmen. The number of graves that we have sought out, and put in a state of repair and furnished with tombstones and flowers, you would hardly believe—Lady Hester Stanhope's in Syria, Jules Jaquemont's in Bombay, a French traveller, and many, many others. It showed the feeling that he had about a traveller coming home to lay his bones to rest in his own land, and the respect he had for their resting-place. It makes me all the more thankful that I was able to bring *him* home to the place he chose himself, and that our friends enabled me to put up such a monument to him.

He brought out, in *Fraser's Magazine*, several letters in February, March, and April, 1863, previous to his "Wanderings." He ascended the Elephant Mountain, and when he came home he lectured upon that before the Geographical Society. I remember so well, when Richard had submitted something he had written to Norton Shaw, at the Royal Geographical Society, the latter saying, "I don't ever remember hearing this word before, Burton! Where does it come from?" He threw back his head and laughed. "I coined it myself of course, and who has a better right?" Norton Shaw laughed heartily. "Well," he said, "it is a good word, a very good word." "Oh!" said Richard, "I always coin one when I have not got one; it is the only way." He visited the line of lagoons between Lagos and the Volta river. He explored the Yellahlah rapids of the Congo river, and while engaged in all this he collected 2859 proverbs in different African tongues, as for example the Wolof tongue, Kanuri or Bornuese, the Oji or Ashanti, the Ga or Accra, the Yoruba; some from the Eun or Dahoman; some from the Isubú, and Dúalla, of the Bight of Biafra; some in the Efik of the Old Calabar river, also Bight of Biafra; some from the Fans or Mpangwe, from the Upper Gaboon river. He held that the object of language-study was to obtain an insight into the character and thought-modes of Mankind, and that it was not only necessary to speak their language, but to investigate their literary compositions.

He thought that in the Semitic dialects, and in other Asiatic and Indo-European tongues—as the Persian, which imitate their style—the habit of balancing sentences naturally produces this parallelism, and he believed that "The Thousand and One Nights" supplies as many instances as can be found in the Hebrew poets. He thought that the whole of Yoruba shows more or less the effects of El Islam. With respect to the Kafirs, he says it must be noticed that they are a mixed race of African, Arab, and perhaps Persian blood. He thought that a collection of proverbs of this sort would make a kind of manual of Asiatic thought. The nations of the East, he said, always delight in the significant brevity of aphoristic eloquence; and the Proverbs of Solomon show their antiquity and their extensive uses by the Jews. The Arabs were equally addicted to proverbs, which passed into the Persian and Indian languages. He therefore produced "Wit and Wisdom from West Africa; or, a Book of Proverbial Philosophy, Idioms, Enigmas, and Laconisms," in 1865, in 1 vol., and his "Mission to Gelele, King of Dahomè" (2 vols., 1864), which should be *now* a very useful book to the French army, as his "First Footsteps in East Africa" or "Harar" should be to the Italians.

CHAPTER XVIII.

HOME.

At last the time came round for a second leave, and we had a second joyous meeting at Liverpool—this time to part no more as previously. It was on the 28th of August, soon after his landing, 1864, that we chose our burial-place in the Mortlake Cemetery. We had been for that purpose to one of the big cemeteries—I think it was Kensal Green—and we had seen with discomfort that there was so much damp, and looking into an open grave we saw it was full of water; so he looked round rather woeful, and instead of saying it was melancholy, as most men would have done, and as *I thought*, he espied a tomb on which the instruments of the Passion were represented, amongst them the cock of St. Peter. So he said, "I don't think we had better be too near that cock, he will always be crowing and waking us up." We were on a visit to my aunts at Mortlake, who had bought Portobello House, close to the station, nearly opposite to where I live now, had been settled there for some years, and where we had had many large family reunions. We walked into the burial-ground where numbers of my people are buried, and he said, "We will have it here; it is like a nice little family hotel;" and he again confirmed the idea in 1882, when we came down to visit my mother's grave.

Whilst Richard had been on the West Coast of Africa, Speke and Grant had been on their Expedition, and returned and had a grand ovation. The labours of the *first* Expedition had rendered the road easy for the *second*. "The line had been opened," Richard wrote, "by me to Englishmen; they had only to tread in my steps." In the closing days of December, 1863, Speke made a speech at Taunton, which for vain-gloriousness and bad taste was unequalled. He referred to Richard as "Bigg," asserted "that in 1857 he (Speke) had hit the Nile on the head, but that now (1863) he had driven it into the Mediterranean." It is not much to be wondered at if the following epigram on one of Richard's visiting cards was left on the table of the Royal Geographical Society—

"Two loves the Row of Savile haunt,
Who both by nature big be;
The fool is Colonel (Barren) Grant,
The rogue is General Rigby."

The first great event was the British Association Meeting at Bath, September, 1864. Laurence Oliphant conveyed to Richard that Speke had said that "if Burton appeared on the platform at Bath" (which was, as it were, Speke's native town) "he would kick him." I remember Richard's answer—"Well, *that* settles it! By God, he *shall* kick me;" and so to Bath we went. There was to be no speaking on Africa the first day, but the next day was fixed for the "great discussion between Burton and Speke." The first day we went on the platform close to Speke. He looked at Richard, and at me, and we at him. I shall never forget his face. It was full of sorrow, of yearning, and perplexity. Then he seemed to turn to stone. After a while he began to fidget a great deal, and exclaimed half aloud, "Oh, I cannot stand this any longer." He got up to go out. The man nearest him said, "Shall you want your chair again, Sir? May I have it? Shall you come back?" and he answered, "I hope not," and left the Hall. The next day a large crowd was assembled for this famous discussion. All the distinguished people were with the Council; Richard *alone was excluded*, and stood on the platform, *we two alone*, he with his notes in his hand. There was a delay of about twenty-five minutes, and then the Council and speakers filed in and announced the terrible accident out shooting that had befallen poor Speke shortly after his leaving the Hall the day before. Richard sank into a chair, and I saw by the workings of his face the terrible emotion he was controlling, and the shock he had received. When called upon to speak, in a voice that trembled, he spoke of other things and as briefly as he could. When we got home he wept long and bitterly, and I was for many a day trying to comfort him.

I reprint a few lines that rushed to my mind in winter, 1864:—

Reprinted from *Fraser's Magazine*, February, 1869.

"'WHO LAST WINS.'

"The following lines were suggested to me in the studio of the late Edgar George Papworth, Esq., of 36, Milton Street, Dorset Square, in the winter of 1864.

"Captain Burton had recently returned from Africa. The annual meeting of the British Association for the Advancement of Science had just taken place at

Bath, and poor Captain Speke's sudden death was still fresh in our memories. We had been invited by the artist to look at Captain Speke's bust, upon which he was then employed. Mr. Papworth said to Captain Burton, 'I only took the cast after death, and never knew him alive; but you who lived with him so long can surely give me some hints.' Captain Burton, who had learnt something of sculpturing when a boy in Italy, took the sculptor's pencil from Mr. Papworth's hand, and with a few touches here and there made a perfect likeness and expression. As I stood by, I was very much impressed by this singular coincidence.

"'A moulded mask at my feet I found,
With the drawn-down mouth and deepen'd eye,
More lifeless still than the marbles round—
Very death amid dead life's mimicry;
I raised it, and Thought fled afar from me
To the African land by the Zingian Sea.

"'Twas a face, a shell that had nought of brain,
And th' imbedding chalk showed a yellow thread
Which struck my glance with a sudden pain,
For this seemed alive when the rest was dead;
And poor bygone raillery came to mind
Of the tragic masque and no brain behind.

"'But behind there lay in the humblest shrine
A gem of the brightest purest ray:
The gem was the human will divine;
The shrine was the homeliest human clay,
Self-glory—but hush! be the tale untold
To the pale ear thinned by yon plaster mould.

"Shall the diamond gem lose her queenly worth,
Though pent in the dungeon of sandy stone?
Say, is gold less gold, though in vilest earth
For long years it has lurked unprized, unknown?
And the rose which blooms o'er the buried dead,
Hath its pinkness paled, hath its fragrance fled?

"'Thus the poet sang, 'Is the basil vile,
Though the beetle's foot o'er the basil crawl?
And though Arachne hath webbed her toil,
Shall disgrace attach to the princely hall?
And the pearl's clear drop from the oyster shell,
Comes it not on the royal brow to dwell?'

"'On the guarded tablet was writ by Fate,
A double self for each man ere born,
Who shall love his love and shall hate his hate,
Who shall praise his praise and shall scorn his scorn,
Enduring aye to the bitter end,
And man's other man shall be called a friend.

"'When the spirits with radiance nude arrayed
In the presence stood of the one Supreme,
Soul looked unto soul, and the glance conveyed
A pledge of love which each *must* redeem;
Nor may spirit enfleshed in the dust, forget
That high trysting-place, ere time was not yet.

"When the first great Sire, so the Legends say,
The four-rivered garden in Asia trod,
And 'neath perfumed shade, in the drouth of day,
Walked and talked with the Hebrew God,
Such friendship was when it first began;
And the first of friends were the God, the man.

"But *we* twain were not bound by such highborn ties;
Our souls, our minds, and our thoughts were strange,
Our ways were not one, nor our sympathies,
We had severed aims, we had diverse range;
In the stern drear Present his lot was cast,
Whilst I hoped for the Future and loved the Past.

"'Twixt man and woman use oft hath bred
The habits that feebly affection feign,
While the common board and genial bed
And Time's welding force links a length of chain;
Till, when Love was not, it has sometimes proved
This has loved and lived, that has lived and loved.

"But 'twixt man and man it may not so hap
Each man in his own and his proper sphere;
At some point, perchance, may the lines o'erlap;
The far rest is far as the near is near—
Save when the orbs are of friend and friend
And the circles' limits perforce must blend.

"But the one sole point at which he and I
Could touch, was the contact of vulgar minds.
'Twas interest's forcible feeble tie
Which binds, but with lasting bonds ne'er binds;
And our objects fated to disagree,
What way went I, and what way went he?

"And yet we were comrades for many years,
And endured in its troth our companionship
Through a life of chances, of hopes and fears;
Nor a word of harshness e'er passed the lip,
Nor a thought unkind dwelt in either heart,
Till we chanced—by what chance did it hap?—to part.

"Where Fever yellow—skinned, bony, gaunt,
With the long blue nails and lip livid white;
With the blood-stained orbs that could ever haunt
Our brains by day and our eyes by night;
In her grave-clothes mouldy with graveyard taint
Came around our sleeping mats—came and went:

"Where the crocodile glared with malignant stare,
And the horse of the river, with watery mane
That flashed in the sun, from his oozy lair
Rose to gaze on the white and wondrous men;
And the lion, with muzzle bent low to earth,
Mocked the thunder-cloud with his cruel mirth:

"Where the speckled fowls the Mimosa decked
Like blue-bells studded with opal dew;
And giraffes pard-spotted, deer-eyed, swan-necked,
Browsed down the base whence the tree dome grew,
And the sentinel-antelope, aëried high,
With his frightened bound taught his friends to fly:

" Where the lovely Coast is all rank with death,
 That basks in the sun of the Zingian shore ;
Where the mountains, dank with the ocean's breath,
 Bear the incense-tree and the sycamore ;
Where the grim fierce desert and stony hill
Breed the fiercest beasts, and men fiercer still :

" Where the Land of the Moon with all blessings blest
 Save one—save man ; and with name that sped
To the farthest edge of the misty West
 Since the Tyrian sailor his sail-sheet spread,
Loves to gaze on her planet whose loving ray
Fills her dells and fells with a rival day :

" Where the Lake unnamed in the Afric wold
 Its breast to the stranger eye lay bare ;
Where Isis, forced her veil to unfold—
 To forget the boast of the days that were—
Stood in dusky charms with the crisp tire crowned
On the hallowed bourne, on the Nile's last bound :—

" We toiled side by side, for the hope was sweet
 To engrave our names on the Rock of Time :
On the Holy Hill to implant our feet
 Where enfaned sits Fame o'er the earth sublime ;
And now rose the temple before our eyes—
We had paid the price, we had plucked the prize ;

" When up stood the Shadow betwixt us twain—
 Had the dusky goddess bequeathed her ban?
And the ice of death through every vein
 Of comradeship spread in briefest span ;
The guerdon our toils and our pains had won
Was too great for two, was enough for one ;

" And deeper and deeper grew the gloom
 When the serpent tongue had power to sting,
While o'er one of us hung the untimely doom—
 A winter's night to a day of spring,
And heart from heart parting fell away
At the fiat of Fate by her iron sway.

" It seems as though from a foamy * dream
 I awake, and this pallid mask behold,
And I ask—Can this be the end supreme
 Of the countless things of the days of old?
This clay, is it all of what used to be
In the Afric land by the Zingian Sea ?"

ISABEL BURTON.

Richard at this time wrote, secretly, a little "squib" of one hundred and twenty-one pages, called "Stone Talk," being some of the marvellous sayings of a petral portion of Fleet Street, London, to one Dr. Polyglot, Ph.D., by Frank Baker, D.O.N., 1865. He kept it quite secret from me, and one day brought it out of his pocket on a

* "Träume sind Schäume."

railway journey, as if he had bought it from a stall, and gave it to me to read. I was delighted with it, kept reading him out passages from it, with peals of laughter. Fortunately we were alone, and I kept saying to him, "Jemmy, I wish you would not go about talking as you do; I am sure this man has been associating with you at the club, picked up all your ideas and written this book, and won't he just catch it!" At last, after going on like that for a considerable time, the amused expression of his face flashed an idea into my brain, and I said, "You wrote it yourself, Jemmy, and *nobody else;*" and he said, "I *did.*" When I showed it to Lord Houghton, he told me that he was afraid that it would do Richard a great deal of harm with the "powers that were," and advised me to buy them up, which I did. He took the *nom de plume* of "Frank Baker" from his second name Francis and his mother's name Baker.

It has been thrown in my teeth, since his death, that he would have married twice before he married me, and as he was between thirty-nine and forty at the time of our marriage, it is very natural that it should be so. I sometimes take comfort in reading passages from "Stone Talk" anent former loves—I do not know who they are:—

"So, standing 'mid the vulgar crowd,
I watched the fair, the great, the proud
That hustled in, when glad surprise
Awaited these my languid eyes.
The pink silk hood her head was on
Did make a sweet comparison
With brow as pure, as clear, as bright,
As Boreal dawn or Polar night,
With lips whose crimson strove to hide
Gems all unknown to Oman's tide,
With eyes as myosotis blue,
With cheeks of peachy down and hue,
And locks whose semi-liquid gold
Over the ivory shoulders rolled.
Not 'low' her dress, yet cunning eye
'Neath gauzy texture could descry
Two silvery orbs, that rose and fell,
With Midland Sea's voluptuous swell,
Intoxicating to the brain
As flowers that breathe from Persian plain
Whereon to rest one moment brief
Were worth a life of pain and grief;
And, though fast closed in iron cage—
Venetian padlock of the age—
The poetry of motion told
Of all by envious flounce and fold
Concealed; each step of nameless grace
Taught glowing Fancy's glance to trace
A falling waist, on whose soft round
No lacing wrinkle might be found
(Nor waspish elegance affright
Thorwaldsen's, Canova's sight),

And rising hips and migniard feet—
Ankle for Dian's buskin meet—
Gastrocunemius——

Cease, Muse! to tell
The things my mem'ry holds too well.
I bowed before the 'Thing Divine'
As pilgrim sighting holy shrine,
And straight my 'chanted spirit soared
To dizzy regions late explored
By Mister Hume—A. B.—C. D.—all
The rout yclept spiritual.
A church of emeralds I see,
An altar-tower lit brilliantly;
A steeple, too, the pave inlaid
With richest tint of light and shade;
A 'deal of purple,' archèd pews;
And all the 'blacks' methinks are 'blues.'
Now throngs the murex-robèd crowd,
A-chanting anthems long and loud,
And children, garbed in purest white,
Kneel with wreathed heads before the light.
I, too, am there, with 'Thing Divine,'
Bending before the marble shrine,
While spirit-parson's sleepy drone
Maketh me hers and her my own.
When sudden on my raptured sight
Falls deadly and discharming blight,
Such blight as Eurus loves to fling
O'er gladsome crop in genial spring.
Fast by the side of 'Thing Divine,'
By spirit-parson fresh made mine,
In apparition grim—I saw
The middle-aged British mother-in-law!!

* * * *

The pink silk hood her head was on
Did make a *triste* comparison
With blossomed brow and green-grey eyes,
And cheeks bespread with vinous dyes,
And mouth and nose—all, all, in fine,
Caricature of 'Thing Divine.'
Full low the Doppelgänger's dress
Of moire and tulle, in last distress
To decorate the massive charms
Displayed to manhood's shrinking arms;
Large loom'd her waist 'spite pinching stays,
As man-o'-war in bygone days;
And, ah! her feet were broader far
Than beauty's heel in Mullingar.
Circular all from toe to head,
Pond'rous of framework, as if bred
On streaky loin and juicy steak;
And, when she walked, she seemed to shake
With elephantine tread the ground.
Sternly, grimly, she gazed around,
Terribly calm, in much flesh strong,
Upon the junior, lighter throng,
And loudly whispered, 'Who's that feller?
'Come! none of this, Louise, I tell yer!'
And 'Thing Divine' averted head,
And I, heart-broken, turned and fled."

DIRGE.

"I also swore to love a face
And form where beauty strove with grace,
And raven hair, black varnished blue,
A brow that robbed the cygnet's hue,
Orbs that beshamed the fawnlet's eyne,
And lips like rosebuds damp with rain.
Ah! where is she? ah! where are they—
The charms that stole my heart away?

"She's fatten'd like a feather bed,
Her cheeks with beefy hue are red,
Her eyes are tarnished, and her nose
Affection for high diet shows;
The voice like music wont to flow,
Is now a kind of vaccine low.
Cupid, and all ye gods above,
Is this the thing I used to love?"

This year, 1864, Richard edited and annotated Marcy's "Prairie Traveller" for the *Anthropological Review.*

Apart from the sad circumstance of Speke's death, we had a very delightful winter. We went to Uncle Gerard's at Garswood, to Lady Egerton of Tatton's, to Lady Stanley of Alderley's (in the present dowager's time), when the now Dowager Lady Airlie and Lady Amberly and all the family were then at home, where we met an immense quantity of distinguished people, and notably Professor Jowett. Then we went to Lady Margaret Beaumont's at Bretton Park, and to Lord Fitzwilliam's; and all these had large house-parties.

This year we became very intimate with Winwood Reade. We went over to Ireland, where we spent a delightful two months. We took an Irish car, and drove by degrees over all the most interesting and prettiest parts of Ireland, at the rate of so many miles a day, stopping where it was most interesting. I had an Irish maid with me, whose chief delight was to see Richard and me clinging on to the car as it flew round the corners, while she sat as cool and calm as possible, with her hands in her muff. "Ye devil," Richard said to her, "I believe you were born on a car; I will pay you out for laughing at me." Some days afterwards, she dropped her muff. There was a great deal of snow on the ground, so Richard said to her very kindly, "Don't get down, Kiernan; I will get your muff for you." He stopped the car, got down, pretended to be very busy with his boot, but in reality he was filling her muff with snow. When he gave it back to her she gave a little screech. "Ah," he said, with glistening eyes, "you'll laugh at me for clinging on the car like a monkey on a scraper again."

We were asked to numbers of country-houses on the way—to the Bellews', Gormanstons', and Lord Drogheda's; and we had the pleasure of making acquaintance with Lady Rachel Butler and Lord James, who were very kind to us. Dublin was immensely hospitable, and at that time very gay. One of our interesting events was making acquaintance with Mr. Lentaigne, the great convict philanthropist. His mania was to reform his convicts, and make his friends take them for service, if nobody else would. He was the man to whom Lord Carlisle said, "Why, Lentaigne, you will wake up some morning, and find you are the only spoon in the house." He took us to see the prisons and the reformatories, and he implored of me to take out with me a convict woman of about thirty-four, who had been fifteen years in prison. I said, "Well, Mr. Lentaigne, what did she do?" "Poor girl! the sweetest creature—she murdered her baby when she was sixteen." "Well," I answered, "I would do anything to oblige you, but I dare say I shall often be quite alone with her, and at thirty-four she might like larger game."

Richard was veritably, though born of prosaic parents, a child of romance. He had English, Irish, Scotch, and French blood in his veins, and, it has often been suggested (though never proved), a drop of Oriental or gypsy blood from some far-off ancestor. His Scottish, North England, and Border blood came out in all posts of trust and responsibility, in steadiness and coolness in the hour of danger, in uprightness and integrity, and the honour of a gentleman. Of Irish blood he showed nothing excepting fight, but the two foreign strains were strong. From Arab or gypsy he got his fluency of languages, his wild and daring spirit, his Agnosticism, his melancholy pathos, his mysticism, his superstition (I am superstitious enough, God knows, but he was far more so), his divination, his magician-like foresight into events, his insight, or reading men through like a pane of glass, his restless wandering, his poetry. From a very strong strain of Bourbon blood (Richard showed "race" from the top of his head to the sole of his feet) which the Burtons inherit—that is, *my* Burtons—he got his fencing, knowledge of arms, his ready wit and repartee, his boyish gaiety of character as alternately opposed to his melancholy, and, lastly, but not least, his Catholicism as opposed to the mysticism of the East, which is not in the least like the Agnosticism of the West. But it was not a fixed thing like my Catholicism; it ran silently threaded through his life, alternately with his mysticism, like the refrain of an opera.

He was proud of his Scottish and North England blood, he liked his Rob Roy descent, and also his Bourbon blood, and he used to laugh heartily when, sometimes, I was half-vexed at something and used to chaff him by saying, "You dirty Frenchman!"

Richard was a regular *gamin*; his keen sense of humour, his ready wit, were always present. He adored shocking dense people and seeing their funny faces and stolid belief, and never cared about what harm it would do him in a worldly sense. I have frequently sat at the dinner-table of such people, praying him by signs not to go on, but he was in a very ecstasy of glee; he said it was so funny always to be believed when you were chaffing, and so curious never to be believed when you were telling the truth. He had a sort of schoolboy bravado about these things that in his high spirits lasted him all the seventy years of his life.

But especially strong were the melancholy, tender, sad hours of the man, full of sensitiveness to pathos in all he said, or did, or wrote. The one paid too much for the other, if I may so express it.

Talking of the Bourbon blood and his *gaminerie*, during this visit to Ireland we were in Dublin, where we had the pleasure of knowing Sir Bernard and Lady Burke, and Richard and he were talking in his study over his genealogy and this Louis XIV. descent. He said, "I want this to be made quite clear." Sir Bernard said, "I wonder, Captain Burton, that *you*, who have such good Northern and Scottish blood in your veins, and are connected with so many of the best families, should trouble about what can only be a morganatic descent at best." I can see him now, carelessly leaning against the bookcase with his hands in his pockets, with his amused face on, looking at the earnest countenance of Sir Bernard and saying, "Why! I would rather be the bastard of a King, than the son of an honest man," and his hearty laugh at the shocked expression and "*Oh!* Captain Burton," which he had been waiting for.

One of the amusing things, and interesting as well, was going to Gerald's Cross by rail, and when we arrived, there was only one car. There was another gentleman and ourselves, and as we had telegraphed for the car, it was ours. Still we did not like to leave him without anything. So we asked him if we could give him a lift. He asked us where we were going, and we told him. So he said, "Well, you pass my house, so I shall be grateful." As we drove along for about half an hour between Gerald's Cross and Cashel, he told us that he was Bianconi, the first inventor of outside Irish cars, that his house was called Longfield, and the whole of his most interesting history. His house was a nice little residence in a garden with a lawn and trees in front, and he insisted upon taking us into it, and giving us afternoon tea, after which we drove on.

We visited Tuam, which we *both* thought a dreadful place; but the name of Burton was big there, on account of the Bishop and the Dean, Richard's grandfather and uncle, and hundreds of the poor crowded round us for *bakshish* (presents). Richard had still some old aunts there, who came to dine with us, his grandfather's daughters. They had a large tract of land here, but Richard's father had made it over to the aunts, and I was very glad of it, as I should have been very sorry to have had to stop there. We were delighted with the fishing population of Lough Corrib, a cross between Spanish and Irish, who have nothing in common with the town; they are called Claddhah, pronounced Clather. We stopped long at the Armagh Cathedral, looking for Drelincourt tombs, of which there are plenty belonging to Richard's people. From Drogheda we went to see the Halls of Tara, the site of the Palace of the Kings, the Stone of Destiny, and then to the site of the Battle of the Boyne, afterwards to Maynooth College, where the boys cheered Richard. Then we proceeded to Blarney and kissed the stone; near Cork to see Captain and Mrs. Lane Fox, now General and Mrs. Pitt-Rivers; and also to Killarney, and thought it very pretty but *very* small. We enjoyed much hospitality at the Castle during our stay. During all our car-driving our little horse used to have a middle-of-the-day feed, with a pint of whisky and water, and she came in at the end of the time in better condition, and looking in every way better, and twice as frisky as when she started.

On the 17th of May the Polytechnic in London opened with an account of Richard's travels in Mecca, and a dissolving view of Richard's picture in uniform. It was arranged by Mr. Pepper of "Pepper's Ghost," and a quantity of little green pamphlets with the lecture were sold at the door. On the 22nd of May we dined with George Augustus Sala, previous to his going to Algiers, and also with poor Blakeley of the Guns, in his and Mrs. Blakeley's pretty little home; he died so sadly afterwards.

Richard was now transferred to Santos, São Paulo, Brazil.

Farewell Dinner to Captain R. F. Burton.

"On Tuesday, April 4th, 1865, there was celebrated an event in London of such importance to anthropological science as to deserve an especial record in these pages. On this day the Anthropological Society of London celebrated the election into their society of five hundred Fellows, by giving a public dinner to Captain Richard F. Burton, their senior vice-president. The Right Honourable Lord Stanley, M.P., F.R.S., F.A.S.L., took the chair, and was supported on the right by Captain Burton. [Here follows one hundred and twenty distinguished names.]

"The noble Chairman, Lord Derby, in proposing 'The health of Captain Burton,' said—I rise to propose a toast which will not require that I should bespeak for it a favourable consideration on your part. I intend to give you the health of the gentleman in whose honour we have met to-night. (Loud cheers.) I propose the health of one—your cheers have said it before me—of the most distinguished Explorers and Geographers of the present day. (Cheers.) I do not know what you feel, but as far as my limited experience in that way extends, for a man to sit and listen to his own eulogy is by no means an unmixed pleasure, and in Captain Burton's presence I shall say a great deal less about what he has done than I should take the liberty of doing if he were not here. (Cheers.) But no one can dispute this, that into a life of less than forty-five years Captain Burton has crowded more of study, more of hardship, and more of successful enterprise and adventure than would have sufficed to fill up the existence of half a dozen ordinary men. (Cheers.) If, instead of continuing his active career—as we hope he will for many years to come—it were to end to-morrow, he would still have done enough to entitle him to a conspicuous and permanent place in the annals of geographical discoverers. (Cheers.) I need not remind you, except in the briefest way, of the long course of his adventures and their results. His first important work, the 'History of the Races of Scinde,' will long continue to be useful to those whose studies lie in that direction, and those who, like myself, have travelled through that unhappy valley—through that young Egypt, which is about as like old Egypt as a British barrack is like an Egyptian pyramid—will recognize the fact that if there have been men who have described that country for *utilitarian* purposes more accurately and minutely, no man has described it with a more graphic pen. (Cheers.) With respect to his pilgrimage to Mecca, that, I believe, was part only of a much larger undertaking which local disturbances in the country prevented being carried out to the fullest extent. (Cheers.) I do not think I am exaggerating when I say that not more than two or three Englishmen would have been able to perform that feat. The only two parallels to it that I recollect in one generation are, the exploring journeys of Sir Henry Pottinger into Beloochistan, and the journey of M. Vambéry through the deserts of Central Asia. (Cheers.) I am speaking only by hearsay and report, but I take the fact to be this, that the ways of Europeans and Asiatics are so totally different —I do not mean in those important acts to which we all pay a certain amount of attention while we do them, but in those little trifling details of everyday life, that we do instinctively and without paying attention to them—the difference in these respects between the two races is so wide that the Englishman who would attempt to travel in the disguise of an Oriental ought to be almost Oriental in his habits if he hope to carry out that personation successfully. And if that be true of a journey of a few days, it is far more true of a journey extending over weeks and months, where you have to keep your secret, not merely from the casual observer, but from your own servants, your own friends, and your own travelling companions. To carry through an enterprise of that kind may well be a strain on the ingenuity of any man, and though, no doubt, danger does stimulate our faculties, still it does not take from the merit of a feat that it is performed under circumstances in which, in the event of detection, death is almost certain. (Cheers.) I shall say nothing in this brief review of that plucky though unsuccessful expedition to the Somali country, which so nearly deprived the Anthropological Society of one of its ablest members. But I cannot pass over so lightly the journey into Harar—the first attempt to penetrate Eastern Africa in that quarter. That journey really opened a wide district of country previously unknown to the attention of civilized man. It led the way indirectly to the Nile expeditions, which lasted from 1856 to 1859. With respect to the labours which were gone through in those expeditions, and the controversies which arose out of those labours, I do not require here to say anything except to make one passing remark. With regard to this disputed subject of the Nile, I may be permitted to say—though those who are experienced in geographical matters may treat me as a heretic—(a laugh)—I cannot help it if they do, for I speak by the light only of common sense—(renewed laughter, and cheers)—but it seems to me that there is a little delusion in this notion of searching for what we call the source of a river. Can you say of any river that it has a source? It has a mouth, that is certain—(cheers); —but it has a great many sources, and to my mind you might just as well talk of a plant as having only one root, or a man only one hair on his head, as of a river having a single source. Every river is fed from many sources, and it does not seem to me that the mere accident of hitting upon that which subsequent investigation may prove to be the largest of its many affluents is a matter about which there need be much controversy. The real test of the value of this kind of work is, what is the quantity of land previously unknown which the discoverer has gone through, and which he has opened up to the knowledge of civilized man? (Cheers.) Judged by that test, I do not hesitate to say that the African Expedition of 1856 has been the most important of our time; the only rival which I could assign to it being that separate expedition which was undertaken by Dr. Livingstone through the southern part of the continent. (Hear.) Where one man has made his way many will follow, and I do not think it is too sanguine an anticipation, negro chiefs and African fevers notwithstanding, to expect that within the lifetime of the present generation we may know as much of Africa, at least, of Africa north of the equator, and within fifteen degrees south of it, as we know now of South America. Well, gentlemen, no man returns from a long African travel with health entirely unimpaired, and our friend was no exception to the rule. But there are men to whom all effort is unpleasant, so there are men to whom all rest, all doing nothing, is about the hardest work to which they could be put, and Captain Burton recruited his health, as you all know, by a journey to the Mormon country, travelling thirty thousand miles by sea and land, and bringing back from that community—morally, I think, the most eccentric phenomenon of our days—a very curious and interesting, and, as far as I could judge, the most accurate description we have yet received. (Cheers.) Now, as to the last phase of the career which I am attempting to sketch—the embassy to Dahomè, the discovery of the Cameroon Mountains, and the travels along the African coast, I shall only remind you of it, because I am quite sure that the published accounts must be fresh in all your minds. I do not know what other people may think of these volumes, but to me they were a kind of revelation of negro life and character, enabling me to feel, which certainly I never felt before, that I could understand an African and barbarian court. As to any theories arising out of these journeys, as to any speculations which may be deduced from them, I do not comment upon these here. This is not the place nor the occasion to do it. All I will say about them is, that when a man with infinite labour, with infinite research, and at the imminent risk of his life, has gone to work to collect a series of facts, I think the least the public can do is to allow him a fair hearing when he puts his own interpretation upon those facts. (Loud cheers.) I will add this, that in matters which we all feel to be intensely interesting, and upon which we all know that our knowledge is imperfect, any man does us a service who helps us to arrange the facts which we have at our command, who stimulates inquiry and thought by teaching us to doubt instead of dogmatizing. I am quite aware that this is not in all places a popular theory. There are a great many people who, if you give them a new idea, receive it almost as if you had offered them personal violence. (Laughter.) It puts them out. They don't understand it—they are not used to it. I think that state of the public mind, which we must all acknowledge, is the very best defence for the existence of scientific societies such as that to which many of us belong. It is something for a man who has got a word to say, to know that there is a society where he will get a fair and considerate hearing; and, whether the judgment goes against him or not, at least he will be met by argument and not by abuse. I think Captain Burton has done good service to the State in various ways. He has extended our knowledge of the globe on which we live, and as we happen to be men, and not mere animals, that is a result which, though it may not have any immediate utilitarian result, we ought to value. (Cheers.) He has done his share in opening savage and barbarous countries to the enterprise of civilized man, and though I am not quite so sanguine as many good men have been as to the reclaiming of savage races, one has only to read his and all other travellers' accounts of African life in its primitive condition, to see that whether they gain much or not by European intercourse, at any rate they have nothing to lose. (Laughter.) But there is something more than that. In these days of peace and material prosperity (and both of them are exceedingly good things), there is another point of view in which such a career as that of our friend is singularly useful. It does as much as a successful campaign to keep up in the minds of the English people that spirit of adventure and of enterprise, that looking to reputation rather than money, to love of effort rather than to ease—the old native English feeling which has made this country what it has become, and which, we trust, will keep this country what it is to be—a feeling which, no doubt, the tendency of great wealth and material prosperity is to diminish; but a feeling which, if it were to disappear from among us, our wealth and our material prosperity would not be worth one year's purchase. (Cheers.) Gentlemen, I propose the health of Captain Burton, and my best wish for him is that he may do for himself what nobody else is likely to do for him, that by his future performance he may efface the memory of his earlier exploits. (Loud cheers.)

"The toast was drunk with three times three.

"Captain Burton, who, on rising, was greeted with loud and protracted cheering, said—My Lord Stanley, my lords and gentlemen, it falls to the lot of few men to experience a moment so full of gratified feeling as this, when I rise to return thanks for the honour you have done me on this, to me, most memorable occasion. I am proud to see my poor labours in the cause of discovery thus publicly recognized by the representative of England's future greatness. (Cheers.) The terms of praise which have fallen from your lordship's lips are far above my present deserts, yet I treasure them gratefully in my memory as coming from one so highly honoured, not only as a nobleman, but as a man. I am joyed when looking round me to see so many faces of friends who have met to give me God-speed—to see around me so many of England's first men, England's brains, in fact; men who have left their mark upon the age; men whose memories the world will not willingly let die. These are the proudest laurels a man can win, and I shall wear them in my heart of hearts that I may win more of them on my return.

"But, however gratifying this theme, I must bear in mind the occasion which thus agreeably brings us together. We meet to commemorate the fact that on March 14, 1865, that uncommonly lusty youth, our young Anthropological Society, attained the respectable dimensions of five hundred members. My lord and gentlemen, it is with no small pride that I recall to mind how, under the auspices of my distinguished and energetic friend Dr. James Hunt, our present president,—and long may he remain so,—I took the chair on the occasion of its nativity. The date was January 6, 1863. The number of those who met was eleven. Each had his own doubts and hopes, and fears touching the viability of the new-born. Still we knew that our cause was good; we persevered, we succeeded. (Cheers.)

"The fact is, we all felt the weight of the great want. As a traveller and a writer of travels during the last fifteen years, I have found it impossible to publish those questions of social economy and those physiological observations, always interesting to our common humanity, and at times so valuable. The *Memoirs of the Anthropological Society* now acts the good Samaritan to facts which the publisher and the drawing-room table proudly pass by. Secondly, there was no arena for the public discussion of opinions now deemed paradoxical, and known to be unpopular. The rooms of the Anthropological Society, No. 4, St. Martin's Place, now offer a refuge to destitute truth. There any man, monogenist or polygenist, eugenestic or dysgenestic, may state the truth as far as is in him. We may truly call these rooms

> 'Where, girt by friend or foe,
> A man may say the thing he will.'

All may always claim equally from us a ready hearing, and what as Englishmen we prize the most, a fair field and plenty of daylight. (Cheers.)

"And how well we succeeded—how well our wants have been supplied by the officers of our society, we may judge by this fact: During the last twenty days not less than thirty members have, I am informed by my friend Mr. Carter Blake, been added to the five hundred of last month. I confidently look forward to the day when, on returning from South America, I shall find a list of fifteen hundred names of our society. We may say *vires acquirit eundo*, which you will allow me to translate, 'We gain strength by our go,' in other words, our progress. This will give us weight to impress our profession and opinions upon the public. Already the learned of foreign nations have forgotten to pity us for inability to work off the grooves of tradition and habit. And we *must* succeed so long as we adhere to our principles of fair play and a hearing to every man. (Cheers.)

"I would now request your hearing for a few words of personal explanation, before leaving you for some years. I might confide it to each man separately, but I prefer the greatest possible publicity. It has come to my ears that some have charged me with want of generosity in publishing a book which seems to reflect upon the memory of poor Captain Speke. Without entering into details concerning a long and melancholy misunderstanding, I would here briefly state that my object has ever been, especially on this occasion, to distinguish between *personal enmities* and *scientific differences. I did not consider myself bound to bury my opinions in Speke's grave; to me, living, they are of importance.* I adhere to all I have stated respecting the Nile sources; but I must change the form of their expression. My own statement may, I believe, be considered to be moderate enough. In a hasty moment, I appended one more, which might have been omitted—as it shall from all future editions. I may conclude this painful controversial subject, by stating that Mr. Arthur Kinglake, of Weston-super-Mare, writes to me that a memorial bust of my lamented companion is to be placed this year in the shire-hall, Taunton, with other Somersetshire heroes, Blake and Locke. I have seen the bust in the studio of Mr. Papworth, and it is perfect. If you all approve, it would give me the greatest pleasure to propose a subscription for the purpose before we leave this room. (Cheers.)

"And now I have already trespassed long enough upon your

patience. I will not excuse myself, because I am so soon to leave you. Nor will I say adieu, because I shall follow in mind all your careers; yours, my Lord Stanley, to that pinnacle of greatness for which Nature and Fate have destined you; and yours, gentlemen and friends, each of you, to the high and noble missions to which you are called. Accompanied by your good wishes, I go forth on mine with fresh hope, and with a vigour derived from the wholesome stimulus which you have administered to me this evening. My Lord Stanley, my lords and gentlemen, I thank you from my heart.

[Here followed twenty-five speeches. Dr. Hunt, the President, concluded:] "He should be very sorry if they were to separate on that occasion, when they had met to bid farewell to Captain Burton, without drinking the health of one on whom they all looked with respect and admiration—Mrs. Burton. (Loud cheers.) He felt it, therefore, to be their duty to join most heartily in drinking long health and prosperity to Mrs. Burton, and may she be long spared to take care of her husband when far away in South America. Those who paid homage to her paid homage also to him, whom they had met to honour, and the more they knew of him the more they respected him. (Loud cheers.)

"Captain Burton: I only hope in the name of Heaven that Mrs. Burton won't hear of this. (Laughter.)

"Dr. Hunt said that as Captain Burton refused to respond to the toast in a proper manner, he must return thanks for Mrs. Burton. She begged him to say that she had great difficulty in keeping her husband in order, but that she would do what she could to take care of him, and to make him as innocent a man as they believed him to be. (Loud laughter.)

"Lord Stanley then left, and the company soon afterwards separated."

Nile.

Richard's speech alluded to the following. I take it from his private, not his published writings:—

"I have five main objections to Jack's theory about the Nile:—

"1. There is a difference of levels in the upper and in the lower part of the so-called lake. This point is important only when taken in connection with the following:—

"2. The native report that the Mwerango river rises from the hills in the centre of the so-called lake.

"3. The general belief that there is a road through the so-called lake.

"4. The fact that the southern part of the so-called lake floods the country for thirteen miles, whereas the low and marshy northern shore is not inundated.

"5. The phenomena that the so-called lake swells during the dry period of the Nile, and *vice versâ*.

"It would of course have been far more congenial to my feelings to have met Jack upon the platform, and to have argued out this affair, openly, before the Association of Science. I went down fairly to seek this contest on September 13th, 1864. The first day was devoted to other subjects, and the second day our grand exposition of onr separate views was to come off, and the rooms of the Section E were crowded to suffocation.

"All the great people were with the Council, I alone was uninvited; so I remained on the platform with my wife, notes in hand, longing for the fray, but when they filed in twenty minutes later, the melancholy announcement was made of his death. I had seen him between one and three p.m., and at four p.m. he was a corpse! I was so shocked, so pained, I could not speak, and remained so for a long while. His death sealed my lips, but I am not bound to bury my opinions in his grave; and when I at last dared to speak, I addressed a public already horribly prejudiced by the partisans of Jack, who know nothing about chivalry, and have spoken of me in terms which I never used towards my dead friend. In short, all my achievements were ignored and forgotten. Everybody is mentioned with honour, but the Pioneer of discovery in these wild regions is carefully ignored. I am now about to leave Europe for some years, and I cannot allow errors which are generally received, to remain as they are, but I do not stand forth as an enemy of the departed. No man better than I, can appreciate the noble qualities of energy, courage, and perseverance which he so eminently possessed, who knew him for so many years, who travelled with him as a brother, till the unfortunate rivalry respecting the Nile sources arose like a ghost between us, and was fanned to a flame by the enmity and ambition of so-called friends. I do not wish to depreciate the services of Jack, nor Captain Grant—they brought us back a new three hundred and fifty geographical miles; but as to the *Nile* sources, I consider the problem wholly unsolved. Jack and Captain Grant seemed to forget that the *more my* expedition did, the better for them, as well as for me. The result of Jack's expedition is a blank space on the maps, covering nearly twenty-nine thousand miles and containing possibly half a dozen waters. Had Jack and Captain Grant really seen—which they did not—three sides of the Nyanza, they would have left unexplored fifty thousand square geographical miles, a space somewhat larger than England and Wales.

"Knowing Jack as I do, I cannot understand why he sent Captain Grant, without valid apparent reason, on July 19th, 1862, to the head-quarters of King Kamrasi of Unyoro, right away *from* the Lakes, unless Jack was determined *alone* to do the work, and to have no one to contradict him. The *Westminster Review* remarks of that: 'Grant will have little to regret, and Burton will be more than revenged should Tanganyika, and not the Nyanza, prove to be the head of the Nile.'

"From Alexandria Jack telegraphed in April, 1863, to the F.O. these big words:—'Inform Sir Roderick Murchison that all is well, that we are in latitude 14° 30′ upon the Nile, and that the Nile is settled.' The startling assertion caused a prodigious sensation at the main meeting, May 11th, 1863. Jack was fêted in Egypt by his Highness the Khedive and by his Majesty of Piedmont, and was presented with a medal bearing the gratifying inscription, 'Honor est a Nilo.' At Southampton he was received by the civic authorities and sundry supporters, including Colonel Rigby of Zanzibar, who, for purely private reasons, had supported Jack against *me.* On June 22nd, 1863, Jack received an ovation in the shape of a special meeting of the Royal Geographical Society, when the windows were broken in by the eager crowd. By-and-by people began to cool their enthusiasm. Despite all that Jack had done to me, I was the first to give flattering opinions of the exploration, until the personal account Jack gave, told me how little had been done. It was something to have passed over three hundred and fifty untrodden miles, but it would take a great deal more than that to settle the Nile problem. Jack tried to crush all expressions of thought. A welcome to Jack was put forth in 1863 by *Blackwood's Magazine*, a periodical from which, for reasons *best known to myself*, I never expected, nor wanted to receive justice. The author of 'The Welcome,' who sought advertisement, wrote: 'We were the first to satisfy ourselves with Captain Speke's geographical views.'

"In January, 1864, Jack's book appeared, 'The Discovery of the Sources of the Nile.' It sold like wildfire at first, and then suddenly dropped, like the stick of the firework. Then Messrs. Blackwood brought out 'What led to the Discovery of the Sources of the Nile,' and people were saying that 'non-discovery would be the fitting term;' and the second stick fell from the rocket. I understood then the danger to which I had exposed myself by *not travelling alone*, when I perceived that a lake, seen only for twenty miles, at the southern edge, was prolonged by mere guesswork to two hundred and forty miles to the north—enough to stultify the whole Expedition. Had we met at Bath, the discussion which *must* have resulted would have brought forth a searching scrutiny upon *both our Expeditions*, and mine would have been found to have been a genuine article; as it is, I am obliged to remain dumb upon many points upon which, if Jack had been alive, I should certainly have spoken. After so long a silence upon the subject, I am justified in drawing public attention as to what was effected by *my* Expedition, in which I was not only unaided, but I may say hindered. I went into the country ignorant of it, its language, trade, manners, and customs, preceded only by a French naval officer, who was murdered almost directly he landed. My friend Hamerton, the Consul at Zanzibar, was dying. Without money, or support, or influence, lacking in the necessaries of life, I led the most disorderly caravan that ever man could gather together, into the heart of Eastern Africa, and discovered the Tanganyika and the Nyanza Lakes. I brought home sufficient information to smooth the path of all who chose to follow me. They had but to read 'The Lake Regions of Central Africa' (2 vols., 1860), and the whole of Vol. XXXIII. of the *Proceedings of the Royal Geographical Society* (Clowes and Sons, 1860), to know all about it. Dr. Beke called mine emphatically 'a memorable expedition;' but, except for a few esteemed friends, my work has been ignored and forgotten. *My* labours rendered the road easy for Jack and Captain Grant. I opened the line to Englishmen, and they had but to follow me.

"I bring no charge against Jack of asserting what he does not believe. In his Taunton speech he declared that, 'as the *real* discoverer, he had in 1857 hit the Nile on the head, and in 1863 drove it down to the Mediterranean,' and he believed these words as firmly and as unreasoningly as he did in his Victoria Nyanza Lake or his 'Mountains of the Moon.' His peculiar habit of long brooding over thoughts and memories, secreting them until some sudden impulse brought them forth, may explain this great improbability. He could not grasp a fact; hence his partial eclipse of the moon on the 5th and 6th of January, 1863, which did not occur. A 'luxurious village' was a mass of dirty huts, a 'king of kings' is a petty chief, a 'splendid port' is a display of savagery. The French of those parts are barbarians, with little more knowledge than their neighbours.

"Captain Grant also has never acknowledged the vast benefits which the second Expedition derived from mine. I therefore mean to produce a small volume, called 'The Nile Basin,'* in which I shall distinctly deny that any 'misleading, by my instructions from the Royal Geographical Society as to the position of the White Nile,' left me unconscious of the vast importance of ascertaining the Rusizi river's direction. The fact is Jack was deaf and almost blind, I was paralytic, we were both helpless, and I may add penniless; we did our best to reach it, and we failed.

"I must also again allude to Jack's 'Mountains of the Moon.' He published a sketch-map in *Blackwood's Magazine*, September and October, 1859, which showed a huge range estimated to rise six or eight thousand feet high. At first the segment of a circle, it gradually shaped itself into a colt's foot, and effectually cut off all access from the Tanganyika to the Nile; then he owns in his book, p. 263, to having built up these mountains on solely geographical *reasonings*, deriving from the same source the Nile, the Congo, and the Zambesi. Now, Captain Grant afterwards said that the mountains were the work of the engraver, and that Jack was amused by them; but if he had looked into the map-room of the Royal Geographical Society, he would have found Jack's own map, showing the lunar horseshoe in all its hideousness. Now, in the map done by Stanford, the Mountains of the Moon are placed in the northern extremity of the Lake Tanganyika; but in his *own* map, published in his *journal*, he altered their position, and inserted them round the western north-sides of the more northern Lake Rusizi, which was manifestly a widening of the river; and again he said, p. 324, 'It was a pity I did not change the course I gave to the Maraungu river, *i.e.* making it an effluent, and not an influent; I forgot my lesson, and omitted to do so;' and when he inquires of the natives whether this river runs *into* or *out* of the lake, he says, 'Because they all say it runs into

* Which he did in 1864.—I. B.

the lake, *I* am quite convinced that it runs out of the lake,' which, to say the least of it, is an extraordinary train of reasoning.

"Mr. Macqueen, an old and scientific geographer, was told by an Arab who had been to Unyamwezi, 'It is well known by all the people there, that the river which goes through Egypt takes its source and origin from the Lake Tanganyika.' Dr. Beke, an old and scientific traveller, quotes De Barros: 'The Nile has its origin in a great lake, the Tanganyika, and after traversing many miles northwards, it enters a very large lake which lies under the equator.' This would, I believe, be the Bahr el Ghazal, or the Luta Nzigé. With regard to the levels, the Tanganyika is allowed but 1844 feet, but during our exploration the state of our vision would, I am sure, explain a greater difference than the fraction of a degree. At Conduci, a harbour on the East African coast, a common wooden bath instrument boiled at 2·14° Fahr.: this would give a difference of about 1000 feet. The Nyanza was made 3550 feet high by my expedition, that of Jack raised it to 3745 feet.

"Mr. Macqueen, F.R.G.S., author of the 'Geographical Survey of Africa,' wrote a very able review on Jack's expedition with Captain Grant, and I shall reprint it in the 'Nile Basin' from the *Morning Advertiser*. In it he speaks in unmeasured terms about the cruelty of the manner in which he crushed Consul Petherick with his ill-temper, vanity, and jealousy, having used him in his own service all he could. Petherick wrote: 'To add insult to injury, flesh and blood cannot bear it, and, whilst not wishing to depreciate the labours of others, I am determined to maintain my own;' and Mrs. Petherick wrote an account of Jack's dining with them. They had a tremendously large ham, which they had brought from England, cooked. They were to wait with boats, well armed and provisioned, until Jack should appear at Gondokoro. They waited long beyond their time, they spent their money, they lost their health, they sacrificed their own trade, and Jack, having helped himself to what he wanted, treated them *de haut en bas*. Mrs. Petherick writes: 'We always meant to open this ham when we met Speke. During dinner I endeavoured to prevail on Speke to accept our aid, but he drawlingly replied, "I do not wish to recognize the 'succour-dodge.'"' She adds, 'The rest of the conversation I am not well enough to repeat. I grow heartsick thinking of it after all our toil. Never mind, his heartlessness will recoil upon him yet. I soon left the table, and would never dine with them again.'

"But when Jack got home, and was in the full fling of his triumph, his unfounded charges influenced the Government, who had employed Petherick to convey assistance and advice to Jack, whose flippant conduct caused this man and his wife to be thrown overboard without pity, his private fortune wasted, his character as a merchant and a public servant blasted, being also deprived of his Consulship. Mr. Macqueen, in his paper, said that Speke left England on a great and noble enterprise. He was patronised and supported by the British Government, by the Royal Geographical Society, and the good wish and sanguine hopes of the public. He says it is incredible that any man, but especially a man who had gone a thousand miles to see the position of the outlet of the Nile supposed to be in that spot, should have remained five months within eight miles of it, without hearing or seeing something certain about the great object of his search, or have found some means to see it. He says, 'All that he brought back was the sacrifice and ruin of zealous associates, first Burton, then Petherick, Grant treated as a cipher, and a mass of intelligence, if such it can be called, so muddled and confused that we do not believe he understands it himself. We regret the miserable termination which the second great African exploration has had; we lament the time that has been lost, and the money that has been spent; but the only person to blame for its poor results is Captain Speke himself.'"

The following five maps, brought up to 1867, are inserted with the kind permission of the Royal Geographical Society, whose property they are.

BURTON and SPEKE, May 1858.

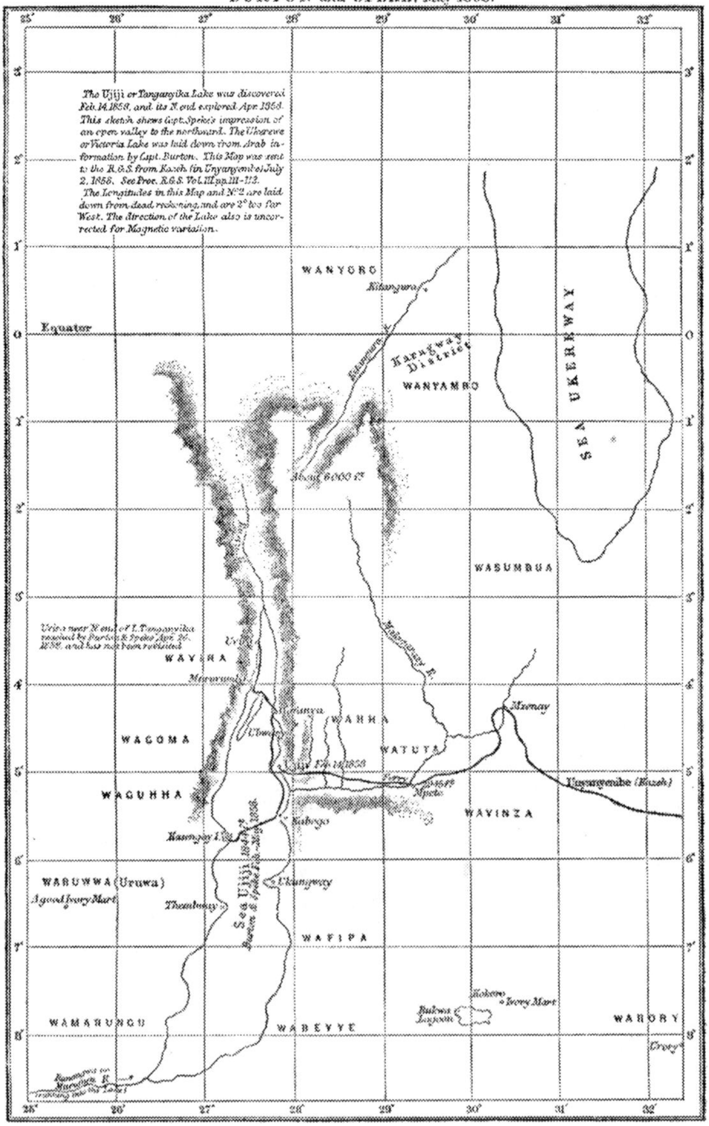

The Ujiji or Tanganyika Lake was discovered Feb. 14. 1858, and its N. end explored Apr. 1858. This sketch shews Capt. Speke's impression of an open valley to the northward. The Ukerewe or Victoria Lake was laid down from Arab information by Capt. Burton. This Map was sent to the R. G. S. from Kazeh (in Unyanyembe) July 2. 1858. See Proc. R. G. S. Vol. III. pp. 111–113.

The Longitudes in this Map and No. 2 are laid down from dead reckoning, and are 2° too far West. The direction of the Lake also is uncorrected for Magnetic variation.

Uvira near N. end of L. Tanganyika reached by Burton & Speke Apr. 26. 1858, and has not been revisited.

Equator

WANYORO

Kitangura

Karagway District

WANYAMBO

SEA UKEREWAY

About 6000 ft

WASUMBUA

Uvira

WAVINA

WAGOMA

WAHHA

WATUTA

Msenay

Ujiji Feb. 14. 1858

Unyanyembe (Kazeh)

WAGUHHA

WAVINZA

Kasengey I.

Kabogo

Sea Ujiji

WARUWWA (Uruwa)

A good Ivory Mart

Thembwy

Ukaungway

WAFIPA

Kokoro

Ivory Mart

Bulwa Lagoon

WAMARUNGU

WABEYYE

WARORY

Crosy

SPEKE. 1858.

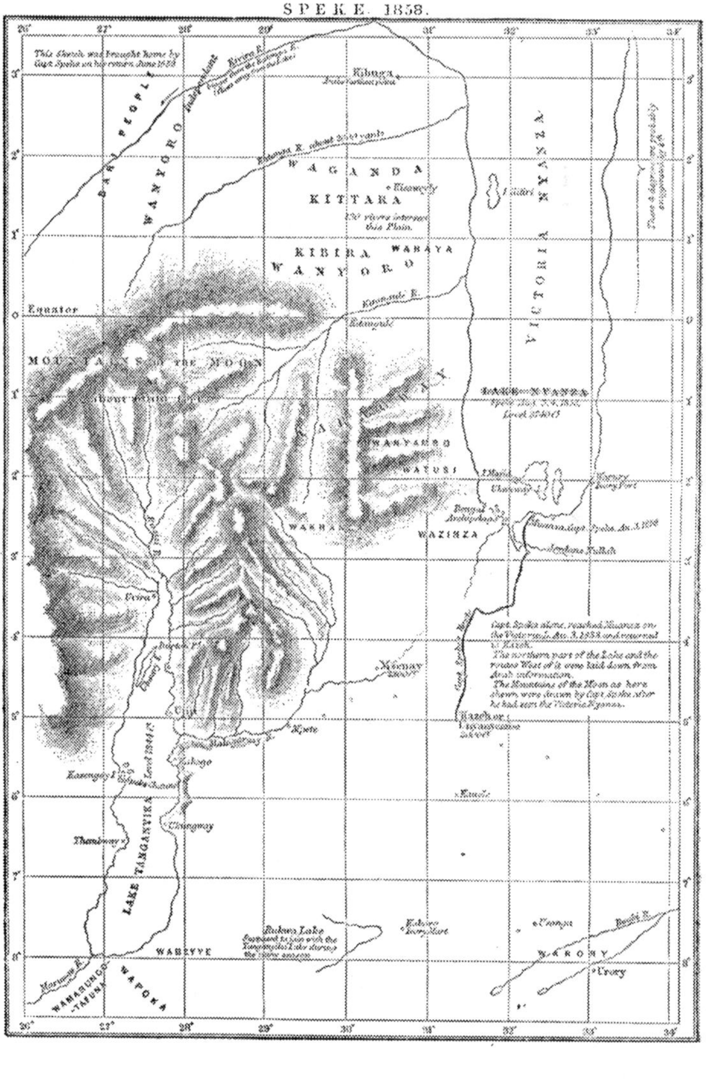

This Sketch was brought home by Capt. Speke on his return, June 1858

BARI PEOPLE

WANYORO

WAGANDA

KITTARA

KIBIRA

WABAYA

WANYORO

Equator

MOUNTAINS OF THE MOON

VICTORIA NYANZA

LAKE NYANZA

WANYAMBO

WATUSI

WAZINZA

Capt. Speke alone, reached Muanza on the Victoria L. Au. 3, 1858 and returned to Kazeh.

The northern part of the Lake and the rivers West of it were laid down from Arab information.

The Mountains of the Moon as here shown, were drawn by Capt. Speke after he had seen the Victoria Nyanza.

Kazeh or Unyanyembe

Uvira

Ujiji

LAKE TANGANYIKA

WAPOKA

WAKORY

Urory

SPEKE and GRANT, 1863.

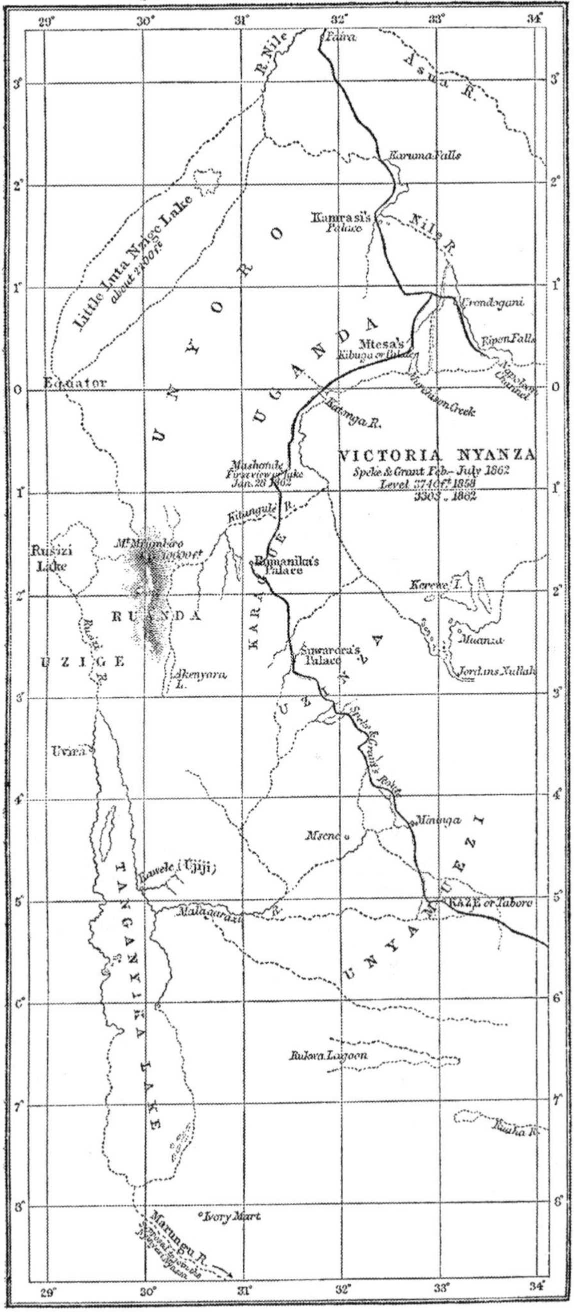

29° 30° 31° 32° 33° 34°

R. Nile
Faira
Asua R.
Karuma Falls
Kamrasi's Palace
Nile R.
Little Luta Nzige Lake about 2,000 ft
U N Y O R O
Urondogani
Ripon Falls
Mtesa's Kibuga or Palace
U G A N D A
Napoleon Channel
Murchison Creek
Equator
Katonga R.
VICTORIA NYANZA
Speke & Grant Feb.–July 1862
Level 3740 ft 1858
3308 „ 1862
Mashonde First view of lake Jan. 28 1862
Kitangulé R.
Rusizi Lake
Mt Mfumbiro 10,000 ft
Rumanika's Palace
K A R A G U E
Kerewe I.
R U A N D A
Rusizi R.
U Z I G E
Muanza
Suwarora's Palace
Akenyara L.
Jordans Nullah
U Z I N Z A
Uvira
Speke & Grant's Route
Msene
Mininga
Kawele (Ujiji)
T A N G A N Y I K A L A K E
KAZE or Tabora
Malagarazi R.
U N Y A M U E Z I
Rukwa Lagoon
Ruaha R.
Ivory Mart
Marungu R.

3° 2° 1° 0 1° 2° 3° 4° 5° 6° 7° 8°

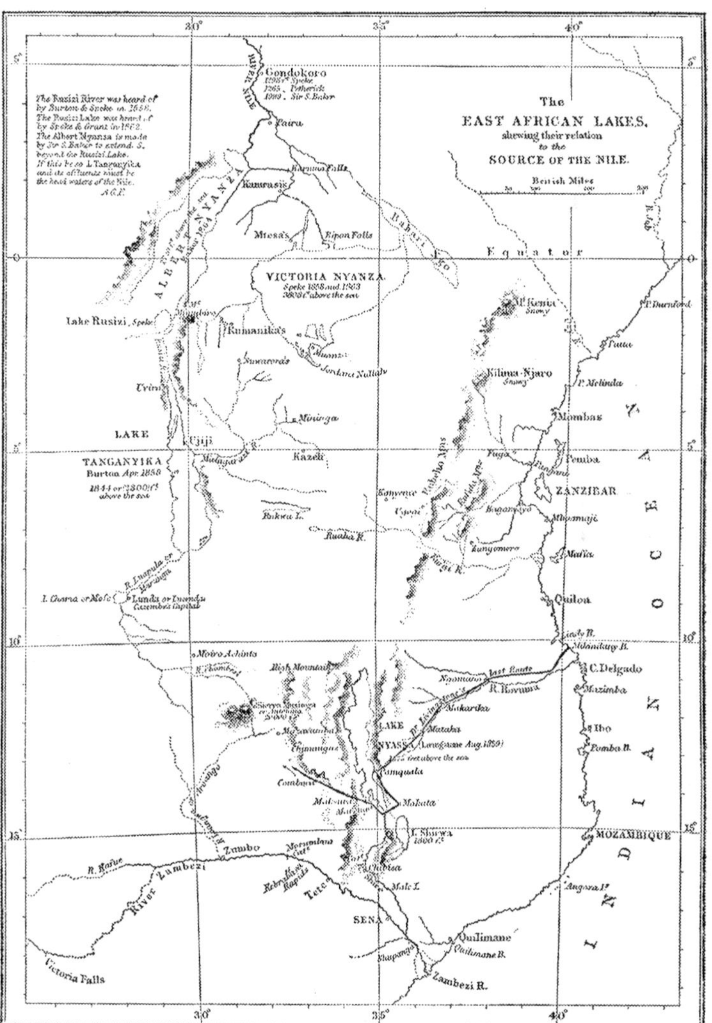

The
EAST AFRICAN LAKES,
shewing their relation
to the
SOURCE OF THE NILE.
British Miles
Gondokoro
Kamrasis
VICTORIA NYANZA
Lake Rusizi
LAKE
TANGANYIKA
Ujiji
Kazeh
Kilima-Njaro
Mombas
Pemba
ZANZIBAR
Quiloa
C. Delgado
LAKE
NYASSA
MOZAMBIQUE
Zumbo
River Zambezi
Tete
SENA
Quilimane
Zambezi R.
Victoria Falls
INDIAN OCEAN
Equator

SIR S.W. BAKER. 1864.

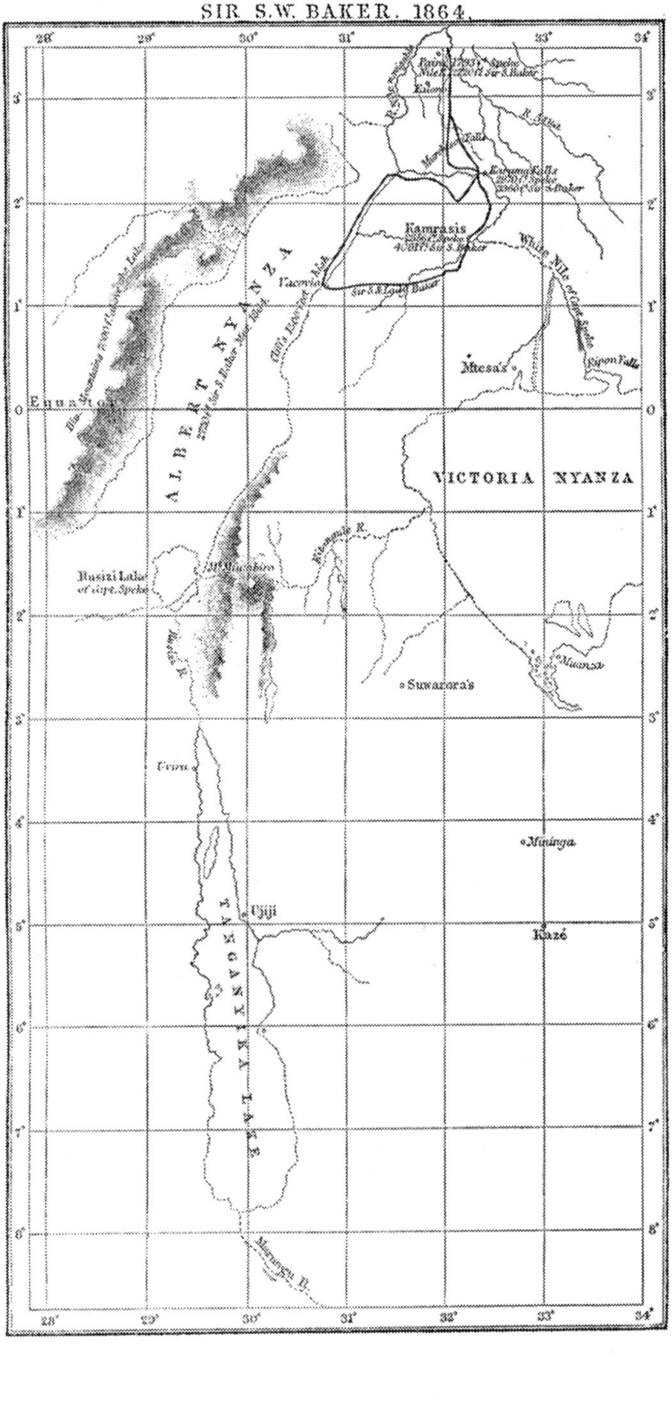

28° 29° 30° 31° 32° 33° 34°

ALBERT NYANZA

VICTORIA NYANZA

TANGANYIKA LAKE

Kamrasis

Vacovia

Karuma Falls

White Nile of Capt. Speke

Ripon Falls

Mtesa's

Rusizi Lake of Capt. Speke

Mt Mfumbiro

Kitangule R.

Suwarora's

Muanza

Mininga

Ujiji

Kazé

28° 29° 30° 31° 32° 33° 34°

CHAPTER XIX.

SANTOS, SÃO PAULO, BRAZIL—RICHARD'S SECOND CONSULATE.

"My native land's the land of Palms,
The Sabiá sings there.
In this drear land no song-birds' notes
With our sweet birds compare.

"More radiant stars bestrew our skies,
More flowers bedeck our fields,
A fuller life teems in our woods,
More love our Home-life yields.

"My wakeful thoughts—alone—at night
Full of sweet memories are,
Of mine own land,—the land of Palms,
Where sings the Sabiá.

"My land has sweetest fruits and flowers,
Such sweets I find not here.
Alone—at night—in wakeful hours
More pleasures find I there,
Mine own dear land,—the land of Palms,
Where sings the Sabiá.

"God, in His mercy, grant I may
To that dear land return,
Ere the sweet flowers and fruits decay,
Which here, alas! I mourn;
That once again, before I die,
I may the Palm-Trees see,
And hear again the Sabiá
Sing its sweet melody."

DANIEL FOX (*translated from the Brazilian of the poet Antonio Gonçalves Dias*).

DURING this stay at home we had represented to Lord Russell how miserable our lives were, being always separated by the climate of Fernando Po, and he very kindly transferred us to Santos, in the Brazils, where I *could* go. So Richard agreed that I should go out with him to Portugal for a trip; that he should go on to Rio de Janeiro; that I should return to London to wind up our affairs, and then join him at Santos; and we set sail in May. I now began to learn Portuguese. We had very bad weather, and on the fourth day we arrived at Lisbon, and went to the Braganza Hotel.

Here was a totally new experience for me. Our bedroom was a large white-washed place; there were three holes in the wall, one at the bedside bristling with horns, and these were cockroaches some three inches long. The drawing-room was gorgeous with yellow satin, and the magnificent yellow curtains were sprinkled with these crawling things; the consequence was that I used to stand on a chair and scream. This annoyed Richard very much. "A nice sort of traveller and companion *you are* going to make," he said. "I suppose you think you look very pretty and interesting, standing on that chair and howling at those innocent creatures." This hurt me so much that, without descending from the chair, I stopped screaming and made a meditation, like St. Simon Stylites on his pillar, and it was, "that if I was going to live in a country always in contact with these and worse things, though I had a perfect horror of anything black and crawling, it would never do to go on like that." So I got down, fetched a basin of water and a slipper, and in two hours, by the watch, I had knocked ninety-seven of them into it. It cured me. From that day I had no more fear of vermin and reptiles, which is just as well in a country where nature is over-luxuriant. A little while after we changed our rooms, we were succeeded by the late Lord and Lady Lytton, and, to my infinite delight, I heard the same screams coming from the same rooms a little while after. "There!" I said in triumph, "you see, I am not the *only* woman who does not like cockroaches."

Here he insisted on taking me to a bull-fight, because he said I ought to see everything *once*. But there is a great difference between a Spanish and a Portuguese bull-fight. In Portugal the bull's horns are knobbed; he does not gore horses nor dogs—he tosses men softly, and if I do not mind that, it is because the men go in for it willingly, are paid for it, and are bred to it as a profession from father to son for endless generations. The only torment the bull has to endure is the darts thrown into the fat part of his neck. If he fights well, they are taken out afterwards and his wounds dressed with oil, and he is turned out loose to fight another day. If he won't fight, he is killed for beef; so you get all the science and the play without the disgusting cruelty. At first I crouched down with my hands over my face, but I gradually peeped through first one finger and then another, until I saw the whole of it; but it awed me so much that I was almost afraid to come out of our box, for fear we should meet a bull on the stairs.

We then went to Cintra, and to Mafra. Richard found an old mosque in Cintra, and we saw Mr. Cooke's beautiful house.* For people who have not been to Lisbon, I may say that Belem Church is, I think, quite the most beautiful thing in the world. It is one of the noted dreams in marble. From Lisbon we went on to Corregado, to Serçal and Caldas, to see Alcobaço, where there is a most beautiful monastery. In the days of rebellion and persecution, the days of Don Miguel, somewhere in the early thirties, the monks had to clear out, and my father took one of them, whose name was Antonio Barboza de Lima, to be our tutor and chaplain, when we were children (and he is now buried at Mortlake); so Richard and I took an extra interest in the details. We then went to Batalha, where there is another beautiful monastery, to Pombal, to Leiria, and to Coimbra. This seat of learning is one of the prettiest, dirtiest, and slowest places imaginable, and we soon made our way to Oporto, and went to Braga to see the Whit-Sunday *fête*, from thence to Malozinhos. This northern part of Portugal is ever so much more beautiful than Lisbon. The more you get into Douro, and the nearer you are to Spain, the larger and handsomer become the people.

However, our time was short, and, after a delightful two months' Portuguese exploration, we had to get back to Lisbon, where we saw another bull-fight, and Richard embarked for Brazil. I promised him to go back by the very next steamer that sailed. As I used to keep my word *very literally*, a few hours after his departure, a very tiny steamer came in, much worse than the West African boats; but I thought myself obliged to go, and we started at 9.20 in the evening, in spite of north-easterly gales, and had a bad time of it in the Bay of Biscay, she being only 428 tons. The route was from London to Lisbon, Gibraltar, Mazagan, Mogador, Canary Islands, coast of Spain, Morocco, and Portugal. On board, besides myself, having made the same mistake, was Dona Maria Rita Tenorio y Moscoso, who afterwards married the Portuguese Minister in London, Count Lavradio. We were in a tremendous fog off Beachy Head, went aground somewhere near Erith in the fog, and were very glad to land on the eighth day, having roughed it prodigiously. I note nothing important except some very interesting experiments at Mr. William Crookes's, both chemically and spiritualistically.

By end of August, *i.e.* in a month, my work was accomplished, and I may as well now say, that whenever we were going to leave England

* One of the lions of Cintra.

for any length of time, he used mostly to like to start *at once* in light marching order, go forward and prospect the place, and leave me behind to settle up our affairs, pay and pack, bringing up the heavy baggage in the rear. It saved time, as double work got done in the space; so, having completed all, I embarked from Southampton in one of the Royal mails. Heavy squalls and thunder and lightning began next day, and at Lisbon the thermometer was 80° in the cabin. We passed Santa Cruz, off Teneriffe, having a good view of the Peak. We got to St. Vincent in ten days, quite the most wretched hole in the world—only barren rocks, and the heat was like a dead wall. We had very charming people on board, mostly all foreigners, except Mr. and Mrs. Wodehouse, and Mr. Conyngham. Neptune came on board on the night of the 24th, we crossed the Line on the 25th, and the ceremonies of "crossing the Line" were gone through, the tubbing and shaving, the greasy pole and running in sacks, and a hair was drawn across the field-glasses, through which you were requested to look at the "Line." The perhaps most striking thing to a new-comer going out, is losing the Great Bear and the Northern Star, and all that one is accustomed to, and exchanging them for the Southern Cross and others.

We arrived at Pernambuco on the 27th, and there I found all the letters that I had written to my husband since we parted, accumulated in the post-office, consequently I did not know what he would think had become of me. Here we had a very rough sea and boiling surf. I passed the evening miserably, thinking about the letters; though everything was looking very beautiful, and the band was playing tunes and everybody waltzing, I sat by the wheel and had a good "boo-hoo" in the moonlight. On the 30th we reached Bahía, and went ashore and lunched with Mrs. Baines, and visited Mr. Charles Williams. The women wanted to sell me small black babies in the market for two shillings. We sailed the same day, and had heavy weather. I rose at five, just before we went into the harbour at Rio. It is about the most glorious sight that a human being can behold, at sunrise and at sunset, the mountains being of most fantastic shapes, and the colours that of an opal. Richard said it beats all the scenery he had ever seen in his life—even the Bosphorus. He came on board at half-past eight in the morning, and we had a joyful meeting, and I handed him all the letters which, by some strange mischance, had accumulated at Pernambuco during our month's separation.

We stayed at the Estrangeiros Hotel, where there was quiet, fresh air, beautiful scenery, and several disadvantages, including cockroaches and mosquitoes. We enjoyed a great deal of hospitality, both Naval and Diplomatic, and had several excursions and picnics. All nations have a "Flagship" and other ships in the harbour; there is a great deal of gaiety and *esprit de corps* amongst the Diplomatic and Consular service. Amongst others here was Mr. Gerald Perry, our Minister, Sir Edward and Lady Thornton, Chevalier Bunsen, the son of the great Bunsen, with whom we used to have learned discussions very often in the evening on "Geist" and other scientific subjects, and German metaphysics generally. Mrs. Elliot, the wife of Admiral Elliot, the Admiral of the Station, was a very kind friend to me, on this my first *début* into this kind of life. We had our first dinner-party at our hotel, and after all the formal people had gone, Richard and the young ones proposed a moonlight walk. We went down to the Botanical Gardens, and tried to get in, but the gates were locked—tall iron gates—and nothing would do but that, as we could not get in, we should scramble over them. It was quite contrary to law, but we had a nice walk about the gardens. There was either no watch-dog, or the guard being unaccustomed to such daring, was not on the look-out; but there were too many snakes about, and particularly the coral snake, of which nobody has any idea in England, because its colours fade as soon as it is put in spirits; so we all came back and climbed over the gate again, and got back without any danger.

But we had come out of hot rooms, and it was dewy and damp, so next day I had my first fever. It consisted of sickness and vomiting, colic, dizziness, faintness, shivering, heat and cold, delirium, thirst, disgust of food. The treatment was calomel, castor oil, hot baths, blankets, emetics, ice, starvation, and thirty grains of quinine. It did not last long, but my being delirious alarmed Richard very much, and he mesmerized me.

In Rio one generally takes a native steamer, which is not very comfortable, to go to Santos, one hundred and twenty miles south of Rio. As soon as I was able to move, Captain Napier took us on board H.M.S. *Triton* for Santos. It was very rough. The captain had given up his quarters to me; the stern ports were not closed, and at night a tremendous sea came in, and swept our cots. It continued very squally, and we anchored at Ilha Grande; next day the men practised gunnery and small-arms, and Captain Napier made me practise with a revolver. It was fifty-eight miles from Rio to Ilha Grande, a pretty mountainous island, which surrounds a lovely bay, with a few huts on it. We then proceeded seventy-eight miles further to St. Sebastian, which is a grand copy of the Straits of Messina (Scylla and Charybdis), and spoils your after-view of what people who have seen nothing bigger, think so wonderful. You steam through an arm of the sea, appearing like a gigantic river, surrounded by mountains (whose verdure casts a green shade upon the water), dotted with houses, small towns, and gardens. The chief town is St. Sebastian, which is very populous. The water is calm; there is a delicious sea-breeze. When Richard went ashore they saluted him with the usual number of guns, and Brazilian local "swells" came off to visit us.

Santos, Brazil, his Second Consulate.

We awoke next morning, the 9th of October, 1865, off the Large. About eleven we were at the mouth, whence one steams about nine miles up a serpentine river, and at one o'clock anchored opposite Santos. We saluted, and the Consular corps came off to see us. We stayed on board that night, and we left the ship at half-past seven next day, loitering about Santos.

Santos was only a mangrove swamp, and in most respects exactly like the West Coast of Africa, the road slushy and deep. Tree-ferns, African mangrove, brown water full of tannin, patches of green light and green dark, in rare clearings here and there houses and fields near town, much water, and good rice. The sand runs up to the mangrove jungle; there is good fishing, and deer in the forests. The heavy sea sometimes washes into the gardens, spoils the flowers, and throws up whale-bones in all directions. At the time of our arrival, the railway from Santos to São Paulo, about eighty miles into the interior, was only just beginning, and a large staff of Englishmen were engaged upon it. Mr. J. J. Aubertin, now, since his freedom, poet, author, and traveller, was then superintendent of it. Richard had been here, and inspected the place before my arrival, although he had met me at Rio, and he had arranged, as there were *two* places *equally requiring the presence of a Consul* (São Paulo on the top of the Serra, and Santos on the coast), that we should live at both places, riding up and down as occasion required, thus keeping our health; and Mr. Glennie, the Vice-Consul—who had gone to Santos as a boy, had been there over forty years, had married there, was perfectly devoted to it, and the only hardship he would have known would have been to live out of it—could remain there. His one ambition of life was to be Consul of Santos, and when we left, some years after, and his nomination was just going out to him, he died—as Richard used to say, "so like Provy."

We therefore, that same day, went in trollies to Mugis, where we lunched. Richard and Captain Napier had started on foot, and soon after Mr. Aubertin and thirteen others joined us. We were twenty-one people. Dr. and Mrs. Hood lived at the foot of the Serra, and they gave us a big tea-dinner. Mrs. Hood, the widow, with her now large grown-up family, strange to say, is now my near neighbour in Mortlake. Next day, what with mules, walking, riding, and occasional trollies, we got at the top of the Serra. There was a huge chasm over which the rail would have to pass on a bridge, with an almost bottomless drop. There were only planks across it; but, as I was on in front, supposing that was what we had got to cross, I walked right across it, about some two hundred yards. When I got to the other side, I turned round to speak, but nobody answered me, and facing round I saw the whole company standing on the other side, not daring to breathe, and my husband looking ghastly; so I turned round and was going to walk back again, when they motioned me off by signs, and all began to file round another way on *terra firma*. It was fortunate that I had such a good head, and did not know my danger.

The train line up the Serra is a very steep incline, one in nine, and is managed by a chain with a stationary engine at the top, a train being hooked on at each end of the rope. On one side was a mountain wall, and the other side a bottomless abyss, but the whole thing was quite beautiful through virgin forest. At this time it was not far advanced enough, and we rode up on mules. At the top a locomotive was kept to take us into São Paulo, which reminded us of Bergamo, in Italy, where we all dined at the little French inn. The next day we took a trip to what was then the end of the line, twelve miles beyond São Paulo, but at this time these trips were part mules, part trollies, part walking ones. We came back to dinner; there were speeches, and we wished the "Tritons" good-bye. Richard went down with them to set up his Consulate, and I remained to look for a house, and set up our *first real home*. After twelve or thirteen days, I went down to Santos by the diligence, by bad roads, but with a lovely panorama. The diligence takes one as far as Cubatão, where a little steamer plies for a couple of hours, first up a fine stream, between banks of tangled magnificence in the vegetation line, then an arm of the sea, or rather lagoons. The journey occupies seven carriage and two boat hours.

The worst of Santos, besides the steaming heat enclosed within and at the bottom of the hills, arising from the mangrove swamps, was the sand-flies and the mosquitoes. Richard was quite impervious to all other vermin, but the sand-flies used to make him come out all over bumps. For the rest, he used to say that he liked to have me near him—it was just like having "catch 'em alive" for flies, as everything came and bit me, and I was not fit to be seen, and spared him.

The fact is, I had fresh English blood, and it was rather a treat to them. The nicest thing was to drive out to the Barra. Captain Richard Hare, R.N., then came in, and we made a large party to stay there. The Barra was our fashionable bathing-place; the sea rolled right in to the strip of sand between it and the mangrove swamps, on the edge of which were (at that time) a few huts, with windows and doors opening on to the sand. In some there were no windows; they only closed by a wooden shutter.

After staying there for some time with Richard, I went up to São Paulo again, because I was getting feverish; it was wet and windy, and it took me eleven hours and a half. On going up, I engaged a very curious little fellow in our service, who deserves a few lines. Chico was thirty-five years of age; he was about four feet high, but perfectly well proportioned, as black as a coal, brimming full of intelligence, and could put his hand to anything. He had just been emancipated. He remained with us the whole time we were in Brazil, and became my right-hand man—more of him anon.

At last I found an old convent, No. 72, Rua do Carmo, which opened on the street in its front, and ran a long way back behind on an eminence, which commanded a view of almost boundless horizon into the country, and was exceedingly healthy. I immediately took it, cleaned it, painted and whitewashed it, and furnished it, and engaged slaves, paying their masters so much, and so much to them, as if they were free men. They were all Catholics, and I made a little chapel for them.

The slaves in Brazil, as a rule, formed, as it were, part of the family, and in ninety-five houses out of a hundred they were kindly treated and happy, but the remaining five out of the hundred were brutal; but, however, in *all* cases, the poor creatures were told, or, if not told, were allowed to believe, that they had no souls, and nothing to look forward to. I, on the contrary, taught them, and had regular lecture and catechism for them, that not only had they souls, but that, although they were condemned by class and colour and custom to be slaves upon earth, just as it was in the Bible, that once dead, they, and we, would stand equal before God. The priest used to come to my little Oratory, where I had the Bishop's leave to have Mass and the Sacraments, and we all received Communion together. They were very happy, the house went upon oiled wheels, and I never had occasion to dismiss a servant the whole time I was there. The differences were chiefly amongst themselves. Richard having settled his Consulate at Santos, and I having prepared our home in São Paulo, he came up and joined me, and for the first time since our marriage we were absolutely settled in a home of our own.

Up the country in Brazil, people always get one or two things in their first few years. You either break out all over boils, so that you cannot put a pin's point between them, and if you have a weak place, they come there in clusters, and you can neither sit nor stand, kneel or lie, and you are an object of misery for some months; but if you have strength, and can pull through it, you bloom out with stronger health than ever after that. This happened to me. I had to be slung up. A friend gave me a barrel of porter, and it was alternately "faint" and a "glass of porter," which revived me for a few minutes, and then more faint and more porter, *ad infinitum.* By the time the barrel of porter was finished, I was convalescent, and when any new ones attempted to break out, a friend gave me two things to try—and I tell it for the sake of those who may follow me; it was to draw a ring of caustic round one, and a ring of laudanum round the other. The caustic ones did not answer, but the ring of laudanum made them disappear, and I got splendid health, which lasted at least seventeen years. Now, people who do not get the boils are bound to get one or more of the complicated diseases of the country, and that is just what happened to Richard. We had no doctors up there, that I am aware of.

On the 17th of January, 1866, we had an awful storm, worse than any known for twenty-five years; there was an awful blackness, the lightning was red, the wind drove in the windows, the hail was jagged pieces of ice one inch in diameter, sharp and long, and made round holes like a bullet, there was a network of flashes, rain from all quarters—a regular cyclone. It drove through the room fronting north, which was like a ship's cabin in a gale. We saw the cathedral struck, the cross knocked off, tiles blown away; the hotel room was like a shower-bath, with a continuous stream of rain. Several houses were struck, some of the doors split, and the streets quite flooded; people were frightened, and lighted candles, and brought out the Madonna. There were sharp rattlings like earthquake; it blew a clock against the walls away; the people all met as after a revolution in Paris. The windows were everywhere broken, and the water looked black. It was quite local, and did not touch the shipping. In the town four were killed and five wounded. The next day was very hot.

Santos is six thousand miles away from Europe, and we only got letters once a month.

Richard's study was the most important feature in the house. It was a long room, running out on an eminence forty feet long, with a good terrace at the end of it, on which we had a telescope, and every convenience for astronomy and observations; and perhaps the other most striking part of the house was a large room, which occupied the whole centre of the house, and opened on the stairs. This was dining-room, receiving-room, and everything. Directly below that was a similar place, that was more like stables than room. It was my refuge for the needy and homeless after dark; they were fed and housed, and turned out in early morning.

On the 27th of July he notes in his journal: "Dream that a bad tooth fell out, followed by five or six big drops of blood; noted the day, and found that my poor friend Steinhaüser had died of heart disease quite suddenly in Switzerland that day." On the 14th of August, 1866, the first through-train went from Santos to Jundiahy. There was a *fête* in consequence, and the company had the bad taste only to omit the Consul and his wife from the invitations to all the English. On the 22nd of August Richard went to stop with the priests of the seminary (Capuchins), which he often did, in their *chacara*, or country-house, where he studied astronomy with Fray João, and metaphysics, physics, and algebra, with Père Germain. Here he was engaged in writing "Vikram and the Vampire," and he got a concession for the lead mines of Iporanga, in São Paulo. On the 21st of December we went down to Rio for our Christmas, which we spent at Petropolis. On the 12th of November some one put a stone on the railway to throw the train off, and on the 19th it was said that a part of the rails was pulled up.

In Santos and São Paulo we remained from 1865 to 1869, and I may say that his career here was equally active and useful, both on the coast and in the interior. We thoroughly explored our own province, São Paulo, which is larger than France. (I do not bore you with two pages of Brazilian names of places, because very few would know where they were, unless they had lived there and had worked in wild places, which is not likely.) We spent a good time at the gold mines and diamond diggings of Minas Geraës. He canoed down the river of San Francisco, fifteen hundred miles. He went to the Argentine Republic of the Páta-Paranà; he went to Paraguay for the purpose of reporting the state of the Paraguayan War to the Foreign Office. He crossed the Pampas and the Andes to Chili and Peru, amongst the dangerous Indians, whilst on sick leave for an illness which brought him almost to death's door. He visited the Pacific coast to inspect the scenes of the earthquake at Arica, returning by the Straits of Magellan, Buenos Ayres, and Rio de Janeiro.

Letters from Richard to *Fraser's Magazine* appeared in three numbers, headed, "From London to Rio de Janeiro." He likewise wrote three books—"The Highlands of Brazil," 2 vols., which I edited and brought out in 1869; "Vikram and the Vampire," one vol. of Hindú tales brought out in 1870; "Paraguay," 1 vol., brought out in 1870. He interested himself immensely in the coffee and cotton produce, Mr. Aubertin being at that time the "father of cotton" in Brazil, but his chief interest lay in the mining and mineral productions of the country. As I have said, he obtained the concession for the lead mines of Iporanga, and Sir Edward Thornton was very angry with him—took it in the sense of Consuls trading, and reported him home. Fortunately, we had the large mind of Lord Stanley (Lord Derby) at the head of the Foreign Office, and he, knowing how caged and misplaced Richard was at such a Consulate, thought he might at least be allowed that little bit of amusement, and sent back a despatch that he did not think that being interested in mineral production could be exactly classed under the head of trading.

Amongst other things, Richard discovered something remarkable. On one of our Expeditions we were stopping at a shanty close to a river, and seeing something glistening, he walked up the bed of the river, which was not deep, and scooped up some of the sand and put it in a jar. On washing it we found that it looked very like rubies. We sent it home to Mr. Crookes, F.R.S., the great chemical savant, and he wrote back, "If you get any more, bigger than this, throw up the Consulate and stick to the rubies." Now, Richard told me that this was only the dust washed down, and that the great stones must lie further up the head of the river. The shanty belonged to an old woman with a right for a good stretch up the river, and she would have joyfully sold it for £50. When I implored Richard almost on my knees to buy it, he would not, saying it would be quite wrong to defraud that poor woman out of her place, when she did not know that rubies were there; that if she *did* know, she would ask him an exorbitant sum; and, what was more, that no one could live there for three days without getting Brazilian fever, so that we should end by being like the dog in the fable, with the bit of cheese and the shadow in the water, and drop the reality for a shadow.

Life in Brazil, if in Rio, was very gay; life at São Paulo was very like a farmhouse life, with cordiality and sociability with the other farmhouses, and some of the good Brazilian society was very charming. The Brazilians are to the Portuguese what the Americans are to us. The Portuguese is heavy; the Brazilian is light, active, nervous, *spirituel*. Their parties are much enlivened by music and dance. They have several native dances, which are danced at the balls—one especial one, which is called the *carangueijo*, which is very active, very amusing, and very significant. The gentlemen and ladies dance it as furiously as the common people, as the Hungarians do the *czardas*. The Music consists of the *modinha*, which answers to our ballad, and is generally mournful; the *lundú*, which is mostly comic, and almost always in the minor key; and the *recitativo*, which consists of playing a flowing melodious accompaniment, and in a voice pitched and attuned to that, reciting a story of love or war or anything, often improvised at the moment. The negroes have their balls in the Plaza, or Square, and they will dance furiously for three consecutive days and nights to the same tune. It is amusing to watch for about an hour out of a window. The negro girls come out *décolletée* in pink or blue cotton—those are the swells—the others dress like natives.

What is so beautiful is Nature, the luxuriance of vegetable and animal life. Everything is so large—the palms, the cacti, and all the things which here are treasured as plants and bushes, are there fine trees. I have seen arums of which one leaf would be six feet long and five broad, behind which a big man could easily hide himself. The virgin forests are unspeakably beautiful, with their wild tangle of creeper and parasite. Orchids, of which (during the rage that lasted in England for them) one single one would have sold for £60, here grow wild—one only had to go out with a knife and grub them up from the trees or rocks; we sent boxes home to our friends. The fir of the country is the araucaria; the gum copaiba is eighty feet high. Flights of gaudy-coloured parrots and all sorts of beautiful coloured birds are on the trees; butterflies, some of which measure ten inches from one wing-tip to the other, when spread, float about the air like large sheets of paper—scarlet, peacock blue, emerald green, cream, white—in fact, every colour; and coming in and out of your room, are little humming-birds the size of a large bee, looking like an emerald or a ruby flitting about, and if you have the sense not to offer to touch them, and put a little wet sugar in a saucer, they will stay there for days; but if you try to catch them, they break their hearts and die. The tints of Brazil are always the tints of the opal in fine weather. The heat is awful, like the damp heat of a conservatory; I flourished in it.

En revanche, Brazil has no history save three hundred years, which relates its discovery and its gradual transfer from Indian natives to the first Portuguese settlers. The Jesuits erected all the buildings on the best sites, made roads, and cultivated; but the Indians are not exterminated—they are only driven inwards—and about ten days from our home our nearest Indians were the Bótacudos. You may see them in the Crystal Palace with their under-lip distended by a bit of wood. The nearest to us were friendly ones, and they would come down to São Paulo on rare occasions. They walk in Indian file, and when they passed our house, or any other friendly house, they threw their arms out towards the house—as if the whole file were pulled by a string—till they had gone by it; and that is their mode of friendly salute. When the railway was opened, they came down out of curiosity to see it. They looked upon the engine as a sort of malignant beetle, but at last they got less frightened, and all clambered upon it; but when it was time to start, and the driver gave the preliminary whistle, they sprang off like mad, and ran for their lives, nor could they be persuaded to mount again.

Another drawback was the reptiles and vermin. There is a large mosquito that fastens its prongs into your hand. I have seen a man let it suck, and then cut half its tail off, and it has gone on sucking and the blood running through—the mosquito being not in the least aware of its loss. Then there is a little grey, almost invisible, mosquito that makes no noise. In Trieste they call them *papataci* (papa-hold-your-tongue). There is the jigger, that gets into your flesh, generally under your toe-nail or under the sole of your foot, and the first time you are aware that there is anything the matter is by your limping, and you then discover that there is a something about the size of a pea in your foot. You send for a negress, who picks at your foot for a few minutes with a common pin—they won't use a needle or any other instrument, because if they did the bag would break, and the eggs would get into your blood—and presently, with a little hurting, she triumphantly holds it up at the end of the pin, puts on a soothing ointment, and you are all right at once. A man thought he should like to take a jigger home to show an English doctor, but it was six weeks from home, and his foot was cut off before he got there.

Another nuisance is the *carapato.* It is everywhere, but chiefly inhabits the coffee plantations. There are three sorts, which only vary in size and colour. It is a cross between a tick and a small crab; the biggest would be the size of a little finger-nail. If you ride through a coffee plantation you come out covered with them. I have more than once taken off my riding habit and found my jacket nailed to the skin from the outside; to pull them is to tear your flesh and produce a festering wound. You have to get into a hot bath, in which you put one or two bottles of *cachaça,* the spirit of the country, and that clears off most of them; and if any obstinate ones remain, you have to light a cigarette, and apply the hot end to their tails till they wriggle their own head and shoulders out from under your skin. Cockroaches you don't count, but you must always look in your sleeves, and dress, and boots, for large horned beetles or spiders or other horrors.

Poor W. H. Bates (the naturalist of the Royal Geographical Society), who was a great friend of ours, was laughed at because he spoke of spiders as big as a toy-terrier; but it is perfectly true—there *are* such spiders, though they are not seen in towns, only out in the forest, and they are the size of a good-sized crab. The body is hairy, and when they are angry they kick up and throw their hairs on you, which are poisonous. I was going to hit one, and a native drew me back and made me run away, for, he said, "it can spring at you, and it is instantaneous death." Richard and I did not go so far as to believe this, unless your blood is in a very bad state, but we did believe in its making people ill for several days. A priest was once going to say Mass, and he took his vestment down from the wall where it was hung up, and put it on, when he suddenly felt something hard in the centre of his back. He called to the servers and asked them to remove his vestment gently, without touching his back, telling them there was something inside. They did so, and it was one of these big spiders; when it was removed he fainted.

The people eat a large black ant, an inch and a half long. They bite off the fat body, which has to them a pleasant acid, and throw the head and legs away. Another use they make of them is to dress them up like dolls and sell them. The *copim*, or white ants, build nests like milestones. The people here believe in a sort of house-that-Jack-built as regards animal feeding. They believe that toads eat ants, that snakes eat toads, that owls eat snakes, also the geese, and that is why they are cheap.

Snakes are eyerywhere—in your garden, in your basement, in your rafters; and there is every description of them, from the boa-constrictor in the wilder parts, to the smallest. It is a common thing to hear the rattlesnake in the grass, and to scamper quickly. Those who kill them cut out the rattle and give it you for good luck. I have one now. At night, when you walk out you go with a lantern at the end of a stick, for the snake called *jararaquassú* lies curled up at night on the road, looking exactly like a heap of dust, and you would certainly put your foot on it; it bites your ankle, and they say that you live about ten minutes.

These things, which sound so wonderful in England, become so common to us who live and travel in Brazil, out of towns and off beaten tracks, that we get quite accustomed to them, as everyday parts of our lives, as you do to showers in April and dying flies in September; so that I should not know now that they had ever happened if I had not written them down at the time. No one who means to write, should ever trust to memory, because scene after scene fades like a dissolving view and is never caught again, whilst others rise to replace them.

The storms were another thing to be somewhat dreaded. For our three summer months, which are December, January, and February (whilst the Thames is frozen over in London), we, maybe, have 115° in the shade, and you see a semicircle of clouds beating up. As our house was on a kind of promontory running out, not to sea, but to grassy plain, we used to have to make "all taut" as if we were on board a ship, because when it did come it was like a cyclone, lasting two or three hours, and then clearing off, leaving everything bright and beautiful, the earth and air barely refreshed; but while it lasted the thunder and lightning were close to you. I have frequently thought that if there was one more clap my head would split—it deafened one. The windows were generally broken, there were balls of fire flying through the air—blue, red, yellow; and on one occasion, on a pitch-black night, perceiving a light from an opposite angle in my husband's room, I thought the house was on fire. The door was locked for the night. I ran down the corridor, unlocked the door, and, going in, found that the lightning had broken a window and had set on fire one of my husband's large rolling atlases on canvas, which hung from the walls. I ran back and called him, and it made him very uncomfortable. He thought that one of these lightning balls of fire must have done it, but there was no aerolite or anything to show. There was no fireplace in the room, not even a box of matches.

At nine p.m. on the 20th of October, a meteor fell with a loud sound, and lit up the City of São Paulo. Martinico Prado and some others were standing near it, and he fell insensible. It fell on the hill near São Bemte; blue flame was seen in our house at the same moment. It was intensely cold, but bright, beautiful weather.

We bought horses—one that had something of the mustang in it, called Hawa, which always carried me, and Penha, a smaller one from Campos for Richard. When we drove, it was in an American buckboard, seat for two, with huge wheels, and a little place to hold a box, with a pair of wild mules that used to pull one's arm off. When Richard did not ride with me, Chico used to take the second horse.

Chico and I never had but one quarrel, and I will give it as an illustration. When I first arrived, Richard used always to laugh at me, because I was so miserable at the way the cruel people treat the blacks—just in the same way that I, and so many others, feel about the treatment of animals—and he kept saying, "Oh, wait a bit, till you have lived with negroes a little; you philanthropic people always have to give in." Well, about six weeks after I got Chico, I heard a tremendous noise, and shrieks of agony proceeding from the kitchen, and rushing in the direction I found Chico roasting my favourite cat at the fire. I made one spring at his wool, and brought him to the ground. Richard, who had also rushed out at the noise, saw me, and clapped his hands, saying, "Brava! brava! I knew it would happen, but I did not think it would be quite so soon." I could only blubber out, "Oh, Jemmy, the little beast has roasted my cat." He then punished him himself, and Chico was a good boy evermore. In begging for forgiveness, he told us that their fathers and mothers always instructed them, that when Christ was thirsty, if He asked a little dog for water, the dog would go and fetch it for Him, but if He asked a cat for water, that it gave Him something in a cup, which I cannot mention in polite society; and that all the little negroes were taught to be cruel to cats, and that he *had* done atrocious things to cats, but he would never do so any more.

A very amusing thing was that this little monkey used to imitate his master in everything. If Richard bought a suit of clothes, he used immediately to take it to the tailor and get it exactly copied in small, and his evening suit especially. To go to a ball he was the *exact* copy of his master—white shirt, white tie, little dress suit, little *gibus*, and all. We used to make him come and show himself to us when he was dressed, to amuse us. Then, unlike his master, he started a toilette-table with mirror, perfumes, and scents, and his pillow was all edged with deep lace. Each of the best families had one of these intelligent negroes; they used to give supper-parties, and then stand up and make speeches, just like us. Mr. Aubertin's used to talk about the railway shares, and the value of cotton, and the coffee produce; another, belonging to a reverend gentleman, used to stand up and speak of the "benighted state of the souls of the black man and the brother;" but our Chico used to declaim on "the Negro's place in Nature," as he had heard Richard do in his lectures, and talk of the progress that they had made from the original ape (Darwinism), and how they might eventually hope to rise into a white man.

Portuguese studies got on very well, and the more I knew of it, the more I enjoyed myself; but it made me quite forget the Spanish I had learnt during my stay at Teneriffe, and whilst Richard occupied Fernando Po. Richard had always known Portuguese from his Goanese *Padre* in India. You cannot speak Spanish, Portuguese, and Italian at the same time; they are so alike, and yet so different.

Portuguese is the most Latin, and the most difficult of the lot, and has much more literature to reward you with than Spanish; but Spanish is the grandest and the most beautiful, albeit with less literature. Still it once happened to me to be in company with a priest, an Italian, and a Spaniard, and we agreed to talk for an hour in each of the four languages. The priest took Latin, the Italian and the Spaniard each their own, and I Portuguese, and we could understand and answer each other, but we could not speak the other three languages. Italians come out to Brazil and can only speak Italian, not a word of Portuguese; they then come to a crisis, when they can speak neither; they then convalesce in Portuguese, speak it perfectly and remain with it—they forget their Italian. I speak of colonists.

We had two very charming picnic-places. One was the Tropic of Capricorn, just five miles from São Paulo; your insurances suffer all the difference, whether you are on this side or that. A boy who was about to pass his examination for the army, who supported a poor widow mother, and consequently was extremely anxious about passing, and with no interest, was destined to be plucked; so the arrogant and ignorant examiner asked the timid, humble boy, "How far is it from the city of São Paulo to the tropical line of Capricorn." The boy, radiant answered, "Between four and five miles, sir." "Go down, sir, you are plucked; it is twenty miles." It was the last question. The boy grew red and white, and turned despairingly to go; suddenly he remembered his mother, turned round, and said nervously, "Please, sir, of course you ought to know better than me, but I lived there five years, sir, and I had to walk it twice a week, to go home from school to mother's house on the Line, from Saturday to Monday." Chorus of laughter at the examiner, and the poor boy passed. (I have already quoted this in my "A.E.I.") Another charming place to picnic, in the mountains, was Nossa Senhora do O.

We occasionally had big dinners, when all the English of Santos and São Paulo assembled to do honour to some railway swell going home. We had for a time some fortnightly balls, at a good-sized hall at the corner of the Plaza, called the Concordia, and we had one curious case of sporadic yellow fever from there. Mrs. Ralston, the young wife of a very nice man (indeed a charming couple), came out of the ball-room with me at five o'clock one morning. I had only to run across fifty yards to my house; they had about twenty minutes to walk home, and she was well wrapped up with shawls. She suddenly drooped her head on her husband's shoulder, saying she felt very queer, and he had to support her home. Almost directly he had laid her on her own bed, she turned round and said, "Oh, is this death?" and died. Next morning, my maid ran in and without any preface said, "Mrs. Ralston's dead." "Oh, nonsense," I said; "I saw her seven hours ago;" and, thinking perhaps it was possible she might be ill, and require some woman-neighbour, I hastily threw on my things, and ran down to her house. The street door opened on to the principal sitting-room, and was unlocked, and to my horror the house was deserted and still, and something was lying covered up on the sofa. I drew back the sheet, and there was my young friend, dead. I knelt down and said a few prayers, and then, feeling rather faint, I stooped to kiss her forehead before covering her up again. The husband and child and servants had all been removed to another house; as I stooped to kiss her a dreadful effluvia knocked me back again, and I perceived that she was covered with large black spots. I fled and ran home again, and told Richard. He looked very grave, and rang the bell, and ordered the horses to the door. He fetched me a large glass of brandy, and made me drink it, with some bread. He said, "It does not matter; I have got to have a long ride to-day on business, and you have got to go with me." We rode about ten miles at a great pace, till I was in a good perspiration. When I got back he gave me a teaspoonful of Warburg drops. He kept me employed all day, and at night he took me to the little theatre, and then he told me that he had done that to save my life, without which I probably should have caught it, if I had not perspired, and partly from sympathy.

One thing I always regret in writing, is that I could recite so many amusing and interesting things that would immensely please a very large portion of English people; but England is so very queer, and I am become convinced it is not the same England that I used to know, that I do not like to venture them. They are not in the least risky, only amusing and adventurous, but being very honest and straightforward, would be sure to tread upon somebody's corns; blame or sneers would be sure to crop up from some quarter or another, and make me regret it. Richard was very fond of quoting the following lines to me over our writing:—

> "They eat and drink and scheme and plod;
> They go to church on Sunday,
> And many are afraid of God,
> And more of Mrs. Grundy."

We had one very curious character at São Paulo. It was the Marchesa de Santos. She was a beauty and a favourite in the time of the present Emperor's father, and led a very brilliant and stormy life. She got finally banished by his Empress (they say) to Santos, with a pension for life, and she lived in a small house a few doors from me. I used to see a great deal of her. She was quite *grande dame*, most sympathetic, most entertaining, full of stories of Rio and the Court, and the Imperial people, and the doings of that time. She had been obliged to adopt up-country habits, and the last time I saw her, she received me *en intime* in her own kitchen, where she sat on the floor, smoking, not a cigarette, but a pipe. She had beautiful black eyes, full of sympathy, and intelligence, and knowledge. She was a great bit of interest to me in that out-of-the-way place.

The Seminary was the most palatial building in that part, and was just beyond the town. It was inhabited by Capuchins, French and Italians from Savoy and Piédmont. One of the monks was a tall, magnificent, and very powerful man, an ex-cavalry officer, Count Somebody, whose name I forget, then Fray G——.

Before he arrived, there was a bully in the town, rather of a free-thinking class, so he used to go and swagger up and down before the Seminary and call out, "Come out, you miserable petticoated monks! come out and have a free fight! For God or the devil!" When Fray G—— arrived, he heard of this, and it so happened he had had an English friend, when he was with his regiment, who had taught him the use of his fists. He found that his brother monks were dreadfully distressed at this unseemly challenge, so he said, "The next time he comes, don't open the gate, but let the porter call me." So the next time the bully appeared, it was so arranged that the gate was opened by Fray G—— (the usual crowd had collected in the road to see the fun), who looked at him laughingly and said, "Surely, brother, we will fight you for God or the devil, if you please. Let us get well into the open, and the public will see fair play." So saying, the friar tucked up his sleeves and gown, and told his adversary to "come on," which he did, and he was immediately knocked into a cocked hat. "Come, get up," said the friar. "No lying there and whimpering; the devil won't win that way." The man stood three rounds, at the end of which he whimpered and holloaed for mercy, and amidst the jeers and bravos of a large crowd, the "village cock" retired, a mass of jelly and pulp, to his own dunghill, and was never seen more within half a mile of the Seminary. Richard rejoiced in it, and used to say, "What is that bull-priest doing in that *galère?*" Richard used to stay a great deal with them, for they were the best-educated men in the province, and knew everything. He said he could always learn something from them.

During the time of the Paraguayan War provisions were very scarce. If muleteers came down to the town, they and their mules were seized for the war. They tried sending their women down with the mules, but then the mules and provisions were seized; the consequence was that the towns were more or less in a state of famine. Chico and I used to sally forth, with paniers and ropes to our saddles, and forage about, and I found that by riding about ten miles out, I came to large flocks of geese and other poultry, and I also ascertained that as the geese were supposed to feed upon snakes, nobody ate them; they were chiefly kept for ornament, and so were cheap. So the first day I came back with both our horses laden with geese, and as I passed through the town the squawking was immense, and most of the Grundy, respectable English tried to avoid me, which made me take an especial pleasure in riding up to them and inquiring after their wives and families, and entering into a conversation, which I, perhaps, should not have otherwise done. When I got up to our house, Richard, hearing the noise, came out on to the balcony, and seeing what was the matter, he threw back his head and laughed, and shook his fist, and he said, "Oh, you delightful blackguard, how like you!" I turned the geese into our poultry-yard and fed them well, and from that, I issued forth to all the country round about, twice a week, and brought in various stocks of other provisions.

Mr. Aubertin, who was the Head of the railway, and whose *chacara* was about a quarter of an hour from us, had opportunities of getting up drinks and having a very tidy cellar, so I used to send down a neighbourly note—"Dear Mr. Aubertin, bring up the drink—I have got the food; dinner seven o'clock." Thus we contrived between us, to feed very well during the whole of the war, while provisions were scarce. Once we managed to give a ball; it was very amusing, and it was kept up till sunrise. We had a delightful American there, who was very witty, and used to keep us all alive, though in after years, for some unknown reason, he blew his brains out. I still recall some of his *bon mots*. I once asked him whether he did not think that a gentleman of our acquaintance was very conceited this morning. "Conceited, ma'am?" he said. "Why, God Almighty's waistcoat would not fit him." On another occasion, there was a rather pronounced flirtation going on, and I asked him if he did not think it would be a case. "A case, ma'am? Why, she nestles up to him like a chicken to a hot brick." He was constantly saying these things that one never forgot.

I think I may say in our own favour, that in this, as well as in all our subsequent Consulates, we never allowed any scandal to be told to us, or uncharitable talk, and we always forbid discussions on religion and politics, which served us in good stead in all our career. Indeed, in this particular place, there *was* a little bit of scandal, and we had seventeen calls on one Monday morning, but every one went away without daring to deliver themselves of their intended tale. "What is the meaning of this?" said Richard to me. I said, "It means that there is some scandal afloat, and nobody dares tell it to us." But a few days afterwards we saw it in the papers. One day a gentleman called upon us, and a few minutes later a lady came, of whom he was rather fond. After a while the lady got up and went down the street, and about five minutes after the jealous husband arrived on the scene, and saw the gentleman sitting there —his supposed rival. Without saying "How do you do?" he turned on me and said, "Have you seen my wife?" "Yes," I said; "I saw her go down the street a few minutes ago." The lover had turned very pale. Richard looked hard at me over the top of his newspaper, and the man had hardly got down the stairs in pursuit of his wife, when my Irish maid poked her face through the door and said, "Well, after that, ye'd swear a hole through a tin p-hot." Now, what on earth would have been the use of making a row and a scandal, and setting on the husband to ill-treat his wife? He did not say, "Has my wife been here?"—he said, "Have you seen her?" Rousseau says, "Mensonge plein d'honnêteté, de fidelité, de generosité, tandis que la verité n'eut été qu'une perfidie;" and without some feeling of this kind—not a lie, but a harmless throwing one's self into the breach to save another's reputation, not one's own, nor from base fear—the milk of human kindness would turn into cream of tartar.

I do not think that a list of the aboriginal tribes of Brazil at the time of its discovery (one hundred discovered by Cabral in 1500) would amuse my readers, or fit in with my subject, but they were mostly destroyed or driven inwards in three hundred and sixty-seven years.

There is an intervening race called the Caboclas; they are the progeny of the Indians and Portuguese settlers. They are a very handsome race, much addicted to superstition and fortune-telling, and the only thing I can remember was learning from them to tell fortunes by the cards, which I afterwards perfected amongst the Mogháribehs in Syria; but it is a practice which, though it interested my husband enormously, and I constantly told them for him, I have long since given up as wicked. For those who tell them ill, it is foolery; for those who tell them well, it is better let alone.

I am not going to give a description of Brazil, because by so doing I should take away from the subject of the book, which is solely Richard Burton, and if I mention incidents, or myself, it is only because I or they are woven up with his life, and cannot well be separated from it, each one showing how he behaved, or what he did or thought on any particular occasion.

The 14th of February was the opening day of the railway, as far as Jundiahy, and this time we were invited and had a very gay time.

Here, in São Paulo, Richard worked hard at Camoens, and we both worked together at our translations—"Iraçema, or Honey-lips," and "Manuel de Moraes, the Convert," and the "Uruguay," all from great Brazilian authors; but we found, although we printed the two first, that they were not well received in England, because they were translations, and I could write a page or two upon the amount of literature and education we lose by boycotting that of other countries.

In spring of 1867 there was fighting in the streets for a couple of nights, about the election time.

The staple food of the people of the country, which takes the place of what the potato would be to the Irish, is a savoury mess of small brown beans, called *fejão;* a very coarse flour, called *farinha*, which looks like a dish of shaved horse-radish, is usually sprinkled over the beans, and then it is called a *fejoada.* It is delicious, and I should have been quite content to, and often did, dine on it. Another favourite dish is a scone of *milho*, the full-grown Indian corn, made hot and buttered. The only way to eat it, is to take it up in your two hands and gnaw it up and down like a bone, which is rather disagreeable, because it covers you with butter. A pepper-pot is also a usual thing, and is kept up *à perpétuité;* it comes on the table in its native earthenware pot, and everybody takes a little bit at the end to digest dinner, in lieu of cheese. Of course Europeans have their own dishes besides.

The greatest difficulty that I found was, that I was obliged to have five relays of every meal. First of all, Richard and I sat down, and our guests, if we had any; after we left the table, succeeded my Irish maid, who had become Donna Maria, and an Irish brother that she had imported, who was very like the "Mulligan" in "Perkinses' ball," and for whom I was fortunate enough to get a good berth on the railway at £200 a year, through the kindness of Mr. Daniel Fox and Mr. Aubertin, and he rose to £600 in course of time, traded, but unfortunately died after some years. After these the food was removed to some other room, where the German servants dined, because they would not sit down with the blacks. When they had finished the emancipated slaves sat down, who would not sit down with the slaves; these being too near their own kind, they obliged them to stand or to sit on the floor in the corners, where they gave them the leavings. But do not let anybody imagine that the slaves suffered, because when they had been about three months with me, from having had a little rice at their old masters', they would sometimes clamour for ducks and chickens, not being content with the good meat and bread and everything else that they got in plenty.

At Rio we met with a very funny and interesting man—a certain Dr. Gunning, with a kind good wife. They lived in a pretty cottage somewhere along the rail up in the forests, and we went to spend a day or two with them. He was a tall gaunt Scotchman, with a good deal of character, and some very curious ideas. He used to do what some people did with horses in Trieste. He used to buy up diseased and useless negroes, treat them well, feed them up, cure them, and then make them work for him; so he got their labour in return for his outlay and his kindness and trouble, and he left in his desk their papers of manumission. Unfortunately, one day in a soft moment he told them so, so the next night they shot him; but as his skull was a good hard one it only gave him a wound, and after that he went on some different tack with them.

He had a curious way of treating snake-bites, of which many thousands die during the year. He told us this himself. He said, "When I am called to attend a negro for a snake-bite, I cauterize the wound, and tie a ligature, and then I give him an awful thrashing, and," he said, "that counteracts the torpor or sleep, produces perspiration, and stimulates the action of the heart; and then I give him spirits or milk in large quantities." However, we all liked him very much. One of the nicest things at Rio was the bathing in the sea. We used to go out of a little gate at the bottom of the garden, and walk along the beach till we came to some circular rocks which acted as bathing-machines, where we could undress, get into the sea and bathe, and come back. In my time there were no bathing-machines in Brazil, only sometimes it was very rough and very deep, and one had to be on the look-out. One day I put my maid to sit upon my clothes, and thought I would swim out to a log of wood, lying apparently about a hundred yards off, when to my horror I saw it move. I swam back for my life, where I found my maid in deadly terror; and, looking, we saw it was a shark, and a good big one too.

One thing that made staying at Rio so very pleasant was the great kindness of the Emperor and Empress to us. The Emperor delighted in scientific men, and the Empress liked good Catholics, so that we were frequently sent for—Richard alone to the Emperor, and I alone to the Empress, or both together. Richard gave two lectures at which all the Imperial family attended. The Imperial family consisted of the Emperor and Empress, the Imperial Princess Isabel, heir to the throne, her husband the Count d'Eu, and the Duke and Duchess de Saxe. These last, however, were less known, less cordial, and less popular in Rio. I can remember on one occasion, when we were sent for to an audience, at which were present the Emperor and Empress, the Princess Isabel and her husband, her Majesty's little dog came in and sat on the rug in the centre of the circle, and sat up begging. They all burst out laughing very heartily. The Emperor was a tall, handsome, fair man, with blue eyes, and brimful of kindness and learning. The Empress was not handsome, but she was the kindest and best of Empresses—very devout, dressed very plainly, but was most imperial in her manners and carriage. The Princess also had the manner of her rank, and was soft and sweet. The Princess Isabel used to give balls every Monday fortnight during the season, to which all persons entitled to go to Court were invited. One night, at one of Princess Isabel's balls, the Emperor walked up to Richard and said, "How is it, Captain Burton, that you are not dancing?" "I never dance, your Majesty—that is, not often; but the last time I did so, it was with the King of Dahomè, to the music of cutting off heads—in pantomime, of course." The Emperor laughed, and he said, "The best of it was, Sir, that the authorities at home were in an awful rage with me, as her Majesty's Commissioner, for dancing with him; but I should like to have seen *them* refuse his dusky Majesty, when, at a single moment of impatience or irritability, he had only got to give a sign, to have fifty spears run into one, or to be instantly impaled."

It was very pretty to see the Princess and her husband go down to the door, the street door, and receive and kiss the hands of the Emperor and Empress. They circulated freely amongst us, and talked to us. The Empress would draw her chair over to me or to any other lady that she had a fancy to talk to, and sit down and chat as affably as any other great lady without ever abating one little bit of her Imperial dignity.

I remember one night Richard and I were giving a large dinner to nearly all the Diplomatic corps at the hotel, after the reception at the palace. At the latter there was a room for the Ministers to wait in, and a room for the Consuls. We were, of course, put into the Consular room. Presently a messenger came and took us into the Ministers' room. This rather offended official etiquette, and *they* said, "Oh, you must not come here; you must go into the Consuls' room." "But," we said, "we have just been fetched out of the Consuls' room and put in here, so we do not know what to do." There was an immense long wait, and several times a messenger came to let in somebody else, and we all stood up in our places, expecting the Emperor. After a long time, when everybody was getting very impatient, a messenger arrived, and said, "This way." They all flocked to the door, and we hung back, thinking we must not have audience with the Ministers. Then the messenger said, "No, no! not for you, gentlemen, but Captain and Mrs. Burton." The poor humble people were exalted; their Majesties had sent for us to their private drawing-rooms, and gave us a long sitting-down audience. As we were driving home, Richard said, "I am afraid all the other fellows will be awfully angry;" and the fact of the matter is, that though we waited dinner for a long time, there were a great many empty chairs that night, which disappointed us sorely; but they were all right next morning.

Whenever we were sickly we used to go down to the Barra, near Santos, which I described before as our fashionable watering-place, where somebody generally lent us a hut. We used to sit in the water and let it roll over us, and walk about without our shoes and stockings (there was not a soul to see us). We took to making collections of butterflies, reptiles, snakes, and ferns, of which there are some four thousand specimens; the orchids we used to send home. I can recollect on some occasions, being down there alone, and being asked to dinner about a mile and a half along the sands from my hut, I used to put my dress and my shoes and stockings up in a parcel, and mounting barefooted, with waterproof on, ride the small pony lent to me; sometimes I used to have to get down and lead him through the streams that were rushing to the sea, to which he had a dislike; so we used to wade through, and then I would get up and ride him on to the next one, and when we reached the hospitable door I was conducted into a room to put on my shoes and stockings and my dinner dress. However, we were not *décolleté*, nor did we wear flowers or diamonds on that lonely coast.

Whenever we went down to Rio, it always meant a great deal of gaiety with the Diplomats and the Squadron, and receptions at the palace. It was especially gay in Sir Edward and Lady Thornton's reign, and I think we all look back to that time as a happy and a very pleasant and lively one.

One of the great charms of Rio, was our little club, numbering about twenty-five intimates, all belonging either to the Diplomatic corps or the Navy. We used to give each other some very nice dinner-parties, and ours was by necessity at the hotel; we mostly dined together at one house or the other every night. Then, besides the frequent palace entertainments, was the Alcazar, where there was a charming French troupe, of which the star was Mdlle. Aimée, and we used to have all Offenbach's music and operas.

One time we went up to Robeio and to Ubá, the end of the railway, and I was given a treat to go on the engine and drive it, with the engine-driver by me.

On the 12th of June we started on a delightful Expedition. We sailed in a steam launch across the Bay of Rio, which is like a beautiful broad lake studded with islands and boulder rocks and bordered by mountains. Two hours brings you to a rickety wharf, where a little railway, running for eleven miles through a mangrove flat, lands you at the foot of the mountains. Here a carriage waits for you, drawn by four mules, and you commence a zigzag ascent for two hours up these most regal mountains, and arrive at a table-land some distance from the summit, where the small white settlement called Petropolis lies. It is a German town with Swiss valleys, pretty views, rides, and drives. The Cascadinha leads down a winding path, or a steep wooded mountain, and as you reach its depths, facing you from opposite, comes the body of water frothing and bounding over the boulders. From the top of the Serra there is a lovely panorama of Rio and its bay, seen as from an inverted arch of mountains. The little settlement of Petropolis possesses a theatre, a Catholic church, the Emperor's palace, and two small hotels; the Court of Ministers and the Diplomats have snuggeries here, and form a pleasant society. The climate is fine and cold when it does not rain, and the scattered houses are like Italian *cascine*.

Here we took coach, which is very much after the fashion of the old diligence, and we drove to Juizdafora. These coaches are drawn by perfectly wild mules; they stand straight on their hind legs. While the passengers are getting in, the coachman is already mounted with reins and whip, and two or three men hang on to each mule. When all is ready the driver shouts "Larga!" The men fall back and the mules rush on at full gallop, swaying the coach from side to side. After three months, when the mules are trained and tamed down, they are pronounced no longer fit for their work, and are sold for carriage-driving.* My pleasant recollection of Juizdafora is of lying all day on the grass under the orange trees, and picking about nine different species overhead, just within reach of my arms. I have never tasted oranges equal, before or since. We then started for Barbaçena, which terminated the coach journey. After this there was no means of getting along except on horseback. We had to discard our boxes and leave them under the care of a trustworthy person, and to make up a pack that we could carry behind us on our saddles, such as a change of linen, tooth-brush, a cake of soap, and a comb. We then mounted and rode twenty

* In travelling, the mules are mostly difficult to treat, and one never passes their noses or their heels without care. I have seen a fine mule spring like a goat on the top of a piano case in the yard, to avoid being saddled. I never before understood the French expression, *Méchante comme une âne rouge.*

miles to Barrozo, a small village with a ranch. We rose at three next morning, and rode twenty-four miles further, and so on, and so on, till we reached San João d'El Rey, where we saw the Mines. We then went on to S. José. Our next place was Cerandahy to Lagos Dourado; here we met a party of English engineers.

On the 24th—a great feast, St. John Baptist—they were laying the foundation for a new railway, and we enjoyed the fun very much. We then, after breakfasting by a brook with the engineers, rode on to an awful place called Camapuão. Here we found the stables better than the house, and we slept by the side of the mules and horses. At one of these shelters that we asked to sleep at, the accommodation was fearful, but the reception was kind and cordial. There was not much to eat. In the middle of the night I woke, and could hear loud hoarse whisperings through the thin partition wall; it sounded like the man and his wife disputing. At length I heard the man say distinctly, "Don't bother me any more; it will be quite easy to kill them both, and I mean to do it." My hair stood on an end, as the saying is, and I softly got up and walked on tiptoe over to Richard, touched him, and said in a whisper, "Hush! don't speak; I have something to tell you." I told him exactly what I had heard. He said, "You will make less noise than I; go softly to that table and take our weapons, hand me mine, and creep into bed with yours. We will sit and watch the door. If it opens, I'll let fly at the door; and if a second comes in, then *you* fire." However, nothing came, though we lay awake till daylight, with our pistols cocked. Next morning they brought us for our breakfast a couple of nice roast chickens, and he said, "My wife and I had a regular quarrel in the night; we had only these two hens, and *she* did not want to kill them, but we had nothing else, and I was determined that you should have them both." So we said to him, "You shall not lose anything by it." Nor did they, for we paid four times the value; but we were glad when he went out of the room, that we might laugh.

Next day we rode on to Sassuhy, to Congonhas do Campo, about twenty-two miles. We saw the church of Congonhas and the seven stations of the Cross. We left at midday, and riding through a difficult country, arrived at Teixeiros. Next day was a very hard day. We started at half-past three in the morning; at half-past ten we breakfasted under a tree by the river. We crossed different rivers about twelve times, wading our horses through. We passed through virgin forests, and up and down scarped rocky mountains till dark, and arrived at Corche d'Agua, a miserable place, where there were no beds or food. We started again before dawn, rode about twelve miles in the dark, passed two villages, and about nine a.m. arrived at

Morro Velho, our destination, where we were most kindly received by Mr. and Mrs. Gordon and family (Superintendent of all the Mines), and soon had bath and breakfast, and our animals quartered in good stables under the care of the host's English groom.

Here we stayed with our kind host for five and a half weeks, making excursions, and seeing most interesting things concerning the Mines. The Establishment consisted of the Superintendent and his family, Mr. and Mrs. Gordon, two sons, and two daughters, and twenty-five officers (English); under them, about three thousand negroes (slaves), who work the mines. On Sunday we went to their church, saw their hospital and the stables, which contained some sixty horses, and we saw an Indian dance.

Here there was much of interest—the muster of the slaves, and pay-day on Saturday. We saw baptisms, and marriages, and burials. We went to see the quicksilver washed in the amalgamation house, and Mr. William Crookes's amalgamation; but this last did not succeed.

We started again after we were rested, passing through interesting mining places, sleeping the night at a friendly *fazenda;* next day we rode on to S. José de Morra Grande, Barro, Brumado, Santa Barabara, and Cates Atlas. There we slept. Next morning we rode to Agua, Queule, Fonseca, Morreia, and Affeixonada; from thence to Benito Rodriguez, then Comargo, then S. Anna, and then Marianna. Here we slept, went to church, visited the Bishop, the Seminary, the Sisters of Charity, hospitals, orphanage, and schools, and rode to Passagem, where we slept. Next day we went down the Passagem mines (gold), forty-five fathoms down, and in another place thirty-two fathoms, and saw the stamps; and then we went and did the same at the S. Anna mines. This day we were so near Mr. Treloar's house, that we gave away all our provisions, saying, "By breakfast-time to-morrow we shall be in a English house." Imagine our horror, on arriving, to find that poor Mrs. Treloar had died the evening before, and that her poor husband was in such a state that it was impossible for him to receive us. He thanked God for Richard's coming, because there was no church, no clergyman, and no burial-ground, and an English Consul performing the burial service is valid; so the sorrowful ceremony was performed, winding up the hill-top, where she was buried, and I was left in charge of all his negroes. They had prepared something for us to eat, for which I had given them five *milreis,* about ten shillings. They all squabbled so violently over this, as to draw their knives, and to begin to stab each other; so, with that ascendency which whites generally have over blacks, I ordered them all to come into my presence and to put their knives down near me, and I asked them if they were not ashamed, when their poor mistress was being carried up the hill to her last burial-place, to behave in so unseemly a fashion, and, ordering them all down upon their knees, I took out my Prayer-book and read the burial service too; and I read it over and over again, until the party came back from the grave.

We then started immediately for Ouro Preto. Here Richard went up the Itacalumi, and I visited the two martyrs of Ouro Preto, the house of Gonzaga. We then slept and dined, and had champagne, and we went to tea at Mr. and Mrs. Spiers', who had a party. Next day we rode on to Casa Branca, S. Vicente, to Rio das Pedras, where we joined some American emigrants. Afterwards we had a very weary and hard ride to Corele d'Agua, our old sleeping-place, where we took a cup of coffee and rode to S. Antonio. We had a pelting rain, and we breakfasted at a *troupeiro's* ranch; thence to S. Rita, and from thence to Morro Velho, six leagues away, arriving like wet dogs.

On the 24th of July we went down the big mine at Morro Velho. Now, this was a great event; few men visitors had been down, and no woman. I forget the positive depth of it, but am under the impression *now* that it was three-quarters of a mile straight down into the bowels of the earth, including the last thirty-five fathoms to the depths. We were dressed in miners' dresses, with the usual candle in our caps, and we got into a basket like a caldron hanging to the end of a long chain, and then we began to descend. It seemed an eternity, going down, down, and down, and of all the things we ever have done, it seemed to me that it was the one that required the most pluck, so dark, so cold, and slimy it looked, and yet suffocating, and if anything happened, you felt that ne'er an arm or leg would ever be found; it realized more than any amount of sermons could do "the bottomless pit." The chain had broken a little while before, and we had seen the poor smashed negroes brought up, and it did break the next day, but *our time was not yet come.* I have got the broken link of that chain now; Mr. Gordon gave it to me, and it is my one relic of those days. After an apparently interminable time we began to see lights below, at a great distance, as you see a seaport town from a mountain as you come down at night, and by-and-by we began to hear voices, and finally we touched ground, and were heartily received by those who had previously gone down to take care of us, including Mr. Gordon himself. They gave us a hearty cheer. We were shown all over the mine, and all its workings, and I must say I think Dante must have seen a similar place wherewith to make his Inferno.

Even Richard notes in his journal, "an awful sight."

RICHARD'S ACCOUNT* OF GOING DOWN THE MINE.

"A small crowd of surface workmen accompanied us to the mouth of Walker's inclined plane, a hot and unpleasant hole leading to the Cachoeira Mine. The negret Chico gave one glance at the deep dark pit, wrung his hands, and fled the Tophet, crying that nothing in the wide, wide world would make him enter such an Inferno. He had lately been taught that he is a responsible being, with an 'immortal soul,' and he was beginning to believe it in a rough theoretical way: this certainly did not look like a place 'where the good niggers go.' Next the descent:—

"Presently the bucket was suspended over the abyss, and we found in it a rough wooden seat, comfortable enough. We were advised by the pitmen not to look downwards, as the glimmer of sparks and light-points moving about in the mighty obscure below causes giddiness and sea-sickness. We did look down, however, and none of us suffered from the trial. More useful advice was to keep head and hands well within the bucket, especially when passing the up-going tub. We tipped and tilted half over only once against a kibble-way drum, placed to fend off the *cacamba*. We had three such collisions, which made us catch at the chains, and describe them as 'moments of fearful suspense;' we had been lowered in a kibble with a superfluity of chain.

"When our eyesight had become somewhat feline we threw a glance round. Once more the enormous timbering under a bar, or to the east of the shaft, called it to every one's attention."

After describing the great extent of the mine, whose vertical height was 1134 feet, and breadth 108 feet, "unparalleled in the annals of mining," and which suggested "a cavern, a huge stone quarry, a mammoth cave raised from the horizontal to the perpendicular," the narrative winds up as follows:—

ON NEARING THE BOTTOM.

"And now, looking west, the huge palace of darkness, dim in long perspective, wears a tremendous aspect; above, at first only, there seemed to be a sky without an atmosphere. The walls were either as black as the grave or reflected slender rays of light glancing from the polished watery surface, or were broken into monstrous projections, half revealing and half concealing the cavernous, gloomy recesses. Despite the lamps, the night pressed upon us, as it were, with a weight, and the only measure of distance was a spark here and there, glimmering like a single star. Distinctly Dantesque was the gulf between the huge mountain sides apparently threatening

* "The Highlands of Brazil." By Captain Richard F. Burton, F.R.G.S.

every moment to fall. Everything, even the accents of a familiar voice, seemed changed; the ear was struck by the sharp click and dull thud of the hammer upon the boring-iron, and this upon the stone; each blow invariably struck was to keep time with the wild chants of the borer. The other definite sounds, curiously complicated by an echo, which seemed to be within reach, were the slush of water on the subterranean paths, the rattling of the gold-stone thrown into the kibbles, and the crash of chain and bucket.

"Through this Inferno gnomes and kobolds glided about in ghostly fashion—half-naked figures muffled up by the mist. Here dark bodies, gleaming with beaded heat-drops, hung in what seemed frightful positions; there they swung like Leotard from place to place; there they swarmed up loose ropes like the Troglodytes; there they moved over scaffolds, which even to look up at would make a nervous temperament dizzy. This one view amply repaid us. It was a place—

> 'Where thoughts were many, and where words were few.'

But the effect will remain upon the mental retina as long as our brains do their duty. At the end of two hours we left this cathedral'd cavern of thick-ribbed gold, and we were safely got out like ore to grass.

"We found the last eighty-three fathoms of tunnel steep and dark, but dry and comfortable. It was well timbered with beams and Candeia trunks wherever the ceiling required propping. At length we reached another vaulted cavern, thirty-five fathoms of perpendicular depth. It was lit up with torches, and the miners—all slaves, directed by white overseers—streamed with perspiration, and merrily sung their wild songs and chorus, keeping time with the strokes of hammer and drill. The heavy gloom, the fitful glare, and the savage chant, with the wall hanging like the stone of Cisyphus, like the sword of Damocles, suggested a sort of material Swedenborgian hell; and accordingly the negret Chico faltered out, when asked his opinion on our return, 'Parece o Inferno!'"

To continue my account. There were the large dark halls with vaults and domes; they were covered with negroes, each with a candle stuck in his black head, hammering in time to some tune to which they were all singing. It would have been a wonderful picture for a painter. How often all my life I have regretted not to have been an artist, instead of musical! The negroes are healthy and well doing; they only work eight hours a day, and have over-pay for anything extra. The mulattoes were the most surly looking ones. After having seen everything we ascended again, and if I may say so, I think the ascent was worse than the going down, and nobody knows, until they have tried that sort of darkness, what daylight and sunlight and fresh air mean. After long mounting, you see at last one star sparkling in the distance like an eye, which appears miles off, and that is the mouth of the shaft.

In the evening there was a concert and a ball amongst ourselves. On the 27th Richard lectured; there were some private theatricals in which I took a part, and forgetting the drop behind the open-air theatre when I backed off, I fell. I sprained my ankle so badly that my leg was all black, and I could not move. Now, the worst of it was that we were going to canoe down the San Francisco river, to come out at the falls of Paulo Affonso, issuing at Bahía, and back to Rio by steamer; but it was impossible to take a woman who could not walk. We could embark at Sabará, a short distance from where we were, and as Richard's time was very short, and he could not take a lame woman, he had to start without me, and I went in the litter to see him embark in the boat *Elisa*.

As soon as I got well, Mr. Gordon, who was an exceedingly liberal, large-minded man, recognized that having three thousand Catholic negroes under him, manned by twenty-five English Protestant officers, it was quite possible that in a religious sense, things might be made more comfortable to them, and he asked me, as an educated English Catholic, to go the rounds of Church and Hospital, and find out if there was anything that could improve their condition. Having been for some time in Brazil, and seeing the wants of the negroes, I thought I could put my finger on the right spot at once. There was one particular ward in the hospital where incurables were put, and a black cross over their beds told them Dante's old words, "Lasciate ogni speranza, voi ch' entrate" ("Leave every hope (outside), all ye who enter (here)"). I dismissed the attendant, for fear they should be afraid to answer, walked round the wards and sat by them, and I will take one case as a specimen of the whole. She was dying of diseases which need not be named here. I said to her—

"Has your case been given over by the doctor?"

"Alas! yes," she said; "I have only got to wait."

"Should you like to live?"

"Yes, of course I should."

"Has the priest been to hear your confession? Have you sent for him?"

"Oh no; I should not dare do that."

"Why not? What is he for?"

"Oh, lady, we must not *ask*, and he doesn't come to us in *this* ward, only to those who go to church."

"Do you mean to tell me that none of you in this ward get the last Sacraments?"

"Oh no; we should be so ashamed to see his Reverence."

"Why, you are not ashamed to see the doctor? What is the difference between the doctor and the priest, except that one is for your body and one is for your soul? You say you are afraid of the priest; will you not be more ashamed of God, whose servant he is?" That seemed to strike them; so, wishing them good-bye, I trotted off to the *Padre.* No matter his name, but he appeared to take things very easy when I told him. He said he "could not administer the Sacraments, because he had not a pyx nor any of the vessels to convey them in."

"Well," I said, "Father, I have been commissioned by the Superintendent to examine into these things, and to report to him what *is* done and what *ought* to be done, and he is going to see it carried out; so will you oblige me by going to hear all those confessions, *now at once*, and taking the holy ingredients in a wine-glass, and administering Viaticum and Extreme Unction, and say a few consoling words to them, and let us see the results? You know that you can break these glasses into little atoms, and you can burn the remnants in one of the furnaces, or keep them for that purpose until I send up the proper things from Rio."

Well, this was done, and, to cut a long story short, that woman was back to work in a fortnight; and when Mr. Gordon saw the immense advantage produced by relief of mind, and the consideration of their feelings, and the action of the brain upon the body, he made it an institution, and commissioned me to send up all the necessary things from Rio.

As soon as I was well enough for a long ride, Mr. Gordon supplied me with horses—one for me, one for Chico, and one for our small baggage—a sail and a few poles to make a tent in the day, a gypsy-kettle on three prongs, a bag of maize for the horses, and rice and other things for ourselves, and taking an affectionate leave of the whole company there, and especially my kind host and family, whom we have always remembered with the sincerest affection, and sadness too, for poor Mrs. Gordon died eventually from a horrible shock (her youngest and favourite son was caught in the machinery in an instant and ground to death—a subject too sad to dwell upon), I commenced my long ride home—a very pleasant ride.

I rose at dawn; we made some tea in our kettle. Replenishing our sack of provisions at every village, and having fed, watered, and groomed the horses, we rode until it was too hot. We put up our bit of sail and rested during the heat, and then we rode on till nightfall; after this we fed again, looked after the horses and picketed them. Some of the country, and especially the forests, were lovely. Whenever we came to a village or a ranch, we and our animals got housed; and when we did not, which was rare, we camped out, for it was very warm. We never met with a single scrap of danger the whole way, nor a rude word; for defence we had only a penknife, our toasting-fork, and an old pistol that would not go off. I had given my weapons to Richard, whose journey was longer and more dangerous than mine.

At one place that we stopped at, we rose at half-past three, and whilst dressing I heard what I supposed was thrashing out grain or beating sacks. It went on for about fifteen minutes, and I did not pay any attention to it, till at last I heard a sob issue from the beaten mass at the other side of the thin partition wall. I knew then what was taking place, and turned so sick I could hardly get to the door. I ran to the room, caught hold of the man's arms, and called for Chico and for everybody in the place, but I was fully ten minutes before I could arouse any one's pity or sympathy; they seemed so used to it they would not take the trouble to get up. The man who was beating only laughed, and beat on. I very nearly fainted. I expected the poor wretch would have been pounded to an ointment, but to my surprise, when he gave it a kick and told it to get up, up rose quite a fine young woman, gave herself a shake, and walked off like a Newfoundland dog. I went after her, and asked her if she was hurt, and she said, "Oh no, not much; he often goes on like that!" "But then," I said, "what did he do it for? What did *you* do?" She said, "Another black woman and I were quarrelling, so he thrashed us both; but as you were sound asleep you did not hear the first."

We arrived in Rio about the fifteenth day. I had never enjoyed anything more; but as I had been out for three months without any change of clothes, I was a very curious object to look at, to say nothing of my face and hands being the colour of mahogany. I had been told before getting in that the Estrangeiros, where I had left my maid and baggage, was full, so I waited till night, and then went straight to the next best hotel in the town. The landlord naturally did not recognize me, and he pointed to a little place on the other side of the street, where sailors' wives went, and he said, "I think that will be about your place, my good woman, not here." "Well," I said, "I think I am coming in here all the same." So, wondering, he took me upstairs and showed me his rooms; but I was so mighty particular, that it was not till I got to his best rooms that I stopped and said, "This will do. Be kind enough to send up this letter for me to the Estrangeiros."

Presently down came my maid, who was a great swell, with my

boxes. After a bath and dressing, I rang the bell and ordered some supper. He came up himself, as I was such an object of curiosity. When he saw me again he said, "Did that woman come to take the apartments for you, madam? I do beg your pardon; I am afraid I was rather rude to her." "Well," I said, "I am that woman myself; but you need not apologize, because I saw myself in the glass, and I don't wonder at it." He nearly tumbled down, and when I had explained my adverse circumstances to him, begged my pardon till I was quite tired of hearing it. I went up to Santos for some time; and when I thought Richard could arrive, I went down to Rio to meet him, and used to go on board every steamer that came in from Bahía in the hopes of his being there. At this time came out to Rio Mr. Wilfrid Blunt and his sister Alice. I went on board ship after ship to meet Richard, but as he never came, I got at last very anxious and miserable, and only used to make a fool of myself by crying when I did not find him. He had been gone over four months. At last the first steamer that I did *not* go to meet, he arrived in, and was quite angry to find that I was not on board to meet him. He had had a very jolly journey, canoeing down the river to the "falls of the Paulo Affonso," and sleeping at different ranches on the banks of the river. It was something like fifteen hundred miles, coming out eventually at Bahía, where he had a great friend, an old gentleman popularly known as "Charley Williams," who gave him hospitality till he embarked, or could catch a steamer to Rio. We then went down to Santos together.

As Richard was canoeing down the San Francisco river, he found a lot of stones called Pingua d'Agua; they are formed by congealed rain in the rocks; they get fossilized, and if polished have the glitter of diamonds. Richard met an Englishman, who told him that he had come over with all he had in the world, £1500, and expended it in diamonds, of which he fondly believed he had got about £30,000 worth, and was going home with them. So Richard told him that he had just come from the diamond mines, and that he should immensely like to see them. When he showed them to him, Richard's face fell, and he said, "What is the matter?" "Well," he said, "I hardly like to tell you, but I am afraid you have been done. Some one has passed off these Pingua d'Agua upon you for diamonds, and I am afraid you have exchanged £1500 for thirty shillings' worth." So the man said, "Oh, you must be a fool!" "Well," said Richard, "if it isn't that I am so sorry for you, I should say 'serve you right,' because I really do happen to know."

About the 17th of April, 1868, Richard, who had been looking queer and seedy for six weeks, but persisting all the time that he was perfectly well, felt feverish and agueish, and went to bed. I gave him calomel and castor oil, and then every sort of thing that I could think of. He got worse and worse, and I was in despair, for there were no doctors; but at last, after some days, a doctor did arrive from Rio, and I sent for him at once, and he passed the night in the house. Of course it was purely Brazilian treatment for a Brazilian disease, and nothing we knew touched it. He had six cuppings, with thirty-six glasses and twelve leeches, tartar emetic, and all sorts of other things, and there was something to be given or rubbed every half-hour, of which a very large ingredient was orange tea. The doctor came twice a day, and the number of remedies was wonderful, every half-hour, and I never left him day or night. They blistered him terribly.

When Richard thought he was dying, he sent me for Fray João, with whom he had been learning astronomy; but Fray João was gone on an expedition up country for two months, and he would not have anybody else for the Sacraments; but he accepted the Scapular, which all Catholics will understand, and to others it is not needful to explain, and he wore it to the day of his death. One night he gave me a terrible fright; he asked me to give him twenty drops of chlorodyne. I objected, but he was so imperative about it that I thought he had been ordered it; fortunately, I only gave him fifteen. He found it too strong, and, also fortunately, he spat it out, and asked me to mix him another of ten, which he drank. He soon frightened me by feeling sick and faint, and I gave him lukewarm water to make him bring it up, and sent for the doctor, who was very frightened about him. He was insensible an hour. He gave ether pills, applied mustard to the calves of the legs and inside the thighs, and then Richard had a calm and good sleep all night, and from that got a great deal better. He was able to go into his study after a month, and took his first drive five weeks after he was taken ill, and at the end of seven weeks I was able to take him down to the Barra, where Mr. Ford had kindly lent us his bungalow, where Richard could sit on the sands and let the sea roll over him, and here he got much better. I may now tell a horrid little story, as it illustrates Richard's power of mesmerizng.

Richard was a great mesmerizer, a thing which everybody who knew him will understand.* He always preferred women, and especially of the blue-eyed, yellow-haired type. I need not say that he began with me as soon as we married; but I did not like it,

* Captain Gambier tells me that he used to mesmerize him when he was a child, and tell him to go up to some room in the dark, and fetch him some particular article or book which he only thought of.

and used to resist it, but after a while I consented. At first it was a little difficult, but when once he had complete control, no passes or contact were necessary; he used simply to say, "Sleep," and I did. He could also do this at a distance, but with more difficulty if water were between us, and if he tried to mesmerize anybody else and I was anywhere in the neighbourhood, I absorbed it, and they took nothing. I used to grow at last to be afraid to be in the same room with a mesmerizer, as I used to experience the greatest discomfort, and I knew if there was one in the room, the same as some people know if there is a cat in the room; but I could resist *them*, though I could not resist Richard. He used to mesmerize me freely, but he never allowed any one else, nor did I, to mesmerize me. Once mesmerized, he had only to say, "Talk," and I used to tell everything I knew, only I used to implore of him to forbid me to tell him other people's secrets, and as a matter of honour he did, but all my own used to come out freely; only he never took a mean advantage of what he learnt in that way, and he used laughingly to tell everybody, "It is the only way to get a woman to tell you the truth." I have often told him things that I would much rather keep to myself.

In the particular instance that I am about to recount, he had mesmerized me to consult about an expedition that he was going to take, as he had previous to his illness meant to start, and I had said to him, "Don't start, because you are going to have a very bad illness, and you will want me and your home comforts;" so he now re-mesmerized me to know what he should do, and I said to him, "Don't take the man that you are going to take with you, because he is a scoundrel; don't buy the things that you are going to buy for the expedition, because you will never use them. You will go a long journey south for your health." I then said to him, "Look! what a curious procession is passing our door, a long procession of people in white, and headed by Maria and Julia" *—who were our old cook and her daughter, aged about seventeen—"they are all in white, with flowers on their heads. What can it mean?" I raved all night about this procession, till Richard got up and shut the shutters, and closed the door, which opened out on to the sands, the night being very hot. The next day this procession made an impression on him, and for curiosity's sake he sent up a mounted messenger to São Paulo to know if anything had occurred, or if there was any news. We had brought no servants with us, had left my maid and everybody behind.

* We were then at the Barra.

Now, on a former occasion, about three months back, he had mesmerized me, and I had had this very cook called to me, and I had said to her, "Maria, go to confession and communion, then send to a lawyer and make your will. You have got a little cottage, and you have saved £150; you have a few boxes of clothes and things. Leave everything to Little Peter"—her son aged six—"and don't trouble about Julia." When I came to, she told me the extraordinary things I had been saying to her, and how frightened she was; but she said, "I will do all that you have told me, only I can't leave Julia without anything;" and I said to her, "I am not conscious of having said anything; but in that case, you had better say that whatever you leave to Julia goes to Peter at her death." Well, this was the news that we got by the mounted messenger: The old cook had died that day in an apoplectic fit, and before the maid had time to call or send for the daughter, she walked in, looking very ill, and sat upon the sofa, rocking and moaning, and she said, "I have come from my mistress to die *here*. I feel so very ill, I will not leave you." From all she told the maid, and the strange way she was going on, the maid inferred that the girl was in a particular kind of trouble, and it would be impossible to keep her there, and she begged of her to let her fetch a carriage and conduct her back to her mistress, where at least if she was ill she could be taken care of, and seeing her in such a state, she was afraid to inform her that her mother was lying dead. One of the slaves fetched a carriage, and they put her into it, and were conducting her home, but she was so bad on the road they had to lift her out, and take her into a little *venda* (a place where they sell wine), and run to fetch a priest, who was just in time to give her the last Sacraments, when she expired. The blood oozed from her eyes, ears, nose, mouth, and from all the pores of her skin. She died very shortly and was buried, and the smell was so bad in the *venda* that the walls had to be scraped and re-whitewashed, although she was only there a few hours. It was afterwards proved that she and the black cook at her mistress's were both in love with the same man, and as she had announced her intention of visiting my house, the cook had given her a cup of coffee before she set out, and had said, "Go! you will never come back." The body was exhumed. It was supposed she had received in the coffee a Brazilian poison, mixed with powdered glass, made of some herbs of which the negroes have the secret. Little Peter would have now become practically, though not theoretically, a Brazilian slave, and his little property would have been absorbed; but by the will made at the Consulate, he was under the protection of the Consul. His education was undertaken, and he was sole inheritor of the cottage, £150, and the boxes of clothes and other property.

At Santos we had a regatta, a separate boat for each nation, about nine or ten in all. The English blustered awfully, and the Americans also—talked a great deal about "Bull's Run," and so forth. All the other people sat very quiet, expecting to be beaten; the consequence was the Portuguese won, and the English came in last, and we sent up and hauled our flag down. The sea was very rough, and surrounded our bungalow; we walked through bare-legged, and went into Santos, and then went back again, and eventually to São Paulo, partly on an engine, and partly walking—butterfly-catching.

When we got back to São Paulo, Richard told me that he could not stand it any longer; it had given him that illness, it was far away from the world, it was no advancement, it led to nothing. He was quite right. I felt very sorry, because up to the present it was the only home I had ever really had quietly with him, and we had had it for three years; but I soon sold up everything, and we came down to Santos, and embarked on the 24th of July, 1868. Here he applied for leave, as the doctors advised him not to go to England at once, but to go down south to Buenos Ayres for a trip, and he asked me to go to England and see if I could not induce them to give him another post. I saw Richard off down south, and taking an affectionate leave of all kind friends, embarked for England.

Our Separate Journeys.

Richard had a splendid journey to the Argentine Republic and the rivers Plata-Paraná and Paraguay, for the purpose of reporting the state of the Paraguayan War to the Foreign Office. He crossed the Pampos and the Andes to Chili and Peru amongst the bad Indians. He went to the Pacific Coast to inspect the scene of the earthquake at Arica, returning by the Straits of Magellan, Buenos Ayres, and Rio to London.

During his delightful trip, which completely recovered his health, he fell in with the Tichborne Claimant, and travelled with him for a week, and never having seen the real man, and as he appeared very gentlemanly, and when he gambled, lost his money and won it without any emotion, he concluded that he was the real thing until he came home. He acquired all the history of the ins and outs of the war, and later produced his book on Paraguay—"Letters from the Battle-Fields of Paraguay," which did not see the light till 1870.

I had, as usual, all my work cut out for me. First I was to try and work the Iporanga mines in London, whole mountains of lead and quicksilver, also gold and copper (twenty-eight square miles). I was to bring out his "Highlands of Brazil," the "Journey of Lacerda," and a second edition of "Mecca," "Uruguay," "Iracema," and "Manoel de Moraes."

I also had a small adventure on the way home at Bahía. I went ashore with a friend from the ship to dine with "Charley Williams," my husband's friend. He was very fond of keeping a menagerie; besides having his garden stocked with wild beasts, his hall contained cages of snakes, amongst them two rattlesnakes. After we had dined in his *chácara*, he insisted on showing me his snakes, and he quietly took one up (out of its cage) near its head. He was used to doing this, but whether he was agitated or what I cannot say, but the snake slipped through his hand, and bit him on the wrist. The friend had bolted upstairs the moment the cage was opened; Mr. Williams just had time to dash it back into the cage and lock it, and staggered against the wall.

Richard had always taught me how to be ready on such emergencies travelling up the country, but the only thing in the hall was a box of wooden lucifer-matches, so I struck them one after another, and kept cramming them into the mark on his wrist made by the snake till I had made a regular little hole. I tied my handkerchief tightly above it, called out loudly for the servants, told them what had happened, and to go and get a bottle of whisky. By degrees I got the whole bottle down his throat, and then my friend and I and the negroes kept walking him up and down for about three hours. We then allowed him to go to bed, and next morning he was no worse for what had happened. I think the bite must have been very feeble not to have done more harm—probably the snake had only time to graze the skin; anyway, the dear old man was so pleased, he brought me home a riding-whip of solid silver up to the lash, which I keep now as a memento.

We had a bad sea and strong trade winds most of the way; the ship was horribly lively off Finisterre, and the hatches down. We found it bitterly cold in August, and on the 1st of September my family met me at Southampton. They were then all puffing and panting and fanning themselves on account of the "tropical weather," as they called it, and I found it so bitterly cold, I had to have several blankets and a big fire, showing the difference of the climates. There was great amusement when my sisters came on board. I took them to my cabin, which was considered the best in the ship. The Captain was showing it off, when one of them, who had never been at sea in her life, turned round to me and said, "Now, Isabel, do you *really* mean to say that you have lived in that housemaid's closet for a month, and slept on that shelf?" The Captain laughed. "Really, ladies," he said, "this is considered a very swell ship, and everybody fights for that cabin."

I did my work well, carrying out everything according to Richard's directions, and Lord Derby, then Lord Stanley, whose sound sense and great judgment knew exactly the man to suit the post, and the post to suit the man, gave him the long-coveted Consulship of Damascus, and was brave enough not to heed the jealousy and spite which did its best to prevent his being allowed to take the post. The Missionaries raised up their heads on the one side, and the people who wanted it for their friends, did all they could to persuade Lord Stanley that it would displease the Moslems, because he had been to Mecca. Richard was delighted when he got the intelligence of his transfer from Brazil to Damascus. He heard it casually in a *café* at Lima, where he was congratulated, having missed most of his letters. He hastened back at once, and he wrote and guaranteed to Lord Stanley that all would be well with the Moslems, as it had ever been from the starting of his career in 1842 up to the present time, 1868—a period of twenty-six years; consequently the appointment was signed, with a thousand a year. Richard's prospects were on the rise, and it was hinted that if he succeeded *there* he might eventually get Marocco, Teheran, and finish up at Constantinople. In fact, we were on the zenith of our career.

I had one very pleasant dinner at Mr. Froude's to meet Giffard Palgrave, Mr. Ruskin, and Carlyle. I brought out Richard's "Highlands of Brazil" for Christmas. I was not successful with the mines, and I found no market for the Brazilian translations, though I published two of them.

Amongst other things I must not forget—

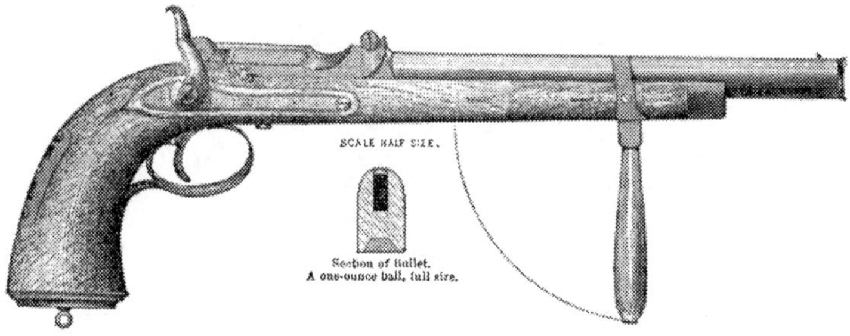

CARBINE PISTOL.

"CAPTAIN BURTON'S CARBINE-PISTOL AND PROJECTILE (PATENTED).

"The principle of the weapon is to avoid the use of the shoulder on horseback. The weapon can be used either as a carbine with both hands, the left arm extended as in archery: in this case the cartridge contains eighty-four grains of gunpowder. Used with one hand, the charge must be reduced to forty-five grains. The projectile serves to blow up ammunition, to fire inflammable articles, and so forth. When explosive projectiles are used with this weapon, a special *safety* bullet has been provided by Captain Burton (see section). It will neither explode if let fall on its point, nor on being fired through brushwood.

"A CAVALRY PISTOL.

"Sir,—Will you kindly allow me to describe in your well-read columns the pistol which is proposed for countries where the traveller's life must often depend upon his weapons?

"I have lately inquired in vain, whilst inspecting stock at half the armouries of the West End, for a single-barrel breech-loading pistol. Of double-barrels there were plenty, but none pleased me. The system of opening the breech is complicated by the presence of two cocks, and it is not what a man requires when looking around at the enemy; he must use the hands without the guidance of the eyes. Moreover, the prices vary from £9 5*s.* to £16. This unconscionable sum is supposed not to include any 'fixings,' even the normal hundred cartridges. I come to the conclusion that the trade prefers the double-barrel simply because the public has to pay double for it. The French are, as usual of late years, well to the fore of us. M. Lefancheux, of Rue Vivienne, has a good single-barrel, throwing a round ball of one ounce (one-sixteenth of a pound); but the breech opening is in a manner which I do not admire, and the price is three hundred francs.

"In conversation with a London gunsmith, I suggested as a holster-pistol a central-fire Albini rifle—the weapon adopted in Belgium—with barrel cut short to about one foot, and the stock changed to a saw-handle; this should, for the purpose of leverage, be made long and heavy. The gunsmith adopted the idea at once, wrote to the Albini Company, and the result was a weapon which, with certain unimportant improvements, will, I believe, presently supplant the popular but uncertain and dangerous revolver, whilst by a tolerably strong wrist it can be used as a pistol. It may be fired at rest on the left arm, or held like a carbine in both hands. With bandolier or cartridge-case bound to his breast, the soldier will readily do with this weapon the work of a succession of revolvers, each holding only five to six shots. The 'Albini pistol' cannot miss fire. How many good lives have been lost by depending upon this revolver! And the pistol deals a one-ounce ball; not the pellets of which many a backwoodsman has taken a cylinderful, and yet has continued 'shyuting' till he killed his man. Finally, it is economical. My weapon, with belt, pouch, and a hundred charges, costs £6 10*s.*; but a large demand will readily bring down the price to £5.

"I am convinced that the Albini, or some similar system, will be the pistol of the future, and I take the liberty of introducing it to you immediately after its birth.*

"RICHARD F. BURTON, F.R.G.S.

"P.S.—In a forthcoming volume upon the Paraguayan War, I hope to show that the pistol will be, *par excellence*, the future arm of cavalry."

FROM THE PRESS.

"A pistol that can kill at five hundred yards has not, we believe, been yet introduced to the public. This boon has been left for Captain Burton to invent, and he has invented, and, what is more, patented it. The butt is that of an ordinary pistol; the barrel is that of a good rifle, cut short, but leaving sufficient 'turn' to send the bullet on its deadly errand with the proper spin. The chief object is to send a rifle-bullet at an enemy or at game without having to use the shoulder, especially when on horseback. And to accomplish this the barrel is fitted with a steel handle to be grasped by the left hand, while the arm is extended as in archery. The left arm is, in fact, formed into a beam of your own flesh and blood, and the carbine-pistol moves freely as on a pivot placed at the end of it, while the butt is directed by the right hand, which takes aim and fires. The recoil is scarcely felt by the rigid left arm; it does not affect the firer so much as the kick to the shoulder would do. The advantage of this arrangement in the case of ladies is obvious. The pistol can also be used with one hand like an ordinary pistol. But in that case it is recommended that the charge be reduced from eighty-four grains of gunpowder to forty-five. The inventor has also provided a patent safety bullet which will explode as a shell when it crashes against the bones of large game, but will pass through brushwood or through the skin of a wild animal like an ordinary ball. It will not explode if let fall upon its apex, but if fired into a box of ammunition it will blow up everything without fail. It is an invaluable projectile, combining the best qualities of the bullet and shell, just the weapon of precision which sends it to its destination, combines the best features of the carbine and the pistol. The carbine-pistol is so light and handy that it will become an indispensable *vade mecum* with people making excursions through jungles in India. No tiger could afford to laugh at it, though in appearance it is as unpretending as a horse-pistol."

This year, before Richard arrived, I had the pleasure of making the acquaintance of Sir Samuel and Lady Baker; I was very much fascinated by the latter, and thought her very pretty. Next day I lunched with them. I also saw a good deal of the Petherwicks,

* I keep two of these pistols in case any one would be willing to order some, so as to push it.—I. B.

and amongst others on his return we dined more than once with my husband's old Egyptian friend, John Larking, at his place, "The Firs," Lea, Kent.

At last the time came round when I got a telegram to say that the *Douro*, Royal Mail, would be at Southampton, with Richard on board; so I went down to Southampton, and at four o'clock in the morning, when Richard looked over the side, I was the first person he saw, and when the plank was thrown across, I was the first to go on board. As far as clothes went, he was pretty nearly in the same condition that I was in, when I arrived from the mines; but for all that, as soon as he had had bath and breakfast, we drove to Netley Abbey, and went to the flower show; then came up to town, and drove to a haberdasher, tailor, and hatter, that he might be fit to dine with my people, who had a party and an enthusiastic reception for him.

He went straight to the Foreign Office next day to report himself, and call on Lord Stanley and Lord Clarendon, who had succeeded to the Foreign Office, and went a round of publishers, mappers, and commissions. That night we had to go to the Admiralty party, and from thence to the Foreign Office party, and the next night, at the Literary Fund, Richard made a speech. He dined with Sir Roderick Murchison, and he went to the Royal Geographical Society Meeting, found it slow, and *was not satisfied with his reception;* he also went to the Levée.

We then went down to Shrewsbury, to stay with Mr. Henry Wace, a bachelor lawyer and a faithful friend, and drove to Uriconium, the Pompeii of Shrewsbury, and then to Haughmond ruins, formerly a Cistercian monastery. Amongst other pleasant things was a lunch-party at Bernal Osborne's, and delightful dinners at Shirley Brookes'.

At last we crossed to France, visited our old haunts where we met as boy and girl. Boulogne, however, was very much changed since our days. She was then "a girl of the period;" she was now "*vieille* and *dévote.*" From here he sent me back, as usual, to "pay, pack, and follow." He was going to Vichy, to take a month's course of the waters, after which he would drop down to Brindisi and go to Damascus.

Soon after Richard had started to Vichy, I began to get unhappy, and wanted to join him, and I did not see why I could not have the month there with him and make up double-quick time after; so I just started off with Mr. J. J. Aubertin (of Brazil memory, whose many works have made him well known, and whose charming "Wanderings and Wonderings" is attracting the literary world now), who was also going there to join him. It was the last *Fête Napoléon.* I never saw Paris so splendid; it was lighter than day —from the Tuileries to the Barrière de L'Étoile it was one mass of light. The Tuileries Gardens were hung with lamps representing huge bunches of grapes, fastened together with festoons and knots the whole length of the Champs Élysées. It was the last blaze of glory; before that day year they were fighting the Germans. As soon as I arrived at Vichy, Richard, with Swinburne, came to the station to meet me, and we were joined by Sir Frederick Leighton, and later on, Mrs. Sartoris.

Vichy is a dull small place, full of sickly people with liver complaints. Like all other places, the baths and the water-drinking fountains are the principal rendezvous. There is the usual band, promenade under the trees, casino, garden, and theatre.

They were very happy days. We made excursions in the day, and in the evenings the conversation, I need not say, was brilliant; everybody contributed something that made him or her valuable. Swinburne recited poetry, Mrs. Sartoris sang to us. All will remember her exquisite contralto voice, and she sang *en intime* without accompaniment.

We went to the Château Bourbonnais at Bussy, and then to Ardoisière cascade and cave, and lovely walks to Malavaux, where there is a châlet at the foot of the mountain and a steep ascent. Here is the ruin of a convent of Templars, who are said to have committed atrocities, who blew up a château containing their only neighbours with gunpowder. There were no roads this way, and they were Lords of the soil. There is a cemetery in the distance, and close to us the Devil's Well, said to have no bottom, and also the Blessed Virgin's Well. Whilst we were at the top, the harvest moon arose; there was a glorious scene of beautiful lights and shadows. Swinburne has lately celebrated this journey in a glorious elegy, of which I quote three verses (the *Fortnightly Review*, July, 1892)—

"The huddled churches clinging on the cliffs
  As birds alighting might for storm's sake cling,
Moored to the rocks as tempest-harried skiffs
  To perilous refuge from the loud wind's wing;

* * * * * *

"Deep down the Valley of the Curse, undaunted
  By shadow and whisper of winds with sins for wings,
And ghosts of crime wherethrough the heights live haunted
  By present sense of past and monstrous things."

The elegy ends—

"But not the soul whose labour knew no end—
  But not the swordsman's hand, the crested head—
The royal heart we mourn, the faultless friend,
  Burton—a name that lives till fame be dead."

From St. Armand there is a splendid view of Vichy, and also for forty-four leagues, if it is clear enough to see around; and the drives are lovely through the mountains and ravines. There was another splendid view from the Montagne Vert. We went to St. Germain des Fosses, and drove all over Clermont, where we visited the Cathedral, all the Churches, Museums, and springs, and bought some of the wonderful petrifactions.* We then made our way to Langéac, from whence we drove thirty-six miles through a most interesting country to Puy. The descent to Puy is very beautiful. It is a curious and striking-looking town; mountains of rock, like huge combs, rise out of its heart. On the top of one of these is a huge statue of the Blessed Virgin, sixteen metres high, cast in iron from the metal cannons of Sebastopol, and we got up into its head to look out of the eyes. When we were in the head we were nearly five hundred feet high from the plain. The Child's head holds three people. The Cathedral has a miraculous black Virgin, and St. Michael has his church too. All these great heights mean climbing five hundred feet, and then ascending two or three hundred steps. On another cone stands an old church. There are basaltic masses just like organ-pipes. We drove to the old Castle and Fortress of Polignac, and to the basaltic rocks, and then we went to see the Museum of Puy. We made our way by the train to Lyons. The country was beautiful, with mountains, gorges, rivers, and old ruined castles, which spoke of feudal times; but two hours before reaching Lyons it is as bad as the black country in Lancashire. Here Swinburne left us for Paris. Richard and I went to Fourvières to make a pilgrimage.† We went to the Cathedral, and the great shrine of Notre Dame de Fourvières. From here Lyons spreads out under your feet like a map; on a clear day you may see Mont Blanc. We visited the source of the Rhone and Saone, and then went on to Culoz; thence to Aix les Bains, where we went to look at the Roman ruins. We changed trains at S. Michel for "Fell's Company" across the Mont Cenis (the railway not being made in those days as it is now). Mr. Bayless, the superintendent, and his secretary met us, and took us on the engine, and showed us everything. The scenery was splendid all day; the rise began from S. Michel to Lanslebourg, which is four thousand four hundred feet high. The ascent was most amusing; we whisked about in the most frolicsome way, close to frightful gorges and over ravines. From inside, you

* Faubourg St. Alyre, "la Fontaine petrifiante" (like Matlock), issues from volcanic tufa on granite. Carbonic acid dissolves calcareous matter.

† There were three things Richard could never resist—a pilgrimage to a holy shrine, mining, and talking with and enjoying gypsies' society.

could sometimes hear little hysterical squeaks, or people taken worse, as the curves were very sharp and the pace good. Lanslebourg is a group of old broken-down châlets, and two broken-down chapels, grouped in a corner. It has a new chapel now. A mountain-torrent sweeps through the village, and the new railway runs by it. Magnificent piles of mountains rose on all sides; the lower range are pine-covered, the higher by snow and glaciers—the snow and fresh mountain air are most exhilarating. I can remember passing this place ten years before, in March, with a carriage and eleven mules, and, owing to the snow, we were five days and nights travelling from Venice to Geneva. It was then a savage country; now every available spot is cultivated in little patches. We had a charming evening at the inn, and dined on fresh mountain trout. The descent next day was marvellous. How little Napoleon I. thought, when he was making a road, that he was only the pioneer for an English railway, thereby making their labour and expense only half of what it would have been! We went from here to Susa and Turin, and from Turin we drove up the Collina, and got a splendid view of the City and of Mount Rosa before going to bed. Here I saw Richard off to Damascus; he was to catch the P. and O. at Brindisi. My train Londonwards left a few hours after, and I did not stop till I reached Paris.

During this short time, Richard's absence permitted a few disagreeables in the geographical line, and as he always relied upon me to answer for him, when he was away, I did so. He said he felt like having a second self on a spot where he could not be, when our affairs compelled us to do double work. Therefore, in answer to a question of Sir Roderick Murchison's, "Where is Livingstone?" I wrote—

"Dr. Livingstone.

"To the Editor of the *Daily Telegraph.*

"Sir,—Will you spare me a little space in your columns to do a service to Dr. Livingstone, by calling attention to Lucenda or Lunda City, the capital of the African chief, known as the Muata (king) Cazembe?

"He is not the least important of the eight negro monarchs—namely, the Muata Ya Noo, vulgarly 'Matiamoo,' in the south; in the eastern tropic, the despots of Karagwáh, of Uganda, and of Unyoro; and, in the western regions, the sanguinary tyrants of Benin, of Dahomè, and of Asiante or Ashantee. And the name of this somewhat obscure potentate has, during the last few weeks, come prominently before the Royal Geographical Society of London.

"Not long ago Sir Roderick Murchison suggested in the *Times* that Dr. Livingstone, having found a discrepancy between the levels of the 'Albert Nyanza' and the Tanganyika lakes, probably turned westward, and attempted to trace the drainage of the latter into the Atlantic Ocean. My husband, Captain Burton, objected to this view of his revered Chief, after whose image—to use the words of the late Lord Strangford—our modern geographers are, so to speak, created. The hydrography of the West African coast is now well known, and it shows no embouchure capable of carrying off so vast an expanse of water as the Tanganyika. The Congo mouth may suggest itself to some, more especially as the north-eastern branch has long been reported to issue from a lake. But the north-eastern is the smaller arm of the two. Moreover, Captain Burton, during his visit to the Yellalah or Rapids, in 1863, ascertained, by questioning the many slaves driven down from the far interior to the Angolan coast, that the Congo lake is distinct from the Tanganyika, and is probably that which figures in old maps as Lake Aquilonda or Achelunda. It will not be forgotten that our good friend Paul du Chaillu made sundry stout-hearted attempts to reach that mysterious basin, concerning which he is also of opinion that it is wholly independent of the Nile Valley.

"The latest intelligence touching Dr. Livingstone suggests the possibility of his having been detained in the capital of the Cazembe, and at once explains the non-appearance of the traveller, and the want of communications, so heartrending to his host of friends. Why are we whispering this to one another as a secret? The report, if we believe in its truth, should be published throughout the length and breadth of England, whose great heart will readily supply men and means to rescue one of her favourite sons from a precarious and perhaps perilous position.

"Unhappily for himself, Dr. Livingstone, unlike Captain Burton, has never made a friend of the Moslem. He has openly preferred to him the untutored African—in other words, the vile and murderous Fetisheer—and his published opinions must be known even at Zanzibar to the religion of the State. The Maskat Arabs are, as my husband reported long ago, all-powerful at the city of Cazembe; and if Dr. Livingstone be detained there, it is doubtless at their instigation.

"I should not have ventured to trouble you with this letter, but Captain Burton is *en route* for Damascus, and I have written to him to supply the public with a complete account of the scene of Dr. Livingstone's supposed captivity, which may tend to suggest the properest measures for securing the safety of a Christian hero who has offered up the flower of his days to the grand task of regenerating the Dark Continent.

"I have the honour to be, Sir,

"Yours obediently,

"ISABEL BURTON.

"October 23, 1869."

I worked in earnest during my few weeks in England, to be able to join him the quicker. First, I had to go down to Stratford, to the Essex flats, to see the tube-wells worked, as Richard was anxious to be able to produce water, if possible, wherever we stopped in the desert. I had many publishers and mappers to see. Not knowing exactly what Damascus was like, I invested in a pony-carriage, and Uncle Gerard gave me a very handsome old family chariot, which was out of fashion in England, and must originally have cost at least three hundred guineas. Lord Houghton made a great many jokes about our driving in our chariot drawn by camels. I very prudently left it in England until I saw what sort of place it was, but took out the pony-carriage. There was only one road in the country, of seventy-two miles, so I sold it, and was actually lucky enough to find a willing customer, who kept it as a curio. I took lessons about taking off wheels and patent axles, and oiling them and putting them together again, and taking my own guns and pistols also to pieces, cleaning and putting them together again. The time passed in buying things to stock the house with. Richard did not receive any of my letters, just as at Pernambuco, so I had to telegraph to him.

During this time Mr. William Crookes and I visited the Mesmeric Hospital, where, I regret to say, I did a good deal of unintentional mischief, by absorbing the mesmerism from the patients; and I attended the meetings of the Royal Geographical Society, and felt very angry with Sir Roderick Murchison, which I expressed in two letters attached to the Nile affair, as follows:—

"The Sources of the Nile.

"To the Editor of the *Times*.

"Sir,—As you daily devote a certain portion of the *Times* to redressing wrongs, I may hope that you will not make an exception to the disadvantage of Captain Burton.

"Five African explorers have pined for the honour of discovering the sources of the Nile, and each one in his turn has believed himself to be that fortunate person, until now that Livingstone (the one who cared the least for that honour) has discovered waters more southerly still. We have all been looking forward with eagerness for this news. Judge, then, of my mortification at the meeting of the Royal Geographical Society on Monday night, to hear all the papers read and discussed almost without reference to Captain Burton, who is *en route* to Damascus. His lake (Tanganyika), which lies the nearest to Livingstone's new discovery, was almost skipped over, and my revered friend, Sir Roderick Murchison, spoke of 'Central, or Equatorial Africa, in which lie those great water basins which, thanks to the labours of Speke, Grant, and Baker, are known to feed the Nile.' After the meeting I went up to Sir Roderick Murchison and asked him *why* Captain Burton had been left out, and he replied in the kindest manner, 'that if it had been so, it was a mere oversight, which he was sorry should have occurred,' and I heard him give the order that it should be rectified in the report before sent to press. I see by your columns of Wednesday, the 10th, *that it was not done*, and I therefore ask you in kindness and courtesy to insert these few lines, that Captain Burton may not be counted for nothing by that large meeting on Monday night in the matter nearest his heart.

"In 1854 and 1855 Captain Burton was employed in heading the Somali Expedition (which ended so fatally), taking with him Captain Speke and two others. From 1856 to 1859 he was occupied in exploring Central Equatorial Africa, taking again Captain Speke as second in command. He was the first to conceive the idea twenty years ago, the first to enter and to penetrate that country, which he did under every obstacle and difficulty, bringing back sufficient information to smooth the path to all who chose to follow him. Lake Tanganyika was his first discovery, Nyanza was Speke's.

"In 1860 Captain Speke started on his own account, taking Captain Grant as second in command, whereby we gained some three hundred and fifty geographical miles, only hitherto known by vague report. Captain Burton spent those three years on the West Coast, at Dahomè and Du Chaillu's country, making ten years, off and on, in Africa.

"Then followed Sir Samuel Baker's Lake, and now Livingstone's.

"It is therefore *impossible* to ignore Captain Burton's services in the Nile question. Dr. Livingstone has undoubtedly discovered *the* sources,* and must rank the first, but no man can claim the second honour, or the water nearest Livingstone's discovery, but Captain Burton, and no one can deny the fact that he, so to speak, opened the oyster for the others to get at the pearl.

"All our friends are asking me why he was left out the other night, and the kind-hearted ones offer me the consoling proverb that 'good wine needs no bush,' which, after all, is nonsense to any but connoisseurs.

"I am, Sir, yours obediently,

"ISABEL BURTON.

"14, Montagu Place, Montagu Square,
"November 12th, 1869."

I then sent to the *Athenæum* the little tracing of 1856, which I have inserted in page 254, with the following letter:—

* Which turned out afterwards to be an error—it was the head waters of the Great Zaire or Congo River that he discovered.

"THE SOURCES OF THE NILE.

"To the Editor of the *Athenæum*.

"November 20th, 1869.

"I enclose you a copy of a small map which I have had for many years in my possession, showing Captain Burton's theory respecting the sources of the Nile as far back as 1856. In that year he left England to command the Expedition for their discovery, which had been the object of his thoughts and studies for many previous years—always a disciple of Ptolemy. Captain Speke joined him, and after three years of unheard-of difficulties and dangers, they returned, having discovered Tanganyika. Whilst they were absent, Captain Burton, being very ill for a short time, and experiencing a yearning to be alone, sent Captain Speke on a twenty days' march to try and find a lake, which his calculations, theories, and inquiries from the Arabs, assured him ought to be there. Speke sighted a water then, and subsequently found on his next expedition, but much farther north, a lake which he called Victoria Nyanza.

"I quote a note from Captain Burton's 'Nile Basin,' p. 37, which is the pivot of the whole affair: 'I distinctly deny that any "misleading, by my instructions from the Royal Geographical Society as to the position of the White Nile," left me unconscious of the vast importance of ascertaining the Rusizi river's direction. The fact is, Captain Speke was deaf and almost blind. I was paralytic, and we were both helpless [he might have added penniless]. We did our best to reach it, and failed.'

"Captain Burton always said from the first that the Nile must have many sources, and that there were probably waters south of the Tanganyika. In his 'Lake Regions' he speaks of a large river, Marungu, draining the southern countries towards the Tanganyika, and entering the lake at its southernmost point, which has now been proved by Dr. Livingstone.* He was misled by Captain Speke's erroneous elevation of the lake, and by the more than probably wrong information received from the African chiefs, as interpreted by his negro servant Bombay. In short, Captain Speke determined to have his own lake at all hazards, and for a time he became master of the field.

"I am anxious, before I sail to join Captain Burton at Damascus—and I have not many days left—to claim Captain Burton's proper position amongst the five explorers of the lakes, having already had a reminder that '*les absents ont toujours tort*.' That position means, *second* to Livingstone as explorer, to whom he has shown the way to the Nile, and *first* as lake discoverer.

"The outlines of the map I refer to were drawn for me in 1856, and where lakes are now correctly marked on maps stood pencil notes, which said, 'Should be water here,' 'Supposed site of a lake.'

* Dr. Livingstone died with this belief, but he had really discovered the head-waters of the Great Zaire or Congo River (1892).

The lakes and names were successively filled up for me in 1859 and 1864. Perhaps you may think it interesting enough to give it a place in your paper, and will kindly allow this letter to accompany it; or the letter by itself if there is no room for the map.

"ISABEL BURTON."

Then appeared in *Punch*—

"A CARD FROM THE ISLE OF AFRICA.

"Father Nile presents his respectful compliments to Mr. Punch, and (with grateful remembrance of the delightful way in which that gentleman depicted saucy Miss Britannia discovering the Father among his rushes, a few years back) begs leave to inform Mr. Punch, and therefore the world, that the Father, at the suggestion of the REVEREND DOCTOR LIVINGSTONE, has removed his head-quarters to a delightful region, about eleven degrees south of the Equator, or Equinoxious line, where for the present he is to be found by his friends. Carriages to set down at Cazembe, a couple of hundred miles or so south of Burton's Lake Tanganyika.

"N.B.—You are heartily welcome to any refreshments which you may bring with you. Niggers about here don't need to be shot."

"NAME! NAME!

"DEAR PUNCH,

"Over the signature 'Isabel Burton,' names belonging to the accomplished wife of the Consul at Damascus, hath appeared (*Times*) a wifely and spirited letter, pointing out that at the great geographical meeting last week, recognition was not made of the discovery, by Captain Burton, of Lake Tanganyika.

"Sir, I am glad of anything that causes Mrs. Burton to publish anything. Unlike some of her sex (and of mine), that lady can think as well as write.

"But I have two reasons for wishing that another system of nomenclature, in regard to places, were adopted.

"(1) I am not good at spelling, even in English, and the barbarous names given by savages worry me much, and send me across the room to atlases, and the like, when it is a bother to me to get off my chair. Perhaps on cold days, like to-day, my style, in the winter, is much more involved than in summer. This is because, to avoid going into the cold, I go into periphrase, and circumvent hard words.

"(2) Injustice, like that indicated by Mrs. Burton (in this case accidental; Sir Roderick is *sans reproche*), would be impossible if new discoveries were stamped properly.

"Henceforth call Lake Nyanza Lake Speke-Grant; the lake above mentioned (which I pray you to excuse me from spelling a second time), Lake Burton; and the new aggregation of water, now believed to be the Nile source, Lake Livingstone, and oblige

"Your faithful friend,

"EPICURUS ROTUNDUS.

"Goneril Villa, Regan Park."

At last the day came round when everything was bought and paid for, and packed and sent off, and I was at liberty to start; and the same night that my arrangements were complete, I left my mother's house for Dover. It was blowing a hurricane, waves mountain high, and a black night, and my brother and sisters, who accompanied me, decided that I must not go on board. I have told that story in my "Inner Life of Syria." Next morning, however, we picked up the poor passengers, who had crossed the night before, and had come to grief. At Paris I found that two of my nine boxes were missing; one contained all my ship comforts, and the other £300 in gold—my little all. I had already taken my passage at Marseilles, and I had to choose between losing my money and losing my passage. I went to the station-master, registered my tale, omitting all about the money, told him where to forward the baggage,* travelled on, and was just in time to catch the P. and O. *Tanjore* before she steamed out, and I immediately, on arrival at Alexandria, took my passage on board the first steamer for Beyrout, which was a Russian, the *Ceres*, which passes or touches at Port Said and Jaffa, and Kaifa, the ancient Helba of the tribe of Aser, St. Jeanne d'Acre, and then I arrived at Beyrout.

* They both arrived five months later, and, strange to say, intact.

CHAPTER XX.

DAMASCUS—HIS THIRD CONSULATE.

THERE was no husband to meet me, and I felt very indignant, just as had happened at Rio last year to him. (Here I met Madame de Persigny.) I at once started for Damascus by road, in a private carriage, and drove for seven hours, putting up at Shtorra, where I was obliged to sleep. Next day I drove on and on, and reached Damascus at sunset; went straight to the inn, which by courtesy was called a hotel, known as Demetri's. It had taken me fifteen days and nights without stopping from London to Damascus. After an hour Richard came in, and I was glad that I had waited for nothing but necessity, as I found him looking very old and ill. He had arrived, and had had a most cordial reception, but he had been dispirited by not getting a single one of my letters, which all arrived in a heap afterwards. He had gone down over and over again to meet me, and I had not appeared, and now the steamer that I had come in, was the only one he did not go down to meet, so that when he came in from his walk, it was a pleasant surprise to him to find me ensconced comfortably in his room; and I found the enclosed scribbled on the corner of his journal, anent my non-arrival—

"'Twas born, thou whisperest, born in heaven,
  And heavenly births may never die;
While truth is pure of leasing's leaven,
  I hear and I believe then—I!
Heaven-born, thy love is born to be
An heir of immortality.

"And yet I hear a small voice say,
  But yesterday 'twas not begot;
It lives its insect-life to-day,
  To-morrow death shall be its lot.
Peace, son of lies! cease, Satan, cease
To mumble timeworn lies like these!"

A few persons who disliked the appointment, and certain missionaries who feared that he was anti-missionary, and have since handsomely acknowledged their mistake, took measures to work upon Lord Clarendon on the plea that he was too fond of Mohammedans, that he had performed a pilgrimage to Mecca, and that their fanaticism would lead to troubles and dangers. On becoming aware that he had lived in the East, and with Moslems, for many years after his pilgrimage, Lord Clarendon, with that good taste and justice which always characterized him, refused to change his appointment until that fanaticism was proved. He had the pleasure of reporting to him a particularly friendly reception.

He wrote before he left London—

"I now renew in writing the verbal statement, in which I assured your lordship that neither the authorities nor the people of Damascus will show for me any but a friendly feeling; that, in fact, they will receive me as did the Egyptians and the people of Zanzibar for years after my pilgrimage to Mecca. But, as designing persons may have attempted to complicate the situation, I once more undertake to act with unusual prudence, and under all circumstances to hold myself, and myself only, answerable for the consequences."

Though he had not received his barat (*exequatur*) and firman till October 27th, he exchanged friendly unofficial visits with his Excellency the *Wali* (Governor-General) of Syria. Then he was honoured with the visits of all the prelates of the Oriental Churches, as well as by a great number of the most learned and influential Moslems, and of the principal Christians. Amongst them were his Highness the Amir Abd el Kadir, his Excellency the Bishop of the Greek Orthodox Church, the Syrian Orthodox and the Syrian Catholic Bishops, the Archimandrite Jebara of the Russian Orthodox Church, the Shaykh el Ulemá (Abdullah Effendi el Hálabi), the Shaykh el Molawíyyeh of Koniah, Ali Pasha el Aazam, and Antun Effendi Shami; Said Effendi Ustuwáneh, President of the Criminal Court of Damascus and its dependencies; Mohammed Effendi el Minnini, Vice-President of the Criminal Court of Appeal; the Mufti Mahmúd Effendi Hamzeh; Shaykh Mohammed Effendi el Hálabi, member of the Lower Court, and several others.

All these dignitaries evinced much pleasure and satisfaction at his being appointed H.M.'s Consul in their City. Some of them, indeed, earnestly requested him to interest the English public in forming a company for making railways through Syria, that being the sole means of bringing about the civilization of the country.

In conclusion, notwithstanding Abdullah Effendi, the Chief of the Ulemá, being the most learned, influential, and Orthodox Moslem, and though it is not consistent with his principles to call upon any

Christian before being visited, he did so; and, after an interview of fifty minutes, departed with a promise to renew the visit.

Owing to the great quantity of fountains and tanks about the house, neuralgia had set in, and Richard had not been getting any sleep; so the following day we cast about for a better sort of living-place, and a quarter of an hour away, through the gardens of Damascus, higher up than Damascus, and just under and on the north of Jebel Kaysún, the Camomile Mountain, in what is *called* a wild and lawless Kurdish village, we found a house that suited us,* and we took it, and moved into it next day, starting with a small quantity of furniture, but soon made it very comfortable. After all said and done, although some of the houses in Damascus were very grand and very romantic, they were all damp; cold in winter; suffocating, from being closed in, in summer. If there is an epidemic, it is like being hived. If there is an *émeute*, you are like a mouse in a trap. If there is a fire at night, you are safely locked within the town gates. Ours was a freer and wilder life; you could mount your horse, and be out in the desert in ten minutes, or in Damascus either.

Mr. and Lady Adelaide Law arrived in Damascus, and I took her to Lady Ellenborough and to Abd el Kadir. It was her father, Lord Londonderry, whose diplomacy with Louis Napoleon delivered this great hero from imprisonment in the Château d'Amboise, and he received her with effusion. Later on came Lord Stafford (present Duke of Sutherland), Mr. Crawley, and Mr. Barty Mitford.

We were soon installed, and bought horses, and I began to study Arabic. The first thing Richard determined to do was to go to Tadmor. This journey was an awfully difficult thing in those days, though I am not aware whether it is now. First of all, six thousand francs used to be charged by the El Mezrab, who were the tribe who escorted for that journey. It was the tribe of Lady Ellenborough and her Bedawin husband, and she was more Bedawin than the Bedawi. There was no water, that is, only two wells the whole way, and only known to them. The difficulties and dangers were great; they travelled by night and hid by day. You may say that camels were about ten days on the road, and horses about eight days. The late Lady Ellenborough was the third of a small knot of ladies, of whom I had hoped to make the fifth—Lady Mary Wortley

* "We were living at the foot of the eastern spur of the Anti-Libanus, upon whose south-eastern slopes lies the large northern suburb of Damascus, El Salahíyyah ('of the Saints'), facetiously changed on account of its Kurdish population into El Talahíyyah ('of the Sinners'). Our friend Bedr Beg was its Chief."—R. F. B.

Montagu, Lady Hester Stanhope, Lady Ellenborough, and the Princesse de la Tour d'Auvergne.

Lady Ellenborough was married to a Bedawin, brother to the Chief, and second in command of the tribe of El Mezrab, a small branch of the great Anazeh tribe. She aided the tribe in concealing the wells and levying blackmail on Europeans who wished to visit Palmyra, which brought in considerable sums to the tribe, whose demand was six thousand francs a head (£240). Richard was determined to go, and we had not the money to throw away; he asked me whether I would be willing to risk it, and I said, what I always did, "Whither thou goest, I will go." Lady Ellenborough was in a very anxious state when she heard this announcement, as she knew it was the death-blow to a great source of revenue to the tribe. She was very intimate with us, and distantly connected by marriage with my family, and she would have favoured us, if she could have done it without abolishing the whole system. She did all she could to dissuade us; she wept over our loss, and she told us that we should never come back—indeed, everybody advised us to make our wills; finally, she offered us the escort of one of her Mezrabs, that we might steer clear of the Bedawi raids, and be conducted quicker to water, *if it existed.* Richard made me a sign to accept the escort, and we did.

From our earliest married days, one of his peculiarities (used rather, I suspect, for training me to observe him, and to understand his wants) would be that he would not tell me directly to do a thing, but I used to find in a book I was reading, or some drawer that I opened every day, or in his own room, marked by a weight, a few words of what he wanted, conveying no direct order, and yet I knew that it was one. I grew quite accustomed to this, and used regularly to visit the places where I was likely to find them, and if I missed there was a sort of "Go seek" expression on his face, that told me that I had not hunted properly, and I knew (by another expression) when I had succeeded. I used to call these "African spoors." We could almost talk before outsiders in this way, without speaking a word out loud.

On the same principle, he used to teach me to swim without my arms, and afterwards to swim without my legs, using either one or the other, but not both, in case of falling out of a steamer and being entangled.

I mention this, because we always talked before people without their perceiving it, and he told me in this way exactly what to say to her; but we provided ourselves with seventeen camels, laden with water, in case of accident. We had each two horses, and everything necessary for tenting out, and were armed to the teeth. We had a very picturesque breakfast, affectionate farewells—the *Mushir* and the whole cavalcade to see us out of the town. We cleared Damascus and its environs by a three hours' march; then Richard, according to his custom, called a halt, and we camped out and picketed, because, he said, it would be so easy to send back for anything, if aught were missing.

We eventually reached Da'as Agha, the Chief of Jerúd, who has a hundred and fifty fighting men. These little villages in the middle of a desert are sometimes very acceptable for the renewal of provisions. This Jerúd was a large one, and was surrounded with salt and gypsum. After this there was only one more village, Atneh, till the Great Karryatayn, in the heart of the desert. Here we were told of some underground curiosities, and we stopped to dig, and discovered an old catacomb. The women only wear one garment; they are covered with coins, and bits of stone made into necklaces and charms against the evil eye. After this we had a long desert ride, and were caught in a dust-storm. A dust-storm is no joke; you may lie down and perhaps make your horse lie, and cover yourself up with rugs, but if it is a bad storm, like a snowstorm, you may be buried. Richard advised our galloping through it, laying the reins on the horses' necks, and letting them go where they would, for, he said, they would know a great deal more than we should; so, covering our faces up in our *kuffiyyehs*—for, as far as heads and shoulders went, we dressed like natives—we gave our horses their heads, and they went at a rattling pace, and about three hours took us out of the storm. Richard and I were alone; all the rest lagged behind. When the horses once got out of the storm (they seemed to understand all about it—one was desert bred and took the lead), they relapsed into a walk till they got cool. We then went by the compass in the direction we meant to take, and were joined eventually by our followers.

We now had to sleep in our clothes, revolvers and guns at our sides, and make our men take turn to watch, in case of an attack from a *ghazú*, or Bedawi raid, and we took off the camels' bells. A *ghazú* may pass you in the night, and if you are quite silent, and a foal does not whinny, nor a dog bark, you are all right; but those are the two things you have to dread. I ought to have said that, though we accepted the escort, we were not hoodwinked. I kept taking stock of our Mezrab between Damascus and our first halt, and I thought he had an uncanny and *amused* look; so I rode up to Richard, and told him, in a language that was not understood, what I thought. Richard gave a grim smile, as Ouida says, "under his moustache," and said, "Yes, I have thought all that out too. Mohammed Agha, come here."

Whatever Richard told Mohammed to do, he did it thoroughly. If he wanted a culprit that had run away, he would say, "Bring me So-and-so, Mohammed." "Eywallah! ya Sidi Beg" (Yes, by Allah, my Lord Beg); and he would go off, saying, "If he were in hell I would have him out." Once he brought a man kicking and struggling under his arm, and put him down before Richard, saying, "There he is, your Excellency."

This faithful Afghan had served him in India, and he had accidentally found him in Damascus, and made him his chief *kawwás*. He now rode up. Richard gave him a few orders in Afghani, which no one else understood. He saluted and retired. When we got about three hours away from Damascus in the open desert, the Bedawin had his mare and his arms taken from him, and was mounted on a baggage mule. Every kindness was shown to him, and he enjoyed every comfort that we had, but two mounted guard over him day and night, and he was thus powerless. We knew quite well that the Bedawin, on his thoroughbred mare, would have curveted off in circles, pretending to look for wells, when in reality he would have fetched the tribe down upon us, and we should have been captured; orders would have been given to respect and treat us well, and then we should have to be ransomed, and this would have *proved* the impossibility of visiting Palmyra without a Bedawi escort at six thousand francs a head, and the Foreign Office would have smartly reproved, and perhaps recalled, their Consul for running such a risk. We stuck our Mezrab up for a show, to prove that we had a Bedawin escort, whenever Bedawi raids were near, but he was not allowed to move or to make a sign. Da'as joined us with ten of his men, and whenever there was the smallest occasion for joy or self-congratulation, they used to do a *Jeríd*. When I say the men are riding *Jeríd*, I mean that they are galloping about violently, firing from horseback at full speed, yelling, hanging over in their stirrups with their bridles in their mouth, playing with and quivering their long feathered lances in the air, throwing them and catching them again at full gallop, picking things from the ground that they have thrown there, firing pistols, throwing themselves under the horses' bellies and firing under them at full gallop, yelling and shouting their war-cry, as Buffalo Bill's cowboys do, only far more picturesque figures, with their many-coloured dresses, and better mounted on their beautiful mares. The wildness of the whole spectacle is very refreshing; but you have to be a good rider yourself, as the horses simply go wild.

On one occasion we saw a large body, apparently of mounted Bedawi. We waved and whistled our stragglers in, and drew up in line; the others did the same. We fully expected a charge. By this time I had transformed myself into a boy (Richard's son)—found it more convenient for riding long distances, and for running away. It *sounds* indecent, but all Arab clothes are so baggy and draping that it little matters whether you are dressed as a man or woman. So he let me ride out with two other horsemen from the ranks forward (it would have been undignified for *him* to do so, being in command of the party); they did the same, and this is what it proved to be—the Shaykh and his fighting men on the part of a distant village, and a priest on the part of the Archbishop of Karryatayn, with invitations. All the men embraced, my hand was kissed, and we were escorted back in great triumph, riding *Jeríd* as before. We rode to the village of the Shaykh, and we sent on others with our letters to Omar Beg, the Brigadier at that time commanding troops at Karryatayn, because they expected a revolt of the tribes.

We eventually arrived at Karryatayn. We were treated with great hospitality by Omar Beg, and when we left he accompanied us a little way with an immense cavalcade, which was very picturesque and pretty. We saw a mirage that day in the desert, and were very tired, and had to sleep with our arms, without undressing. We then had a somewhat dangerous defile to pass through mountains, where we found a well. I had invented a capital way of watering the beasts. Man can always draw water, but nobody thinks of the horses, and in a cup or tin pot you cannot get enough water for them. I had bags made of skins, exactly like a huge tobacco-pouch with ropes, and whenever we came to inaccessible water *these* were lowered until every animal had drank its fill. At each of these places, Jerúd, Atneh, and Karryatayn, several who had been longing to go to Tadmor wanted to join us, secure of protection, of food for themselves, and corn for their animals without paying a farthing for it. We increased to a hundred and sixty persons, and some had one and some two animals. I had one man with me as my own servant, a Syrian Christian, who gave us a great deal of trouble. He was very clever, and the best dancer; but the second or third day after a hard day's ride, the horses were dead beat, and instead of taking his horse and watering and feeding it, and putting it in shelter as I desired, he drew his sword and cut its throat, in hopes of being allowed to ride my second horse, so I ordered him off to the baggage in the rear. No Moslem would have done such a thing. I never liked him after. We could not turn the man out to die in the desert, but the day that we got back to Damascus, my husband sent him to prison, for that and thefts in the houses where we stayed.

We met with another *ghazú* before we arrived, but we imposed on them by calling a halt, planting the flag, showing our Bedawin, and ordering breakfast to be spread. We then improvised a *tir* by planting a lance in the sand at a good distance, with a pumpkin at the top, or an orange, and showed them how far our rifles would carry, and the *ghazú* being mounted on mares, not camels, we were not attacked. A few of ours curveted about, preparatory to bolting, but my husband called out to the men to form into line, and then he shouted, "The first man who leaves this line, I'll shoot him in the back as he rides away." That made them settle down.

The first sight of Palmyra makes you think it is a regiment of cavalry drawn out in single line on the horizon; it was the most imposing sight I ever looked upon, though I have seen plenty of other ruins. It is so gigantic, so extensive, so bare, so desolate, rising out of, and partially buried in a sea of sand. There is something that almost takes your breath away about this splendid City of the Dead. When you are alone and gazing in silence upon her solitary grandeur, you feel as if you were wandering in some unforgotten world, and respect and wonder bid you hush like a child amidst the tombs of a long-closed and forgotten churchyard. This was the Tadmor built by Solomon, as a safe halt for the treasures of India and Persia passing through the desert (2 Paralipomenon or Chronicles viii. 4), "And he built Tadmor in the wilderness, and all the store cities, which he built in Hamar." Read also 3 Kings or 1 King ix. 18.

I shall never forget the imposing sight of Tadmor. There is nothing so deceiving as distance in the desert. At sea you may calculate it, but in the desert you never can. A distant ruin stands out of the sea of sand, the atmosphere is so clear that you think you will reach it in half an hour; you ride all day and you never seem to get any nearer to it, just as if it receded in proportion as you advanced. We camped outside, close to the great colonnade. We had five tents, our free-lances ten, the rest of the party theirs, and the animals close by. There were four sulphurous streams; we kept one to drink, and one to bathe, and two for the animals. There is a height of rock on which is a castle; the mountain-top was cruised all around with an infinity of labour to form a drawbridge and moat. The ascent is exceedingly steep. On two sides is a fine range of mountains, on the other two a desert of sand, stretching far away like a yellow sea. The ruins and a small oasis caused by the foundation lie at our feet. It is possible that Tadmor once spread over all the irrigated part of the plain. A few orchards, and the splendid ruins, and a handful of wretched people have huts plastered like wasps' nests within them. The whole City must have been composed of parallel streets, and similar streets crossing them, some formed by immense columns, and stretching far over the plains, and cornered by temples and castles. The Temple of the Sun was carved from great blocks of rock from the mountains; has some fine cornices, some still perfect. In one direction there is a falling wall on the slant, as if it was arrested in falling. It has a square court of seven hundred and forty feet each side, encompassed by a wall seventy feet high. The central door is thirty-two feet high and sixteen wide. The temple still has one hundred columns standing. The few people who live there are disgusting and ophthalmic.

The tombs are a great interest—tall square towers with a handsome frontage. Inside are four stories. The ceilings are beautiful; the entrances are lined with Corinthian columns and busts. There are tiers to the very top for bodies. One contained one hundred bodies. One bore a 102 B.C. date, one Anno Domini 2—evidently a very swell family, and all speaking of sad ruined grandeur. The ruins are enormous and extensive, and simply splendid. I cannot describe the sensation of being in a great City of the Dead, and thinking over all the story of Zenobia and her capture, especially by moonlight. The simoom blew our tents nearly down part of the time. Richard discovered caves, and he spent several days excavating. We found human curios, human bones, and skulls with hair on them, which we brought home. There is a sulphurous river, bright as crystal, and tepid with the properties of Vichy. Water issues from a cavernous hole in the mountain, and streams through Palmyra. A separate spring, of the same quality, bubbles up in the sand near it. The Damascenes send for Vichy water; why don't they get it from here? We also found some Greek statues; one of Zenobia, life size. Some of our men were taken with *wahteb*, a disease peculiar to Syria, and hereditary—a sort of convulsions or hysteria. They generally get a firstborn to tread up and down the back, but I brought them to quicker with doses of hot brandy and water. We returned by a different route part of the way. There is a well-known river and outwork six hours' ride away from Palmyra, called Selamíyyah, and bearing east-south-east of the Mount of Hamah. Here begins a high rolling ground called El Aláh, which we come to later on. We had very bad weather, and our tents were nearly carried away at night. We had a wild-boar hunt on the way. We fell in with fifty Bedawi; they were not strong enough to attack us, but we had to stick to our baggage. Our usual day in the desert (in which we lived off and on) was as follows:—

The usual travelling day is that those who had anything to do rose two hours before starting, but those who had not got into their saddles at dawn. Being, as one may say, head *sais*, or groom, I saw the horses groomed, fed, watered, and saddled. Our dragomans * attended to striking the tents and the baggage. We started at dawn, and rode until the sun was unbearable; we then halted for one or two hours. The animals were ungirthed, fed, and watered, and we had our food and smoke, and perhaps a short sleep; after which we mounted, and rode till near sunset. We then halted for the night. The tents were pitched. If we were near an inhabited place Richard sat in state on his divan and received the Chiefs with *narghíleh* and sherbet; I saluted, and walked off with the horses. I had drilled my people so well that they were all drawn up in line; at one word of command, off with the bridles, and on with the head-stalls; at another word the saddles off, the perspiring backs rubbed with a handful of *raki*, to prevent galls, and the horse-cloths thrown on. They were then led about to cool for a quarter of an hour, then ridden down to water, if there was any, or watered out of the skins if there were not, and their nose-bags put on with *tibn*—straw chopped up as fine as mincemeat, the hay of this country—then picketed in a ring, heels out, heads in, hobbled fore and aft, and grooms in the middle.

I would then go back to my husband, and sit on the divan at a respectful distance and in respectful attitude, speak little, and be invited to have a sherbet or *narghíleh.* I then saluted, and went to see the horses groomed for the night, and get their suppers; then I returned to my husband's tent, supper and bed, and to-morrow *da capo.* The baggage animals, with provisions and water, are directed to a given place so many hours in advance by the compass. One man of our riding-party slings on the saddle-bags, containing something to eat and drink; another hangs a water-melon or two to his saddle, another the skins to draw water for the horses, and another or two, nose-bags with corn. We ride on till about eleven, and dismount at the most convenient place, and water as we go along, if there is any. The horses' girths are slackened, their bridles changed for halters; they drink, if possible, and their nose-bags are filled with one measure of barley. We eat, smoke, and sleep for one hour or two; we then ride on again till we reach our tents.

We are supposed to find them pitched, mattresses and blankets spread, mules and donkeys free and rolling to refresh themselves, baggage stacked, the gypsy-pot over a good fire, and perhaps a

* If any one wants dragomans, let them give preference above all to Melhem Wardi, of Beyrout, and consult his brother Antun.

glass of lemonade or a cup of coffee ready for us. It does sometimes happen that we miss our camp, that we have the ground for bed, the saddle for pillow, and the water-melon for supper. Richard used to take all the notes, sketches, observations, and maps, and gather all the information. The sketches and maps were Charles Drake's business, when with us. I acted as secretary and aide-de-camp, and had the care of the stable and any sick or wounded men; I could also help him with the sextant, and with some of his scientific instruments.

A short day's riding would be eight hours, a very long one would be thirteen, and we generally stayed at any place of interest till it was exhausted. In this way we saw all Syria, Palestine, and the Holy Land off the beaten tracks, and through the deserts, the Haurán and wild places included. I do not like to say too much about it, because my two volumes of "Inner Life of Syria," which were published in 1875, and "Unexplored Syria," written by Richard, Charley Drake, and me (2 vols., 1872), have mostly told everything. These will be republished in the Uniform Library.

Camping out is the most charming thing in the world, and its scenes will always live in my memory. It is a very picturesque life, although hard, but one gets so used to it, as quite to dislike a house. I can never forget some of those lovely nights in the desert, as after supper we all sat round in circles; the mules, donkeys, camels, horses, and mares picketed about, screaming, kicking, and holloaing; the stacked loads, the big fires, the black tents, the Turkish soldiers, the picturesque figures in every garb, and wild and fierce-looking men in wonderful costumes lying here and there, singing and dancing barbarous dances (especially the sword-dance); or stories told, or Richard reciting the "Arabian Nights," or poor Palmer chanting Arab poetry, or Charley Drake practising magic to astonish the Moghâribehs, though neither of these two were with us *then*. A glorious moon lights our tripod and kettle; the jackals howl and chatter as they sniff the savoury bones, and if you can remain breathless, it is the prettiest thing to see them gambol in the moonlight, jumping over one another's backs, but if one, smelling food, runs round your tent when all are asleep, the shadow on the white canvas is so large that it frightens you. A distant pack coming along sounds like the war-cry of the Bedawi booming down upon you; their yell is unearthly as it sweeps by you, passes, and dies away in the distance. I used to love the sound, because it told me I was in camp, by far the most delightful form of existence when the weather is not too cruel.

Madame Omar Beg's two pets were a hyæna, which received me

at the gate, and a lynx that lay upon the divan. The first put its fore-paws on my shoulders and smelt my cheek, and did "pouf" (like a bellows blowing in your face) to frighten me; and the other sprang at me and mewed and lashed its tail. For sheer fright I stood stock still and they did nothing to me, and amused Madame Omar immensely when she came in.

Camel-riding is very pleasant, if it is a *delúl* with a long trot, but a slow walk is horribly tedious, a baggage animal is bone-breaking, and a gallop would be utter annihilation. A *shugduf* or *takhtarawán* shakes you till you are sore. The nicest mount is horse or mare—mare safer; but Richard did a very wise thing—he chose *rahwáns.* They run an American trot, and there is no more fatigue in riding them than sitting in an armchair. You have only to sit still and let them go, and they cover enormous spaces in the day; so he used to arrive perfectly fresh when we were all tired out. I possessed a couple of stallions. I was headstrong and foolish, and I would ride them, because I hated the *rahwáns'* paces; so I took a great deal more out of myself than I need have done, as they generally danced for a couple of hours before they settled down to their work. However much you may love the desert and camp life, when you have had your fill of it, I cannot tell how refreshing it is to see the first belt of green, like something dark lining the horizon, and to long to reach it. When you enter by degrees under the trees, the orchards, the gardens of Damascus, you smell the water from afar, and you hear its gurgling long before you come to the rills and fountains; you scent and then see the fruit—the limes, figs, citron, water-melon; you feel a madness to jump into the water, to eat your fill of fruit, to go to sleep under the delicious shade.

Such is entering Damascus. You forget the bitter wind, the scorching sun, the blistering sand; you wonder if it is true that you are going to have a bath, to change your clothes, to sleep in a real bed, without having to watch against Bedawi, or if your brain is hurt by the sun, or if your blinded eyes are seeing a mirage. Your tired, drooping horse tells you it is true; he pricks his ears, he wants to break out into a mild trot; done up as he is, he stops to drink at every rill, and, with a low whinny of joy, gathers a mouthful of grass at every crop. You who have never travelled in the desert do not know what *water* means. I have seen forty Bedawi race to a hole in a rock where as much rainwater had gathered as would fill a hand-basin, fling themselves off their horses, bend and put their lips to it, and then courteously make way for each other. You will see people in the East sitting, in what would appear to you a placid idiotcy of delight, by a little trickling stream not a foot wide, with a *narghíleh*, and calling it *kayf*, which means *dolce far niente*, or "sweet do-nothing."

Our House.

"Though old as history itself, thou art fresh as the breath of Spring, blooming as thine own rosebud, as fragrant as thine own orange flower, O Damascus, Pearl of the East!"

Our house in Damascus overhung the road and opposite gardens, with projecting lattice windows, was bounded on the right by a Mosque, on the left by a *Hammám* (Turkish bath), and front and back by gardens. On the other side of the road, among the apricot orchards, I had a capital stable for twelve horses, with a good room for *saises* (grooms), and a small garden with the river running through it. As soon as you got out of our village there was a bit of desert sand, and a background of tall yellow-coloured mountain, called Jebel Kaysún, or the Camomile Mountain, and that was what our village smelt of. When you entered our house, you came into a square courtyard, coarsely painted in broad stripes of red, white, and blue. All around were orange, lemon, and jessamine trees, a fountain playing in the middle, opposite the *liwán*, a raised room with one side taken out of it, open on to the court, spread with carpets and divans, and the niches filled with plants. Here, on hot days, one receives and offers coffee, lemonade, sherbet, chibouques, *narghílehs*, and cigarettes. On one side is a dining-room, on the other a cool sitting-room; all the rest is for servants and offices. Upstairs, six rooms run round two sides of the courtyard; a long terrace occupies the other two sides, joining and opening into the room at either end. There is a cool house-top with plants, to spread mats and divans, to sit amongst the flowers under the trees and by the Mosque-minaret, to look either towards our mountain, or over Damascus and the gardens, and inhale the desert-air from the other side of Damascus.

We also made a beautiful arbour in the garden opposite, which contained chiefly roses and jessamine. By lifting up the overladen vines and citrons, and branches of the lemon and orange trees, and supporting them on a frame-work, so that no sun could penetrate their luxuriance; we had a divan made under them for the cool summer evenings near the rushing river, and many happy hours of *kayf* we passed there. The Mosque next door to us, seemed to be built round and clung to a huge vine tree, which spread up and down all over it and its terrace, and the *Muezzin's* Minaret and my study window were cheek by jowl. The village was charming—

Vincent Brooks Day & Son lith.

OUR DESERT-CAMP.

FROM A PAINTING BY CHARLES TYRWHITT-DRAKE

domes and minarets peeping out of trees, bubbling streams, the music of the water-wheel.

Whenever we were in Eastern life, whether in Syria or elsewhere, we always made a point of being thoroughly English and European in our Consulate; but, when *not* obligatory, we used to live a great deal *with* the natives, and *as* the natives, for the purpose of experience. We wore European dress in Damascus and Beyrout, and we wore native dress up the country or in the desert. It was as easy for me to wear men's dress as my own, because it was all drapery, and does not in the least show the figure. There is nothing but the face to tell by, and if you tuck up your *kuffiyyah* you show only half a face, or only the eyes. Thus we would eat what they ate. If I went to stay with a harem, I always went in my own clothes; but if I went to the bazar, I frequently used to dress like a Moslemah with my face covered, and sit in the shops in the bazar, and let my Arab maid do all the talking lest I might be suspected, that I might hear all the gossip, and enter something into their lives. And the women frequently took me into the mosques in the same way, knowing who I was.

We attended *every sort* of ceremony, whether it was a circumcision, or a wedding, or a funeral, or a dervishes' dance, or anything that was going on, or any religious ceremony—my husband to the Cafés and the Mosques, the evening story-tellers' haunts; I to the charm shops, where the *khosis* (fortune-tellers) hang out and administer love philters or, in short, every sort of thing, and mix with all classes, religions, and races and tongues. My husband's friendship with Mohammedans, and his knowledge of Arabic and Persian, the language of literature, put him in intimate relation with the Arab tribes and all the chief authorities, and the *only man* who could not get on with him was the Turkish *Wali*, or Governor-General, Rashíd Pasha.

I cannot do better than copy Spyr. R. Lambros's letter describing the Arabic Library at Damascus, which was a rich find for Richard :—

"The library was founded by the Ommayads. The building is situate near the stately Djami which bears their name. It has a great stone vault supported upon four columns, and ornamented with mosaics. Not so long ago it was restored with much taste under the superintendence of the Governor of Syria, Achmet Hamdi Pasha, a favourite of the Sultan Abdul Hamid. There is no proper catalogue of this library, nor is it arranged. Several of the manuscripts are moth-eaten and much injured by damp. Still there exist in it valuable papyri, as well as manuscripts on parchment and paper. Among them, according to M. Papadopulos, a conspicuous place is due to a history of Damascus in nineteen large volumes. A great deal that is new is to be found in them regarding the City and its walls, as well as about the fine arts in Damascus. This codex is a jewel of Arabic literature, and an inexhaustible source for the whole annals of the city.

"The collection of old Arabic papyri is rich. There are several that throw light on obscure periods of Arabic history and poetry, or deal with the general history of Arabs and their literature. 'Some of these papyri are as late as the fifteenth century, and may be considered,' says M. Papadopulos, 'as copies of various monuments in stone.' On papyrus rolls are to be found whole collections of poems by celebrated Arab authors, of whom Ibn Khaldoun is the most notable. Others contain decrees of the Emirs of Damascus.

"M. Papadopulos mentions also a history on parchment of the Tartars, by Abulghazi Bahadur, and a history and geography of Damascus and Palmyra, by Abulfeda. Although M. Papadopulos gives no details regarding these writings, one can identify the history of Abulghazi as that which was discovered by Swedish officers in the captivity after the battle of Pultowa, 1709, and translated into German, and subsequently (1726) into French, and published in two volumes under the title of 'Histoire Généalogique des Tatars.' Regarding the work of Abulfeda one cannot, from the brief notice that M. Papadopulos supplies, come to any certain conclusion, whether it be a portion of the 'Annales Moslemici' or an unpublished production of the celebrated Mohammedan prince and polyhistor.

"Among the other treasures of the library are a treatise of Abul-Hassan, the Arabian astronomer of the thirteenth century; a roll of Abumazar, the astronomer (*circa* 855), on the observatories at Bagdad and Damascus; a medical treatise of the teacher of Avicenna, Abu-Sahaal; a meteorological bulletin relating to Damascus, by Abul-Chaiz; papyrus rolls containing the Pentateuch, the Psalter, and the Gospels, in Kufic characters; papyrus rolls and others, consisting of Plato's 'Laws,' in Arabic, the 'Organon' of Aristotle, the work of Hippocrates, 'De Aëre, Aquis, et Locis,' and one containing some portions of the 'Birds' of Aristophanes (in Arabic?), and presenting variants from the received text, and the Bible, in Syriac.

"But the great prize of the library, so far as one can judge from the inadequate description given of it, is a Greek manuscript of the Old and New Testament, comprising the Epistle of Barnabas and a portion of the Shepherd of Hermas. As the discovery of it is highly interesting, I will give an exact translation of the passage referring to it.

"'One of the most important of the so-called uncial manuscripts, which contain the whole of the New Testament complete, is as follows:—

"'The manuscript is written on well-prepared parchment, and is 12½ inches wide and 13¾ inches tall. It consists of 380½ leaves, of which 200 contain the Old Testament (in the Septuagint version) incomplete; but 180 the whole of the New Testament, the Epistle of Barnabas, and a large portion of the Shepherd of Hermas. The manuscript is divided into four columns, and in each column there

THE BURTONS' HOUSE IN SALAHÍYYAH, DAMASCUS.

Bv Sir Frederick Leighton.

are fifty lines. This manuscript may be regarded as similar to the Codex Sinaiticus, and consequently is worthy of a searching inquiry and investigation. The discovery of this gem is due to us.'

"Every reader will see that it is really a gem. Not only is the mere antiquity of the manuscript a point of importance, but also the fact that it contains a portion, and a considerable portion, of the Shepherd of Hermas, which has lately been seen in a new light, thanks to the researches and criticisms of scholars like Hilgenfeld and Harnack. It is well known that Hilgenfeld maintained that he had found the Greek conclusion, still missing, of Hermas, in a London publication of the well-known forger, Constantin Simonides (Nutt, 1859). This supposed conclusion was, after the appearance, simultaneously with Professor Hilgenfeld's conjecture, of the collation of the Athos Codex by Lambros, accompanied by an introduction by Mr. Armitage Robinson, utterly rejected by Professor Harnack, and declared to be a pure forgery of Simonides—an opinion in which I concur. Now comes the ancient manuscript from Damascus as a new document. Does it contain the conclusion of the Shepherd? Unfortunately the meagre notice supplied by M. Papadopulos neither throws light on this point nor affords us sufficient information, nor does it allow us to form any certain opinion on the whole question of the importance of the Damascene Codex and its similarity to the Sinaitic, which also contains, besides the Testament, a small portion of the Shepherd. I hope, however, to be soon in a position to give further intelligence on this important discovery.

"SPYR. R. LAMBROS."

ENVIRONS OF DAMASCUS.

The small rides and excursions round Damascus are innumerable and beautiful; they lead through garden and orchard with bubbling water, under the shady fig and vine, pomegranate and walnut. You emerge on the soft yellow sand, and you throw off your superfluous strength, by galloping as hard as you will. There is no one to check your spirits; the breath of the desert is liberty. There is Mizzeh, a village placed exactly on the borders of the green and yellow; one side looks into trees and verdure, and the other side in the bare sand. After that, you get into the desert, and to Kataná, a village three hours away, and Hámah. Jeramánah is a Druze village. Jobar is a Moslem village with a synagogue, dedicated to Elijah, and is a pilgrimage for Damascus Jews, and built over a cave, where they believe the prophet used to hide in time of persecution. A railed-off space showed where he anointed Hazael. When the prophet was at Horeb, "the Lord said unto him, Go, return on thy way to the wilderness of Damascus, and when thou comest, anoint Hazael to be King over Syria" (1 Kings xix. 15). Burzeh is a beautiful little village almost hidden under the mountain, nestling in verdure, and partly hidden by a cliff at the mouth of the glen. A Moslem Wely, called Makám Ibrahím (place of Abraham), assembles thousands of pilgrims on its festival day, where they practise the *Da'aseh*, meaning the treading—that is, the Shaykh riding over the prostrate bodies of the Faithful without hurting them—as at Cairo. Josephus, or rather Nicolaus of Damascus, says, "Abraham reigned at Damascus, being a foreigner who came with an army out of the land above Babylon, called the land of the Chaldean, but after a long time he got up and removed from that country, also with his people, and went into the land of Canaan, but now the land of Judea. Now, the name of Abraham is still famous in the country of Damascus, and there is shown a village named from him 'the habitation of Abraham,' and Burzeh is this village." It is still disputed whether Burzeh or Jobar is the true site of Hobah. These rides will take you from our mountain in a semicircle all round Damascus (at the distance of about an hour and a half from Damascus during the whole time), which is in our centre.

The longer excursions are the Convent of Saídnaya, considered by the Greeks to be Ptolemy's Danaba. There are also the Rock-tombs and temples of Menin Helbon, said to be the Chalybon of the Bible, once famed for its wine, exported to Tyre, noted by Ezekiel and Strabo, and horrible stuff it is, if it was the same as it is now. Then there is the village of Dhumayr, which contains a well-preserved temple, built in A.D. 246. This is the first day's station for the Baghdad camel-post, which Richard was responsible for. About two miles eastward of that, and at the foot of the lowest range of Anti-Lebanon, called Jebel el-Kaus, are the ruins of a little town and fort deserted for centuries. The desert of Arabia stretches right away to the east and south-east.

These are the little and middling runs. It was very pleasant for us, as we used to get acquainted with all the Shaykhs and people for two or three days' ride all round Damascus, and if we felt dull—which, by the way, we never did—we could run out and pay them a visit, such as Shaykh Sali's camp, passing El Bassúleh to Hijáneh. Lakes are marked on the maps a day's journey from Damascus. There are four lakes supposed to receive the Abana and Pharphar, but they are generally dry, the rivers evaporating or disappearing in the sand. You ride across the Ghutah plain, the Merj, and Abbs (the plains of Damascus) into the Wady el Ajam. It is also pleasant to ride down to the coast, seventy-two miles, and take a steamer going to Tyre, Sidon, and other coast places.

Richard's day, as I said, was divided into reading, writing, studying, and attending to his official work. There was one kind of duty within the town, another without the town, to scour mountain and desert, to ride hard, and to know everything that is going on in the country, and *personally*, not through dragomans only. His talents were particularly Eastern, and of a political and diplomatic kind; his knowledge of Eastern character was as perfect as his languages. He was as much needed out of the town as in it, and very often when they thought he was far away, he was amongst them, and they wondered how he knew things. I interested myself in all his pursuits, and I was a most fortunate woman that he allowed me to be his companion, his secretary, and his aide-de-camp. I looked after our house, servants, stables, and animals. I did a little gardening. I helped my husband, read and wrote, studied Arabic, received and returned visits, saw and learnt Damascus through, till I knew it like my own pocket, looked after the poor and sick of my village and its environs. Sometimes I galloped over the plains, and sat in the Bedawi tents, sometime went up all the mountains. Summer times I smoked *narghílehs* by the waterside in a neighbour's garden. Sometimes I went to pass two or three days with a harem. Our lives were wild, romantic, and solemn. After sunset the only sounds were the last call to prayer on the Minaret top, the howling of the wild dogs, the cries of the jackals in the burial-ground outside the village, the bubbling of the fountains, the hootings of the owls in the garden, the soughing of the wind through the mountain gorges, and the noise of the water-wheel in a neighbour's orchard. There was often a free fight in the road below, to steal a mare, or to kill. We have often gone down to take some poor wretch in, and bind up his sabre-cuts.

I used to have a large reception every Friday, and not only of the Europeans, but the Authorities as well as the natives of every tongue, race, and creed, who used to assemble in our Divan for *narghílehs*, sherbet, and coffee. It used to begin at sunrise, and go on till sunset. How I look back to those romantic days when the assembled party, being afraid to remain in our quarters after the sun was down, used to file down through the orchards and gardens to the safe shelter of the Damascus gates at sunset, and the mattresses and cushions of the divans were spread on the housetop, backed by the romantic Jebel Kaysún, with a bit of desert sand between it and us, and on all the other three sides a view over Damascus, and its surrounding oasis, and the desert beyond!

Then the supper was prepared on the roof, and there remained with us the two most interesting and remarkable characters of Damascus, the two who never knew what fear meant—the famous Abd el Kadir and Lady Ellenborough, known there as the "Hon. Jane Digby el Mezrab." Abd el Kadir was a dark, handsome, thoroughbred-looking man, with dignified bearing and cool self-possession. He dressed in snowy white, both turban and burnous. Not a single ornament except his jewelled arms, which were splendid. If you saw him on horseback you would single him out from a million; he had the seat of a gentleman and a soldier. He was every inch a Sultan. His mind was as beautiful as his face. He spoke the perfection of Arabic, he was a true Moslem, and he and Richard were both Master-Sufi. All readers will know his history. He was the fourth son of the Algerine Marabout Abd el Kadir Mahi ed Din, and was born in 1807. You all remember his hopeless struggles for the independence of Algeria, his capture, his imprisonment in France from 1847 to 1852—a treacherous act, and a tarnish to the French Government. Lord Londonderry earnestly entreated Louis Napoleon to set him free, which he did, going to the prison himself to let him out, and treating him with the greatest honour. He pensioned him and sent him to Damascus, where he was surrounded by five hundred faithful Algerines. He divided his time into prayer, study, business, and very little sleep. He loved the English, but he was loyal to Louis Napoleon. When the massacre in 1860 took place, he used to sleep at his own door, lest any poor Christian wretch should knock and petition to be saved from slaughter, and for fear his Algerines, being Moslems, should turn a deaf ear; and he saved many, sending guards down to the convents of women, and to his friends.

Our other friend was the Hon. Jane Digby, of the family of Lord Digby, married to Lord Ellenborough, and divorced. She made her home in Damascus, and eventually married a Bedawin Shaykh (Mijwal el Mezrab), the tribe of Mezrab being a branch of the great Anazeh. She was a most beautiful woman, though at the time I write she was sixty-one, tall, commanding, and queen-like. She was *grande dame au bout des doigts*, as much as if she had just left the salons of London and Paris, refined in manner and voice, nor did she ever utter a word you could wish unsaid. My husband said she was out and out the cleverest woman he ever met; there was nothing she could not do. She spoke nine languages perfectly, and could read and write in them. She painted, sculptured, was musical. Her letters were splendid; and if on business, there was never a word too much, nor a word too little. She had had a most romantic, adventurous life, and she was now, one might say, Lady Hester Stanhope's successor. She lived half the year in a romantic house she had built for herself in Damascus, and half her life she and her husband lived in his Bedawi tents, she like any other Bedawin woman, but honoured and respected as the queen of her tribe,

SALAHÍYYAH, DAMASCUS IN THE OASIS—THE DESERT BEYOND.
Bv Charles Tyrwhitt-Drake.

wearing one blue garment, her beautiful hair in two long plaits down to the ground, milking the camels, serving her husband, preparing his food, giving him water to wash his hands and face, sitting on the floor and washing his feet, giving him his coffee, his sherbet, his *narghíleh*s, and while he ate she stood and waited on him, and glorying in it; and when in Damascus they led semi-European lives. She looked splendid in Oriental dress, and if you saw her as a Moslem woman in the bazar you would have said she was not more than thirty-four years of age. She was my most intimate friend, and she dictated to me the whole of her biography, beginning 15th March, 1871, and ending July 7th.

After I left a report came home that she was dead. I answered some unpleasant remarks in the Press about her, throwing a halo over her memory, in which I stated that I being the possessor of the biography, no one had a right to say anything about her except myself. She reappeared again, having only been detained in the desert by the fighting of the tribes. Her relatives attacked her for having given me the biography, and she, under pressure, denied it in print through one of the missionaries, and then wrote and asked me to give it back to her; but I replied that she should have had it with the greatest pleasure, only having "given me the lie" in print, I was obliged for my own sake to keep it, and she eventually died. I have got it now, but I shall never publish it.

After this episode of my being publicly attacked about her biography, *Chambers' Journal*, September 9th, 1876, produced the following notice:—

"Jane Elizabeth, Lady Ellenborough, if we may trust the matter-of-fact pages of Lodge's 'Peerage,' is the only sister of the present Lord Digby, being daughter of the late Admiral Sir Henry Digby, G.C.B., great-grandson of the fifth Lord Digby; her mother was a daughter of Thomas William Coke, of Holkham, the veteran M.P. for Norfolk, and well-known agriculturist, afterwards created Earl of Leicester. She was born in April, 1807, and when little more than seventeen, was married to the late Lord Ellenborough (the Governor-General of India); but the union was dissolved by Act of Parliament in 1830.

"The rumour of her death was effectually contradicted a few months later by a letter in her own handwriting, addressed to an English lady, who was well acquainted with her in Damascus. This lady and her husband had mourned old Lady Ellenborough for two or three months as having died in the desert, and had quite given up all hope of ever seeing her again, when one day she received from her a letter stating that she was alive and in the best of health, and asking her to contradict the rumour of her decease.

"Lady Ellenborough was fortunate in the possession of at least one sincere friend, generously eager to defend her when attacked, and to make out the best case possible for her. Mrs. Isabel Burton, who had been intimately acquainted, and in the habit of daily intercourse with this extraordinary woman, during a residence of some years in Damascus, while her husband, Captain Burton, was the English Consul at that city, appears to have contracted a warm attachment for her, and speaks of her, in spite of all her faults, in terms of the highest praise. To Mrs. Burton Lady Ellenborough confided the task of writing her biography, and dictated it to her day by day until the task was accomplished. In a letter to the *Pall Mall Gazette*, written in March, 1873, when under the belief that Lady Ellenborough was dead, Mrs. Burton says, in allusion to this biography, 'She did not spare herself, dictating the bad with the same frankness as the good. I was pledged not to publish this until after her death and that of certain near relatives.'

"Mrs. Burton subsequently adds, 'I cannot meddle with the past without infringing on the biography confided to me; but I can say a few words concerning her life, dating from her arrival in the East, as told me by herself and by those now living there; and I can add my testimony as to what I saw, which I believe will interest every one in England, from the highest downwards, and be a gratification to those more nearly concerned. About sixteen years ago, tired of Europe, Lady Ellenborough conceived the idea of visiting the East, and of imitating Lady Hester Stanhope and Lady Mary Wortley Montagu, not to mention a French lady, Mdme. de la Tour d'Auvergne, who has built herself a temple on the top of Mount Olivet, and lives there still. Lady Ellenborough arrived at Beyrout and went to Damascus, where she arranged to go to Baghdad across the Desert. A Bedouin escort for this journey was necessary; and as the Mezrab tribe occupied the ground, the duty of commanding the escort devolved upon Shaykh Mijwal, a younger brother of Shaykh Mohammed, chief of this tribe, which is a branch of the great Anezeh tribe. On the journey the young Shaykh fell in love with this beautiful woman, who possessed all the qualities that could fire the Arab imagination. Even two years ago she was more attractive than half the young girls of our time. It ended by his proposing to divorce his Moslem wives and to marry her; to pass half the year in Damascus—which to him was like what London or Paris would be to us—for her pleasure, and half in the Desert to lead his natural life. The romantic picture of becoming a Queen of the Desert and of the Bedouin tribes exactly suited her wild fancies, and was at once accepted; and she was married, in spite of all opposition made by her friends and the British Consulate. She was married according to Mohammedan law, changed her name to that of the Honourable Mrs. Digby El Mezrab, and was horrified when she found that she had lost her nationality by her marriage, and had become a Turkish subject. For fifteen years she lived as she died,* the faithful and affectionate wife of the Shaykh, to

* This was written at the time when the report of Lady Ellenborough's death was generally believed to be true.

whom she was devotedly attached. Half the year was passed in a very pretty house, which she built at Damascus just without the gates of the City; and the other six months were passed, according to his nature, in the Desert in the Bedouin tents of the tribe.

"'In spite of this hard life, necessitated by accommodating herself to his habits—for they were never apart—she never lost anything of the English lady, nor the softness of a woman. She was always a perfect lady in sentiment, voice, manners, and speech. She never said or did anything could wish otherwise. She kept all her husband's respect, and was the Mother and the Queen of his tribe. In Damascus we were only nineteen Europeans, but we all flocked around her with affection and friendship. The natives did the same. As to strangers, she received only those who brought a letter of introduction from a friend or relative; but this did not hinder every ill-conditioned passer-by from boasting of his intimacy with the House of Mezrab, and recounting the untruths which he invented, *pour se faire valoir*, or to sell his book or newspaper at a better profit. She understood friendship in its best and fullest sense, and for those who enjoyed her confidence it was a treat to pass the hours with her. She spoke French, Italian, German, Slav, Spanish, Arabic, Turkish, and Greek, as she spoke her native tongue. She had all the tastes of a country life, and occupied herself alternately with painting, sculpture, music, or with her garden-flowers, or poultry, or with her thoroughbred Arab mares, or in carrying out some improvement. She was thoroughly a connoisseur in each of her amusements or occupations. To the last she was fresh and young; beautiful, brave, refined, and delicate. She hated all that was false. Her heart was noble; she was charitable to the poor. She regularly attended the Protestant church, and often twice on Sundays. She fulfilled all the duties of a good Christian lady and an Englishwoman. She is dead. All those who knew her in her latter days will weep for her. She had but one fault (and who knows if it was hers?), washed out by fifteen years of goodness and repentance. Let us hide it, and shame those who seek to drag up the adventures of her wild youth to tarnish so good a memory. *Requiescat in pace.*'

"But Lady Ellenborough was *not* dead. It will, of course, be obvious that, along with Lord Brougham, she has been privileged to read the obituary notice of her own career; and she is probably destined to see many more summers and winters in her Arab home.

"It is evident, from the tenor of the last few sentences of the foregoing letter, that the 'one fault' to which the writer alludes was the elopement of Lady Ellenborough with Prince Schwartzenberg, and that Mrs. Burton entirely disbelieves in the half-dozen or more of apocryphal husbands intervening between Lord Ellenborough and the Arab sheikh. At any rate, the eccentric lady is entitled to the benefit of the doubt; and public curiosity respecting this extraordinary woman must remain unsatisfied until the period shall arrive when her friend and confidante, Mrs. Burton, will be at liberty to publish the autobiography committed to her charge.

"It would be possible, without difficulty, to draw at once a parallel and a contrast between the eccentric Lady Ellenborough and the scarcely less eccentric niece of the younger Pitt, Lady Hester Stanhope, whom I have named above, and who, more than half a century ago, exchanged English life, habits, and sentiments, and possibly also to some extent her faith as well, for those of the wild and romantic East."

The others, besides Richard and myself, on the house roof were frequently Charles Tyrwhitt-Drake, an indefatigable worker in the Palestine Exploration; and E. H. Palmer, afterwards professor of Arabic at Cambridge, and in 1882 murdered by the Bedawi in Arabia. We were six, and I need not say how romantic those evenings were, what a halo my memory throws around them, what conversation, what real adventures, real life, real wit, real spirituality we enjoyed; and we often stayed there till the moon was on the wane. The two Englishmen were living with us, and Abd el Kadir, with an escort of his Algerines, who were picketed in our court, would see the lady home on his road to his own palace. Now I am the only survivor of those happy meetings.

Richard and Children.

Richard's love for children was quite extraordinary. If there was a child in the room, even a baby in arms, no one could get a word out of him; but you would find him on the floor, romping with them, and they were never afraid of him. I do not think there could possibly be a better illustration than the very admirable and striking account given by Salih, who was one of the missionaries in Damascus:—

"*Burton at Damascus.*

"My first sight of Captain Burton revealed not only the man in his complex character, but supplied the key to the perplexing vicissitudes of his extraordinary career.

"On his arrival in Damascus, Burton called at my house. My study adjoined the drawing-room, into which he was shown by a native servant. I heard him command the Arab to fetch me in harsh, peremptory tones, which were meant to be obeyed. The servant, not thinking that I was in the study, went to seek me elsewhere. I advanced, in noiseless Damascus slippers, to the drawing-room door, and I came upon a scene never to be forgotten.

"At one side of the room stood my curly-headed, rosy-cheeked little boy of five, on the other side stood Burton. The two were staring at each other. Neither was aware of my presence. Burton had twisted his face into the most fiendish-like aspect. His eyes rolled, exposing the whites in an alarming manner. The features were drawn to one side, so as to make the gashes on his jaw and brow appear more ghastly. The two cheeks were blown out, and Burton, raising a pocket-handkerchief to his left cheek, struck his right with the flat of his right hand, thus producing an explosion, and making the pocket-handkerchief fly to the left as if he had shot it through his two cheeks.

"The explosion was followed by a suppressed howl, something between the bark of a hyæna and a jackal. All the time Burton glared on the little fellow with the fiery eyes of a basilisk, and the child stood riveted to the floor as if spell-bound and fascinated, like a creature about to be devoured. Suddenly a very wonderful thing happened. The little boy, with a wild shout of delight, sprang into the monster's arms, and the black beard was instantly mingled with the fair curls, and Burton was planting kisses all over the flaxen pate. The whole pantomime was gone through as quick as lightning, and Burton, disentangling himself, caught sight of my Arab returning without me, and, instead of waiting for an explanation, hurled at him a volley of exasperating epithets, culled from the rich stores of spicy and stinging words which garnish Arabic literature. Burton had revealed himself to me fully before he saw me. The child's clear, keen instinct did not mislead it. The big, rough monster had a big child's heart behind the hideous grimaces. The child's unerring instinct was drawn by affinity to the child's heart in the man."

During our time a very interesting episode occurred at Damascus—a sad one, too. Lord and Lady Langdale had a daughter who was married to Count Téleki. It was not a very happy marriage. She made a journey to Syria and Palestine with her mother, a very nice cousin, and a young friend of his, for diversion. Like many travellers, unused to sun, hard riding, bad water, exposure, and fatigue, she got the usual fever and dysentery, and was brought down in a dying state to Damascus. She was of Agnostic principles, but in her last few hours she desired to be baptized a Catholic. I did all I could for her in the way of nursing, and Richard as far as his power went. When she died, her desk was found to contain a letter which had been written years before, when she had been very much excited by reading Buckle's "History of Civilization," and she wrote, "Should I die at Damascus, I should like to be buried by Buckle." It so happened that there was place for two next to Buckle, and she was buried there—a most impressive and touching funeral. Her coffin was covered with the Union Jack; Richard and all his dragomans and *kawwáses*, in full uniform, were present; and some time after, appeared the following note in a newspaper :—

Buckle's Grave.

"The London correspondent of the *Manchester Guardian* says, 'A traveller just arrived in London from Damascus gives some rather interesting details about the present condition and surroundings of Buckle's grave. Though it was left for so long after his death, without a stone even to mark it, that it had the altar-tomb of white marble and black basalt that was at length erected, and was now enclosed in a high wall with a padlocked gate. Next to Buckle's tomb are the tombs of two rather remarkable women. The first is that of the Countess Téleki (a daughter, I believe, of Lord Langdale), who especially desired that her grave should be next to Buckle's; and the next tomb is that of Lady Ellenborough, erected by her brother, Lord Digby, with an Arabic inscription from the Korán, placed on it by her later husband, the Arab sheikh, in singular proximity to the cross which forms part of the monument. On Buckle's tomb also, on which, however, there is no cross, there is an Arabic inscription, suggested by the famous Emir Abd el Kadir.'"

Syria.

Each year in January we rode out with the Meccan Caravan, or Haj, as far as Ramsah, the third station, and one year returned to Damascus *viâ* Izra (the Edhra of the Handbook) and the celebrated Haurán valley plain, inspecting the chief settlements and making acquaintance with the principal Shaykhs. Richard writes—

"I had business at Hums (Emesa), generally written Homs, and Hamáh (Hamath Epiphaneia), on the northern borders of the consular district of Damascus. From there I examined and sent home native facsimiles of the four unique basaltic stones, whose characters, raised in cameo, apparently represent a system of local hieroglyphics peculiar to this part of Syria, and form the connecting link between picture-writing and the true syllabarium. A friend was kind enough to give me some valuable papers, amongst them two maps noting the most important of the three hundred and sixty villages, which he had traced himself by aid of native information. These stud the plain known as El'Aláh; the same number of villages are allotted to the Lejá. This plain is a high rolling ground beginning at Selamíyyah, the well-known ruin and outwork of Palmyra, six hours' ride from, and bearing east-south-east of the Mound of Hamáh. It extends five days' journey to the north, and from east to west two or three days'. Some call it the 'Great Syrian Desert;' but the Seleucidæ here kept their immense studs of elephants and horses. The whole is virgin ground, as are also the eastern slopes of the Jebel Kalbíyyah, on the left bank of the Orontes, and of the country extending from the parallel of Hums to that of Selamíyyah. In the

THE BURTONS' HOUSE-ROOF AT DAMASCUS AND THE ADJOINING MOSQUE-MINARET.

By Charles Tyrwhitt Drake.

first five hours we had examined five ruins; and the basaltic buildings are exactly those of the Giant Cities of Bashan. We returned to Damascus by Jebel el Húlah; saw the fine crusading castle called Husn el Akrád, the plain of the Nahr el Kabír, the Eleutherus river. Our hardships were considerable; the country was under water, and the rushing torrents and deep ditches caused long detours. We had heavy and continuous rains, furious blasts, snow and sleet like Norway. One of the followers sickened and died, and we were all frostbitten. In all my trips and peregrinations, I had business to do as well as pleasure.

"Throughout Syria, when the basaltic soil runs to any depth, the earth is loose and treacherous, fatiguing to traverse in summer, and impassable in winter. In some places the water is sulphurous or brackish, but in most places without any unpleasant taste; it is strongly diuretic."

Unexplored Syria.

Taken from Richard's journals of excursions to the Libanus with Charley Drake and me, and once with Drake alone, the Tulúl el Safá, the Anti-Libanus, the Northern Libanus, and the 'Aláh. We collected eighty-one original Greek inscriptions in the Haurán mountain, and in the 'Aláh, a collection of Alpine plants from the Libanus, shells, and geological specimens. Charley Drake did the plans and sketches and maps, Richard and I the writing.

Richard wrote—

"The fact was we had long been tantalized by the sight of the forbidden Tulúl el Safá, or Hillocks of the Safá Pyramids, looking at the distance like baby finger-tops, dotting the eastern horizon within sight of our housetop, and, thinning out northwards, prolonged the lumpy blue wall of the Jebel Durúz Haurán, which appears to reflect the opposite line of the Anti-Libanus. Many also were the vague and marvellous reports which had reached our ears concerning a cave called by the few who knew it Umm Nírán, the mother of fires. The difficulty and danger of visiting these places arose in my time simply from the relations of the *Wali's* government with the hill tribes of Bedawin, who, mixed up with the Druzes, infest the Trachonic countries. The hill tribes proper are Agaylát, the Hasan, the Shurafát, the Azámát, and the Masá'id. The Safá is tenanted by the Shitayá, the Ghiyás, and the Anjad, whilst the Lejá belongs to the Sulút, as clients of the Druzes. These are nine hordes intermarried, who combine together in the warfare of the tribes. They are the liege descendants of the refractory robbers of the Trachonitis, who, to revenge the death of their Captain Naub, rose up against the garrison of three thousand Idumæans stationed in their country by Herod, son of Antipater. Their prowess as plunderers is still famous.

"To the scandal of every honest man, they are allowed to scour the plains, carry off the flocks, and harry the flocks and herds of the peasantry. They served as ready implements of revenge against all those disaffected to or disliked by the petty autocrat [Rashíd Pasha] who then disgraced the land by his rule. They are small and slightly made, with oval face, bright brown eyes, and restless roving look of the civilized pickpocket. The features high and well formed, the skin a clear olive yellow. They wear long love-locks of raven-wings' tint, well buttered. Their dress scanty and irregular. The action, like the eyes, is wild and startled; the voice is a sort of bark. When attacked, they put the women, children, and cattle in the rear, form a rude line, carefully guard against being out-flanked, and advance file-firing with great regularity. They attack strangers, and they have no sense of hospitality, and for this reason it was not really safe to ride alone three hours beyond the Eastern gate of Damascus. The Subá'a, therefore, made the plain of Damascus a battle-field, and the Wuld Ali levied black-mail in Cœle-Syria.

"Dust was thrown in the eyes of the civilized world whilst the *Wali* employed hordes of banditti to plunder its own hapless subjects, whilst the satellites had the audacity to publish, 'Le désert est cultivé, les Bedouins sont soumis, et le brigandage anéanti.' So it came to pass that all the broken-down Gassanian convents had never to our knowledge been visited by any European traveller. Mr. Porter was told that a hundred horsemen would not attempt a journey to El Diyúrá. We received no damage, and nighted in the old temple of Ba'al, called Harrán el 'Awámid. However, the Ghiyás found us out, advanced in a steady line, treated us to a shower of bullets, severely wounding in the leg our gallant companion and friend, Bedr Beg. As we were well mounted and armed, and the riding ground good, we could have brought down as many of them as we pleased, for we were all armed with six-shooters, and eight shot rifles, but, as we wanted to avoid a blood-feud, we did not return fire. After Rashíd Pasha was gone, the mystery of their attacking us was cleared up.

"These convents are in an excellent state of preservation. What we have to complain of is that the spirit of clique too often succeeds in ignoring the real explorer, the true inventor, the most learned writer, and the best artist. The honour is denied to the right man. Party is successful against principle. The Pharisee, with his aggressive, vigorous, narrow-minded nature, with his hard thin character, all angles and stings, with his starch inflexible opinions upon religion, politics, science, literature, and art, with his broad assurance that *his* ways are the only right ways, rules with a rod of iron the large herd of humanity, headed by Messrs. Feeblemind and Ready-to-halt. We find in our national life, when the Battle of the Creeds, or rather of 'Non-Credo' *versus* 'Credo,' has been offered and accepted; when every railway station is hung with texts and strewed with tracts for the benefit of that British-public-cherished idol the working-class; when the South Kensington Museum offers professional instruction in science and art for women before they become mothers, suggesting that creation by law may be as reasonable as creation by miracle; when Secularism draws the sword against Denominationalism; briefly, when those who 'believe' and those who do not, can hardly keep hands off one another in a *mêlée*, it suggests a foretaste of the mystical Armageddon."

Richard and Charley Drake sketched and fixed the positions of some fifty ruins which are fated to disappear from the face of the earth. They took squeezes of from twenty to twenty-five Greek inscriptions, of which six or seven have dates, and explored the Harrah, or 'Hot-Country,' the pure white blank in the best maps, and took hydrographic charts, as they found that the guide-books and the maps teemed with mistakes.

"I thought," he said, "when I came here that Syria and Palestine would be so worn out that my occupation as an explorer was clean gone, but I soon found that although certain lines had been well trodden, that scarcely ever a traveller, and *no tourists*, have ever ridden ten miles off the usual ways. No one knows how many patches of unvisited and unvisitable country lie within a couple of days' ride of great cities and towns, such as Aleppo and Damascus, Hums, and Hamáh.

"Where the maps show a virgin white patch in the heart of Jaydur, the classical Ituræa, students suppose that the land has been examined, and has been found to contain nothing of interest. The reverse is absolutely the case. Finally, as will presently appear, there are valid reasons for that same, for the unexplored spots are either too difficult or too dangerous for the multitude to undertake. To visit carefully *even* the *beaten* tracks in the Holy Land occupies six months, and none *except a resident* can afford leisure or secure health for more, and the reason that these places have escaped European inspection is, that they do not afford provisions, or forage, or water; they are deadly with malarious fever, they are infested by the Bedawi. They do not often detain you for ransom, nor mutilate you; but they will spear you. They will not kill you in cold blood; that is only done for a *Thar*, which is the blood-feud between tribes. Still, under these mitigated circumstances, travellers may know that their escorts will turn tail, and will hardly care to expose themselves, their attendants, and baggage to a charge of Bedawin cavalry. Indeed, the running away of the escort is the traveller's safeguard. If the tribe could seize all, it knows that dead men are dumb, but it knows that the fugitives have recognized them, and that before evening the tale will be known through all the land.

"There is no reverence in this ancient place for antiquity. Syria would *willingly* change from ancient and Oriental to modern and European. The ruins of the 'Aláh are pulled to pieces to build houses for Hamáh. The classical buildings of Saccæa are torn down and made into rude hovels for the Druzes, who fled from the Anti-Libanus and Hermon. Syria, north of Palestine, is an old country, geographically and technologically and other ways, but it is absolutely new. A land of the past, it has a future as promising as that of Mexico or the Argentine Republic. The first railway that spans it will restore the poor old lethargic region to rich and vigorous life. 'Lazare, veni foras!'—it will raise this Lazarus of Eastern provinces, this Niobe of nations, from a neglected grave. *There is literally no limit that can be laid down to the mother-wit, the ambition, the intellectual capabilities of its sons. They are the most gifted race that I have as yet ever seen, and when the curse shall have left the country—not the bane of superstition, but the bane and plague-spot of bad rule—it will again rise to a position not unworthy of the days when it gave to the world a poetry and a system of religion still unforgotten by our highest civilization.*

"My object was to become acquainted with the Haurán and its Druzes, to see the Umm-Nírán Cave, called the 'fire cave,' of which one hears such extraordinary legends, and the Tulúl el Safá, which is the volcanic region, east of the Damascus swamps.

"The South Pacific Coast, and Mediterranean Palestine, are two pendants in the world, only the East is on a much smaller scale. The lakes and rivers, plains and valleys, cities and settlements, storms and earthquakes, in fact, all the geographical, physical, and the meteorological, as well as the social features of the two regions, show a remarkable general likeness with a difference of proportion.

"The world is weary of the past. In these regions there is hardly a mile without a ruin, hardly a ruin that is not interesting, and in some places, mile after mile and square mile after square mile of ruin show a luxuriance of ruin. There is not a large ruin in the country which does not prove, upon examination, to be the composition of ruins more ancient still. The mere surface of the antiquarian mine has only been scratched; it will be long years before the country can be considered explored, before even Jerusalem can be called 'recovered,' and the task must be undertaken by Societies, not by *individuals.*

"Of history, of picturesque legend, of theology and mythology, of art and literature, as of archæology, of palæography, of palæogeography, of numismatology, and all the other 'ologies and 'ographies, they have absolutely no visible end. If the New World be bald and tame, the Syrian old world is, to those *who know it well,* perhaps a little too fiery and exciting, paling with its fierce tints and angry flush the fair vision which a country has a right to contemplate in the days to be. There is a disease here called 'Holy Land on the Brain,' which makes patients babble of hanging gardens and parterres of flowers. The 'green sickness' attacks tourists from Europe and North America, especially where the sun is scarce. It attacks the Protestant with greater violence than the Catholic (the Catholic from long meditation is prepared for it). The Protestant fit is excited and emotional, spasmodic and hysterical, ending in a long rhapsody about himself, his childhood, and his mother. It spares the Levantine, as 'yellow Jack' does the negro. His brain is too well packed with the wretched intrigues and petty interest of material life to have any room for excitement at 'the first glimpse of Emmanuel's Land.' The sufferer will perhaps hire a house at Siloam, and pass his evenings in howling from the roof, at the torpid little town of Jebus, 'Woe! woe to thee, Jerusalem!' Men fall to shaking hands with one another, and exchange congratulations for the all-sufficient reason that the view before them 'embraces the plain of Esdraelon.'

"*A long and happy life should be still before it. The ruined heaps show us what has been; the appliances of civilization, provided with railways and tramways, will offer the happiest blending of the ancient and the modern worlds. It will become another Egypt, with the advantages of a superior climate, and far nobler races of men.* Time was when I dreamt of the Libanus as my future *pied à terre.* When weary with warfare and wander, one could repose in peace and com fortable ease. I thought of pitching a tent for life on Mount Lebanon, whose *raki* and tobacco are of the best, whose *Vino d'oro* is *compared* with the best, whose winter climate is like an English summer, whose views are lovely, a place at the same time near and far from society—it was *riant* in the extreme;* but in the state of Syria in *my* time, the physical mountain had no shade, the moral mountain no privacy, the village life would have been dreary and monotonous, broken only by a storm, an earthquake, a murder, a massacre. Such is the rule of the *Wali* in this unfortunate time, when drought and famine, despotism and misrule, maddens its unfortunate inhabitants.

"We now determined the forms and bearings of the Cedar Block, the true apex of the Libanus. We then went to the unknown and dangerous region called Tulúl el Safá, the Hillocks of the Safá district, a mass of volcanic cones lying east of the Damascus swamps called lakes. Then we explored the northern Anti-Libanus, a region which is innocent of tourists and traveller, and appears a blank of mountains upon the best maps. Of my fellow-traveller Charley Drake I can only say that every one knows his public worth. At the end of my time here came three tedious months of battling unsupported, against all that falsehood and treachery could devise; the presence of this true-hearted Englishman, staunch to the backbone, inflexible in the cause of right, and equally disdainful of threats and promises, was our greatest comfort: I can only speak of him with enthusiasm. Our journey to the northern slopes of Lebanon, and the 'Aláh or the highland of Syria, is an absolute gain to geography, as the road lay through a region marked on our maps 'Great Syrian Desert,' and the basaltic remains in the extensive and once populous plain lying north-east and south-east of Hamah have been visited, sketched, and portrayed for the first time. We found lignite, true coal, bituminous schists and limestone, the finest bitumen or asphalt, mineral springs of all sorts, and ores of all kinds, and plants and rhubarb. And then the duty of a

* Ah, what a beautiful life it would have been!—I. B.

Consular officer in Syria is to scour the country, and see matters with his own eyes, and personally to investigate the cases which are brought before him at head-quarters, where everything except the truth appears.

"After our visit to Ba'albak and the northern Libanus, we 'did' the southern parts of the mountain, the home of the Druzes as opposed to that of the Maronites; then we ascended Hermon, then we had our gallop to the Waters of Merom, that hideous expanse of fetid mire and putrefying papyrus. We paid a visit to the only Bedawin Amir in this region, the Amir Hasan el Fa'úr of the Benú Fadl tribe, and then we visited most of the romantic and hospitable Druze villages which cling to the southern and eastern folds of Hermon."

We used to spend all the summers in the Anti-Lebanon. Bludán is a little Christian village, Greek orthodox, which clings to the Eastern flank of the mountain overlooking the Zebedáni valley, which is well known to travellers, because it leads from Damascus to Ba'albak. In it we found the *official* sources of the Barada, the river of Damascus, but its *real* source is a pool just behind our quarters, fed in winter by the torrent of Jebel el Shakíf. The Bludán block is a few miles north of the site of Abila, the highest summit of Anti-Lebanon, and is fronted on the west by Jebel el Shakíf, or "Mountain of Cliffs," with gaps and gorges. Bludán lies twenty-seven miles to the north-west across country, away from Damascus.

Ours was a large claret-case-shaped house of stone; the centre was a large barn-like limestone hall with a deep covered verandah; a wild waste of garden extends all round the house, a bare ridge of mountain behind; a beautiful stream with two small waterfalls rushes through the garden. It is five thousand feet high—an eagle's nest, commanding an unrivalled view. The air was perfect, only hot at three p.m. for an hour or two, and blankets at night. There was stabling for eight horses; no windows, only wooden shutters to close at night. We see five or six ranges of mountains, one backing the other, of which the last looks down upon the Haurán. We can see Jebel Sannin, which does not measure nine thousand feet above sea-level, monarch of the Lebanon, and on the left, Hermon, king of the Anti-Lebanon. The Greek villages cling like wasps' nests to our mountain, and Zebedáni, on the plain beneath, contains thirty-five thousand Mohammedans.

The utter solitude, the wildness of the life, the absence of *luxe*, and no society, the being thoroughly alone with Nature and one's own thoughts, was all too refreshing; we led half-Eastern lives and half-farmhouse life. We made our own bread, we bought butter and milk from the Bedawi, we bought sheep or kids from passing flocks. We woke at dawn, and after a cup of tea, we used to take the dogs, and have long walks over the mountains with our guns.

The game were bears (very scarce), gazelles, wolves, wild boars, and a small leopard called *nimr*, but for these we had to go far, and watch in silence before dawn. But Richard had opinions about sport; he only wanted to kill a beast that would kill us if we did not kill it, and the smaller game, partridges, quails, woodcocks, hares, and wild duck, we never shot unless we were hungry, and we would not have the gazelles hunted. He had the greatest contempt for the Hurlingham matches, and the battue slaughters in English parks, where, instead of honestly walking for your game, and bringing it home to eat, the young men of to-day have a gentle stroll to eat *pâté de foie gras*, drink champagne, and the keeper hands them a gun with a pheasant almost tied to the end of it to blow to pieces. And what Richard thought about sport I heartily agreed with. The hot part of the day was spent in reading, writing, and studying Arabic. He sent home from Bludán, during 1870, "Vikram and the Vampire" (Hindú tales), "Paraguay," and "Proverbia Communia Syriaca" (Royal Asiatic Society, 1871)—three works he had been long preparing.

His three literary necessities were Shakespeare, the Bible, and Euclid, and they were bound up together, with three large clasps, like a breviary, and went everywhere. *His* method of language-learning he has described in his autobiography. He taught me this way. He made me learn ten new words a day by heart. "When a native speaks, then say the words after him to get his accent. Don't be English—that is, shy or self-conscious—if you know five words, air them wherever you can; next day you will know ten, and so on till you can speak. Don't be like the Irishman who would not go into the water until he could swim. Then take a very easy childish book, in the colloquial language of the day, and translate it word for word underneath the original, and you will be surprised how soon you find yourself unconsciously talking."

At twelve we had our first meal; in the afternoon native Shaykhs, or English from Beyrout or Damascus, came to visit us, or rare tourists would crawl up to see what sort of people we were, and how we lived. They all used to say, "Well, it is glorious, but the thing is to get here." We set up a *tir* (shooting-place) in the garden, and used to practise pistol or rifle shooting, or fence, or put on the *cavesson*, and lunge the horses if they had had no exercise. When the sun became cooler, all the poor within sixteen miles round would come to be doctored;

the hungry, the thirsty, the ragged, the sick and sorry, filled our garden, and Richard used to settle grievances, and they all got money or clothing, food or medicine, and sympathy. Before dinner we used to assemble in the garden to eat a few mouthfuls of *leban* salad and drink a liqueur glass of *raki*, which was quite necessary to give us sufficient appetite. Divans were then spread on the housetop, and we used to watch the moon lighting up Hermon, whilst we smoked the after-dinner *narghíleh.* The horses were picketed out all these summer nights, and the *saises* slept with them. The last thing was to have night prayers, and then to go the rounds to see that everything was right, turn out the dogs on guard, and then to bed.

The mails came once a fortnight, and Richard would ride into Damascus and see that all was well. Sometimes we used to give a picnic to some of our Moslem neighbours, and we would gallop out in the plain, and stay in the black tents of the Arabs. I used to have to ride down to the Moslem village Zebedáni every Sunday for church. The path was steep, and covered with rolling stones, so that the horses used mostly to slide down, and it occupied about an hour and a half. The most curious part was that the Shaykhs and chief Moslems always accompanied me to Mass. The thing that astonished the Shaykhs the most, was the small acolytes being able to read and sing in Latin, and they constantly exclaimed, "Máshálláh!"

We were much grieved about this time to hear the sad news of poor Lord Clarendon's death. Few amongst us that have not some happy recollection of that kind, true heart. He belonged to a breed of gentlemen that with one or two exceptions may be said to have died out. R.I.P. At this juncture Mr. E. H. Palmer and Charley Drake had come back from Sinai and the Tih Desert, and came to stay with us.

We wandered about for a long time together. On a long day we might easily zigzag forty or fifty miles, and thirty or thirty-six on a short day. We never rode straight to a place, and always rode two horses, as there is so much to be seen on both sides of a direct way.

Ba'albak is far more beautiful, though much smaller than Tadmor, and can be seen without any danger. Tadmor is more romantic, picturesque, more startling, and there is the attraction of the danger, and being in the absolute desert. Londoners and Parisians would consider Ba'albak in the desert, but we from Damascus do not. This was the holy place of the old Phœnicians, and I do not know a finer sight, from a distant height, when Ba'albak is lit up by the setting

THE BURTONS' HOUSE AT BLUDÁN, IN ANTI-LEBANON.

By Charles Tyrwhitt-Drake.

sun. The fertile plain of the Buká'a, with its black Turcoman tents and camels, lies in the distance. There is a big stone still lying there, which would weigh eleven thousand tons. The Hajar el Hablah, or pregnant stone, is a huge unfinished block. Our measurements were seventy feet long, fourteen feet two inches high, and thirteen feet eleven inches broad. The extraordinary sight makes you exclaim, "Something must have frightened them before they had time to carry it off."

Riding about, you come to the Turcomans' tents, who have wandered about Syria since the days of the Crusaders, and have preserved, like their neighbours the *Nuwar* (gypsies), their ancestral language and customs. We then went to live for a short while with the Maronites, two hundred thousand people, under the rule of their Patriarch, and we camped for some time under the cedars of Lebanon. There are only nine of these large and ancient trees left; the four largest are in the form of a cross, and three smaller. There are 555 trees (newer than these nine), all told, and they are 7368 feet above sea-level. While stopping with his "Beatitude the Maronite Primate of Antioch, and of all the East," whom his flock calls "our Patriarch, our Pope, and our Sultan," we saw for once the simplicity and sincerity of the Apostolic ages.

B'sherri, Jezzín, and Sadád produce a manly, independent race of Christians, fond of horses and arms, with whom I am not ashamed to own community of faith. In all my life I have never seen worse riding than the Kasrawán; it consists of nothing but *débris* of rock, fields, valleys, and mountains, all of the largest jagged stones. Our horses had to do the work of goats, and jump from one bit of rock to another, and it lasted over twelve hours at once. We lost our camp, but after seeing our exhausted horses groomed, fed, watered, and tethered in a warm spot, we were glad to eat a water-melon, and sleep on our saddle-cloths in the open. The next day was just as bad until we reached Affka, but the scenery was glorious. We had three days of this awful riding, which the Syrians call "Darb el Jehannum," the "road of hell." We visited Mr. Palgrave's old quarters, a monastery of fifty or sixty Jesuits, where Mr. Palgrave was a Jesuit for seventeen years. Here we all got fever.

Upon the 26th of August, Richard received at night, by a mounted messenger, the two following letters from Mr. Wright, Chief Missionary at Damascus (No. 2), and from Mr. Nasif Meshaka, Chief Dragoman of the British Consulate (No. 1). I give them as they were written:—

No. I.

"DEAR SIR,

"The Christians in Damascus are in great alarm; most of them have left for Saídnayah, and others are about to leave for elsewhere. Their alarm was occasioned from the following facts: signs of crosses were made in the streets in the same way which preceded the massacre of 1860. On the 23rd instant a certain Mohammed Rashíd, a Government inspector *(teftish)*, being in disguise, caught a young Jew, twelve years old, in the service of Solomon Donemberg, a British-protected subject, making signs of crosses in a cabinet of a mosque at Súk el Jedíd. Yesterday another young Jew, in the service of Marco, a French Jew, was caught also. Both of these two boys were taken to the Government; being under age, they were at once released by order of Mejlis Tamiz Hukúk. It is believed that the Moslems are the authors of these signs, either directly or indirectly, to stop the Government from taking the Redíf (militia), which is managed in a very oppressive manner, that is, leaving many families without males to support them. Such kinds of Redíf prefer rather to be hanged than seeing their haríms without support or any one to maintain them in their absence. A certain Nicolas Ghartous, a Protestant from Ain Shára, reported to me yesterday that while waiting on Mr. Anhouri, near the barracks of the Christian quarter, being dressed like a Druze, three soldiers of the same barracks came to him and said, 'Yakík el 'ijl,' a technical term used by the Druzes, meaning, 'Are you ready for another outbreak?' Ghartous replied, 'We are at your disposal.' The soldiers replied, 'Prepare yourself, and we will reap our enemies from here to the Báb Sharki' (the Christian quarter), and thus they departed. Hatem Ghanem, a Catholic member in the Haurán, came here to recover some money due to him by Atta Zello of the Meydán Aghas. While claiming the money he was beaten, and his religion and Cross were cursed by his debtor, who was put in prison at the request of the Catholic Patriarchate. Twenty to thirty Redífs of the Meydán ran away to the Lejá'a, to take refuge there. The Redífs will be collected next Saturday, the 27th instant, some say at the Castle of Damascus, others at Khabboon and Mezzeh. The report is current that on that day there will be no work in town, and that there will be an outbreak. Although Ibraham Pasha, the new Governor, arrived on the 23rd instant, he will not undertake his duties till the return of the *Wali*. The Governor, as well as some Frenchmen, through M. Roustan, who is now at Jerusalem, intend to propose to the *Wali* to leave Holo Pasha to continue occupying his present function under the present circumstances. The *Mushir* left on the 19th instant. The *Wali* is absent. The *Muffetish*, whom you know his inefficiency, is the Acting Governor-General. Consuls are absent (that is, the French and English). The presence of the high functionaries, and especially the Consuls, is a great comfort to the Christians in general."

No. 2.

"Dear Sir,

"I have just got in from Rasheiya, and before I sat down several Christians and one Moslem came in to ask if I knew what was coming. They seemed to be very much afraid; but, except that people don't act logically, I see no reason for fear. The fear, however, *does* seem *very* great. I know nothing. Any English of us here should be ready at the worst to fight our corner. Many thanks for your prompt action in our affairs. It is something to have

'One firm, strong man in a blatant land,
Who can act and who dare not lie.'

"W. W."

It appeared that one of those eruptions of ill-feeling, which are periodically an epidemic in Damascus, resulting from so many religions, tongues, and races, was about to simmer into full boil between Moslem and Christian. The outsiders are fond of stirring up both, for they reap all the benefit. It appeared that a slaughter-day was fixed for the 27th of August, 1870; all the Chief Authorities, by an accidental combination of affairs, were absent as well as the Consuls. Wednesday is the Moslem's unlucky day, and also, I believe, the 23rd; it is thought it will be the day of the end of the world. There would be nobody to interfere, and nobody to be made responsible. It was the night of the 26th when he got these letters. Richard ordered the horses to be saddled, the weapons to be cleaned. In ten minutes he told me what his plans and arrangements were. He said, "We have never before been in a Damascus riot, but if it takes place it will be like the famous affair of 1860. I shall not take you into Damascus, because *I* intend to protect Damascus, and you must protect Bludán and Zebedáni. I shall take half the men, and I shall leave you half. You shall go down into the plain with me to-night, and we shall shake hands like two brothers and part; tears or any display of affection will tell the secret to our men."

So it was done, and at six o'clock the next morning he walked into the *mejlis* (council chamber). He was on good terms with them all, so he told them frankly what was going on, and said, "Which of you is to be hanged if this is not prevented? It will cost you Syria, and unless you take measures at once, I shall telegraph to Constantinople." This had the desired effect. "What," they asked, "would you have us to do?" He said, "I want you to post a guard of soldiers in every street; order a patrol all night. I will go the rounds with Holo Pasha. Let the soldiers be harangued in the barracks, and told that on the slightest sign of mutiny the offenders will be sent to the Danube (their Cayenne). Issue an order that no Jew or Christian shall leave the house till all is quiet." All these measures were taken by ten o'clock a.m., and continued for three days. Not a drop of blood was shed, and the frightened Christians who had fled to the mountains began to come back. There is no doubt that my husband saved Damascus from a very unpleasant episode. Mr. L. Wright, Mr. Scott, and the other missionaries, his own dragomans, and a few staunch souls who remained quietly with him, appreciated his conduct, and he received many thanks from those on the spot. The diligence was so much in request (nearly all the Christians and Europeans had tried to leave) that a friend of mine could not get a seat for three weeks; yet these people, so soon as they sighted the Mediterranean, were brave and blatant. "Oh! *we* were not at all frightened; there was *no* danger whatever!" Mr. Eldridge, who had lived for ten years safely on the coast, and had never ventured up to Damascus in his life, a civilian whose dislike to the smell of powder was notorious, wrote me a pleasantly chaffing letter, hoping I had recovered my fever and fright, and giving Richard instructions how to behave in time of danger. When Richard had gone I climbed back to our eyrie, which commanded the country, and collected every available weapon and all the ammunition. The house was square, looking every way. I put a certain number of men on each side with a gun each, a revolver, and bowie-knife. I put two on the roof with a pair of elephant guns carrying four-ounce balls, and took the terrace myself. I planted the Union Jack on the flag-staff at the top of the house, turned our bull-terriers into the garden, locked up a little Syrian maid, Khamoor (the Moon), who was very pretty (Richard used to say her eyes were of the owlified largeness of the book of beauty), in the safest room, and my English maid, who was as brave as a man, was to supply us with provisions. I knew that I could rely upon our own men, so I filled all the empty soda-water bottles full of gunpowder, and laid fusees ready to stick in and light, and throw amongst the crowd. I then rode down to the American mission—the only other people near—to tell them if there was the slightest movement to come up and shelter with me; and then into the village of Bludán, to tell the Christians there to come and camp in our garden; and lastly to Zebedáni, where there were a few Christians living amongst the thirty-five thousand Moslems, and I sent them up at once, because there would be no time for *them* to reach me if danger came suddenly. The others were close by. I then rode down to the Moslem Shaykhs, and asked them what *they* thought. They told me there *would* be a fight. "One half of our village will fight *with* you and yours, the other half will destroy the Christians here and at Bludán. They will hesitate to attack *your* house, but if matters are so bad as that, they shall pass over our dead bodies, and those of all our house, before they reach *you*." And every night they came up and picketed round the garden till my husband came back.

This lasted three days, and all subsided without accident. At this time also there was a tremendous row between a Moslem and a Christian woman; he tore the woman's ear down, smashed her black and blue, bruised her, and took all her gold ornaments from her. The case of Hassan Beg, on whose account my husband was reported, by the British Syrian School missionaries, to be recalled *on account of my conduct*, happened a whole year before my husband's recall. After this, when we rode desert-wards, the tribes used in the evening to dance especially for Richard. The men formed a squad like soldiers; they plant the right foot in time to tom-tom music, with a heavy tread, and an exclamation like that used by our street-menders when the crowbar comes down with a thud upon the stones. When they are numerous it sounds like the advance of an army, and they would burst out into song, of which the literal translation would be—

"Máshálláh! Máshálláh! At last we have seen a man!
Behold our Consul in our Shaykh!
Who dare to say 'Good morning' to us (save Allah) when he rules?
Look at him, look at the Sitt!
They ride the Arab horses!
They fly before the wind!
They fire the big guns!
They fight with the sword!
Let us follow them all over the earth!"
(Chorus) "Let us follow, let us follow," etc., etc.

We were very fond of animals, and especially of wild ones. Holo Pasha had given us a panther cub trapped in the desert to show his appreciation of what Richard had done. We brought him up like a cat. He grew to be a splendid beast, and never did any of us harm, but he frightened the other animals a little sometimes. We kept him very well fed, in order that he might never attack them. Our cat was very frightened of him, and the only animals that he was frightened of were the bull-dogs. He used to sleep by our bedside. He had bold bad black eyes, that seemed to say, "Be afraid of me." He used to hunt me round the garden, playing hide-and-seek with me as a cat does a mouse. When he bit too hard, I used to box his ears, when he was instantly good. But he grew up and was large. There was a certain baker that the bull-terriers used to bite, and the panther, who also saw in him what we did not, worried him. At last the peasantry, who were frightened of him, gave him poison in meat. He withered away, and nothing we could do did him any good, and one day, when I went to look round the stables, he put his paw up to me. I sat down on the ground, and took him in my arms like a child. He put his head on my shoulder, and his paws round my waist, and he died in about half an hour. Richard and I were terribly grieved.

There are charming rides across the Anti-Lebanon through a mountain defile to Ain el Bardi, where we found black tents and flocks feeding by the water. There is very much to be seen in the plain of El Buká'a, beginning at Mejdel. Anjar is a little village on a hillock standing alone; on its top is a small gem of a temple built by Herod Agrippa in honour of Augustus, with a very graceful broken column; below it are the ruins of Herod's Palace, and a twenty minutes' further ride in the plain lie the ruins of Chalcis. From the temple above named we could see the greater part of the Buká'a, walled in at either side by the Lebanon and the Anti-Lebanon, and dotted with seventy-two villages. Anjar is bisected by the Litani river, falsely called the Leontes. Having feasted our eyes, we rode on to the square ruins of Chalcis in the plain, and to Neby Za'úr to see the tomb, and we carried off skulls and bones. We crossed the plain, ascended the Lebanon, and when near its summit turned to our left across a mountain called Jebel Barúk, in the territory of El Akkúb.

A favourite ride was into the Druze country, beginning at Barúk, a stronghold in a wild glen. They are a fine, tall, strong, and manly race, who can ride and fight and shoot, and are fit to be our allies. There is no cant about them; they are honest and plain-spoken, and do not know intriguing, lying, stealing, or spying. A Druze house has huge black rafters in the ceiling, and straight tall columns down the middle; there is a private room for council. The women have one blue garment, and one white veil showing one eye. They are chaste, and good wives and mothers. They have clean, comfortable homes, and give a warm welcome, and we rested here for some time. People often say, "What is the real religion of the Druzes?" No one ever knew who was not a Druze; they conform to the national religion, the Moslem. In speaking to you or me, they would appear to have a particular leaning to our respective faiths. They have a secret creed of their own, which, although women are admitted to the council chamber, is as mysterious as Freemasonry. Some Moslems pretend that they worship Eblis, and some Christians say the bull-calf El Ijl.

On our road we came to another stronghold, like an ancient

convent, where lives Melhem Beg Ahmad, a Druze chief, a dare-devil-fine-old-man, who, when he mounts, takes his bridle in his teeth, puts his musket to his shoulder, and charges down a mountain that an English horse would have to be led down. He lives in great style; he threw his cap in the air, drank to our health a thousand times, and his sons waited on us at dinner. Muktára hangs on a declivity in a splendid ravine in wild mountains in the territory of Esh Shuf. The house we were going to is like a large Italian *cascine*, nestled amidst olive groves, that are, so to speak, the plumage of the heights. It is the Syrian palace of the Jumblatts, the focus and centre of the Lebanon Druzes. Here reside this princely family, headed then by a Chieftainess, the "Sitt Jumblatt."

Long before we sighted Muktára, wild horsemen, in the rich Druze dress, came careering down, jeriding on beautiful horses, with guns and lances, the sons and retainers of the house heading them. They were splendidly mounted, and one of the sons had a black mare, so simply perfect I infringed the tenth commandment. We descended into a deep defile, and rose up again on the opposite side, the whole of which was lined with horsemen and footmen to salute us, and the women trilled out their joy-cry. Ascending the other side was literally like going up stairs cut in the rock; it was a regular fastness. We rode our horses up the flight of stairs into the court. We received the most cordial and gracious hospitality from the *Sitt*, who had all the well-bred ease of a European *grande dame*. Water and scented soap was brought in carved brass ewers and basins to wash our hands, incense was waved before us, we were sprinkled with rose-water, whilst an embroidered gold canopy was held over us. Coffee, sherbet, and sweets were served. The next morning the palace was filled with grey-bearded and turbaned scribes, with their long brass inkstands, and the *Sitt* explained to Richard that her affairs were entirely neglected at Beyrout, and asked him to do something for her. He explained that it was a great embarrassment to him, as he was subordinate to Mr. Eldridge, but that, whatever she chose to write, he would make a point of going himself to present her wishes to Mr. Eldridge. Richard notes in his journal that day among others, "Eldridge does nothing, and is very proud of what he does. Consular office awfully careless; sick of dyspepsia; nothing to do body and mind."

We sat down to a midday meal equivalent to a dinner, and then went to the *Jerid* ground, where the sons and their fighting men displayed their grace and skill. The stables are solid, and like tunnels with light let in, containing sixty horses, all showing blood, and some quite thoroughbred. At nightfall there was a big dinner, to which all the retainers flocked in; there was dancing and war-songs between the Druzes of the Lebanon and the Druzes of the Haurán, ranged on either side of the banqueting hall; they performed a pantomime, they sang, and recited tales of love and war far into the night.

An amusing thing was, that after the *Sitt* had dined with us, I found her shortly after sitting cross-legged on the floor of the kitchen, devouring a second dinner. I said, "Ya Sitti, I thought you had eaten your dinner with us; what are you doing?" She laughed, and said, "My dear child, you don't suppose for an instant that I got a bit into my mouth with those knives and forks; I was only doing pantomime for the honour of the house. Now I am getting my *real* dinner with my fingers!" We were accompanied out with the same honours as those with which we were ushered in. How sorry we were to leave! Our friendship always lasted. We used to begin, "My dearest sister," and she used to say all those sweet things which only Easterns can say, such as—"My eyes sought for you many days till my head ached; when will you come to repose them, that I may not see your empty place?"

We went on to Deir el Khammar to the palace of Bayt el Din (B'teddin), where Franco Pasha (the best governor the Lebanon has ever known) lived, and was restoring this ruined castle of the late terrible Amir Beshir Sheháb, from whence the view is splendid. He had about five hundred soldiers, and was doing enormous good. He had a band, a school, was planting pine trees and wheat, teaching carpet-making, tailoring, shoemaking, making roads, teaching religion and loyalty to God, to the Sultan, with liberality and civilization. He produced an electric shock upon us by the invisible band playing "God save the Queen." We sprang to our feet, and in that wild place it made me cry. In this region we met the only real *prince* in Syria, the Emir Mulhem Rustam. We had an immense quantity of deputations of Druze Shaykhs; those of the Haurán were something like bears, with huge white turbans, green coat, massive swords, some in red, and all exceedingly wild-looking. We then went to Ali Beg of Jumblatt, at Baderhan. We passed innumerable Druze villages, until we came to Jezzín, one of the three manly Christian villages. Usuf Beg, their Chief, was a delightful Shaykh.

Sometimes these breakfasts on the march were very amusing, where there were a mixture of races and religion. You would see forty intrigues round a dish of rice. At Rasheya there was no water; here we were on Druze ground again. From this we went to the top of Mount Hermon, *i.e.* it has three tops, and we put a *kakú* of stones on the highest for a remembrance. The view is immense. We found a cave and saw a hare. When we got to the bottom, there was hardly a shoe or a rag left amongst us. Here we met some very charming Druze chiefs, and went with them to Hasbeya, because Richard was convinced that the sources of the Jordan were not as they are given in books; and he was perfectly right. There is a slanting rock with some figs growing out of it, and oleanders growing in luxurious clumps in the sand all around, and out of this rock rushes a stream, which we traced to the Jordan. Near is a mine of bitumen.

From thence to Kefayr, another Druze village, after which we rode to Banias. Of course, there are loads of things to see all the way—caves or temples, or what not; but, then, all those can be got in books. The sources are supposed to be here, at Banias, and are made much of; and all visitors go to the fountain of Jordan, the cave of Pan, the temple of Herod and Augustus, with the three niches. The water trickles from beneath under the stones, separating into eight or nine streams, but they are not the real source.

We had a large escort to-day. Ali Beg Ahmadi and his cavalry, Shaykh Ahmad, and many others, came to escort us, and we had a delicious gallop over the plain of Ghyam, which is part of the Ard el Húleh, through which runs the Jordan, and another portion of the same is called the Abbs. We came to Arab tents, and drank milk with the Bedawi; we found many of them down with fever, and stopped to doctor them with Warburg's drops. We had to ride all day, and at last through marshy, rushy places under a burning sun, without a breath of air.

This valley of the Jordan, if drained and planted, would be immensely rich, but it teemed now with luxurious rankness, fever, and death. We pitched our tents under a large tree, divided from the lake by papyrus swamps; a most unwholesome spot, where we were punished by every sort of insect and crawling thing in creation; and we all got headache and sore throat at once.

The Bahret el Huleh, or the Waters of Merom in Josh. xi. 5–7, anciently called Lake Semachonitis, is a small blue triangular lake, the first and highest of the three basins of the Jordan. We had all our escort with us; we had scarcely any food; there was none for the horses. We had to turn them all loose to forage for themselves, except the stallions, and they had to be led. It was a hideous expanse of fœtid mire and putrefying papyrus. We had a frightful night, a stifling heat, a very blizzard of wind, rain, thunder, and lightning, and we were camped under the only tree in the plain. It was black dark; the ground was bad-smelling black mud; we passed the dark hours in holding our tent-pole against the wind, and digging trenches outside to let the water off. There were no dry clothes to be had, and the various vermin would not let one rest. We were like that for three days; so we piled up the trunks and sat at the top of them, and read "Lothair," by Disraeli, which we had brought with us. The description of the great houses of England read so funnily sitting in this black mud in the centre of desolation, surrounded by feverish swamps.

In spite of the difficulties of moving in such weather, Richard and I were agreed that if we stayed there any longer, we should all perhaps get in such a state as not to be able to move at all; so we saddled our horses, and ordering our followers and escort to strike tents, pack, load, and follow, we mounted and waded our horses through the water, scrambled over stones and slippery rocks, and in and out mud and slush for two hours, often sinking deep, till we reached the mountain roots and began to ascend.

After some hours' climbing we arrived at the seventy-two tents of the Shaykh Hadi Abd Allah; he instantly gave us hospitality, barley for our horses and food for ourselves. They were all yellow and sickly, and, even at this height, dying like sheep of fever from the miasma arising out of the plain that we had been in for three days. They had lost many children, and double sorrow when sons. One boy was dying as we entered. Our tents came up to us late that day with all our belongings. Our animals and people were fed. We stayed with the tribe long enough to doctor them all round, and to leave remedies and directions; and I baptized the incurables and the dying children.

Then came down the Amir Hasan el Fá'ur of the Benú Fadl, or Fazli tribe. He heard of our being in the neighbourhood, and took us off to his camp on the summit of a mountain called Jebel Haush, a day's ride away, where we found his three hundred tents. The whole tribe turned out to meet us, mounted and couching their lances, and jeríded the whole way back. The reception tent was fifty feet long, and each divan was twenty-five feet long. The retainers cleared a space for our camp, corn was brought, horses picketed; an excellent dinner on a large scale in the big tent was cooked, lambs and kids roasted whole, stuffed with pistachios and rice, bowls of *leban*, unleavened bread, honey, and camels'-milk butter, bowls of clear sparkling water. I love to think now of those dark, fierce men, in their gaudy flowing costumes, lying about in different attitudes, the moon lighting up the scene; the lurid glare of the fire on their faces, the divans and pipes, *narghílehs* and coffee, their wild and mournful songs, their war-dances, their story-telling; and on that particular night, and on all these sort of nights, my husband would recite to them one or another tale out of the "Arabian Nights"—those tales which he has now translated literally for the London world; and I have seen the gravest and most reverend Shaykhs rolling on the ground and screaming with delight, in spite of their Oriental gravity, and they seemed as if they could never let my husband go again.

I can remember that night, when he and I went to our tent and lay down on our respective rugs, he called me over, for he was stung by a scorpion, but when I struck a match there was nothing but a speck of blood, as though from a black ant; so we lay down again, and he called out, "Quick, quick! I *know* it is a scorpion." I ran over and struck another light, and plunged my hand into the shirt by the throat, and the scorpion caught my finger. I drew it out and shook it off, and killed it; but it did not sting me, being, I supposed, exhausted. I rubbed some strong smelling-salts into the wounds, and, seeing he was pale, ran off to the provision-basket and got a bottle of *raki*, and made him drink it, to keep the poison from the heart, and he woke in the morning quite well.

I now discovered that though they were treating us with this splendid hospitality, that behind the scenes they were also dying in their tents of fever, although they were in the purest air; so here we again stayed to doctor, and nurse, and baptize, and leave directions and remedies.

We then went on to most of the romantic and hospitable Druze villages which cling to the southern and eastern folds of Hermon—Mejdel Esh Shems to Birket er Ram, or Lake Phiala,* a little round lake which we found interesting enough to come back to afterwards. Mejdel is on a declivity of a mountain defile—their favourite position—a Druze stronghold, very fighting and turbulent, where we were received and treated like relations. Then we got to Beyt-Jenn, where we had a mixed Druze and Christian place. We came in for a very interesting Druze wedding at Arneh, at the foot of Hermon, just above which rise the sources of the Awaj, which waters El Kunayterah. We then went to a Druze village called Rimeh, to look for a stone with an inscription, which we found in a stable, and then to the Bukkásim, which is the Druze frontier. Here our Druze cavalcade took an affecting leave of us. As we rode away I could see them for three-quarters of an hour standing on a high rock to watch us out of sight, one or two of them with their faces buried in their mares' necks.

---

* The cave near Affka forms the Orontes, the Jura sends forth the Bárada of Damascus, and Lake Phiala Josephus makes the highest water of the Jordan.

The Wuld Ali.

Our escort of free-lances one day, as we were riding to some of our usual environs, soon perceived that we were making for the desert, towards the direction where the dreaded Mohammed Dúkhi was known to camp, and they began the well-known dodges of making their horses curvet and prance and wheel in circles as if they had become unmanageable, and every round became so much larger that they gradually dropped out of sight. Presently some cast a shoe, or another had broken a girth, and stopped to rectify it. The fact is, Richard had been determined to make friends with the Wuld Ali tribe, of which Mohammed Dúkhi is the Chief, and rules five thousand lances. At last we found ourselves alone, so we rode on all that day, slept by our horses at night in a ruined *khan*, and got in sight of the Wuld Ali encampment late next day. Richard said to me, "Now mind, when they see us two horsemen, they will come galloping across the sand in a body with their lances couched; if we were to turn and run, they would spear us; but if we sit our horses, facing them like statues on parade, just as the Life Guards sit in their sentry-boxes at the Horse Guards at home, they will take us in with great applause, and our horses will stand it, because they are used to desert manners."

I said "All right," as I always did when he gave me an order, and I was glad he put me up to it, for, sure enough, when they saw our two dusky figures galloping from a distance across the sand towards them, the whole tribe charged with their lances couched, and we reined in and stood stock still, facing the charge; but as soon as they got within a few yards, they seemed by instinct to recognize the man they were charging. They lowered their lances, opened their ranks to enclose us, and with one cry of "Ak-hu Sebbah!" (Brother of the Lion), jumped off their horses, kissed our hands, galloped in with us jeriding, and held our stirrups to alight. I need not say that we were treated with all the true hospitality of real Bedawi life, and we remained several days with them. My husband's object was to make peace between the Wuld Ali and the Mezrabs. We visited the lakes which are near them, and they were all dried up except a bit of water in the sand about the size of a small duck-pond. "What, then," said Richard, "becomes of the Bárada and the Awaj, the so-called ancient Abana and Pharphar?" They have been partly drawn off, and partly evaporated before reaching their basements at 'Utaybah and Hijánah, where we then were.

The Arabic of Damascus, *especially* the Christian Arabic, Richard found so grating to the ears after the pure speech of the Bedawi—and that of the Nejd and El Hejaz.

Richard writes an account of a trip—

" A little later on Charley Drake and I again started to revisit the Tulul el Safá,* and our first eight days was over the old ground. This trip added considerably to our scanty geographical knowledge of these regions off the tracks. In one week we collected some hundred and twenty inscriptions, and three lengthy copies of Greek hexameters and pentameters from the Burj, a mortuary tower at Shakkah, a ruin long since identified as the Saccæa of Ptolemy. We went to the top of Tell Shayhán, whose height is 3750 feet, which showed us that the Lejá, the Argob of the Hebrews and the western Trachon of the Greeks and Romans, is the gift of Tell Shayhán.† It is a lava bed, a stone torrent poured out by the lateral crater over the ruddy yellow clay and the limestone floor of the Haurán valley, high raised by the ruins of repeated eruptions, broken up by the action of blow-holes, and cracked and crevassed by contraction when cooling, by earthquakes, and the weathering of ages. 'The features are remarkable. It is composed of black basalt, which must have issued from the pores of the earth in a liquid state, and flowed out until the plain was almost covered. Before cooling its surface was agitated by some powerful agency, and it was afterwards shattered and rent by internal convulsions and vibrations' (Porter). Two whole days were spent at Kanawát, the ancient Canatha, a city of Og.

"There are now hundreds of Druzes, and we may remark for the first time 'the beauty of Bashan,' the well-wooded and watered country. We then went along the Jebel Kulayb and visited the noble remains of Sí'a, where we met with three Palmyrene inscriptions, showing that the Palmyra of Ptolemy extended to the south-west far beyond the limits assigned to it. We then got to Sahwat el Balát, where lives my influential friend, Shaykh Ali el Hináwí, a Druze Akkál of the highest rank; and here they gathered to meet me and palaver. We crossed the immense rough and rugged lava beds which gloom the land. Jebel el Kulayb was bright with vetch, red poppy, yellow poppy, mistletoe with ruddy berries, hawthorn boughs, and the vivid green of the maple and the sumach, the dark foliage of the ilex oak scrub, and the wild white honeysuckle. There was cultivation; the busy Druze peasantry at work, the women in white and blue. The aneroid showed 5785 feet, the hygrometer stood at 0°, the air was colder than on the heights of Hermon in June, and the western horizon was obscured by the thickest of wool packs. Here we made two important observations. The apparently confused scatter of volcanic cratered hill and

* I was not well, and was left at home.—I. B.

† This answers something to the Karst above Trieste.

hillock fell into an organized trend of 356° to 176°, or nearly north-south. The same will be noticed in the Safá, and in its out-layers the Tulul el Safá, which lie hard upon a meridian; thus the third or easternmost great range, separating the Mediterranean from the Euphrates desert, does not run parallel with its neighbours, the Anti-Libanus and Libanus, which are disposed, roughly speaking, north-east 38°, and south-west 218°.

"The second point of importance is that El Kulayb is not the apex of the Jebel Durúz Haurán, though it appears to be so. To the east appeared a broken range, whose several heights, beginning from the north, were named to us. Tell Ijaynah, bearing 38°, back by the Umm Haurán hill, bearing 94°; the Tell of Akriba (Wetz Stein), bearing 112° 30′; Tell Rubáh, bearing 119°; and Tell Jafnah, bearing 127° 30′. We believed that Tell Ijaynah was 6080 English feet high, and we thought that Jebel Durúz must be greatly changed since it was described by travellers and tourists.

"Here the land, until the last hundred and fifty years, was wholly in the hands of the Bedawi, especially of the Wuld Ali, and the nine hill tribes already named. At last the Druzes, whom poverty and oppression drove away from their original home, the Wady Taym and the slopes of Libanus and Hermon, settled here. In Rashíd Pasha's reign seventeen mountain villages have been repeopled, and in 1886 some eight hundred families fled to this safe retreat; nor can we wonder at the exodus, because of half the settlements of the Jaydur district, the ancient Ituræa, eleven out of twenty-four have been within twelve months ruined by the usurer and the tax-gatherer, and at one time a hundred and twenty Druze families went in one flight from their native mountains to the Haurán.

"They found here a cool, healthy, but harsh climate, a sufficiency of water, ready-made houses, ruins of cut stone, land awaiting cultivation, pasture for their flocks and herds, and, above all things, a rude independence under the patriarchal rule of their own chiefs. In short, the only peaceful, prosperous districts of Syria are those where home rule exists, and there is scarcely any interference by the authorities. It is a short-sighted and miserable management which drives an industrious peasantry from its hearths and homes to distant settlements where defence is more easy than offence.

"This system keeps the population of the whole province to a million and a half, which in the days of Strabo and Josephus supported its ten millions and more. The European politician is not sorry to see the brave and sturdy Druze thrown out as a line of forts to keep the Arab wolf from the doors of the Damascene, but the antiquary sighs for the statues and architectural ornaments broken up, the inscribed stones used for building rude domiciles, the most valuable remnants of antiquity white-washed as lintels, or plastered over in the unclean interiors. The next generation of travellers will see no more 'mansions of Bashan.'

"At Shakkah (Saccæa) there are still extensive ruins and fine specimens of Hauránic architecture, especially the house of Shaykh Hasan Brahím with its coped windows and its sunken court.

Here we were received by the Druze Chief, Kabalán el Kala'áni, who behaved very badly to us, and when we tried to go, refused to let us unless we paid him forty napoleons for ten horsemen. We laughed in his face, told him to stop us if he dared, and sent for our horses. However, as we were going into a fighting country, I sent back all the people who would have been in the way.

"The Druzes had been quarrelling amongst themselves; fifteen men had been killed, and many wounded. We had to doctor three; one had a shoulder-blade pierced clean through. We were joined *nolens volens* by ten free-lances, and escorted as far as Bir Kasam, their particular boundary. Finally, it appears that our visit to the 'Aláh district, lying east of Hamáh, has brought to light the existence of an architecture which, though identical with that of the Haurán, cannot in any way be connected with that of Og. Although only separated by seventy miles from the southern basaltic region, the northern has also its true Bashan architecture, its cyclopean walls, its private houses, low, massive, and simple in style, with stone roofs and doors, and huge gates, conspicuous for simplicity, massiveness, and rude strength. Moab has the same, only limestone is used instead of basalt.

"Dumá Ruzaymah is occupied by three great houses, and the Junaynah hamlet is the last inhabited village of this side towards the desert. We now got to the Wady Jahjah, thence to El Harrah, 'the Hot or Burnt Land,' and to the Krá'a, which we crossed in fifty-five minutes, and got into or entered the Naká, *and were surprised to see a messenger mounted on a dromedary, going at a great pace, and evidently shunning us.* We had descended 3780 feet; the passage occupied two hours.

"We then ascended into the Hazir, and from the top we had our first fair view of the Safá,* a volcanic block, with its seven main summits. They stood conspicuously out of the Harrah, or 'Hot Country.' In the far distance glittered the sunlit horizon of the Euphrates Desert, a mysterious tract, never yet crossed by European foot. We eventually arrived at the stony, black Wa'ar, a distorted and devilish land, and we then got to a waterless part, where our horses were already thirsty, and into the Ghadir, where we had been promised water, and it was bone dry. After long riding, we came to a ruined village, El Hubbayríyyah, where we found yellow water forming a green slime. It was again the *kattas* which led me to the water, as in Somali-land. Here we spent an enjoyable fifty minutes at the water, refreshing ourselves and beasts; it lies 3290 feet above sea-level. We presently fell into the Saut on return; it was good travelling, and we saw old footmarks of sheep, goats, and shod horses.

"The only sign, as we turned out of the Saut and swept down from the Lohf, that human foot had ever trod this inhospitable wild, was here and there a goat-fold, with a place for the shepherd on a com-

* "This is a term used at Damascus to the northern offsets; these are the southern."

manding spot, or more probably a Bedawin sentinel or scout (you often see a solitary tribesman perched on a hilltop). The road was simply a goat-track, over the domes of cast-iron ovens, in endless succession. It was a truly maniac ride. *At the Rajm el Shalshal we again saw traces of our friend on the dromedary.* That day at 4.20 p.m. we were surprised by our advanced party springing suddenly from the mares, and hearing the welcome words, 'Umm Nirán!' (the mother of fire). Late as it was, we rejoiced, because a night march over such a country would have been awful. The cave is as dry as the land of Scinde, and in the summer sunshine the hand could not rest upon the heated surface, but after rain there is a drainage from the fronting basin into the cave. We crawled into it and entered a second tunnel, and after two hundred feet we came to the water, a ditch-like channel, four feet wide. The line then bent to the right from north-north-east to the north-east. Here, by plunging our heads below water and raising them further on, we found an oval-shaped chamber, still traversed by the water. We could not, however, reach the end, as shortly the rock ceiling and the water met. The supply was sweet, the atmosphere close and damp, the roof an arid fiery waste of blackest lava. The basalt ceiling of the cave sweated and dripped, which could not have been caused only by simple evaporation. The water began by a few inches till it reached mid-thigh. The length was a total of three hundred and forty feet; the altitude was 2745 feet.

"A water scorpion was the only living thing in the cave. This curious tunnel reservoir is evidently natural. There are legends about a clansman going in with black hair, and coming out after the third day with white hair, and one of our lads declared he had taken an hour to reach the water; but we, on all fours, took three minutes. We set out again next day for the great red cinder-heap, known as Umm el Ma'azah, where we halted for observation, and then fell into the trodden way which leads from the Ghutah section of the Damascus plain to the Rubbah valley.

"We had long and weary desert rides, seeing everything to the Bir Kasam. Bedawi never commit the imprudence of lingering near the well after they have watered their beasts, because that is the way to draw a *ghazú*, or raid, down upon you.

"Now I have every reason to be thankful that I did not bring my wife on this journey, as she was not very well. In this country fever and dysentery seize upon you with short notice, and pass away again, and she, though in no danger, was not in a state for hard riding at the time. At Bir Kásam, a Druze greybeard, on a *rahwán*, rode up to the well, and took the opportunity of making me a sign: pretending to question him, as to the name of a mountain on the horizon, I led him away, and he cautiously pulled out of his pocket a medicine bottle, which he handed to me, from my wife. I then knew there was something up, and I thanked him, giving him some money, and asked him if he had anything to say. He said, 'If I may advise you, get rid of all your party. They want to go to Damascus or Dhumayr; announce that you are going to neither, and they will probably forsake you, as this is not a safe spot. I shall ride on, till out of sight, and then turn round and ride back to Damascus, by slow degrees, sleeping and eating on the road. You and your friend ride into Jebel Dákwah; but first read the directions about the medicine.'

"I uncorked the bottle, saw my wife's warning in writing, and carefully put them in my pocket not to leave a 'spoor.' I then paid him still more handsomely, and told him to go back to my wife, and tell her it was 'all right,' and not to fear. As evening fell, they asked us what our intentions were. We said we were not going either to Damascus or Dhumayr, and, as our messenger had prophesied, they all disappeared in the night, to our great relief. As soon as the last man had disappeared, we went into the Dákwah Mountain (hid our horses in a cave), from the cone of which you command a view of the whole country, and after a few hours we saw a hundred horsemen and two hundred dromedary riders beating the country, looking for some one in the plains. At last they turned in another direction, towards some distant villages, and when we were consoled by not seeing a living thing, we descended from our perch, galloped twenty miles to Dhumayr, where we were well received by faithful Druzes, whose Chief was Rashíd el Bóstají. We were just in time. The Governor-General had mustered his bravos; they missed us at Umm Nirán, at the Bir Kasam, and again upon the *direct* road to Dhumayr, having been put out by our *détour* to Dákwah. They were just a few hours too late everywhere; so, to revenge themselves, they plundered, in the sight of six hundred Turkish soldiers, the village of Suwáydah, belonging to my dragoman Azar, whose life they threatened, and also Abbadáh and Haraán el Awáníd. So we rode into Damascus, escaping by peculiar good fortune a hundred horsemen and two hundred dromedary riders, sent on purpose to murder *me*. I was never more flattered in my life, than to think that it would take three hundred men to kill *me*. The felon act, however, failed."

Rashíd Pasha's Intrigue with the Druzes—My Account from Damascus.

"I wish each man's forehead were a magic lantern of his inner self."

About this time the Druzes wrote and asked Richard to come to the Haurán. He wished to copy Greek inscriptions and explore volcanoes. He was not aware that the *Wali* had a political move in the Haurán, which he did not wish him to see. Mr. Eldridge knew it, and encouraged him to go, as his leave would be short. Richard knew that if he went to one man's house, he must go to everybody, therefore he asked them all to meet him at the house of the principal Shaykh. When the *Wali* was told by Richard that he was going, his face fell, but he suddenly changed, and said, "Go soon, or there will be no water." Mr. Eldridge, who never left Beyrout, and had at that time never seen Damascus, had talked a great deal about going there; so Richard wrote and asked him to go with him, but to that there was no answer. It was providential that I was weak with fever and dysentery, and could not ride, so that I was left at home. As soon as he was gone the *Wali* wrote to me, and accused my husband "of having made a political meeting with the Druze Chiefs in the Haurán, thereby doing great harm to the Turkish Government." Knowing that Richard had done nothing of the kind, I told him so, but I saw there was a new intrigue on. The *Wali* had only let my husband go in order to be able to accuse him of meddling, and by Mr. Eldridge's not answering I suspected he knew it too. An old Druze from the Haurán came to our house, said he had seen my husband, and began to praise him. I said, "Why, what is he doing?" He replied, "Máshálláh! we never saw a Consul like him. He can do in one day what the *Wali-Pasha* could not do in five years. We had a quarrel with the Bedawi, and we carried off all their goats and sheep, and the Government was going to attack us. Our Chiefs, when they saw the Consul (Allah be praised!), told him the difficulty, and asked him what we ought to do. He told us we ought to give back the goats and sheep to the Bedawi, and to make up our quarrel, and submit to the Government, for that the war will do us great harm. The Shaykhs have consented, and now we shall be at peace. Máshálláh! there is nobody like him!" I now began to wonder if the *Wali* had intended a little campaign against the Druzes, and if my husband had spoilt it by counselling submission. If he had intended to reduce the Druzes of the Eastern Mountains, and if a campaign took place in Jebel Durúz Haurán, the inhabitants would have been joined by the fighting men of the Lebanon, Anti-Lebanon, and Hermon. The country is eminently fitted for defence, and the Druzes, though badly armed, are brave, and animated by the memories of past victories. In short, the same disgraceful defeat of the Turkish Government would have taken place as that which occurred in 1874, and which caused the *Wali*, Mustafa Beg, and nine high officials to be dismissed.

The *Wali* then employed somebody—who I need not name—to inform him what day my husband was coming back. On being questioned about it, my suspicions were aroused; I immediately gave the wrong date (it was God's own blessing that I had for once been unable to go with him). I got the faithful old Druze to start at once, with a pretended bottle of medicine. I wrote, in a cipher that my husband and I composed and understood together, the whole history of the case, and I tied it round the cork of the bottle, covering it with leather and a bit of oil-skin, and sent my messenger straight out to meet him. It was just in time. He noticed with his keen desert instincts the fresh spoor of one solitary dromedary; the rider was bound like them from Shakkah to the north-east (where the Bedawi encamped), not for exploration, but with a message. He divined the ill-omened foot-prints which he saw twice in different localities, and so soon as the medicine bottle reached him, with what Ouida would call "a quiet low laugh under his moustache," he altered his course, and from a concealed shelter in the rocks was able to watch the progress of a hundred horsemen and two hundred *Redifs*—dromedary riders, two in each saddle—beating the country and looking for some one. Now, these were not *real* Bedawi, but the jackals who call themselves Bedawi, who surround the Cities, and are to be hired like bravos for any dirty work. They went off on a false scent, and he arrived home all right. Now, the day of his arrival I had been obliged, more or less officially, to attend a ceremony, where the *Wali* and Authorities and the Consuls would be present with their wives. I was determined to go, and to put on a perfectly calm exterior, though I felt very heart-sick, and a well-known Greek in the *Wali's* pay said to me, with a meaning, unpleasant smile, "I fancy there will be important news for you in a short while." I felt very faint inside, but I said coolly, "Oh, will there? Well, I suppose I shall get it when it comes." Almost immediately afterwards, Richard's Afghan walked in, and saluting said, "The Consul has returned and wants you." The faces of the *Wali* and his Greek were a study. I saluted them all, went out, jumped on my horse, and rode back. Had the *Redifs* fallen in with Richard, the verdict would have been, "Fallen a prey to his wild and wandering habits in the desert." The *Wali* then forged a letter from Richard to the Druzes, and forwarded it through Mr. Eldridge to the Foreign Office. Here it is:—

REAL COPY (TRANSLATED) TO THE SHAYKHS OF THE RENOWNED DRUZE MOUNTAIN.

"After the usual compliments we want to inform you that this time the wish to visit you has moved us, and to take the direction of your country.

"For which reason we will leave Damascus on the Wednesday, and sleep at Hijaneh; the second day at Lahtah, and the third at Kanawát.

"We therefore hope that you will meet us in the above-mentioned place, that we may see you."

FALSE COPY (TRANSLATED) AND SENT TO ENGLAND.

"Traduction d'une lettre addressée par le Consul Britannique, en date du 22 Mai, 1871 (3 Jui), aux Cheikhs Druzes Haurán.

"'Après les compliments d'usage, *je m'empresse* de vous informer que, animé du désir *de m'entretenir avec vous*, je quitterai Damas mercredi *pour vous rejoindre*, et que j'arriverai ce jour même à Hedjan, et le lendemain à Lahita, et le troisième à Finvate. Je nourris l'espoir que vous ne manquerez

This is a simple general *return visit* to the visits of the Druzes, not to waste time in going to each man's house, nor to make jealousies by singling out some and neglecting others.

pas *tous* de venir me recontrer, au dit village de Finvate, *afin de prendre part à cette entrevue.*'"

This *adds* all the words that are dashed, to give it a semblance of a secret political meaning.

Richard and I and Charley Drake made another pleasant journey exploring the Anti-Libanus. Everybody thinks, even professional geographers, if you speak of the Anti-Libanus, that you are going over trodden ground, filling up details upon the broad outlines traced by other people; but it is very far from being the case. Now the best maps only show a long conventional caterpillar, flanked by acidulated drops, and seamed with a cobweb of drainage. They never name a valley north-east of Zebedáni, nor a summit, except Jebel el Halímah, which is not its name. The northern half of the Anti-Lebanon is arid and barren, the southern is very fertile, and it is far superior to the Lebanon. Weird, savage, like parts of Moab, the colouring is richer, forms more picturesque, contrasts of shape and hue are sharper, and the growth is more like thin forest. "That ravines of singular wildness and grandeur furrow the whole mountain side, looking in many places like huge rents," is true of Anti-Lebanon, but not of Lebanon. The views are superior; it is richer and more remarkable.

Some of our followers will not forget some of our day's work, for we ascend successively every height, taking angles, laying down altitudes, and building up *kakús* to serve for a theodolite survey. Charley Drake mapped and sketched whilst we wrote.

The Convent of Nabi Baruh is ruinous in the extreme, but it gave us the idea of being the most ancient which we had seen throughout Syria and Palestine. The reception in these wild places is always the same, if they are not Christians, who—why, it is impossible to say—generally receive one badly, except of course the Maronites in their stronghold, and more especially the splendid Christians of Jezzín, Sadád, and B'sherri, who are marked exceptions to the generality of Christians, and who are equal, if not better than the rest.

All the Chiefs and notables meet the stranger at a distance beyond the houses. As the two parties meet, he reins in his horse and touches hands, snatching away his with a jerk if they attempt to kiss it, reproachfully ejaculating "Astaghfir 'Ullah!" (I beg pardon of Allah, *i.e.* God forbid that such a thing should happen). If you permit it they kiss your hand, and ridicule you in their minds as a fool, who delights in such homage as a priest, whose right it is. Guided by the Shaykhs, each in a strict precedence as at a London dinner-party, he rides leisurely, not hastening the pace, lest he cause his host to run; he dismounts at the door, and the Chiefs and notables rush to hold his horse, his stirrup, and his back under the shoulders. He must be sure to ride into the courtyard, no matter how broken be the gate threshold, nor how slippery the pavement, or up the steps, or they will suspect him of not knowing how to ride. He is led to the *salamlik*, but he will not enter till the women who have been sprinkling the floor have made themselves scarce. He sits down, doubling his legs a little if he cannot cross them, whilst the others form a semicircle upon humbler rugs before him. Each salaams, and is salaamed to, as he takes his place, squatting ceremoniously on his shins, till his visitor says, "Khuz ráhatak" (Take your ease), suggesting a more pleasant posture. If he fails to do this they will watch an opportunity to change seat, but if disposed to be impertinent they will stretch out their shanks and require a reproof. Water pipes, sherbet, lemonade, and coffee are brought, after which the Shaykh will retire and beg you to repose.

A breakfast is served about noon of cheese, soured milk, grape syrup, raw green onions, boiled rice, wheaten scones, and eggs fried in clarified butter. It is vulgar for the stranger to produce his own wine and cold meat from the saddle-bags. At sunset meat is served. A whole kid is a prime sign of honour. During meals one of the family stands up, holding a metal pot full of drinking water. Pipes and coffee conclude. The correct thing is to compel the Shaykh and the Chiefs to eat with you; the followers and retainers will eat afterwards, the trays being removed to another part. At night there will be a *samrah*, or palaver, in which the state of the country in general, and the village in particular, is discussed, grievances are quoted, the usurer and creditor complained of, the Government and Governor abused. Local legends are told, and the traveller can gain any amount of information if he can speak the language. They press him to stay next day, and his excuses are received with a respectful and regretful unwillingness.

Before leaving next morning he will find out privately what he has cost them, he will find out that his animals have been well fed, and he will manage to slip it and something more into the hands of one of the women or children. Before the departure the women of the family will offer excuses for their poor fare, saying, "La tawákhizná" (Don't be offended with us), and he will hasten with many "Astaghfir 'Ullahs" to express his supreme satisfaction. He mounts as ceremoniously as he dismounted, preceded by his escort, but every now and then he reins in, dismissing them—"Arja'ú ya Masháikh" (Return, O Shaykhs). They persist in walking to the last house, and often much farther; they again try to kiss his hand, which he pulls away as before, and the visit ends. The visited then retire and debate what has caused the visit, and what will be the best way to utilize it.

We divided and visited every section of the northernmost line of Anti-Libanus from the Halímat el Kabú, 8257 feet above sea-level. We enjoyed an extensive and picturesque view far superior to anything seen in the Libanus, especially southwards. From here we might write a chapter on what we could see. The weather being clear, we could even see the long-balled chine of the Cedar Block of the Libanus, and its large spots of snow, which glowed like amethysts in evening light. We could see the apex of the Libanus, which falls into the Jurd of Tripoli. We could see the Jebel el Huleh, which defines the haunts of the mysterious Nusayri; the glance falls upon the Orontes Lake, upon the rich cultivation of Hums and Hamáh, one of the gardens of Syria upon the ridge of Salámiyyah, that outpost of ancient Tadmor, and upon the unknown Steppe el Huleh, and the Bedawi-haunted tracts which sweep up to the Jebel el Abyaz, whilst the castle of Aleppo bounds the septentrional horizon. The end of this day was a remarkable one. "It was the only occasion," said Richard, "during my travels in Syria and Palestine that I felt thoroughly tired. My *rahwán*, though a Kurd nag, trembled with weakness, and my wife jogged along sobbing in her saddle, and if it had not been for the advice of Charley Drake we should have spent the night on the mountain-side; but we did arrive. Habíb had built a glowing fire, beds were spread, tea was brewed, and presently a whole roast kid appeared, and restored us all in the best of humours; and our horses, after plenty to eat and drink, and being well rubbed down, lay down. We had had fifteen hours very hard work, not counting the before and after the march."

We next determined to prospect the third part of the east-west section of Anti-Libanus, including the Ba'albak crest, and then to ride up the Cœle-Syrian valley so as to fill in the bearings of the western wady mouths. We had forage for our beasts, water the whole way, and we were excited by the account of inscriptions and ruins. The Wady el Biyáras was splendid in scenery, and though our road was horrible, we congratulated each other in not missing it, and we descended into the Wady Atnayn.

It is very curious to observe the goats and sheep; they don't mix much, though in the same flock. The goats prefer difficult and venturesome places, the sheep browse in the lower lands. The goat is curious and impudent—he goes out of the way to stare and sneeze at you; the sheep is staid and respectable, like the "good young man." Here Richard did nothing but quote a piece of poetry which amused him intensely—

> "In Teneriffe, for a time brief,
> I wandered all around,
> Where shady bowers and lively flowers
> Spontaneously abound.
>
> "Where posies rare perfume the air
> In festoons o'er your head,
> Brave sheep and cows in pastures browse
> Without remorse or dread." *

Some of the goatherds are rather bullying. The Kurdish dog is shaggy, with cropped ears, large head, brindle coat, rough hair, bushy tail, as big as a St. Bernard, and looks like a bear; but if he is a soldier's dog, he is always civil. I took one from a Bedawi tent as a pup; he was christened "Kasrawán," which soon became "Cuss." From his earliest puppyhood he played watchman, and led our horses by the halter. As he grew up he would hardly allow a native to pass along the road at night. He wrangled with and made love to our English bull-terriers, he appeared to be sorely oppressed with the seriousness of life, and could never get fighting enough. A Fellah threw him some meat with a needle in it, a favourite style of revenge of one who has been once bitten, and does not care to be bitten again; we were obliged to put him out of his misery, and he was honourably buried in the garden of Bludán.

We carried out all our prospected journey, gathering information, inscriptions, and ruins everywhere, till we reached Yabrud, where the Shaykhs gave us a picnic, to show us the Arz el Jauzah.

There is a temple known as Kasr Namrúd; the water flows through a conduit of masonry, and is said to pass into a large underground cistern below, round the ample stone troughs and scattered fragments of columns. All through Syria Nimrod represents the Devil, and 'Antar the Julius Cæsar of Western Europe. The picnic, under the shade of this venerable building, passed off happily enough. The *kabábs* of kid, secured instantly after sudden death, were excellent; the sour milk and the goat's cheese were perfection; and the Zahlah wine had only one fault—there was only half a bottle, and we could have drank a demijohn. We were very much struck by the similarity of plan which connects the heathen temple with the Christian church. It was late in the afternoon when we shook hands with our good host. It is pleasant to think upon happy partings—we never saw them again.

On our way home we passed ruins, arched caves, and sarcophagi,

---

* Lines by a West African poet.

whilst a wall displays a large rude crucifix. We were received later at Talfíta with all honours by the Shaykh el Balad Mahfúz, whose pauper homes had been destroyed and the rest threatened by the villainous usurers under British protection, and next day we rode into Damascus. During this excursion, we had seen in a range of mountains, supposed to be impracticable, four temples, of which three had been hitherto unvisited; we had prepared for the map of Syria the names of five great mountains; we had traced out the principal gorges, all before absolutely unknown to geography; we had determined the disputed altitudes of the Anti-Libanus, and we proved that it is much more worthy of inspection than the much-vaunted Libanus.

Another Trip, described by Charley Drake.*

"It is curious to see even what discrepancies there are in the heights of the Lebanon, which have been visited by scientific men. It shows that it must have been guess-work. There is one height which the goatherds know by the name of Tizmarún; but the aneroids, uncorrected for temperature, gave a reading of barely nine thousand feet, and this is the highest, though not generally acknowledged so.

"We wonder whether England will ever look upon Syria as anything else than a land for tourists to amuse themselves in; whether she will ever see that a *pied à terre* there, would secure her not only an uninterrupted passage to India, but wealth incalculable in mineral and agricultural produce; that both may yet be drawn from this fertile land, whose soil needs no manure, and whose mountains teem with ores.

"The prettiest scenery we had seen in the Lebanon was at the head of a large *wady*, called El Nakrah; wild deep gorges, overhung by fantastic rocks, and in some places thickly wooded, are alternated by open grassy Alps, contrasting well with the deep rich purple of the basalt, and the yellow sandstone which was never far from it. When we got to the head of the Wady Mimnah overlooking the entrance to Hamath, the comparatively level tract that stretches from Tripoli to Hums, and divides the Lebanon from the Jebel Nusayri, we got to Akkar, to Kala'at el Husn and to Hums, crossing the river Orontes. When we were in the 'Alah, all the Arabs agreed that it contained three hundred and sixty-five ruins, and that if a man travelled for a year, he might never sleep twice in the same village; and we quite believed it. The number of Bedawi who infest this region, the want of water, the loose basaltic soil, so tiring to horses, and want of reliable information, is, doubtless, the reason why this district has never been explored.

* Most of these descriptive scientific journeys are more for geographers and antiquaries.

"The Pasha of Hamáh worried us with a large escort, which meant piastres. The troop would have made the fortune of any theatre as a gang of bandits in a burlesque. There were horses of all sizes and colours—some had bridles, some had none—half-starved beasts, not able to keep up with ours; pistols that would not go off, swords that would not come out of the scabbards; but one of them, a short-bodied, long-legged fellow, was mounted, without stirrups, on a year-old colt, his only arm a lance sixteen feet long. He looked like a monkey, armed with a broomstick, riding a small dog. On the road we found several ruined, deserted, fortified camps. The Circassians are come into this part of the country, and have taken a village from the Nusayri, and ousted the rightful owners, and we think there will be mischief later on. We reached the edge of the plain, in which stands Salamíyyeh, whose chief, Amir Ismail, is a patriarchal old gentleman. Holo Pasha sent us a large escort without our asking him; but when we explained to them our intention of striking across the desert to Shakún, they declined to go, which delighted us. Going along, we found the Haddidín Arabs encamped all along the desert.

"It is a curious thing to say, but there are sheep and goats where there is apparently nothing to eat, yet they are always fat. The soil is rich, but very tiring to horses, because it gives way beneath their weight, letting them sink in to the hock. At Shakún we found a quarantine for travellers from Baghdad. We were now on the ordinary travelling road from Hamáh to Aleppo. In these deserts the Haddidín go to the wells, which are a great depth, a hundred to a hundred and fifty feet. A horse is attached to the end of a rope, and trots away, bringing the leathern bucket to the surface. If the well be not very deep, they sometimes harness two women in it. El Háthir is in a marsh which has been dry for two years, and abounds in a large and troublesome horse-fly, whose bite is so severe that the horses were streaming with blood.

"We passed through a salt-pan which becomes a lake in the winter months, and is a source of considerable revenue to the Government. Soldiers are placed here to prevent contraband trade in salt.

"The refraction induces mirage. It seems impossible that one is not looking upon a pellucid and unruffled lake, in which both the houses of Jabúl and the outlines of an insular Tell are clearly reflected by the mirage.

"Akrabeh must have been a place of importance from the extent of ground over which the ruins are spread. The resemblance borne by the mounds on which the castles are built in Hums, Hamáh, and Aleppo is very striking; they are quite identical, Aleppo being the largest. At Hamáh particularly we find monuments of greatest possible value. History is silent about the construction of these three sister castles, but we thought that the five blocks of basalt at Hamah, covered with hieroglyphics in excellent preservation, may be the opening page of a new chapter in history."

Richard took copies and Charley Drake took squeezes of them.

At Aleppo, in the south wall of the Jam'ia el Kahan, is a block of basalt with an inscription similar to those of Hamáh. Though much defaced, Charley Drake made out nineteen characters identical with the above-mentioned, and a doorstep bore the same. Charley Drake thought that the key to these characters must be looked for in *beth* (house), *kaf* (hand), *gimel* (camel), *ain* (eye), etc., of the Semitic alphabet. Hands, flowers, and teeth, and other unmistakable signs occur. If Richard was right, the well-known Moabite Stone would be modern in comparison, and we shall see these remarkable monuments deposited in the Louvre or the St. Petersburg Museum; and, as Charley Drake said, "there will be the usual gnashing and weeping of teeth after it is too late." But for my own part, in 1892, I begin to doubt that England is sufficiently interested in anything, except money, to have the energy to gnash its teeth at all.

"The ironwork of the gates of the castle of Aleppo is very good. The upper gate bears the name of Melek el Dhaher and the date 645 A.H. Having been officially informed that the mosques of Aleppo might not be visited by any Christian, we thought that something interesting might be found; but we managed to see them, and we did not find much, and the Shaykhs were only anxious to give all the information they could. We crossed the Nahr el Kowwáyyik, which does not run thirty miles to the south of Aleppo, as said in maps, but loses itself at a distance of two and a half hours from the City. On our road a row was going on between the Kurdish shepherds and the Fellahín of this place. The shepherds bring sheep down from Mesopotamia and Diarbekr by easy stages, and sell them at Aleppo and Damascus. The Fellahín envy and dislike these itinerant pastors. We rode seven and a half miles from Aleppo, arriving at Serákib.

"If you listen, the Fellahín are always talking about money, and prices, and transactions. The Bedawi only delights in listening to or telling stories of travelling and adventure, or smokes his pipe in placid enjoyment, while another of them sings an endless romance to the stirring tones of a one-stringed fiddle. We rode on to Mo'arrat el No'aman, where we visited some very interesting ruins in Jebel el Zowi. We then went to Jirjinnáz, as we found we could make it a head-quarter, and visit all the ruined cities within reach and then move on to Temányeh. The natural features and ruins of the 'Aláh are nearly all alike—a rolling plateau varying from thirteen hundred feet at the north-eastern, to sixteen hundred feet at the south-western above sea-level.

"From Damascus to Aleppo, one only meets with a few favoured villages whose supply of water is just sufficient to irrigate a patch of land and a few trees. The first ruin in the 'Aláh was Abu Mekkeh, and it was exactly like the uninhabited cities of the Haurán and the Lejá. The ruins of Surr'Aman are a mere collection of rude shelters piled up with old materials. The ruins of Tarútín el Tujjar are the most important in the 'Aláh. The village of Harráken was repeopled by Fellahín four years ago. Happily they have not the organ of destructiveness, as have their brethren in Palestine, and what was broken was accidental, and not wilful damage, like in the Haurán. At Burj el Abiadh ruins of considerable extent surround the white tower after which it is named. At Kufayr we found a ruined tower two stories high. The tower and ruins at El Fárajeh are of the usual type, but more solid. Nearly all the ruins bear crosses, Greek or Latin. At El Ikhwayn there is good water, but at Temányeh the villagers have to go a mile distant, to a hill with a well at the top. We then went to Atshán, passing the mounds and pillars which mark the site of S'kayk el Rubyíet. We next visited El Ma'an, which has the largest guard-house in the 'Aláh, built by Justinian. Of the ruins of Duwaylíb little has been left; the stones have been carried off for building purposes. We got water for our thirsty horses at the shallow well of Arúneh, beside which and around were encamped the Bedawi Mowáyleh. We rode through the ruins of Kefr-Ráa, and then descended into the valley of Orontes to Hamáh.

"There is a pyramidal-roofed tomb at El Barah. The roofs of these curious sepulchral monuments are built of massive stones, open inside up to the apex. One rock-hewn cave contains six loculi, five and a quarter feet long, by three and a quarter feet deep, and two and a quarter feet wide, with semicircular arches above them. On one of the rounded pillars we remarked that two crosses had been obliterated. A round-about road took us to Kefr Omar, where we saw a ruined monumental column built with circular stones upon a square base. We then went to Hass, where there was every kind of style of tomb—a square tower supporting a pyramidal roof, and all kinds of other shapes. The number of ruined villages in this district is surprising. During the day's ride you could count from six to eight with not a mile between them. Near Mo'arrat el No'aman is a castle similar to that near Salamíyyeh. At Danah there are very extensive ruins, and one building called the 'Church' resembles that near Hass. The stones used in these buildings are commonly six feet long, by two wide, and two deep. Here the Shaykh told us that twenty years ago a tomb had been opened, and a small gold image, a sword, a dagger, and some glass and pottery vessels had been found. There were one or two tombs in imitation of rock-hewn sepulchres. We felt certain that the ruined cities of Jebel el Zowi would amply repay any one with time and opportunity to make excavations. We then went to examine the Hums Lake, whose position, considering the rapid fall of the Orontes Valley, had always been a puzzle.

"We eventually came to a dam of masonry five hundred yards in length, and twenty feet high in the centre, built across the northern end of the lake. A small square tower stands at the west of it, and the water leaks through it in several places, but the dam looks as if it would last many centuries. The lake is now four or five feet lower than in winter, yet the surface of the water is about twelve feet higher than the river at the base of the dam, and many feet higher than the housetops of Saddi. Were the barrage ever to give way the destruction to life and property down the valley of the Orontes would be terrible. The ruins of Wajh el Haja afforded little of interest. We passed through many villages till we came to Tell Nebi Mand, a conspicuous mound. The native Moslems think that this prophet was related to the patriarch Joseph, but the Shaykh assured Richard that the tomb was that of Benjamin. The place marks the site of the ancient Laodicea and Libanum. At the south-east end of the lake is a large building standing at the water's edge, called Kasr Sitt Belkis ('Queen Belkis' Castle'), and near (*i.e.* about two miles distance) is an old entrenched camp some four hundred yards square, called Tell S'finet Núh, or 'the Mound of Noah's Ark.' It was probably a Roman post of observation to guard the entrance of the Buká'a. From Tell Nebi Mand we rode back to Damascus."

"Fais ce que dois, advienne que pourra."

"Caused by the moon's veering orb, what tumult and strife I see!
Wherever I view the earth, iniquity rife I see.
Daughters of turbulent mind, awaking their mother's ire,
And sons who of froward mood wish ill of their sire, I see.
Sherbets of sugar and rose the world to the fool supplies;
But nought save his heart's blood the food of the wise I see.
Galled by the pack-saddle's weight, the Arab's proud steed grows old;
Yet always the ass's neck encircled with gold I see.
Master, go forth and do good;
The counsel of Háfiz prize;
Far better than treasured pearl
This counsel so wise—
I see."

Ode composed when Persia was invaded by Taimur.

Unofficially speaking of official things, we had rather a lively time, in an unpleasant sense, during these summer months. I always say "we," because I enter so much into my husband's pursuits, and am so very proud of being allowed to help him, that I sometimes forget that I am only as the bellows-blower to the organist. However, I do not think that anybody will owe me a grudge for it.

No. 1.

The first shadow upon our happy life was in 1870–71. An amateur missionary, residing at Beyrout, came up to Damascus, visited the prisons, and distributed tracts to the Mohammedans. It was the intention of the Governor to collect these prints, and to make a bonfire of them in the market-place. Damascus was in a bad temper for such proselytizing. It was an excitable year, and it was necessary to put a stop to proceedings which, though well meant, could not fail to endanger the safety of the Christian population. The tract-distributor was a kind, humane, sincere, and charitable man, and we were both very sorry that he had to be cautioned. He had an enthusiasm in his religious views which made him dangerous outside a Christian town. At Beyrout he was well known, but at Damascus he was not, and the people would have resented his standing on bales in the street haranguing the Turks against Mohammed. I believe this gentleman would have gloried in martyrdom; but some of us, not so good as he is, did not aspire to it. His *entourage,* also, was not so humble or so kind as himself.

Richard was obliged to give the caution, to do his duty to his large district, thereby incurring at Beyrout most un-Christian hatreds, unscrupulously gratified. Richard, with the high, chivalrous sense of honour which guided all his actions, redoubled his unceasing endeavours to promote the interest and business of these persons, amidst the hailstorm of petty spites and insults—which justice and greatness of mind on his part they themselves were obliged *eventually* to acknowledge, however reluctantly. We were decidedly destined to stumble upon unfortunate circumstances. Since that, a gentleman told off to convert the Jews in one of Richard's jurisdictions, insisted on getting a ladder and a hammer, and demolishing a large statue of St. Joseph in a public place of a Catholic country, because he said it was "a graven image." Why are the English so careless in their choice? and why have other foreign Consuls no *désagrémens* on this head?

Richard writes—

No. 2.

"The Druzes applied early in 1870 for an English school. They are our allies, and we were on friendly terms with them. As two missionaries wished to travel amongst them, I gave them the necessary introductions. They were cordially received and hospitably entertained by the Shaykhs, but on their road home they were treacherously followed by two *mauvais sujets* and attacked; they were thrown off their horses, their lives were threatened, and their property was plundered.

"Such a breach of hospitality and violation of good faith required prompt notice: firstly, to secure safety to future travellers; and, secondly, to maintain the good feelings which have ever subsisted between the Druzes and the English. To pass over such an act of treachery would be courting their contempt. I at once demanded that the offenders might be punished by the Druze chiefs themselves, and twenty napoleons, the worth of the stolen goods, were claimed by me for the missionaries. The Druzes went down to Beyrout to try to pit Consulate-General against Consulate, and refused to pay the claim. I then applied for their punishment to the Turkish authorities, knowing that the Druzes would at once accede to my first demand—a proceeding approved of by her Majesty's Ambassador at Constantinople. After three months the Shaykh el Akkál, head religious chief, brought down the offenders, who were recognized by the missionaries. They confessed their guilt, and the Shaykh, who was staying as a guest in our house, assured me [Richard] that I was perfectly right in acting as I had done, and that every Druze was heartily ashamed of the conduct of these two men."

No. 3.

"In June, 1870, I prepared a despatch for our Ambassador at Constantinople, on the system of defrauding the poor and of 'running' villages by the Damascus Jewish money-lenders.

"I will now try to explain how these matters stood.

"In former days, when not a few Europeans were open to certain arrangements which made them take the highest interest in the business transactions of their clients, a radically bad system, happily now almost extinct, was introduced into Syria. The European subject, or *protégé*, instead of engaging in honest commerce, was thus encouraged to seek inordinate and usurious profits by sales of the Government and by loans to the villagers. In such cases he, of course, relied entirely upon the protection of a foreign Power, on account of the sums to be expended in feeing native functionaries before repayment could be expected. Thus the Consuls became, as it were, *huissiers*, or bailiffs, whose principal duties were to collect the bad debts of those who had foreign passports.

"Damascus contained a total of forty-eight adult males protected by H.B.M.'s Consulate, and of these there were a triumvirate of Shylocks. Most of them are Jews who were admitted to, or whose fathers acquired, a foreign nationality, given with the benevolent object of saving them from Moslem cruelty and oppression in days gone by. These *protégés* have extended what was granted for the preservation of their lives, liberties, and property, to transactions which rest entirely for success upon British protection. The case of No. 1, whom we will call Judas, is a fair example. He has few dealings in the city, the licit field of action. But since the death of his highly respectable father, in 1854, he had been allowing bills signed by the ignorant peasantry of the province to accumulate at simple and compound interest, till the liabilities of the villagers have become greater than the value of the whole village. A——, for instance, on the eastern skirt of Mount Hermon, owed him 106,000 piastres, which were originally 42,000. He claims 5000 purses from the B—— family, upon a total debt of 242,000½ piastres, in 1857. We have not yet passed through a single settlement where his debtors did not complain loudly of his proceedings; and to A—— may be added C——, ——, and D—— el X——, a stronghold of the Druzes. Some villages have been partly depopulated by his vexations, and the injury done to the Druzes by thus driving them from the Anti-Lebanon to the Haurán, may presently be severely visited upon the Ottoman authorities.

"The British *protégé* is compelled every year, in his quality of *shúbasi* (farmer of revenue), to summon the village Shaykhs and peasantry, to imprison them, and to leave them lying in jail till he can squeeze from them as much as possible, and to injure them by quartering *hawali*, or policemen, who plunder whatever they can. He long occupied the whole attention, though it had other and more important duties, of the Village Commission (*Kumision Mahasibat el Kura*), established in A.H. 1280 (1863). For about a year a special commission (*Kumision Makhsus*) had at that time, 1870, been sitting on his case, whose intricacies, complicated by his unwillingness to settle anything, wearied out all the members. At different times he quarrelled with every person in the Court—from the *defterdar*, who is its President, to the Consular Dragomans, who composed it. Even felony was freely imputed to him by various persons. He was accused of bribing the Government *khatibs* (secretaries) to introduce into documents sentences of doubtful import, upon which he can found claims for increased and exorbitant interest, of adding lines to receipts and other instruments after they have been signed, and of using false seals, made at home by his own servants. One of the latter publicly denounced him, but was, as usual, paid to keep silence. He is reported again and again to have refused, in order that the peasants might remain upon his books, the ready moneys offered to him for the final settlement of village liabilities. His good management had baffled all efforts at detection, whilst every one was morally certain that the charges were founded on fact. He corrupts, or attempts to corrupt, all those with whom he has dealings.

"I wanted to inform them that British protection extends to preserving their persons and property from all injustice and violence, but that it would not assist them to recover debts from the Ottoman Government, or from the villages of the province, and that it would not abet them in imprisoning or in distraining the latter. To such general rule, of course, exceptions would be admissible, at the discretion of the officer in charge of H.B.M.'s Consulate; in cases, for instance, when just and honest claims might be rejected, or their payment unduly delayed. The sole inconvenience which would arise to such creditors from their altered positions would be the necessity of feeing the Serai more heavily; and even they openly communicated with the local authorities, reserving the Consulate as a forlorn hope. The change might possibly have directed their attention to a more legitimate commercial career. Such a measure would have been exceedingly popular throughout the country, and would have relieved us from the suspicion of interested motives—a suspicion which must exist where honesty and honour, in an English understanding of these words, are almost unknown; and from the odium which attaches to the official instruments of oppression. Finally, the corruption of Damascus rendered me the more jealous of the good name of the Consulate, and the more desirous of personal immunity from certain reports which, at different times, have been spread about *others* in office. I therefore posted on the door of H.M.'s Consulate, Damascus, the following notice:—

"'Her Britannic Majesty's Consul hereby warns British subjects and *protégés* that he will not assist them to recover debts from the Government or from the people of Syria, unless the debts are such as between British subjects could be recovered through H.M.'s Consular Courts. Before purchasing the claims, public or private, of an Ottoman subject—and especially where Government paper is in question—the *protégé* should, if official interference be likely to be required, at once report the whole transaction to this Consulate. British subjects and protected persons are hereby duly warned that protection extends to life, liberty, and property, in cases where these are threatened by violence or by injustice; but that it will not interfere in speculations which, if undertaken by Syrian subjects of the Porte, could not be expected to prove remunerative. British subjects and protected persons must not expect the official interference of the Consulate in cases where they prefer (as of late has often happened at Damascus) to urge their claims upon the local authorities without referring to this Consulate, and altogether ignoring the jurisdiction of H.B.M.'s Consul. Finally, H.B.M.'s Consul feels himself bound to protest strongly against the system adopted by British subjects and protected persons at Damascus, who habitually induce the Ottoman authorities to imprison peasants and pauper debtors, either for simple debt, or upon charges which have not been previously produced for examination at this Consulate. The prisons will be visited once a week. An official application will be made for the delivery of all such persons.

(Signed) "'R. F. BURTON,
"'H.B.M.'s Consul, Damascus.

"'Damascus, June 20th, 1870.'"

I have already related how, on August 26th, Richard received a letter from the Rev. W. Wright, and likewise one from the Chief Consular Dragoman, Mr. Nasif Meshaka, which induced him to ride at once to Damascus (from Bludán, the summer quarter); how he found that half the Christians had fled, and everything was ripe for a new massacre; how he sought the authorities, and informed them of their danger; induced them to have night patrols, to put guards in the streets, to prevent Jews or Christians leaving their houses, and to take all measures needful to convince the conspirators that they would not find every one sleeping as they did in 1860. The *Wali* and all the Chief responsible Authorities were absent. The excitement subsided under the measures recommended by him, and in three days all was quiet, and the Christians returned to their homes.

I affirm that, living in safety upon the sea-coast, no man can be a judge of the other side of the Lebanon, nor, if he does not know some Eastern language, can he be a judge of Orientals and their proceedings. Certain Jewish usurers had been accused of exciting these massacres, because their lives were perfectly safe, and they profited of the horrors to buy up property at a nominal price. It was brought to Richard's notice that two Jewish boys, servants to British-protected subjects, were giving the well-understood signal by drawing crosses on the walls. Its meaning to him was clear. He promptly investigated it, and took away the British protection of the masters temporarily, merely reproving the boys, who had acted under orders. He did not take upon himself to punish them. Certain ill-advised Israelitish money-lenders fancied it was a good opportunity to overthrow him, and with him his plan of seeing fair proceedings on the part of the British *protégés;* so they reported to Sir Moses Montefiore and Sir Francis Goldsmid that he had tortured the boys. His proceedings were once more proved just. The correspondence on the subject was marvellously interesting, but being official I cannot use it.

"The Jews," he writes, "from all times held a certain position in Syria, on account of their being the financiers of the country; and even in pre-Egyptian days Haim Farhi was able to degrade and ruin Abdullah Pasha, of St. Jean d'Acre. In the time of Ibrahim Pasha, about forty-four years ago,* when the first Consuls went there, a few were taken under British protection, and this increased their influence. Then came the well-known history of the murder of Padre Tomaso. After this had blown over, all the richest people of the community tried to become British-protected subjects, or *protégés* of some foreign Consulate. In the time of Mr. Consul (Richard) Wood, (1840), they were humble enough. In the massacre of 1860 they enriched themselves greatly, and men possessing £3000 rose suddenly to £30,000. Then they had at their backs in England Sir Moses Montefiore, Sir F. Goldsmid, and the Rothschilds † and others, who doubtless do not know the true state of the Jewish usurers in this part of the world. The British Consul became the Jews' bailiff, and when we went to Syria we found them rough-riding all the land. I speak only of the few money-lenders. When I arrived in 1869, Shylock No. 1 came to me, and patting me

* Now sixty-four years in 1893.

† Now, in 1893, the Sassoons, the Oppenheims, and Bischofheims.

patronizingly on the back, told me he had three hundred cases for me, relative to collecting £60,000 of debts. I replied, 'I think, sir, you had better hire and pay a Consul for yourself alone; I was not sent here as a bailiff, to tap the peasant on the shoulder in such cases as yours.' He then threatened me with the British Government. I replied, 'It is by far the best thing you can do; I have no power to alter a plain line of duty.' Shylock then tried my wife's influence, but she replied that she was never allowed to interfere in business matters. Then Sir Francis Goldsmid, to our great surprise, wrote to Head-quarters—a rather unusual measure—as follows: 'I hear that the lady to whom Captain Burton is married is believed to be a bigoted Roman Catholic, and to be likely to influence him against the Jews.' In spite of 'woman's rights' she was not allowed the privilege of answering Sir Francis Goldsmid officially; but I hope to convince him, even after years, that he was misinformed."

I think that religion certainly is, and ought to be, the first and highest sentiment of our hearts, and I consider it my highest prerogative to be a staunch and loyal Catholic. But I also claim to be free from prejudice, and to be untrammelled in my sentiments about other religions. Our great Master and His Apostles showed no bigotry, and it is to them that I look for my rule of life, not to the clique I was born in. Many amongst us Old Catholics, who live amongst our own people, and are educated men and women, go forth into the world and are quite unbiased against other faiths; we take to our hearts friends, without inquiring into their religion or politics. And if sometimes we sigh because they are not of our way of thinking, it is not from any bigotry or party feeling; it is because we love them, and we wish that we could give them some of our happiness and security. I appeal to my enemies—if I have any—to say whether I have any prejudice against race or creed.* At all events, I have an honest admiration and respect for

* Although a staunch Catholic, I was an ardent disciple of Mr. Disraeli—I do not mean Mr. Disraeli as Prime Minister of England, but the author of "Tancred." I read the book as a young girl in my father's house, and it inspired me with all the ideas, and the yearning for a wild Oriental life, which I have since been able to carry out. I passed two years of my early life, when emerging from the school-room, in my father's garden, and the beautiful woods around us, alone with "Tancred." My family were pained and anxious about me—thought me odd; wished I would play the piano, do worsted work, write notes, read the circulating library—in short, what is generally called improving one's mind; and I was pained because I could not. My uncle used to pat my head, and "hope for better things." I did not know it then, I do now: I was working out the problem of my future life, my after mission. It lived in my saddle-pocket throughout my Eastern life. I almost know it by heart, so that when I came to Bethany, to the Lebanon, and to Mukhtára—when I found myself in a Bedawi camp, or amongst the Maronite and Druze strongholds, or in the society of Fakredeens—nothing surprised me. I felt as if I had lived that life for years.

the Jewish religion. They were the chosen people of God. They are more akin to us than any other faith.

Jesus Christ was a Jew, the Apostles were Jews. He came not to destroy the Law, but to change the prescriptions necessary for the times. The Great Reformer was the connecting link between us. He made Christianity, or Judaism, for the multitude, a Syro-Arabian creed. He parted the creation into two divisions—those who accepted the new school, and those who clung to the old. We are of the former, and the Jews of the latter fold. It would be madness to despise those who once ruled the ancient world, and who will rule again—do we not see signs of their return to power every day? It would be more than folly not to honour the old tribes of the chosen people of God. In Syria only the Jews, Druzes, and Bedawi can boast of their origin. In the Syrian world we know, only the Jews and Catholics can boast of antiquity of religion. An Eastern Jew cannot but be proud of his religion and his descent. As I turn over my old Damascus journal, my heart warms to think that some of our dearest native friends at Damascus were of the Jewish religion. We were on good terms with them all, and received sincere hospitality from them. At Trieste, again, the enlightened and hospitable Hebrews were our best friends. It is the Jews who lead society here, the charities and the fashion; they are the life of the town. When I call to mind how many Jews I know, and like, and have exchanged hospitality with, here and in the East, I do not know how to speak strongly enough on the subject.

But now let us turn to the dark side of the picture. Even those who are the proudest of their Semitic origin speak contemptuously of their usurers. And, let me ask, do we pet and admire our own money-lenders? Let a Damascus Jew once become a usurer, back him up with political influence, and see what he will become. He forgets race and creed; that touching, dignified, graceful humility changes into fawning servility, or to brutal insolence and cruelty, where he is not afraid. He thirsts only for money. The villanies practised by the usurers, especially the Shylocks in Damascus, excite every right-minded person to indignation; and if I had no other esteem for my husband, I should owe it to him for the brave manner in which he made a stand against these wrongs at every risk. He knew that no other Consul had ever dared—nor would ever dare—to oppose it; but he said simply, "I must do right; I cannot sit still

---

I felt that I went to the tomb of my Redeemer in the proper spirit, and I found what I sought. The presence of God was actually felt, though invisible. The author possesses by descent a knowledge that we Northerners lack (a high privilege reserved to his Semitic blood).—I. B.

and see what I see, and not speak the truth. I must protect the poor, and save the British good name, *advienne que pourra*, though perhaps in so doing I shall fall myself." And he did—but not for this.

He is not what is *called* a religious man, but he acts like one; and if he did nothing to win respect and admiration, that alone should give people an insight into his character, whilst I, like Job's wife, incessantly said, "Leave all this alone, as your predecessor did, as your Consul-General does, and as your successor will do, and keep your place, and look forward to a better." If the usurers had been Catholics instead of Jews, I should like them to have lost their "protection," to have been banished from Damascus, and *excommunicated* as long as they plied their trade. More I cannot say. Nay, I prefer the Jew to the Christian usurer. The former will take my flesh and blood, but the Christian will want my bones too.

Richard writes—

"One man alone had ruined and sucked dry forty-one villages. He used to go to a distressed village and offer them money, keep all the papers, and allow them nothing to show; adding interest and compound interest, which the poor wretches could not understand. Then he gave them no receipts for money received, so as to be paid over and over again. The uneducated peasants had nothing to show against the clever Jew at the Diwán, till body and soul, wives and children, village, flocks, and land, became his property and slaves for the sake of the small sum originally borrowed. These men, who a few years ago were not worth much, are now rolling in wealth. We found villages in ruins, and houses empty, because the men were cast into jail, the children starving, and women weeping at our feet; because these things were done in the name of England, by the powerful arm of the British Consulate."

My husband once actually found an old man of ninety, who had endured all the horrors of the Damascus jail during the whole of a biting winter, for owing one of these men a napoleon (sixteen shillings). He set him free, and ever after visited the prisons once a week, to see whether the British-protected subjects had immured pauper Christians and Moslems on their own responsibility. One of the usurers told him to beware, for that he knew a Royal Highness of England, and that he could have any Consular officer recalled at his pleasure; and my husband replied that he and his clique could know very little of English Royalty if they thought that it would protect such traffic as theirs. The result of this was that they put their heads together, and certain letters were sent to the Chief Rabbi of London, Sir Francis Goldsmid, and Sir Moses Montefiore.

They sent telegrams and petitions, purporting to be from "all the Jews in Damascus." We believe, however, that "all the Jews in Damascus" knew nothing whatever about the step. Richard said, "They are mostly a body of respectable men—hard-working, inoffensive, and of commercial integrity, with a fair sprinkling of pious, charitable, and innocent people." These despatches, backed by letters from the influential persons who received them, were duly forwarded to the Foreign Office. The correspondence was sent in full to Richard to answer, which he did at great length, and to the satisfaction of his Chiefs, who found that he could not have acted otherwise.

Richard wrote: "I am ready to defend their lives, liberty, and property, but I *will not* assist them in ruining villages, and in imprisoning destitute debtors upon trumped-up charges. I would willingly deserve the praise of every section of the Jewish community of Damascus, but in certain cases it is incompatible with my sense of justice and my conscience." They bragged so much in the bazars about getting Richard recalled, that a number of sympathizing letters were showered upon us.

I quote the following *verbatim* :—

"DEAR MRS. BURTON,

"We desire to express to you the great satisfaction which Captain Burton's presence as British Consul in Damascus has given us, both in our individual capacities and in our character of missionaries to Syria.

"Since his arrival here we have had every opportunity of judging of Captain Burton's official conduct, and we beg to express our approval of it.

"The first public act that came under our notice was the removing of dishonest officials, and the replacing them by honest ones. This proceeding gave unmixed pleasure to every one to whom the credit of the English name was a matter of concern. His subsequent conduct has restored the *prestige* of the English Consulate, and we no longer hear it said that English officials, removed from the checks of English public opinion, are as corrupt in Turkey as the Turks themselves. As missionaries we frankly admit that we had been led to view Captain Burton's appointment with alarm; but we now congratulate ourselves on having abstained, either directly or indirectly, endeavouring to oppose his coming.

"Carefully following our own habitual policy of asking no consular interference between the Turkish Government and its subjects, we stand upon our right as Englishmen to preach and teach so long as we violate no law of the land, and we claim for our converts the liberty of conscience secured to them by treaty. In the maintenance of this one right we have been firmly upheld by Captain Burton.

"A few months ago, when our schools were illegally and arbitrarily closed by the Turkish officials, he came to our aid, and the injustice was at once put a stop to. His visit to the several village schools under our charge proved to the native mind the Consul's interest in the moral education of the country, which it is the object of those schools to promote, and impressed upon the minds of local magistrates the propriety of letting them alone.

"Within the last few days we had occasion to apply to Captain Burton regarding our cemetery, which had been broken open, and it was an agreeable surprise to us when, after two days, a police-officer came to assure us that the damage had been repaid by the Pasha's orders, and search was being made for the depredator.

"Above all, in view of any possible massacre of Christians in this city—the all but inevitable consequence of a war between Turkey and any Christian Power—we regard as an element of safety the presence among us of a firm, strong man like Captain Burton, as representing the English interests.

"When, not long ago, a panic seized the city, and a massacre seemed imminent, Captain Burton immediately came down from his summer quarters, and by his presence largely contributed to restore tranquillity. All the other important Consuls fled from Damascus, and thus increased the panic.

"We earnestly hope that Captain Burton will not suffer himself to be annoyed by the enmity he is sure to provoke for all who wish to make the English name a cover for wrongs and injustice, or think that a British subject or *protégé* should be supported, whatever be the nature of his case.

With kindest respects, we are, dear Mrs. Burton, yours very truly,

"(Signed) JAMES ORR SCOTT, M.A., Irish Presbyterian Mission.

"WM. WRIGHT, B.A., Missionary of the Irish Presbyterian Church.

"P.S.—By-the-by, on one occasion one of the most important Jews of Damascus, when conversing with me [Wm. Wright] and the Rev. John Crawford, American missionary, said that Captain Burton was unfit for the British Consulate in Damascus; and the reason he gave was that, being an upright man, he transacted his business by fair means instead of by foul.

"Damascus, November 28th, 1870."

"MY DEAR ISABEL,

"I was calling at a native house yesterday, where I found assembled some leading people of Damascus. The conversation turned upon Captain Burton and the present British Consulate. One word led to another; and I heard, to my surprise and consternation, that men famed for their *various pecuniary* transactions are boasting about everywhere 'that, upon *their* representations, *the Consul is to be recalled*,' and all Damascus is grieved and indignant at them. For my part I cannot, will not, believe that her Majesty's Government would set aside a man of Captain Burton's standing, and well-known justice and capacity in public affairs, for the sake of these Jews, who are desolating the villages and ruining those who have the misfortune to fall into their clutches. He is also so thoroughly adapted for this Babel of tongues, nations, and religions, and is so rapidly raising our English Consulate from the low estimation in which it had fallen in the eyes of all men, to the position it ought to and would occupy under the rule of an incorruptible, firm, and impartial character like Captain Burton's.

"At the risk of vexing you, I must tell you what I now hear commonly reported in the bazar, for several merchants and others have asked me if it was true. [Here follows the history of the complaints.] Our present Consul is too much a friend to the oppressed, and examines too much everything *himself*, to suit their money transactions. The Consulate for an age has not been so respectable as now; and should you really go, I should think any future Consul would shrink to do his duty, for fear of his conduct being misrepresented at home. You must write me a line to tell me the truth, if you may do so without indiscretion; and people are wanting to write to the Foreign Office and the *Times*, so provoked are they at the lies and duplicity. The day I was with you and you refused to see Judas and the other Jew, who seemed to dodge you about like a house cat, and looking so ill at ease and in a fright, did you then suspect or know anything about all this?

"With regard to the Arab tribes, they too have an admiration for Captain Burton's dauntless character and straightforward dealing, so different from others. You know that Shaykh Mohammed el Dhúky and Farés el Mézyad openly say so in the desert.

"I had intended to scribble but two lines, and I have been led on till my note has become a long letter. So, good-bye; and I truly hope all these machinations will end in the discomfiture of their inventors.

"Your affectionate cousin,
"JANE DIGBY EL MEZRAB.

"Damascus, November 28th, 1870."

"MONSIEUR LE CONSUL,

"C'est avec le plus plaisir nous venons vous exprimer notre satisfaction at les sentiments de notre amour envers votre amiable personne, ayant toujours devant les yeux les belles qualités et les grands mérites dont vous êtes orné.

"Il y a plus d'un an que nous avons eu l'honneur de vous connaître, et nous sommes en même de pouvoir apprécier votre bonne disposition pour le soutien de la cause chrétienne sans distinction de religion; et, par conséquent, nous sommes extrêmement reconnaissants au bienfait philanthropique de Gouvernement de S.M. Britannique, qui a daigné nous envoyer à Damas un représentant si digne et si mérité comme vous l'êtes, Monsieur le Consul.

" C'est avec regret que nous avons appris que des gens malicieux de Damas se sont plaints contre vous pour des causes qui vous sont très-honorables.

" Nous venons vous exprimer notre indignation pour leur conduite inexplicable at méprisable en vous témoignant notre reconnaissance pour le grand zèle et l'activité incessante que vous déployez toujours pour le bien at pour le repos de tous les Chrétiens en général.

" Nous espérons que vous continuerez pour l'avenir comme pour le passé à nous accorder les mêmes bienfaits.

" C'est avec ce même espoir que nous vous prions, Monsieur le Consul, d'agréer nos sentiments de haute considération.

" (Signé) EROTEOS, Patriarche Grec d'Antioche.

" A M. le Captaine Burton, Consul de S. M. Britannique à Damas.
" Damas, le 15 Décembre, 1870."

" MONSIEUR LE CONSUL,

" Nous avons entendu avec beaucoup d'inquiet que certains gens malicieux à Damas se sont plaignés de vous pour des causes qui vous sont très-honorables.

" Nous désirons vous exprimer combien leur conduite es méprisable et inexcusable à nos yeux.

" Nous vous avons connu maintenant plus qu'un an ; nous vous avons trouvé toujours prêt à assister la cause chrétienne, sans égard pour les differences de la religion at à nous appuyer quand nous aurions été peut-être traités durement.

" Dans les circumstances actuelles de cette année nous aurions beaucoup d'inquiétude s'il y avait une chance même que vous nous quittiez. Nous ésperons que vos bons offices seront continués pour nous dans l'avenir comme dans le passé. Nous vous prions de vous servir de notre regard pour vous comme Consul et ami aussi publiquement que possible.

" Daignez agréer, etc., etc.

" (Signé) L'EVÊQUE MACARIOS, Le Vicaire du Patriarcat à Damas. (L.S.)
" GREGOIR JACOB, Archev. Syrien Catholique de Damas. (L.S.)
" Le Vicaire du Patriarcat Maronite à Damas. (L.S.)
" Le Vicaire du Patriarcat Armenian Catholique à Damas. (L.S.).

" A Monsieur R. F. Burton, Consul de S. M. Britannique à Damas.
" Damas, le 13 Décembre, 1870."

To conclude: the effect of their conduct in Damascus will fall upon their own heads, and upon their children. Do not purposely misunderstand me, O Israel! Remember, I do not speak of you disparagingly as a nation, or as a faith. As such I love and admire you; but I pick out your usurers from among you, as the goats from the sheep. You are ancient in birth and religion; you are sometimes handsome, always clever, and in many things you far outstrip us Christians in the race of life. Your sins and your faults are, and have been, equally remarkable from all time. Many of you, in Damascus especially, are as foolish and stiff-necked as in the days of old. When the time comes, and it will come, the trampled worm will turn. The Moslem will rise not really against the Christian—he will only be the excuse—but against you. Your quarter will be the one to be burnt down; your people to be exterminated, and all your innocent tribe will suffer for the few guilty.

A Druze of the Haurán once said to me, "I have the greatest temptation to burn down A——'s house. I should be sent to Istambúl in chains, but what of that? I should free my village and my people." I begged of him not to think of such a crime. A sinister smile passed over his face, and he muttered low in his beard, "No, not yet! not yet! Not till the next time. And then not much of the Yahúd will be left when we have done with them." I quote this as a specimen of the ill-feeling bred over the interior of Syria by their over-greed of gain. And I only hope that the powerful Israelite Committees and Societies of London and Paris will—and they can if they will—curb the cupidity of their countrymen in Syria.

We were present at a very grand review, where a splendid mare, ridden by Omar Bey, was the centre of attraction, and the newspapers afterwards noticed her in the following manner:—

Cutting from the *Boomerang.*

"Lady Burton mentions a very fine mare which Omar Bey, a Turkish brigadier-general at Damascus, bought from some Arabs after a free fight in the desert. She was so handsome that at a grand review, the only one held while Sir Richard Burton was Consul at Damascus, neither Lady Burton nor her husband could look at anything else. Omar Bey was subsequently ordered to leave the district, and sold the mare for £80, being all she would fetch at the time. It does seem a pity that, in a great horse-breeding country like Australia, there are not men to be found patriotic enough to secure specimens of these famous breeds of antiquity. We have plenty of breeders willing and anxious to secure and continue the breed of the English thoroughbred, but although we are possessed of some of the finest areas in the world for horse-breeding, and in a climate analogous in many respects to Mesopotamia, the original home of the horse, we have unfortunately no one among all those who have amassed wealth who will, either for pleasure or profit, take in hand the formation of a pure Arabian stud. There can be no question that in this country, where feed is not a matter of consideration, the Arabian would grow to a very much larger size."

We at last determined to thoroughly do Palestine and the Holy Land, and we went down in an awfully rough sea, in a very tiny and dirty little Egyptian steamer, as far as Jaffa. There were great doubts as to whether we could land, but at last boats were put out, and we got in on the top of a truly alarming surf, shooting through a narrow hole in the rocks just wide enough to admit the boat. The plain of Sharon was looking beautiful—meadows of grass land, wild flowers, cultivation, and orange groves all along our forty mile-ride.

I shall not say much about this pilgrimage, because it is too well known, except that we remained long enough to see and learn everything by heart about every place where our Saviour and His followers ever were in Syria, not only with the Bible and "Tancred," but learning all the legends, and the folklore handed from father to son. I have given a very long account of this in my "Inner Life of Syria" (2 vols., 1875), so that I don't want to repeat it again.

With Richard it was a constant matter for thought whether the sites and the tombs were the correct ones; and the sword of Godfrey de Bouillon and the Crusaders' arms, also those of the Knight Templars, were always of immense interest to him. We visited all the Patriarchs, and principally Monseigneur Valerga, a man of brilliant education, with the *savoir faire* of the diplomat or courtier, blended with religion. We went through all the ceremonies of *all the numerous religions* during the Holy Week, the Mohammedan as well as the fourteen Christian sects, and Jewish, of which not the least touching thing is the wailing of the Jews outside the wall of the Temple on Fridays, and the Greek fire on Holy Saturday. A Jewish friend took us in for the Passover. We visited all the country of St. John, Bethlehem, Hebron, where Abraham, Sarah, Isaac, Jacob, Rebecca, and Leah are buried; to Mar Saba, where is the Convent of Penitent Monks, in a most wonderful ravine. From there we got down to the Dead Sea, and swam in it, and saw fish. It receives daily seven million tons of water, and has no outlet; but its evaporation forms the desert of salt, called the Ghor, all round its southern shore, which fact Richard compares with Tanganyika. From there we went into Moab; we visited Moses' Tomb on the return journey. At Bethábara we bathed, and brought home bottles of the water of the Jordan; thence we went to Jericho, but we took care to visit every spot where tradition and folklore says our Saviour touched at, *off the tracks* besides. We encamped on the supposed sites of Sodom and Gomorrah, and so on to Bethel, and Hai, the most ancient site in

Palestine, the camping-ground of Abraham, where he and Lot parted and divided their flocks; and we gradually made our way to Nablus, which is the boundary between the Damascus and Jerusalem Consular jurisdictions. We ascended Mount Ebal and Mount Gerízim, and stayed with the Samaritans, who then numbered a hundred and thirty-five. We then went to Samaria, and through the plain of Esdraelon; and we camped at ancient Engannin, where Christ cured the ten lepers. From thence to Scythopolis into the Ghor, and to as many sites of the towns of the Decapolis as we could realize. We went to Naim, and Endor, and Tabor, and Nazareth—at Nazareth we were stoned (a little political manœuvre); thence to Cana. About Nazareth Richard wrote in his private journal—

"I rode down the country by the vile Kunayterah road to Tiberias, where the Jews protected by our Government were complaining that the *Wali* had taken from them and had sold to the Greek Bishop Nifon, at Nazareth, a cemetery and synagogue, which for the last four hundred years had belonged to their faith, and to visit a few men who held British passports, which ought to have been annually changed, but had through carelessness not been renewed since 1850. For these acts, I was destined to the same honour as my Master, namely, being stoned out of Nazareth; and because I did good to the Jews, they also betrayed me to the Authorities, and asked for my recall."

We went up the Mountain of Precipitation to Hattín, and ascended to Tiberias, the second and the middle sea which feeds the Jordan, and we visited the site of the eight towns so much frequented by our Saviour. From thence we went to Sáfed, which is a very fanatical Jewish Holy City, from which we could see the Jaulán and the Haurán stretching right away into the Arabian desert of the ancient kingdom of Báshan; and from here we again made our way to the plain of Huleh, which we remember of old, and the Waters of Merom, where we camped before under difficulties, and so nearly got a bad fever. This time it was black from a recent prairie fire. The best amusement on these occasions is to laugh at one another's miserable, unrecognizable faces, all swollen with bites and stings, like the face one sees in a spoon. After a lot of other places, we got back to Birket er Ram or Lake Phiala, which I remember saying a while ago we determined to revisit. Richard found something that excited his attention about it, so we emptied the water out of all our goat-skins, blew them up with air, strapped them to our camp-table, made a raft, and used the tent-poles for oars. It is supposed to have no bottom, is six hundred yards broad, and about nine hundred wide. We sounded with the lead, and the deepest part proved to be seventeen feet and a half. It has a weed bottom and leeches below, no shells; but the air began to whistle out of the skins, and Richard and Charley Drake only just got back in time to save themselves a swim.

Whilst at Jerusalem and its environs Richard did two very graceful things. He saw a monk conducting a party of Catholics, who wanted to say prayers in the Sepulchre itself at three o'clock on Good Friday. It was invaded by the usual class of tourists. The monk shrunk back with his people, and the particular time for these prayers was slipping away. Richard stepped forward, and, touching his cap, said, "What is the matter, Father?" He said, "The Sepulchre is full of tourists, who are not Catholics. We have no right to turn them out, and we don't like to push in and begin our devotions." Richard said, "Leave that to me." He went in and explained to them, and they came out. Richard then passed the monk and his party in, and he stood guard himself outside the whole time they performed their devotion, and would not let any one pass. These little acts used to win him the heart of everybody.

Another day we were riding in rather a desert place about a mile from a small village; we met a solitary priest and his acolyte. I was about to ride up to speak to him, when he gave me the sign—I mean the sign the priest gives you when he is secretly carrying the Blessed Sacrament. I told it to Richard, who ordered his men to draw up in two lines for the priest to pass through and salute. He jumped down from his own horse, and offered it to the priest, asking to accompany him. The priest declined it, but he blessed him as he passed. I always thought of this afterwards in Austria, when I saw the large picture in the Palace at Innsbrück, of Rudolph the Second of Hapsburg doing the same thing.

At Jerusalem we explored the Mágharat el Kotn; these are enormous quarries, also called the Royal Caverns. The entrance looks like a hole in the wall outside the town, not far from the Gate of Damascus. Creeping in, you find yourself in endless caves and galleries unexplored. We used to use magnesium fusees, and take plenty of ropes to have a clue.

CHAPTER XXI.

RELIGION.

"Men don't believe in a devil now, as their fathers used to do;
They've forced the door of the broadest creed to let his Majesty through.
There isn't a print of his cloven foot, or a fiery dart from his bow,
To be found in earth or air to-day, for the world has voted it so.

"But who is mixing the fatal draught that palsies heart and brain,
And loads the bier of each passing year with ten hundred thousand slain?
Who blights the bloom of the land to-day with the fiery breath of hell?
If the devil isn't, and never was, won't somebody rise and tell?

"Who dogs the steps of the toiling saint, and digs the pits for his feet?
Who sows the tares on the fields of time, wherever God sows His wheat?
The devil is voted not to be, and of course the thing is true;
But who is doing the kind of work that the devil alone should do?

"We are told that he does not go about as a roaring lion now;
But whom shall we hold responsible for the everlasting row
To be heard in home, in Church and State, to the earth's remotest bound,
If the devil, by a unanimous vote, is nowhere to be found?

"Won't somebody step to the front forthwith, and make his bow and show
How the frauds and crimes of a single day spring up? We want to know.
The devil was fairly voted out, and of course the devil's gone;
But simple people would like to know who carries his business on."

ALFRED J. HOUGH, *in the Jamestown (N.Y.) Journal.*

IT must not be supposed that Richard was the least insincere, because he tried religions all round. He wanted to get at the highest, the nearest to God, the nearest to other worlds, and in that respect he was like Cardinal Newman. He always spoke the truth, and if he changed every other day, he would have said so. Every time he was disappointed with a religion he fell back on mysticism. It was the soul wandering through space, like the dove out of the ark, and seeking a place whereupon to rest. In each religion he found something good, and much that disappointed him; then he took the good out of that religion, and went away. He was sincere with the

Mohammedans, and found more in that religion than in *most.* He hoped much from spiritualism, and studied it well; but he could make nothing of it as a religion. It never seemed to bring him any nearer; but he believed in it as in the light of a future frontier of science. *His* Agnosticism, which in his case is a misapplied word, was of a much higher cast; it was the mysticism of the East. It was the tired soul or brain that said, "Oh, my God, I have studied all things, and I am still no nearer the point of closer connection with Thee, whom my soul longs for and aims at. I know nothing; I can touch nothing. Faith is a gift from Thee; give it to me!" He became impressed with one fact here in Syria, as he had done at Baroda in his youth, and that is that Catholicism is the highest order of Spiritualism, having no connection with jugglery, or table-turning, or spirit-rapping; that we cannot call it up at our pleasure, nor pay for it; but that, when something *does* happen, it is absolutely *real*, only we are not allowed to speak of it, except amongst ourselves, and then with bated breath. Richard, however, had opportunity enough of seeing all this for himself in Syria, in Damascus, where some very extraordinary things were going on, that were, without a doubt, genuine.

> "Demand of lilies wherefore they are white,
> Extort her crimson secret from the rose."
>
> WILLIAM WATSON.

> "Brave as a lion, gentle as a maid,
> He never evil word to any said;
> Never for self, but always strong for right,
> He was a very perfect gentle knight."

During the time we were at Damascus, there was a "mystery" going on in the lower quarter, called the Maydán—the tail of Damascus, which runs out towards the desert—amongst a certain sect of the Mohammedans, called the Shádilis, or Sházlis. They used to assemble at nights together at the house of one of them for Moslem prayer and reading and discussion, when they became conscious of a presence amongst them that was not theirs. They used to hear things and see things which they did not understand, and this went on for two or three months before they came to an understanding. I let my husband tell the story in his own words, and you will all understand later on how it found its way into my "Inner Life of Syria."

Fray Emanuel Förner, who figures largely in this history, was a friend Richard used to study with. He confided his troubles relative to these people to us. He asked us whether, as Richard had more influence with the Moslems than any one else, he could be induced to protect them. Richard felt that it was going beyond the boundary of his Consular prerogative to interfere in a matter which concerned the national religion; he therefore answered him that his position obliged him to abstain from interfering in so interesting a matter, although he could do so in cases where the *Protestant* schools or missions formally claimed protection against the violation of the treaties and concessions of the Hatti-Sheríf. He added that the Spanish Consul was the proper person for him to apply to, being *his* Consul, and that it was his duty likewise to restrict me from any active part which might compromise the Consulate.

But this interested him enormously. He thought he saw his way in it to the highest kind of religion, and he followed it up *unofficially*. Disguised as a Shâzli, and unknown to any mortal except me, he used to mix with them, and pass much of his time in the Maydán of Damascus with them; and *he saw what he saw;* and when, as in reading this account you will see, Fray Förner was the guide who was pointed out to them by that spiritual Presence, Richard stuck to him, and with him used to study the Shházlis and their history. This gave him an enormous interest in Damascus, but it was his ruin; and the curious Spiritualism, *if you like to term it so*, that was developing there was almost like a "new advent," and though he did not then *mean* it, he ended by sacrificing his worldly career entirely to it.

It was not for a whole year after the event of my disagreement with the Shaykh's son at Zebedáni (which missionaries of the British Syrian schools have since reported as the cause of my husbaná's recall, after which the same Shaykh had become one of my most faithful followers, but which had nothing to do with my husband's misfortunes), that twelve of the most favoured of these Shházlis had been seized, transported in chains, and partially martyred. Fray Förner died curiously, and Richard came and told me all this, with a great deal more than I had known, or than *has*, or *ever will be* published, about the Shházlis, and he was filled with remorse that he had not taken up their case and protected them.

He had written up their case. He said, "If I should write to Lord Granville, and tell him that there are at least twenty-five thousand of secret Christians longing for baptism, and if I were to say, as I know I can, that I can arrange it with the Moslems to *give them to me*, and not to touch them because they are *mine;* supposing I were to buy a tract of land and give it to them, and build a village, and that I took no taxes from them in repayment, they could settle there unmolested, and supposing that I should request the Patriarch Valerga of Jerusalem to come and baptize them, would *you* be afraid to stand godmother for them with *me* on guard?" and I replied that "I would be only too proud to do it." It was then settled that these letters should be written and sent.

Lord Granville communicated with the Patriarch Valerga, who at once sent *openly* and *clumsily* to the Turkish *Authorities* at Damascus to know the truth, thereby *starting an evil;* and, *even so*, four hundred were found who were willing for martyrdom, but the Patriarch was evidently in *no* hurry for martyrdom. The affair, instead of being confided to Richard, was hopelessly mismanaged, and his recall followed within the month; and Richard said, "This is suffering persecution for justice' sake; *no more of this, till I am clear of a just and enlightened Government.*" It broke his career, it shattered his life, it embittered him on religion; he got neither Teheran, nor Marocco, nor Constantinople. I may be wrong, but I have always imagined that he thought that Christ would stand by him, and see him through his troubles, but he did not like to speak of it. Richard never asked a single word at the Foreign Office—he was too proud; and he let me do it in a Blue Book of our own. My friends in the Foreign Office, of whom I had about thirteen, gave me *each* a *different* reason for the recall; but when I got an audience with Lord Granville, I got the true one. Syria and Christianity lost one of England's greatest men, who was ruined, and her descent in prosperity and happiness commenced; and I never heard that the Government, or the Foreign Office, or the Service, or the British name in the East, was any better for it. I humbly venture to think the contrary. He wrote himself the history of the "Revival of Christianity in Syria."

When I brought out my "Inner Life of Syria," Richard brought me the following account, blushing like a schoolboy, and asked me if I would insert it in my own name—if I would mind, as I could not be godmother to the Sházlis, being godmother to *it.*

"The Christian Revival in Syria.

"'Men are four. He who knows not, and knows not he knows not, he is a fool—shun him; he who knows not, and knows he knows not, he is simple—teach him; he who knows, and knows not he knows, he is asleep—wake him; he who knows, and knows he knows, he is wise—follow him.'—*Arab Proverb.*

"'What I tell you in darkness, that speak ye in light: and what ye hear in the ear, that preach ye upon the housetops. And fear not them which kill the body, but are not able to kill the soul; but rather fear him which is able to destroy both soul and body in hell.'—MATT. x. 27, 28.

"'Have pity on me, have pity on me, at least you my friends, because the hand of the Lord hath touched me.'—JOB xix. 21.

"Christianity was born and grew in Syria. She gave the light of the Gospel to the world. The grace of God has returned to Syria. Shall she struggle single-handed with Moslem cruelty and oppression, unaided by the Christian Powers who owe to her the Light of Faith?

"The heading of these pages will not a little surprise many, but not all of my readers, who will be divided into two classes—those familiar with old prophecies, and those who are not. The first will expect, the others will not expect, to hear that Christianity has revived spontaneously, unaided by Missionaries, Catechists, or Consuls, in this fanatical Moslem land, especially in Damascus, the 'Gate of the Holy City,' the ancient capital of the Caliphs, where, even at present, Christian representatives of Great Powers are not allowed to fly their flags. But the movement has taken place; it grows every year; its consequences are difficult to see, impossible to calculate. The conversion of the Mohammedans has begun at last, without England's sending out, as is her custom, shiploads of Bibles, or spending one fraction upon it; and in this great work, so glorious to Christianity, England, if old traditions are about to be verified, is to have a large share. She must now decide whether the Revival of Christianity, in the land which gave it birth, shall spread its goodly growth far and wide, or whether it shall be cut down by the hand of the destroyer.

"The first step in this movement, taken as far back as 1868, was heralded by signs and tokens and graces, which partake of the miracle and of the revelation. And here, at the beginning, I may remind my readers, especially Protestant readers, that the Lord has a mighty arm—'*brachium Domini non est abbreviatum*'—and that in this same City of Damascus, the terrible persecutor, Saul of Tarsus, became St. Paul, not by reading, nor by conversations with Christians, but by the direct interposition of Jesus Christ. The visions and revelations which I am about to record rest upon the same solid basis as Christianity itself—that is to say, upon the unanimous testimony borne to them by sincere and devout men, who have no purpose to serve, and who have risked their all in this world without any possible object but to testify to mankind the truths revealed to them. We need not delay to consider whether the graces and tokens which have been vouchsafed are natural, preternatural, or supernatural; objective or subjective. Suffice it for us that they have been submitted to crucial tests, and that even this philosophic and incredulous age cannot deny that they have taken place.

"About four years ago a small body of Moslems who inhabit the Maydán, or southern suburb of Damascus, had been initiated into the Shádili Order of Moslems by one Abd el Karim Matar, of Darayya, whose touching end will presently be recounted. This man, a mere peasant, left his wife, his family, and his relations in his native village, in order to become Shaykh of the Dervishes, and he hired a house in the Sukhkháneh quarter of the Maydán. It is bisected by the long street through which the annual Hajj Caravan passes out *en route* to Mecca, and its inhabitants, with those of the Shaghur quarter, are held to be the most bigoted and fanatical of their kind. Through the influence of the Shádilis, however, not a Christian life was lost in their quarter during the dreadful massacre of 1860; many, indeed, were hidden by the people in their houses, and were sent privily away without the walls after the three days of bloodshed had passed. Our Lord, who promises to remember even the cup of cold water given in His name, did not, as will presently appear, forget these acts of mercy to the terrified Christians.

"I am going to assume that all my readers are not perfectly *au courant* of the many subdivisions of the influential and widespread religion—El Islam.

"The Order of Shádili Dervishes was founded by Abd el Husayn Shádili, who died at Mecca in A.H. 656 (A.D. 1258). They are not, therefore, one of the twelve originally instituted, and for that reason they are rarely noticed by writers upon Eastern Spiritualism (for instance, 'The Dervishes,' by John P. Brown. London: Trübner, 1868). They obtained fame, however, by introducing to the world coffee, so called from the Abyssinian province of Kafa. The use of coffee in Yemen, its origin and first introduction into that country, are due to the learned Ali Shádili Abu Omar, one of the disciples of the learned doctor Nasr Ood Deen, who is regarded as one of the Chiefs, and whose worth attests the high degree of spirituality to which they had attained ('First Footsteps in East Africa,' p. 78. London: 1856).

"The Shádili are Sufis or Mystics, esoterics from El Islam, who have attempted to spiritualize its material portions. This order, like all others, admits of two main divisions, the Sharai or orthodox, and the Ghayr-Sharai, who have greatly departed from the doctrines of El Islam.

"The vital tenets of the heterodox are—

"1. God alone exists. He is in all things and all things are in Him—evidently mere pantheism.

"2. All things visible and invisible are an emanation from Him, and are not really distinct from Him—this is the Eastern origin of the classical European '*divinæ particula auræ*.'

"3. Heaven and hell and all the dogmas of positive faiths are allegories, whose esoteric meaning is known only to the Sufi.

"4. Religions are a matter of indifference; that, however, is the best which serves as a means of reaching true knowledge, such as El Islam, whose philosophy is Tasawwuf (Sufi-ism).

"5. There is no real distinction between good and evil, for all things are one, and God fixes the will of man, whose actions therefore are not free.

"6. The soul existed before the body, and is confined in it as a bird in a cage. Death therefore is desirable to the Sufi, whose spirit returns to the Deity whence it emanated. Evidently the

'Anupadishesha Nirvana' of the Hindu, absolute individual annihilation.

"7. The principal duty of the Sufi is meditation on the unity which advances him progressively to spiritual perfection, and which enables him to 'die in God."

"8. Without 'Fayz Ullah' (Grace of God) this spiritual unity cannot be attained; but God favours those who fervently desire such unification.

"The general belief in these tenets has given the Shádili Order a doubtful name amongst the multitude, who consider it to profess, like the 'Babis' of Persia, opinions of a subversive and anti-Islamitic nature. The orthodox portion, however, is not blamed, and at Damascus one of its members is a conscientiously religious Moslem, the Sayyid Abd el Kadir of Algerian fame, whose name is still so well known in Europe, and who is beloved and respected by all. The Syrian Shádilis are distinguished by white robes and white skull-caps and turbans, of which they allow the inner flap to protrude a little from the folds behind the ears.

"Abd el Karim Matar and his Shádili acolytes used to meet for private worship at his house in the Maydán suburb, and they spent nights and days in praying for enlightenment before the throne of Grace. Their numbers varied from sixty to seventy, and even more. Presently, after persevering in this new path, some of them began to be agitated by doubts and disbelief; the religion did not satisfy them, they anxiously sought for a better. They became uncertain, disquieted, undetermined, yet unable, for fear of being betrayed, to declare even one to another the thought which tormented them. Two years had been spent in this anxious, unhappy state, each thinking himself the only one thus subject to the tortures of conscience.

"At length they were assured by a vision that it was the religion of Christ which they were seeking. Yet such was their dread of treachery that none could trust his secret with his neighbour till they had sounded one another, and had found that the same idea was uppermost in every mind. Presently about forty of them, headed by Abd el Karim Matar, met for their usual night-prayers; after prolonged devotional acts, all fell asleep, and our Lord was pleased to appear to all of them separately. They awoke simultaneously, and one, taking courage, recounted his vision to the others, when each responded, 'I also saw Him!' Christ had so consoled, comforted, and exhorted them to follow His faith, and they were so filled with a joy they had never known, that they were hardly dissuaded from running about the streets to proclaim that Christ is God; but they were admonished that they would only be slaughtered, and rob the City of all hope of entering the same fold.

"They wanted a guide, director, and friend who could assist their tottering steps in the new way which they were now treading, and they heartily prayed that God would be pleased mercifully to provide them with the object of their desire. One night, after again meeting, as before, for acts of devotion, sleep overcame them, and they saw themselves in a Christian church, where an old man with a long white beard, dressed in a coarse brown serge garment, and holding a lighted taper, glided before them, and smiling benignantly never ceased to cry, 'Let those who want the truth follow me.'

"On awaking each told his dream to the other, and they agreed to occupy themselves in seeking the person who had appeared to them. They searched in vain through the City and its environs for a period of three months, during which they continued to pray. One day it so happened that one of the new converts, H—— K——, now at J——, entered by chance the monastery of the R.R. Fathers of the Terra Santa, near Bab Tuma, the north-eastern gate of Damascus. This is an establishment of Spanish Franciscans, who enjoy French protection by virtue of a Papal Bull and of immemorial usage. What was his astonishment to see in the Superior, Fray Emanuel Förner, the personage who had appeared to him in his dream. This saintly man, Latin Curé and Franciscan of the Terra Santa, approached and asked the Moslem what he was seeking. The Neophyte replied by simply telling his tale and that of his comrades, and then ran speedily to inform the others, who flocked next day to the monastery. The poor padre was greatly perplexed. He reflected that visions do not happen every day. He feared some political intrigue, of which Damascus is a focus; he doubted their sincerity, and he dreaded to endanger the City, and to cause for the sake of the forty another massacre like that of 1860. On the other hand, he still more dreaded to lose forty sincere souls by refusing to them baptism. However, concealing his agitation, he received them with touching kindness; he gave them books which taught them all the Christian doctrine, and he instructed them how to meet in prayer for mutual comfort and support. Lastly, he distributed to each a crucifix, the symbol of their new faith. This event took place in the early spring of 1870. Fray Emanuel remained for about four months in this state of dilemma, praying to know the will of God, and he was admonished as to what he should do. Having performed his task on earth, he fell asleep quietly one day about three months afterwards. Some said the death was caused by climate, but many of his most intimate friends, living a few hours from the convent, did not hear of it till late in November, 1870, and then they had cause to suspect treachery.

"The converts, now numbering some two hundred and fifty, held regular prayer-meetings in one another's houses, and these could not fail to attract the notice of the neighbouring Moslems. Later still a crucifix or two was seen, and suspicions ripened into certainties. The local authorities were at once informed of what had happened. The Ulemá, or learned men, who in El Islam represent the Christian priesthood, were in consternation. They held several sessions at the house of Shakyh Dabyan, a noted fanatic living in the Maydán suburb. At length a general meeting took place in the town-house of the Algerine Amir Abd el Kadir, who has ever been held one of the 'Defenders of the Faith' at Damascus.

"The assembly consisted of the following Ulemá:—

"1. Shaykh Riza Effendi el Ghazzi.

"2. Abdullah el Hálabi.

"3. Shaykh el Tantáwi.

"4. Shaykh el Khání.

"5. Shaykh Abdu Razzak (el Baytar) and his brother.

"6. Shaykh Mohammed el Baytar.

"7. Shaykh Salím Samára.

"8. Shaykh Abd el Ghání el Maydáni.

"9. Shaykh Ali ibn Sa'ati.

"10. Said Effendi Ustuwáneh (the Naib el Kazi, or assistant judge in the Criminal Court of the Department at Damascus), and other intimates of the Amir.

"Riza Effendi, now dead, was a determined persecutor of the Nazarene, and Abdullah el Hálabi, also deceased, had pronounced in 1860 the Fatwa or religious decree for the massacre of the Christian Community, and had been temporarily banished instead of being hanged as high as Haman. These specimens will suffice. Still let us be just to the President of this assembly, Abd el Kadir. He was carrying out a religious duty in sitting in judgment upon renegades from his faith, and he was acting in accordance with his conscience; but during the massacre of 1860 he not only extended his protection to the Christians, but he slept across his own threshold on a mat, lest any terrified and supplicating wretch might be turned adrift by his Algerine followers.

"The assembly, after a long discussion, pronounced the sentence of death upon the converts. The only exceptions were the Amir Abd el Kadir and the Shaykh Abd el Ghání el Maydani, who declared 'that a live man is always better than a dead man.' The Shaykhs Tantáwi and El Khání declared 'that to kill such perverts was an act more acceptable to Allah than the Friday prayer.'

"If there be one idea more strongly fixed than any other in Moslem brain it is this—the renegade from El Islam shall surely die. His death must be compassed by any means, fair or foul: perjury and assassination are good deeds when devoted to such an end. The Firman of February 12th, 1856, guaranteed, it is true, life and liberty to *all* converts; it was, in fact, a perfect system of religious toleration on paper. But it was never intended to be carried out, and the local Turkish authorities throughout the Empire have, doubtless acting under superior instruction, ignored it as much as possible.

"The usual practice in the Turkish dominions when a convert is to be convicted, opens with a preliminary imprisonment, either on pretence of 'counselling' him, or upon some false charge. The criminal tribunal then meets; witnesses are suborned; the defence is not listened to; a *mázbatah*, or sentence, is drawn out, and the victim is either drafted off with the Nizam (regular troops), or sent to the galleys, or transported to some distant spot. The assembly, however, not daring to carry out the sentence of death, determined that the perverts must be exiled, and that their houses and their goods must be destroyed or confiscated. A secret *Majlis* was convened without the knowledge of the Christian members of the tribunal, and this illegal junto despatched, during the night, a squadron of cavalry and a regiment of infantry, supported by a strong force of police, to occupy the streets of the Maydán. Some fifty Shádilis were known to have met for prayer at the house of one Abu Abbas. At four o'clock Turkish time (10 p.m.) they rose to return home. Many of them passed amongst the soldiery without being alarmed, and whilst so doing fourteen were separately arrested and carried to the *karakuns* (guard-houses) known as El Ka'ah, and the Sinnaníyyeh. Here they were searched by the soldiery and made to give up their crucifixes. They were then transferred, some to the so-called great prison in the Serai, or Government house, others to the *karakun* jail in the Government square, and others to the debtors' jail, then at the Maristán, or Mad-house, now transferred to Sidr Amud, near Bab el Baríd.

"I hasten to record the names of the fourteen chosen for the honour of martyrdom. All were sincere and inoffensive men, whose only crime was that of being Christians and martyrs; the rulers, however, had resolved upon crushing a movement which, unless arrested by violence, would spread far and wide throughout the land.

"1. Abu Abbas (the man in whose house the prayer-meeting was held).

"2. Sáid Isháni.

"3. Abu Abduh Bustati.

"4. Abd el Ghani Nassás and his son,

"5. Mohammed Nassás.

"6. Ghanaym Dabbás.

"7. Salih el Zoh.

"8. Abdullah Mubayyad.

"9. Ramazan el Sahhár.

"10. Salih Kachkul.

"11. Mohammad Nammúreh.

"12. Bekr Audaj.

"13. Mohammad el Dib.

"14. Marjan min el Kisweh.

"After some days they were brought to the great secret *Majlis* (tribunal), at which presided in person his Excellency the *Wali*, or Governor-General, of Syria, Mohammed Rashíd Pasha. This officer, a *protégé* of the late Aali Pasha, Grand Vizier at Constantinople, has been allowed to rule the province of Syria for the unusual term of more than five years, and the violence and rapacity displayed by him and his creatures have doubtless added an impulse to the Revival of Christianity—it was evil working for good. With a smattering of Parisian education, utterly without religion, but determined to crush conversion because it would add to that European influence which he has ever laboured to oppose, Rashíd Pasha never conceals his conviction that treaties and firmans upon such a subject as Moslem conversion are so much waste paper, and he threatens all who change their faith with death, either by law or by secret murder —a threat which, as the cold cruelty of his nature suggests, is not spoken in vain. And he uses persecution with the more readiness as it tends to conciliate the pious of his own creed, who are greatly scandalized by his openly neglecting the duties of his religion, such as prayer and fasting, and by other practices which may not be mentioned here.

"The Governor-General opened the sessions by thus addressing the accused—

"Are you Shádili?

"Answer: We once were, we now are not.

"Gov.-Gen.: Why do you meet in secret, and what is done at those meetings?

"Answer: We read, we converse, we pray, and we pass our time like other Damascus people.

"Gov.-Gen.: Why do you visit the Convent of the Faranj (Franks or Europeans)?

"Abu Abbas: Is it not written in our law that when a Moslem passes before a Christian church or convent, and finds himself hurried by the hour for prayer, he is permitted to enter and even pray there?

"Gov.-Gen.: You are Giaours (infidels)!

"Abu Abbas (addressing one of the Ulemá): What says our law of one who calls a faithful man Giaour?

"Answer: That he is himself a Giaour.

"The Governor-General was confounded by this decision, which is strictly correct. He remanded the fourteen to their respective prisons. Here they spent three months awaiting in vain the efforts of some intercessor. But they had been secretly tried, or their number might have attracted public attention; the affair was kept in darkness, and even two years afterwards not a few of the Europeans resident at Damascus had ever heard of it. The report reached the Consular corps in a very modified form—persecution had been made to assume the semblance of political punishment. The Russian Consul, M. Macceef, succeeded in procuring their temporary release, but this active and intelligent officer was unable to do more. The British Consul could hardly enter into a matter which was not brought officially before his notice. The Consul of France and the Spanish Vice-Consul took scant notice of the Shádili movement, perhaps being unwilling to engage in open warfare with the Governor-General, possibly deeming the matter one of the usual tricks to escape recruitment or to obtain a foreign passport. The Neophytes, however, found an advocate in Fray Emanuel Förner, before mentioned. This venerable man addressed (March 29, 1870) a touching appeal to the General of his Order, and his letter appeared in the *Correspondance de Rome* (June 11, 1870). The Franco-Prussian War, however, absorbed all thoughts in Europe, and the publication fell still-born from the Press.

"Fray Emanuel relates in his letter that one day, when visiting the Neophytes before their imprisonment—he modestly passes over the important part which he had taken in receiving them—he asked them if they could answer for their constancy. The reply was: 'We believe not simply through your teachings of the Word, and through our reading the religious books which you gave us, but because the Lord Jesus Christ has vouchsafed to visit us and to enlighten us Himself, whilst the Blessed Virgin has done likewise!' adding, 'How could we without such a miracle have so easily become Christians?' The good priest would not express his doubts, for fear of 'offending one of these little ones.' He felt an ardent desire to inquire into the visions and the revelations to which they alluded. But he did not neglect to take the necessary precautions. Assembling his brethren, and presiding himself, he began with the unfortunate Salih, and he examined and cross-questioned the converts separately. He found them unanimous in declaring that on the first night when they witnessed an apparition, they had prayed for many hours, and that slumber had overcome them, when the Saviour Jesus Christ appeared to them one by one. Being dazzled by the light, they were very much afraid; but one of them, taking courage, said, 'Lord, may I speak?' He answered, 'Speak.' They asked, 'Who art Thou, Lord?' The apparition replied, 'I am the Truth Whom thou seekest. I am Jesus Christ, the Son of God.' Awakening agitated and frightened, they looked one at the other, and one took courage and spoke, the rest responding simply, 'I also saw Him.' Christ had once more so consoled, comforted, and exhorted them to follow His path, and they were filled with such ineffable joy, love, faith, and gratitude, that, but for His admonishing them (as He used to admonish the disciples), they could hardly restrain themselves from rushing into the streets and from openly preaching the Gospel to the Infidel City. On another occasion the Blessed Virgin stood before them with the Child Jesus in her arms, and, pointing to Him, said three times in a clear and distinct voice, 'My Son Jesus Christ, Whom you see, is the Truth.' There are many other wonderful revelations whose truth I can vouch for, but I feel a delicacy of thrusting them before unbelievers. Indeed, I have kept back half of what I know, and I am only giving the necessary matter.

"Of the fourteen Christian converts remanded to prison, two were suffered to escape. The relations of Mohammad Dib and Marjan bribed the authorities and succeeded in proving an alibi. Abd el Karim Matar, the Chief of the Shádilis, who had been placed in confinement under the suspicion of being a Christian, fell ill, and his relations, by giving bribes and by offering bail, carried him off to his native village, Darayya. There, as he was now bedridden, the family gathered around him, crying, 'Istash'had!' That is to say, 'Renew the faith (by bearing witness to Allah and his prophet Mohammad).' The invalid refused, turning his face towards the wall whilst his cruel relations struck and maltreated him. The cry was incessantly repeated and so was the refusal. At last such violence was used that the unfortunate Abd el Karim expired, the protomartyr of the Revival.

"On the night of Ramazan 1, A.H. 1286 (December, A.D. 1869), the 'twelve' (a curious coincidence that it was the number of the first Apostles in this very land) who remained in prison were secretly sent ironed, *viâ* Beyrout, to the dungeons of Chanak Kalessi (the Dardanelles fortress). Thence they were shipped off in a craft so cranky and dangerous that they were wrecked twice, at Rhodes and at Malta. At last they were landed at Tripoli in Barbary, and they were finally exiled to the distant interior settlement of Murzuk. Their wives and children, then numbering sixty-two, and now fifty-three, were left at Damascus to starve in the streets, but for the assistance of their fellow-converts and of the Terra Santa Convent. It is a touching fact that if one of these poor converts has anything, he will quickly go and sell it, and use the profit in common, that all the brethren may have a little to eat. The Porte is inexorable; even H.I.M. of Austria was, it is reported, unable to procure the return of the exiles. Yet probably the 'Commander of the Faithful,' Sultan Abdul Aziz, will ere long expect Austria, as well as England and the rest of Western Europe, to fight his battles.

"I call upon the world that worships Christ to punish this high-handed violation of treaty, this wicked banishment of innocent men. Catholic and Protestant are in this case both equally interested. The question at once concerns not only the twelve unfortunate exiles and their starving families. It involves the grand principle of religious toleration, which interests even the atheist and the infidel throughout the Turkish Empire, throughout the Eastern world.

"Upon the answer depends whether Christianity shall be allowed free growth and absolute development. Let England demand of the Porte the removal of this Governor-General. Deliver us from this modern Herod! Let Abdul Aziz call off his dog from worrying the followers of Christ for the sake of the bones thrown to him by Aali Pasha, his Grand Vizier. Send us an honest man, unlike Rashíd Pasha, who will not dare to rend asunder the most solemn ties that can bind nations, who will have the courage to do his duty.

"Amongst the Shádili converts was a private soldier of the Nizam or Regulars, aged twenty-three, and bearing the highest character. About five months after the movement commenced, the soldier Ahmed el Sahhár being in barracks retired to a corner for prayer and meditation, when suddenly our Saviour stood before him, and said, 'Dost thou believe in Jesus Christ, the Son of God? I am He.' The youth at once replied, like the man blind from his birth, 'Lord, I believe.' Jesus said to him, 'Thou shalt not always be a soldier; thou shalt return free to thy home;' upon which Ahmed inquired, 'How can I set myself free?' Jesus again said, 'I will deliver thee,' and with these words the beatific vision disappeared.

"The young soldier had fallen into a state of ecstasy. Presently he arose and passed through the barracks, exclaiming, 'Jesus Christ is my God! Jesus Christ is my God!' His comrades were scandalized. A crowd rushed up; some covered his mouth with their hands; others filled it with dirt, and all dealt out freely blows and blasphemies. At last it was decided that Ahmed had become possessed of a devil, and, whilst he preserved perfect tranquillity, heavy chains were bound upon his neck, his arms, and his legs. At that moment Jesus Christ again appeared to him, and said, 'Break that chain!' He said, 'How can I break it, it being of iron?' and again the voice spoke louder, 'Break that chain!' He tore it asunder as though it had been of wax. A heavier chain was brought, and the same miracle happened once more. This was reported to the officers, and by them to their Bey or commandant; the latter sent for the private, and, after heaping reproaches, abuse, and threats upon him, ordered him to be imprisoned without food or water, and to be carefully fettered. Still for a third and a fourth time the bonds fell off, and supernatural graces and strength were renewed to the prisoner, who made no attempt to move or to escape from his gaolers.

"The soldiers fled in fear, and the commandant no longer dared to molest the convert. The case was represented to Constantinople, and orders were sent that Ahmed must appear at the capital. He was despatched accordingly under an escort, and with his wrists in a block of wood acting as handcuffs. Reaching Diurat, a village three hours from Damascus, he saw at night the door of his room fly open, and the Blessed Virgin entering, broke with her own hands the block of wood and his other bonds. By her orders he walked back alone to Damascus and reported himself to his regiment. It was determined this time to forward him with a party of soldiers, but without chains or 'wood.'

"Arrived at Constantinople, the accused was brought before a court-martial; a medical man was consulted as to his sanity, and the prisoner was not a little surprised to find himself set at liberty, and free to go where he pleased. Thus the promise of Jesus Christ was fulfilled. The neophyte took the name of 'Isa,' which is Jesus, and returned to Damascus, where his history became generally known. The Turks pointed him out as the 'soldier who broke four chains.' Some term him the 'Majnún,' the madman, though there is nothing about him to indicate the slightest insanity; but most of the people held him in the highest respect, calling him Shaykh Ahmed, and thus raising him to the rank of 'Santon,' or saintly man.

"The terrible example of the Shádili families has not arrested the movement—persecution never does. The blood of the martyrs is still the seed of the Church. But the converts now conduct their proceedings with more secrecy. They abstain from public gatherings, although they occasionally visit Fray Dominic d'Avila, Padre Guardiano, or Superior of the Terra Santa. The society has now assumed a socialistic character, with private meetings for prayers, and with the other precautions of a secret order. The number of converts has greatly increased. At the end of 1869 the males in the City of Damascus amounted to 500; in 1870 it had risen to 4100; and in 1871 it represents 4900, of whom some 700 have been secretly baptized. Moreover, I have been assured by the converts with whom I associate and converse frequently, some of them being men highly connected and better educated than their persecutors, that a small tribe of freebooters living in and about the Druze mountain (Jebel Druze Haurán), having been troubled and threatened by the local Government, has split into two parties—Moslem and Christian, the latter known by crosses hoisted upon their tent roofs. The converts described to me the Bukâa (Cœlesyria) as a field in which the gospel has lately borne fruit, and this was unexpectedly confirmed. The peasantry of B——, a little village on the eastern slope of the Lebanon, and near Shtora, the central station of the French road, lately became the property of a certain M. A—— T——. He owned two-thirds of the village, but by working the authorities he managed to get into his hands the whole of the houses and fields, the crops and cattle—in fact, all the village property. The wretches, after being nearly starved for months, lately came up to Damascus, and begged to be received as Christians. In early July it was whispered that the Latin Patriarch of Jerusalem, Mgr. Valerga, is expected to meet, at his summer residence in Beyrout, Mgr. Franchi, the Papal Envoy; that both these prelates will visit Damascus, and that then these poor souls will ask for baptism.

"Protestantism has also had its triumphs. About ten months ago a certain Hanifi Moslem, named Abd el Razzak, having some misgivings about his faith, left his native city Baghdad in order to visit the Bab or head of the Babi sect, who lies in the galleys of S. Jean d'Acre—what a place for such a purpose! The interview not being satisfactory, he travelled to Damascus, where he came under Protestant influence. Thence he was removed to Shtora on the French road, and finally to Suk el Gharb in the Maronite mountains. There he was enabled to study, and he was publicly baptized under the name of Abdallah. The Turkish authorities had no power over him; but the second case did not end so well.

"A certain Hajj Hassan, a coachman in the service of a Christian family at Beyrout, M. Joachim Najjar, began about 1869 to attend the Protestant service, and for two months before his incarceration he professed himself a Christian, although he had not been baptized. He is described by all who know him as a simple and sincere man, gifted with great strength of will. He was waylaid, beaten, and finally cast with exceeding harshness into prison at Beyrout by the Governor, Rauf Pasha, who replied to all representations that he was unable to release him; he acted, in fact, under superior authority. The convert was not allowed to see his family, and on Thursday, June 29, he was sent in charge of a policeman to the Capital: this, too, despite the remonstrances of the Consuls-General for the United States and Prussia.

"The superintendent of the British Syrian school, where the convert has a child, took the precaution of despatching to head-quarters one of the employés, the Rev. Mr. Waldmeier, so that energetic action began even before the arrival of Hajj Hassan. Rashíd Pasha commenced by treating with contempt her Majesty's Consul's strong appeals to his justice; he openly ignored the Treaty, blaming me for not having quoted the actual article, and he declined to permit the interference of strangers in the case of a subject of H.I.M. the Sultan. He maintained that he had a right to send for the Neophyte in order that the latter might be 'counselled;' and for that purpose he placed him under arrest in the house of the most bigoted Moslem in Syria, the chief of police, Mir Alai (Colonel) Mustafa Bey. He complained strongly of the conduct of Protestant missionaries in Syria, accusing them of secretly proselytizing, though he admitted in the same sentence that the convert Hassan had openly attended a Christian church for some time. On the next day he ungraciously refused my request that the Presbyterian missionaries (Rev. Messrs. Wright, Crawford, and Scott) might be allowed access to the Neophyte. About midday on Friday, June 30, Rashíd Pasha sent for Hajj Hassan, who had been duly disciplined by the police, and locking the door, he began to ask whether the convert was not in fear of being strangled—words which, in his mouth, had a peculiar significancy. He then proceeded to offer a price for apostasy, which rose to thirty thousand piastres. This was stoutly refused by the Neophyte, who was returned to arrest. Presently the Governor-General heard that I had telegraphed for permission to proceed to Constantinople to represent to my Ambassador the state of things in Syria within my district, and Hajj Hassan was ordered to return under the charge of a policeman to Beyrout. The new Christian, however, was warned that he must quit that port together with his family within twenty days, under pain of being sent to Constantinople handcuffed, or, as the native phrase is, 'in wood.'

"The case of Hajj Hassan came to a lame and impotent conclusion. He had been delivered out of the Moslem stronghold, Damascus, to the safe side of the Lebanon. The Protestant Christians of Beyrout, with their schools, missions, and Consuls-General to back them up, should have kept him at Beyrout, and Rashíd Pasha should have been compelled either to eat his own words or to carry out his threat. In the latter case the convert should have been accompanied to Constantinople by a delegate from the Missions, and the Sublime Porte should have been compelled to decide whether she would or would not abide by her Treaties and Firmans. The plea that exile was necessary to defend the convert from his own co-religionists, that banishment was for his own benefit, is simply absurd. Either the Porte can or she cannot protect her Christian converts. In the latter case they must be protected for her. Never probably has there been so good an opportunity for testing Turkey's profession of liberalism, and the Turks are too feeble and too cunning to let another present itself.

"In their first fright the Beyrout European Christians withdrew their protection from Hajj Hassan. On the diligence arriving at the 'Pines,' a forest about an hour before reaching Beyrout from Damascus, the convert was ordered to dismount, and his wife and five children (one at the breast) were turned adrift from the house which had protected them for some days, at nine o'clock at night, to wander whither they could. Hajj Hassan was subsequently removed from Beyrout to Abeigh, an Anglo-American (U.S.) Mission station in the Lebanon, probably by the exertions of Dr. Thomson, author of 'The Land and the Book,' who distinguishes himself in Beyrout by daring to have an opinion and to express it, though unfortunately he stood alone and unsupported. On July 20th, Hajj Hassan was to be shipped off by night to Alexandria, where he was expected to 'find good employ.' Suddenly his passport was refused by the local authorities, and he was hidden in the house of a Consular Dragoman. The Porte had sent a secret despatch, ordering him to be transported to Crete, Cyprus, or one of the islands in the Archipelago, where his fate may easily be divined. At length a telegram arrived from Constantinople, and the result was that, after a fortnight's detention by sickness, Hajj Hassan was sent off by the French mail of Friday, August 11th. Verily, the Beyroutines are a feeble folk. They allowed themselves to be shamefully defeated by Rashíd Pasha when he was grossly in the wrong.

"When the depositions of Hajj Hassan were taken at the Consulate, Damascus, he declared that a Moslem friend of his, named Hammud ibn Osman Bey, originally from Latakia (Laodicea), but domiciled at Beyrout, had suddenly disappeared, and had not been heard of for twelve days. Presently it became known that Hammud, about two years ago, when in the employ of Mr. Grierson, then Vice-Consul of Latakia, was drawn for the Army, but had not been called upon to serve. He was in the habit of hearing the missionaries preach, and on more than one occasion he declared that he would profess Christianity—a course from which his friends dissuaded him.

"Hammud determined, in the beginning of 1871, to visit Beyrout, and Mr. Grierson gave him letters of introduction to the missionaries and to the superintendent of the British Syrian schools, requesting that he might be taken into the service of some European family. Here he again openly committed himself by declaring that he was a Christian. His former master, knowing that the eyes of the police were upon him, made immediate arrangements for his leaving by the steamer to Latakia, where he had been recruited, giving him at the same time a note for the colonel commanding the regiment. Hammud, however, on the evening before his journey, imprudently walked out in the direction of the barracks: he was seized and put in irons —probably to be 'counselled.'

"Mr. Grierson, when informed of this arrest, at once addressed Toufan Bey. This officer is a Pole commanding one of the regiments of the 'Cossacks of the Sultan,' the other being quartered at Adrianople. Visiting the Military Pasha of Beyrout, he begged that as Hammud's passage had been taken for Latakia, where his name had been drawn, the convert might be allowed to proceed there. The two officers sent for the man and gave the required directions respecting him. But Hammud was already in the enemies' hands; and the normal charge of desertion was of course trumped up against him. He was sent with a number of other conscripts to the capital, with tied hands, and carrying the rations of his fellow-soldiers; and presently a report was spread that he had been put to death.

"Hajj Hassan on returning to Beyrout informed Mr. Johnson, Consul-General for the United States, that during his arrest at Damascus the soldiers had threatened to 'serve him as they had served

Hammudeh.' He went at once to Rauf Pasha, who replied that the man had been arrested and sent to head-quarters because he had been conscripted two years before at Latakia and had deserted. This was directly opposed to the statement made by Mr. Grierson, namely, that the man had never been called upon to serve. Mr. Johnson could do no more, as Hammud had made himself amenable to the law of the land, and he seems not to have taken any steps to decide whether it was a *bonâ-fide* desertion. He inquired, however, what the punishment would be, and was told that it would depend upon circumstances.

"Several people at Beyrout wrote to me at Damascus, begging of me to institute a search for the missing man. Shortly afterwards letters were despatched from Beyrout, stating that Hammud had been found in the barracks alive and well, and contented with his condition as a soldier. What process he has been through to effect such a wonderful change we are not informed, nor where he has been hidden during its operation. The 'counselling' has probably compelled the convert by brute force to conceal his convictions.

"Another story in the mouths of men is that a young man, the son of a *kázi* or judge, had lately suffered martyrdom at Damascus for the crime of becoming a Christian. This may possibly be a certain Said el Hamawi, who disappeared three or four years ago. Said was a man of education, and a Shaykh, who acted *khatíb* (or scribe and chaplain) to one of the regiments. He was convicted of having professed Christianity, and was sent for confinement to the Capital. When let out of prison he repeated his offence, and he has never been heard of since.

"On the morning of the Saturday (July 1) which witnessed the unjust sentence of exile pronounced upon Hajj Hassan, a certain Arif Effendi ibn Abd el Ghani el Nablusi was found hanging in a retired room of the Great Amáwi Mosque at Damascus, where he had been imprisoned. No inquest was held upon the body, which may or may not have shown signs of violence; it was hastily buried. Some three years before this time, Arif Effendi, a man of high family, and of excellent education, had become a Greek Christian at Athens under the name of Eustathius. Presently he reappeared in Syria as a convert, a criminal whom every good—that is to say, bigoted—Moslem deems worthy of instant and violent death. He came to the Capital, and he introduced himself as a Christian to the Irish-American Presbyterian missionaries; to Monseigneur Yakub, the Syrian Catholic Bishop, and to others; nor did he conceal from them his personal fears. He expected momentary destruction, and presently he found it, being accused, truthfully or not I am unable to say, of stealing fourteen silver lamp-chains, and a silver padlock. The wildest rumours flew about the City. The few declared that the man had hanged himself. The Nablusi family asserted that, repenting his apostasy, he had allowed himself to be hanged, and the vulgar were taught to think that he was hanged by order of Sayyidna Yahya, our Lord John (the Baptist), whose head is supposed to be buried in the Great Mosque. It was currently reported that the renegade had been sent to the Algerine Amir, the Sayyid Abd el Kadir, who, finding him guilty of theft, had ordered him to receive forty stripes and to be arrested in the Mosque, at the same time positively refusing to sanction his execution as his accusers demanded. This proceeding, though irregular, is not contrary to Moslem law; the Ulemá claim and are allowed such jurisdiction in matters concerning the Mosque.

"I, suspecting foul play, applied on the 3rd of July for information upon this subject to the *Wali*, who rudely refused to 'justify himself.' Eight days afterwards the Governor-General thought proper to lay the case before the Tribunal. The result may easily be imagined. That honourable body cast the blame of the illegal imprisonment upon the Amir Abd el Kadir, whom they hate because he saved so many Christian lives in 1860. They delivered a verdict that the convert had been found hanged by his own hand, they antedated a medical certificate that the body bore no marks of violence, and they asserted contrary to fact and truth that the deceased was decently washed and buried, whereas he was thrust into a hole like a dog.

"And now I will answer the question prominent in every reader's mind: 'These men are Turks; are we bound to protect them?'

"I simply reply we are.

"It is obviously our national duty to take serious action in arresting such displays of Moslem fanaticism as those that have lately taken place in Syria. Mr. Gladstone cannot forget his own words: 'We would be sorry not to treat Turkey with the respect due to a Power which is responsible for the government of an extended territory, but with reference to many of her provinces and their general concerns, circumstances place her in such a position that we are entitled and, indeed, in many cases, bound to entertain questions affecting her internal relations to her people, such as it would be impertinent to entertain in respect to most foreign countries. . . . All that we can expect is that when she has contracted legal or moral engagements she should fulfil them, and that when she is under no engagements she should lend a willing ear to counsels which may be in themselves judicious, and which aim solely at the promotion of her interests. . . . As regards the justice of the case, we must remember that as far as regards the stipulations of the Hatti-i-Humaioun, we are not only entitled to advise Turkey in her own interest, in her regard to humanity, in her sense of justice, in her desire to be a civilized European Power, to fulfil those engagements, but we are also entitled to say to her that the fulfilment of those stipulations is a matter of moral faith, an obligation to which she is absolutely bound, and the disregard of which will entail upon her disgrace in the eyes of Europe. . . . We are entitled to require from Turkey the execution of her literal engagements' (Debate on Crete and Servia. Mr. Gregory's motion for correspondence and Consular Reports on the Cretan Insurrection, etc., as reported in the *Evening Mail* of Feb. 15–18, 1867).

"These memorable words deserve quotation the more, as throughout the nearer East, especially among the Christian communities,

England still suffers under the imputation of not allowing the interests of Christendom to weigh against her politics and her sympathy with the integrity of the Turkish Empire. Even if we care little for the propagation of Christianity, or for the regeneration of Asia, we are bound to see that treaties do not become waste paper.

"The first step to be taken in North Syria, and to be taken without delay, would be to procure the recall and the pardon of the twelve unfortunates who were banished in 1870 to Tripoli of Barbary, and to Murzuk in Inner Africa. This will be a delicate proceeding; imprudently carried out, it will inevitably cost the lives of men whose only offence has been that of becoming Christians, and it will only serve to sink their families into still deeper misery. But there should be no difficulty of success. Our Consul-General at Tripoli could easily defend the lives if not the liberties of the Neophytes. Her Majesty's Ambassador Extraordinary and Plenipotentiary at Constantinople should be directed firmly to demand that an officer of high rank be sent from Head-quarters, and that he should be made duly responsible for landing the exiles in safety at Beyrout. Thence they should be transferred to Damascus; their pretended offences should be submitted to a regular tribunal, whose action would be watched by me or my successor, and when publicly proved to be innocent these men should be restored to the bosoms of their families, whilst the police should be especially charged with their safety.

"This step taken, the next will naturally be to urge the instant recall of the unjust *Wali*, or Governor-General, of Syria, Mohammed Rashíd Pasha, together with those members of the Secret Tribunal, more especially the Mufattish Effendi, Mahommad Izzat, who made themselves his instruments in carrying out illegal and tyrannical measures against a body of twelve innocent men. And when the head and front of the evil shall have been removed and the limbs formally impeached, a consummation devoutly to be desired, unless due prudence be exercised much evil may be the result. Rashíd Pasha has filled every important post with his familiars and creatures; he will doubtless leave directions after his departure for all manner of troubles to be excited, especially between Christians and Moslems, Greeks and Latins, in order to stifle the outcry which will rise from the length and breadth of the land. The remedy will be a High Commissioner, and a Firman from Constantinople couched in the strongest terms, and holding all Governors and Judges (*muftis* and *kázis*) personally responsible for any disorderly proceedings. And should they not be able to keep the peace, should any threat of repeating the horrors of 1860 be heard, the nations of Europe must prepare to keep it for them.

"Thus will the unhappy province—a land once flowing with milk and honey, now steeped to the lips in poverty and crime—recover from the misery and the semi-starvation under which it has groaned during the last five years. Thus also Christianity may again raise her head in her birthplace and in the land of her early increase. Thus shall England become to Syria, and through Syria to Western

Asia, the blessing which Syria in the days of the early Church was to England, to Europe, and to the civilized world. Let her discharge her obligations before her God.

"RICHARD FRANCIS BURTON."

* * * * * * *

I saw at the Mission in Damascus, and obtained leave to copy, the following testimonial addressed to Richard, and his reply.—I. B.

"Damascus, July 12, 1871.

"To Captain Burton, H.B.M.'s Consul at Damascus.

"Sir,—We beg to tender to you our heartiest thanks for your prompt decisive action in the case of Hassan the converted Moslem, and also to congratulate you on the result of your determination and firmness.

"For some time past we had heard that a Moslem converted to Protestantism at Beyrout had become subject to considerable persecution. A convert more obscure than himself has been put out of the way and has not since been heard of, and Hassan had been subjected to a series of arrests and imprisonments, and had several times narrowly escaped assassination. The chief Consulates, however, had become publicly interested in him, so that his safety from legal execution seemed ensured; and as he was always accompanied by some one to protect him from assassins, he seemed for the time to be safe. But on the 29th of June we were surprised to find that he was being transported to Damascus, having been arrested and bound in chains. The English colony in Beyrout became alarmed, as they declared that none so transported to Damascus ever returned again. Two agents of the Mission were despatched from Beyrout, one preceding the prisoner to give us information as to what had taken place, and the other accompanying the prisoner to watch what became of him. On receiving intelligence of the convert's transportation to this City, the missionaries of the three Missions at Damascus resolved to lay the case before you, but on doing so found that you had with your usual energy already taken up the case, and categorically demanded the release of the prisoners. And though the authorities ignored the Firman granting civil and religious liberty to the people of this Empire, and denied your right to interfere on behalf of the prisoner, the unflinching stand you took by the concessions of the Hatti-Sherif secured the release of the prisoner: you have thus vindicated the cause of humanity, for on the day on which the prisoner escaped through your intervention, the Moslem authorities strangled in the Great Mosque of Damascus a Moslem convert to Christianity. The man had made application to the Irish American Mission for protection, and declared that he lived in daily fear of strangulation. He was imprisoned in the Great Mosque, and strangled as they say by St. John the Baptist, and then carried away by one man and thrown into a hole like a dog.

"This accident proves that your uncompromising firmness with the authorities was an act of pure mercy, and that the worst apprehensions of the Beyrout missionaries were not unfounded. But more important still, you have asserted the binding character of the spiritual privileges of the Christian subjects of the Porte, contained in the Firman of 1856, and which, according to Fuad Pasha's letters to Lord Stratford de Redcliffe, comprises 'absolutely all proselytes.'

"We are sure, Sir, that your conduct in this affair will receive the unqualified approbation of the best public opinion in Christendom, and we have no doubt it will receive, as it merits, the warm approval of your own Government.

"We who were near and anxious spectators of the proceedings in this affair cannot too warmly express our sense of the satisfaction with which we witnessed the fearless, firm, and efficient manner in which you conducted this important case until the convert was permitted to leave this city.

(Signed) "E. B. FRANKEL, Missionary of the London Jews' Society.

"JAMES ORR SCOTT, M.A., Missionary of the Irish Presbyterian Church.

"FANNY JAMES, Lady Superintendent of the British Syrian Schools, Damascus.

"WILLIAM WRIGHT, A.B., Missionary of the Irish Presbyterian Church, Damascus.

"JOHN CRAWFORD, Missionary of the United Presbyterian Church of North America at Damascus.

"ELLEN WILSON, Lady Superintendent of the British Syrian Schools, Zahleh."

Captain Burton's reply to the Rev. E. B. Frankel, Rev. J. Orr Scott, Miss James, Rev. W. Wright, Rev. John Crawford, Miss Wilson.

"Beludan, July 19, 1871.

"I have the pleasure to return my warmest thanks for your letter this day received, in which you have formed so flattering an estimate of my services as H.M.'s Consul for Damascus. Nor must I forget to express my gratitude to you for the cordial support and approval of my proceedings connected with your Missions which you have always extended to me. This friendly feeling has greatly helped to lighten the difficulties of the task that lay before me in 1869. You all know, and none can better know, what was to be done when I assumed charge of this Consulate; you are acquainted with the several measures taken by me, honourably I hope to our national name, and you are familiar with the obstacles thrown in my way, and with the manner in which I met them. My task will encounter difficulties for some time. Still the prospect does not deter me. I shall continue to maintain the honest independence of H.M.'s Consulate, to defend our rights as foreigners in Syria, and to claim all our privileges to the letter of the law. Should

I meet—and there is no fear of its being otherwise—the approval of my Chiefs, who know that an official life of twenty-nine years in the four quarters of the world is a title to some confidence, I feel assured that we may look forward to happier times at Damascus, when peace and security shall take the place of anxiety and depression.

"Meanwhile I recommend to your prudent consideration the present state of affairs in Syria. A movement which I cannot but characterize as a Revival of Christianity, seems to have resulted from the peculiar action of the authorities, and from the spirit of inquiry awakened in the hearts of the people. It numbers its converts by thousands, including men of high rank, and it is progressing even amongst the soldiery.

"I need hardly observe that it is the duty of one and all of us to labour in the grand cause of religious toleration, and to be watchful lest local and personal interpretations are allowed to misrepresent the absolute rights of all converts to life and liberty. And I trust that you will find me, at the end as in the beginning, always ready to serve your interests, to protect your Missions and Schools, and to lend my most energetic aid to your converts.

"I am, with truth and regard, yours faithfully,

(Signed) "RICHARD BURTON,

"H.M.'s Consul, Damascus."

This was the time that Richard was nearest making a public declaration of Catholicity, but it was his "recall." I cannot tell it better than in his own words:—

"I took the part, and espoused the cause of these forty martyrs, and wrote home offering to be security for them if the Latin Patriarch Valerga might be sent down to baptize them. I promised to stand guard, and my wife would be godmother to them all. I asked her if she were afraid, and she said, 'Afraid! No, indeed, only too proud.' Lord Granville wrote to inquire into the matter, and the reply was, 'that Valerga would not come, that the matter was very much exaggerated, that there were only four hundred.' I have copies of the letter now. Then my seven enemies clubbed together, and represented most falsely that my life was in danger, that I was very unpopular with the Moslems, which only meant the corrupt Rashíd Pasha."

Lord Granville, like many another easy-going, pleasant diplomat (to please God knows who), ruined the life of the best man under his rule with the stroke of his pen. That *did* put the whole of Syria in a blaze of revolt and indignation, and it required the utmost prudence not to put a match to it. It is a pitiful tale, and was a revolting sight to see seven jackals trying to rend an insulted and martyred lion.

One fine day a bombshell fell in the midst of our happy life. It was not *only* the insult of the whole thing, it was the ungentlemanly way in which it was carried out from Beyrout. This was our position and the way it was done :—

We were surrounded by hundreds who seemed to be dependent upon us; by villages which, under our care, consular or maternal, seemed to be thriving, prosperous, peaceful, and secure; by friends we had made everywhere. Our lives, plans, and interests were arranged for years; we were settled down and established as securely, we thought, as any of you in your own houses at home. Our *entourage* was a large one—dragomans, *kawwáses*, servants; our stud, various pets, and flowers; our home, and our "household gods;" our poor for thirty miles around us. And so surrounded, our only wish was to stay, perhaps for life, and do our duty both to God and our neighbour; and we were succeeding, as I mean to prove. You, through whose evil working the blow struck us on this day, examine your hearts, and ask yourselves why you did this thing, because God, who protects those who serve Him, will allow this cruel deed to follow you, and recoil upon you some day, when you least expect it. It was useless to mislead the Authorities and the public at home, by laying the blame upon the Moslems. Richard always has been a very good friend to the Moslems, and the Moslems have always liked him; but in this instance, local and individual weakness, spite and jealousy, overthrew him.

The horses were saddled at the door, in the Anti-Lebanon, and we were going for a ride, when a ragged messenger on foot stopped to drink at the spring, and advanced towards me with a note. I saw it was for Richard, and took it into the house for him. It was from the Vice-Consul of Beyrout, informing him that, by the orders of his Consul-General, he had arrived the previous day (15th of August), and had taken charge of the Damascus Consulate. The Vice-Consul was in no way to blame.*

Richard's journal says—

"*August* 16*th.*—All ready to start—rode in.

"*August* 18*th.*—Left Damascus for ever; started at three a.m. in the dark, with a big lantern; all my men crying; alone in *coupé* of diligence, thanks to the pigs. Excitement of seeing all for the last time. All seemed sorry; a few groans. The sight of Bludán mountains in the distance at sunrise, where I have left my wife. *Ever again?* Felt soft. Dismissal ignominious, at the age of fifty, without a month's notice, or wages, or character.

* Lord Granville, a courteous and easy-going peer, complaisant to the great and unmindful of the little officials, soon found an excuse to recall him. When he did recall him, he did so without the trial usually allowed to accused people to prove their guilt or innocence, or to defend themselves, and from that date began the ruin of Damascus and the visible and speedy decline of Syria.—I. B.

"The Turkish Government has boasted that it would choose its own time, when Moslems may become Christians if they wish. The time has now come."

Richard and Charley Tyrwhitt-Drake were in the saddle in five minutes, and galloped into town without drawing rein. He would not let me accompany him. A mounted messenger returned on the 19th with these few written words, "Don't be frightened; I am recalled. Pay, pack, and follow at convenience." I was not frightened, but I do not like to remember what I thought or felt.

I could not rest on the night of the 19th; I thought I heard some one call me three successive times. I jumped up in the middle of a dark night, saddled my horse, and, though everybody said I was mad, and wanted to put me to bed, I rode a journey of nine hours across country, by the compass, as if I were riding for a doctor, over rocks and through swamps, making for the diligence halfway house. Three or four of my people were frightened, and followed me. At last I came in sight of Shtora, the diligence-station. The half-hour had expired; the travellers had eaten and taken their places, and it was just about to start; but God was good to me. Just as the coachman was about to raise his whip, he turned his head to the part of the country from whence I was coming, hot, torn, and covered with dust and mud from head to foot; but he knew me. I held up both my arms, as they do to stop a train. He saw the signal, waited, and took me in, and told the ostler to lead my dead-beat horse to the stables.*

I reached Beyrout twenty-four hours before the steamer sailed. When Richard had once received his recall, he never looked behind him, nor packed up anything, but went straight away. It is his rule to be ready in ten minutes to go anywhere. He was now a private individual in misfortune. I passed him in the diligence, walking alone in the town, and looking so sad and serious. Not even a *kawwás* was sent to attend on him, to see him out with a show of honour and respect. It was a real emblem of the sick lion. But *I* was there (thank God) in my place, and he was so surprised and glad when he saw me! I was well rewarded for my hard ride, for when he saw me his whole face was illuminated, and he said, "Thank you, *bon sang ne peut mentir.*" We had twenty-four hours to take counsel and comfort together.

Everybody called upon us, and everybody regretted. The French Consul-General made us almost take up our abode with him for those twenty-four hours—our own Consul-General cut us. At four o'clock I went on board with my husband, and on return I found his

* Men who know the ground will know what that ride means over slippery boulders and black swamps in the dark.—I. B.

faithful servant Habíb, who had also followed him, and arrived just ten minutes too late—only in time to see him steam out; he had flung himself down on the quay in a passionate flood of tears.

Any Consul, in any part of the Eastern world, with one drop of gentlemanly feeling, would have gone to meet his comrade in distress, and sent a couple of *kawwâses* to walk before and behind him. Mr. Eldridge's action was as big a thing as if he had posted handbills all over Beyrout to announce to the world that no notice was to be taken of him. The disgrace was to himself, not to Richard.*

The only notice Richard took of *this* tragedy in his life is one sentence in his journal: "After all my service, ignominiously dismissed, at fifty years of age"—and at whose instance, do you think? (1) A Pasha so corrupt that his own Government was obliged to recall him a month later, threaten him with chains, and throw him into a fortress, and his brains were blown out a short while after by a man he had oppressed. (2) His own Consul-General, whose memory is only known to his once immediate acquaintances by the careful registering of his barometers, and the amount of beer which helped that arduous task, and who exactly suited the Foreign Office by confining himself to so narrow a circle. He was fearfully jealous of his superior subordinate, and asked for his removal through Mr. Kennedy, who was not commissioned for that business. Mr. Eldridge said afterwards, "If Burton had only have walked in *my* way, he would have lived and died here." Thirdly, an aggressive schoolmistress, who altered, or *allowed to be altered*, some words in a letter he wrote her, changing "mining" into "missionary," to be shown at Exeter Hall. Fourthly, fifthly, and sixthly, three unscrupulous Jewish usurers. Seventhly, an elastic Greek Bishop, who began a crusade against the Protestants of Nazareth, and prevented them from cultivating their land, and who had snatched away a synagogue and cemetery from British-protected Jews.

When we were in camp there, he caused his people, who were about a hundred and fifty against six, to pick a quarrel with our people, and they stoned us. "Stoning" in the East means a hailstorm the size of melons, which positively seems to darken the air. As an old soldier accustomed to fire, Richard stood perfectly calm, collected, and self-contained, though the stones hit him right and left, and almost broke his sword-arm; he never lost his temper, and never fired, but was simply marking the ringleaders to take them. I ran out to give him his two six-shot revolvers, but when I got within stones' reach, he made a sign to me not to embarrass his movements; so I kept near enough to drag him out if he were wounded, putting his

* All Consuls, especially men who live in the East, will understand me.—I. B.

revolvers in my belt. When three of his servants were badly hurt, and one lay for dead on the ground, he drew a pistol from a man's belt, and fired a shot in the air. That was my signal. I flew round to the other camps, and called all the English and Americans with their guns. When they saw a reinforcement of ten armed English and Americans running down upon them, the cowardly crew turned and fled. This was followed by a *procès-verbal* between Richard and the Bishop, which Richard won.

I was left to pack, pay, and follow; so I took the night diligence back, and had, in spite of the August weather, a cold, hard seven hours over the Lebanon, for I had brought nothing with me; my clothes were dry and stiff, and I was very tired. On the road I passed our honorary dragoman, Hanna Misk. I called out to him, but I had no official position now, so he turned his head the other way, and passed me by. I sent a peasant after him, but he shook his head and rode on. "There," I said, "goes the man who has lived with us, travelled with us, and shared everything we had, and for whose rights concerning a village my husband has always contended, because his claims were just." The law of "Le Roi est mort, vive le Roi!" extends, I suppose, everywhere; but probably the king's widow always feels it.* I wonder how old one has to grow before learning the common rules of life, instead of allowing every shock the world gives one to disturb one, as if one were newly born? It is innate in cool natures, and never learnt by the others, who take useless "headers" against the dead wall of circumstances, until they grow old and cold and selfish. Disraeli told us that "no affections and a great brain form the men that command the world; that no affections and a little brain make petty villains;" but a great brain and a great heart he has no description for. Here he stops short; but I can tell him those are the men for whom there is no place. The nineteenth century will have none of them.

Richard was a general favourite, but he was too powerful to suit the Turkish *Wali*, or Governor-General, who for once found a man he could not corrupt. To give some idea of *how* incorruptible, he was once offered £10,000 on the table, which the man in question brought with him, to give an opinion which would have swayed a public transaction, which would have been no very great harm, but yet it would not have been quite "square" for such a man as Richard, and a promise of £10,000 when the thing was done—"for," said the man, "I can get plenty of money when I like, and this will pay me well." My husband let him finish, and then he said, "If you were a gentleman of my own standing, and an

* I have had to endure the same since I have been a real widow.—I. B.

Englishman, I would just pitch you out of the window; but as you are not, you may pick up your £10,000 and you may walk down the stairs. But don't come here again, because if the thing is right, I shall do it without your paying me; and if it is not, there is not enough money in the world to buy me." He then called me, and he told me about it, and said, "This man's harem will be offering you diamonds; mind you don't take them." "There is not the slightest chance," I said; "I don't want them." Now, it is a perfect fact that, although I am a woman, jewellery is no temptation to me; I therefore take no credit to myself that I have refused enough to enable me to wear as many as any woman in London; but when they brought me horses, it was quite another sensation, and I had to screw up my courage hard—and bolt.

It is perfectly true that Richard is the only man not born a Moslem and an Oriental who, having performed the Hajj to Mecca and Medinah, could live with the Moslems in perfect friendship after. They considered him a *personâ grata*—something more civilized than the common run of Franks; they called him Haji Abdullah, and treated him as one of themselves. During Richard's time in Syria he raised the English name, which was going down rapidly, to its old prestige in the time of Sir Richard Wood and Lord Strathnairn, and the old days of Lord Stratford de Redcliffe. He explored all the unknown parts of Syria, Palestine, Holy Land, Haurán, the 'Aláh and Nejd; he stood between the poor peasantry and the usurers; he advanced and protected the just claims of British subjects. When a massacre appeared imminent he kept the peace. The fanatical persecution of the Christians was stopped; he stood between them and his friends the Mohammedans; he said, "They are mine, and you must not touch them;" he saved innumerable villages from slavery. In fact, he was just the man whom Rashíd Pasha, the corrupt Turkish Governor-General, could not stand; he was an avenging angel in his way. His own Consul-General was jealous of him. The Beyrout missionaries, or *rather* the British Syrian schools missionaries—for we were friends with several Beyrout missionaries, notably Dr. Thomson and Dr. Bliss—poisoned Exeter Hall against him, although they got more help from him than from any one, simply because neither he nor I were, what I believe the technical term is, "practical Protestants." The three foremost Jews set Sir Moses Montefiore and the illustrious Jewish families of London against him, because he could not stand by and see the poor plundered twice and thrice over, never getting a receipt for their money, never being allowed a paper to show what they had paid, till (when England is paying millions to suppress Slave-trade in various parts of the world) she was unconsciously abetting it, and aiding it, and protecting it, all over the Syrian villages, by the power of complaisant Consuls. The Greek Bishop abetted our being stoned at Nazareth, because he had advanced and protected the Protestant missionaries' just claim in his jurisdiction. These seven hornets were sufficient to kill and break the heart of St. Michael the archangel. They say three hornets kill a man, and six will kill a horse.

* I am now going to suppose that *all* my readers are not familiar with Syria and its Cities, its native and foreign officials, or its various Religions and Races. As a wanderer in that land, now free and independent of all employments and Governments, an impartial looker-on and a student of its politics, religions, and peculiar mode of Government, I will diverge for a moment from my subject to explain a few facts.

On arriving in Syria, one lands at Beyrout, a pretty town of no very great importance to the world. It is the concentration of all that Syria knows of comfort, luxury, and pleasure. Christian and semi-civilized, it has its soldiers and policemen, its ships and sailors under the windows, its semi-European mode of living and manners, and its free communication with Europe by telegraphs and regular mails. Steamers anchor in the open roadstead (there is no harbour, pier, or landing-place, save a few broken unclean steps leading to a small, dirty custom-house quay), an occasional merchant-ship appears, and at times some wandering man-of-war. It is ruled by a Governor subject to the *Wali*, who rules Syria, being in fact Viceroy to the Sultan. This great official lives at Damascus, and visits Beyrout for sea-bathing and to make holiday. It is also the residence of the Consuls-General, who represent foreign Powers and European influence, and are very great people in their way; and also of a large European society of the middle classes. Beyrout is backed by the high range of the Lebanon, which is inhabited by Druzes and Maronites, and ruled by a separate Governor, Franco Pasha, an able officer, independent of the *Wali*. After crossing the Lebanon and descending into the plain of the Bukâa (Cœle-Syria) Civilization, Christianity, and all free communication with the outer world, are left behind; as are comforts, luxuries, and Society, whilst the traveller is completely at the mercy of Beyrout as to how much or how little he may receive of the necessary help such as man should give to his fellow-man. For safety he is self-dependent on his own personal courage and his knowledge of the East, and woe betide the hapless one who has no friend at Beyrout, or whose Consul-General may be a little sick, or selfish, or ill-tempered, or otherwise ill-disposed.

* I wrote this on the spot, end of 1871.—I. B.

He steps forth into the solemnity of Orientalism, which increases upon him during the sometimes dreary and barren seventy-two miles journey, and he finds himself in the heart of Oriental life in the City of Damascus. This Orientalism is the great charm of "the Pearl of the East." She is still pure and innocent of anything like Europeanism. However much the wanderer may dislike it at first, the life so grows upon him that, after a time, to quit it would be a wrench. But this is what makes the demi-semi-fashionable of Beyrout hate Damascus, with a spice of fear, knowing nothing of her attractions; whilst she, on her side, lazily despises the effeminate and, to her, luxurious and feeble Beyroutine. Damascus, I have said, is the heart and capital of Syria, the residence of the *Wali* and his *entourage*, who rule Syria, who fear the strong and who oppress the weak, who persecute Christians, who starve the people, and who fill their own pockets. If his Excellency died to-morrow the voice of Syria would go up to heaven in one loud cry of execration, embodying the popular curse upon a departed tyrant's soul, "May the Lord have no mercy upon your resting-place!" Here also are the head-quarters of the Army and Police, the chief *Majlises* or Tribunals, which represent our Courts of Law; business institutions and transactions have also their place in Damascus, and, being a "Holy City," I need not say that it is the religious *chef lieu*.

Syria has always been cursed with races, tribes, and faiths enough to split up the country, and to cause all manner of confusion. For instance, the Moslem is the national religion. There are the Moslem Sunnites, or orthodox of four schools, viz. the Hanifi, Shafí, Hanbeli, Maliki; the Shí'ah heresy, locally called Metáwali (of these most are Kurds); the Nusayri (also Shiites), but their faith is little understood. The Nowar, or Gypsies, are self-styled Mohammedans. Besides these there are Shádilis or Sházlis (Dervishes and Sufis), Persian "Babis," Chaldean Yezidis, Ismailiyehs (Shí'ahs) from different parts of the East, and Wáhhabis, who keep themselves in the background. The Bedawi, who are as the sands of the desert they inhabit, are also Moslems.

After the Moslems, but conforming with them, come the Druzes, who are divided into Akkal and Juhhal; which simply means "the wise men" and "the foolish (young) men," as the former lead a more rigid life than the latter. Their belief is more or less a mystery; for policy's sake they affect the national religion, and they will lean towards the faith of whatever person they may happen to address.

The Jews are divided into Sephardim, Askenazim, Samaritan, and Karaite.

Then we come to the Christians, who number fourteen sects—Maronite (Catholic), Greek Catholic, Greek Schismatic (styled "orthodox"), Armenian Catholic, Armenian Schismatic (styled "orthodox"), Syrian Catholic; Jacobite, which is Syrian "orthodox" or non-Catholic, Latin Catholics (like the French, etc.), a few Protestants (from the missions and schools of England, Chaldea, Prussia, and the United States, and their converts), Copts, Abyssinians, Chaldean Catholic and Chaldean Schismatics (styled "orthodox"). The Catholic rites have each a liturgy different from the Latin Catholic Mass, and said in their own language; they communicate under both kinds, but there is no heresy in their belief. A French Catholic satisfies his obligations of hearing Mass on Sunday with them, but of course he cannot receive their communion under both forms.

Nineteen Europeans reside at Damascus. This is the residence of the Consuls, whose districts extend to Baghdad on the east, and to Nablus on the south, and who have all the real work to do. Some suppose that they are subject to the Consulates-General at Beyrout, but this, though the Turks desire it, is highly unadvisable, as Damascus work requires prompt and decided action and no loss of time; moreover, any order which might apply to Beyrout would be totally inapplicable at Damascus; finally, in nine cases out of ten it would proceed from the advice of a dragoman interested in the case, his superior not knowing Arabic, or perhaps never having seen Damascus.

Upon the English Consul devolves the responsibility of the post for Baghdad, and the protection of commerce, of travellers, and of some half-dozen English residents. There are, besides the Consular corps, four missions each with its school, three European religious houses (Lazarists, Franciscans, and Sisters of Charity), an English engineer, a French sanitary officer under his own Government, and, lastly, the *employés* of the French Road Company.

Whoever lives in Damascus must have good health and nerves, must be charmed with Oriental life, and must not care for society, comforts, or luxuries, but be totally occupied with some serious pursuit. Should he be a Consul—an old soldier is best—he must be accustomed to command a strong hand. The natives must be impressed by him, and know that, if attacked, he can fight. He must be able to ride hard and to rough it in mountain or desert, in order to attend to his own work, instead of sending a dragoman or a *kawwás*, who probably would not really go, or if he did might be bribed. He must have the honour and dignity of England truly at heart, and he should be a gentleman to understand fully what this means; not a man risen from the ranks, and liable to be "bullied or bribed." He should speak Arabic, Persian, and Turkish, as well as English, French, and Italian, so as not to take the hearsay of his dragomans. He must be able to converse freely with Arabs, Turks, Bedawi, Druzes, Kurds, Jews, Maronites, Afghans, and Persians, and understand their religious prejudices. He must have his reliable men everywhere, and know everything that goes on throughout the length and breadth of the country. He should have a thorough knowledge of Eastern character. He must keep a hospitable house. He should be cool, firm, and incorruptible. He must not be afraid to do his duty, however unpleasant and risky, and having done it, if his Chiefs do not back him up, *i.e.* his Consul-General, his Ambassador, and the Secretary of State for Foreign Affairs, the Turkish local authorities know he has done his duty at his own risk; they admire and they fear the individual, but they despise his Government whilst they fawn and cringe to it. Thus the interests of England, and English pride, are trampled in the dust. Such a man is Richard, and such a man is like a loadstone to the natives. Were he in no authority the country would flock to him and obey him of their own accord from his own personal influence amongst them.

But this is exactly the man who does not suit the present *Wali* and his creatures, upon whose misrepresentations and falsehoods the Porte has demanded his recall; it is no secret, for all Syria is ringing with it, and the *Wali* has it proclaimed in the bazars. I may add that all Syria is looking on with anxiety and distress lest he *should* be removed. No other class of man could hold his own against the present local Turkish authorities, and they would treat him like a kind of upper servant. If the Porte knew its own interests, it would ask to keep Richard, and discharge its own faithless *employé*. That troubles will follow his removal, I may safely prophesy; and that his successor will be insulted in the streets, and compelled by terror and sickness to run away from his post, is very possible. That is what we may come to. Let the name of England nevermore be mentioned—let her sons be incorporated with the Turkish subjects, whilst Prussians and the French keep their proper position and their national dignity.

P.S.—A month later Mohammed Rashid Pasha was *recalled, and Richard was in England.*

This, then, was the moment to press for the immediate return of the twelve unfortunates exiled to Murzuk, and to impress upon the Ottoman Authorities, who, since the death of Russia's friend, Aali Pasha, the Grand Vizier of pernicious fame, appear ready to reform a host of abuses, that the friendship of England can be secured only by scrupulous fidelity to treaties, especially to those which concern religious toleration.

An Account of Richard Burton by Salih (nom de plume of an English Missionary at Damascus).

"Burton was sound at heart. The more I saw him alone the better I liked him. At Damascus he was truly 'a brave, strong man in a blatant land.' When you got down through the crusts, you found a fearless and honest friend.

"But Burton was given to pantomime. He was always saying things to frighten old women of both sexes, and to make servant-maids stare. He took great delight in shocking goody people, and in effecting his purpose he gave free rein to his imagination. People who knew Burton partially, from meeting him at public dinners or in clubs, have generally a number of gruesome stories to retail about his cruelty and immorality. They often say truly that Burton told the horrible stories against himself. I have no doubt he did, just as he represented himself in the guise of a monster to my little boy. At the same time I am certain that Burton was incapable of either monstrous cruelty or gross immorality. I go farther, and I state it as my firm conviction that Burton was constitutionally and habitually both humane and moral. I knew Burton well, in sickness, in trouble, in disappointment, in his home, in the saddle, under fire, and in the presence of almost every condition of savage life, and I have noticed that acts of cruelty and immorality always drove him into a white heat of passion. A young English lady had been treated rudely at Damascus by a Persian, and when Burton failed in securing official redress, I was in dread for months that he would with his own hand kill the ruffian if he met him. The scoundrel, however, met his fate at other hands. Shielding the weak from cruelty and protecting the poor from oppression, constituted Captain Burton's chief work at Damascus.

"Noticing the difference between Burton's real character and that for which he got credit in many quarters, I often asked him how certain specific stories had originated. It was interesting to learn how the legends had grown. Some of them had been told of old Castilian Hidalgos and 'British sea-dogs' before Burton's grandfather was born. Others were founded on facts, but they had received so many artistic touches at camp-fires and in mess-rooms that incidents innocent in themselves had grown to monstrous dimensions. From observation and much inquiry I have long come to the conclusion that the wild stories in circulation about Burton were bogeys, partly borrowed and partly invented—mere adaptations and travellers' yarns to shock and stun and create a little boisterous fun.

"The impatience with which Burton treated my servant revealed a characteristic that had much to do with his career. 'Genius is patience,' said Sir Isaac Newton. If this definition be correct, Burton must have lacked genius. 'The Prime Minister's secret is patience,' said Pitt. If Pitt be right, Burton had no chance of ever finding his way to the Premiership, for he never learned the secret. I think Burton was not without genius. He was certainly a very clever man, but he could not put up with stupidity in others. I am afraid he sometimes delighted to stick pins in Government officials who mistook the region of the world in which he was located, or who failed to apprehend the facts communicated in his last despatch. I am afraid he never got sufficiently into diplomatic training as to overlook the weakness of his immediate superiors, and hence the higher rounds of the diplomatic ladder were not to be trodden by his feet. He was shuttle-cocked about from one pestiferous region to another till at last the Foreign Office, in a lucid moment, sent the Oriental enthusiast to Damascus.

"Burton's quarrel with missionaries was also an open sore. I do not know the full merits of the original strife, but I believe it was a somewhat mixed affair. Certain benevolent gentlemen have always had a tendency to do proxy beneficence as cheaply as possible. In picking up missionaries they have sometimes been guided more by the price than the quality. Burton, it seems, came upon some of these job-lots, and found them jobbing, as was to be expected, and, with his usual impatience, 'went for them.' Then a great uproar ensued, in which the original cause was lost sight of, and Burton received the stamp of an anti-missionary Consul. The Consular dog had got a bad name, and that was enough for some.

"When it became known that Burton was destined for Damascus, there was a kind of panic among the missionaries of Syria, and active steps were taken to prevent the appointment being carried out. The Damascus missionaries held aloof from the organized opposition. The moral character of some of Burton's immediate Christian predecessors had not been of a sort to reflect much credit on Christian missionaries, or even on British subjects; and from the missionary point of view it seemed that a moral Consul who made no religious professions might, on the whole, prove as satisfactory as an immoral one who read the service to English travellers on Sundays. Besides, it was known to be the constant aim of the Damascus missionaries to steer clear of all diplomatic interference, and to keep the Consular finger out of their pie. They gave Burton a cordial welcome as their Consul, but they also gave him clearly to understand that any action of his, friendly or unfriendly, bearing on their work, would be regarded by them as an impertinent and unfriendly act.

"Burton appreciated their kindness, and frankly accepted their conditions, and missionaries and Consul maintained the most cordial relations, and it was understood that the whole missionary body at Damascus deeply regretted Burton's recall. One fact regarding this agreement may be noticed. The restless and energetic Burton maintained the compact in the spirit, but broke it in the letter. He visited all the mission schools in the most gracious manner, examined the children thoroughly, and afterwards made some valuable suggestions to the missionaries as to the perfecting of their educational organizations. He ever after spoke of the teachers and the schools with great cordiality and unstinted praise.

"The other missionaries of Syria, with solitary exceptions, maintained their attitude of hostility to Burton, and never lost an opportunity of speaking against him, and some of them not only embellished old stories to his discredit, but invented new ones, *furor ministrat arma*, to prove his deep-seated hostility to the missionary cause. Many influential travellers pass yearly through Syria, deeply interested in the splendid educational and religious efforts that are being made to elevate that land. Everywhere they heard of the anti-Christian Consul, and the constant drip made a deep impression. Almost the only honest and praiseworthy efforts being made to lift the Holy Land out of the slough of Oriental degradation stood to the credit of the missionaries, and it was intolerable that their efforts should be thwarted by a British Consul.

"Burton might, by patience and well-doing, have worn down and outlived the hostility of these missionaries, but he had the misfortune to come into sharp conflict with the Jews, and he had thus on his flank an active, persistent, and powerful enemy.

"It would be interesting to narrate how a number of Russian and other Jews at Damascus became British subjects, but the by-paths and crooked ways would be too long and intricate for our space. Burton found himself the official head and protector of a colony of British Jews. Some of these were men of great wealth and affluence, and it was well known that the official virtue of helping them was seldom left to be its own reward.

"Burton, though always posing as an Oriental, thought fit to hew Oriental prejudice against the grain. He might have seen his beautiful wife flashing in brilliants, roped in pearls, and riding the best blood Arab of the desert; but he threw away all these tokens of appreciation in obedience to an occidental prepossession in favour of common honesty.

"Burton found that his Jews were living by usury. Some of them were known to charge as little as thirty per cent., but rates ran up to sixty, or more. 'His mouth is full of water * and he cannot bark' is a common Arab proverb, but Burton had nothing in his mouth, and he barked ferociously. His official duty was to urge the recognition of British claims, and insist on their being paid. That was the form that 'law and order' took at Damascus. What did it matter if the people were starving! At the word of the Consul a band of Bashi-Bazouks would swoop down on the defaulting villagers, eat their food, lie in their beds, insult their wives and daughters, until the usurer was satisfied. Should the villagers be unable to pay, they were not only evicted, but driven like cattle to prison, there to rot till they had paid the uttermost farthing. Burton did not like the business. He grew fierce, declared in the strongest language at his command that he would not be 'Bumbailiff' in such transactions. I am inclined to think that in this case, as in most

* Meaning bribes.—I. B.

others, Burton's impatience led him into doing the right thing in the wrong way. He was indignant, his blood was up, and on being asked gently what was the use of a Consul at Damascus if he did not enforce British claims, he lost the composure befitting the diplomatic service.

"The storm broke. The *Alliance Israelite* took up the case of '*poor Israel.*' Noble, and humane, and generous Jews in England ranged themselves on the side of 'their persecuted brethren.' Some of them would have been more fierce than Burton had they known the truth. Correspondence followed, and the archives of the Foreign Office now contain Burton's splendid vindications, which may some day see the light."

"The Recall of Captain Burton.

"To the Editor of the *Civil Service Gazette.*

"Sir,—I have just seen some letters from Damascus, from which I learnt a few facts that may interest you with reference to the recall of Captain Burton.

"The Consulate was left in charge of Mr. Jago, who, however, was so alarmed at certain demonstrations of dissatisfaction on the part of the natives that he prudently took advantage of an opportune fever, and left the town and the Consulate to take care of itself. The English Government is, therefore, entirely unrepresented in Damascus.

"The Kurds who inhabit the suburb of Damascus, called the Salahíyyeh, say that now Captain Burton has gone, there is no one who can protect them from the extortions of the Governor-General, and have notified their intention of leaving *en masse.* As they are about ten thousand fighting men, they will not improve the pacific aspect of the country when they are let loose over it, feeling that they have no protector but their sword.

"The Mohammedans, whose 'fanatical aversion to Captain Burton' is the ostensible pretext for his recall, have been holding mass meetings, and even praying publicly in the mosques that God will send him back to them. Letters are flowing in every day from village sheikhs and Bedawin chiefs, asking that he may return to Damascus, as there is no one else to whom they can appeal for help or succour.

"So strong is the feeling, that Mrs. Burton was obliged to slip away secretly, as the people wished to retain her as a hostage in order to make sure that Captain Burton would go back to them.

"In addition to these facts, which I can vouch for, I can tell you that, from my own experience of the country, I feel sure that Captain Burton's absence will be a source of great inconvenience (to put it mildly) to intending travellers this next winter. If you have any friends who propose visiting Syria, you cannot do better than advise them not to do so, as there will assuredly be troubles before long.

"I cannot pretend to enter into the real reasons for this blunder on the part of the Foreign Office (though they are not hard to guess), but of one thing I feel assured, and that is that the mistake would never have been made had Lord Stratford de Redcliffe been still at Constantinople.

"I am, Sir, yours truly,
"E. H. PALMER.

"St. John's College, Cambridge."

"THREATENED TROUBLES IN SYRIA.

"To the Editor of the *Standard*.

"Sir,—Forewarned will not be forearmed in this case, for the mischief is half done already by the actions of her Majesty's Government.

"I came to Syria in February last with a special mission from the Palestine Exploration Fund. I have since been travelling over the length and breadth of the land, and this, with several years' previous acquaintance with the East, enables me to see more of the real state of the country than falls to the lot of the ordinary tourist.

"In the early spring I found Syria in an abnormal state of excitement, arising from many causes. That excitement has gone on increasing, chiefly for five reasons: 1. The injustice and rapacity of the Governor-General (*Wali*), Mohammed Rashíd Pasha, who now misgoverns Syria. 2. The agitation kept up by Egypt, with whom Syria and its Governor sympathize only too strongly, and with whom they will act the moment opportunity offers. 3. The ruin of the peasantry, crushed by exorbitant taxes, starved by a bad season, and devoured by Jewish money-lenders. 4. The way in which the *Wali* pits sect against sect for his own political ends; and in this land, where party feeling runs so high, nothing is easier. And, 5. The strong Christian movement, none the less strong for being under the surface—this has already been noticed in some English papers.

"There was but *one* man in Syria who both saw and protested against the many and glaring acts of injustice done by the *Wali*, and this was her Britannic Majesty's Consul at Damascus, Captain R. F. Burton, whom her Majesty's Foreign Office have thought fit to remove, giving ear to the tale raised two years ago, by certain missionaries and others, that Moslem fanaticism was working against him. Knowing the people and the country as well as I do, I hesitate not one moment to say that this is a deliberate lie (and I am ready to prove it such) invented by Captain Burton's enemies. Few men, if any, would have got on as well as he has with all classes here, Mohammedans and Metaweli, Greek Catholics and Syrians, Protestants and Latins. He visited and was visited by the religious sheikhs, and especially by the Emir Abd el Kadir of Algerian fame. This prince is looked upon as the leader of Mohammedan religion here. These facts are sufficient to show how false is the plea of Captain Burton's not being able to deal with Mohammedans on account of their fanaticism. Only to-day I have heard numbers of Moslems deplore his removal, which pleased only the *Wali* and his creatures, and a few Jews engaged in nefarious usury. I dwell upon these points, as I feel convinced that unless his successor be a man of *his* stamp—which will be hard to find—he will sink to that state of subserviency to the *Wali* to which the Consuls of other nations at Damascus have sunk. They are weak and timid, and completely under the *Wali.* The English Consul was the only man of independence, but now that Syria is becoming of vital importance to us on account of the Euphrates Valley Railroad, our name and *prestige* must go, through her Majesty's Government recalling, at the instigation of a Turkish Pasha, the only man fit to represent Great Britain in Syria. The *Wali*, having succeeded by his vile intrigues in displacing one of the most efficient of her Majesty's Consular officers, will feel that there is no one to check his malpractices; the peasantry, sooner or later, must rise; the great Christian movement will be crushed, not without bloodshed, for the converts now number many thousands of resolute men of all classes, and we must be prepared for the worst. I venture to predict that before many months have passed, the troubles of Syria will have drawn upon her the eyes of Europe, and when blood has been shed England will see the error she has committed in throwing her influence here to the dogs, and obeying the wishes of Rashíd Pasha.

"I am, Sir, etc.,

"CHAS. F. TYRWHITT-DRAKE.

"Damascus."

"THE DAMASCUS CONSULATE.

"The following letter, to which we have alluded in a leading article, on the subject of Captain Burton's recall, has been addressed to the Editor of the *Times*, by a well-known Syrian traveller:—

"Sir,—In a letter I addressed to you, dated August 17th, on the state that Syria, especially in the Damascus district, was likely to fall into in consequence of the recall, from his post as Consul at Damascus, of the only man who had the courage to resist and check the malpractices of the notoriously corrupt and cruel Governor-General Mohammed Rashíd Pasha, I predicted that troubles would quickly ensue. On the 18th of August—the day that Captain Burton left Damascus—a raid was made into the Christian quarter by Mustafa Bey, Mir Alai of Zabtiyeh (Chief of Police), a most fanatical Mahomedan, with two hundred men, for the purpose of arresting certain Moslems suspected of a leaning to Christianity, and who had been decoyed from their own quarter by a police spy, Mahmud Bey Adham, a man who had by some means become possessed of their secret. Happily, these suspects were able to take refuge in the house of an English consular dragoman just as they were being arrested, and though the *gérant* of her Majesty's Consulate ordered them to be given up, yet the matter became so public that the *Wali* feared to proceed to extreme measures, and released them after a day's imprisonment. The affair, however, will not stop here, though it may lie dormant awhile.

"On August 23, three days after Captain Burton's leaving Beyrout, the Protestant missionaries were prevented by the *Kaimakam* (Governor) from making some small additions to their school at Rasheyya. The Rev. Messrs. Wright and Scott requested the *gérant* of her Majesty's Consulate to procure them an order from the Government to enable them to go on. A so-called order was immediately procured, but, of course, it was utterly useless; a second produced no better effect.

"This is but the commencement, yet it serves to show the way in which English missionaries will be hindered, and how English influence is to be crushed. It would be, to any one unacquainted with Syria, an incredible matter if I were to say how our national *prestige* has fallen since the last ten days. I have some twenty letters from Moslem sheikhs of towns and villages, religious sheikhs and men of influence, as well as from Druzes and Christians, which I have been asked to forward to Captain Burton, as the writers think that their urgent entreaties may favour his return.

"The Government organ, *El Hadikat el Akhbar*, has written a most shameful article on Captain Burton's recall, stating that he was not only on bad terms with the authorities, but also with his colleagues and all British-protected Jews, and other lies equally base. A few Jews, whom he refused to help in scandalous and illegal transactions, of course detest him, and have been secretly aiding the *Wali* against him. A most fulsome article, too, appeared in another paper, *El Suriva* (The Syria), from the pen of the *Wali* himself in praise of the gentleman now in charge of her Majesty's Consulate here.

"I fear to take up too much of your valuable space by dilating on the subject, but I am every day more convinced that there will be great trouble in this unhappy land of misrule.

"I am, Sir, etc.,

"Chas. F. Tyrwhitt-Drake.

"Damascus, September."

"Revival of Christianity in Syria.

"To the Editor of the *Tablet*.

"Sir,—I have just seen the account published in the *Tablet* of the 16th and 23rd of September, of the revival of Christianity in Syria. I can only say that you have an exceedingly well-informed correspondent, but one who seems hardly aware what enormous proportions this movement is assuming in the districts of Hums, Hamáh, and even Aleppo. The number of these diverts from Islam is almost impossible to calculate, but I believe that in the whole of Syria twenty to twenty-five thousand is a moderate computation.

"Now that Rashíd Pasha, of infamous memory, is removed from Syria, can nothing be done to bring back the twelve Sházlis banished to Africa? Will neither England nor any other Christian Power say one word in their favour? Is the policy of maintaining the unity of Turkey to be so strictly adhered to, that not even a harsh word is to be said to her though she deliberately breaks her treaties and solemn obligations: when, after promising religious freedom to all her subjects, she invariably persecutes those who dare to leave the religion of Mohammed, not perhaps directly, but by some subterfuge, as bringing against the so-called 'renegades' a charge of evasion from conscription, or desertion from the army.

"Hoping that your advocacy may do something to bring about the return of these twelve martyrs, whose wives and families would have been starved here long ago had it not been for the liberality of their co-sectarians,

"I remain, Sir, etc.,

"CHAS. F. TYRWHITT-DRAKE.

"Damascus, November 13."

Richard wrote at the end of his time in Syria, just before his recall—

"My time here is marked and rendered bitter by contact with tyranny and an oppression which even this land of doleful antecedents cannot remember. The politics of the unworthy *Wali*, Rashíd Pasha, are alternately French and Russian, and, like all Orientals educated in Europe, he hates Europeans. I have been brought into collision with him, by his utterly ignoring the just claims and rights of British subjects and *protégés*, and he was supported by those whose duty it was to oppose him, so I had to battle alone with hands bound."

Later on, after his recall, he writes—

"But they, his powerful protectors, failed, and truth from my poor pen and tongue prevailed, and Rashíd was recalled in disgrace and degradation, and threatened with irons and fetters. Every measure which I had ventured to recommend during my time was ordered to be carried out. The reform was so thorough and complete that her Majesty's Ambassador at Constantinople was directed officially to compliment the Porte upon its newly initiated line of progress. But Pashas soon fall into bad ways, and it is always the case of 'new broom.' The irony of events is extraordinary. Damascus is the civil, military, and ecclesiastical Capital of the country, the head-quarters of the Government and the High Courts of Appeal, the residence of the chief dignitaries, where the Consul-General ought to live, and the Vice-Consul for the shipping duties at Beyrout. But Beyrout is safe; Damascus is not always so. Persia has observed this long ago, and have a Consul-General. Russia, Prussia, France, and Italy do not speak to the Capital through Vice-Consuls, but Consuls; yet, to gratify the F.O.'s most *un*distinguished servant Mr. Eldridge, as soon as I was gone, a Vice-Consul was appointed for the Capital—a creature of his own. Therefore, to the detriment of British interest, to the injury of English residents, missionaries, and school-teachers, we took rank after Spain, Portugal, and Greece, because their representatives are often *rayyàhs*, or subjects of the Porte, and take precedence of the British Vice-Consul. Yet the English public is now surprised to hear from my successor that English travellers have been made prisoners at Kerak."

I must now return, and finish my own Eastern career, more for the sake of showing the goodness of the Syrian heart, than for any other interest. I am bound, though late, to bear testimony to them.

After seeing Richard off, I had a cold eight hours' drive over the Lebanon, arrived at the *khan* at Shtora, found my horse in excellent condition, and slept for a few hours. Early in the morning I rode to see Miss Wilson, who kindly insisted on my remaining a day with her. Mr. Tyrwhitt-Drake, a *kawwás*, and servants and horses, met me here, and escorted me back to Bludán; but we lost our way in the mountains, and had an eleven hours' hard scramble. I was ill, tired, and harassed, and was thankful to find my friend Mrs. Rattray, who came over to keep me company. She was as much troubled as I was myself. I do not care who says to the contrary, but the world *in general* is a good place; for, although a *few* bad people make everything and everybody as miserable as they can—permitted, I infer, by an all-wise Providence, like mosquitoes, snakes, and scorpions, to prevent our becoming too attached to this life, and ceasing to work for the other, where they cannot enter—the general rule is good, and whoever is in trouble, as I have said, will always meet with kindness, comfort, and sympathy, from some quarter or other.

I had every right to expect, in a land where official position is everything, where love and respect accompanies power and Government influence, where women are of but small account, that I should be, morally speaking, trampled underfoot. I do not know how to describe with sufficient gratitude, affection, and pleasure the treatment I met with throughout Syria. The news spread like wild-fire. All the surrounding villages poured in. The house and the garden were always full of people—my poor, of course, but others too. Moslems flung themselves on the ground, shedding bitter tears, and tearing their beards, with a passionate grief for the man "whose life" they were reported to wish to take. The incessant demonstrations of sorrow were most harassing, the poor crying out, "Who will take care of us now?" The Moslems: "What have we done that your *Díwan* (Government) has done this thing to us? They sent us a man who made us so happy and prosperous, and protected us, and we were so thankful; and why now have they taken him from us? What have we done? Were we not good and thankful, and quiet? What can we do? Send some of us to go over to your land, and kneel at the feet of your Queen." This went on for days, and I received, from nearly all the country round, little deputations of Shaykhs, bearing letters of affection, or condolence, or grief, or praise. These sad days filled me with one gnawing thought—"How shall I tear the East out of my heart by the roots, and adapt myself to the bustling, struggling, everyday life of Europe?"

I broke up our establishment, packed up my husband's books, and sent them to England, settled all our affairs, had all that was to accompany me transferred to Damascus, and parted with the mountain servants. Two pets—the donkey that had lost a foot, and a dog that was too ill to recover—had to be shot and buried in the garden.

When all these sad preparations were finished, I bade adieu to the Anti-Lebanon with a heavy heart, and for the last time, choking with emotion, I rode down the mountain, and through the plain of Zebedáni, with a very large train of followers. I found it hard to leave the spot where I had hoped to leave my mortal coil.

I had a sorrowful ride into Damascus, and I met the *Wáli* driving in State, with all his suite. He looked radiant, and saluted me. I did not return his salute, and he told his Staff that he was afraid I would shoot him. Somebody did that a little later on. He looked less radiant when the news of his own recall reached him a few days later, with a special telegram, that if he delayed more than twenty-four hours, he was to be sent in chains. He fought hard to stay, and I do not wonder, for he had a splendid position, and had bought lands and built a palace, which he never lived in; and he had to give up all his ill-gotten goods, lands, and palace, squeezed out of the peasantry.

At Damascus I had to go through the same sad scenes, upon a much larger scale than I had gone through at Bludán. All our kind friends, native and European, came to stay about me to the last.

I saw that Richard's few enemies were very anxious for me to go, and that all the rest were equally anxious to detain me as a kind of pledge for his return. I reflected that it would be right that I should coolly and quietly perform every single work I had to undertake—to sell everything, to pay all debts, and arrange every liability of any kind incurred by my husband, to pack and despatch to England our personal effects, to make innumerable friendly adieux, to make a provision or find a happy home for every single being—man or beast—that had been dependent upon us. This was rendered slow and difficult, as the Government left us *pro tem.* without a farthing. A servant generally gets a month's notice with wages and a character, but without any defence we were annihilated as if by dynamite. At last I made our case known to Uncle Gerard, who telegraphed to the Imperial Ottoman Bank, "to let his niece have any money that she wanted." Before I left I went and dressed our little chapel with all the pious things in my possession.

On the day of the sale I could not bear to stay near the house, so I went up to Arba'in, or "the Forty Martyrs," above our house, on Jebel Kaysún, about fifteen hundred feet high, and I gazed on my dear Salahíyyeh below, in its sea of green, and my pearl-like Damascus, and the desert sand, and watched the sunset on the mountains for the last time. I also met some Mogháribehs, who came up to pray there, and who prognosticated all sorts of good fortune to me.

In one sense I was glad, because I was a kind of hostage, giving the lie to his enemies. If there had been anything wrong, I should assuredly have paid the forfeit. I had no anxiety, for though I had magnificent offers—two from Moslems to shoot certain official enemies, as they passed in their carriage, from behind a rock, and another from a Jew to put some poison in their coffee—I slept in perfect security, amongst my Moslem and Kurdish friends, with my windows and doors open, in that Kurdish village, Salahíyyeh. Between us and the City was a quarter of an hour's ride through orchards that were wild and lawless—at least, in my time, no one would come there from sunset to sunrise, and timid people, not even in the day, without a guard. We had the house on a three years' lease, and my bedroom window and the *Muezzin's* Minaret were on a level, and almost joined, so that we could talk to each other. I used to join him in the "call to prayer," and he used to try not to laugh. I never missed a pin; I never had anything but blessings. All my work took me some time, but I resolved, whatever the wrench would cost me, I would set out the moment it was finished. My husband being gone, I had no business, no place there; I knew it would be better taste to leave.

We all began to perceive that the demonstrations were beginning to be of an excitable nature; the Moslems assembling in cliques at night, a hundred here and a hundred there, to discuss the strange matter. They were having prayers in the mosques for Richard, and making promises of each giving so much to the poor if they obtained their wish. They continually poured up to

Salahíyyeh with tears and letters, begging him to return, and I felt that my presence and distress only excited them the more. I left more quickly because I was informed that my presence was exciting the people, who lived in hopes of his return, and his non-appearance was causing an irritability that might break out into open mutiny and cause another massacre. They were beginning with the usual signs of meeting in clusters in the streets, in discussing the affair in the mosques, in the bazaars, in the *cafés*, and putting up public prayers for his return.

As half the City wanted to accompany me on the road, and I was afraid that a demonstration might result, I thought I should be wise to slip away quietly. My two best friends, Abd el Kadir and the Hon. Jane Digby el Mezrab (Lady Ellenborough), were with me till the last, and, accompanied by Charley Drake and our two most faithful dragomans, who had never deserted me and put themselves and all they possessed at my disposal, Hanna Asar and Mr. Awadys, I left Damascus an hour before dawn, sending word to all my friends that parting was too painful to me.

> "Linger not out the hours of separation's day
> Till for sheer grief my soul to ruin fall a prey." *

I felt life's interest die out of me as I jogged along for weary miles, wishing mental good-byes to every stick and stone. I had been sickening for some days with fever. I had determined not to be ill at Damascus, and so detained. Pluck kept me up, but having braved the fatal 13th, and set out upon it, I was not destined to reach Beyrout.

When I reached that part of the Lebanon looking down upon the sea, near Khan el Karáyyeh, my fever had increased to such an extent that I became delirious, and had to be set down on the road-side, where I moaned with pain and could not proceed. Half an hour from the road was the village of my little Syrian maid. I was carried to her father's house, and lay there for ten days very ill, and was nursed by her and by my English maid. Many kind friends, English and native, came to see me from Beyrout and from the villages round about.

Mr. Tyrwhitt-Drake took our house, part of the furniture, the faithful Habíb, and the *sais*, my two horses, which I could not bear to sell into stranger hands, the dogs, and the Persian cat, "Tuss," who, however, ran away the day after I left, and has never been seen or heard of since. All the other servants and animals were well provided for in other ways. I was offered £15 for my white donkey,

* Charles T. Pickering, "The Last Singers of Bukhára."

but I could not bear to sell him, so I left him also with Mr. Tyrwhitt-Drake, and he eventually found a good home with our successor, Mr. Green (afterwards Sir W. Kirby Green), and died. The bull-terriers also died natural deaths with Mr. Drake. It was a great relief to know that the former would never become a market donkey, nor the latter pariahs, nor be beaten, stoned, and ill-used. I was obliged to sell Richard's *rahwán*, and I sent it to the purchaser, the Vice-Consul who succeeded, from the village where I was ill. He came to pay me a visit. Although the poor horse had only been there one night, this gentleman told me he had no trouble in finding the house, for as soon as the *rahwán* got near the turn leading off the diligence road, he started off at full gallop, and never stopped till he reached the door, nor would he go anywhere else.

I went down to Beyrout as soon as I was well enough to move, and, assisted by Mr. Watkins of the Imperial Ottoman Bank, Mr. Drake, and Mr. Zal Zal, embarked in the Russian ship *Ceres*, the same that had brought me formerly from Alexandria to Beyrout. As we were about to steam out, an English Vice-Consul in the Levant gaily waved his hand to me, and said laughingly, "Good-bye, Mrs. Burton. I have been sixteen years in the service, and I know twenty scoundrels in it who are never molested; but I never saw a Consul 'recalled' except for something disgraceful, and certainly never for an Eastern Pasha. You'll find it's all right; they would hardly do such a thing to such a man as Burton." We were a fortnight at sea, detained by fogs and two collisions.

On reaching London I found Richard in one room in a very small hotel. He had made no defence—had treated the whole thing *de haut en bas*, so I applied myself for three months to putting his case clearly before the Foreign Office in his own name. I went to the Foreign Office, where I had thirteen friends, and knew most of its Masters, and I asked them to tell me frankly what was the reason of his recall.

Firstly, I was told it had been represented that he was in danger from the Mohammedans. That was *too easily* disproved by fifty-eight letters from every creed, nation, and tongue of the thirty-six in Syria, from Bedawi tribes, Druzes, Moslems of all categories, from the Ulemá, from Abd el Kadir; and, like proverbs, this homely correspondence sprung from the heart illustrated the native character better than books, and was a fair specimen of local Oriental scholarship. What the Press and the Public thought about it in various nations was the same—in forty-eight articles chiefly from the English Press and the Levant, and five leaders. All that England has ever done to *him* of neglect and slight has never touched him in any man's mind. He was the brightest gem in his country's crown, and his country did not deserve him. I went the rounds of my friends repeatedly in the Foreign Office, and insisted on having a reason for the recall.

When the Mohammedan question was disposed of, it was found that it was because "Burton had written a letter to convoke the Druzes to a political meeting in the Haurán." I asked if I might have a copy of that letter, and, having kept the *original* copy, I was able to put them side by side in the report, showing it was forged by Rashíd Pasha. He was then accused of opposing missionary work, because he had written advising a schoolmistress, in the kindest spirit, to try and prevent her husband entering into *mining* speculations: as there was so much cheating going on, he was afraid he would drop several thousand pounds. "Mining" was *somehow* changed to "missionary;" but that fact was disposed of by the regretful and indignant letters at his recall from all the *other* missionaries. He was accused of being influenced against the Jews because he protected the poor villagers from paying their debts twice and thrice over to the usurers, who took their money and refused receipts, leaving nothing to show. Amongst the letters one Jew wrote home that Captain Burton "was influenced by his Catholic wife against the Jews." I am proud to say that I have never in my life tried to influence my husband to do anything wrong, and I am prouder still to say that if I *had* tried I should not have succeeded, and should have only lost his respect. The Jews have never had a better friend than me. I distinctly divide the usurers from the Jews, just as I divide the good, honest, loyal half of the Irish Catholic nation from the Fenians and the moonlighters, who are mostly Irish living in England and America, and who go over for the purpose of fomenting disturbance. I have suppressed many a thing that civilized and idealized Jews would be ashamed to have known of their lower and fanatical brethren in the East and elsewhere. He was accused by the Greek bishop of firing into "harmless Greeks at play," because he fired a shot in the air to call assistance when we were being stoned to death.

Mr. Eldridge, who was quite a Russian at heart, went on the plan of never compromising himself by writing an official order to Richard; he never wrote him anything but private notes. Richard said he could not use private notes in official life as proofs. I thought this very wrong. I saw a *plan* in this mode of action, so I used to keep them in a portfolio till wanted, so that when I put the case together I was able to state the facts very correctly. I have got several packets of that Blue Book now, if anybody wants to see one. It ended by Richard getting the *nearest thing* to an apology that one could expect out of a Government office, and an offer of several small posts, which he indignantly refused. In his journal I find he was offered Pará, but would not take it—"Too small a berth for me after Damascus."

Shortly after, Mr. L—— offered him, that if he would go to Iceland to inspect some sulphur mines, he would pay his passage there and back, and his expenses, and if he found he could conscientiously give a good report of the sulphur mines, that he would give him £2000. He went, and as we were at a very low ebb, and as Mr. L—— did not pay for *me*, I was left with my father and mother, which was a very fortunate circumstance, because my mother died shortly after. I may put in a parenthesis that, though Richard was able conscientiously to give a *splendid* report of the mines, Mr. L—— did not pay him the £2000. The trip resulted in a book called "Ultima Thule: a Summer in Iceland" * (2 vols.), which was not published till 1875, and his "Zanzibar City, Island, and Coast" (2 vols., 1872); and he wrote a lecture for the Society of Antiquaries, a "History of Stones and Bones from the Haurán," and "Human Remains and other Articles from Iceland." We had ten months of great poverty and official neglect (but great kindness from Society), during which we were reduced to our last £15, and after that we had nothing to do but to sit on our boxes in the street, for we had *nothing*, not a *prospect* of anything; but we let nobody know that. He remarked one day when we were out on business—

"Lunch, one shilling,
Soup not filling."

And I noticed afterwards, in his journal, that he had longed for some oysters, and looked at them long; but he says, "They were three shillings a dozen—awful, forbidden luxury!"

At last my uncle, Lord Gerard, asked us up to Garswood, and we debated if we had a right to accept it or not. I begged him to do so, as I thought it might bring us good luck. We were alone in a railway compartment, when one of the £15 rolled out of my purse, and slid between the boards of the carriage and the door, reducing us to £14. I sat on the floor and cried, and he sat down by me with his arm round my waist, trying to comfort me. Uncle Gerard kept us one month, paid our fare up and down, and, without knowing that we wanted anything, gave me £25, and from that

* It is a valuable book, chiefly for its philosophical transactions, antiquarian proceedings, and philological miscellanies, and the mineral resources of the island. —I. B.

time one little help or another came to keep us alive without our asking for anything. We sold some of our writings, and it was discovered that some back pay was due to Richard.

During this ten months at home, we saw a great deal of Winwood Reade, whom all know by his travels in Africa, his many literary works, of which the cleverest, but the most harmful, was the "Martyrdom of Man," of which he presented Richard with a copy, which was carefully treasured till about six months before Richard's death. He told us the following account of a ghost story :—

There was a place in Africa or in India (I forget at this distance of time), where there was a haunted bungalow, and Winwood Reade was longing to see a ghost, as he was very sceptical about the existence of such things. In this particular bungalow there was a room on the ground floor, with folding doors of glass that opened to the ground, leading out into the compound. Every night at twelve o'clock these glass doors (being locked) slowly opened outwards, and the ghosts of three surgeons who had died of cholera appeared in their winding-sheets. Winwood Reade engaged the bungalow for the night, it being quite empty, but he could not induce anybody, for love or money, to go with him. At last he tempted a black boy, by large promises of money, to pass one night there, and the boy said *if he might sleep on the roof* he would, but nothing would induce him to go inside the house. So they started forth, and Winwood took with him a good novel, his gun, his watch, and plenty of brandy and water, and towards eleven o'clock made himself very comfortable on some cushions in a corner of the room in full view of the window. As his watch pointed to twelve, the doors slowly opened, he seized his gun, and in a moment the three white figures appeared. I said, breathless with excitement, "And what did you do, Winwood?" He smiled and hesitated, and said, "To tell the honest truth, I dropped my gun and fainted, and when I came to I got out of the house as quick as I could, called the boy, went away, and never went back." He was such a brave man he could afford to own this.

Richard writes at this time in his journal, "I called on some old friends, and as I came out of the house I heard the servants whisper, 'Why, Captain Burton looks like an old gypsy.'" This was after his recall.

We had one very pleasant evening at Lady Marian Alford's. She had been building her house at Prince's Gate, and Miss Hosmer had sculptured her fountain; it was the opening night. Lady Marian wanted to prepare a little surprise for her friends, so she made Richard dress as a Bedawin Shaykh, and Khamoor (my Arab girl) and me as Moslem women of Damascus. I was supposed to have brought this Shaykh over to introduce him into a little English society. He spoke Arabic to Khamoor and me, and broken English with a few words of French to the rest of the party. It was a delightful little party, and we enjoyed it very much, and—though they all knew him—nobody recognized Richard, which was very amusing; but presently the Prince of Wales and the Duke of Edinburgh were announced, and Lady Marian had to go out to prepare them for this little joke, which amused them immensely, and so it gradually had to ooze out. There was a delightful supper, three tables each of eight. Khamoor in her Eastern dress came in with coffee on a tray on her head, and presented it kneeling to the Prince and the Duke, and to the others standing. Everything that Lady Marian Alford did was so graceful.

I see that Richard notices in his journal a correspondence between himself and the Rev. Herbert Vaughan, D.D. (our present Cardinal), which I imagine was about the Sházlis. And he also notices that his name is again left out of Sir Roderick Murchison's address, and asks, "Why? Old Murchison hates me."

Again speaking of Sir R. Murchison, Richard writes, "He was anxious to pay due honour to our modern travellers, to Livingstone and Gordon, Speke and Grant. He has done me the honour of not honouring me." Later on: "Received a card from him to go and see him."

We also went to Ashridge, Lord Brownlow's, on a visit to Lady Marian Alford, which visit we enjoyed immensely, where we met Lord Beaconsfield and numbers of other delightful people.

He also notices in his journal: "Had the satisfaction of hearing of Rashíd Pasha's disgrace and removal. Wonder if he wishes he had not crossed swords with me."

This year was the Tichborne trial, and Richard was subpœnaed by him, but his evidence did more good to the family. Amongst other things the Claimant said to Richard, "That he had met me in Rio de Janeiro, and that I had recognized him as a long-lost cousin; but, on fixing the dates, it was proved that I had sailed from Rio for London a week before the Claimant arrived there." We had one very lively meeting at the Royal Geographical Society. He writes—

"Rassam stood up about a native message to Livingstone. Colonel Rigby contradicted, and said there were no Abyssinians in Zanzibar. They began to contradict me, so I made it very lively, for

I was angry, and proved my point, showing that my opponents had spoken falsely. My wife laughed, because I moved from one side of the table to the other unconsciously, with the stick that points to the maps in my hand, and she said that the audience on the benches looked as if a tiger was going to spring in amongst them, or that I was going to use the stick like a spear upon my adversary, who stood up from the benches.* To make the scene more lively, my wife's brothers and sisters were struggling in the corner to hold down their father, an old man, who had never been used to public speaking, and who slowly rose up in speechless indignation at hearing me accused of making a misstatement, and was going to address a long oration to the public about his son-in-law Richard Burton. As he was slow and very prolix he would never have sat down again, and God only knows what he *would* have said; they held on to his coat-tails, and were preparing, in event of failure, some to dive under the benches, and some to bolt out of the nearest door."

We went a great deal into Society those ten months, and we saw much of the two best literary houses of the day, where one always met *la haute Bohème*, the most interesting Society in London, mixed with the best of everything, and those were Lord Houghton's and Lord Strangford's.

About this time we went to visit Mr. ——, our then publisher, at his country-house, where he showed us all that was comfortable and luxurious, with ten horses in the stable—everything else to match. He gave us a large literary dinner, at which Lord Houghton, with his quiet chuckle, called out across the table, "I say, Burton, don't you feel as if we were drinking out of poor authors' skulls?" Upon which Richard laughed, and tapped his own head for an answer.

Richard was very anxious that Alexandretta should be the chief port in Syria, into whose lap the railway would pour the wealth of the province, for it is the only good port the country possesses on the eastern coast of the Mediterranean. Alexandretta, if freed from its stagnant marshes, would be magnificent; the railway should go to Damascus, Jerusalem, and Aleppo.

With regard to Sir Roderick Murchison, his journal again contained the following, speaking of one of his books:—

"Since these pages went to print Sir R. I. Murchison has passed away, full of years and of honours. I had not the melancholy satisfaction of seeing for the last time our revered Chief, one of whose latest actions was to oppose my reading a paper about the so-called Victoria Nyanza before the Royal Geographical Society; whilst

* I never saw Richard so angry in my life; his lips puffed out with rage.—I. B.

another was to erase my name from the list of the Nile explorers when revising his own biography. But peace be to his manes! I respect the silence of a newly made grave."

We went, for the first time in our lives, and the last, to a great banquet at the Mansion House, which amused us very much. Whenever we wanted to make any remarks at dinner-time we made them in Arabic, thinking that probably no one would understand us. Curiously, the people who sat next to us turned round, and said in Arabic, "Yes, you are perfectly right; we were just thinking the same thing;" and Richard said, "We spoke Arabic thinking nobody would understand us;" and they said, "It is most probable that out of all this huge crowd we are the only four people who happen to speak Arabic, and happen to sit together."

Another very interesting visit we paid was to the Surrey County Lunatic Asylum, Wandsworth Common, where the doctor, who was a friend of my husband's, invited us to spend the day and dine with him, and he showed us over everything; but I know that I, for one, felt awfully glad when we left it; some of the faces that I saw there I can see now if I shut my eyes and think.

In 1872, we were on a visit at Knowsley, the Earl of Derby's, and we planted there a cedar of Lebanon, which we had brought; and we went over the alkali works at St. Helen's, very interesting to Richard, who did not know so much of the "Black Country" as we did. We then went to Uncle Gerard's, where we met the Muriettas (now Marchesa de Santurce), and many other pleasant people. Here we went down some coal-pits (265 fathoms) for further information, and we planted more cedars of Lebanon and a bit of Abraham's oak, which we brought from Mamre, some distance from Hebron.

That year my mother got very ill, and we all assembled in town to be with her. She had been paralyzed for nine years, and, nevertheless, had been strong, active, and cheerful, and enabled in some fashion to enjoy life. Her strong brain kept her alive.

At this time the public, answering an appeal of mine in the *Tablet*, describing the poverty and destitution of the Syrian Inland Churches, sent me wherewith to furnish six of them, which has never been forgotten out there.

In 1872, poor General Beatson died at New Swindon. Richard sent thirty-two species of plants from the summit of the Libanus to the British Museum; and this year he got the news from Syria that he had gained his cause about the stoning at Nazareth. The

Greek Bishop had brought an action against him before the Tribunal, and Richard won it with honour.

He wrote and lectured on the "Stones and Bones of the Haurán," March, 1872, and "Human Remains in Iceland" in late 1872.

I attended the Tichborne trial, and saw Sir John Coleridge examine my cousin, Katty Radcliffe. Richard whispered to me, "The next thing plaintiff will do, will be to call himself Lord Aberdeen." I came home from there, and found the other brother, Father Coleridge, S.J., giving my mother Communion. At this time, too, we attended all the learned societies, where Richard generally made speeches. We also went down to the Duke and Duchess of Somerset's, where we met Lady Ulrica Thynne, the Brinsley Sheridans, and afterwards, at their house, brilliant and fascinating Mrs. Norton.

Charles Reade, the well-known author, who was a great friend of ours, gave us a delightful dinner and pleasant evening, asking a great many actors and actresses to meet us. Sir Frederick Leighton began to paint Richard on the 26th of April, and it was very amusing. Richard was so anxious that he should paint his necktie and his pin, and kept saying to him every now and then, "Don't make me ugly, don't, there's a good fellow;" and Sir Frederick kept chaffing him about his vanity, and appealing to me to know if he was not making him pretty enough. That is the picture that Sir Frederick has now, and is going to leave to the nation; and both Richard and I always retained the pleasantest memory of the many happy hours we passed in his studio. Richard was examined on the Consular Committee, and made them all laugh. He complained that the salary of Santos had been very inadequate to his position; he had been obliged to use his own little capital to supplement. He was asked how his predecessor (a baronet) had managed, and he answered, "By living in one room over a shop, and washing his own stockings." Richard attended the Levée on May 13th.

We went to a Foreign Office party, where Musurus Pasha explained to Richard why he was obliged to go against him, by the order of the Turkish Government about Syria, and Richard said to him, "Well, Pasha, I did not know that you had; but I can tell you that, though I never practically wish evil to my enemies, they all come to grief, and you are bound to have a bit of bad luck on my account." The next day Musurus Pasha fell down and broke his arm. It is an absolute fact that everybody who did my husband an injury had some bad luck.

Richard tried to get Teheran, which was one of the places that he longed for and was vacant, and we knew that three names were sent up to her Majesty for approval; but we also knew, *sub rosa*, that Mr. (afterwards Sir Ronald) Thompson, a personal friend in their youth of Mr. and Mrs. (afterwards Lord and Lady) Hammond, of the Foreign Office, was to get it.

I brought out "Unexplored Syria" (2 vols.), in which Richard and I and Charley Drake collaborated, on the 21st of June, 1872, while Richard was in Iceland.

Richard sailed on the 4th of June from Leith for Iceland. The 5th of June was one of my most unhappy days. I got up early, and passed the day with my mother. She received Communion at a quarter to one; at 9.30 p.m. she asked to see everybody. We said prayers to her, but did not think her in any danger. At eleven some instinct made me refuse to go home to my lodging. We were summoned suddenly. I ran in and took her in my arms; she turned her head round upon my shoulder, looked at me, breathed a little sigh, and died like a child at a quarter to twelve p.m. All the week she lay in state, the room dressed like a chapel, with flowers and candles, and we, her children, passed all day by her, and had all our religious services in her room. (Richard notes in his journal, "Poor mother died about midnight, June 5th.")

On the 12th of June, attended by all the people she liked best, we buried her at Mortlake.

At last, Lord Granville wrote to me, and asked me if I thought Richard would accept Trieste, Charles Lever having died; and he also advised me to urge him to take it, because they were not likely to have anything better vacant for some time. And I was able to send Richard's acceptance of Trieste to Lord Granville on July 15th. We knew that after a post of £1000 a year, with work that was really diplomatic, and with a promise ahead of Marocco, Teheran, and Constantinople before him, that a commercial town on £600 a year, and £100 office allowance, meant that his career was practically broken; but Richard and I could not afford to starve, and he said he would stick on as long as there was ever a hope of getting Marocco.

Finally we were taken into some sort of favour again. Lord Granville *had not understood* Richard's letter about wanting to have the Sházlis baptized, and feared that it might result in a *Jehád*, or religious war, if the baptisms had taken place. Richard told him "he knew it *would not*." He knew he could carry it through; he was not a man to risk such a matter. His plan was to buy a tract of land, to give these people the means of building themselves cottages, choose their own Shaykh, their own Priest, and make for themselves a little Church. The village *was to belong to him*, and he would have put it under the protection of his friends amongst the Mohammedans. He would have taken no taxes from them, and no presents or provisions, as other people do, and the consequence is they would have been now a flourishing colony. *That was the real cause of the recall;* and, as I have said before, Richard said, "That is suffering persecution for justice' sake with a vengeance; but we won't have anything more to do with this subject until I am free from an enlightened and just-minded Government in March, 1891."

On the 26th of August I was going a round of country-house visits in Richard's absence, and arriving at ten o'clock at night at Uncle Gerard's, met the sad news that our youngest and favourite brother, the flower of our flock, Jack Arundell, commanding the *Bittern*, had died of rheumatic fever between the West Coast of Africa and Ascension, where he is buried—that is to say, he did not die of rheumatic fever, but it was a question of sleep saving him. A very slight dose of opiate had been administered to him to ensure this boon. He had never mentioned the peculiarity in our family of being very sensitive to opiates; he went to sleep and never woke again, to the grief and distress of all on board. He was only thirty-one years of age, was bright and good-looking; he was a dashing officer, with his heart in his profession, and a fine career was before him. He had not had time to hear of our mother's death before he joined her. It was a terrible blow to us.

Richard arrived on the 8th of June in Iceland, embarked for return on 1st of August, and arrived in England from Iceland at eleven at night on the 14th of September.

On the 5th of October, 1872, the day was fixed for Richard to have a tumour cut out of his shoulder or back. He had got it from a blow from a single-stick, when he was off guard and his back was turned. It was an unfair blow, only the man did it in fun; anyway, he said so. He had had it for a long time, and it had frequently opened and discharged of itself, but now it was getting troublesome. Dr. Bird, of 49, Welbeck Street, performed the operation. It was two inches in diameter, and from first to last occupied about twelve minutes. I assisted Dr. Bird. He sat astride on a chair, smoking a cigar and talking all the time, and in the afternoon he insisted on going down to Brighton. He did not wish me to go with him, but I accompanied him to the station. I always liked to wait on him, so I got him his ticket, had his baggage put in, and took him a place in a *coupé* whilst he went off to buy his book and paper, and then I called the guard. I said, "Guard, my husband is going down to

Brighton. I wish you would just look after him, he is not very well;" and I gave him half a crown. Presently an old man of eighty hobbled by on crutches, "Is that him, ma'am?" "No," I said. Next a consumptive boy came by, "Is this him, ma'am?" "No," I said; "not yet." Many passed, and of all those who he thought looked as though they wanted taking care of, he asked the same question, and he got the same answer. Presently Richard came swaggering along, as if the whole station belonged to him—all fencers know the peculiar walk a soldier has who is given much to fencing and broadsword —and I whispered to the guard, "There he is," and I stood by the carriage till the train went, and I heard him whisper to a comrade, "She would never ask me to take care of such a chap as that, unless he was a raving lunatic. I'll take devilish good care I don't go near him; he would probably pitch me out of the carriage."

After this we had a large family party at Wardour Castle, which we enjoyed immensely.

A Greek priest from Syria came to see us, and we took him to a spiritualistic *séance.* He was dreadfully frightened, and said his prayers out loud all the time.

On his way up to Iceland he went to see Holyrood in Edinburgh, and, visiting Queen Mary's room, exclaimed, "No wonder she sighed for France." He went to the Levée held there by Lord Airlie (the present Earl's father).

Before I finish with Syria, there is a question I want to set at rest on behalf of both Richard and myself. During my husband's life, from his journey to Mecca in 1853, till his death in 1890, a period of thirty-seven years, a story was current about him, which he had no idea of, and when he did hear it, treated it as a good joke—that when he was on the road to Mecca he killed two Mohammedans, who suspected him of being a Frank and a Christian. He told me it was absolutely false; and, if any one knew what a horror he had of any one taking the life of *anything,* they would not doubt it for a moment. He would not allow even an animal to be killed, saying that "we had no right to destroy life." One of his greatest remorses was shooting a monkey in his younger days; "it cried like a child," he said, "and I can never forget it." This story did happen to two Englishmen, who were travelling in the desert about this time; and who, in consequence of their unfortunate necessity, never appeared before the public, nor gave an account of their travels.

Now, I mention this incident in connection with Syria (instead of Mecca), because, after my husband died, his mantle in this respect descended upon my shoulders. Mrs. Mentor Mott had assured me on leaving Syria "that I did not leave a single enemy behind me," but it issued from the British Syrian schools long afterwards, that the cause of my husband's recall was that I had shot two men, and wounded a third, because they did not stand up and salute me, and that I was afterwards abandoned and neglected; though it never reached my ears till five days after Richard's death, and that through a missionary's letter to the *Newcastle Daily Chronicle*, owing, I suppose, to my being a Catholic. He waited twenty years, till my husband could not contradict it, and then did not lose a single instant in publishing this utter fabrication. The fact is, these missionaries get to know a little Syrian Christian Arabic—some more, some less—and perhaps unintentionally they get hold of some wonderful stories, and make mistakes and mischief. This is the true story.

It was in a time of great excitement between Moslems and Christians. I was riding through a village of about thirty-five thousand Moslems. There was a feud between two local Shaykhs, the two principal men of the village. The Consulate favoured one and not the other, who were bullies. I rode through this village alone, having sent the men in attendance on me to do a commission. The son of the *un*friendly Shaykh, a youth of twenty-two, wanted to commence the row by attacking me—spat at me, and tried to pull me off my horse. This in the East means volumes, my position there being that of a very great personage. If I had been cowardly, fainted, and screamed, there would not have been a Christian left alive by the evening in that village. In fact, as it was, all the villagers were upon their knees in deprecation of the outrage, but were afraid to interfere with the village bully; so I reined in my horse, and slashed him across the face with my hunting-whip, and he howled and roared as if he were about five years old. The noise brought my men up sharply, whom he had not seen, having thought I was alone; seeing what was going on, they flung themselves upon him, and I think he was very sorry for himself when they had done with him. There was a general scuffle, in which somebody's pistol went off in his belt, because they have the bad habit of keeping the trigger down on the hammer, instead of at half-cock; but the ball fortunately went into a wall, and nobody was hurt.

When I got home, a strong body of people from the village came up to tell me that the youth, to revenge his beating, had collected all the most riotous people of the village and was coming up at night to burn our house (Sir Richard Wood's house in the Anti-Lebanon, by the way, which he lent to Richard). I had not enough people about me for defence, my husband having ridden a little distance in the desert and taken most of our men; so I sent a mounted messenger over to the *Wali*, and the next morning at dawn I was horrified at my husband's confidential Afghan, in full *kawwás* uniform, armed to the teeth, coming to tell me that my horse was saddled at the door, and that I must get up and ride down to the plain; he would explain as we went. I found the plain covered with troops, who saluted me as I rode down, and then the Colonel rode up to me, and told me that the *Wali* had ordered him to burn and sack the village. I told him that if he did such a thing my husband and I would leave the country at once; that these things were quite contrary to our English ideas. He said, "Then I put myself at your orders." I told him that since he was so kind as to let me have what I wanted, he was to assemble the principal Moslems of the village, and to bind them over by an oath not to touch the Christians, who were chiefly very poor, Greek Orthodox by religion, and Fellahín of the Anti-Lebanon, and he should take the youth and put him in prison for a while—say, a month.

This was carried out, and at my request he drew off the troops, and there was great rejoicing in the village. For this conduct, for which the writer to the *Newcastle Daily Chronicle* has induced many people to believe that my husband was recalled, I received a complimentary letter from the Consul-General, Mr. Eldridge, who did not like me because I hated his way with Richard, and the thanks of the Governor-General, the Wali Rashíd Pasha, for having saved them a great deal of trouble, both then and in the expected riot which Richard prevented. Richard was also very pleased with me. I should be ashamed to mention these things, but I do not mean to die and to leave any attack upon my husband not cleared up, nor any on myself, if I happen to hear of them.

When the youth was let out of prison, he became my most devoted servant. The year after we left, his mother, who was very fond of me, did some trifling thing which he had forbidden her; they say it was selling eggs in the market. His father was absent, and, be the offence what it may, we received a letter to tell us that he called his mother into the courtyard, assembled the household, and with his own hands he strangled her, and buried her in the courtyard under the stones. I never heard whether his father said anything when he came home, but I did hear that while she was dying, she extended her arms to our house, and that she called piteously, "Ah, Ya Sitti! ah, Ya Sitti! if thou wert here this abomination never could have been done."

It is monstrous for any missionary of the British Syrian schools or otherwise, to pretend that my husband was recalled, because I defended myself against the man who attacked me. The real cause was very different; it was his one endeavour to do what England professes to admire (theoretically, anyway), what Richard did in practice, namely, sacrifice himself for Christianity's sake!

And here I must be allowed a by-word. People in small official life are always subject to these trials, and, knowing this, how careful a Minister at home should be in listening to complaints! The lower an officer's grade, the lower the people he has to contend with. The Consul deals with all classes; when he rises to be Minister or Ambassador, he is above the mob, which cannot touch him. The enemies of the Consul will crawl in the dust to the Minister. Meantime the junior official has to run the gauntlet of the mud pelted at him, and if his Chief at home listens to it, a weak man dare not do his duty for fear of losing his post; the strong man does his duty, but he knows he has no chance of rising. Only the bad man succeeds.

He arrives at a new place, and all the bad people make a dead set at him to take up and protect their evil doings and to join them against their local enemies. If he does it he is upheld by them, but loses caste with the decent classes; if he does not, they form a cabal, and even pay people to write home complaint after complaint against him, till the Minister for Foreign Affairs, who knows nothing of these matters, says, "There must be something wrong about this man, or I should not get bad reports of him right and left. It is evident he won't do for the place." He recalls his good, honest, brave servant, who was doing his Master credit, and he puts him on a shelf to pine in useless inactivity, and breaks his spirit, and sends out another, who naturally says, "I am duly warned what to do. I will take care not to do what my unfortunate predecessor did, but the reverse." He has learnt that the "decent people" only looked on, or if one or two did take his part, they were not believed, or not listened to. He does as the others bid him—"wins golden opinions" —and the Minister at home thinks it is all as it should be. Who shall blame the man? He has, perhaps, a wife and children to support, and he yearns for promotion. If he sees but one road to his Chief's favour, that of "hearing no complaints of him," what shall he do? What consolation has he when he is driven out of the world by penury, and has to earn his pittance in some out-of-the-way settlement? How easy are the sacrifices of an independent man, who can afford to bide his time!

I have seen many cases of this kind during thirty years of Consular life, and personally I was always acting the part of Job's wife, but unsuccessfully. Richard had no chance of rising to his proper position; he was much too good. The "light of God" was upon him. The Home Authorities heard all the complaints; *he* did not report to them the good he did, but *I* will cry it from the house-tops until all hear it. He gained respect and influence over all classes. All the good and the poor loved and trusted him; the bad feared him. He had pre-eminently the Divine gift of pity. He had some talisman for attracting the people; and when they got a written order from him, they would kiss it and put it on their heads as if it were a Sultan's Firman. He was more than equal to his position if he had been only commonly backed up at home.

With so many races, creeds, and tongues, all at variance, in an Oriental intriguing focus, it is impossible to please everybody. You cannot well walk down the street without treading upon somebody's toes. It is difficult for a man who does his duty in a hotbed of corruption to be universally popular, and there are *some* whose *disapproval* is a *proof of integrity*. One must have a straight line of duty. If a person wants you to do something wrong, and you act uprightly and refuse, they are sure to write to some great personage at home, to ask them to complain at head-quarters. They never mention what *they asked you to do*—what bribe they offered—but invent something against you. If they are listened to, they can always keep you in hot water, as *cela encourage les autres.*

"To R. F. B.

"Ever remember, 'tis Pretension rules
Half men, three-thirds of women—to wit, the fools.
In yonder coterie see, my friend, yon pair
Of vapid witlings waging wordy war,
While female senates hear, in trembling awe,
This thing and that thing laying down the law.
Murmured applause shall fill each greedy ear,
Of 'Charming man!' 'Delightful, clever dear!'
And Lady Betty lends her sweetest smile
T' inflame their ardour and their toils beguile.
Yet those same lips no word of worth afford
To thy true heart, strong brain, quick pen, sharp sword.
Pine not, brave soul! he whom such trifles vex,
Unfit to serve, much less can rule the sex.
Ask not the remedy—go, win a name,
Famous or infamous, 'tis much the same;
For silly girls and shallow youths make game
Of God-like nature, all unknown to fame;
But souls select, instinctive, recognize
Congenial spirits unmarked to vulgar eyes.

You asked what caused this egotistic strain—
The fit is on me; let me here explain.
Fools, seeing in youth a hero's value spurned,
Ignored a heart and soul that fondly yearned
And burned for honours honourably earned;
His teens long passed, exiled in distant land,
A noble heart held out the long-sought hand,
Taught him to labour, strengthened him to wait
The turn of fortune's tide that makes us great.
Nor years' long lapse, nor change, nor fate can raze
From Mem'ry's page those words of kindly praise.
If one man's name on our heart's page be penned,
'Tis his—no need to name our true best friend." *

ISABEL BURTON.

Some of us are left in the world to fight our battle. There are strong souls who can resist all attacks; nothing overthrows them, nothing can even hurt them. The devil makes war upon the world, but especially upon them. Nevertheless, it is as hard for a brave spirit to hold its own, and see its fancied treasures falling away from it in the hour of need, as for a gallant and successful general, on the eve of victory, in the turn of the battle, to be deserted by his troops, and left, in spite of his own qualities, to disgrace and death.

Richard's character presented a singularity in the Levant, wondered at by all, condemned by many, approved of or not by those who would suffer or rejoice under his rule. He was a perfectly honest man—I do not allude only to money. His enemies rejoiced at it, his friends trembled for him, whilst indifferents were only astounded at his folly. An attempt was made to console him with the hazy promise of a future, which seemed, however, rather to consist in the good opinion of good men than in anything tangible or useful. For him, truth to a principle meant self-annihilation. He had always done the noble thing, and now, because he did those noble things, he was virtually regarded as unfit for the very employment for which God and Nature and his own life had peculiarly fitted him.

My old friend Charles Reade told us that "in less than two hundred years the first stone of *honesty in biography*" will have to be laid, and then he proceeds to relate how *his* "hero and martyr" has been treated by the world; how he had earned the gold medal of the Humane Society twice, and the silver twelve times; how he has never received either, but is a blind and destitute old man, living in a chimney corner, deserted and forgotten by the world, and shunned by those he has saved; how his only public honour is being permitted to cross a certain bridge without paying the common toll, from whose

* The just departed Earl of Derby.

waters beneath he has saved so many lives at the risk of his own. He describes his hero as one of Nature's gentlemen, fit company for an Emperor, a man without his fellow, who adorns our country. He was earning thirty shillings a week when charity towards his fellow-creatures induced him to throw away his sight for the public good, and the parish allows him three and sixpence a week. He tells us that he better deserves every order and decoration the State can bestow than does any gentleman or nobleman whose bosom is a constellation; "yet," he says proudly, "not a cross or ribbon has ever ascended from the vulgar level. Why? because," he adds, "this world, in the distribution of glory, is a heathen in spite of Christ, a fool in spite of Voltaire." I quote Charles Reade's story to show that nowadays England does not confer honour on merit in any class of life. The higher and lower orders share the same fate. Honours follow a certain red-tape routine, not noble deeds, and often mock their wearer; whilst many a noble brow looks up to heaven with patient, uncomplaining dignity, adorned only by God and Nature, and by a life of chivalrous actions. The English public are, however, seldom wrong *when once they know the truth*, and perhaps the best and truest honour is their good verdict.

* * * * * * *

Whilst here, we saw the Oriental papers every fortnight, and all the accounts we read of our old home were of "Arab raids, of insults to Europeans, of miserable, starving people, of sects killing one another in open day, of policemen firing recklessly into a crowd to wing a flying prisoner, and a general fusilade in the streets; of sacked villages, and plundered travellers." We read of Salahíyyeh spoken of as a "suburb of Damascus, which enjoys an unenviable reputation;" of innocent Salahíyyeh men being shot down by mistake for criminals, "because the people of Salahíyyeh are such confirmed ruffians, that they are sure to be either just going to do mischief or just returning from it." That is the place where for two or more years we slept with open doors and windows, and I freely walked about alone throughout the twenty-four hours, even when my husband was absent, and left with Moslem servants.

* * * * * * *

Having lifted any possible cloud which may have hung over the real history of Richard's removal from his Eastern post—the only suitable one he ever held—it is unnecessary for me to enter into any further explanation of the causes of the base detractions from which he has suffered. His case is not altogether a new one in the human history, and the true explanation—the only real explanation—

of it, which can face the light of day, has been admirably expressed in the lines written by the most brilliant statesman the Foreign Office ever sent to the East—the "great Eltchi," whom I and all lovers of the Orient speak of with admiration, respect, and pride—Lord Stratford de Redcliffe—and which are applicable to Richard in every sense, except that, so far from ever "spurning the gaping crowd," he always sacrificed himself for the poor, the ignorant, and the oppressed.

"Nay, shines there one with brilliant parts endowed,
Whose inborn vigour spurns the gaping crowd?
For him the trench is dug, the toils are laid,
For him dull malice whets the secret blade.
One fears a master fatal to his ease,
Or worse, a rival born his age to please;
This dreads a champion for the cause he hates,
That fain would crush what shames his broad estates.
Leagued by their instincts, each to each is sworn;
High on their shields the simpering fool is borne." *

* From Lord Stratford de Redcliffe's "Shadows of the Past."

END OF VOL. I.

PRINTED BY WILLIAM CLOWES AND SONS, LIMITED, LONDON AND BECCLES.

Made in the USA